THE PRICE OF
NATIONHOOD

The
PRICE OF
NATIONHOOD

THE AMERICAN REVOLUTION
IN
CHARLES COUNTY

JEAN B. LEE

W·W·NORTON & COMPANY
New York   London

FRONTISPIECE MAP: *The Chesapeake, "The Best Laid Out for Trade of Any [Country] in the World." Detail from* A New Map of Virginia, Maryland and the Improved Parts of Pennsylvania and New Jersey, *by J. Senex (London, 1719). Courtesy of the Maryland Historical Society.*

The text of this book is composed in Van Dijck,
with the display set in Caslon 471
Composition and manufacturing by The Haddon Craftsmen, Inc.
Book design and cartography by Jacques Chazaud

Library of Congress Cataloging-in-Publication Data
Lee, Jean Butenhoff.
The price of nationhood : the American Revolution in Charles County / Jean B. Lee.
p.   cm.
Includes bibliographical references and index.
1. Charles County (Md.)—History.   2. United States—History—Revolution,
1775–1783—Social aspects.   I. Title.
F187.C4L44   1994
975.2′4702—dc20   93-42536

ISBN 0-393-96847-2

W. W. Norton & Company, Inc., 500 Fifth Avenue, New York, N.Y. 10110
W. W. Norton & Company Ltd., 10 Coptic Street, London WC1A 1PU

2 3 4 5 6 7 8 9 0

For Chris

My dear and loving husband

CONTENTS

———⟨∞⟩———

PART THREE: POSTWAR ADJUSTMENTS

ILLUSTRATIONS

MAPS

ACKNOWLEDGMENTS

Encouragement for this study has come from many persons and institutions. I wish especially to thank Merrill D. Peterson, whose scholarship long has inspired me and who has always given generously of his counsel and time. Stephen Innes's graduate colloquium in early American social history awakened my enthusiasm for that field, and he offered valuable appraisals along the way. To William W. Abbot, I am thankful for his unwavering encouragement and understanding, his insightful suggestions, and the conversations we have shared. Armstead L. Robinson has done much to support and forward the project, for which I am deeply grateful. The late Stephen Botein advanced suggestions that proved crucial in helping me conceptualize the book. As it neared completion, advice from Rhys Isaac, Pauline Maier, and Lorena S. Walsh was invaluable. And I remember and appreciate the roles that John E. Butenhoff and Donald Ziegler had, long ago, in decisions that led ultimately to this book.

Many others freely shared their perceptions and raised penetrating questions as the manuscript evolved. Charles L. Cohen, Iris Heissenbuttel, Orva W. Heissenbuttel, Christine L. Heyrman, Cynthia A. Kierner, J. Richard Rivoire, Sharon V. Salinger, and students in my graduate seminar at the University of Wisconsin read drafts of the entire manuscript. Don Higginbotham and Fred Anderson offered much appreciated critiques of material on the wartime experiences of people in Charles County, as did participants at a session of the 1992 meeting of the Organization of American Historians and at seminars sponsored by the Philadelphia Center for Early American Studies, the Washington Area Seminar on Early American History, and the Institute of Early American History and Culture. Papers presented at Morgan State University and the Carter G. Woodson Institute for Afro-American and African Studies, at the University of Virginia, enabled me to try out ideas related to the black population. So, too, a paper delivered at the 1989 United States Capitol Historical Society Symposium gave me an opportunity to explore dimensions of revolutionary leadership. The chapters on the postwar years are stronger than they otherwise would have been because of Edward L. Ayers, Ronald Hoffman, Linda K. Kerber, and members of the Boston Area Seminar in Early American History and the Early American Study Group at the University of Wisconsin. Lois Green Carr, A. Roger Ekirch, Richard Hamm, Carey Howlett, William E. Jackson, Joseph C. Miller, Thomas L. Purvis, and Thad W. Tate also contributed to this effort in significant ways.

Many depositories made their manuscript and rare book collections available, and I am especially grateful for assistance from the staffs of the Maryland State Archives at the Hall of Records, the Maryland Historical Society, the Southern Maryland Studies Center at Charles County Community College, the University of Virginia Library, the Library of Congress, Georgetown University Library, the Virginia Historical Society, the William R. Perkins Library at Duke University, the Historical Society of Pennsylvania, and the New York Public Library. At the Maryland State Archives, Susan R. Cummings was patient and persevering, and Phebe R. Jacobsen, Susan A. Collins, and Diane Frese helped make the many hours I spent there both pleasant and productive. Donna Ellis and Marcia Miller did the same at the Maryland Historical Society. Archivists and librarians at the Colonial Williamsburg Foundation, the Virginia State Library, the College of William and Mary, and the State Historical Society of Wisconsin also were unfailingly helpful.

Thanks are owing to those who assisted me in locating historic buildings, portraits, and other illustrative materials. J. Richard Rivoire has been wonderfully generous in sharing information, drawings, and photographs. Sarah L. Barley has been indefatigable in locating items at repositories and in private hands, and her enthusiasm for this project has been uplifting. With good humor and a spirit of adventure, Thomas N. Lee, camera in hand, followed me hither and yon across Charles County. Other photographs are the work of John C. Kopp, staff photographer at Charles County Community College. To all who have allowed me to use illustrative materials, I am grateful.

This study has received generous and much-appreciated financial support. While I pursued graduate work in Charlottesville, Virginia, fellowships from the Danforth Foundation and the Thomas Jefferson Memorial Foundation enabled me to commence the research. In 1982–83 a Dissertation Fellowship awarded by the Educational Foundation of the American Association of University Women gave me an entire year of uninterrupted research and writing. Assistance also came from the Society of the Cincinnati in the State of Virginia and from the Carter G. Woodson Institute for Afro-American and African Studies. The American Association for State and Local History, the National Endowment for the Humanities, and the Charles Ulrick and Josephine Bay Foundation, through the grant-in-aid program of the AASLH, underwrote the costs of research and analysis of the activities of propertied women in the county. During 1984–86 a postdoctoral fellowship from the Institute of Early American History and Culture, which was funded in part by the National Endowment for the Humanities, enabled me to undertake additional research. Finally, a faculty research grant from the Graduate School of the University of Wisconsin and a senior research fellowship supported by the College of William and Mary and the Colonial Williamsburg Foundation afforded me time to complete the manuscript. I shall always be grateful that these institutions helped me realize my vision of tracing one society through the formative years of the nation.

In Steven Forman I have been blessed with an enthusiastic, kind, and amiable editor. The book has benefited greatly from his attention and support. Beverly A. Smith's devotion to the project, and her friendship, have sustained me. She, Barbara C. Hiler, and Sarah Campany helped prepare the manuscript with great good patience and care. Sarah Marcus checked many a citation. James J. Baker, John S. Barr, John M. Cooper, George Craddock, Ann Gephart, Ronald M. Gephart, John M. Hemphill, Dennis O'Toole, Marjorie Sidebottom, Robert Stanley, Gail S. Terry, and David Waters—each in his or her own special way—enabled me to persevere.

The members of my family alone know how much they contributed during the years of research and writing. I owe much to my husband and intellectual companion, Christopher F. Lee, for his unflagging confidence and encouragement, for his incisive criticisms and suggestions at every stage of the undertaking, and for the grace and good humor with which he listened to unending details about the lives of the people of Charles County. To Daniel, Brad, and Deborah, I am thankful for their patience and their understanding that this work occupied a small part of the house and a large part of my thoughts.

J. B. L.

Madison, Wisconsin
June 14, 1993

God dwells among the details, not in the realm of pure generality. We must tackle and grasp the larger, encompassing themes of our universe, but we make our best approach through small curiosities that rivet our attention—all those pretty pebbles on the shoreline of knowledge. For the ocean of truth washes over the pebbles with every wave, and they rattle and clink with the most wondrous din.

—STEPHEN JAY GOULD
Wonderful Life:
The Burgess Shale and the Nature of History

THE PRICE OF
NATIONHOOD

Introduction

T HE EIGHTEENTH CENTURY REMAINS A PRESENCE IN CHARLES COUNTY, Maryland. Tobacco fields still dot the land, and narrow country roads wind through woodland to the Anglican parish churches of Durham, Trinity, and William and Mary, all built before 1800 and still in use. The traveler coming upon St. Ignatius Church encounters a scene that has retained its striking pastoral beauty through the centuries: Below the hillside where Jesuit fathers have laid generations of the faithful to rest, the broad Potomac and Port Tobacco rivers join and continue on to Chesapeake Bay and the sea. A profound quiet prevails. All that is lacking from an earlier day are sailing vessels out of Liverpool or Glasgow, Bristol or the West Indies, bound for nearby river landings.

Place-names and dwellings also evoke memories of another era. The county's four rivers, the Wicomico, Potomac, Patuxent, and Port Tobacco (formerly Portobacke), call to mind Indian peoples long since departed, as do Zekiah Swamp and several tidal creeks: the Mattawoman, Nanjemoy, Chicamuxen, Pomonkey, and Piccowaxen. The names of early white families persist in roads and country crossings named for the Smallwoods, Dents, Marburys, and others. The towns of Port Tobacco, Newport, and Benedict date from prerevolutionary days. And most of the early houses that have survived, about two dozen built before 1800, are those of the gentry that once domi-nated life in the county.

The careers of some among them extended well beyond the county's bor-ders, not only to the statehouse in Annapolis but also to the nation's first capital in Philadelphia. On a ridge near Port Tobacco stands Mulberry Grove, where John Hanson, president of the Continental Congress, once lived. Fol-low the narrow road north from the town, just as eighteenth-century travelers did, and one comes upon Rose Hill, home of Gustavus Richard Brown, the physician and botanist who helped found the hospital department of the Continental Army and who, on a cold night in December 1799, crossed the Potomac to Mount Vernon in an unsuccessful effort to save its owner's life. Brown's neighbor was Thomas Stone, signer of the Declaration of Indepen-dence and a member of the state Senate throughout the revolutionary and Confederation periods. Not far away is the plantation of his uncle, Daniel of St. Thomas Jenifer, whose political career took him from colonial official to member of the Constitutional Convention of 1787. Finally, tucked away in the northwestern corner of the county is Smallwood's Retreat, to which Maryland's highest-ranking officer in the Continental Army, Major General William Smallwood, retired after the War for Independence.

One never sees, when traveling through the county today, the wooden slave quarters whose occupants constituted a major share of the wealth of men like Smallwood and the others. A common sight in the eighteenth century, the quarters have long since fallen into decay. So, too, have the dwellings in which the majority of white inhabitants—small and middling planters and their families—passed their lives.

In the years before the American Revolution, Charles County was a ter-minus for transatlantic commerce. It was part of the Tobacco Coast, that labyrinth of land and water, rivers and bays, that made Maryland and Virginia renowned for unsurpassed navigable waters and "the best laid out for trade of any [country] in the world." Letters from British correspondents to persons living in the county needed only an address such as "Port Tobacco, Potomac River" or "Patuxent." At riverain landings and in towns sited at the water's edge, residents exchanged tobacco and other agricultural products for the wares of local artisans and shopkeepers, as well as for English manufactured goods, African slaves, and West Indian sugar.[1]

The county also was a principal crossroad of America. Contemporary maps show the intercolonial post road passing through Port Tobacco, which served as the county seat, locus of an Anglican parish, and a center of the Potomac Valley tobacco trade. To the north along the road lay Annapolis and Philadel-phia. To the south, via ferries that plied the Potomac, lay Williamsburg and Charleston.[2] Whether travelers came overland or arrived on oceangoing ves-

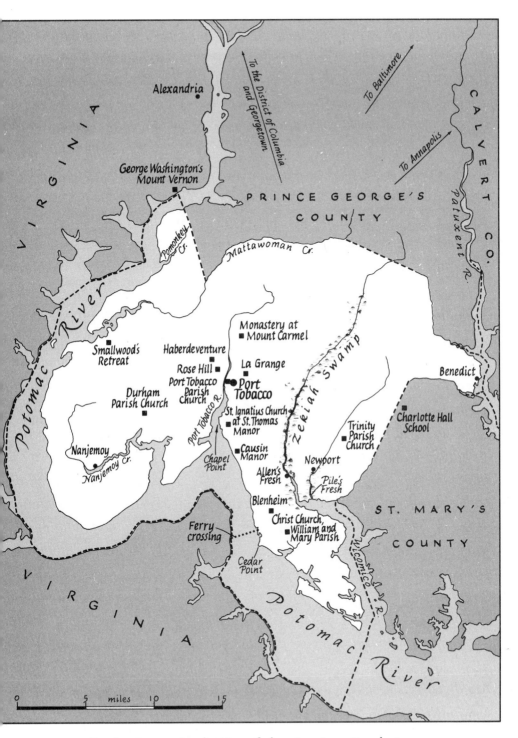

Charles County in the Era of the American Revolution

sels, many stopped at local plantations or ordinaries, and a few recorded their impressions of the county and the people who lived there.

One of those travelers, a young Englishman named Nicholas Cresswell, managed to capture much of the essence of life in Charles County on the eve of the Revolution. He came to the New World in 1774 because he believed that "a person with a small fortune may live much better and make greater improvements in America than he can possibly do in England." During five weeks at sea, Cresswell became acquainted with Alexander Knox, a Scotsman bound for the village of Nanjemoy, in the southwestern part of the county, where his brother was a merchant and storekeeper. Although Cresswell intended to settle in Virginia, his friendship with Knox drew him to the county four times between May 1774 and the following winter. There he first saw tobacco cultivated, and there he fought the "excessive heat" and fevers that preyed upon newcomers to the region. Taking tea, dining, and dancing at the "pleasant Houses" of the gentry; attending a "reaping frolic . . . a Harvest Feast," where "the people very merry" danced barefoot, "the Girls without stays"; and watching slaves laboriously plant tobacco seedlings in hillocks, Cresswell observed the gamut of the county's social strata. He also experienced the world just beyond the plantations: Scottish traders and their stores, ships lying at anchor to take on tobacco, excursions along Maryland's Potomac shore or across the river to Virginia, and church services and dining in Port Tobacco. A discerning observer, he characterized the inhabitants as hospitable, civil, kind, and obliging. People "appear to live very well, and [to be] exceedingly happy," he wrote. And even the slaves, in their leisure hours together, seemed happy and "as if they had forgot or were not sensible of their miserable condition."[3]

Other travelers during the late colonial period, although they spent less time in the county and left briefer accounts than Cresswell's, also described an inviting scene. A British officer who arrived after the Seven Years' War found the landscape "extremely pleasant and very open for America," with gently rolling hills that reminded him of England except that they were better timbered. About the same time, a Frenchman who ferried across the Potomac to the county noted that "on my arival in maryland, I thought there was something pleasanter in the Country than in Virginia, it is not a Continual flat as the latter, there is a greater variety, and fine prospects from the riseings . . . the land seems beter Cultivated and setled, the roads are not so sandy." Others, too, found the main road good and, beside it, "ma[n]y fine streams of pure water—and many beautiful hills."[4]

Even as these impressions were set down in wayfarers' journals, the people and place they described were being drawn into the momentous events—revolution, war, and the creation of a new nation—that swept across America between the 1760s and 1800. This book explores how the inhabitants of Charles County—the illustrious and humble, free and slave, male and female, Protestant and Catholic—experienced those events and how their lives and society changed as a result. My focus encompasses the immediate and ongoing impact of the war, which is perhaps the least explored area of the Revolution. After two centuries we have a vast literature on the background and causes of the Revolution and on military operations, diplomatic affairs, and the creation of the American political system. We know least about how the majority of men and women, in their communities, experienced and responded to the war and its consequences. The historical literature, moreover, has so emphasized the political and national gains of the era that few have stopped to ask (other than for the loyalists) what was lost.[5]

People in Charles County shared in the gains, but they also paid a tremendous social and economic price for political independence and nationhood. And while in many ways their history is unique, in other ways what happened to them also occurred elsewhere in America. This local study, then, can serve as a window through which to glimpse, sometimes with striking clarity, at other times only dimly, the generation that lived through, and helped shape, the formative years of the nation. To do so requires abandoning the traditional landmarks at which most studies in the period begin or end (especially Independence in 1776, peace in 1783, or establishment of the federal government between 1787 and 1789) and, instead, treating the time through which the revolutionary generation passed, the time from the late colonial period to the Age of Jefferson, as a whole.

During the 1760s and early 1770s, people in Charles County witnessed the fullest flowering of Maryland's plantation society, something akin to the concurrent golden age of Annapolis. A secure, self-confident, forward-looking elite dominated a complex, hierarchical, and stable social order. An expanding and modestly diversified economy, which was in harmony with the British scheme of empire, offered white inhabitants a level of well-being not surpassed during the colonial period. Even enslaved blacks—by comparison with both earlier and subsequent eras—were experiencing an interlude of relative stability. Problems and tensions existed, to be sure. Yet, tellingly, they were manageable and never shook the foundations of the mature social order. The late colonial county is the subject of Part One of this study—and the baseline for assessing the dramatic changes that followed.

Part Two examines revolution and war. In the decade before Independence, imperial policies and proprietary politics created unusual, rapidly mounting opportunities for people to challenge constituted authority. Individually and through communal efforts, they experimented with everything from solemn statements of their rights to crowd action. Like the vast majority of colonial localities, Charles County was not at the forefront of the Revolution, but by 1776 its people were overwhelmingly in the patriot camp. Two chapters devoted to the coming of the Revolution trace their transit from disaffection to rebellion, from words to action. These same chapters show how political upheaval invited white men of all social ranks to become involved in shaping the course of events, even as the colonial elite, with a few exceptions, continued to exercise leadership.

By the time people celebrated Independence, they were thoroughly enmeshed in the war that would secure it. Wars are flash points that provide unusual access to past communities. They throw into graphic relief the contours of the societies involved: their resilience and fragility, their capacity both to endure and to change. The War for Independence elicited immense communal efforts—to provide for the Continental Army and protect home territory—and it tested the American population as never before. What the war required of individuals and communities—everything from labor to loyalty—and what it left them to work with after peace was declared in 1783, fundamentally affected their hopes and circumstances and profoundly influenced the subsequent development of the United States.

Together, Charles County inhabitants ultimately proved effective at supporting the war effort. They strove to meet seemingly endless requests for Continental troops and supplies, and they also grew adept at minimizing damage from British raiders operating on the Potomac and its navigable tributaries. Plantations, towns, and warehouses suffered damage, but compared with the destruction and havoc wreaked in the Carolinas and parts of Virginia, Charles County survived the war relatively unscathed. Throughout the long and difficult conflict, the elite continued to lead, but only by being sensitive to the populace and by mediating between national military needs and local residents' capabilities and inclinations to meet those needs.

The period between the end of the war and the beginning of the nineteenth century is the subject of Part Three. With peace, optimism coursed through the county. Having cooperated as never before during the war, many people afterward turned their energies to improving their society by promoting religion, education, and private and civic virtues. Even the enslaved had cause for a measure of hope because private manumissions and successful freedom suits created the county's first sizable free black population. In addition, men who had served in the army and in Congress returned home knowing more of America, firsthand, than any previous generation. Their sense of a new nation, and their hopes for the future of the United States, found tangible expression in the political careers they launched, the trading connections they formed with Philadelphia and Baltimore merchants, and their promotion of the economic development of the Potomac river valley. During the 1790s local men also worked to seat the national capital just a few miles upriver.

Yet, as one century drew to its close and another dawned, Charles County increasingly showed the social and economic strains of Independence and nationhood. The economy, which had fit well within the British Empire, suffered protracted decline in the new nation. The war devastated the tobacco trade, peace did not restore its earlier structure and vitality, and no one found an adequate substitute. Economic distress had social and political repercussions. During the depression of the mid-1780s, Port Tobacco was the scene of the principal riot that occurred in postwar Maryland. At the same time, because people did not pay their taxes, a succession of local tax collectors, sheriffs, and some of their sureties, all members of the elite, found themselves driven into insolvency. Public officeholding suddenly lost much of its attraction. Finally, ties among blacks were severed as planters, hard pressed to pay their debts and taxes, sold off slaves. So rapid was their dispersal that the extent of slaveholding among white households jumped by one-third between 1782 and 1790, and Charles County earned the dubious distinction of having the highest proportion of slaveholding households in all of Maryland.

Beyond the county, owing to the favorable peace treaty and the creation of a national domain, millions of acres of virgin land beckoned to both the propertied and the poor, as did the rising towns of Alexandria, Georgetown, Washington, and Baltimore. And that brought major demographic change to the county. After having grown throughout the eighteenth century, the white and black populations peaked at 20,600 souls in 1790 and then immediately entered long-term decline. People just moved away—to towns and to the backcountry of Maryland, Virginia, and North Carolina, across the mountains to Kentucky, and onto the fertile Gulf Coast. Outmigration siphoned off some on the margins of the society, but it also lured away substantial property holders, well-educated members of the elite, and even a few of the county's principal revolutionary leaders. On the eve of the Civil War, Charles County had 20 percent fewer people than when George Washington became president, and not until after World War II did the total population surpass the peak year of 1790.

The society left behind lacked the air of well-being, and the self-confident gentry leadership, of the late colonial period. In their place were abandoned plantations, a decaying county seat, vacant public offices, rising costs for poor relief, and a population that shifted during the 1790s to a black, enslaved majority. "The country . . . appears as if it had been deserted by one half of its inhabitants," wrote a lonely wayfarer who realized that once, and not long ago, the landscape had been more inviting, the people more hospitable and prosperous.[6] Many of the opportunities released by the Revolution lay largely beyond, not in, Charles County. From a broader vantage, however, the county's loss was the nation's gain, for those who migrated from the Potomac shores after the war joined thousands of their countrymen and -women from the eastern seaboard, and together they spanned the continent.

This book pursues some large themes: the American Revolution as a transforming, ongoing phenomenon, civilians' responses to the War for Independence, the tenor of the nation's formative years, and the nature of Chesapeake society. In pursuing these themes while simultaneously attempting to evoke the sights and sounds of the eighteenth-century county, I have adopted a narrative style of presentation. As a result, much statistical data on everything from literacy rates to the distribution of slaves among plantations are contained in the notes and appendix at the end of this volume. So, too, references to ongoing scholarly debates have been kept to a minimum in the text but appear in the notes. Where warranted, the text does establish larger settings—regional, imperial, or national—that influenced conditions and events in Charles County or that illustrate commonalities and differences between it and other places in revolutionary America.

This study has taught me the value of seeking the general through the particular—of finding in the close examination of one place the outlines of an entire era. The rich evidence for the county sometimes reinforces, sometimes extends, and at other times contravenes interpretations advanced for other localities or the nation as a whole. Again and again, the people of the county seem typical of the Chesapeake tidewater and of America generally—in their social order extending from slaves to squires, for example, or the general steps they took to protest British imperial measures, problems associated with army recruiting, and postwar activities directed toward individual and communal improvement. The postwar years in the county also impart enhanced meaning to the idea that the 1780s constituted a critical period, a time of crisis and danger in the political and economic life of the new nation. In these and other ways—even as the blend of persons and place was unique—much of what happened in the county resonated across America.

But the evidence also reveals an instructively distinctive place. For example, when compared with other recent depictions of late colonial Maryland and Virginia, the late colonial county seems more socially stable and harmonious, with a more secure, less threatened gentry. Charles County women who eschewed marriage and maintained economic independence serve as counterpoints to female dependency in early America. Civilians' contributions to the

War for Independence seem greater, their failings more understandable, when viewed from the local level instead of the more common national perspective. The Revolution itself appears less tumultuous than in some other places, even in other parts of Maryland. Many of the differences were real. Others no doubt reflect our incomplete comprehension of the past.

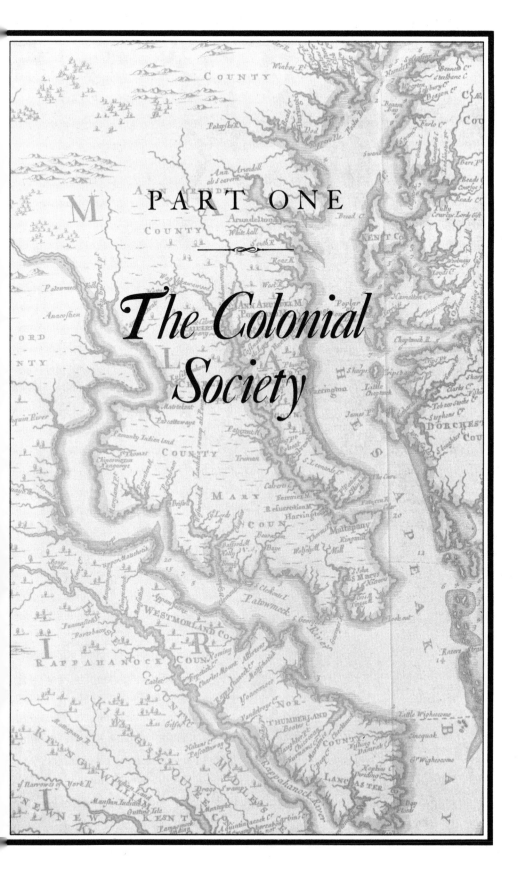

PART ONE

The Colonial Society

Prologue:
Within
the Bounded Oaks

Jesuit missionaries were harbingers of permanent white settlement in what was to become Charles County. In 1642, when the colony of Maryland was less than a decade old, priests settled near the Indian town of Portobacco, or Portobacke, and proselytized among the neighboring Piscataways, Nanjemoys, Mattawomans, Yaocomicos, and related Indian peoples. Maryland was a proprietary province, the gift of the English monarch to the second Lord Baltimore, a Roman Catholic who in turn gave the Jesuits four thousand acres of land along the Potomac and Port Tobacco rivers. There they established St. Thomas Manor, which today is the oldest surviving Jesuit mission founded in the English mainland colonies. Also during the 1640s a handful of other men took up tracts on the west side of the Wicomico River, and within a few years settlement spread up the Potomac and along the streams and runs that drained the land. Throughout the colonial period the county faced outward, toward the rivers whose waters flowed into Chesapeake Bay and the sea beyond.[1]

In 1658, when approximately four hundred white settlers were living west of the Wicomico, the proprietary government established Charles County, named for the third Lord Baltimore. It lay adjacent to Maryland's oldest county, St. Mary's, was bordered on the south and west by the Potomac, and had a variable northern boundary coterminous with the extent of white settlement. In 1695 the colonial legislature rearranged county lines on the lower Western Shore, and except for one subsequent addition, Charles thereby acquired its permanent dimensions. Lying entirely within the tidewater, the county remained adjacent to St. Mary's and the Wicomico but now also jutted east between Indian and Swanson creeks, thereby affording access to the Patuxent River. The great bend of the Potomac defined about 75 miles of the western and southern border, and on the north the county ran along Matta-woman and Swanson creeks, with a straight line connecting their headwaters. Beyond lay a new jurisdiction, Prince George's County. In 1748 a nub of the latter lying north of Mattawoman Creek was annexed to Charles, and at that point the county encompassed approximately 460 square miles. Wherever water did not define the perimeter, surveyors marked a double line of bound-ary trees, often oaks, "That the same may be known and perceived by all persons."[2]

The men and women who settled in the county during the seventeenth century began a task—transforming the landscape from extensive woodlands into hundreds of plantations and several market towns—that would require several generations to complete. And they did so under exceedingly trying circumstances. As elsewhere in the Chesapeake, the disease environment was lethal; tobacco, the only cash crop, was labor-intensive; many early immi-grants arrived as unfree, indentured laborers destined for the fields; and most immigrants, whether free or indentured, were males.[3]

In combination, these factors brought profound demographic and social consequences. The alien disease environment subjected newcomers to a pe-riod of "seasoning," during which they contracted and often succumbed to a host of debilitating illnesses against which they had no immunities. Among those who survived entry into the Chesapeake, disease and harsh working conditions produced such high mortality rates that few immigrants lived beyond their forties. Servants could not marry before they worked out their indentures, typically over four or five years, and many free men probably had to delay marriage because the sex ratio was heavily skewed toward males (as much as three to one). Delayed marriage and early death meant that few children were born to most couples. Pregnancy and childbirth increased fe-male mortality, and children died in droves, one-third before their first birth-day, more than one-half before age twenty-one. Owing to these circum-stances, the county's population neither grew by natural increase nor achieved a balanced sex ratio during the seventeenth century. Most inhabi-tants were immigrants from England.

This abnormal demographic situation made family life both complicated and fragile. Death usually carried off one or both parents before a child reached maturity. Grandparents were an anomaly. Widows and widowers quickly remarried. Thus households often included children from several different marriages and, sometimes in addition, a few field workers, whether unrelated orphans, free laborers, indentured servants, or, toward the end of the century, a black slave or two. All crowded together in the serviceable but small and rude wooden dwellings characteristic of early Maryland plantations.[4]

[handwritten margin note: COLLAGE-FAMILY]

Neither towns nor, for most newcomers, nearby relatives relieved the isolation of the early settlements. Building networks of friends and neighbors took time. Community-wide institutions were fragmentary. Courts performed essential services such as recording deeds and punishing the wayward, and Catholic priests living at St. Thomas Manor ministered to their scattered flock. Protestant inhabitants, however, waited until the end of the century for Anglican parishes to be organized. Schools were nonexistent.[5]

The social order that evolved during the seventeenth century was highly stratified, with the indentured servants, unfree and impoverished, at the bottom. Above them was an expanding group of freed servants. Some became tenants on other people's property, but those who managed to acquire land of their own, a few head of cattle, and perhaps an indentured servant or two, entered the ranks of small or middling planters. The planters' ranks also included men who had arrived in Maryland both free and able to buy property in the county. At the apex of the hierarchical society stood a handful of individuals, the gentry, whose wealth or services to the proprietary government enabled them to acquire large tracts of land ranging up to five thousand acres. Few men advanced alone. A sure path to upward mobility was marriage to a woman, usually a widow, who brought property to the union and contributed her labor to the household.[6]

*[handwritten margin note: SOCIETY STRUCTURE *]*

By 1700, when the county's population reached twenty-eight hundred souls, the contours of the social order that would characterize the eighteenth century were emerging. The white population finally was growing by natural increase, and the native-born, who were more likely than immigrants to live longer and have stronger economic and family ties to the area, would soon constitute a majority. Although men still outnumbered women, the sex ratio was gradually assuming a more normal balance. Also by the turn of the century, a transition from white servitude to black slavery was under way because fewer Englishmen and -women were entering Maryland as bound laborers. Planters who could afford the higher purchase price of blacks converted to slavery, and this transition dramatically intensified social stratification. For slavery created a new tier of permanently enslaved blacks at the bottom of the social scale; additionally, it increased economic disparities among whites—by dividing slaveowners from planters who farmed without bound labor.[7]

Also fundamental to the eighteenth-century social order was the growth of

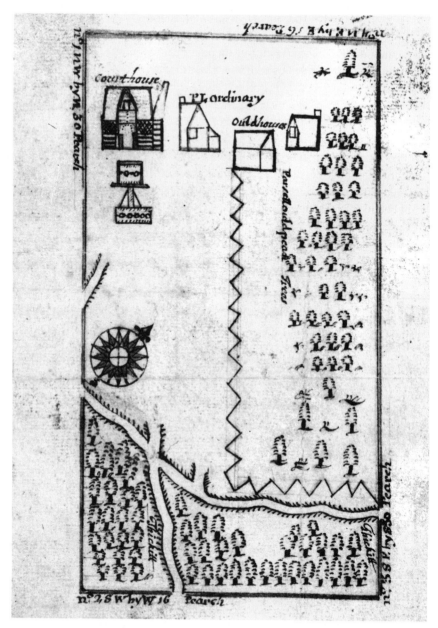

CHARLES COUNTY SCENE, 1697. *The landscape depicted in this rare sketch was typical of the early county. The timber and clapboard courthouse, originally planned as a substantial planter's dwelling, is surrounded by more modest structures, a fenced orchard, and woodland. The site lay inland from the Potomac River and west of Zekiah Swamp. In 1729 the courthouse was abandoned, and the county seat relocated to Chandler Town (later Port Tobacco), at the head of the Port Tobacco River. Charles County Court, Court Records (C658), Lib. V1, fol. 277, Maryland State Archives.*

the gentry to the point where they dominated the political life of the county. Before 1700 their numbers were too small and their lives too brief for them to monopolize the offices that came with government on the English model. Furthermore, few lived long enough to have sons old enough to succeed them in office. Men of lesser means filled the void. But by the third generation, greater longevity and intermarriage among daughters and sons of elite families had created a self-perpetuating squirearchy able to pass its political power, in addition to its status, from one generation to the next.[8]

By then, however, only Protestant gentlemen reaped political gains from their wealth, connections, and social standing. For between 1689 and 1718 Maryland, the only English colony founded as a refuge for Roman Catholics, came under the control of a Protestant Lord Baltimore, accepted an established Church of England, and adopted the legal exclusion of Catholics from officeholding and voting.[9]

Protestant ascendancy, gentry dominance, planters great and small, an economy tied to the production and marketing of tobacco, and the increasing use of slave labor were to characterize Charles County for the remainder of the colonial period. Yet while these conditions were the warp and woof of life, the whole piece of cloth gradually took on patterns that the early immigrants scarcely could have imagined.

CHAPTER ONE

John Elgin's World

In 1769 John Elgin of lower Durham Parish, in the southwestern part of the county, witnessed a will, and beside his name he wrote "1708," the year of his birth. Aged sixty-one and rapidly growing "old and full of Days" by the standards of his time, he had lived through the transition from a roughhewn to a rapidly maturing colonial society. During his threescore years an ever-greater proportion of his neighbors and friends was native-born and thus escaped the hazards of the Atlantic crossing, the seasoning, and, for many whites, long years of servitude. Between 1700 and the Revolution, the county's population increased nearly sixfold, a process Elgin knew well because he kept the register of births in Durham Parish. With four siblings and assorted nieces and nephews living near his plantation, he had seen, in his own family, the development of an extensive kin network upon which people could call for everything from extra hands at harvesttime to a home for an orphaned child. Similar, complicated networks existed throughout the county. During his lifetime, too, the local population became more ethnically diverse, more plantations were seated, and the labor force grew increasingly black. Commerce and marketing arrangements improved. And the country road that passed Elgin's plantation led to a church, tobacco warehouse, market town, and school. In the twilight of his years, he was living in a stable society, one whose economy was prospering within the British scheme of empire.[1]

No one can any longer recount John Elgin's life in great detail, but the extraordinarily rich and revealing documentary records for Charles County allow us to evoke much of the world he knew: the people among whom he passed his days, the landscape his gaze took in, the rituals and rhythms of ordinary life, how he and his neighbors made their livelihoods, and their commercial ties to the empire. The following pages do not present a detailed history of the colonial county. Rather, they are meant to set the stage for the revolutionary period that followed. They allow us to appreciate the full force, and the transforming nature, of revolution and war.

THE PEOPLE

John Elgin's world was inhabited by persons of English, Scottish, Irish, and African heritage. About 90 percent of the county's white population was of English stock. Although an occasional newcomer might portray himself as "banished into the remotest corner of the world amongst Indians, Negroes and Slaves, and separated by the Atlantic from my dearest friends," by the late colonial period most whites were of English ancestry, not nativity, and infrequently spoke of England as "home." Yet English ways surrounded them, from the Book of Common Prayer read at Anglican church services, to the reduced rights that married women suffered under the common law, to county government administered by justices of the peace, sheriffs, and constables.[2]

The Scots were known for their mercantile ways, for Charles County was an integral part of the Scottish marketing system that, by sending agents to America, penetrated and transformed the trade of the Potomac Valley after the 1740s. Like men and women of English blood, Scots were found throughout the white social order, from convict rebels forcibly transported to the colonies after the Battle of Culloden (1746), to a few clergymen, physicians, and merchants who belonged to the elite. Yet in the aggregate the Scots ranked below the English, often faced resentment for their sharp trading practices, and seldom attained high local office as justices of the peace or sheriffs. Then, too, they were sometimes believed slovenly even by the casual hygienic standards of the day. Nicholas Cresswell spoke of "Scotch cleanliness" that would have "disobliged" his stomach had it "been of a squeamish nature."[3]

The Irish, who never constituted more than a few hundred residents, were far below the Scots in social standing, so much so that a local priest once advised a prospective Irish immigrant named Sutton to conceal his nationality. "I do not see his name can hurt him," wrote Father George Hunter, the superior at St. Thomas Manor, "but I fear his Country may as my B[rothe]r tells me he's an Irish-man, therefore if he comes as indeed I hope he will . . . I must begg you'l caution him against discovering his Country." The Irish contributed to the county's substantial Catholic minority.[4]

The ethnic origins of the black population are more obscure than those of the whites for whom they toiled. Yet there is no reason to believe that the pattern deviated from what is known about Maryland as a whole. The province was on the outer rim of the slave trade to the Western Hemisphere and never, so far as has been determined, the recipient of more than a thousand Africans in any single year. The African homeland of most slaves carried to the northern Chesapeake was somewhere in Senegambia, along the Guinea Coast, or, less frequently, in Angola. The trade took up war captives, political adversaries of local rulers, criminals, and, in much larger numbers, victims of organized slaving and excess people during times of famine. Africans themselves procured the slaves, carried them to the coast, and there traded them to Europeans, who dared not enter the interior because the disease environment was lethal to them. Colonial demand and African supply factors accounted for the predominance of males in slave cargoes, for Chesapeake planters wanted male field workers and many African peoples preferred not to export large numbers of women.[5]

By the mid-eighteenth century, most Africans destined for plantations in Charles County left their homeland on ships outward bound from the Gambia River or the Windward and Gold coasts. Weeks later they entered the county via the Potomac and Patuxent rivers. Because slaves experienced their own version of seasoning, which was mildest in warmer months, and because planters wanted to begin working them soon after they were brought ashore, the majority of involuntary immigrants reached Maryland between May and October.[6]

From 1700 to 1775 the number of people in the county increased from twenty-eight hundred to about sixteen thousand. The black population grew more rapidly than the white: Whereas blacks constituted one-fifth of the inhabitants during the decade after 1700, they accounted for two-fifths in 1755 and nearly one-half as of 1775. Notwithstanding continuing influxes of newcomers from Africa and the British Isles, immigrants made up a diminishing proportion of the entire population because natural increase became well established for whites at the beginning of the eighteenth century and for blacks by about 1730. In sum, then, the prerevolutionary population was largely native-born, although Europeans and Africans continued to arrive; featured a white majority, although its proportion of the entire population was gradually declining; and experienced a growth rate for blacks exceeding that of whites.[7]

For most people living during the 1760s and 1770s, these demographic developments meant that the isolation of the early settlements was no more and that kin, neighbors, and friends likely were close at hand. Even recent immigrants—white immigrants at least—found that "The people are remarkably hospitable" and often delighted in introducing newcomers to the "customs and manners" of the country. What kind of welcome newly arrived Africans received at local slave quarters, no one knows.[8]

THE BOUNTIFUL LAND

Hundreds of plantations carried the names of early settlers, places in Great Britain, or Christian saints. Others evoked feelings of hope (Tompkins Long Lookt For, The Widows Venture, Promise), disappointment (Robeys Vexation, Good for Little, Hard Shift), or resignation (All I Cou'd Get, The End of the Scuffle, Perrys Last Chance). Still others stirred memories of human compassion (The Captains Friendship to the Poor Widow) or meanness (Hamill Outwitted, The Orphans Loss). Slightly more than seven hundred people owned land in the county as of 1774, but the number of producing units was greater because of separate quarters, tenancies, and plantations on which parents had settled their children without relinquishing title. Almost everyone—landowning and tenant families, hired hands, slaves, and indentured servants—lived on plantations. Land was the foundation of the economy and a significant indicator of socioeconomic status.[9]

Land also served as a reminder that Maryland was a proprietary province, the possession of an absentee Englishman. With seventeen thousand acres leased to tenants, the incumbent Lord Baltimore was the largest landowner in the county. In addition, he received quitrents on another 251,000 acres in private hands. The rents were small—varying from a few pence to a shilling or two per acre each year—but Marylanders periodically chafed at them because they drained hard currency from the colony. Charles County planters annually emptied their coffers of about £350 sterling when the proprietary collector came by.[10]

Among the private landowners as of 1774, 95 percent held at least 50 acres, the minimum needed for a viable plantation, while 75 percent held more than 100 acres. That pattern had persisted for a generation, suggesting that land distribution had achieved a state of equilibrium notwithstanding sales, gifts, and bequests. If one arbitrarily defines a small plantation as 100 acres or less, a middling one as 101 to 500 acres, and a large one as anything above that size, then three-fifths of the landowners possessed middling plantations. Less than 10 percent of owners had truly extensive holdings of 1,000 acres or more. The largest of these, at 5,200 acres, was owned by the Jesuits of St. Thomas Manor.[11]

Despite the crucial importance of land, Maryland planters never could be sure just where their property lines lay because of what one observer called "the preposterous custom of marking only the beginning tree of the tract." The result, a Marylander once explained to an English correspondent, was as follows:

> Our boundaries are perpetually fluctuating: this I know will seem strange, but the fact is really so—we are permitted to have but one fixed boundary at the beginning of each tract of land, from there we run such a course & so many perches & so on as many courses & distances as will include the quantity we choose to take up, always closing the survey with this expression, then with a straight line to the beginning; the [compass] needle by which all our courses are directed being subject to a continual variation, the courses must also vary, and there being but one given boundary, the exterior lines of our lands are constantly shifting.

Since no one knew the rate at which the earth's magnetism caused the compass needle to deviate from due north over the years, the original survey of any tract could never be duplicated. Thus "it happens not seldom that a survey new-made after a good many years cuts off from the neighbor's plantation a piece of arable and tilled land, giving him instead, at some other corner, a piece of woods . . . or swamp land or other barren strip."[12]

Nor was variation of the compass the only problem. The single fixed point in a survey might vanish if the original boundary tree decayed or was felled. Another problem was the irregular shape of many tracts, since land warrants specified only the number of acres to be patented, not their configuration. Patentees therefore attempted to engross the best land, even if oddly shaped plantations resulted. To complicate matters further, the original surveys were not always accurate, and a landowner might be ignorant of the number of acres he or she actually possessed. In one case, that of Poynton Manor on Nanjemoy Creek, the confusion lasted more than a century. Originally granted in 1658 to William Stone, the first Protestant governor of Maryland, the tract was supposed to contain 5,000 acres. Stone willed what he thought were 2,900 acres to his eldest son, but a resurvey in 1666 indicated that the legacy came to only 1,400 acres. Several generations later the size of Poynton Manor remained uncertain, for a resurvey in 1783 showed that a section supposedly containing 1,000 acres actually amounted to 1,736.[13]

County residents therefore lived on plantations that had just one fixed survey point apiece, that often were irregularly shaped and sometimes of uncertain size, and whose original borders could not be verified because of the variation of the compass. Under such circumstances, "discords" and lawsuits over boundaries sometimes occurred, and they contributed to the "litigious spirit" for which the province was known.[14] Nonetheless, what seems remarkable are the measures people took to preserve boundary markings and the infrequency with which one neighbor sued another. People did the best they could with an archaic, ill-conceived system of land survey.

To begin with, they tried to designate their plantation lines with several boundary trees, and to do so as permanently as nature would allow. Said one resident to another: "If this tree Should Stand a hundred year[s] these marks which you See on the tree will be Seen." Once trees were marked, inhabitants tried to preserve them and, if they disappeared, to replace them with stones or wooden posts. John Ensey and his brother were raccoon hunting one night and saw something in a tree, "and in order to get their game Set the tree on fire and burnt it down when they went home they Informed their father of what they had done and he Said twas well if they had not burnt the bound tree of Sanders Land." After daybreak Ensey discovered that his sons indeed had destroyed the boundary tree, and he immediately ordered them to build a pile of stones in its place.[15]

As people went about their daily activities—clearing new ground, building a road, hunting, searching the woods for livestock, riding to a reaping—it was not unusual for one person to turn to another and point to or touch a boundary marker. By the time children reached their teens, they were instructed on the location of plantation lines. "Ever since he was a Lad," a sixty-four-year-old man recalled, he had frequently been told that a certain red oak designated the beginning of a neighbor's property. Nor could the Ensey brothers soon forget that when they were boys, their father took them to a boundary tree, "and Francis Green being in Company said the Boys had better be Whiped[.] Mr. Chandler answered they had better Give em a Dram which he did and told em to remember that . . . the tree was the Second bound tree of his the said Chandlers Land."[16]

Despite such neighborly attention and concern, markers nevertheless decayed unobserved in the woods or were destroyed, as when a boundary tree was "worked up in Coopers Timber." If memory also failed, then property lines grew "precarious" or were lost, as John Elgin's father experienced firsthand. When asked to identify the bounds of his own plantation, he could not; nor could anyone he asked. In such circumstances a landowner's usual recourse was to petition the county court and request "a Commission to Perpetuate the memory of the bounds of the . . . Land." The court thereupon appointed at least two substantial planters to conduct an inquiry. They in turn posted notices at the parish church and other public places throughout the county, which stipulated a time when citizens could come to the land-owner's property, attest to their knowledge of its borders, and witness the placing of new markers.[17]

So it was that, on a winter's day in 1776, twenty-five men gathered where three tracts of land came together. Only memory guided them. An elderly man recalled that thirty years earlier he had been shown "a White Oake standing . . . about five yards from the Main Road . . . on a level near the head of a valley," and he remembered seeing another boundary tree at the crest of a hill. Stones were seated where the man thought the trees had stood. The survey lines, if not restored with complete accuracy, at least were settled to the landowners' satisfaction, and costly litigation was avoided. Remembering boundary markers, and testifying to their location when need arose, were valuable acts of neighborliness in Charles County.[18]

The quality and use of the land whose boundaries caused such concern varied from one plantation to another, depending on location, soils, and hus-bandry. Soils ranged from some that "with good Husbandry would last for ever" to others that seemed "but indifferent," according to late colonial

1735 BOUNDARY STONE MARKING "THE END OF THE 5TH COURSE OF GREENWEIGH." *This stone and several others marked the lines of Greenweigh plantation, which is on the Potomac River in northwestern Charles County. Courtesy of J. Richard Rivoire.*

travelers. Much of the best acreage, and the most valuable plantations, lay adjacent to the rivers and navigable creeks. Land along the Potomac was "good and Strong," its "Rich & Sandy" soils devoted to tobacco and grain cultivation. Equally valuable were the light soils adjacent to Nanjemoy Creek and, in the eastern sector of the county, the "black & good" soils beside the Wicomico and Patuxent rivers and Zekiah Swamp. In the southeastern tip of the county, an observant newcomer found "a kind of dry earth mixt with a great deal of clay as small as flower and thickest of any thing I can compare it to . . . it produces wheat very well." Inland, many tracts contained middling mixtures of sand and clay, sometimes interlaced with stones, but bottomlands might be "very rich land" because they were catch basins for topsoil from the surrounding terrain. The worst soils were stiff, "mean," and "full of gullies," and while tenant farms were not inevitably inferior, Lord Baltimore's acreage was among the least desirable. Once it had "been good, kind Land," but long occupancy and lack of care had rendered hundreds of acres "So poor that the People who live near it say they wou'd not give one/ [shilling] p hundred [acres] Rent for it."[19]

The earliest white settlers in the county had come upon nearly unbroken forests generously endowed with hardwoods—red, white, and Spanish oak, tulip, hickory, and beech. By the Revolution the landscape was dotted with croplands and meadows, orchards and woodlots. People constantly cut timber to fuel their hearths and to build their houses and outbuildings, their rail fences, and the hogsheads and barrels in which they shipped their commodities to market. Most plantations retained substantial woodlots, but owners, aware of a dwindling resource, often tried to conserve timber for their own use, rather than sale, and to cut as much as possible in swamps. Newly cleared land usually was planted in tobacco, which was notorious for depriving the soil of nutrients. Working oystershells into the earth improved its fertility, but when yields declined after successive tobacco crops, planters sowed corn or wheat and, later, allowed their "old fields" to revert to scrub and woodland until fertility was restored. Then the agricultural cycle began anew. This long-fallow method of cultivation was ecologically sound but imparted an unkempt look to parts of the landscape.[20]

Much of the rhythm of life was tied to the unending cycles of planting and cultivation, harvest, and consumption or marketing of the land's bounty. As planters reckoned the passage of time, Christmas Day marked the end of one year and the beginning of the next. On December 25 many a worker's wage or a tenant's rent was paid, many a slave's contract for hire begun or completed, and many a plantation changed hands, its vacating occupants having had time to harvest their crops and ready them for market.[21]

More than any other single factor, the tobacco cycle paced the tempo of

life. Oronoco tobacco was sown in beds in early spring, then transplanted to the fields in late May or June. When Nicholas Cresswell watched the process at a plantation near Nanjemoy in 1774, he discovered that "the Land is first hoed into small round hills about the size of Molehills and about 4000 of them in an acre." Taking seedlings that "are something like small Cabbage plants," field hands "make a hole with their fingers or a small stick and put them in, one in each hill. Two Negroes will plant three acres in one day." Thus they performed their monotonous tasks twelve thousand times between dawn and dusk. And that was merely the beginning, for tobacco cultivation required regular weeding, deworming, and suckering from June through harvesttime in late summer. Workers spent long hours under the Chesapeake sun, each with only a hoe to turn the soil and a sharp thumbnail to remove suckers from the plants. The intensity of effort involved meant that a single person usually produced no more than a thousand pounds per year, so that substantial profits in tobacco came only through harnessing the labor of others, whether slaves, servants, hired hands, or wives and children. In September, after the plants had begun drying in the field, they were cut and then cured for several weeks in tobacco houses. Finally, leaf was stripped from stalk and packed, or prized, into hogsheads for shipment overseas, a process that continued through the winter. October was "the dealing time," when planters and merchants haggled over what the year's crop would bring.[22]

Tobacco made the Chesapeake the jewel of the British Empire because the mother country derived more revenue from it than from any other colonial commodity. Yet the region's agricultural economy was considerably more diverse than the term "Tobacco Coast" implied, and to this generalization Charles County was no exception. Bounty from the land fed and partially clothed the growing population, provisioned ships drawn to the Potomac and Patuxent, put grain and meat on West Indian tables, and seeded Irish fields

(facing page) SARUM. *The oldest surviving plantation house in Charles County, Sarum is of great architectural interest because it documents the evolution of building design and carpentry techniques in eighteenth-century Maryland. Scientifically dated to 1717, the original structure (top) features a high-pitched roof, stair tower, and gabled dormers, which are reminiscent of English styles. Materials included riven oak clapboards and chestnut shingles. About 1760 the original structure was incorporated into a much-enlarged house, in the attic of which the 1717 roof framing remains visible (longitudinal section). Shortly thereafter a shed-roofed porch was added across the front, giving Sarum the appearance shown in this early-twentieth-century photograph. The house is on the north side of the Wicomico River. Drawings by J. Richard Rivoire. Photograph courtesy of the Maryland Historical Society.*

with flax. In addition to tobacco, plantations produced cereal crops and legumes, vegetables and fruits, livestock and dairy products, hides, and fiber—wool, flax, and even cotton. For the diligent, work was never done, no matter what the season of the year.[23]

The growing cycles of cereal crops—wheat, corn, oats, rye, and barley—complemented that of tobacco. Wheat, for instance, was harvested about the beginning of July, after the time-consuming task of setting out tobacco seedlings was finished. Oats ripened shortly after the wheat, tobacco in September, Indian corn about the beginning of October. Whereas tobacco cultivation was done by hand, some planters used horses to plow their grain crops.[24]

Much of the grain produced in the county was consumed locally. Indian corn, the most plentiful, grew "as high as a man and as thick as one's Shackle bone and generally [with] three heads each of which is about six or eight inches long." Made into hasty pudding laced with pig fat or fried as cakes,

JOHNSONTOWN BARN. *In such structures planters dried newly harvested tobacco until it was ready to be packed into hogsheads and moved to a public warehouse for inspection and storage until export. This late-eighteenth-century tobacco barn, enlarged ca. 1818, exhibits seventeenth- and eighteenth-century construction techniques. Reflecting the increasing importance of grain production in Charles County, the building had a wooden floor used for threshing. Since this picture was taken, the barn was dismantled and later reassembled in St. Mary's County. Courtesy of J. Richard Rivoire.*

cornmeal constituted a dietary staple for "the lower rank of people," both poor whites and slaves. An immigrant alleged, however, that corn mush was so incompatible "with an English constitution" that local residents "never pretend to offer it" to recently arrived whites.[25]

Only "those that have got Estates" served bread made from wheat. This grain was not more plentiful locally for several reasons: It was readily marketed in the West Indies; insects reduced yields; "of late years a distemper they call the rust sometimes seises and withers it all . . . before it gets ripe"; and if Nicholas Cresswell's observation of one plantation was generally true, Charles County planters were wasteful, at least when judged against the intensive cultivation practices he was familiar with in England. "Went to see them reap Wheat," he wrote in his journal. "The greatest slovens I ever saw, believe that one fourth part is left on the Field uncut. Some . . . mow it with sticks fixed on the scythe in parallel lines to lay the grain straight. This makes worse havoc than the reapers." Cresswell pronounced local planters' wheat "but indifferent and their crop very light, seldom that they get seven bushels from an acre, but they put it into the ground in such a slovenly manner without any manure, it is a wonder that they get any." Whatever the quality of the husbandry, large plantations, using slave labor, produced substantial crops. For example, in July 1774, the same month when Cresswell watched the reaping, a few plantations between the Wicomico and Potomac rivers reportedly marketed over six thousand bushels of wheat.[26]

People either ground their grain by hand or carried it to one of several mills. The "Great Mill" near Port Tobacco, established before 1715, was run by the Jesuits. Perhaps the largest operation, at least in the 1760s, was Benjamin Fendall's. On a dam at the head of the Wicomico River, he operated three mills equipped with large stones "of the best *Cullen* Grit"; a sixteen-by-thirty-foot brick bakehouse in which "the Hearth of the Oven is laid with fine Stone from *Britain*, and draws 150 wt. [pounds] of Ship Bread at a Draft, and bakes extremely well"; a kiln for drying malt; a two-story granary; and houses for a miller and a baker. The site, Fendall explained, was "the most convenient Place" for ships "to take in their Bread."[27]

On soils ill suited for grain or tobacco, "plenty of fine Orchards" were planted. Peach trees were common, probably because they bore fruit even on the poorest land. Some orchards yielded so abundantly that hogs were fed "with peaches that would sell very dear" in English markets. An impression of the frequency and variety of fruit-bearing trees can be gleaned from descriptions of the plantations belonging to eighteen underage orphans, which were filed with the local orphans' court between 1777 and 1782. On their estates stood some thirty-six hundred fruit trees, primarily apple and peach but also cherry, pear, and damson plum. People pressed the fruit into cider, the "Common Country Drink," and they also turned it into bunnell (made from the mash that remained after extracting the juice), brandy, and vinegar. The brandy distilled from lower Western Shore peaches and aged five or six years reputedly surpassed "every other kind of ardent spirits, in the delicacy of its flavour. Many people prefer it to the best Jamaica spirits, or Cogniac brandy."[28]

Meat, fish, and fowl were available in variety and abundance in the fields and forests and from the rivers and streams. Livestock both supplied important dietary protein and was shipped to the West Indies. Wildlife abounded. Cresswell spent a day in February 1775 shooting wild ducks and geese, "of which there is incredible numbers. I am told 60 ducks have been killed at one shot." He also dined on roast swan, which he found to be "black, but eats very well." Father Joseph Mosley described plentiful supplies of deer, wild turkeys, raccoons, and squirrels, as well as possums that were "the fatest animal in winter on the face of the earth, and at that time fine eating." Pheasants, hawks, partridges, and eagles, too, thrived in the county. Mosley said that an eagle kept in the garden at St. Thomas Manor was "as big, if not bigger than myself: it will kill any dog that attacks it." Edible aquatic life— turtles, fish, crabs, and oysters—added to the bounty of the land. The Potomac River, for example, was filled with "excellent fish of many different kinds, as sturgeon, shad, roach, herrings, &c. which form a very principal part of the food of the people living in the neighborhood." A traveler who crossed the river in the 1790s claimed that "in a very few minutes" the ferrymen gathered nearly a bushel of succulent oysters from a bank lying off the county.[29]

In addition to producing foodstuffs, tobacco, and timber, plantations yielded leather, which was turned into shoes, and fiber—wool, flax, and cotton—which was spun and knitted or woven into country cloth. Surpluses of these and other commodities were exchanged locally, forming an important domestic economy.[30] But for many manufactured items, households turned to nearby stores stacked with European imports. For just as they were a planting people, the inhabitants of Charles County were a trading people.

TRANSATLANTIC COMMERCE

In 1733, when the Chesapeake was mired in one of the periodic depressions that plagued the tobacco trade, Governor Samuel Ogle reported that Maryland's commerce was "greatly Decay'd," nearly at a standstill, and that planters had not found a viable export crop to replace tobacco. "The Inhab[ita]nts still supply themselves with what Manufactures are needful for them f[ro]m

G: Britain only, so far as they can possibly find means to purchase the same," he informed British officials, "but the exceeding Poverty of the People in general, occasion'd by the low price of Tobaco, hath driven the poor Familys to make some few course Woollens & Linnens, to cloath themselves, without which they must go naked." Not only was commerce stagnant, but marketing arrangements had advanced little since the early days of English settlement. Throughout the province most import-export trade involved direct transactions between ship and shoreline. That is, a ship or servicing craft moved from one plantation landing to another, discharging European manufactures and taking on hogsheads of tobacco for the return Atlantic voyage.[31]

After the 1730s the county's external trade grew more diverse and, on balance, more prosperous. Commerce became quite centralized because import merchants established stores and coincidentally fostered town life and also because after 1747 planters were required to take their leaf to a public warehouse for inspection and storage until shipment. Thereafter most transactions were conducted at the market towns of Port Tobacco, Benedict, Newport, and Nanjemoy, each of which had an inspection warehouse nearby; at warehouses on Chicamuxen and Pomonkey creeks; and at Cedar Point. While tobacco remained the prime export crop, a valuable trade in foodstuffs developed with the sugar islands of the West Indies. By the 1760s Charles County, like Maryland generally, teemed with trade. Furthermore, a vibrant, expanding merchant community ranged from resident factors, or agents, of Scottish tobacco firms to a handful of men who were reaching for greater commercial independence and prosperity within the British Empire.[32]

Every ship trading anywhere along the north shore of the Potomac River had to register and subsequently clear for departure at the provincial Naval Office on Cedar Point. Lying some forty-five miles above the river's mouth, the point is the first place where the Potomac narrows significantly, to a width of about two miles. Because of convenient ship anchorage and ferries that carried people over the river, the area had long been a center of trade. Many slaves, indentured servants, and convicts were first exposed to sale from the decks of vessels riding at anchor off the point. There, too, ships took on provisions and cargo. Most then moved on to towns and warehouses upriver, while others dropped down to the mouth of the Wicomico River and entered it to trade.[33]

The largest of the county's market towns was Port Tobacco, which contemporary maps rightly depicted as a threshold along the Tobacco Coast. The busiest river port on the Maryland side of the Potomac, Port Tobacco was known as the "County-Town" because of the many services it afforded the public. On or adjacent to the public square, people bartered produce at the marketplace, worshiped at Port Tobacco Church, registered deeds and wills at the courthouse, and watched country justice meted out at the jail, the whipping post, and the gallows. Radiating from the square were St. Andrew's and St. George's streets, constant reminders of the crosses of St. Andrew and St. George on the British national flag. Bordering the square, and along streets strewn with oystershells that lessened the mire when it rained, stood dwellings and merchants' and artisans' shops. These buildings in turn were surrounded by an assortment of fences, gardens, kitchens, storehouses, and other outbuildings. Through the nearby inspection warehouse, the largest in the county, annually passed at least a thousand hogsheads, containing more than a million pounds of tobacco, during the late 1760s. It was shipped to Britain, France, Holland, and Russia.[34]

Although Port Tobacco never grew large, as early as the 1740s it boasted several inns, a goldsmith's shop, and even a brewery with a kiln and a two-story, sixty-foot-long malthouse. By the 1750s, when approximately seventy people resided in the town, some of them asked the General Assembly to pass a law "to prevent Fires being made in wooden Chimneys, in Houses situated near Store-Houses and public Buildings" and also to prohibit swine and geese from being raised within the town limits. And a resident staymaker advertised wares of the latest fashion as well as workmanship unsurpassed "by any Master Stay-maker now in Being."[35]

Twenty years later, in the early 1770s, Port Tobacco was busier than at any other time during the colonial period. In addition to the courthouse, the "pretty Church of Free stone with an Organ in it," and the tobacco warehouse, the streets were lined with twenty to thirty dwellings, most of them one-story structures. Weary travelers and local planters in search of food and drink, a game of cards, and fodder for their horses could choose from half a dozen ordinaries, or tippling houses, whose proprietors were legally bound not to "Suffer Idle loose or disorderly Persons to Tipple Game or Commit other Disorders or Irregularities." The ordinaries had their drawbacks. One guest complained in 1774 that "For company all the night in my Room I had Bugs in every part of my Bed—& in the next Room several noisy Fellows playing at Billiards." Although furnishing bed and board was the primary purpose of the town's ordinaries, planters also found them convenient places for auctioning off a parcel of slaves or a tract of land.[36]

Most of the town's trade was conducted elsewhere, in the artisans' shops and merchants' stores. Port Tobacco seems never to have supported an extensive settled community of craftsmen, which made it a typical southern country town. Thus one could not be sure that a goldsmith, clock and watch repairman, or staymaker, having opened a business, would still be in residence when needed later. Import-export merchants were another matter, for by the 1770s at least eight, and probably more, operated stores. John Glassford and

Company, the largest Scottish firm trading to the Chesapeake, had its Maryland headquarters in the town, as did John Semple and Company, another Scottish firm. To their stores, and the others, came what must have been an unending stream of men and women, for on their ledgers the merchants of Port Tobacco carried the accounts of hundreds of persons.[37]

In 1771, apparently with the aim of siphoning off some of the town's commerce, Father George Hunter announced that "at the Request and for the Convenience of the Inhabitants of Charles County," he had drawn up a plan for a new town. It would be named Edenburgh, in honor of the proprietary governor, Sir Robert Eden, and would be located on St. Thomas Manor near the mouth of the Port Tobacco River. But the merchants and innkeepers of Port Tobacco, a mile or so upriver, need not have worried. Questions arose as to whether Hunter could alienate land granted to the Roman Catholic Church, and the provincial Assembly refused his petition for such authority. Edenburgh remained a cornfield.[38]

Within a ten-mile radius of Port Tobacco were two smaller towns. Newport, on Pile's Fresh, which drained into the Wicomico River, served the county's southeastern corner, while Nanjemoy, "a small Village of about five houses, all Planters except Knox and Bayley, who keep a store," drew people from the area west of Port Tobacco. Small as it was, Nanjemoy boasted a "famous and notable Ship Harbour." These three towns, from whose warehouses more than two million pounds of tobacco were shipped annually, were part of the Potomac Valley trade network.[39]

Benedict, the second-largest town in the county, was nestled in the Patuxent river valley. Lying nineteen miles due east of Port Tobacco, Benedict had at least three sizable stores and was the commercial center for the county's northeastern sector. European and East Indian goods "much too tedious to particularize" filled merchants' shelves, and through the inspection warehouse passed some of the best tobacco grown on the lower Western Shore. Every year about seven hundred hogsheads were exported.[40]

In the organization of its trade, Charles County was the Chesapeake in microcosm. All principal trading arrangements found in the region were evident in the county by the 1760s and 1770s, which indicated the increasing vitality, diversity, and competitiveness of the local export economy. Large planters might correspond directly with British commission merchants to whom they consigned their tobacco for sale and who, in return, filled orders for goods and extended credit, all for a fee, of course. The majority of planters, however, turned to local marketing facilities, to indigenous merchants or to stores owned and operated by Scottish mercantile firms. Lines of trade linked the county to the West Indies, Africa, the European continent, and the British Isles. However they traded, white families were participating in what has

RIDGATE (CHIMNEY) HOUSE
(CA. 1770). *Overlooking the town square at Port Tobacco, the house served as both home and store for merchant Thomas Howe Ridgate and is thought to be the oldest surviving commercial structure in the county. Courtesy of J. Richard Rivoire.*

MAXWELL HALL
(CA. 1768). *George Maxwell (d. 1777), a Scottish immigrant who became a successful Chesapeake merchant, built the house on the proprietary manor of Calverton and lived there with his wife, Elizabeth, and their children. Standing above the Patuxent River near the town of Benedict, the house is comparable to those of other local merchants and planters of similar status. Photograph by John M. Wearmouth. Courtesy of the Southern Maryland Studies Center, Charles County Community College.*

been called an "empire of goods," which presented them with a wide array of consumer items and contributed generally to a rising standard of living in the late colonial Chesapeake.[41]

The 1771 voyage of the ship *Molly* exemplified much about the operations of Scottish firms. When the *Molly* slipped down the Clyde and out to sea that year, it was bound for the Potomac with a cargo consigned to George Gray of Port Tobacco, a factor for Jamieson Johnston and Company. The company was one of many Glasgow firms that, after 1740, brought to the Potomac Valley the most efficient marketing system in the colonial Chesapeake. Through chains of stores located along the river and its tributaries, resident factors bought tobacco and sold imported goods for their firms and, in the process, redirected a lot of trade from England to Scotland. Several circumstances contributed to their success: large-scale credit and marketing facilities in Scotland, especially Glasgow; the Scots' ability to supply oronoco tobacco to the French market; their willingness to advance credit, which attracted many small planters to their stores; and savings in operating costs gained by buying tobacco in advance, which reduced the turnaround time of merchant vessels.[42]

The Scots attempted to correlate the flow of goods with the price and demand for tobacco. When the *Molly* reached the Potomac in 1771, for example, the Chesapeake economy was booming, and George Gray learned that his store soon would be cluttered with merchandise imported in about fifty barrels, bales, and casks. The large cargo he received that year carried an invoice value of £1,597 sterling, including freightage and insurance. In other years, when the demand for leaf slackened, Jamieson Johnston and Company sent him much smaller cargoes.[43]

The 1771 shipment also underscored the colonial nature of the Charles County economy: It consisted entirely of European manufactured goods, nearly all of which would be exchanged for just one agricultural commodity, tobacco. The shipment included over eighteen thousand yards of cloth. Ticking would be sewn into feather bed mattresses and pillows; Irish linen, Holland and Glasgow cloth, osnaburg, and printed cotton would be fashioned into clothing and household furnishings; and fine garments could be made from lawn and cambric, sewn and adorned with newly arrived thread, stays, ribbons, buttons, and lace. Several thousand yards of coarse German cloth probably was destined for the backs of slaves. In ready-made apparel there were stockings, handkerchiefs, gloves, felt hats for men and boys, and black satin hats for women and girls. People would keep their records and conduct correspondence with the ledgers, paper, ink, and two thousand quills in the shipment. When the box containing books was uncrated, they would purchase spellers, primers, histories, and *Aesop's Fables*, in addition to assorted testa-

SAMUEL HANSON (1716–94) and ANN HAWKINS HANSON (1726–ca. 73). *The fine fabrics and lace shown in these matched portraits almost certainly were imported from Europe and exemplify the increasing use of consumer goods during the late colonial period. When the portraits were painted in 1765, Samuel Hanson was a merchant, planter, and county court justice. The couple lived at Greenhill plantation, about three miles north of Port Tobacco, and belonged to one of the county's most prominent gentry families. Samuel's brother Walter (1712–94) also was a county court justice, while another brother, John Hanson, Jr. (1721–83), served as president of the Continental Congress in 1781–82. Artist: John Hesselius. Courtesy of the Corcoran Gallery of Art, bequest of Gertrude B. Merritt in memory of Juliana Hanson Bibb.*

ments, prayer books, and Bibles. Some customers would also ride with new saddles, bridles, and whips, buy metal spoons, teakettles, and brass candlesticks for their tables, and add new hoes, garden spades, rope, twine, and nails to their plantation equipment.[44]

Dealing at a Scottish-owned store offered planters several advantages. Credit and merchandise usually were immediately available, and they were relieved of further risk and expense in bringing their tobacco to market. Therefore, when ice cut through the hull of the Glasgow ship *Susanna* in January 1749 and it sank off Nanjemoy with 219 hogsheads on board, planters who had sold their leaf to Scottish factors were not out a shilling. Likewise, those who traded locally need not worry about losing a year's work to Atlantic storms or, during the many years when England and France were at war, capture on the open sea. They also avoided shipment, insurance, and storage charges, which could easily equal the purchase price. If buyers in Maryland paid "dear" for leaf, only to have overseas markets decline before it reached Europe, then buyers, not planters, took the loss. So, too, when Chesapeake producers glutted the market and tobacco could not be reexported from Scotland "at any price as there is more made than all Europe can consume." For all these reasons, many planters were willing to accept Chesapeake tobacco prices that frequently were lower than those in Britain. Given the credit arrangements that underpinned the trade, planters also frequently ran up debts, usually small debts, at factors' stores. In good times, such as the late 1760s and early 1770s, they could reasonably hope that the next crop would enable them to settle their accounts.[45]

To hedge against losses and turn a profit for their firms, Scottish factors strove to buy tobacco low and sell their goods high, decided whether settling debts "in Tobacco or Currency will be most for our Int[e]rest," and attempted to manipulate the exchange rate between British sterling and Maryland tobacco or currency. Such practices hardly endeared them to the local citizenry. James Lawson, a Glasgow merchant, once told Alexander Hamilton, a young Scotsman who entered Charles County about 1760, that "I greatly approve . . . of your Settling our Mary[lan]d debts in [provincial] Currency at 150 p Cent advance upon the Sterling Cost . . . As it is highly probable the Exchange will fall rather than rise after this." He also detailed how the factor's real cost of tobacco could be lowered by raising planters' costs for merchandise by 25 percent, then warned Hamilton that "In case this calculation should be Seen and do you any hurt, please destroy this letter or tear it [the calculation] away."[46]

On another occasion Lawson claimed that invoices he sent to Charles County were inflated with bogus insurance charges: "As to the Insurance of your goods p the Nancy . . . there was none made for you tho I mentioned it at the foot of the Invoice that was only to Show the Charges that in case you had Sold them by the Invoice the buyer would have seen that charge—I do the same with all the Invoices I send." With no apparent realization of the incongruity of his remarks, Lawson subsequently assured Hamilton that to cheat him "would in my opinion [have] been an unpardonable Sin."[47]

Planters who neither dealt with Scottish factors nor corresponded directly with British merchants could transact their business with independent local traders. Almost to a man, they enjoyed an advantage the Scottish factors could not match: Through birth or marriage they belonged to the county's elite. Most were planters and slaveowners as well as merchants, and their activities signaled the maturing of the colonial economy. They forged connections with British firms, amassed capital to expand their operations, and traded to the West Indies and across the Atlantic.[48]

Philip Richard Fendall of Port Tobacco and James Forbes of Benedict operated a modified form of the consignment system as independent agents for James Russell. In the 1760s Russell headed the largest London firm trading to Maryland and was thoroughly acquainted with the lower Western Shore. Having emigrated about 1730 from Scotland to Maryland, he subsequently married remarkably well. His wife, Ann, was the daughter of Philip Lee of Charles County, an influential member of the governor's Council and the naval officer for the entire north shore of the Potomac River. Through his marriage to Ann, therefore, Russell gained access to the highest levels of the plantation society. He prospered, then about 1753 moved his family to London and became a commission merchant. But instead of corresponding directly with planters, he worked through a few merchants like Fendall and Forbes, his principal agents on the Potomac and Patuxent rivers, respectively. They persuaded planters to consign their tobacco to Russell, took orders for manufactures, and oversaw his ships when they were in Chesapeake waters. For these services Russell paid his agents commissions and advanced them credit.[49]

Whereas Russell came to the Chesapeake, prospered, and left, another Scotsman, George Maxwell, settled permanently at Benedict and by the 1760s had built a complicated trading empire. He had stores in Benedict and Annapolis, on the upper Patuxent, and across Chesapeake Bay on Maryland's Eastern Shore. Besides exporting large amounts of tobacco, he owned three vessels in partnership with the Glasgow firm of Buchanan and Simson, was a minor partner in slaving voyages that the firm organized, and imported African slaves.[50]

Maxwell and Russell each experimented with the cargo system, an innovation that became somewhat common as oceanic commerce expanded dramatically and also grew more competitive after the Seven Years' War ended in 1763. Essentially the cargo system was a reverse of the traditional consignment trade, in which planters shipped their tobacco to Britain and waited for payment in goods. With the cargo system, an English or Scottish merchant first consigned goods to the Chesapeake, then waited to be paid. A Marylander like Maxwell ordered merchandise from his British correspondent, who, functioning as a wholesaler, obtained the items on credit from the manufacturer and shipped them to America. The Chesapeake merchant was supposed to sell the cargo and remit tobacco or bills of exchange before the British correspondent and manufacturer settled their accounts. The entire process usually took twelve to fifteen months.[51]

Just as Maxwell's mercantile success caused him to look beyond Charles County, in his case to Annapolis and the Eastern Shore, other local merchants did the same. Perhaps none more successfully enlarged their sphere of operations than Daniel of St. Thomas Jenifer, Robert Townshend Hooe, and Frederick Stone, who eventually entered a partnership. Jenifer began his mercantile career in the county and by the 1760s had expanded his horizons to Annapolis, where he solicited tobacco for Glasgow, Liverpool, and London markets, imported fine clothing and fabrics, and sold slaves and indentured servants. About 1765 he formed a trading partnership with his nephew Frederick Stone, who soon was transacting business at Port Tobacco and Annapolis, selling West Indian rum, and offering the ship *Jenifer*, of two hundred tons burden, for charter to any European port. After 1768 Stone and Hooe carried on extensive importing activities as Hooe, Stone and Company. Jenifer joined the firm in 1771.[52]

When Jenifer looked beyond the county for widening opportunities in the early 1760s, he logically set his sights on Annapolis, Maryland's busy capital. In the early 1770s Frederick Stone and Robert Townshend Hooe looked in an opposite direction, upriver from the county, to Alexandria, Virginia. Located near the Great Falls of the Potomac and accessible to the largest sailing vessels of the day, Alexandria was better situated than any other town on the river for marketing large amounts of grain grown in the Virginia backcountry. At Alexandria, Hooe, Stone and Company operated a store and shipped flour and barreled pork to Barbados. In Port Tobacco the firm traded mostly for tobacco. Thus, by maintaining stores in both places, the partners were nicely situated to profit from the principal agricultural products of the Chesapeake. Their imported merchandise came in cargoes consigned by Osgood Hanbury and Company, an affluent and well-established London firm.[53]

When Hanbury shipped Hooe, Stone and Company goods worth £565 sterling in 1770, the invoice carried additional charges amounting to £71 for packaging, freight, shipping, customs fees, insurance, and Hanbury's commission. On the eve of the Revolution a handful of Maryland merchants moved to London with the intention of eliminating the British supplier, and his commission, from their trading connections. This step carried several potential advantages: The colonials might live in England for less than the commissions they had been paying, would personally select and contract for merchandise, and hoped to establish direct banking connections in London. Still, it was a risky venture because American traders could not match the capital and credit resources of their large British competitors and were less capable of riding out a severe depression. To prosper, they needed to conduct a sufficient volume of business and receive timely payment for the goods they dispatched to Maryland. And it remained to be seen how effectively they could deal with the linendrapers and ironmongers whose wares they sought.[54]

Two merchants who decided that the potential rewards justified the risks were John Barnes and Thomas Howe Ridgate of Charles County. Barnes began trading in 1764 with financial backing from his father, a prominent merchant and legislator from St. Mary's County. Within five years he formed a partnership with Ridgate, who had emigrated from England. Like Hooe, Stone and Company, they were well situated: They tapped the tobacco trade at their stores in Port Tobacco and Benedict and the grain trade at another store in Georgetown, Maryland, at the Great Falls of the Potomac. The two men also imported slaves direct from Africa and sold them on the Patuxent and Potomac rivers. By "moderate calculation," according to Ridgate, who was inclined to exaggeration, the firm annually shipped eight thousand hogsheads of tobacco and imported goods worth £12,000 to £14,000 wholesale.[55]

In August 1771 Ridgate, with £4,000 cash in hand, set himself up as a merchant in London. The time seemed propitious, for he found "not a Cold H[ogs]h[ea]d in London[,] its bought as soon as it arrives." Confident that "our concern is too large to be trifled with" and that "its in my power by settling here to make our concern very Valueable & in a course of years . . . make a Fortune," Ridgate seemed to have boundless aspirations. He wanted to expand operations to Virginia and perhaps the Eastern Shore of Maryland, cut out Scottish competitors, buy tobacco outright if necessary but preferably have planters consign it to him, and transport it in ships owned by Barnes and Ridgate. In return, he intended to select the cargoes of goods he sent out to the Chesapeake, have a stake in several slaving voyages each year, and deal in West Indian sugar and rum. To help him realize his far-flung goals, he hoped to forge a profitable connection with a London mercantile house. He kept his plans to remain in London secret lest he provoke opposition from British competitors, and he fully expected, in the autumn of 1771, that the venture would succeed. In a letter written to a Charles County merchant, Ridgate boasted that "I know every buyer of Tob[acco] & every branch of the Trade as well as any of the Houses here & I find our Credit here as good as the best[,] every Tradesman trusted us for the Goods with as much pleasure and satisfaction as they would any persons whatever."[56]

Although Ridgate's aspirations and optimism exceeded that of other Charles County merchants—as his address on Bishopsgate Street, London, attested—they, like he, had cause to feel expansive that fall. They had never known better tobacco markets, trade with the West Indies was growing, and the British Empire was at peace. For customers who patronized the merchants, the state of the county's economy meant good prices for their tobacco and grain, ready buyers, easy credit, and stores brimming with goods from beyond the sea.

CHAPTER TWO

Degrees of Freedom

ENGLISH PEOPLE WHO SETTLED THE CHESAPEAKE BROUGHT WITH THEM complementary concepts about the nature of human society, and these profoundly shaped the social order and promoted stability in Charles County. The first concept was centuries old in Western culture and envisioned societies as hierarchically organized—that is, people occupied different ranks or levels extending from the lowliest slave woman to the most powerful gentleman. The second condoned the practice of some people holding property rights in others. Slaves and servants were a "species" of property, to use the contemporary term, because they were bought and sold and because the fruits of their labor belonged to their masters. Apprentices, too, had masters and were said to be "in servitude." Even on the eve of the Revolution, this traditional social organization was considered divinely ordained, not just humanly constructed. Wrote the Reverend Jonathan Boucher in a sermon prepared for delivery at Port Tobacco: "[A]ccording to the subordination of conditions (which, for the good of all, our Maker has established among mankind), some must toil and drudge for others." He could anticipate knowing listeners, for both law and custom significantly constrained the personal freedom of a majority of the county's inhabitants. Stability was founded on an ordered, not an egalitarian, society.[1]

Recent interpretations of Chesapeake history argue that its hierarchical arrangements nevertheless were being tested and challenged, overtly or implicitly, during the late colonial period. For example, members of Protestant dissenting sects—Separate Baptists, Presbyterians, and Methodists—undermined the secular authority and pretensions of the gentry by living and worshiping plainly and by advocating the spiritual equality of everyone, even slaves, before God. In Virginia some gentlemen allegedly were deeply troubled over the prospect that mounting indebtedness to British merchants threatened their autonomy and way of life. In Maryland political conflict supposedly was both pervasive and evidence of democratic strivings that called elite rule into question.[2]

Yet such challenges did not resonate uniformly across a region so vast and varied. From the vantage of Charles County, neither nascent democrats nor dissenting Protestants endangered social stability. The gentry, moveover, appear self-confident, their privileged status and lifestyle unthreatened by neighbors close at hand or merchants far away. Stresses and strains certainly existed and sometimes surfaced. Local Anglicans and Catholics occasionally squared off at each other. And harsh punishments meted out to slaves intimate whites' apprehensions that, without such severity, the chattel labor system might be undermined. Still, almost everyone in the county either accepted or at least acquiesced in an order founded on inequality. It was the only order they had ever known.

Chesapeake hierarchy often is depicted in terms of wealth and the visual evidence of it. A rude plank dwelling or a stately Georgian mansion reveals much about its occupants' status. Equally illuminating is a sketch of blacks at work or the stylized portrait of a gentlewoman at leisure. For an entire population, the distribution of wealth can be plotted using data from tax, land, and probate records. The result is a neat pyramid with clearly defined layers labeled gentry, middling and small planters, tenants, servants, and, at the base, slaves. Wealth *was* a primary indicator of status, but the social reality was much more complicated.[3]

A different, albeit related, way to conceptualize the region's social order assesses the degree to which individuals and groups enjoyed or were denied fundamental civil liberties. Here a useful place to begin is a 1755 census for Maryland, which designated four gradations of liberty or lack of it: free, indentured and hired servants, convicts, and slaves. Of the 13,056 people then living in Charles County, close to 60 percent were classified as free, and nearly all of them were white. (Only 13 black persons and 239 mulattoes were free.) Servants constituted another 4 percent of the population, while 2 percent were convicts transported to the Chesapeake, the dumping ground for the dregs of British society. These whites (854 people), bound to labor for a specified term, formed a narrow band between the overwhelmingly white free population (7,493) and the thoroughly African-American slave population (4,520 blacks and 189 mulattoes).[4]

Yet freedom was much more a matter of degree than the census indicated. "Free" white married women, for example, were subject to severe disabilities under both English common and Maryland statutory law, while the county's sizable Catholic minority was politically disenfranchised and religiously circumscribed. Among slaves, some masters allowed their bondmen and -women a measure of autonomy, whereas others were unspeakably cruel. Planters great and small, women married and unmarried, Protestants and Catholics, tenants and contract laborers, apprentices and indentured servants, convicts and slaves—all occupied different niches along a broad social spectrum. One's status and options, legal and otherwise, depended upon a montage of factors, including ethnicity, gender, marital status, religion, family, age, wealth, and conditions of labor. In addition, the extent of one's personal freedom might change several times over the course of a lifetime—as, for example, slaves were alternately subject to kind or inhumane masters; servants, apprentices, and convicts began or completed their terms; and women married or buried their husbands. Even so, whether white or black, the great majority of people living in the late colonial county were deprived of important liberties, including the right to come and go at will, to reap the profits of their own labor, to worship as they pleased, to receive full legal protections, and to participate in the political process.

Schematic representations of the many degrees of freedom, something similar to pyramidal representations of wealth distribution, are impossible to construct because individuals' circumstances were complicated and surviving evidence leaves too many questions unanswered. That said, it is possible to aggregate the many dimensions of freedom, of personal autonomy, by examining five groups: the male gentry, economically independent women, white "laboring hands," enslaved African-Americans, and Roman Catholics.

MEN OF "GREAT INFLUENCE"

The major beneficiaries of the county's complex, even kaleidoscopic social order were the male gentry, and several characteristics set them apart from the county's "plain Country people." Gentlemen had "fortunes"; other men, a "competency." Whereas most local plantations were family operations, a few large planters utilized 20 or more adult laborers, mostly slaves. And while 585 men owned land in the county as of 1774, only 37 held tracts of 1,000 acres of more, and fewer than 1 in 5 had at least 500 acres. Although Charles County gentlemen were no match, financially, for the great planters of the

South Carolina lowcountry, much less the English aristocracy, even a visiting Englishman could appreciate that they were "people of considerable property."[5]

For most, a plantation was their greatest economic asset and the center of their world. No one described the vista more euphorically than William Hanson, who lived near St. Thomas Manor. Like the best estates in the county, Hanson's stood on high ground overlooking water. "The situation is high, dry, and healthy," he said, and "the prospect delightful, having a fine view of Patowmack river, Virginia, Port-Tobacco creek, and the neighbourhood all round." At this "seat" was "every advantage to make life delightful and happy," beginning with his two-story, twelve-room house. Surrounding it was a pastoral scene permeated with evidence of the manual labor from which the gentry itself was exempt. The world of field hands and stockmen: rich land "capable of producing any commodity suited to the climate," two tobacco houses, a large granary, a cornhouse, and a cow barn and stables. The world of domestics and artisans: a brick kitchen, dairy, and spinning room, a weaver's house, and a lumber-working room. If the scene was not the creation of Hanson's own hand, he nonetheless could account it a product of his managerial skills. It represented, in the words of another gentleman, the result of "a life of Industry and care."[6]

Standing today atop bluffs and ridges, or preserved in photographs when fire and time have worked their ways, are houses of the late colonial elite, visual evidence of their world and their place within it. Haberdeventure, a five-section structure north of Port Tobacco, uniquely combined the principal house types then common in southern Maryland: frame, frame with brick gable ends, and brick. The house belonged to Thomas Stone, a young lawyer who married well (his bride's dowry was £300 sterling). If the design of Haberdeventure was quintessentially southern Maryland, La Grange, built shortly before the Revolution, was Georgian and both architecturally and socially more imposing. Located east of Port Tobacco, La Grange was home to James Craik, a Scottish physician who had served in George Washington's Virginia Regiment during the Seven Years' War. La Grange, with its air of formality, spacious proportions, and imported mahogany woodwork, reflected the relative prosperity of the years during which it was built. Even more imposing was Blenheim, home of the Lees. The mansion reportedly featured red Flemish bond brick, stained glass windows, marble and slate flooring, and a cupola. Standing beside an iron railing that surrounded the roof, family members and guests scanned the countryside and the heavens with a telescope.[7]

While most inhabitants of the county lived amid much humbler surroundings, received little or no formal education, and seldom traveled farther than a

LA GRANGE (CA. 1765). *This gracefully proportioned Georgian home of Dr. James Craik is one of the largest dwellings built in Charles County during the colonial period. The pavilion and porch were added in the 1830s. Courtesy of The Maryland Independent.*

DR. JAMES CRAIK
(1730–1814). *After serving with Virginia troops commanded by George Washington during the Seven Years' War, Craik, a Scotsman, moved to Charles County, established a medical practice there, and was appointed a county court justice. During the War for Independence he helped organize the hospital department of the Continental Army. Thereafter, at Washington's urging, Craik moved to Alexandria, Virginia, just a few miles from Mount Vernon. Photograph by John C. Kopp. Courtesy of Sarah Craik Dupree and the Southern Maryland Studies Center, Charles County Community College.*

HABERDEVENTURE, *the home of Thomas Stone and Margaret Brown Stone. Construction of the central section of the house began about 1771; hyphens and wings were added later. The two-story kitchen-service wing at the right dates from the mid-nineteenth century. Courtesy of the A. Aubrey Bodine Photographic Collection, The Peale Museum, Baltimore City Life Museums.*

MARGARET STONE (1751–87), *the daughter of Dr. Gustavus Brown and sister of Dr. Gustavus Richard Brown, grew up at Rich Hill plantation, several miles east of Port Tobacco. In 1776 she accompanied her husband to Philadelphia, where she underwent smallpox inoculation and became so ill that he wrote to a friend in Maryland, "[t]he illness of a wife I esteem most dearly preys most severely on my Spirits." Rarely in good health thereafter, Margaret died in 1787, and her grief-stricken husband died a few months later. Artist: Robert Edge Pine. Courtesy of the National Portrait Gallery, Smithsonian Institution, gift of Mrs. Frank J. Clement.*

THOMAS STONE (1743–87), *a signer of the Declaration of Independence, was one of the county's most prominent revolutionary leaders, as both Continental congress-man and member of the Maryland Senate. He was elected to the Constitutional Convention of 1787 but did not attend because of poor health. Artist: Robert Edge Pine. Courtesy of the National Portrait Gallery, Smithsonian Institution, gift of Mrs. Frank J. Clement.*

(*facing page*) RECEPTION ROOM OF HABERDEVENTURE. *Fully paneled in southern yellow pine, this room, with its flanking corner cupboards and carved details, is an unusually fine example of an eighteenth-century interior from the county. The paneling was removed from the house about 1928 and is now on permanent display at the Baltimore Museum of Art. Whereas the Stone family used the room to receive guests, the museum shows it as a dining area. Courtesy of the Historic American Buildings Survey, Prints and Photographs Division, Library of Congress.*

few miles from home, the gentry's world was, collectively, much broader. No group was better educated or more widely traveled. In a society where one of every three white men signed his name with a mark, elite males seem to have been uniformly literate, and a few had access to the best formal education available in their day. The Jenifer and Hanson families enrolled sons in the grammar school and college at Princeton. William Smallwood and Philip Thomas Lee were educated in England, at Eton. And Dr. Gustavus Brown sent his son, Gustavus Richard Brown, to the University of Edinburgh for medical training.[8]

The elite was acutely conscious of its status. When five men, all justices of the county court, felt slighted in the allocation of church pews, the governor heard about it. Various gentlemen also cherished their riding chairs, blooded horses, militia commissions, and honorific titles, whether whimsical, ceremonial, or official. One of the Smallwoods, who were among the wealthiest families in the county, was "commonly called King of the woods." When the Virginia Lees referred to Richard Lee, Sr., patriarch of the Maryland branch of the family, they called him "Esquire Lee." John Hanson, a local merchant, proudly preserved a 1748 certificate from the guild council of Glasgow, Scotland. It bestowed upon him the title of "Burgess and Gild Brother" of that city. Charles County even had a genuine Scottish laird, the elder Dr. Brown. The social distance that the elite cultivated and enjoyed did not mean social isolation, however. As a ditty published in *The Maryland Almanack for the Year of our Lord, 1761* ran, "Let not the Great the Least disdain, All, all are Links of Nature's Chain."[9]

Gentry hospitality was legendary. An illiterate neighbor of Richard Lee's related what happened when he called at Blenheim about 1766: "Squire Lee according to Custom asked me if I would drink a Dram or some Cyder, I in a merry Humour used freedom enough to say I had not eat my Breakfast, Mr Lee laugh'd and said I must wait 'till it was dress't, the Squire asked me if a cut of Bread and Cheese would do? I answered very well, which was ordered to be brought and Mrs Lee at the same time went out and presently returned with a Plate of Fresh Beef, hashed as good as ever I saw." Nicholas Cresswell's journal contains a litany of gentry attentiveness, which began as soon as he reached Nanjemoy in 1774. His host introduced him at every house in the village, and thereafter Cresswell dined at plantations, danced nearly all night with "young ladys," watched "diverting plays" (which "seems very strange to me, but I believe it is common in this Country"), got drunk ("Sick with my last night's debauch"), and visited Annapolis with several gentlemen.[10]

By the time the newcomer returned to Nanjemoy he was suffering from "a Fever with some cussed physical name." After Gustavus Richard Brown, the Edinburgh-trained physician, prescribed "some slops" (physic), Cresswell

kept to his room, "very weak" but in good spirits because "the whole neighbourhood behaves with the greatest kindness to me, some of them has attended me constantly all the time." Just as he began regaining strength,
Brown's apprentice sent some pills that caused a desperate progression from
"constant thirst and a very bad taste in my mouth" to loose teeth, a "throat
and tongue much swollen," and "spitting and slavering like a mad dog."
Rightly, Cresswell deduced that "I am poisoned." Brown was summoned,
made "a truly physical face" when he saw the medicine, and apologized
because the apprentice had sent "strong Mercurial Pills, in the room of cooling
ones." The sick man promptly gave Brown "as hard a blow as I could with my
fist over the face, and would have given him a good trimming had I been
able." The gentleman physician merely made "a most formidable frown.
. . . Begged I would moderate my passion," and predicted that brimstone and
salts would effect a cure. Unconvinced, Cresswell verbally "abused" Brown so
"unmercifully" that he stopped visiting his patient. Still, he monitored Cresswell's progress, and when the "much reduced" Englishman, clothes hanging
about him "like a skeleton," came to pay the bill, Brown refused to accept any
money until the recovery was complete. Nor would those who took "every
possible care" of Cresswell accept payment for their trouble.[11]

In addition to being hospitable, members of the elite were powerful. What
was said of one gentleman—that he wielded "great influence among his
Neighbours"—applied to many. In the county's semiliterate society, where
people reportedly had an "extreme partiality for oratory, and speech-mak-
ing," gentlemen were most skilled at oratory and rhetoric, most knowledgeable about important developments within and beyond the county, and therefore best positioned to influence popular perceptions. The elite, moreover,
were able to offer lesser folk valuable assistance. Squire Lee—allegedly possessed of "a liberal education . . . a cultivated mind . . . strong understanding,
and a judgment comprehensive and perspicuous"—"counsel[ed] his neighbours in their litigious contests, and he was always ready to give them his
mature and best advice." Dr. Brown, in addition to treating both rich and
poor, secretly ameliorated "honest poverty." Such occasions involved more
than altruism, as Cresswell realized. They created "obligations." People of
lower social rank had more incentive to support a hierarchical system if they
benefited from it.[12]

The gentry also promoted learning and in other ways acted as public
benefactors. Except for a gift from the elder Dr. Brown, the church at Port
Tobacco would not have had an organ. "Public-spirited Gentlemen" in
Charles and adjacent counties paid for a rider who carried mail to Annapolis at
least once a fortnight. When a lending library was founded in the provincial
capital in 1762 to disseminate "a Spirit of Science thro' the Country," gentle-

men in the county subscribed and paid a substantial annual fee. Such efforts undoubtedly made life more convenient and satisfying for elite families, but they also redounded to the benefit of others who used the mail, were admitted to gentlemen's libraries, or sang hymns to the sounds of the organ, an instrument not usually found in parish churches at the time.[13]

The gentry's most concerted effort at beneficence involved the free school, which the legislature had chartered in 1723 "for the liberal and pious Education of the Youth." Governed by a self-perpetuating board of visitors and

DESK AND BOOKCASE (MID-EIGHTEENTH CENTURY). *Fine furnishings distinguished gentry families from "plain Country people." This piece, made of American walnut, belonged to the Barber family of Port Tobacco. The imported Vauxhall glass used on the bookcase doors was exceedingly costly and therefore rare in the colonies. Courtesy of the Museum of Early Southern Decorative Arts, Winston-Salem, N.C.*

situated on a hundred acres overlooking the Potomac River, the school offered Latin, Greek, writing, arithmetic, and other subjects. Student fees and profits from the land supported the schoolmaster. Yet by the early 1770s neither the school nor its counterparts in St. Mary's, Calvert, and Prince George's counties were generating enough income "Separately [to] afford a sufficient encouragement for Proper Masters," whereupon "sundry Gentlemen" stepped in to revitalize education in the area.[14]

After obtaining more than £1,200 in private pledges, they secured Assembly approval to sell the old free school properties and establish a consolidated academy. It was named Charlotte Hall, almost certainly in honor of the wife of King George III. The legislature lent prestige—but no money—to the venture when it appointed a board of trustees headed by Governor Robert Eden and composed of seven prominent men from each participating county. Those from Charles included Squire Lee, who stood second only to Eden in the proprietary government; the local delegation to the legislature; two county court justices; and the Reverend Isaac Campbell of Trinity Parish, who operated a "justly celebrated school." The site chosen for the new academy was at Cool Springs in St. Mary's County, where the waters allegedly had curative powers.[15]

Gentry influence and power found stark expression in officeholding. Whether appointed or elected, the elite dominated public offices. More correctly, some of the elite did so, for even within the upper echelon of the society, dramatic differences of freedom and status prevailed. No Catholic gentleman—no matter how great his wealth, advantageous his marriage, or ancient his lineage—legally could vote or hold office. Among Protestants, only those of English descent realistically could hope to serve in the most important posts: justice of the county court, sheriff, delegate to the Assembly, and proprietary placeman. Scotsmen, members of the largest white ethnic minority, rarely attained high office. When they did, there was some extraordinary circumstance, such as the elder Gustavus Brown's lordship and wealth or James Craik's fame for having served in the Seven Years' War.[16]

Civil government within the county was entirely appointive, and it reinforced, politically, the hierarchical social order. The magistrates who tried suits and oversaw everything from poor relief to the condition of the roads, the sheriff who collected taxes and punished the convicted, the clerk who kept the public records, the constables who apprehended men and women accused of fornication, bastardy, and assault, the collector of proprietary quitrents, the deputy commissary who administered the probate of estates, and even the men who inspected planters' tobacco and declared what was marketable—these and others were appointed, not elected. The proprietary filled the chief offices—justice, sheriff, clerk, deputy commissary, and quitrent collector—and always chose members of the gentry. In turn, the justices controlled most of the lesser offices.[17]

The locus of political power was the court at Port Tobacco, where twelve to fifteen "worshipfull justices" heard civil cases involving no more than £100 sterling, tried all criminal cases except those against whites accused of capital crimes, and handled many administrative matters affecting the populace. In the fifteen years after 1760, just twenty-six men sat on the court, and all but one sheriff was first a justice. These "principal Gentlemen" were planters and merchants rather than lawyers. Theirs was country justice, and they insisted upon conducting it with appropriate decorum. By the 1760s the court employed a man to beat the drum at the quarterly sessions and to "wash the Court house the Saturday before the Court," sweep it daily during the session, and "Attend the Chief Justice at his Lodgins every morning by 9 O Clock and also at Dinner time." When a juryman "much in Liquor" fell asleep in the middle of a trial, he was fined, as was anyone found guilty of throwing balls against the courthouse.[18]

Bound by common and statutory law, the magistrates nevertheless exercised a good deal of discretion. The court punished one man for "waylaying" Richard Pile "in the night . . . and attacking him with a Clubb," fined another for abusing an indentured servant woman, and rewarded a third for disbanding a "tumultuous meeting" of slaves. Among its administrative duties, the court granted licenses for ordinaries, apprenticed orphans and stipulated whether they should receive schooling and learn a trade, and decided whether slaves and adult white men were too old or disabled to be taxed.[19]

To the extent that public money was dispensed for welfare purposes, the court dispensed it. The idea was to provide essential services, but at minimal cost to taxpayers. Thus one inhabitant received five hundred pounds of tobacco for nursing and burying an impoverished woman, while another collected two thousand pounds for keeping a "Madman" for a year. In 1762 Nancy Simpson stated that she had "languished under a Disorder in her head and throat this year Past," had lost her palate, and was so wasted that she could not walk. Her parents had "sustained" her as long as they could, but, she told the justices, "as I now am almost Seventeen Years of Age . . . and being born in this County humbly begs your worships to Extend your Charity." They directed a physician to "use his Indeavours to Cure her."[20]

Once the court spoke, individual justices often personally implemented its orders. No matter seemingly was too trivial to escape their involvement. Hence they served on the commissions that the court appointed to mark landowners' boundaries. When Mary Marshall complained that the road leading from her plantation to the inspection warehouse at Cedar Point "is very hurtfull to her," two justices investigated, agreed that the road was too steep for rolling hogsheads of tobacco, and recommended construction of an alternate route. When an indigent woman petitioned that she was "in a most Deplorable Condition in as much as She Cannot get any thing Towards a Lively Hood," and when a visitor to the county said that he had only enough money "to go home to his own Country or to get him Cured of his many Infirmities here," the court ordered two of its members to obtain medical help. Between quarterly sessions the magistrates handled such matters and helped keep the peace in their neighborhoods. A few even had private jails at their plantations, where persons accused of crimes could be held until the next meeting of the court.[21]

If the gentlemen justices behaved imperiously—as they sometimes were accused of doing—little could be done about it because they were proprietary appointees. Occasionally, very occasionally, someone complained to the House of Delegates, the popularly elected branch of the Maryland legislature. It usually summoned several justices. One would deign to appear, whereupon the house would examine the complaint and was likely to conclude that the

CLERK'S STOOL FROM THE CHARLES COUNTY COURTHOUSE, PORT TOBACCO. *Notwithstanding "worshipfull" justices' efforts to impart proper decorum to county court sessions, this walnut clerk's stool suggests the rather rustic ambience of country justice. The courthouse itself dated from about 1730 and probably was constructed of brick. No contemporary description survives. Courtesy of the Museum of Early Southern Decorative Arts, Winston-Salem, N.C.*

justices had been inattentive or negligent or, in one instance in 1751, had stretched "your Power to the utmost Limits of the Law." After the attending justice ritually apologized and "submitted to the Lenity and Determination" of the house, it ritually recommended "more Caution and Circumspection for the future." And that was the end of it.[22]

Charles County also was home to a few proprietary placemen who held high and lucrative provincial offices. If anyone had stopped about 1760 to ask a local planter who, among the gentry, was most advantageously situated within the proprietary regime, the answer surely would have been Squire Richard Lee. His father had migrated from Virginia to Maryland in the early eighteenth century and subsequently served as justice and sheriff of Prince George's County, member of the upper house of Assembly (which was also the governor's Council), Provincial Court justice, and naval officer of the north shore of the Potomac River. The latter office brought him to Charles County, where he began building Blenheim near Cedar Point. When the elder Lee died in 1744, Richard succeeded to the Council seat and naval position, both of which he retained until the end of the colonial period. In 1773 his own son, Philip Thomas Lee, joined him on the Council. As much a part of Annapolis society as that of southern Maryland, Squire Lee referred to Blenheim as "my Country Seat on No[rth] Potomack."[23]

Charles County residents were governed not only by appointed officials but also by the only men they elected: delegates to the lower house of Assembly and vestrymen and church wardens of the Anglican parishes. Protestant males who owned at least fifty acres or any property worth at least £40 sterling could vote. Landholding alone probably enfranchised less than one-third of them. Of the rest, many no doubt were landowners' sons who could claim enough personal property, such as slaves, livestock, and artisans' tools, to qualify. (A prime field hand was worth enough to entitle his master to vote.) Other men almost certainly owed their voting rights to property that had been their wives', for under the common law a husband owned all personalty his wife brought to the marriage. With their dowries, dower rights from previous marriages, and legacies, local women often added appreciably to their husbands' assets. All this suggests that a majority of white Protestant men could vote.[24]

Freemen habitually chose members of the elite as vestrymen and Assembly delegates, an outcome no doubt influenced by voice voting. Annual vestry elections seem to have been sedate affairs in which men's votes directly affected their purses. For vestrymen could ask the legislature to levy local taxes for church repairs and construction of chapels in outlying sectors of the parish, and they also selected the public tobacco inspectors. This nonecclesiastical duty made sense socially because the vestry was the only governmental body in each parish. Denied to everyone at the local level was the right to choose the Anglican minister. The proprietary zealously guarded that prerogative.[25]

Compared with vestry elections, much more power was at stake in those for the House of Delegates. Called at the governor's pleasure, lower house elections were held infrequently, sometimes five or more years apart. When they did occur, campaigns and polling were moments of high drama. Only the elite battled one another for the county's four Assembly seats, but they needed the freemen's votes. To get them, candidates called in the "obligations" of lesser planters, which was easy to do because of viva voce balloting. If that was not enough to gain them the highest elective office in Maryland, some gentlemen were willing to use raw, coercive power.[26]

Two elections held in the middle of the eighteenth century exposed the nonbeneficent side of the gentry. When Arthur Lee, an incumbent member of the House of Delegates, county court justice, and son of Squire Lee, ran for reelection in 1754, he lost. "Poor Arthur," wrote Michael Earle, another member of the legislature, "he had not Interest [influence?] enough to be ret[urne]d." But Lee had a different perception of his defeat "& complain'd heavily of a Bull Dogg that was made use of to terrifie his People." Although he and his supporters challenged the legality of the election, the House of Delegates narrowly decided not to overturn it. Dejected, Lee left Annapolis. Recounted Earle: "Sam the Barber when he came to take our Wiggs told us poor Mr. Lee was just gone out of Town & that Land a Mighty he looked as [bad?] as a Stuck Pigg."[27]

Peter Dent may have preferred a bulldog to what actually happened in the Assembly election of 1749. Dent was at Bryantown, not far from Benedict, when Justice Robert Yates "came to him . . . and abused him very grossly, by calling damn'd Rascal, damn'd Lyar, and impudent Fellow; and told him, he should never get his Ends at the Election, in carrying those he wanted," meaning the candidates he supported. When Yates bragged that he "always did Justice to all mankind," Dent retorted "that he could not say so," for Yates "had made him ride to Port-Tobacco very often for nothing." At that the magistrate took great offense, turned to another magistrate named Allen Davis, and demanded that Dent be referred to the next session of the court. Davis refused, whereupon Yates "swore he would have a Bench-Warrant, and do his [Davis's] job."[28]

Trying to mediate the situation, Davis invited Dent to drink with him and attend militia muster a few days later, and there he promised to "screen" Dent "from what had happened between him and Mr. Yeates" if he would change his allegiances. Determined not to be intimidated or cajoled, Dent voted for the candidates of his choice. Then, when the county court met, the sheriff arrested him on the promised bench warrant and took him before the justices, who "informed him, he was sent for, for abusing Mr. Yeats; and demanded of him, if he would confess the Thing or stand Tryal." Confident that witnesses would testify that Yates had hurled the first insult, Dent demanded a jury trial. The court ordered him to post bail, but when he left to obtain it, he "was called back by the Sheriff, and upon his Return was told by Mr. Davis, the Court did not think fit to let him stand Tryal; and thereupon proceeded to fine him 1000 lbs. of Tobacco."[29]

Fortunately for the beleaguered voter, his candidates won election to the House of Delegates, which promptly investigated the incident and summoned four justices to appear before it. One of them, William Eilbeck, eventually arrived. He confessed to the truth of Dent's allegations, admitted that "he was involved in passing the said Judgment, by the Majority of the Opinions of the said Justices, and omitted entering any Protest thereto." Powerless to discipline a proprietary appointee, the house resolved that Eilbeck's behavior "proceeded from an Inadvertency, and not from any evil Design," but nevertheless lectured him sternly. "It plainly appears," the speaker of the house intoned, that the Charles County magistrates "did not use that Caution which is absolutely necessary, in all Cases for the due Administration of Justice, which consists in hearing coolly, fully, and impartially, both Sides of the Question, before they proceed to Judgment." Stopping just short of accusing the court of breaking the law it was sworn to uphold, the speaker "recommended" that the justices should exercise greater caution and avoid "Complaints of the like Nature hereafter."[30]

They did, but electioneering, gentry-style, continued, as the bulldog tactics of Arthur Lee's opponents subsequently proved. In time, however, candidates relied on more subtle tactics to gain votes. In 1771 the lower house expelled Francis Ware and Josias Hawkins because "sundry" inhabitants of the county proved that their "treating" voters to alcoholic beverages had resulted in an "undue Election." Unoffended, the voters reelected both men within a month.[31]

WOMEN OF CONSEQUENCE

All women were excluded from the political rituals and rights enjoyed by and guaranteed to propertied Protestant men. And that was but one dimension of an inferior female status created and sustained through custom and law in Charles County, as throughout the colonies. Whereas local children of both genders were admonished to behave "Dutifully and Submissively," to be "dutiful & obedient" to their parents, only women were counseled about

being obedient to their spouses. Even after his death, according to one husband's will, his wife was to follow his dictates "as if I myself had lived and
remained as intended at the head" of the family. Education, too, set females
apart from males. Girls did not attend the local free school, much less travel
abroad for instruction. Females also were more likely to be illiterate, even in
gentry families (approximately two-thirds of white women could not sign
their names, compared with about one-third of the men). And while the
orphans' court regularly directed that boys should be taught basic arithmetic,
thereby probably revealing minimal societal expectations, the court was un-
concerned whether girls learned the same skill.[32]

Gender, too, lay at the core of a distinct, and dependent, female legal
status. Single women (femes sole) legally were free to come and go as they
pleased and to earn income. They could acquire and dispose of property, enter
contracts, and use the courts to enforce them, just as any freeman could. But
the moment a woman spoke her wedding vows, she became civilly dead, a
nonperson under the law, a feme covert. Any real estate she brought to the
marriage became her husband's to manage and exploit during his lifetime, and
he gained outright ownership of all her personal property, from slaves to
household goods to clothing. The law also accorded him the right to determine how the couple's children would be raised and educated, even to the
extent that he could unilaterally bestow custody of their minor offspring upon
whomever he pleased. Should misery plague a marriage, it endured nonetheless because divorce was unheard of in Maryland. Small wonder, then, that
Squire Lee's daughter Alice once wrote, "happily I am little more than 12
Y[ea]rs Old & not so eager to tye a Knot which Death only can Dissolve."[33]

The broad range of constraints upon "free" women is undeniable. Yet,
another and telling dimension of female experience emerges from the activities
of single women who exercised considerable autonomy over their lives, probably the maximum possible for their time and place. Always a minority among
white women, they controlled substantial property and garnered enough income to survive and even prosper without husbands, without the abject legal
subordination of marriage. Occasionally proclaiming their status as "planter,"
they managed landed estates and corresponded with British merchants.
Women also ran ferries and mills, lent money, invested in land, hired out their
slaves, practiced midwifery, and, in one instance, operated a tobacco inspection warehouse and, in another, served as the collector of Lord Baltimore's
quitrents. Some belonged to the gentry; the rest ranked lower in wealth and
status.[34]

A few of these female entrepreneurs were spinsters, but most often they
were widows. Marriages created household economies to which wives often
brought not only their labor but also property. Their dowries, inheritances,

and other assets typically included household goods, slaves, and even land. Within marriage the wife's material contributions, added to her husband's property and to the productivity of the entire household, promoted the family's well-being. If the husband died first, his wife had dower rights to a share of his estate.[35]

A Maryland widow legally was entitled to hold, use, and profit from one-third of her deceased spouse's land, but she could not dispose of it because she had only a lifetime interest. In addition, she regained control of any land she had contributed to the marriage, and she had a right to full ownership of one-third of her husband's personalty. Through their bequests men often provided more generously for their wives than the law required, and they sometimes expressed confidence that their spouses' "wisdom," "discretion," and "judgment" would enable them to use their inheritances well. But any widow who did not receive at least her dower "thirds" was entitled to renounce her husband's will, thereby publicly rejecting his final wishes, his conception of what was best for her. Simultaneously she also asserted the primacy of her legal rights over his desire to distribute assets among other heirs.[36]

July 4, 1776, was a day of independence in more ways than one for Elizabeth Martin. On that day she went before the probate officer of Charles County "and Quitted her Claim to the Several bequests and Devises made to her in the Will of her said husband and Elected in lieu thereof her Dower or third part of the Deceasts Estate both Real & personal." Between the years 1740 and 1784, nearly one-fifth of the widows whose husbands' wills were probated in the county renounced them. As one woman asserted, that was "Justly my Right."[37]

Often it is apparent why a widow acted, or it is at least possible to discern the choices that confronted her. For some the decision must have been obvious: Their departed spouses' wills either ignored them completely or left them pittances. Robert Knox, a wealthy Nanjemoy merchant, set aside £800 sterling for the child his pregnant wife was carrying and then bequeathed his other children more then five thousand acres of land in Virginia, his estate in Scotland, all his Maryland realty, and his livestock and slaves. Almost as an afterthought he decided to "give unto my Wife Rose Townsend [Knox] whatever is customary given to Widows in the part of the World where my Estate lyes." Just as Rose Knox renounced her husband's will, so did Rebeccah Perry, whose landowning spouse left her only the use, not even ownership, of a feather bed and bedding, and Sarah Maddox, whose husband had stipulated "that she shall not Debar or hinder any of my Sons from Setting on the Lands" he granted her.[38]

Other widows faced less clear-cut choices because their spouses were willing to be more generous than the law required, but only during their widow-hood. When Cornelius Norton died in 1741, he left his wife a lifetime estate in his plantation, slaves, and everything else he owned, "provided she doth not marry." She could either enjoy use of the entire estate while she was single and trust that if she remarried, her new husband would provide at least as well for her, or she could take her dower rights. In choosing the latter course, she received the use of only one-third of Norton's land but would have it throughout her life, and she owned her third share of the personalty, including slaves, outright. These assets she could mortgage or sell, options denied her under a lifetime estate. In purely economic terms, moreover, the widow Norton enhanced her attractiveness as a potential marriage partner because she would be able to bring property to any future union. Other women, whose spouses granted them all or nearly all of their estates for use during life, with no remarriage restriction, chose not to renounce the wills but to enjoy use, if not full ownership, of more than their dower.[39]

Because Maryland law permitted women separately to renounce land or personalty, some widows used that privilege to their advantage. Under the terms of one man's will, the wife received half his slaves, nearly all the livestock, all household furnishings, but no land. She kept the personalty but claimed her dower rights in realty. When a husband left his spouse his entire plantation but only the use of two slaves during her lifetime, she retained the plantation but claimed ownership of her third share of the personalty. Another woman did likewise because, while her husband willed her more than half of his land, he encumbered her third share of his personal property with a lifetime estate. She abided by the will regarding the realty but claimed full ownership of the personalty. Each of these women, and others, gained more than their dowers by renouncing just a portion of their husbands' wills.[40]

By the eve of the Revolution a propertied group of single women, mostly widows, lived in Charles County. Among its most marriageable females, at least in economic terms, they chose the freedom of feme sole rather than the civil death awaiting them if they married or remarried. Because each controlled land and/or slave labor, she had no need of a husband to provide for her in exchange for surrendering everything she possessed and also losing important civil rights. Time and again in the records, one comes upon a woman whose husband had died years before and who had remained single, all the while conserving and enlarging the assets she had received at his death. Her wealth accorded her status and financial security beyond that enjoyed by many white men (although no political rights). These women were different from widows in the seventeenth-century Chesapeake, who, historians believe, almost always remarried, and quickly. Nor were they like many widows in New England, who were forced to live dependent, constricted lives, usually in adult children's households, because they could not farm by themselves. The propertied widows of Charles County were more like the *signares* of the African coast and Brazil, women who profited from owning and trading slaves, than they were like their sister colonists in New England or the early Chesapeake.[41]

When Elizabeth Hanson's husband died in 1740, he left her a lifetime estate in four hundred acres of land, the profits of his water mill, ownership of five slaves, use of two more, and additional personalty. She lived on for another twenty-four years but never remarried. At about age sixteen, in 1755, Judith Dent married Jeremiah Chase but almost immediately was "left a childless Widow, w'th a very considerable Fortune," according to the Reverend Jonathan Boucher's version of the story, because her husband "was cut off by a very shock'g Casualty (poisoned by a Negro)." When Boucher was courting Judith Chase in the late 1760s, he estimated her savings at about £1,500 sterling, "Enough . . . to make two reasonable People happy." He failed in his efforts to obtain her hand, however, as did any other man who sought her company and fortune. When her property was assessed at the end of the War for Independence, she held nearly twice as much land as her husband had owned and more than double the number of slaves.[42]

Sometimes a woman relied upon more than her share of her deceased husband's assets in order to remain feme sole. Rachel Forry Lemmon was already a widow with several children in 1771 when she inherited her brother's estate. A decade later, having reverted to her maiden name, she had sufficient capital to buy the most valuable piece of real estate in the town of Port Tobacco. Ann Halkerston needed more than family assets after she was left with three young sons and no relatives in America who might help her. In 1762 several local men organized the "PORT-TOBACCO LOTTERY, for Relief of a distressed Widow," sold hundreds of tickets, and thereby helped her achieve economic independence. Soon she was the proprietor of a "noted and well-frequented tavern in Port-Tobacco town" (Thomas Jefferson stayed the night in 1775, while on his way to attend the Continental Congress in Philadelphia). By the time Halkerston died in 1777, still feme sole, she owned seven slaves and enough property that she could afford to send a son abroad to be educated.[43]

In Ann Halkerston's case it is not known how the proceeds of the charitable lottery were used, but the experience of another widow suggests an answer. Anne Horner, a daughter of the gentry, married a county court justice. At his death about 1772 his financial affairs were in ruins, valuable assets were subsequently seized for the benefit of his creditors, and his widow bound out at least one son for whom she could not provide. In 1774 a group of local residents, out of "Love and Regard" for Anne and her five children, each donated as much as £50 sterling toward their care and comfort. The money was to be used for one purpose only: to purchase slaves.[44] Anne Horner's well-being and freedom as feme sole were to be secured with the labor of the unfree, a common occurrence among the propertied women of Charles County.

LABORING HANDS

The great majority of white people ranked not as economically privileged unmarried women or as members of gentlemen's households. Rather, they comprised a kaleidoscopic mixture, including middling planting families who lived reasonably comfortably; poor families who occupied rustic dwellings and harbored little hope of becoming prosperous; blacksmiths and housekeepers; schoolmasters and seamstresses; wage laborers and indentured servants; newcomers on the make and longtimers slipping into insolvency. What unified these and other "plain Country people" was their need to labor in order to survive. What significantly divided them were the terms and conditions under which they did so. The more people could control or substantially influence when they worked and how, the more free they were in comparison with the bound-out whites and enslaved blacks all around them.[45]

Assessing the autonomy of any white laboring hand ("as we commonly Call it") defies easy categorization. Who, for example, was more autonomous, a small landowner eking out subsistence on poor soil or a craftsman who possessed little more than tools and clothing but whose skills were in demand? A substantial landowner mired in debt or a smaller operator able to turn a modest profit? And what about married women, whose coverture effectively conceals whatever latitude they exercised? At this distance no one knows.[46]

Yet, without oversimplifying, we can isolate several fundamental distinctions among laboring hands that signaled much about the extent of their self-determination. People whose energies benefited mainly themselves and their families were distinct from those subordinated to a master. Workers who entered contractual relationships with employers might find their daily routines much more regulated than those who simply agreed to accomplish specific tasks at agreed-upon prices. And people who controlled substantial property, especially land and slaves, were set apart from those who, in the words of a storekeeper, had to rely "altogether upon his own Industry for a Maintenance and support."[47]

Arguably the best-positioned nonelite whites held sizable producing plantations, in the range of one hundred to five hundred acres (three-fifths of recorded landowners as of 1774). Besides the gentry, they were most able to grow a variety of marketable crops, support crafts such as smithing and shoemaking, exchange plantation surpluses for domestic and imported products, and ride out hard times. Slaves, who were common on the larger units, added to the owner's wealth through both production and reproduction. And if not needed for other purposes, some of the acreage could be rented to tenants. Amid such surroundings middling planters enjoyed the status that went with a landed Chesapeake estate. Their dwellings and outbuildings might be "exceedingly good" or in disrepair, their lands well tended or not, but they alone decided when they worked and how. And if they were both male and Protestant, they were entitled to vote and might also attain lesser offices such as constable, keeper of the roads, and undersheriff.[48]

Small planters, inhabiting less than a hundred acres, had fewer options and operated on a smaller scale. Plantation buildings tended to be humbler, absent was the craftworking often associated with larger units, and bound and slave laborers were not much in evidence. Still, a fifty-acre tract, which represented the lower limit of viable plantation size in the county, conveyed voting rights (albeit not much chance of petty officeholding). And however they labored, small planters, too, set the terms.[49]

So did tenants, but within prescribed limits. A lease specified annual rent payments and, commonly in addition, restricted land use and designated improvements to be made on the property. Few tenants were so unrestrained as the skilled carpenter who agreed to repair a gentleman's house and deliver an ear of corn annually in exchange for a ninety-nine-year lease on thirty acres of land. More typical were provisions about how much timber could be cut, how the land was to be improved, the number of hands who could work it, and in what form the rent was to be paid. One St. Thomas Manor tenant basically worked as he pleased, so long as he paid a yearly rent of two thousand pounds of tobacco and a hundred pounds of pork and, in addition, planted "100 good apple trees and 100 oaks or locust every yeare." Tenants sometimes also had to furnish the Jesuits' table with "fatt" hens and capons.[50]

Success for tenant families was measured by how much they produced beyond the landlord's share. If they were unable both to support themselves and to abide by their leases, if they worked depleted and eroded soils as on the proprietary manors, then their material lives were meager, their futures unpromising. But tenancy had a positive side as well: It offered persons with little property of their own a chance to advance economically. John F. D. Smyth eagerly took that chance after arriving in the county about 1772 "in a State of Indigence." At first he boarded with a planter and attempted to practice surgery—"but with[ou]t the Confidence of any one," it was said, because he had only the rudiments of medical training. Smyth then rented a plantation and slaves to work it, but his tenancy proved an abysmal failure,

THE HOUSE OF A MIDDLING CHARLES COUNTY PLANTER. *Small clapboard dwellings such as this sheltered many white families. Windows and frames were modified ca. 1840. Photographed about 1930, the building no longer exists. Courtesy of the Early American Architecture Survey, Prints and Photographs Division, Library of Congress.*

LUM JACKSON HOUSE. *Poor planting families and slaves lived in small structures built with readily available materials. This plank dwelling, dating from the late eighteenth or early nineteenth century, had a clapboard roof and wooden chimney. The attached shed was probably a later addition. Drawing by J. Richard Rivoire.*

doubtless because his pretensions exceeded his practical knowledge of husbandry. In contrast, the tenants of St. Thomas Manor, who usually held long-term leases, accumulated substantial personal property and achieved reasonably comfortable standards of living. And the leaseholds enfranchised male tenants.[51]

Among landless laborers, some informally managed to barter their services for necessities—tanned hides and shoes traded for corn and wheat, for example, or weaving exchanged for a place to live. Others entered specific written agreements governing their work. A roofer hired at St. Thomas Manor in 1742 promised to "work from break of day or its Light Till . . . 8 at night," twenty-six days per month. A mulatto bricklayer agreed in 1760 to work beside a white man and to "conform to his way of working," also twenty-six days in every month. About the same time Father Hunter, the Jesuit superior, contracted to employ a workman as a joiner, glazier, or at "whatever business he's accustom'd to as I shall choose to employ him . . . both winter & Summer as long as I shall please to employ him: on these terms, he's to be allow'd one bottle of Rum p[er] week whilst he works & at no time to be condemn'd to Homini for a meal." This arrangement presumably satisfied both men's needs.[52]

Employers tried to hire people known for their "Sobriety, Industry, and Integrity," their "knowledge and fidelity," but performance did not necessarily match expectations, as Daniel of St. Thomas Jenifer learned to his dismay. As a proprietary official Jenifer frequently was absent from the county, and in 1769 he hired an overseer to manage his plantation there. The man signed a contract in which he promised to be "Dilligent, faithful, honest, and Industrious." Yet he repeatedly rode off on Jenifer's horses and "left all the Negroes without any Controul or Direction"; embezzled hogs, corn, and tobacco; and "Corrupted one of the Slaves" by convincing him to lie about who owned the tobacco. Even when at the plantation, the overseer managed poorly—or so Jenifer thought after once finding him "Shut up in the House at ten O'Clock in the Day time after being out all Night" and on another day discovering him "playing at Cards with Negroes" from the neighborhood.[53]

Below the level of hired hands was the lowest stratum of white workers: indentured servants and convicts who lived and labored at the behest of their masters. Variously advertised as farmers and wagoners, weavers and tailors, carpenters and cabinetmakers, painters and farriers, these bound laborers, constituting but a small segment of the county's population, continued to arrive from Britain until the Revolution. One ship alone dropped anchor in the Potomac during the 1760s with seventy-five servants and fourteen convicts on board. A few local people also fell into servitude, for two reasons. The occasional white woman convicted of bearing a mulatto child was sold to labor for seven years, her child until it reached age thirty-one. Secondly, unmarried debtors who were "languishing" in jail, unable to "redeem their Bodies" by satisfying their creditors, risked being sold into servitude for up to five years.[54]

Most interactions between servants and masters are unretrievable today. While surely not representative of all masters' attitudes, ads for runaways betray no empathy for white bound laborers: "a very imprudent Fellow," "an *Irish* woman . . . very fleshy," "an *English* Convict Servant Man . . . very swarthy . . . has a quick artful Way of talking," "a servant lad . . . [having] light coloured hair, which he generally wears in a slovenly manner," and finally, a Highland Scottish "servant girl . . . speaks bad English." Abuse also undoubtedly occurred. In 1760 a coroner's jury viewed Joseph Grant's body, which showed "fresh marks of Violence such as Several Stripes on his back & hands and one of his thighs and one Stripe on his face," and concluded that beatings from his master, added to general "weakness," had caused the death. No charges were filed, however, because the jurymen doubted that Grant's master "had any Intention of killing" him. Not surprisingly, few servants asked the county court to intervene and stop harsh treatment. The court customarily helped only when servants completed their terms and were "Sett at their Liberty" but could not collect agreed-upon freedom dues (usually clothing and tools) from their *former* masters.[55]

Whatever their discontents, servants' most effective means of seizing autonomy for themselves was by running away, a not uncommon approach to escaping difficult situations in the county. On occasion, spouses abandoned each other, sons "absconded" from their parents, sailors jumped ship and disappeared into the countryside, hired hands "went away," men who sank hopelessly into debt ran away from their creditors, and slaves took flight from their masters. So, too, did indentured and convict servants. If captured, they endured whatever punishment their masters applied and served additional time. On the other hand, successful runaways crossed the threshold to freedom.[56]

Whether they ran away or completed their terms, the fate of most Charles County servants is unknown. But one lonely image suggests how little they carried with them when they took or earned their liberty. Upon leaving the household in which she had served her time, one woman "walked about the County" followed by her two-year-old daughter.[57]

SLAVERY

"Charity to Negroes is due from all[,] particularly their Masters," wrote Father Hunter during a spiritual retreat in 1749. "As they are members of Jesus Christ, redeemed by his precious blood, they are to be dealt with in a charitable, Christian, paternal manner, which is at the same time a great means to bring them to do their duty to God, & therefore to gain their Souls." At the time Hunter recorded these thoughts, from New England to South Carolina fortunes were being made in the Atlantic slave trade, and the morality of owning black people was neither seriously nor widely questioned. The Jesuit priest's prescription for the treatment of enslaved blacks, although implicitly accepting chattel slavery, was benevolent and humane by mid-eighteenth-century standards.[58]

In contrast, a slave named Peter experienced bestial brutality. According to one of the most graphic descriptions preserved in the county court records, a small planter named John McAtee allegedly murdered "negroe Peter Slave of Ann Berry by tying his hands with a cord and Stretching and hoisting him up theirby to the Beams of a house for the Space of Six hours and Cruely beating and Whipping him with Burch Rods to wit thirty five Rods and giving him one hundred Stripes therewith by Reason whereof he died." At McAtee's trial in 1772, people summoned to testify offered further gory details: the slave "off his feet in the air" at McAtee's house; a birch rod measuring four feet long and an inch thick; wounds six inches long and half an inch deep; lashes on "the back Shoulders Sides and Belly." Unconvinced that McAtee was guilty of murder, a jury of his peers acquitted him.[59]

Peter's unpunished killing and Father Hunter's admonitions about charitable treatment mark the spectrum of whites' attitudes and behavior toward the slaves of Charles County. These examples also illustrate the futility of conceptualizing slavery in monolithic terms. Just as freedom was a coat of many colors, slavery came in differing hues. Within bondage, conditions varied. This is not to deny, however, the powerful constants of British colonial slavery: coercive extraction of labor from people of African descent, legal systems that imposed lifelong bondage and ensured its passage from generation to generation, and denial of any legal rights or protections. Enslaved blacks inhabited a world where their condition and skin color were the most negative social references one could invoke. Father Hunter himself characterized sinners as "slaves to Satan," and a woman whose neighbor called her "a negroes whore" went into court and sued for slander.[60]

Some of the most intriguing questions about slavery in the county, as in other places, elude answers for lack of evidence. Most elusive: How did slaves perceive their lives during the colonial period? Colonial slavery could not have been the same institution that it was between the Revolution and the Civil War. Was slavery any easier to bear in the days when some whites also were held in servitude, the liberties of the majority of people were significantly circumscribed, and memories of Africa probably included memories of African slavery? Was bondage more palatable before Thomas Jefferson proclaimed that all men were created equal, before slavery became an explosive, divisive moral and political issue, and before the growth of free black populations offered an alternative vision of existence? No slave living in the county during the eighteenth century left a single document that broached these matters. In fact, everything recorded about the slaves, even when they provided the information, is the work of whites and was shaped by their purposes and perceptions. They did not write of blacks' attitudes toward bondage.

But whites counted slaves, for tax and other purposes, and the best records yield information about gender, age, and the number who lived on individual plantations and within local parishes. Using such data from Charles and other Chesapeake tidewater counties, scholars have inferred that in the century before the Revolution, slave life underwent a profound transition from isolation to community. For several decades after planters began converting to slave labor in the late seventeenth century, most blacks were imported— "Saltwater negroes"—people from diverse ethnic and language groups. Few in number and predominantly males, cut off from their African cultures, the newcomers toiled in an alien and lonely environment, usually on small plantations, and had to adopt new ways of life and labor. Over the course of the eighteenth century, as a sizable and increasingly native-born, more gender-balanced population developed, and as many plantation labor forces grew larger, slaves found ever more opportunities to interact with one another, establish somewhat stable family and communal ties, and create a distinctive African-American culture. All these enabled the most deprived members of Chesapeake society to endure.[61]

To the extent that forming settled slave communities in Charles County depended upon population density and gender parity on homeplaces and in surrounding neighborhoods, the process must have been prolonged and uncertain. Even as the number of slaves grew from about six hundred to nearly five thousand during the first half of the century, most lived and worked in small groups. As late as the mid-1750s, half the adults belonged to plantations with no more than five adult black laborers, three-quarters to units with no more than ten. The male to female ratio among adults remained so skewed (127:100) that many men probably lacked mates. In addition, the slave population was unevenly dispersed across the county. The highest density occurred on the neck of land between the Potomac and Wicomico rivers, where two-thirds of the plantations utilized chattel labor. The lowest was in Durham Parish, where only one-third of producing units did so.[62]

Still, demographic conditions conducive to slave family formation and communal activities unquestionably were better in the 1750s than in preceding generations. And in succeeding years—as the population grew rapidly, the average size of plantation groups gradually increased, and the gender imbalance disappeared—slaves' opportunities to share work and leisure, tribulation and joy, dreams and despair, presumably grew in tandem. From a purely demographic perspective, the possibilities for reasonably stable black family and community life reached a peak on the eve of the Revolution. (One must speak of possibilities because kin and communal connections seldom can be ascertained.)[63]

Even so, hundreds of people were not particularly well situated. At some quarters children were the only slaves present. At others, men and women returning from the fields did not hear the voices of black children, and elderly slaves had no audience of young listeners to whom they might pass along memories of Africa, religious instruction, or advice about getting by in bondage. Where women and children or, less commonly, men and children were the only occupants of quarters, young African-Americans missed continuous contact not only with one parent but with any black adult of the absent gender. Kin and friends may have lived nearby, but most *regular* social interaction centered on the fields and meadows, the quarters and woods, of the home plantations.[64]

On those homeplaces, slaves labored under the watchful eye of master or overseer and with only as much control over their work as they could negotiate or manipulate. Until they were old enough to be sent to the fields, boys and girls waited on masters' tables, hauled water and firewood, and ran errands. Most adults were field hands "brought up to Plantation Business," and even females learned to "Plough well, and cut pretty well with an Ax." When men were assigned other jobs, their physical exertions varied according to the tasks they performed: carpentry, brickmaking, blacksmithing, coopering, building boats, or laboring as wheelwrights, sawyers, tanners, shoemakers, and colliers. During the fishing season on the Potomac, men also worked seines day after day. Women relieved of field work served as domestics, the most skilled of whom combined in the same person "a fine Cook Wench, who is a good Seamstress, and can do any kind of House-work." A few women, like Bennett Neale's Hannah, were known and respected as healers. Hannah's reputation was so widespread that she reportedly traveled "great distances f[ro]m home to visit sick people." Whether healers, domestics, or field hands, female slaves had another occupation that candid masters acknowledged: They were "breeding Women."[65]

Jenny, a mulatto, is one of the few slaves for whom even a cursory biography can be constructed. The daughter of a black father and a white mother, Jenny and several siblings belonged to the Neale family. She managed her master's grain mill despite being so remarkably short that she needed help hoisting bags of flour onto horses' backs, and she also was a proficient "Flux Doctor." In the 1740s, when "doubled with age" and considered "past labour," Jenny nevertheless "used to go about doctoring for the Flux and used to raise Poultry, & take care of negro Children." One who knew her recalled subsequently that she "had great liberty in going about & attending people sick with the Flux in the Neighbourhood" and that people customarily approached Jenny, not her master. Although some "said she was a witch," probably because of her healing skills, those skills afforded her an unusual measure of autonomy within bondage.[66]

However they labored, blacks coped with enslavement—and in ways that drew on elements of their African heritage. Some Charles County slaves played the banjo, an African instrument fashioned from a gourd, and many retained the rhythmic and emotional music and dance of their homelands. Not that whites necessarily appreciated slaves' distinctive folk art. Nicholas Cresswell, the recently arrived Englishman, judged their music and song so "Rude and uncultivated," their dancing "most violent exercise . . . irregular and grotesque" that "I am not able to describe it." As he wrote, African languages were spoken and ritual body markings seen on local plantations, some blacks had names that hearkened back to Africa, and some families' precise knowledge of their lineages continued oral traditions common in African societies. As late as the 1780s whites mentioned a conjurer and "Chief of his Colour in the Neighbourhood" as if his presence were not unusual, and even today a descendant of Charles County slaves demonstrates thatching techniques handed down within his family and said to be African in origin. All such manifestations of African customs undoubtedly helped foster a sense of black identity.[67]

Slaves also coped with bondage by maintaining contact, as best they could, with family members and friends living on nearby plantations. Considering masters' propensity to buy, sell, mortgage, hire out, and give away slaves, knowing people in the neighborhood must have been a nearly universal phenomenon. Sunday was the day for gathering, as Cresswell noted after attending what he called a "Negro Ball" near Nanjemoy, and his journal contains a rare glimpse of communal interactions. "Sundays being the only days these poor creatures have to themselves," he wrote, "they generally meet together and amuse themselves with Dancing to the Banjo" and singing songs in which "they generally relate the usage they have received from their Masters or Mistresses in a very satirical stile and manner." The slaves made "very droll music," and, said Cresswell with a hint of disbelief, "all appear to be exceedingly happy at these merry-makings and seem as if they had forgot or were not sensible of their miserable condition." One can imagine that Sunday gatherings offered young slaves lessons in complaining safely and enduring well.[68]

Enmeshed in a world largely defined by whites, blacks persevered by partially assimilating to white culture, including Christianity, although the extent of assimilation and the meaning that slaves gave to cultural adaptations elude description. Those who somehow managed to forge reasonably under-standing relationships or attachments with masters might benefit substan-tially—through receipt of privileges or property or even intercession on their behalf. Hence, after George Washington had gained title to a Charles County slave in payment for a debt, his former master asked that the man not be taken away to Virginia, on the grounds that "the Negroe you Attach'd was brought up in the Family, has always been a favorate Negroe in the Family, and has been much Indulg'd. He has now a Wife and Several Children, which he seems to have a great Affection for, and has declar'd Several times that he will Loose his life, or had rather Submit to Death then go to Virginia to leave his Wife & Children, and do immagine from his declirations that he has made he will be Troublesome to any master in Virginia, tho as fine a Slave as any in Maryland." The plea and delicately phrased threat proved unavailing, but when Washington's farm manager came to collect the slave, he kept "out of the way" while his protectors opined that they "suppose'd he was looking out for some one to purchase him, or hire him." In the end, entreaty and evasion merely bought some time, for the slave was removed to Virginia. More fortu-nate were Cate, whose dying master provided that she could "go to which of my Sisters she shall chuse to goe to," and Joe, who was offered the choice of becoming a joiner or mason.[69]

The ultimate act of benevolence for a master—one only rarely under-taken—was manumission. When it happened in the county, freedom was granted to individuals, not groups, and without commentary on the morality of slavery. The small free mulatto population probably originated in masters' manumissions of either children they had fathered with slave women or descendants of white women. And a few blacks gained their freedom through exemplary service, as when a mistress released a bondman and bequeathed him her entire estate because he "has been a faithful Servant." Linking manu-mission with a grant of property, however modest, was not unusual. When the mulatto Ann was freed, she also received a chest, a bed, a spinning wheel, and her mistress's "meanest" clothes. Ann did not, however, begin her life in freedom with her eight-year-old daughter, who, although never to "work at the hoe," was to remain a slave until her sixteenth birthday.[70]

While masters commonly exacted a price for manumission by not freeing a slave until she or he had labored for some years, one widow continued to extract labor even after releasing a bondwoman. Esther Harrison was respon-sible for seven orphaned grandchildren and wanted to provide for them after her death, but she also wanted to manumit a slave named Judah. She did both. In 1776 Judah became "free for the Residue of her days saving that she shall and must live with and take Care of my Grand Children . . . so far as washing mending and Cooking for them during their minority." Judah learned first-hand that freedom is a matter of degree.[71]

For every person manumitted in the county during the colonial period, hundreds more remained in bondage. Although growing kin networks afforded them diversion and companionship, and skilled tasks sometimes offered alternatives to monotonous field work, blacks' labor was becoming more onerous. Over the course of the century, masters required longer workdays and permitted less respite, even in winter. In addition, the more successful slaves were in establishing families and communities, the more they had to lose.[72]

When the tobacco crop was in the shed, when a master needed to pay a debt or educate a child, when children in slaveholding families came of age, daughters married, or a widow died, when a slave mother weaned her infant or became "a very great scold," then blacks who had endured bondage together were torn apart. In disposing of slaves, some masters respected kinship ties and attempted to keep at least some family members together. In 1768 Roger Smith bequeathed his wife two slave families—a couple with seven children and a woman with two—and at her death they descended intact to Smith's brother. (Yet when the latter died, just six years after the initial bequest, the slaves were parceled out in four lots.) Other masters probably broke up slave families and friends with no more disquietude than merchant Thomas Howe Ridgate, who wrote, "so adieu to [the] Negro's."[73]

Masters even planned to dispose of children still in the womb or not yet conceived. Cebberamous was destined to lose "the first Child that . . . [she] shall bring to good." Sue was similarly to be stripped of "the first Child that . . . [she] Brings that liveth a year & if in Case it Dieth in a year then the next Child." Mothers—and fathers, too, if they were present—abruptly lost children just as they were beginning to explore the world on foot. Venus kept her infant until it could babble and toddle but then had to relinquish it to a white couple who were to "take the Child . . . under their own immediate Care so soon as it . . . shall arrive at the Age of two years." Almost as if he were dealing out cards, a master gave the first child of Henny to his daughter, the second to his wife, and the third to his son, "and so Alternatively and respectively for all the increase that the said negro Henny may have."[74]

Slaves dispersed among members of the same white family could hope to see one another, at least occasionally, if they lived within accessible distances. And those temporarily hired out might look forward to returning to the slave quarter on the home plantation. But sales, especially auctions advertised widely in the *Maryland Gazette* and Virginia newspapers, were a different matter. Blacks on one large plantation learned this firsthand after their owner's death in 1764. Sold at public auctions held six months apart, which surely prolonged anxieties in the quarter, twenty-nine men, women, and children went to seventeen different masters.[75]

Involuntarily constrained in so many ways and consigned to the bottom of the social order, slaves had limited, though not ineffective, means to ease their labors and protest their status and treatment. They could lay down their tools at opportune moments (one disgruntled master complained that nothing was accomplished when his overseer left slaves unsupervised for several days at a time). They could better their material circumstances by taking food, clothing, and other property from their owners or neighboring planters—and risk severe punishment if discovered. Or they could run away.[76]

Indirect evidence (namely, the paucity of newspaper advertisements for runaways) suggests that flight usually was temporary and over fairly short distances during the colonial period. In such circumstances, acquaintances on other plantations might provide food and other assistance. Long-distance flight among strangers had to be more problematic, a point underscored by runaways from Virginia and elsewhere who made it as far as Charles County, only to be captured and jailed at Port Tobacco until masters retrieved them.[77]

So well entrenched was slavery, so well protected by white society, that local blacks almost never struck out violently against masters. When Nann allegedly poisoned fish prepared for her master's table and Jane set fire to her mistress's house, those were rare, isolated acts of resistance. And although such episodes surely unnerved whites, they did not shake the foundations of the county's hierarchical social order.[78] Until late in the colonial period, however, there was a perceived threat, real or imagined, to the social hierarchy. It came not from the slaves but from the county's large Catholic minority. But whenever concerns about Catholics intensified, so did fears that they would enlist slaves for their own purposes.

The Catholics

In the summer of 1765 a French traveler visited St. Thomas Manor and talked with Father Hunter, who stated that, of approximately ten thousand Roman Catholics living in the province, "Charles County has more of the Cathol. religion than any other [county]. . . . [H]e has generally from 800 to a th[ousan]d at his Sundays mass." The number seems surprisingly large because, under Maryland law, Catholics could hear mass only in what was deemed a private chapel, meaning a chapel attached to a residence. Nor was that the sole religious impediment they faced. Catholics also were taxed to support the Church of England. And while Protestants sent their children to

local Anglican schoolmasters, including rectors, priests were barred from operating schools. These restrictions, and political disenfranchisement, took
effect when seventeenth-century Catholic rule in Maryland gave way by 1715
to a Protestant Lord Baltimore and a state-supported Anglican establishment.
After talking with Hunter in 1765, the Frenchman concluded that "the poor
Catholiques have lost most of their privileges."[79]

Nonetheless, during much of the colonial period the Anglican majority of
Charles County distrusted and feared their Catholic neighbors because they
constituted a separate community within the larger society. Catholics did not
want their children to "apostatize from their Religion or marry Contrary to
Roman Religion." On their plantations and at St. Thomas Manor, they had
more private chapels than the Anglicans had churches. And in those chapels
the Jesuits decried the Protestant Reformation that the Anglicans extolled.
Martin Luther, in Father Hunter's preaching, was a heretic at "war ag[ain]st
the true Church, aiming at nothing less than its total overthrow & a total
abolishing of all religious worship & veneration instituted & establish'd by
the Redeemer of mankind." Hunter's hero, a man to be emulated for his
"unbounded zeal," was Ignatius Loyola, pillar of the Counterreformation and
founder of the Jesuit order.[80]

In tending their flock, the Jesuits seemed indefatigable. Father Joseph Mosley, who spent six years in Charles and St. Mary's counties beginning in 1758,
relished his calling. "I've care of above fifteen hundred souls," he wrote soon
after arriving from England. "No Prince in his Court can have more satisfaction and enjoy himself more, than I do in instructing those that are under my
charge. I am daily on horseback, visiting the sick, comforting the infirm,
strengthening the pusillanimous." He regularly rode 150 to 300 miles a week
because "We have many to attend, and few to attend them. . . . and in our
way of living, we ride almost as much by night as by day, in all weathers, in
heats, cold, rain, frost or snow." After riding nearly 400 miles on his last
"Mass fare" through the area, in 1764, he mused that "Swamps, Runs, miry
holes, [and being] lost in the night . . . ever will in this country" attend the
Jesuit mission.[81]

In following the dictates of their religious convictions, priests and laity
alike pushed against the limits of the law. In 1752 a committee of the lower
house of the Assembly complained of "Popish Priests, or Jesuits," who "build
and erect public Mass Houses, Plantations, and Edifices, for the public Exercise of their Functions." Anyone passing by St. Thomas Manor could see for
himself. The octagonal chapel adjoining the priests' dwelling house may not
have accommodated the hundreds of people who reportedly heard Hunter say
Sunday mass, but it certainly held more than the handful of Jesuits in residence.[82]

Catholics also thwarted the law by giving children a parochial education. More than once the Assembly heard complaints that priests were "corrupting the Minds of Youth by teaching School publicly" and by illegally sending children to convents and "Popish Seminaries" in France and Flanders, where they were "out of the King's Obedience and Allegiance" and trained in papist "Superstitions and dangerous Principles." Charles County parents who wanted to send their children abroad to Catholic institutions contacted Father Hunter, who arranged the voyages and admission fees. The cost was substantial. William Neale, a wealthy planter, set aside both the cash in his estate and the rents of his tobacco warehouses near Port Tobacco so that two sons could "be sent home to be educated." Despite the demands of a large family, the father of Mary Ann Semmes was willing to give her a "fortune" of £150 if it gained her admittance to a nunnery. Because Mary's health made her acceptance questionable, he thereby offered 50 percent more than the usual entrance fee "rather than she shou'd fail."[83]

If a family had to "count every farthing" and could not afford the entire cost of sending a child abroad, Hunter was not deterred. He persuaded Benedictine nuns to admit Marianne Hagan for a reduced fee, perhaps because they trusted his assertion that she was "as valuable I believe in most or all respects as I have hitherto sent over." The young woman's father had suffered financial reverses, Hunter explained, and had the Benedictines refused to take her, "God knows how matters wou'd have gone w[i]th her, but heaven ever

LANCASTER FAMILY CHALICE (CA. 1600). *This English communion chalice was long used in the Lancaster family of Charles County. For nearly a century before the Revolution, Maryland Catholics could hear mass only in private chapels and homes, and the portable slate altar stone made any table an altar. Georgetown University Art Collection, Washington, D.C.*

provides for its elect." Even abject poverty did not deter the Jesuit superior. When an orphan who had no immediate family wanted to enter a convent, Hunter managed to find an English noblewoman willing to donate the £100 entrance fee.[84]

So parents watched as vessels carrying their "very little ones" and the older children disappeared from view. Many were "great sufferers" until they learned that sons and daughters were safely in Europe and with "Countrymen" who had preceded them. Once abroad, the youths remained for several years or a lifetime. By his father's orders, Jonathan Boarman had to "stay his time out wh[ich]ever way his thoughts may turn as to a state of life, the money being all payd & the F[athe]r having none to throw away." Parents could ease the separation with the thought that, in France and Flanders, Catholics had more religious freedom than they knew in Maryland.[85]

Had Catholics contented themselves solely with individual piety and mutual encouragement, they might not have provoked the wrath of the county's Protestant majority. But the Catholics were not silent. They proselytized, even among black slaves. Anglicans charged that Catholics, especially the Jesuits, were disputatious and unrelenting in their attempts illegally "to withdraw our People from the Communion of the Church of England." From the early days of Protestant rule in Maryland, complaints arose that priests made "it theire business to go up and down the County to persons houses when dying and phrantick and endeavour to Seduce and make proselytes of them." Intermarriage, too, was hazardous, and not only because priests reportedly made the non-Catholic partner swear that the couple's children would be reared in the Church of Rome. He or she also was pressured to convert. Once, after a local priest had published the banns for a Catholic man and a Protestant woman, he reportedly "turned them both violently out of the Chapel, in the Presence of the Congregation"—on their wedding day!— because the would-be bride adamantly refused to forsake her creed. Then, too, the priests' "public Preaching is so notorious and unreserved," a committee of Anglican ministers asserted in 1753, "that there are known Instances of their Preaching publicly to large mixed Congregations in Port Tobacco Court House." What the Anglicans feared, the Jesuits applauded. "Our discourse ought to be chiefly of the progress of our Missions," Hunter wrote during his spiritual retreat in 1749, to which he added, "where & how greater good may be done, more conversions be made, what methods to be taken for the catechising of Children and Negroes."[86]

Catholic separateness and proselytizing were bad enough, from the Anglicans' point of view, but their worst fears had an imperial dimension. For so long as Catholic France vied with Protestant England for control of the North American continent or aided the Catholic Pretender to the English throne,

Anglicans in Charles County worried about the Jesuit citadel and the "papists" in their midst. As the case was phrased at a meeting of the provincial Anglican clergy in 1753, Protestantism could not survive where Catholicism prevailed, and English liberties would wither should a Catholic gain the throne. Especially between the Scottish uprising of the 1740s and the outbreak of the Seven Years' War a decade later, Anglicans in Charles County had little difficulty conjuring up visions of Catholics conspiring with the hated French, cutting Protestant throats, and inspiring slaves to foul deeds. As the Frenchman visiting St. Thomas Manor noted, the minority was "much threatened" by the majority.[87]

The year 1746 was especially tense. For months the *Maryland Gazette* was filled with news of British efforts to put down the forces of the Pretender in Scotland and with lurid anti-Catholic tracts designed to affirm "*what Detestation all true Protestants ought to have of the* Popish Religion." At such a time, when Catholics on the lower Western Shore were accused of supporting the "unnatural Rebellion" with heart and purse, and when some in St. Mary's County allegedly boasted "very frequently . . . [that] they would wash their Hands in the Blood of Protestants" and preach in the Anglican churches, Bowlen Speak could not contain himself. The Charles County planter "did, in a public Manner, drink the Pretenders Health, and good Success in his Proceedings." For that indiscretion he was hauled before the county court and then the Provincial Court in Annapolis, fined, and required to post bond "for his . . . keeping the Peace, and being of good Behaviour."[88]

Yet Speak's transgression paled when compared with the "suspected treasonable Practices" of Richard Molyneux, a "Popish Jesuit" and Hunter's predecessor at St. Thomas Manor. In March 1746 Molyneux was brought before the governor's Council and admonished about his alleged disaffection and seditious activities. Although the priest had been "remarkably unguarded" since his arrival in Maryland, Governor Thomas Bladen intoned, his behavior since the outbreak of the Scottish rebellion "exceeded all the Bounds of Prudence and Decency, and has not preserved the least Appearance of any Respect for that Government, under which your self and those of your Communion have been treated with the Greatest Tenderness and Lenity."[89]

Planters living near St. Thomas suspected Molyneux of consorting with the enemy. He was away from the manor for several months at the time of the rebellion, and "by the Neighbourhood it was supposed he . . . was gone among the French" in the backcountry. He returned with several strangers who spoke either French or Dutch—probably French, people decided. When Molyneux took the strangers into St. Mary's County to buy them horses, he aroused the curiosity of a Catholic named John Jones, who "enquired what they were, at the Priest's, who answered they were Wappalow Priests, but . . . Jones said they were no more Priests than he was, being too gay drest."[90]

Even more ominously, the Jesuit superior allegedly permitted, even encouraged, "frequent Meetings of People and Negroes under Pretence of divine Worship." However benign these gatherings may have been, they were not calculated to ease the minds of colonists who were already wary of their Catholic neighbors and suspicious that Molyneux was harboring agents of the French. Meetings that included slaves aroused "Suspicion of something else being designed than a bare Exercise of Religion."[91]

The end of the rebellion in 1746 did not end religious strife in the county. Priests' "Traiterous Practices" continued and invited prosecution—or so a proclamation from the governor asserted. In September of that year, Molyneux took the precaution of temporarily deeding St. Thomas Manor and all other Jesuit property in the province to a Charles County layman, in exchange for five shillings sterling and a barrel of corn. A few months later convict rebels who were remnants of the Catholic Pretender's forces arrived in the Potomac and were set to work in the fields. And more than a year after the rebellion ended, religious animosity flared once more. As the *Maryland Gazette* reported in September 1747, "We hear from *Charles* County, that as two Men were lately debating about Religion, they got to such a heat of Passion, that one of them stabb'd the other, of which wound he died soon after."[92]

Antipathy between Anglicans and Catholics subsided thereafter, only to be rekindled during the final British-French struggle for control of North America. In the 1750s, as tensions along the frontier mounted and ultimately touched off the Seven Years' War, accusations about Maryland Catholics increased. All the old charges about the growth of popery, the evil intents of the Jesuits, and the Catholic foment of slave insurrection were raised anew. This time one of the accusers was the Reverend Isaac Campbell, a young Scotsman who had lived through the uprising in his homeland and had since emigrated to America. By 1753, when clergymen of the established church gathered in Annapolis to consider "the dangerous Encroachments of Popery, and its Growth in this Province," Campbell was the rector of Trinity Parish, just a few miles from St. Thomas Manor. From him the clerics (and in due time the governor and lower house of Assembly) heard about Jesuit proselytizing activities in the county. And from him they learned of priests who preached in the courthouse "at public Times" when convicted criminals who were Catholics were on their way to the gallows. The practice gave "great Offence," although Campbell did not say who was offended, and, he charged, the justices and sheriff were most imprudent to tolerate such preaching.[93]

Others may have been more willing to allow the condemned the comfort of a last sermon and a few moments of repentance, but Campbell's was not the only local voice raised against Catholics. In 1756 "the Freemen, and the Electors of Charles County" faulted the Assembly for not stopping the immigration of priests and laity, and they also complained about the Jesuits' "public Churches," their efforts to convert non-Catholics, and their wealth. Not only was St. Thomas Manor the most valuable estate in the entire county, but the priests there occupied a residence so fine that even some Jesuits considered it "a palace unbecoming a religious order."[94]

The barrage of accusations against Catholics coincided with the outbreak of war. In the summer of 1754, Virginia troops led by George Washington went down to defeat against the French. The following March a large flotilla carrying General Edward Braddock and a British army sailed up the Potomac and past the county's shoreline, en route to their sad destiny in the American wilderness. Within a few weeks the people who watched the ships glide by that day were caught up in the worst episode of alleged servant and slave conspiracy in the county's history. The court records of the affair are mute as to how it began or whether Catholics were thought to be involved. The timing nonetheless suggests deep anxiety in the society, an anxiety fed by fears of Catholics near at hand and Frenchmen on the frontier.[95]

The episode began with a bowl of boiled milk and bread. In January 1755 a white servant named William Stratton served it to his master, Jeremiah Chase, an Anglican and "Gentleman of considerable Eminence in the Law" newly elected to the House of Delegates. Although Chase reportedly became ill before he had time to set down his spoon, and "Languished" thereafter, he was well enough to attend the Assembly in February. Then, at the beginning of April, he suddenly died. Stratton was jailed, as were Chase's slave Jemmy and several others who belonged to different masters. The charges were conspiracy and poisoning, and Stratton was said to have confessed to the deed. By the time a special court of oyer and terminer convened at Port Tobacco in June, two more slaves were indicted for attempting to poison their masters, allegedly within days of Chase's death.[96]

In separate trials presided over by the senior justices of the county court, all the defendants pleaded not guilty. Convinced that knowledge of events extended well beyond the accused, the court called more than thirty witnesses, white and black, including slaves brought in specifically to testify against the slave defendants. In the end the white servant Stratton, the bondwoman Jemmy, and Anthony ("the Poison Doctor") were hanged. Upon the order of the governor, their bodies were strung up in chains along the public road, silent testimony to the consequences of slave conspiracies. A bondman named Jack was hanged for attempting to poison his master in a plot that reportedly backfired when two slave children accidentally ate the potion

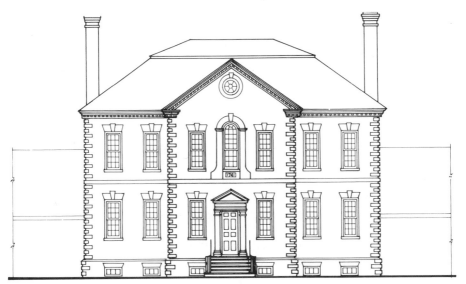

THE JESUIT RESIDENCE AT ST. THOMAS MANOR (EARLY 1740s). *An eighteenth-century traveler found this building, one of the finest and most imposing examples of Georgian architecture in Charles County, "exceedingly handsome, executed in fine taste, and of a very beautiful model . . . imagination cannot form the idea of a perspective more noble, rich, and delightful, than this charming villa in reality is." The roof originally was hipped, and the chimneys were freestanding at roof level (top). Drawing by J. Richard Rivoire. Photograph by Thomas N. Lee.*

and died. Yet another slave was acquitted of attempting to poison his master. And bondwoman Hannah suffered Moses's law: Her ear was chopped off, and she received thirty-nine lashes for giving false testimony in court. Her punishment, and the executions on July 4, ended the episode. It served a social purpose. A few months later, in response to the governor's request for information about "Reports of the tumultuous Meetings & Cabaling of Negroes, the Misbehaviour of the Roman Catholicks in some Countys and the absence of some of the Priests," the Charles County magistrates reported that patient and circumspect inquiries in their neighborhoods had not turned up anything of note.[97]

Britain's victory in the Seven Years' War swept the French from North America, and this immensely relieved religious tensions in Charles County. Not that Protestants were any more accepting of Catholic doctrine. An occasional Anglican still fortified himself by reading *The Morning Exercises against Popery* and *The Moderation of the Church of England*, while a newcomer gossiped that the Jesuits "seem to have a haram of female slaves, who are now become white by their mixture" and "absolutely slaves in every sense to these priests." Yet the political climate had changed. With France defeated, greater tolerance was possible and social stability was enhanced. No one protested when, during the mid-1760s, Hunter and several French seamstresses operated a "School de la haute ville" that trained students to dress flax, spin, and weave. Nor did anyone complain when Gerard Blackstone Causin, a wealthy Catholic, became foreman of the county's grand jury in 1770. And when Hunter tried to establish the town of Edenburgh at the Jesuit manor, he found the local delegates to the Assembly, all Anglicans, willing to help present his petition to the legislature.[98]

In retrospect, the Catholic threat was more imagined than real, especially after Richard Molyneux, who seemed to be the Counterreformation incarnate, passed from the scene. The number of planters daring or drunk enough to toast the Pretender's health was small, as were the numbers of Jesuits in residence and of children dispatched to European convents and seminaries. Yet, as the coming of the Revolution itself showed, fear of conspiracy can be as powerful as the real thing. French departure from the continent dampened fears and thereby helped unify the society. In the next war, the county's Catholics would have every reason to stand shoulder to shoulder with their Anglican neighbors against the British, for then their political and religious liberty would hang in the balance.

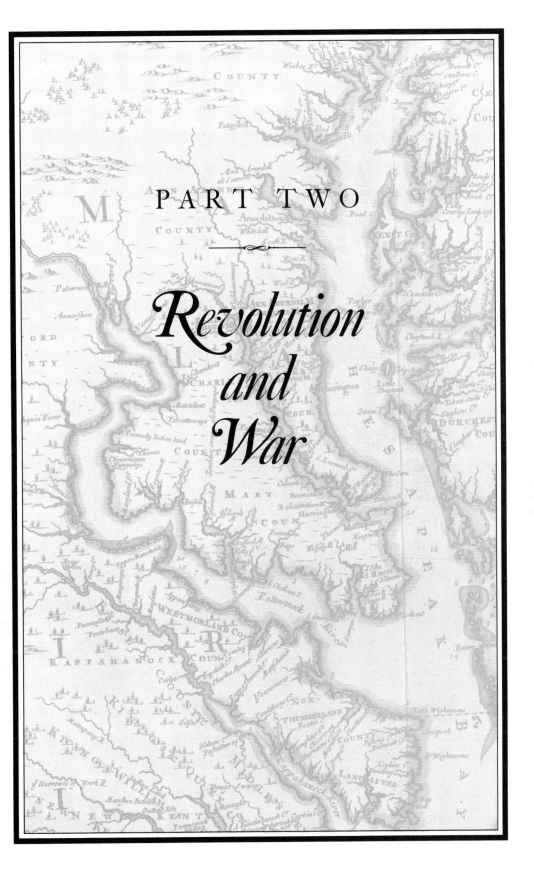

PART TWO

Revolution
and
War

CHAPTER THREE

Primed for Revolution

AT THE END OF THE SEVEN YEARS' WAR, NO SAGE COULD HAVE PRE-
dicted that British colonists in North America shortly would stage the first
successful anticolonial revolution in modern history, manage to win a war
against the strongest naval power on earth, and found a nation out of thirteen
disparate colonies extending more than twelve hundred miles along the Atlantic seaboard. Nor could any sage have foreseen that the Declaration of Independence would usher in the most politically creative period in American
history—during which were laid the foundations of government based upon
popular consent, written constitutions, and division of powers between the
states and the national government—or, indeed, that the American Revolution would be the first in an age of revolutions that swept across much of
Europe and Latin America by the middle of the nineteenth century. The
colonies at the close of the Seven Years' War in 1763 seemed far too diverse
and fractious for all that, despite common membership and pride in a victori-
ous British Empire. "Such is the difference of character, of manners, of religion, of interest, of the different colonies," wrote one traveler, that if they
were "left to themselves, there would soon be a civil war from one end of the
continent to the other; while the Indians and negroes would, with better
reason, impatiently watch [for] the opportunity of exterminating them all
together." John Adams, a native son of New England, added that "inter-

course" among the colonies was "rare, and their knowledge of each other so imperfect."[1]

Among the many remarkable features of the American Revolution are the speed with which it developed and the momentum it attained between 1765, the year of the Stamp Act crisis, and 1776, the year of Independence, when "Thirteen clocks were made to strike together." During that period British government ministers intended a series of measures—including the Stamp Act, the Townshend Revenue Act, rigorous enforcement of customs collections, and the stationing of British army units in Boston—to be rational, fair policies for tightening imperial administration and raising revenues for the colonies' defense and support. Increasing numbers of colonists, however, came to regard these measures as violations of their fundamental rights as Englishmen and, in their darkest musings, as a deliberate ministerial conspiracy to reduce them to slavery. Beginning with the Stamp Act crisis, they protested and resisted—with learned pamphlets and simple songs, with humble petitions to Parliament and mob actions aimed at royal officials in America, and with a potent economic weapon, the embargoing of trade with the mother country. For its part, Parliament consistently claimed, in the words of the Declaratory Act of 1766, that the colonies "have been, are, and of right ought to be, subordinate unto, and dependent upon the imperial crown and parliament of Great Britain" and subject to British law "in all cases whatsoever."[2]

At one level all was cacophony while colonists vigorously debated one another and the British government about the extent of their rights and liberties, the nature of the connection between mother country and colonies, and what forms of resistance were justified. Yet out of the cacophony emerged the powerful ideology of the Revolution, with its emphasis on inalienable rights (including the right of revolution) and limited government founded on popular consent. Out of the cacophony, too, emerged an intercolonial communications network composed of individuals and committees that exchanged information, interpreted events and motives, and attempted to coordinate and unify colonial resistance. This network became the central means for disseminating revolutionary ideas and tactics.[3]

Resistance might not have ripened into rebellion, at least not as soon as it did, without the Boston Tea Party and the retaliatory Coercive Acts. Convinced that the wellspring of disaffection and disobedience lay in Massachusetts, and that conciliatory moves like repeal of the Stamp Act and Townshend duties had only emboldened the dissidents, Parliament in early 1774 reacted sharply to the destruction of tea in Boston Harbor. It closed the town's port until restitution was made, and it radically altered civil government in the colony by making the upper house of the legislature appointive (as in all other royal colonies) and by curtailing the powers of town meetings. That in turn galvanized men at the forefront of the revolutionary movement elsewhere, for if Parliament succeeded in unilaterally changing the Massachusetts form of government, no colony was safe. During the summer of 1774 extralegal popular meetings and conventions throughout America elected delegates to the First Continental Congress, which was to fashion a unified response to the Coercive Acts and other colonial grievances. Meeting at Philadelphia that autumn, Congress asked the colonists to embargo trade with Britain once more and to prepare for their own defense. By 1775, the year in which the battles of Lexington and Concord touched off the Revolutionary War, towns, counties, and colonies from New Hampshire to Georgia were part of a vast network of extralegal committees—of observation, correspondence, and safety—as well as provincial conventions that enforced the trade embargo, began mobilizing military manpower, and otherwise usurped many functions of the established colonial governments. This "system of action," to invoke John Adams's phrase, was the organizational base of the Revolution.[4]

No colony, no community traveled the road to revolution in exactly the same way. Local political dynamics, economic interests, lofty ideals and petty quarrels, as well as a host of other factors, ensured that the experience of each was distinctive, even as all ultimately arrived at Independence. Because Maryland, as a proprietary province, was the possession of the lords Baltimore, the great political issues during most of the colonial period had centered on proprietary, not royal, prerogatives. The major divide within the government ran between two groups. The proprietary establishment included the governor and his Council (which was also the upper house of the Assembly), officials who served at the pleasure of the proprietary regime, and Anglican clergymen. Members of the second and more fluid group, often called the country party, tended to oppose proprietary interests and rhetorically cast themselves as guardians of the people's interests—understandably so, since the country party's primary arena was in the House of Delegates, the elected lower house of Assembly. Out of the party came the core of revolutionary leadership in Maryland, while the proprietary establishment had a vested interest in preserving the old regime.[5]

Maryland politics in the decade before Independence, like the Revolution generally, displayed a pattern of provocative events following in rapid sequence and building a momentum never known before. Sometimes British measures, particularly the Stamp and Coercive Acts, drew the sharpest reactions. At other times the context was proprietary, especially between 1770 and 1773, when Marylanders were embroiled in a multifaceted conflict over officeholders' fees, Anglican ministers' salaries, and public tobacco inspection.

Whatever the focus, the course of events offered many opportunities for people, both prominent and obscure, to articulate dissatisfactions, join in the heady experience of challenging constituted authority, and participate in extralegal activities ranging from deliberative public meetings to mob action.[6]

Accounts of the coming of the Revolution in Maryland have traditionally taken a province-wide perspective, which includes events in local communities only sporadically, when they demonstrate or add detail to some broader theme. The result is an interweaving of events within and among several levels—local, provincial, continental, and imperial—with the sharpest focus on the provincial level, primarily at Annapolis. This approach, while valuable, ignores the ways in which local populations individually moved toward rebellion, as well as the pace at which they entered the revolutionary mainstream. A sharp focus on the local level reveals the blend of indigenous and external, unique and shared circumstances so characteristic of the Revolution everywhere. This same vantage, moreover, is essential to understanding how rural areas, where the vast majority of colonists lived, were drawn into a movement whose initial flash points were in urban centers, particularly colonial capitals. Without the support of rural communities, the Revolution could not have succeeded.

INVITATIONS TO CHANGE

In Charles County, several long-standing circumstances undergirded the revolutionary movement. The nature of proprietary rule and the condition of the Anglican church created grievances and encouraged alienation from two of the most important institutions in the colony. On the other hand, ideas about fundamental civil rights and even about alternatives to proprietary and monarchical forms of government prepared men to resist what they interpreted as infringements of their rights, and, eventually, to entertain thoughts of abandoning traditional allegiances. These were sturdy foundations upon which revolution could be built.

To begin with the proprietary regime, few people had much affection for their absentee lord. The last Lord Baltimore (who was proprietor from 1751 to 1771 and was to be succeeded by a bastard son) had a reputation for debauchery and rapacity and was "much Dispised in Maryland." Viewing the colony mostly as a source of place and profit, he habitually appointed favorites, sometimes men of invisible merit, to lucrative government and clerical offices. For every one he sent to America, moreover, a native-born gentleman was bypassed, as Daniel of St. Thomas Jenifer of Charles County learned firsthand. Between 1766 and 1768 Jenifer vaulted into the inner circle at Annapolis and gained major offices under the patronage of Governor Horatio Sharpe. When Sharpe lost the governorship, however, Jenifer's political fortunes sank, and he had to make way for proprietary favorites dispatched from England.[7]

If Jenifer was disenchanted with the vagaries of patronage, other county residents were discontented about proprietary revenues, which enabled Lord Baltimore to live in considerable splendor in England. His annual income from the province came to the immense sum of approximately £12,500 sterling, including quitrents on every tract of land and duties on every trading vessel and hogshead of tobacco. Occasionally the county's representatives in the House of Delegates, in concert with fellow legislators, protested these levies. Sometimes freemen themselves complained, as they did in 1756, when they counted the duties among the "Aggrievances, Extortions, and Oppressions" suffered under the proprietorship.[8]

Other grievances concerned the established Church of England. In structure the church was as hierarchical as the planting society of which it was a part. Its financial foundation was broad: Every taxpayer, whether an Anglican or not, paid to support his or her neighborhood parish. And every freeholder was expected to appear on Easter Monday to choose vestrymen and church-wardens. Yet the power to make major decisions lay not with the communicants or even the vestry, but with the Assembly in Annapolis and the proprietor in London. If a congregation and vestry wanted to build a new church or chapel or substantially repair an existing structure, they had to petition the Assembly for authority to assess taxpayers for the cost. Similarly, only the Assembly could redraw the boundary lines of parishes, which might markedly alter their tax base. And only Lord Baltimore could appoint the Anglican minister, or rector, of each parish, a power he guarded zealously. Congregations therefore had no say about the men who occupied their pulpits and were supposed to lead them in piety. Nor could they discipline or remove wayward shepherds. Once installed in a parish, a rector remained until he left voluntarily or died.[9]

[margin annotation: LORD BALTIMORE IN CONTROL FROM LONDON ↓ PROBS. W/ CHURCH]

Clerical livings in Maryland ranked among the most lucrative in the British Empire because they were pegged to the number of taxables, or polls, in each parish and because the proprietary government seldom created new benefices in response to population growth. Charles County entered the eighteenth century with four parishes and a population of twenty-eight hundred souls. On the eve of the Revolution, the same four parishes included more than fifteen thousand people. Rectors' salaries in 1767 ranged from £138 sterling in Durham Parish to £254 in Port Tobacco Parish, which made it the fifth most

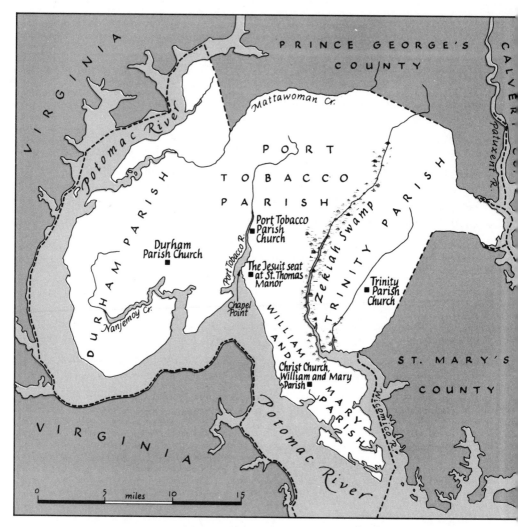

The Anglicans and the Catholics. The exact boundary lines of the Anglican parishes are unknown, owing to official but unspecific descriptions such as "beginning at Phillip Hoskin's Quarter, soe with a straight line to the head of Joseph Bullett's Mill Branch. . . ." Durham Parish lay west of Nanjemoy Creek and south of Mattawoman Creek. Port Tobacco, the largest parish in the county, extended from Nanjemoy Creek on the west, to the Prince George's County line on the north, to Zekiah Swamp on the east. William and Mary Parish mostly occupied the neck of land between the Potomac and Wicomico rivers. These three parishes dated from 1692, when the Church of England was originally established in Maryland. Trinity Parish, organized in 1744 out of two earlier parishes, ran southeast from Zekiah Swamp to the St. Mary's County line, northward to that of Prince George's County, and eastward to the Patuxent River. The northwestern corner of Charles County, above Mattawoman Creek, was, for religious purposes, part of a parish church in Prince George's County.

St. Thomas Manor, owned by the Society of Jesus, served the Roman Catholic population. The Jesuits maintained their headquarters on five hundred acres of land on the east side of the Port Tobacco River. On the west side, another thirty-five hundred acres were leased to tenant farmers. Other holdings lay scattered about the county.

valuable benefice in the entire colony. By the following year, because tobacco growers had to pay in leaf and the price was rising, each local rectorship was worth at least £300. The provincial clergy, a jocular observer once mused, "minded hogsheads of tobacco more than points of doctrine, either orthodox or hetrodox."[10]

Clergymen seated in Charles County during the eighteenth century were a mixed lot. As elsewhere in Maryland, a substantial number of them were Scotsmen, "the Generality" of whom spoke English so poorly, in Governor Sharpe's estimation, that "near half the Inhabitants have some Room for complaint that they are obliged to pay their Minister for preaching to them in an unknown Tongue." The language problem nevertheless paled when compared with the behavior of some divines. William Maconchie occupied both PARISH Port Tobacco and Durham parishes for three decades until his death in 1741, SCANDALS and although a "Mere Nusance" compared with other "Rascally Clergy," he was bad enough. "He fights & drinks on all occasions," a visiting Englishman alleged, and, in sum, "makes the church stink." Maconchie's successor at Port Tobacco reportedly was a man of "much Levity, no Learning and [is] Supposed to be a Free thinker or Deist; he gives himself great Liberties in ridiculeing religion." About the same time, William and Mary Parish was scandalized by the "many Irregularities" of its minister, who was indicted in the county court for assault and for "being Drunk on the Sabbath day" and who was characterized in a letter to the bishop of London as "the most absolute sot in nature."[11]

By the Seven Years' War, less colorful men were serving the county's Anglicans. An Irishman installed at Port Tobacco Parish was merely "a very poor heavy Preacher." And John MacPherson, the Scottish-born rector of William and Mary Parish, was merely negligent and insolvent. No later than 1762 he returned to Britain for a protracted stay. Although his parishioners diligently searched for a temporary curate, an assistant clergyman, they still lacked a resident minister, despite paying for one, in August 1763. When MacPherson learned that the congregation intended to complain to the governor about his long absence, he quickly wrote to a confidant in Maryland: "Shou'd this be the case, I hope you'll endeavour to make Interest with the Governor, for continuance yet of Indulgence. Had I not confidence in his favour, I know not but I shou'd be in danger of deprivation: for the people, I must own, have had too much reason for exclaiming."[12]

MacPherson eventually returned to his benefice and by 1768 was languishing in the county jail as an insolvent debtor, notwithstanding his clerical salary, profits from glebe lands and slaves, and other assets. After the county's delegation to the Assembly decided that he could not possibly extricate himself from debt or jail, the Assembly ordered MacPherson's release; allowed

CHRIST CHURCH, WILLIAM AND MARY PARISH. *Founded in 1692, William and Mary is one of the original Anglican parishes in Charles County. The current church, built after 1810, retains vestiges of an eighteenth-century structure. Photograph by Thomas N. Lee.*

COMMUNION CHALICE, DURHAM PARISH CHURCH. *At his death in 1704 William Dent bequeathed £5 sterling "to purchase necessaries or ornaments" for the parish where he had served as a vestryman since its founding in 1692. This communion chalice and its paten cover bear the markings of a London silversmith and the inscription "The Gift of William Dent Esquire to Durham Parish." During the last years of his life Dent was both a county court justice and speaker of the lower house of the Maryland Assembly. Information provided by Margaret Shannon. Photograph by John C. Kopp. Courtesy of Christ Church, Durham Parish.*

him to retain his clothing, library, and less than half of his salary; and directed that three county justices use his remaining assets to liquidate his debts. He was still insolvent on the eve of Independence.[13]

While MacPherson's parishioners carried on without him during his protracted stays in Britain and the local jail, Isaac Campbell's tenure in adjacent Trinity Parish offered them an example of the best that could be expected of the Anglican divines assigned to Charles County. Campbell, another Scotsman, became rector at Trinity in 1751 and for more than three decades labored to meet the spiritual needs of a parish that he described as "upwards of twenty Miles extent." In addition, by 1763 he had founded "a justly celebrated school" where, to judge from his personal library, he offered students both a classical education and instruction in geography, surveying, and navigation.[14]

During the 1760s and 1770s, Campbell joined other rectors on the lower Western Shore in trying to improve the quality of the clerics appointed to Maryland parishes. They identified several local young men believed to be sober, honest, pious, and well affected to the English church and constitution, sent them to England with recommendations for ordination, and promised to make each a curate until some parish needed a rector. Campbell offered a curacy to one man, if he was ordained, "knowing of none that would be so agreeable . . . to my Parishioners or myself."[15]

The laity of Trinity Parish, therefore, might count themselves fortunate in having a rector whose moral conduct was never cause for complaint, who was dedicated to their intellectual as well as their spiritual growth, and who tried to improve the local Anglican priesthood by sponsoring native Marylanders. Yet the parishioners' good fortune was not of their own making. They had not chosen Campbell. When he passed from the scene, Trinity might well have to accept a successor with low morals and little concern for the congregation's welfare, if the travails of other parishes in the late colonial period were any guide. Such men, grumbled a former local rector, "give great offence to many devout People," encouraged laity to regard the clergy with contempt, and fostered both Catholicism and unbelief.[16]

Because the provincial Church of England lacked any means of disciplining errant rectors, its hold on the Anglicans of Charles County was tenuous. For non-Anglicans, it was an institution to which they did not belong but which they were required by law to support financially. Catholics added that burden to the other religious and political disabilities they endured under the proprietor. The situation of the Anglican church was ripe for change.

Political ideas current in the county also suggested the possibility of change. From gentlemen to paupers, white men talked freely about their supposed fundamental rights as English subjects, rights that, they were quick

TALK OF ENGLISH RIGHTS

to assert, protected their persons and property. Some men also contemplated what form of government would best secure those rights and, in so doing, drew upon classical and Enlightenment ideas that helped fuel the American Revolution. The Reverend Campbell, for one, was conversant with the writings of Aristotle, Plutarch, Cicero, and Caesar; the Christian humanism of Erasmus; the scientific thought of Newton; the political theories of Locke, Montesquieu, Grotius, and Pufendorf; and the Scottish common sense philosophy of Francis Hutcheson. Such an intellectual brew encouraged educated men to question their own institutions and habits with an eye to improving or even supplanting them.[17]

For example, Thomas Stone, who became one of the county's foremost revolutionary leaders, received a classical education at Port Tobacco, then read law in Annapolis during the mid-1760s. He also attended the Forensic Club, whose gatherings, unlike those of other clubs in the provincial capital, involved more than imbibing Jamaica rum and Madeira wine, smoking tobacco, and trading witticisms. Founded in 1759, the Forensic Club included legislators and law students, and each monthly or fortnightly supper featured a formal debate. Is democracy or monarchy the better form of government? Should soldiers who doubt the justice of a war nevertheless fight? Can sovereignty be acquired through conquest? Do people "have a right to dethrone a King when he degenerates into a Tyrant?" And, at the height of colonial resistance to the Stamp Act, can "used & approved privileges . . . be taken from a particular Set of people for the Advantage of the Major Part of the State?" In this convivial atmosphere Stone, a future signer of the Declaration of Independence, debated questions that he soon heard urgently raised in revolutionary committees and conventions and in the Continental Congress.[18]

Not everyone approved of the ideas that Stone and other young men encountered as part of their formal educations. When Charlotte Hall School was founded in 1774, Jonathan Boucher decided to mark the occasion with a lengthy sermon on "education among ourselves," which he planned to deliver at Port Tobacco Church. Rector of an Anglican parish in Prince George's County and a strident, contentious supporter of king, church, and proprietor, Boucher also had a penchant for telling others what he thought was wrong with them. His intended audience would be no exception. By allowing children to study the writings of ancient Greeks and Romans, he charged, parents and schoolmasters were exposing them to the dangerous and erroneous doctrine of republicanism, of self-government. When classical writings were held up as models of composition, rhetoric, and oratory, students tended to accept "the sentiments and principles of our great masters in the art, who were republicans." Therefore, "as subjects, intended to live under a monarchy, we are at least preposterously, if not dangerously, educated, when we are taught to prefer republicanism." To remedy the problem as he defined it, Boucher wanted the first schoolmaster of Charlotte Hall to be a devout Anglican, take an oath that the British sovereign was the only rightful ruler of the American colonies, and do nothing to lessen his students' esteem for and obedience to the British government. For their part, students should diligently read the history, constitution, and laws of England at least as assiduously as the classics.[19]

Boucher never delivered his castigation. By the time he was ready to mount the pulpit in Port Tobacco, inhabitants of the county were "much exasperated at the proceedings of the [British] Ministry and talk as if they were determined to dispute the matter with the sword." A decade of intermittent conflict between England and America had given new life to the abstract ideas contained in the schoolbooks. "Owing to some embarrassments in Government," as Boucher delicately phrased the matter, his sermon was postponed and ultimately canceled.[20]

PREPARATION, 1765–70

Between 1765 and the early 1770s, white residents of Charles County had an unusual number of opportunities to question and resist established authority. In limited, modest ways, they mimicked actions undertaken elsewhere to protest the Stamp Act and the Townshend duties, manifestations of tightened British imperial policy. Then, beginning in 1770, political and economic problems within Maryland sparked individual and organized resistance and the circumvention of proprietary government. The prime sources of local discontent were the collapse of the public tobacco inspection system and a related furor over Anglican rectors' salaries and proprietary officers' fees. In this provincial context, inhabitants moved from disaffection to outright disobedience, and they experimented with a wider range of protest tactics than they had used against Britain. Throughout the period the county's elite, especially the magistrates, played a leading, though not an entirely unified, role. In addition, ordinary men and women saw that the proprietary government, the established church, and Parliament itself could be successfully challenged. By 1774, when news of the Coercive Acts reached the county, people were primed for revolutionary thoughts and deeds. With their attention suddenly focused on the rapidly escalating imperial crisis, they hurriedly embraced those extralegal tactics with the most revolutionary potential: politics out of doors and crowd action. Having taken longer than urban areas, whether Annapolis, Boston, or Charleston, to reach this point, the county swiftly caught up and moved into the revolutionary mainstream.

The Stamp Act offered the first lessons in resistance. Between double mourning bars, the April 18, 1765, issue of the *Maryland Gazette* announced "melancholy and alarming" accounts, soon confirmed, that Parliament intended to tax the colonies directly for their own defense beginning November 1. The act required that contracts, bills of sale, newspapers and almanacs, ship clearances, civil court documents, and many other papers essential to government, commerce, and the exchange of information be printed or written on stamped paper distributed by a crown agent. Although stamp taxes were common in England, American colonists quickly interpreted the 1765 law as a dangerous innovation, a threat to their property and the powers of their legislative assemblies to levy internal taxes. In Maryland everyone from the governor to protesters in the streets became aroused, while the *Gazette* barraged the public with news of resistance in other colonies. After mobs in northern colonies forced stamp distributors to resign, thus ingeniously making implementation of the act impossible there, a crowd coursed through the streets of Annapolis. When it hanged the Maryland distributor in effigy and destroyed his warehouse, the panicked man fled the province. More subdued protest prevailed when Governor Sharpe, worried about possible further violence and aware that the Stamp Act threatened Lord Baltimore's prerogatives under the Maryland charter, allowed the legislature to meet. The lower house promptly branded the act an unconstitutional violation of the Assembly's "sole right to levy taxes and impositions on the inhabitants of this province, or their property and effects" and, for good measure, argued that Parliament had no right to tax the colonies because they were not represented in it.[21]

Although Annapolis was the center of activity in Maryland, information about the crisis reached rural areas through word of mouth, correspondence, and the pages of the *Maryland Gazette*, which cast the act as a mortal threat to liberty and property. No one rioted in Charles County—neither a stamp distributor nor stamped paper was to be found there—but people rankled at Parliament's determination to tax them. Their first tactic was avoidance.

News of the Stamp Act arrived in Port Tobacco at a difficult time, when "it hath pleased almighty God to send a hard winter & scarsity by a Defissient summer" and just after desperate men had secretly posted notices threatening to kill the sheriff, magistrates, and constables if they issued warrants or attempted to apprehend delinquent debtors. Undeterred by this threat to their lives and authority, the magistrates actually accelerated proceedings against debtors in an effort to clear the court docket while use of unstamped paper was still legal. Entered into the records during the August court session were an extraordinary 210 judgments for debt, substantially more than all judgments entered during the preceding three sessions. Individuals, too, hastened to put their affairs in order before November 1. Beginning attorneys like Thomas Stone usually were rather leisurely about establishing their circuits, the string of courts in which they practiced. But in 1765 Stone had no time to lose if he was to avoid the highest stamp duty of all, £10 sterling for admission to any single court. From late April to the end of summer, therefore, he rode hundreds of miles across Maryland and was admitted to practice before the bars of the Mayor's Court in Annapolis and the courts of Anne Arundel, Prince George's, Frederick, Charles, and probably several other counties. That October, the month before the act was to take effect, men and women hurried to the probate officer in Port Tobacco to file wills and take out letters testamentary. All of these actions legally avoided stamp duties. None of them directly contested the act.[22]

[margin note: CHARLES CO. STAMP ACT RESISTANCE]

The first known episode of overt resistance in Charles County came when the court, in concert with others throughout Maryland, refused to hold its November session. Because duties did not apply to criminal proceedings, the justices might have met for that purpose alone and yet not recognized the Stamp Act. Closing the court thus signaled resistance, not merely reluctance to conduct business because stamped paper was unavailable.[23]

By March 1766 several county courts, including the one in Charles, had reopened. Although this is generally interpreted as a radical step, premised on the novel idea that an act of Parliament was unconstitutional and therefore void, the Charles County court records tell a more cautious story. At its March session the court heard only criminal matters. Besides indicting twenty-two whites for bastardy, breach of the peace, or theft, the grand jury charged three slaves with murder. The slaves were immediately tried for knifing a white man in the back, and two of them went to the gallows. Public order had to be preserved; a society thoroughly committed to slavery could not afford to let slave crimes go unpunished for long. If anyone pressed the court to hear civil cases or attend to community needs such as poor relief, the justices refused. The court never openly violated the Stamp Act by handling civil matters.[24]

One of the most effective protest methods that American colonists hit upon in 1765 was nonimportation of British goods. That caught the attention of British merchants and enlisted their influence in securing repeal in early 1766. Here, too, the Charles County experience was anything but extreme. Initiated by merchants in New York and Philadelphia, nonimportation was in effect only briefly in Maryland and scarcely affected the county. Yet embargoed trade evidently turned people's thoughts to replacing British manufacturers with domestically produced goods. Hence two local planters brought fifty yards of homespun linen to the courthouse in August 1766 so that the justices could inspect and reward these examples of colonial self-sufficiency.[25]

[margin note: NON IMPORTATION 1765]

Although actual resistance was mild, the lingering effects of the crisis were profound. The county was inundated with information about the full panoply

[margin notes: IDEAS OF REV. FROM OTHER COLONIES IMPORTANT TO MINDS OF CHARLES CO.]

of colonial actions—ranging from arid constitutional arguments to the systematic destruction of the governor's house in Massachusetts—which formed a reservoir of ideas and tactics that might be tapped later. Just as important, the crisis diminished the authority of government, whether royal or proprietary. The Frenchman whose visit to the lower Western Shore during the summer of 1765 took in St. Thomas Manor and noisy taverns marveled at how vehemently people, even in high proprietary circles, castigated the act. "It is Certain that this act has made a great alteration in the americans Disposition towards greatbritain," the Frenchman observed after attending a dinner at which the "rage" of Daniel of St. Thomas Jenifer and other gentlemen increased as the wine flowed. The company raised a huzzah at the thought of taking up arms to defend their liberties and property, and seemed convinced that "if the americans took it in head[,] they were able to cope with Britain in america." Wrote one dismayed proprietary official a few years later: "[T]he People have become sensible of their Power ever since the cursed Scheme of the Stamp Act."[26]

When Parliament in 1767 passed the Townshend Revenue Act, which circumvented constitutional issues about internal taxation by levying duties on external trade, Charles County was drawn a bit further into colonial protest efforts. Buoyed by the prosperity of the late 1760s, Marylanders took their time adopting nonimportation once again. Eventually notices in the *Maryland Gazette* asked every county to send representatives to Annapolis "to consult on the most effectual Means to promote Frugality, and lessen the future Importation of Goods from Great-Britain." However chosen or self-selected (the majority who attended were legislators), these representatives agreed upon a weak, colony-wide nonimportation association in June 1769. Four Charles County men signed it: Assembly delegates John Hanson, Jr., and William Smallwood, magistrate Walter Hanson, and Philip Richard Fendall, who was clerk of the court.[27]

Implementation proceeded slowly, even unenthusiastically, and not until late October was nonimportation organized in Charles and several other counties. Then, according to a letter published anonymously, "the people" of Charles met "to appoint a Committee of Twelve Gentlemen, placed in different parts, to keep a lookout that no British, or other goods, should, contrary to the intention and spirit of our association, be landed any where in the county." A few weeks later, when merchandise was landed "contrary to the Tenor of the Association," a "Committee of Merchants" made sure that the goods were returned to Britain. Apparently this was the county's first extralegal, popularly chosen body dedicated to resisting British policy. It was still operating the following summer.[28]

In reacting to the Stamp and Townshend Acts, people in the county selectively borrowed methods of protest initiated elsewhere and took the first steps toward coordinated action with other localities. Beginning in 1770, they turned to provincial issues, drew upon what they had learned—and sometimes took the lead within Maryland. Popular initiative grew more common. A much larger segment of the population became actively involved in protest efforts, resistance expanded, and momentum mounted.

PERFECTING PROTEST, 1770–74

In October 1770 the tobacco inspection act, an omnibus law vital to the government and economy of Maryland, expired. First enacted in 1747, the law not only established public inspection warehouses but also regulated British customs collections in the province, authorized the Assembly to set maximum fees that proprietary officials could charge for services rendered the public, and levied taxes of thirty pounds of tobacco per taxable, or poll, for Anglican rectors' salaries. The act failed because members of the country party in the House of Delegates, allegedly trying to "distinguish their Zeal for popular Regulations, to recommend themselves to the Suffrages of the People," wanted to reduce the fees and salaries. The upper house refused.[29]

Having grown familiar with popular politics by now, planters and merchants immediately organized an extralegal inspection system patterned after the defunct law. On November 15 traders from throughout the Western Shore gathered at Port Tobacco, centrally located in the tobacco-growing region, and established a voluntary association to protect the quality of the staple and prevent "the Exportation of Virginia Trash from Maryland." Other meetings soon enacted similar arrangements, and the transition from public to private inspection was accomplished with little disruption. High tobacco prices no doubt "prevented the Planters from being sensible of the Loss" of the act, according to Maryland's new governor, Robert Eden.[30]

Much more volatile was the subject of fees that proprietary officers charged for scores of government services, such as having a court summons delivered, an estate settled, or a land warrant issued. When the inspection act died, so did statutory authority for the fees, and that locked proprietary and country politicians in fierce debate for the remainder of the colonial period. On the proprietary side, Eden issued a carefully worded proclamation forbidding charges higher than those listed in the expired law. In effect, he reissued the fee schedule through executive decree. For its part, the House of Delegates stridently claimed exclusive jurisdiction over fees by equating them with taxes (an argument it did not extend to royal customs fees, however). Both echoing and exceeding its earlier stand on the Stamp Act, the house also branded the proclamation unconstitutional, arbitrary, and oppressive. The opposing views were aired at length in a famous newspaper debate between Daniel Dulany, a high proprietary placeman, and Charles Carroll of Carroll-ton, a young Catholic who, although disenfranchised, forged close connections with the country party. Despite the clamor, the controversy directly affected only people who needed government services. Most paid, but "some under the Influence of Our *Patriots*" refused.[31]

In contrast, the Anglican levy personally affected every taxpayer, and therefore, the controversy that erupted over it was laden with opportunities for ordinary men and women to flout proprietary authority. Unlike the offi-cers, who suddenly lacked statutory grounds for their fees, the rectors could fall back on Maryland's original church establishment act (1702), which in-cluded a *higher* tax of forty pounds of tobacco per poll. Some people ac-quiesced. Others tendered the lapsed rate. And still others refused to pay at all on the disingenuous ground that a technicality rendered the 1702 statute invalid. The clergy reacted by instituting a test case in Anne Arundel County court in 1772, but when the court refused to rule on the statute's legality, the question was appealed to the Provincial Court at Annapolis. To opponents of the poll tax, appeal was not an encouraging development because a majority of the judges also sat in the upper house of Assembly, where they habitually protected clerical interests.[32]

At that point the litigation stalled. While taxpayers enjoyed free rein in deciding whether or not to support the established church, two leaders of the country party, William Paca (an attorney in the stalled litigation) and Samuel Chase, attacked the 1702 statute in a vitriolic newspaper debate, mostly with the Reverend Jonathan Boucher. After several months of sparring, an exas-perated Boucher claimed that the clergy were ready to proceed to trial over the establishment act. "Whether they shall, or not, it seems, rests entirely with you. If, then, you really be the patriots you wish to be thought, approve yourselves such, by concurring in the necessary measures to obtain a speedy, and a *decisive*, determination of this unhappy dispute."[33]

Paca and Chase were seeking more favorable terrain on which to contest the act, and they found it in Charles County. On February 25, 1773, they announced that their attendance at the county courts would interrupt their debate with Boucher but that, within two weeks, they expected to furnish "ample compensation for their delay." Then they departed for Port Tobacco, where neither practiced law, to argue what may have been a contrived case. Certainly it was not the judicial confrontation the clergy envisioned. *Harrison v. Lee* was a criminal action instituted by a member of the House of Delegates against the county sheriff, Richard Lee, Jr. Without question, they were two of the more colorful characters in the county.[34]

The plaintiff, Joseph Hanson Harrison, was a magistrate who had a pronounced distaste for the proprietary regime. Ten years before, saying that he was "determined to be no longer a Slave," he offered to sell his property in Charles County. He wanted to move to Virginia, he advertised, "where all loyal Subjects are well Rewarded for any of their Services, and where all Animals of the voracious and vulture Disposition are detected, despised, and suppress'd, and above all, where the Liberty and Property of the Subject, is, with the greatest Care and Tenderness, duly and impartially supported and protected, and where Religion is propagated with equal Zeal and at much less Expence, and that under the immediate Notice of one of the best of Sovereigns on the Face of the Earth." Whatever vexed him, Harrison eventually calmed down, perhaps discovered that Virginia was not the paradise he imagined, and remained in Maryland. In 1768 he was elected to the House of Delegates and, not surprisingly, compiled a strong antiproprietary voting record. Without exception he supported reduced clerical salaries.[35]

The defendant in the case, Richard Lee, Jr., was equally flamboyant but for different reasons. The proprietary government customarily chose sheriffs from among incumbent county court justices, but not so with Lee. No doubt because his father was Squire Lee, the inexperienced younger man was appointed sheriff in 1768. Upon taking office, he transferred the county prisoners to a private jail within sight of his father's house at Blenheim and at some point erected a forbidding stake fence. A curious traveler described it as follows: "A Ditch & low mud fence was cast up, on the top of which was drove in Stakes 3 feet high & a foot asunder, between which was wove green Branches of Cedar as close as possible." According to some of the prisoners, Lee's jail was overcrowded, open to the wind and rain, dank, unheated in winter, and stifling in summer. Seventeen people were packed into one room and an adjoining dungeon in July 1769: "[T]he heate of oure Bodeys and Breth of 17 men Confined in so Small a place it is imposable to Describe wh[a]t wee all Suffer."[36]

Such accusations might have been dismissed as exaggerated jailhouse grumbling except for an incident that had happened the previous February. Apparently it started when the sheriff learned that a runaway slave had tried to break out of the jail. Lee suddenly appeared with a "gang of Negros," ordered them to whip the runaway, and then, because he suspected others of being accomplices, turned the slaves onto a free mulatto woman and two white men, one of whom was William Wright. With the lash marks on his back, Wright recounted that "the Sheriff Ordered the Negroes to come into the Goal [Gaol] and Tye me accordingly they Tyed me around the Wrists and carried me out of Goal stripped my Shirt over my Head and Tyed me up to a Walnut Tree before his Father's Door and there gave me a Severe Whipping . . . when I was carried back to Goal they fastened me by the Hands and Feet with a Rope like an Ox led to be slaughtered." The episode earned Lee the epithet Whipping Dick and ended only after he had threatened to subject every prisoner to the lash. At March court the county grand jury indicted him for Wright's whipping, which obviously caused special umbrage because slaves had laid hands on a white man. Lee pleaded no contest and was fined.[37]

For months thereafter prisoners and former prisoners mounted a barrage of allegations about deplorable conditions at the jail and the barbarity and tyranny of the sheriff, whom one of the men likened to the Roman emperor Nero. By enlisting members of the county's governing elite, moreover, they carried the accusations to the governor and legislature. Assemblymen Joseph Hanson Harrison and Francis Ware, magistrate Samuel Hanson, and proprietary placeman Daniel of St. Thomas Jenifer made sure that Lee's behavior was widely discussed. In November 1769 the House of Delegates ordered the sheriff to bring several prisoners to Annapolis for questioning. Lee, however, fled Charles County—"where by the Duty of his Station he ought at all Times to be found," an insulted lower house asserted—and went to Virginia. The aggrieved delegates cited Lee for contempt, satisfied themselves that he had unduly increased his prisoners' miseries, and urged Governor Eden to remove him from office for being "unworthy of and unfit for so important a Trust."[38]

Eden asked his Council, of which the sheriff's father was the senior member, to conduct an inquiry, and the Lee forces mobilized to save what the errant sheriff called "a place as well profitable as honorable." To hear their accounts, all the prisoners and their visitors, including wives who stayed the night, were treated most tenderly. The Lees allegedly had slave children run errands for the prisoners; served them copious amounts of good meat, bread, cheese, cider, beer, and rum; fed them broth or gruel when they were ill; sent them clean bedding when they had "the Itch"; and repaired the jail when the roof leaked. Prisoners, claimed the sheriff's supporters, responded to these kind ministrations by shouting to visiting gentlemen that they were starving, by calling the elder Mrs. Lee "old Jezable dry bones" and Squire Lee an "old Damned Roguish son of a Bitch," and by so verbally abusing the family housekeeper that she did not stay long during her frequent trips to inquire after their welfare. Supporters also argued that the complainers were inveterate liars and jailbreakers. Unpersuaded, the Council did not exonerate the sheriff, but it also decided in May 1770 that it had insufficient evidence to justify removing him from office.[39]

Lee's career as sheriff made him persona non grata in much of Charles County. Because his father ranked second only to the governor among proprietary officials, he had been named sheriff ahead of local magistrates. He had broken the taboo against slaves' assaulting whites and allegedly mistreated prisoners terribly. After some of the gentry placed the accusations before the House of Delegates, he had ignored its summons and left the province. Still, the Council that would not exonerate him nevertheless protected him.

Rather than avoid further confrontation with members of the elite, as prudence should have suggested, Lee soon sought one out. Sometime in 1771 he went to the plantation of Joseph Hanson Harrison, the antiproprietary legislator who had helped publicize the sheriff's transgressions, and arrested Harrison for not paying the poll tax specified in the church establishment act. Although Harrison relented, paid the tax, and thereby avoided a stay in Lee's jail, he brought charges of assault and battery and false imprisonment against Lee and asked £60 sterling in damages. This was the case that came to trial in February 1773 and caused Samuel Chase and William Paca to break off their newspaper debate with Boucher so that they could ride to Port Tobacco to represent their fellow legislator. Indicative of the importance attached to the case, seven attorneys argued it. Harrison's were all antiproprietary men. Defending Lee were Thomas Stone and two lawyers from outside the county, none of whom was a legislator.[40]

The sheriff pleaded not guilty and invoked the 1702 establishment act to justify his actions. Had the court allowed that justification, it would have been forced to rule on the validity of the statute, and that it had no intention of doing because the issue was still before the Provincial Court. Therefore, the justices ordered a twelve-man jury to consider only the *facts* of the Harrison-Lee case, not whether the sheriff's actions were legal. The fact was that Lee had arrested but not jailed Harrison; no one denied it. "No such aggravating Circumstance as dragging the Plaintiff to Jail or ill Treatment of him" occurred, according to an anonymous writer who may well have been one of Harrison's attorneys. "Yet such was the Idea which the Jury entertained of the Liberty of the Subject, that they looked upon the Sheriff's Arrest . . . of the Plaintiff for the oppressive and illegal Demand of the *Forty per Poll* as an Offence of the First Magnitude against the Rights of *Englishmen*." Although the justices refused even to consider the validity of the church establishment act, the jury forged ahead of them and concluded that Harrison's arrest constituted a primary assault on the rights of Englishmen *because* the act was illegal and oppressive. The jury thereupon convicted Lee and awarded Harrison the full £60. When Lee's attorneys objected, the justices stayed the judgment until the Provincial Court ruled on the establishment act. It never did because of the onrushing Revolution. Hence the Charles County jury was the only judicial entity in Maryland ever to pass judgment on the act.[41]

By the time the jury offered its unsolicited opinion, resistance to the poll tax was widespread in the county. Many people chose to ignore the act, while others tendered their rectors the old rate of thirty pounds of tobacco per poll. Then, in the summer of 1773, four men were indicted for a more forceful mode of resistance: They refused to reveal their taxable assets—namely, the number of persons for whom they were liable. One resister was accused of "denying and Refusing to give in himself and 10 Negroes As Taxables"; another of "not giving in his Wife (a Slave hired to him) as a Taxable." In each of these indictments the action was initiated by a constable, the officer of the court charged with compiling a list of the taxables in his district. But at the same court session at which the Harrison-Lee case was tried, a constable himself was indicted for joining the resistance. He simply did not produce a list, and that act of omission prevented *any* taxes from being collected in his district.[42]

The court moved swiftly to define the limits of acceptable resistance. If the ministers agreed to reduced levies, that was fine. The justices took a dim view, however, of any threat to the entire tax structure. Therefore, they promptly fined the evaders five hundred pounds of tobacco for every taxable concealed, removed the wayward constable from office, and, for good measure, fined him five hundred pounds. Still, even as the poll tax controversy revealed the potential for people in the lower ranks of society to surge ahead of the magistrates, those officials also responded to the public mood. In late 1773, when the rector of Port Tobacco Parish petitioned the court to levy his salary at the rate specified in the establishment act, the court summarily rejected the request.[43]

Thomas Stone, the only local attorney who represented Lee, also felt the weight of public sentiment, and he paid a price for defending his unpopular client. County sheriffs were responsible for collecting attorneys' fees, but after the Harrison-Lee trial the sheriffs on Stone's court circuit either could not or would not collect his. "I should be extremely sorry that you should want one moment what is due from me," he wrote to a creditor in 1774, but "I have been almost ruined this year by the scandalous conduct of Sheriffs towards me. Otherwise no gentleman should have asked me twice for cash owed him." Not surprisingly, when Stone became a revolutionary leader he advocated listening to the "vox populi."[44]

Depression

Stone was not alone in apologizing to his creditors. After six years of high tobacco prices, plentiful imports, and easy credit arrangements, the Charles County economy entered a steep decline in late 1772. One cause of the downturn was a financial panic that began in England and Scotland and rapidly reverberated across the Atlantic. Markets vanished, tobacco prices plummeted, and lawsuits mounted because merchants and factors called in outstanding debts in a desperate attempt to stave off bankruptcy. A second cause of the downturn originated in the county, with the quality of the tobacco brought to market. In 1770 merchants had helped organize the voluntary inspection system because they knew that without it, the reputation of Maryland leaf would suffer. "Be cautious," Thomas Howe Ridgate wrote from London to his agent in the county. "Never [buy] any Tobacco but whats inspected." Yet the voluntary system could not keep trash off the market. In 1773 the Assembly, faced with a severely depressed tobacco trade and intense popular pressure, reinstated public inspection (even though the issues that had caused its demise, officers' fees and Anglican salaries, remained unresolved). The public warehouse system quickly revived. The tobacco trade did not.[45]

Boom and bust cycles were nothing new in the Chesapeake, of course. They were endemic to the export trade. Yet the trough of the 1770s seemed particularly severe because the peak had been so high. Between 1766 and 1769 the average price per hundredweight of tobacco shipped out of the inspection warehouse at Port Tobacco jumped 50 percent, and comparable spectacular increases were recorded at all public warehouses in the county. Although official records were not kept during the period of voluntary association, 1770–73, other evidence suggests that peak prices held well into 1772. By 1774 the average price at every warehouse was lower than at the start of the boom cycle. Furthermore, whereas an average of more than four thousand hogsheads left the county each year between 1766 and 1769, just twenty-nine hundred hogsheads were shipped in 1774. Behind these figures was the stark reality that many people, from small planters to entrepreneurs like Ridgate, could not pay their debts.[46]

Indebtedness was a way of life to Marylanders. If you advanced them credit or money, "they clearly understand that you are also lending them all the time that they consider necessary to pay it back," observed a traveler soon after the Revolution. He might have added that the cost of recovering debts through the courts often deterred creditors from filing suit. During the prosperous years between 1766 and 1772, buyers competed for tobacco by extending planters unusually generous amounts of credit. Most planters accumulated small debts, which they could expect to pay off so long as tobacco prices remained high. Merchants like Athanasius Ford were more ambitious: When Ford marketed tobacco valued at £210 sterling in 1771, a London firm advanced him merchandise worth nine times that amount. Most ambitious of all, perhaps, was the firm of Barnes and Ridgate, which in early 1772 owed about £10,000 to one London firm alone, Osgood Hanbury and Company.[47]

When the financial panic struck, the convention of waiting for debtors to settle their accounts was abandoned. Instead a chain reaction began in British mercantile houses and ended at the courthouse and plantations of Charles County. To satisfy creditors who were pressing them, merchants in England and Scotland pleaded with their agents in the Chesapeake to collect all outstanding debts. The latter in turn pressured the planters and, if payment was not forthcoming, brought suit. Independent operators did the same. The number of debt cases filed in the county courthouse mounted during 1773 and escalated sharply the following year. Not since 1765, when the justices had hurried to clear the docket before the Stamp Act went into effect, were they so preoccupied with issuing debt judgments. Even so, at the end of the August 1774 court session, more than three hundred cases remained on the docket.[48]

The firm that won the most judgments was not a large Scottish mercantile house like John Glassford and Company. Nor did the American agent of a major London trader like James Russell press planters the hardest. Rather, the Maryland firm of Barnes and Ridgate exceeded all other merchants in the number of suits filed and judgments obtained.[49]

For the two partners, the ambitious and risky attempt to establish their firm in London, eliminate British commission merchants from their operations, and trade with Africa, the West Indies, and the Chesapeake ended in disaster. Inadequate capitalization and inexperience in the labyrinthine trading customs of the metropolis undoubtedly contributed to their downfall. Equally, Osgood Hanbury and Company and other English competitors, regarding the Marylanders as interlopers, pushed them "devilishly" and spared no effort to force them to stop trading. Then too, manufacturers to whom Barnes and Ridgate owed money behaved with "extreme inveteracy." The provincials consequently were utterly incapable of riding out the panic of 1772. No sooner had it begun than they ceased their operations and "Ridgate offered their business to several merchants here, all of whom refused it."[50]

Powerless to prevent Hanbury from seizing a ship and cargo they were about to dispatch to the Chesapeake, Ridgate ignominiously took passage for home and left Barnes, who arrived in England in the fall of 1772, to face the firm's creditors. Soon he was confined to King's Bench prison. "The Lord only knows when he may be released," lamented Joshua Johnson, another Maryland trader trying to succeed in London. "I go and mingle a tear of condolence with him every now and then." Having been forced into bankruptcy, Barnes finally was released from King's Bench in the summer of 1774.[51]

Across the Atlantic the firm's assets were in the hands of bankruptcy trustees. In 1774 they successfully prosecuted sixty-two debt cases in the Charles County court, yet the amounts recovered scarcely touched the firm's liabilities. Nor did nearly £1,000 sterling realized from sale of the Barnes and

Ridgate headquarters at Port Tobacco and the store at Benedict. The trustees therefore continued to prosecute many more lawsuits. As they proceeded, planters who lost suits bought a little time by mortgaging to the trustees everything from cooking utensils to land. Prospects of satisfying those mortgages dimmed, however, when the colonies plunged into war and Independence.[52]

To John Barnes's compatriots in England, he was a terrifying example of what might befall Chesapeake merchants should their striving toward greater commercial autonomy fail. Whenever Joshua Johnson felt especially insecure, as happened often during the depths of the prewar depression, he raised the specter of himself as a "companion with poor J[ohn] B[arnes] in the King's Bench."[53] Yet what Barnes and Ridgate had attempted of their own volition—to trade without British middlemen—the War for Independence forced upon every exporter in America. And more.

REFLECTIONS

Between 1765 and 1774, Charles County residents learned through example and personal experience how to resist both proprietary and imperial power. They did so even if their actions were of questionable legality, as when they refused to pay Anglican poll taxes or Thomas Stone's legal fees and when they haggled over ministers' salaries. In response to the Townshend duties and especially to the demise of public tobacco inspection, merchants and planters also formed extralegal organizations to control their trade. Although these efforts were not entirely successful, they offered valuable lessons in cooperative local ventures. Moreover, whether in the Stamp Act crisis or the Harrison-Lee trial, and even in the shrill complaints about Sheriff Lee, men were quick to invoke their conceptions of the rights of Englishmen to justify the positions they took. These experiences were to serve them well in the impending break with England.

Throughout these years, members of the gentry remained in the forefront of protest. It was they who shut the courthouse doors in 1765 and reopened them in 1766, who brought the nonimportation association of 1769 home from Annapolis, who helped organize the extralegal inspection system, and who fined and fired the men whose resistance to the poll tax threatened the system through which all local public monies were collected. Except for Sheriff Lee, the governing elite were not threatened with loss of their power during these years, and they were the ones who carried the accusations against Lee to the governor and legislature and who later brought him to trial for arresting Assemblyman Harrison.

Local people, like other Marylanders, nonetheless had "become sensible of their Power ever since the cursed Scheme of the Stamp Act."[54] By 1773, as events quickly unfolded in the county, there were hints that popular resistance could threaten the local power structure as well. For the freemen, the possibilities were just dawning. Yet during the final imperial crisis—beginning with the Boston Tea Party and culminating in the Declaration of Independence—the freemen did not seize the occasion to topple the elite. Rather, the elite, with sensitivity to the popular mood, continued to lead in an increasingly revolutionary, and economically precarious, environment.

CHAPTER FOUR

"*Liberty Mad*"

I<small>N THE EARLY MORNING OF</small> M<small>AY</small> 21, 1774, N<small>ICHOLAS</small> C<small>RESSWELL, NEWLY</small> arrived in America from England, first set foot in Charles County. At Elizabeth Laidler's ferry-house he stopped for breakfast with his traveling companion and three black oarsmen who were rowing them up the Potomac River. Their stomachs filled, the men returned to their small boat and spent much of the day gliding along the county's shoreline until, in the afternoon, they docked at Nanjemoy. Cresswell soon was dining and dancing at the plantations of the gentry. At Mrs. Leftwick's and Colonel Richard Harrison's he drank tea. Bostonians may have dumped tea into their harbor, but in Charles County, during what another visitor called "this loveliest month" of May, men and women were drinking the beverage with pleasure.[1]

But not for long. On May 30, eight days after first visiting Colonel Harrison, Cresswell returned for dinner and found the assembled company much agitated by news from the north. Indeed, the *only* topic of conversation that evening was the British naval blockade of Boston Harbor, Parliament's response to the Tea Party. Cresswell found that "the people seem much exasperated at the proceedings of the Ministry and talk as if they were determined to dispute the matter with the sword." That same day Philip Richard Fendall, the merchant and court clerk, wrote from Port Tobacco that "The Continent in General or at least so far as we have had accounts are greatly Alarmed."[2]

When word reached Boston that Parliament intended to choke off the town's maritime commerce until the inhabitants paid for the destroyed tea, a committee of the town meeting immediately tried to enlist sympathy and support in other colonies. Every colony, the committee argued, should stop trading with Britain until Parliament recanted. An express rider brought this request to Baltimore on May 24—during the interim between Cresswell's visits to Harrison's plantation—and on the following day Annapolis "inhabitants" (reportedly not the "most respectable" of them) took the lead in formulating Maryland's response. Meeting "out-of-doors," meaning without official status or sanction, they proposed to "preserve North America and her liberties" with a total trade embargo enforced by "associations" in the counties and towns. The colonies should stop exporting to Britain immediately and cease importing soon thereafter. The meeting also recommended a moratorium on debt litigation filed by British creditors, which would distress them while benefiting Maryland debtors. Endeavoring "to give the strongest Impressions of the Sufferings of Boston in the Common Cause," and hoping that public gatherings throughout Maryland would follow their lead, the Annapolitans appointed a committee of correspondence responsible for encouraging the counties to embargo trade.[3]

Fendall expected that the province, at a minimum, would adopt nonimportation and that probably nonexportation was in the offing, too. The latter, he warned James Russell, his kinsman and mercantile correspondent in England, would cause British merchants to "suffer greatly by having your Ships return in Ballast, as it will not be in the power of your Agents here to fill them up . . . before such Resolves take place." Enthusiasm for hasty measures was not running as high in the countryside as in the provincial capital, however. In Charles County, people were no more eager for a total, immediate trade boycott than they had been in the wake of the Townshend Revenue Act. "Our Patriots are blazing away about the Boston affairs," observed another Port Tobacco merchant on June 5, "but I think they will not resolve upon non-exportation." For planters had no intention of forgoing the income from tobacco growing in the fields, not when the year's crop, the first to be marketed under the revived inspection system, might reinvigorate stagnant commerce.[4]

Therefore, rhetoric exceeded proposed remedies when unnamed and unnumbered inhabitants gathered at the courthouse on June 14 to contemplate the latest imperial crisis. After electing Walter Hanson, senior justice of the county court, to preside, those present denounced the blockade of Boston as "a violent attack upon the liberty and property of the [town's] inhabitants . . . [which] in its consequences tends to render insecure, and destroy the rights and privileges of all British America." That said, the proposed methods of resistance were "by much the most moderate of any I have heard of," according to Fendall. Yes, Charles County would join a nonimportation association encompassing everything except medicines, but it would not implement the measure for six weeks, thus giving ships loading in Britain or already coursing toward the Chesapeake time to arrive. And yes, the county would join in nonexportation, but not for another sixteen months, during which planters would continue marketing their staples. On the subject of debt litigation, the record of the meeting was silent, perhaps because a moratorium was depicted as personally dishonest rather than politically desirable.[5]

The meeting also created the county's first committee of correspondence, thereby forging a vital communications link with other localities. A majority of its eighteen members were Assembly delegates, magistrates, and prominent merchants. Half of the committee also was named to attend an extralegal Provincial Convention in Annapolis: Assemblymen William Smallwood, Josias Hawkins, and Francis Ware, Justices Walter Hanson, Joseph Hanson Harrison, John Dent, and Daniel Jenifer, merchant Robert Townshend Hooe, and lawyer Thomas Stone, who had somehow managed to redeem himself after the Harrison-Lee trial. At the convention, representatives of all the counties were to elect delegates to the First Continental Congress and frame a "rational . . . and practicable association for this province." There was hope in Port Tobacco that the provincial plan would come close to the one drafted in the courthouse—and concern that it should be "fit," "reasonable," "rational," and "effectual."[6]

Although the pronouncements of June 14 were the most strident that residents were willing to approve, they nevertheless promised, vaguely, to adopt other measures that would "protect and secure the liberties of this county according to the true principles of the English constitution, and thereby shew themselves loyal and faithful subjects to his majesty king George the third." Fendall, for one, did not doubt local resolve, for Parliament's treatment of Boston alarmed "All Ranks of people." At the moment they were concentrating on nonimportation: "The general Crye among the people here is, we will suffer any hardships till we can manufacture Cloaths for ourselves." Unless Parliament relented, he predicted, the British "will certainly loose the most beneficial Branch of their trade to America[,] I mean that of their Manufactures, for if some [of] the people get into a way of Manufacturing for themselves they will not again leave it off."[7]

Moderate though it may have been on the scale of revolutionary politics, the June 14 meeting at Port Tobacco ushered in a two-year period of intense extralegal politics in Charles County, which carried it from disaffection to rebellion. At first, popular meetings and extralegal committees functioned alongside the legally established local government. On some days the courthouse was used for revolutionary politics; on others, for business conducted under the proprietary regime. Then, during the summer and autumn of 1775, the traditional government all but collapsed. The patriot element meanwhile coalesced and gained strength, grew ever more assertive, and demonstrated just how thoroughly it embraced revolutionary rhetoric and tactics, including intimidation. By June 1776 the county's free population was overwhelmingly patriot and alienated from Parliament, King George III, and the entire British nation. Throughout these two years, as the theater of politics changed dramatically, many of the key players remained the same.

"Entering into Associations"

For several months after the June 1774 meeting in Port Tobacco, men and women watched and waited for developments beyond the county's borders. Although the Provincial Convention at Annapolis called for a trade embargo, it did not implement one and instead waited to see what the First Continental Congress would do when it convened at Philadelphia in September. Meanwhile, Marylanders became aware of the full extent and severity of the Coercive Acts. Parliament not only had blockaded Boston Harbor but had unilaterally altered the Massachusetts colonial charter by strengthening the royal establishment and diluting the powers of the town meetings and the lower house of the legislature. Furthermore, Massachusetts had a new governor: General Thomas Gage, commander of the British Army in America. To British politicians, "The constitutional authority of the Kingdom over the colonies must be vindicated, and its laws obeyed." To shocked Americans, these measures threatened every colony. "The troubles in America," wrote a lower Western Shore resident, loomed "Ten times worse than at the time of the Stamp Act."[8]

ANTI-
BRITISH
SENTIMENT
RUNS HIGH

No more popular meetings were called in the county that summer, yet anti-British sentiment ran high. The public was distracted "owing to the D——d unjust acts of Parliament respecting America." Joseph Hanson Harrison predictably emerged as "a violent opposer of the [British] Government." And in August the committee of correspondence reacted vigorously when the brig *Mary and Jane*, from London, appeared in the Potomac River with chests of tea stowed in its hold. Suspicious that some of the tea was destined for the Cunninghame, Findlay, and Company store at Port Tobacco, the committee summoned the firm's chief factor in Maryland. He promised not to land the "detestable Article," and the ship's captain agreed to carry it back to England. To prevent other tea from being delivered, the committee alerted its counterparts in counties along both shores of the Potomac.[9]

As Charles County entered the vortex of political revolution, people maneuvered as best they could, to gain what advantages they could, while they were still able to trade. Everyone expected a nonimportation agreement of some kind, and soon. While one man hurriedly ordered goods from England with a plea that they be sent to him "with quick Dispatch," another would not place an order because "we are Just Entering into Associations . . . when that is settled if they will allow us to send for any thing [I] shall write." Faced with the prospect that the flow of European manufactures was about to end, Fendall struck upon an ingenious plan: In lieu of importing trade goods, import tradesmen, especially weavers, shoemakers, tailors, carpenters, joiners, and masons. In mid-August he asked James Russell to send him forty or fifty indentured servants, "the fewer women the better," by the first ship bound for the Potomac. Two weeks later, convinced "there is money to be made by it," he requested as many skilled servants as Russell's ships could transport.[10]

The specter of nonexportation suddenly gave planters economic rewards they would not otherwise have received in 1774. When Robert Carter of Nomini Hall plantation in Virginia heard that some planters in southeastern Charles County had about six thousand bushels of unsold wheat, he immediately offered to buy all of it at "the highest price I shall give for wheat of the growth of this Year." Instead of the usual arrangement of paying half the cost upon delivery and the rest in money and goods sometime later, Carter offered to pay the full price, in cash, when his boats loaded the grain.[11]

Tobacco growers, too, found themselves in an unexpectedly favorable trading position. Original projections called for a large 1774 crop and, consequently, low prices (about 10s. provincial currency per hundredweight). But at midsummer the tobacco in the fields seemed "by far the worst we have had for many years" because of bad weather. At the same time, some planters, convinced that cessation of trade was imminent, talked of not saving any seeds for 1775. Should nonexportation be adopted, "there will be little or no tobacco planted next year, this Joined to the Very bad prospect of a Crop this year must raise the price of that Commodity very considerably." Eager buyers soon offered 20s. currency per hundredweight at Port Tobacco and nearly that much at Benedict. They got few takers, for growers anticipated even higher prices.[12]

To the chagrin of their Scottish competitors, the local agents of several English consignment firms adopted an extraordinary tactic in order to persuade planters to ship with them rather than accept the Scots' country price. Fendall and others *advanced* cash, as much as £6 sterling per hogshead (about 12s. sterling per hundredweight). By the end of the first week in August more tobacco had been shipped out of Port Tobacco warehouse on consignment than in any other year since the 1740s. Growers thereby stood to profit from what might be spectacular advances in European tobacco prices if nonexportation were enacted. Meanwhile, with their substantial cash advances, they purchased imported manufactures locally. "Were we clear of these Politicks," explained one consignment agent, "the people would readily ship to have goods in Return, but they dread a Non-Importation Scheme will take place before they can have their Goods." Therefore, they were intent "upon supplying themselves with Money to purchase Goods here."[13]

Customers lined up to buy what they could before everything disappeared from merchants' shelves. Merchandise was becoming increasingly scarce at Port Tobacco and in general on the lower Western Shore—not only because the possibility of an embargo caused people to stock up while they could, but also because, since the financial panic of 1772, British suppliers had shipped smaller cargoes to the Potomac. Another year of imperial strife, the prediction ran, and "the poor people and all those who could not lay in more Goods than would answer their present Necessitys will be in the Utmost Distress." Scarcity preceded the war.[14]

The Continental Congress, which met from early September until late October, ended the suspense over the mode of colonial resistance and, for the county, marked a turning point from anticipation to action. On September 22 Congress asked Americans to stop ordering goods from Britain. The *Maryland Gazette* announced the request on September 29, the day Walter Hanson directed his English correspondent to send him some cloth. The following day he canceled the order because "I find it is the Sense of the General Congress Now held at Philadelphia that we send for no goods from Brittain Until Matters are better Settled Between the Mother Country & the Colonies." Hanson's neighbors reacted similarly, although one gentleman could not resist ordering a new watch from England.[15]

Soon after Congress disbanded, local people learned the details of the Continental Association, a full-fledged trade embargo to be implemented by committees of correspondence and of observation in every county, city, and town in America. Unless Parliament repealed the Coercive Acts, all imports from Britain were to end on December 1, 1774, and all exports to Britain, Ireland, and the West Indies on September 10, 1775. The terms of the association were quite close to the resolves adopted at Port Tobacco the previous June.[16]

In the year after Congress met, revolution came to Charles County. When Cresswell returned to Port Tobacco for church services and dinner on October 16, 1774, having been away from the county for three months, he discovered "Nothing talked of but War with England." In the ensuing months proprietary government faltered and extralegal committees and politics flourished. As the colonial crisis deepened in 1775 with the battles of Lexington, Concord, and Bunker Hill and with formation of the Continental Army, the movement toward a complete break with Britain assumed an inexorable quality, even if people were not yet ready to contemplate, much less call for, Independence. Drawn more and more into revolution by the onrushing events and through newly forged links with other Maryland counties and other American colonies, the people of Charles County, from one autumn to the next, rigorously enforced the Continental Association, watched their trans-ocean economy grind to a halt, offered men more opportunity than ever before to participate in the body politic, flushed out the loyalists among them, and began preparing for war in earnest. All this was accomplished before the year of Independence.[17]

"The Lord Protect this . . . Country"

In June 1774, during the first days of excitement over the renewed imperial crisis, people described only as "inhabitants" had gathered at Port Tobacco and decided how to respond to the Coercive Acts. The following November 18, when men again crowded into the courthouse, this time to implement the recommendations of Congress, participation in the local revolutionary movement both narrowed and expanded. It narrowed because the meeting was restricted to legally enfranchised voters, meaning Protestants with estates worth at least £40 sterling, and because the county's committee of correspondence, which maintained communications with other localities, was cut from eighteen to ten members. The scope of revolutionary politics expanded because the meeting established the largest political entity the county had ever had: a committee of observation of ninety men who were charged with enforcing the Continental Association.[18]

In choosing members of the committees of observation and correspondence and a delegation to the next Provincial Convention in Annapolis, the voters signaled several things about the local leadership of the Revolution as of late 1774. First, the colonial power structure—that is, the governing elite on the county court and in the Assembly—was largely intact and prepared to lead. Second, whether out of preference or deference, the freeholders were willing to entrust the highest positions of leadership to that elite, both elected and appointed. Thus they chose twelve men, all legislators and justices, to attend the convention and gave them "full power to represent and act for this county." So, too, the committee of observation revealed how much the revolutionary leadership emanated from a society founded on deference and ranked social orders. Listed first among the ninety members—an indication that they received more votes than other candidates—were the incumbent assem-

[handwritten margin notes: ELITE READY TO LEAD — DEFERENCE TO ELITE]

blymen and a majority of the justices. In addition, the names of all four Anglican rectors not only lent ecclesiastical support to political protest but also intimated the extent of dissatisfaction with British policies.[19]

Finally, in a county with about seventy-five miles of Potomac River shoreline and many other miles of navigable tributaries, the Continental Association would succeed only if a large body of men were mobilized to watch, listen, set an example, and prod the wayward in their neighborhoods. Hence the great size of the committee of observation. In constituting it, the freeholders had to reach beyond the governing elite, and when they did, they demonstrated a strong tendency to choose substantial property holders or younger sons of such holders. For some wealthy men like Warren Dent, owner of twenty-two hundred acres of land, Gerrard Fowke with twenty-seven hundred, and Henry S. Hawkins with sixteen hundred, the burgeoning revolutionary movement offered access to power that they might never have attained under the proprietor because of the small number of local offices. The same held true for men of lesser means. As early as 1774 the resistance to Great Britain was creating political opportunities—for the propertied as both electors and wielders of authority—far in excess of what the colonial system offered.[20]

Considering this portrait of the men at the forefront, it is worth asking who was notably absent, either by choice or because he was unacceptable to the freeholders. The county's highest proprietary placemen, Squire Richard Lee and Daniel of St. Thomas Jenifer, were not elected to any committee or to the convention. Also left out were the factors of the major Scottish tobacco firms. And except for Gerard B. Causin, the names of prominent Catholics were missing, suggesting that the Protestant majority saw no need just then to integrate them into the political process.[21]

The drift of revolutionary politics—toward extralegal governance and increased political participation—created consternation among the Lees at Blenheim plantation. The best surviving statement of dismay comes from Squire Lee's daughter Alice. Writing confidentially in early 1775 about "a subject very unfit for a female pen," she chastised the "dangerous" innovation of electing, in her estimation, "Ignorant or designing Men into these Committees." Almost certainly anxious about her unpopular father and brother Richard, she vaguely alluded to committeemen whose "evil views . . . under the Marque of Patriotism, may freely vent the private Venom that has been long rankling in their hearts" and to "the mischiefs that popular Rage (mingled as it to[o] frequently is with private gall)" might cause. "Many of the measures that are adopted by at least *part* of every Committee," she fervently believed, were "destructive of those very rights they profess to protect, & if generally pursued will probably introduce as much violence & oppression as we can possibly apprehend from the Mother Country."²²

With a touch of disdain, Lee spoke of "the noble ardor of Liberty," which "seems so essentially necessary in the catologue of American Virtues, at this present alarming Crisis." All about her, neighbors demonstrated such ardor during the winter of 1774–75. The convention at Annapolis called for money and supplies for the relief of Boston and also recommended increased production of wool, flax, and cotton to replace European textiles. Inhabitants of the county responded favorably on both counts, although they had great difficulty finding a boat to transport about twenty-five hundred bushels of grain to Massachusetts. When the convention asked freemen from sixteen to fifty years old voluntarily to enroll in militia companies, choose officers, and begin drilling, local men soon were "learning the military exercise, and forming companies with great diligence and alacrity." Finally, when the convention asked each county to raise money to arm its militia, inhabitants gathered at the courthouse on January 2, 1775, and elected "gentlemen" in every hundred (the civil jurisdictions into which the county was divided), who were to approach every free man and woman for a contribution. All the while, watchful residents made sure that the Continental Association was "most religiously adhered to." With events in Charles County partly in mind, William Fitzhugh in nearby Calvert County remarked that "We hear of Nothing now, but Raising Companys, Military Exercises, Meetings of Committees, Siesing Goods, Advertising Delinquents &c &c."²³

Just as some men earlier had surged ahead of the county's justices during the Anglican poll tax controversy, a few surged ahead of Maryland's revolutionary leadership centered in the Provincial Convention. The convention, rejecting the idea that all debt litigation should cease, advised only that the courts should not prosecute cases brought by factors who violated the Continental Association. But just before Christmas of 1774, with the association newly in effect, several members of the Charles County committee of observation attempted to shut down the court at Port Tobacco entirely. Two versions of the incident exist. According to Fitzhugh, "The Committee of Charles County I am told, Went to the Court when Setting & Order[e]d them to Adjourn, forbidding them to proceed to any Business Except Criminal. This the Magistrates thought most Prudent to Obey. The Lord Grant a Speedy End to this Democratical Confusion." With greater passion, tobacco factor Alexander Hamilton identified the instigators as Francis Ware, Dr. John Parnham, and the ever-troublesome Joseph Hanson Harrison, whom he characterized as "a few Men of desperate fortune." They approached the bar, Hamilton recounted, "and made a motion that the Courts of Justice should be immediately stopped. . . . One of Parnham's arguments . . . was 'that by continuing to administer Justice impartially, the Trader would receive the payment of his debts and of course be enabled to make remittances to his Constituents, and which would be furnishing our enemies with weapons to fight us, and which we ought by every Method in our power to prevent them from receiving.' " The court opposed the three men, "though very faintly," and although the justices refused to "close" the court, they did adjourn it until the following February. Hamilton warned that "If this example is followed . . . adieu to Liberty and everything that is desirable in Life," yet he also contended that the justices were "greatly blamed" for their action. When the full committee of observation met in mid-January, it resolved "by a great majority, that no further restraint should be laid upon the bringing suits at law in this county, than is done by the last provincial convention." As in the poll tax controversy, the more enthusiastic protesters were checked.[24]

In this expanding revolutionary movement, one can see at work the beginnings of polarization, a process that within months divided the populace into a very large patriot and a very small loyalist camp. No middle ground was tenable. Holding the undecided or the recalcitrant up to public scrutiny was a potent way to spur cooperation, and the inhabitants who crowded into the courthouse for the January 2 meeting did just that: They instructed the men chosen to collect money for the militia also to inform the committee of observation "of such persons (if any there be) who are *able*, and on application refuse to subscribe, that their names and refusal may be recorded in perpetual memory." Fumed Alice Lee: Those "seeming desirous of depriving people of the privilege of even thinking differently from themselves certainly savours more of a Roman Inquisition, than a Society of Men combined to assert the Cause of Freedom!"[25]

In February the increasing stridency of the populace caused Nicholas Cresswell to take his final leave of the county. Men were arming and mustering everywhere, and to criticize the Continental Congress was "as much as a person's life is worth." Fearful that the local committee of observation was about to arrest him as a spy, he decided to "save them the trouble by decamping immediately." Just nine months before, his first impression of Charles County people had been that they were "remarkably civil and obliging." His last: "They are all liberty mad."[26]

Liberty mad or not, planters and merchants were turning their thoughts more and more to their last chance to market tobacco. Although nonexportation was not scheduled to take effect until September 10, many people believed that, as soon as Congress reconvened in May, it would resolve to shut down transocean trade. Even so, planters hesitated to ship hogsheads on hand for fear "that if they Ship their Tobacco and these [Coercive] Acts are not

Repealed, that they may in the confusion loose their property." In order to attract cargoes, therefore, consignment agents once again advanced up to £6 sterling per hogshead and, furthermore, guaranteed to pay planters "whatever the Sales [in Britain] may exceed that Sum, this is the only Scheme we could fall on to get any Tobo. at this time." Even the Scots were forced to pay cash in advance.[27]

Amid such trading, news arrived of the fighting between British army regulars and the minutemen of Lexington and Concord, Massachusetts, on April 19. At so critical a juncture, reports were confused and incomplete. Daniel of St. Thomas Jenifer reacted to the first account reaching the Potomac with, "I hope it is not true[,] if it should [be,] the Lord Protect this . . . Country." On May 4 Philip Richard Fendall wrote from Squire Lee's: "The times are dreadfully Alarming there has certainly been an engagement between the Kings Troops and the Provincials in the Massachusetts Government, Various are the Reports. . . . Some say the Kings Troops are all Cut off except 500 but the last Account goes so far as to say that they are all Cut off to a man." A month after the battles Fendall lamented that "every thing relating thereto is vague and uncertain." From Philadelphia, where he was the first Charles County man to serve in the Continental Congress, Thomas Stone told his wife, Margaret, "Pray God preserve you, and bless our little ones. We are like to see times, which will require all our fortitude to bear up against." Lexington and Concord, he was convinced, would "reduce both England and America, to a state to which no friend of either, ever wished to see."[28]

News of the fighting energized people. By the time Stone's letter reached his plantation north of Port Tobacco, his neighbors, and their neighbors, and so on all across the county no longer were reluctant to part with tobacco. Certain that Congress would end exportation within days or, at most, weeks, freemen and slaves worked at a frenzied pace to ready leaf for market, while ships in the Potomac took on hogsheads as fast as they could be brought from the warehouses. Apprehensive lest there not be enough tonnage to carry them all away, merchants scanned the horizon for sails heaving into view, scrambled to charter any available vessel, and bargained among themselves for cargo space. Cooperation among competitors suddenly became advantageous. Hence, about 180,000 pounds of Glassford and Company tobacco left the county on James Russell's ships, prompting his agent to explain, "I thought it better to do this than Risque the Ships being detained or going home dead freighted."[29]

No one had the time or inclination to concentrate on tobacco cultivation that year. Planters concentrated on subsistence and converted some fields to corn, cotton, and flax. In others, large crops of wheat stood ripening. If Congress adhered to its original nonexportation deadline of September 10 (as

ultimately it did), the grain might yet be marketed in the West Indies. To be
sure, some tobacco was planted in 1775, but not much; many growers had
kept their promise not to save seeds from the previous crop. "Add to this the
. . . anxiety of the times [and] the greatest part of our time and thought is
taken up in Consulting the proper means to Support our Suffering Brethren to
the North-ward and to prepare for our own Safety. the Dreadfull alternative
of death or Slavery held forth to us by the Ministry does not Require a Single
moment to an honest Mind to determine on, So that very Little attention will
be paid to the Cultivation of a plant we Can Expect no Profit from." In
rhetoric as well as deed, Charles County had reached the revolutionary mainstream.[30]

While the export economy ground to a halt, the strength and effectiveness
of the patriot forces grew, as John Baillie and Patrick Graham learned to their
chagrin. Baillie, a Scotsman who arrived on the ship *Lady Margaret*, intended
to sell merchandise that he had stowed on board without the captain's knowledge. He found a willing accomplice in Graham, a tailor who secretly helped
unload the goods, stored them at his house in Port Tobacco, and sold a
portion to unsuspecting buyers "in a daring and direct violation of the continental association." When the ship's captain learned of the plot, he, for
reasons unknown, told a member of the county committee of observation,
who in turn called for the entire committee to meet on June 3.[31]

Few members made it to Port Tobacco for the hastily arranged meeting,
but a large crowd did. When someone suggested turning the occasion into a
general meeting of the inhabitants, "a very full and respectable number attended at the court-house, in Port-Tobacco, to make enquiry into this affair."
With the magistrate George Dent presiding, the throng satisfied itself of the
men's guilt and then "*RESOLVED*, That the said John Baillie and Patrick
Graham, for their infamous conduct, ought to be publicly known and held up
as foes to the rights of British America, and universally contemned as the
enemies of American liberty; and that every person ought henceforth to break
off his dealings with the said John Baillie and Patrick Graham." Since the *Lady
Margaret* had already put out to sea, the illicit cargo could not be returned to
Britain just then. So the unsold goods, together with what could be retrieved
from buyers, were stored at Port Tobacco. The unpopular tailor had to
relinquish the money he had received for merchandise not recovered.[32]

The freemen's resolution to shun the would-be profiteers was not empty
rhetoric, for people in the county visited upon them total economic and social
ostracism. Graham discovered that no one brought him tailoring, paid money
owed to him, or sold him provisions to feed his family. Baillie received comparable treatment. Their only chance to be reinstated into the community lay in
a public ritual of confession, contrition, and humble petition for forgiveness.

Each man chose that course over the life of an outcast, and each appealed for absolution to the highest revolutionary body in Maryland, the Provincial Convention.[33]

Confessing that he had "very justly incurred the displeasure and resentment of the County," Graham lamented his "imprudence & ill conduct." Then, "with contrition . . . and his most solemn promise & assurance never more to do, or encourage any thing inimical to American Freedom," he humbly pleaded (referring to himself in the third person) to be "restored to his former rights of a Citizen, as he has already suffered greatly, not only in his own Person, Property, and reputation, but should he continue much longer in the present situation, his Offence must reduce an innocent wife & four young children to beggary & ruin."[34]

Baillie was somewhat less contrite. True, he had "willfully though in some degree ignorantly broke the Association." And yes, public censure was justified. But he complained that censure was "executed with such rigour, it has been with the most extreme and hazardous difficulty he could obtain the necessary food to support a life rendered miserable by his conduct, and the above mentioned sentence."[35]

In deciding the men's fate, the convention clearly took into account local public sentiment. Appended to Graham's petition were the signatures of 120 Charles County men of all ranks, who said that they were convinced of his "hearty repentance" and supported his plea for clemency. On the other hand, Baillie managed to persuade just four men, all of them undistinguished, to sign his plea. The convention decided that Graham should be allowed to practice his "former" trade and to provide for his family—so long as he avoided selling merchandise. Baillie's petition was rejected without comment.[36]

The same Provincial Convention session that weighed the fate of Graham and Baillie also took Maryland far down the path of revolution. On August 14 the delegates adopted two measures—the Association of the Freemen of Maryland and a call for all able-bodied men to enroll in the militia—which became "the principal criterion whereby we discriminate a whig from the most detestable of beings, a tory." All free males except the governor were asked to sign the association, a document written soon after the American defeat at Bunker Hill and laced with references to "uncontroulable Tyranny" and "arbitrary," "vindictive," "unlimited," and "cruel" imperial policies. By signing or making their marks, men engaged to unite "as one Band . . . and pledge ourselves to each other and to America, that we will, to the utmost of our power, promote and support the present opposition" to Britain. Besides signing the call to arms, every freeman was supposed to answer it by joining a militia company within thirty days and by mustering regularly thereafter.[37]

With these measures the line between patriot and loyalist was starkly, effectively drawn. Directly confronted with the choice of either endorsing the Association of the Freemen and joining the militia or, conversely, standing forth as British sympathizers, most men in Charles County took up a pen and a gun by mid-September.[38] For the fainthearted and the uncommitted, the example of Graham and Baillie's ostracism must have been a compelling incentive to move into the patriot camp.

The Association of the Freemen of Maryland, the Continental Association, and the full activation of the militia were the most dramatic signs among many that proprietary government was disintegrating throughout the province. In Charles County the quitrents were not collected in 1775. After an estate inventory was entered in the public records on February 2, more than two years elapsed before another was recorded. And although the court continued to punish criminal offenses, frequent adjournments slowed debt litigation, which evoked grumbling among merchants that the county's debtors "have taken advantage of the times." To fill the void, the committee of observation emerged as a full-fledged extralegal governing body, within guidelines established in the convention.[39]

As envisioned by the convention, the county committees of observation were the organizational base for a widening revolution. From them authority extended upward to the convention, then onward to the mutual will of the colonies expressed in the resolves of the Continental Congress. From Congress and the convention, directives and authority turned back to the committees, whose actions everyone was called upon to "pay obedience to and acquiesce in." In August 1775 the convention expanded the committees' responsibilities. In addition to their original task of enforcing the Continental Association, they were charged with overseeing the signing of the Association of the Freemen, with arresting loyalists deemed dangerous to the American cause, with receiving voluntary contributions to purchase arms and build "Manufactories," and with issuing licenses thenceforth required before debt cases could be filed and prosecuted in the county courts.[40]

To men still loyal to king and proprietor, "all was lost in Maryland" by the time the convention completed its session on August 14: "The proprietary government was compleatly overturned, though the Officers were permitted to remain in degraded Stations." Thomas Johnson, who was to become Maryland's first state governor, agreed: "We yet retain the forms of our Government, but there is no real force or efficacy in it." Richard Lee, Jr., described the situation differently: "[A]ll *written* law [was] prostrate."[41]

For Lee and a handful of other Charles County men, the events of the late summer forced them into the open as unyielding loyalists. They refused to condone rule by popular meetings, committees, and conventions, refused to sign the Association of the Freemen and join the militia, and refused to forsake their allegiance to king and proprietor. Instead they chose self-imposed ostracism, either in or beyond the county. Foremost among them was Squire Richard Lee, Sr.

As the old councillor watched his world, and his place and power within it, dissolve, he blamed the Bostonians. In an unguarded moment he "damned them for destroying the tea." Depending on who told the story, several hundred "sons of liberty" or a mob marched to within three miles of Blenheim and demanded, in a most undeferential manner, that Lee come to them. Convinced this was his only chance to save Blenheim and the lives of his family, he left his wife and daughters "in fits" and accompanied the "rebel chiefs" to the waiting crowd. Someone thrust a document at him—a retraction of his uncharitable opinion of the Bostonians—and then the demand rang out that he should drop to his knees, slavelike, and sign it. The squire, however, launched into an oration that allegedly silenced his listeners and kindled resolve in loyalists' hearts:

Take the poor remains of a life almost exhausted in your service. I have lived among you upwards of seventy years, and with reputation; but if at this advanced age the malice of my enemies can drag me at their pleasure from the peaceable enjoyments of domestic felicity; or if the blind and uninformed rage of party, which contends for liberty and the rights of humanity, at the very instant it is imposing the greatest and most disgraceful of all slavery, *a restraint upon the mind*, can with impunity . . . force me to a concurrence in measures against the conviction of my conscience; it is time to take an eternal farewel of the world. You may indeed kill me, but you shall not force me to make an ignominious denial of the truth, or to retract *one* syllable I have asserted. . . . Act as you please; I have *lived a freeman*, and it is my unalterable resolution to *die one*.

With that, Lee turned on his heel, rode home unimpeded, and, in "poignant distress," went into self-imposed exile on his plantation. He never again held public office.[42]

Other loyalists abandoned place and property and boarded the last ships to leave the Potomac River when exportations ceased. Francis Walker and Richard Lee, Jr., surely were forced out. Walker, the last master of the county free school, was so overtly sympathetic to the British government that the trustees refused to pay his salary and students withheld their tuition. For him, the request to enroll in the militia came with an ultimatum: Take up arms or leave the province. Walker left so hastily—some would claim he was "driven away"—that he was unable to liquidate his property in land and slaves and therefore boarded ship without enough money to pay for his passage. Richard

Lee, Jr., departed under similar circumstances. In several petitions for compensation that he subsequently filed with the British government, he disingenuously attempted to portray himself as a popular, respected man. Yet, other words betrayed the truth: "[O]rdered to take up a Musquet in defence of a cause I reprobated," the "obnoxious" former sheriff was "driven from Maryland in Sep[tembe]r 75."[43]

A third man, Philip Richard Fendall, left less dramatically. Of the fourth generation of Fendalls to live on the lower Western Shore, he was the nephew of Squire Lee. Unlike the Lees, Fendall initially participated in the revolutionary movement. He signed Maryland's nonimportation agreement in 1769 and later served on the county's committee of observation and in the Provincial Convention. Soon after returning from the eventful convention of August 1775, however, he gave a "faithful friend" power of attorney to collect his debts and oversee his Maryland property. He sailed on the *Potomac*, the last ship to leave Maryland or Virginia when the trade links to Britain were completely severed.[44]

Only one other loyalist is known to have left Charles County that fall— not by ship but overland, toward the backcountry—and he did so with a haughty flourish, one that bespoke shattered dreams and pretensions. Orphaned at an early age and unable to complete medical training in Scotland, John F. D. Smyth nevertheless paid for his voyage to the Chesapeake by acting as a ship's surgeon. By about 1772 he boarded in Charles County, *"rather in a State of indigence,* and attempted to practise Surgery." Soon he rented a plantation, but the owner—alarmed that Smyth might abscond with the slaves—successfully sued him for failure to pay rent. Thus it was that Smyth assigned all his worldly goods to two creditors on September 29, 1775, "in the fifteenth year of the Reign of George the third," language that appears nowhere else in the local records. Included in the property was a colt named General Gage, foaled at the time of Lexington and Concord.[45]

In the years ahead, a few more loyalists abandoned Charles County and the lives they had made there. The wonder is not that they left but that they found so few compatriots prepared to do the same. The completeness with which people shunned the smugglers Graham and Baillie offers testimony to a public consensus, a consensus to resist the Coercive Acts and other British measures until they were repealed. In Thomas Stone's words, "War, any thing is preferable to a Surrender of our Rights." If some preferred the old political order, they kept silent, no doubt intimidated by the rigor with which those bent upon resistance organized themselves and then enforced the Continental Association and the resolutions of the Provincial Convention.[46]

Unlike the Eastern Shore of Maryland, which was much more exposed to

British naval power and where a loyalist insurrection was crushed only with military force, Charles County was solidly in the patriot camp before war came to the Chesapeake. The fact that all of the county's representatives to the Assembly and a majority of the magistrates were actively involved in resistance from 1774 forward no doubt smoothed the transition. So, too, did greater opportunities for political participation. Under the proprietary government, elections had been infrequent. Once each year freemen chose their parish vestry, and at irregular intervals of two years or more, substantial property holders voted for assemblymen. In contrast, between June 1774 and September 1775, enfranchised inhabitants, and sometimes those with lesser estates, met at least six times at the courthouse and elected more than one hundred men to a variety of committees. Such frequent, broad participation was without precedent in the county. And through such participation, freemen became vested in the revolutionary cause.[47]

Beyond political considerations were those of family and property. None of the four loyalists known to have left the county in the fall of 1775 seems to have had a wife or children there. Leaving, moreover, entailed abandonment of property to an uncertain fate. When Fendall boarded ship, he turned his back on his mercantile career, his income as county clerk, and the profits of a seven-hundred-acre plantation on the Potomac, which he later said was in "a beautiful healthy situation, and commands an extensive view up and down the river." There he had lived in a "large elegant brick dwelling house" surrounded by woodland and meadows, rich upland that yielded "the best tobacco, wheat, and Indian corn," gardens and orchards, and, at his landing, fish in abundance. Fendall's chances of duplicating his Maryland lifestyle in England were virtually nonexistent. Most people, in fact, had little economic incentive to retrace the ocean voyage their forebears had made, for, in Nicholas Cresswell's words, "a person with a small fortune may live much better and make greater improvements in America than he can possibly do in England." Between 1776 and 1783, whenever British vessels cruised the Potomac and raided the county, white inhabitants almost uniformly sought to repel rather than run to the fleet. Their roots, their families, their property, and their opportunities were in America.[48]

Except for property, much the same could be said for twenty-two-year-old William Thomas, a black man. He belonged to John Barnes, of the venturesome mercantile firm, and accompanied his master to England in 1772. Two years later Thomas was baptized in St. Mary White Chapel in London, and on July 16, 1774, Barnes set him free "from all manner of Slavery and Servitude whatsoever," because of his "Great Fidelity and Meritorious Services." Drawn back to Charles County, Thomas entered his manumission in the public records in December 1775. He chose to spend the war years amid the rolling hills and the plantations where he had toiled as a slave—perhaps because family and friends still did.[49]

HOW MUCH REVOLUTION?

The intensifying Revolution that appalled Maryland loyalists also worried many patriot leaders. One can perceive their concern in the convention's appeals for public order and for obedience to the county committees, and again in its call for every county to elect a new committee of observation during September 1775. The convention limited the size of each one, directed that polling proceed under the watchful eyes of local convention delegates, and restricted the electorate to men who met the colonial property qualification. The latter provision extended suffrage to Roman Catholics.[50]

On September 12, therefore, freemen once again converged on Port Tobacco, this time to place thirty-two of "the most discreet and sensible" freeholders on the committee of observation. In the voters' choices one can glimpse a search for stability in the midst of revolution, for a controlled transition from the old to a new political order. Only four of the successful candidates had not served on the original committee of ninety chosen nearly a year before. Furthermore, because the new committee was only a third the size of its predecessor, the colonial governing elite—ten assemblymen and incumbent or former justices—constituted a much larger proportion of the membership. When, in turn, the committee (not the "inhabitants" and electors as in months past) balloted for convention delegates, the winners already had sat in that body: Assemblymen William Smallwood, Francis Ware, and Josias Hawkins; Continental Congressman Thomas Stone; and merchant Robert Townshend Hooe, who was rapidly emerging as a major procurer of military stores for Maryland. These men became distinguished wartime leaders from the county.[51]

Almost at the moment the new committee of observation was elected, Continental nonexportation closed off access to the British commercial system. For a few weeks before exporting stopped on September 10, the price of tobacco soared to 30s. Maryland currency per hundredweight, triple what it was before the crisis over the Coercive Acts arose. On September 11 tobacco remaining in the county was worthless, as were commodities normally traded in the West Indies.[52]

No matter how long the Continental Association lasted, inhabitants could count on the bountiful land and the waters surrounding the county to feed and even clothe them. No longer, however, could they count on any income from exports. Buying imported manufactures was not at issue, since the association had ended that sector of trade nearly a year before. Rather, the most pressing economic problem was unsettled debts. For months the magistrates had expedited some uncontested cases but, conversely, had used court adjournments to slow other debt litigation. Then, in August, the convention—in a convoluted series of resolves that revealed the delicacy with which it approached interfering with the county courts—denied creditors direct access to them. Instead each committee of observation was to establish a subcommittee for licensing certain *new* debt cases. The convention did nothing, however, about cases that creditors already had won. They were free to seek "executions" (court orders for collection), which made debtors' property subject to seizure and insolvents subject to jail.[53]

Within days after nonexportation took effect, "riotous proceedings" erupted at Port Tobacco. Relatives and friends of a debtor "who was in on execution for a very considerable Sum of Money" broke into the jail and set him free. "They did not pay any regard to the resolves of the Convention, nor to the Committee of the County then sitting," alleged Alexander Hamilton. Alarmed committee members quickly canvassed the public mood and concluded that unless they seized control of debt collection, mob rule would supersede theirs.[54]

Because "vast numbers" of executions had been issued or were expected— "to the great vexation of some and ruin of others, who have it not in their power to pay their just debts, at this time of general stoppage of our trade"— the committee on September 27 ordered the clerk of the court not to issue, and the sheriff not to serve, executions. Creditors, moveover, were to countermand those already served unless the debts in question could be collected "without oppression." These actions were necessary, the committee insisted, "for the ease and quiet of the people" and to avoid "much distress, disorder, and ruin, [which] may happen before the provincial convention can have the particular situation of this county under their consideration, and grant relief."[55]

Until early 1777 the local justices continued officially to describe their tribunal as "a Court of the . . . absolute Lord and proprietary of the province of Maryland," but the words rang hollow after September 1775. When the committee of observation—including a majority of the justices—unanimously moved to prevent the court from enforcing debt judgments, it drained what little power remained, locally, in the proprietary regime. Within months, country justice came to a standstill. In March 1776 the court neglected to empanel a grand jury, ceased criminal prosecutions, and conducted almost no business save for one telling exception: Resolutions of the Provincial Convention were entered in the official record. During the summer of Independence, as Marylanders mobilized men and resources for a long war and turned to writing a state constitution, the court—the locus of authority in colonial Charles County—did not meet at all.[56]

Yet if the court became moribund as the Revolution proceeded, the justices did not. In fact, as committee members and chairmen of popular meetings, most of them helped guide the county from colonial status to Independence. In the process the source of their authority changed. As justices they were proprietary appointees; as committee members and chairmen of meetings they were elected by the freemen. The justices qua committeemen also had to share local governance as never before—with mass meetings and with men newly elevated to decision-making roles. The colonial elite was being transformed.[57]

Until February 1777, when county government was revived and reorganized under the Maryland Constitution of 1776, the committee of observation was the only viable governing body in the county. It continued to oversee the Continental Association, guarded against loyalism, nominated militia officers, helped gather military stores and provision troops stationed at Port Tobacco, and conducted a census of all inhabitants. Not least, it announced the Declaration of Independence.[58]

The months leading up to the Declaration were filled with anticipation and anxiety in the county. King and Parliament alike turned a deaf ear to Congress's protestations of American grievances and, instead, declared the colonies in a state of rebellion. Thousands of British troops and German mercenaries reportedly were on their way to force the colonies into proper subordination to the mother country. In early 1776 British warships entered Chesapeake waters. Virginia already was in turmoil, since its royal governor, Lord Dunmore, was rallying loyalists and had even promised freedom to every slave and indentured servant who joined him and fought for the king. Ousted from the colony, Dunmore and his followers took to a flotilla of vessels that shelled the town of Norfolk in January 1776 and began marauding along the shores of the bay.[59]

Charles County seemed endangered, for rumor had it that Dunmore planned to sail up the Potomac River to Alexandria, where he would rendezvous with John F. D. Smyth, the ne'er-do-well loyalist who had only recently fled the county and allegedly was recruiting Indian allies in the backcountry. Loyalists and Indians, governor and ne'er-do-well, they would ravage the Maryland and Virginia countryside. Thomas Stone confided to General Washington, commander of the Continental Army, that Dunmore "seems determined to extend the Calamities of War to every defenseless place within his

Compass." Feeling militarily vulnerable, their commerce gone, and the proprietary regime near total collapse, Charles County people contemplated Independence.[60]

On May 10, 1776, the Continental Congress recommended that the colonies provide for themselves "such government as shall . . . best conduce to the happiness and safety of their constituents in particular, and America in general." The Maryland delegation, whose instructions did not encompass such a fateful step, withdrew from Congress until the Provincial Convention could address this question. Although personally distraught over what he regarded as Congress's precipitous and premature action, Stone, writing from Philadelphia, urged that "the Vox Populi must in great measure" guide the Provincial Convention. Wisdom and prudence required that the "fair and uninfluenced sense" of *"the people at large"* must be heard. And heard they were, at popular meetings across Maryland. In mid-June Daniel of St. Thomas Jenifer, who was about to make the leap from proprietary placeman to revolutionary politician, noted that "we are verging fast towards independence."[61]

"A great number of the inhabitants of CHARLES county" met during June to take "into our most serious consideration the present state of the unhappy dispute between Great-Britain and the United Colonies, and the very great distress and hardships they [*sic*] have brought upon us." Claiming all colonial grievances as their own, the assembled freemen detailed the "insult and injury" Britain had visited upon them, including "all the colonies being declared in actual rebellion . . . slaves proclaimed free, enticed away, trained and armed against their lawful masters. . . . [A] formidable fleet of British ships, with a numerous army of foreign soldiers, in British pay, are daily expected on our coast to force us to yield the property we have honestly acquired, and fairly own, and drudge out the remainder of our days in misery and wretchedness, leaving us nothing better to bequeath to posterity than poverty and slavery."[62]

Then, rising to further rhetorical heights, the freemen renounced their allegiance to Britain and instructed their convention delegates to push for immediate Independence:

[O]ur affection for the people, and allegiance to the crown of Great-Britain, so readily and truly acknowledged till of late, is forfeited. . . . And as we are convinced that nothing virtuous, humane, generous, or just, can be expected from the British king, or nation, and that they will exert themselves to reduce us to a state of slavery, by every effort and artifice in their power, we are of opinion that the time is fully arrived for the colonies to adopt the last measure for our common good and safety, and that the sooner they declare themselves separate from, and independent of the crown and parliament of Great-Britain, the sooner they will be able to make effectual opposition, and establish their liberties on a firm and permanent basis.[63]

In more ways than one, this landmark meeting broke with the past. For as the freemen renounced their allegiance to Britain, they simultaneously embraced a decidedly less deferential politics than of old. For two years they had trusted the county's convention delegates to use their own good judgment and had sent them to Annapolis with "full power to represent and act for this county," even to "bind" the inhabitants to uphold convention resolves. Now, in the heady days of mid-1776, "WE the . . . freemen of Charles county," who had not even elected the delegates, insisted upon a right to "charge and instruct" *their* representatives "in certain points relative to your conduct in the next convention." The practice of explicitly instructing people's representatives on important questions came later to the county than to other places in revolutionary America, but no less powerfully. "The Instructions of our constituents," wrote Stone, "are sacred."[64]

Asserting a "right to hear, or be informed what is transacted" at Annapolis, the freemen also told the county's delegates to ensure that the convention admit the public to its sessions, record all votes, and publish its proceedings. Furthermore, they called for a new form of government for Maryland, suitable to a "free and independent" state "for time to come." As they cast off British rule, the freemen of Charles County sought to exercise some power of their own.[65]

During the last days of June, Governor Robert Eden departed for England, and the Provincial Convention promptly authorized the Maryland delegation in Congress to vote for Independence. The next step was to frame republican state government *"by the authority of the people only."* Here was the great constitutional inversion of the revolutionary period: Instead of Maryland's government emanating from a charter granted by the king, it would henceforth be rooted in the sovereignty of the people. Or at least some of them. Certainly women and slaves would have no voice in how they were governed. And while allowing every freeman his say on the question of Independence was fair enough—since he might need to defend it with his life—forming a government was a different matter, at least in the opinion of a majority in the convention. Amid the uncertainties of the summer of 1776, when none knew but many feared how far the course of Revolution might carry them, the convention ordered that only free adult males with at least a fifty-acre freehold or other property worth £40 sterling—"and *no others*"—should vote in the forthcoming elections.[66]

That decision threw the fledgling state "into much Confusion." Arguments were bandied about "that every Man who bears Arms is intitled to Vote" and that "the ultimate end of all freedom is the enjoyment of a right of free suffrage." Election officials in a few counties were sympathetic and permitted any militiaman or soldier to vote. But in most counties, including Charles, officials enforced the property qualifications and, in the process, upheld the traditional view that suffrage derived from property holding and from the attachment to the community that such holding implied.[67]

On election day, August 1, the county's voters registered their displeasure with the convention by refusing even to cast their ballots at the polling place it had designated. Assembled elsewhere, they then refused to elect Thomas Stone to the forthcoming state Constitutional Convention, despite his being "a friend to universal liberty" who was "famous for *Moderation*" and who had represented them in the Provincial Convention and all Maryland in the Continental Congress. He allegedly "would not stoop to rascals." In Stone's stead, the voters chose John Parnham, the radical who had helped force the county court to close in 1774.[68]

The state's first constitution, which was not submitted to popular ratification, caused some uneasiness in Charles County, but not much. Measured against the future, the Constitution of 1776 and the Maryland Declaration of Rights did not anticipate a nation that would adopt universal suffrage for white men during the nineteenth century. Measured against the colonial past and the county's thoroughly hierarchical social order, the new frame of government promised substantial change. Catholics regained the civil and political liberties denied them for nearly a century, and the Church of England was disestablished. "Grievous and oppressive" poll taxes (essentially a per capita levy on all adults except white women) were eliminated in favor of ad valorem taxation (whereby a fixed rate was applied to the assessed value of property). The suffrage qualification dropped to fifty acres or property valued at £30 currency (the worth of a slave boy in 1776), although high property qualifications for candidacy to the Assembly were established (£500 for the lower and £1,000 for the upper house). Still, since the county's four Assembly delegates now stood for election annually, they were more regularly accountable to their constituents. On the other hand, although the upper house of the legislature, christened the Senate, was an elective body, it was not subject to direct public control. At five-year intervals the voters of each county chose two electors, who then balloted for the senators.[69]

In structure the revived county court closely resembled its colonial predecessor. Besides handing down justice in accord with common and statutory law, it once again became the center of local government. As before, the justices were appointed. They, and the judges of a newly constituted county orphans' court, received their commissions from the governor. Conversely, the voters henceforth elected the sheriff for a three-year term. He could not succeed himself.[70]

By May 1777 the new system described in the state constitution had come to life through elections and appointments. Scanning the names of those who occupied the judges' chairs at Port Tobacco and the legislators' seats in Annapolis, one can grasp what had happened to the governing elite during nearly three years of extralegal politics. Almost to a man, the colonial elite was intact. Of the thirteen justices who presided in 1774, ten were returned to the court in 1777, and all but one of them had served on the committee of observation in the interim. In the revolutionary crisis, power had flowed from court to committee and then, with statehood, back to the court.[71]

The composition of the last colonial and first state delegations to the Assembly seems, at first glance, to belie the argument about continuity, for none of the colonial assemblymen was returned in 1777. But their absence was entirely unrelated to any rejection by the voters. William Smallwood, Francis Ware, and Josias Hawkins, who had been at the forefront of the revolutionary movement in Charles County, had obtained military commissions: Smallwood as commander of the Maryland Line of the Continental Army, Ware as colonel of the First Regiment of the Line, and Hawkins as a colonel in the militia. Under the state constitution their military positions rendered them ineligible to sit in the legislature. Local freemen did not vote for them but marched to their commands.[72]

Although the colonial elite remained intact in 1777, it was also augmented and, more than that, significantly transformed. Many other men had gained political responsibilities and prominence since 1774. Edward Boarman won election as sheriff and thereby became the first Catholic in nearly a century to occupy that post. The revived county court was twice the size of its predecessor, and that created places for some of the newly prominent (and ensured that even in wartime a quorum could be obtained). Although appointed, the post-Independence court could legitimately claim public approval and support in a way that its colonial predecessor could not. For in the years surrounding Independence, the freemen had elected nearly every justice, old and new, to the committee of observation. This expanded, experienced—and responsive—elite, a revolutionary elite, was poised to exercise leadership through the coming years of war.[73]

CHAPTER FIVE

War on
the Potomac

BEFORE FIGHTING BROKE OUT AT LEXINGTON AND CONCORD, TALK OF
war came easily to Marylanders' lips. In 1765 men boasted, "Damn . . . but
they would fight to the last Drop of their blood before they would Consent to
any such slavery" as the Stamp Act. They also cheered at the idea of "takeing
up arms" to defend their liberties, and they predicted that Americans could
"Cope [militarily] with Britain." Nearly a decade later in Charles County,
"people . . . talk as if they were determined" to contest the Coercive Acts
"with the sword." By October 1774 "Nothing talked of but War with England," or so it seemed in Port Tobacco.[1]

But if, on the eve of the long struggle for Independence, Marylanders freely
talked of war, they had little actual *experience* with it, either on their own
territory or by strengthening British arms during the imperial conflicts of the
eighteenth century. In the Seven Years' War (1756–63), the greatest of those
conflicts and the only one that involved extensive fighting in North America,
Maryland's contribution of men and supplies was modest at best. A few
militiamen, including some from Charles County, patrolled the western frontier and skirmished with French troops at Fort Duquesne, but that effort
paled when compared with those of the Virginia Regiment, commanded by
young George Washington, or the provincial forces of Massachusetts. As the
War for Independence approached, Maryland scarcely even had a militia. The

home guard—reportedly "very ill supplied with Arms, and for want of a proper Militia Law not under good Regulation or Command"—was "far from . . . formidable."[2]

During the war, therefore, Marylanders for the first time were called upon simultaneously to defend their homes and communities as necessary, provide thousands of recruits for the American Army, and generate substantial amounts of war matériel. Not surprisingly for a society little acquainted with warfare, responses to military needs sometimes were halting, disorganized, and inadequate. Yet civilians also accomplished a good deal, although their accomplishments frequently went unapplauded at the time and unnoticed in the historical literature. How local communities actually mobilized human and material resources for the army and also met enemy threats to their own territory is a little explored aspect of the revolutionary experience.[3]

"THEY WILL ALL BE SOLDIERS BY AND BY"

Charles County entered the war years with important advantages, not least of which were continuities in political leadership, the absence of a loyalist threat, and the success of prewar protests in generating organized communal actions. The inhabitants also had the capacity to feed themselves and contribute military supplies, so long as their lands were not laid waste by rival armies.

On the other hand, economic and geographic circumstances potentially impeded civilians' abilities to support the Continental Army and also defend their home territory. The prewar depression and the loss of trade within the empire meant that families began the war financially buffeted and with dwindling amounts of imported clothing, bedding, and other items upon which they and the army depended. Stagnant trade, currency shortages, and massive inflation lay ahead.

The county was geographically vulnerable because Chesapeake waters were ideal for "predatory," "Piratical" warfare. When a British fleet first entered the bay in early 1776, its commander, Andrew Snape Hamond, ordered his forces to "annoy the Rebels by every means in your power" and "seize and detain all American Vessels you may meet with, as well as those of any other Country that may be trading with the Americans." He was soon convinced that "on account of the navigable Rivers of this Country, there is no part of the Continent where ships can assist land operations more than in this." A thousand men and eight or ten small ships could "distress the Colonys of Maryland & Virginia to the greatest degree, and employ more than ten times their numbers to watch them." The colonial avenue of trade had become an avenue of war.[4]

People along both shores of the Potomac River were acutely aware of their vulnerability and, as early as the fall of 1775, tried to do something about it. Their first thought was to sink vessels in the ship channel somewhere off Charles County "so that no ship of Force coud get up the River" beyond that point. They also hoped to build an onshore battery that could rain down gunfire on enemy intruders. General Washington's farm manager at Mount Vernon, situated opposite the northwestern shore of the county, reported, however, that "most people say it is impractible & I fear it will be found to be so." He was right. Determined that "something should be done," the Charles County committee of observation had dispatched men to measure the width and sound the depths of the channel. Unfortunately they discovered that wherever it was narrow enough for erecting a sunken barrier, it was too deep for the barrier to do any good. And wherever the channel was shallow enough for such a barrier, it was so wide that the cost of scuttling many ships was prohibitive. Explaining all this to Washington at army headquarters in New England, his farm manager concluded that "I believe we must defend our plantations upon Potowmack with our Musquets—I believe the gentlemen are ready & willing to turn out & defend any mans property—but the common people are most Hellishly freightened."[5]

The next idea that seemed worth trying, considering "the importance of that great river," was to build warning beacons from its mouth all the way to Alexandria, more than one hundred miles inland, on the assumption that shoreline beacons would transmit intelligence of approaching warships "in a more speedy manner than can be done by land." This project, too, would require coordination among people on both sides of the river. Therefore, in April 1776 a small delegation of Marylanders and Virginians met in Port Tobacco and planned for twenty beacons, nine of them in Charles County, spaced approximately five miles apart. To be visible at that distance, each would be large, "a kind of Iron Grate suspended by a Chain on the end of a Sweep fixed with a Swivel so as to be turned." Because these "Alarm-Post[s]" would be visible only in clear weather, lookout boats would need to patrol the river, ready to fire warning shots, whenever the area was shrouded in fog and mist. Although the Maryland Council of Safety, the executive arm of the Provincial Convention, approved the project, it seems never to have been built. During the war, therefore, boats cruising ahead of enemy raiders fired their guns to alert inhabitants to impending danger. Failing that, they discovered their peril when they spotted columns of smoke rising from plundered plantations and tobacco warehouses or, at even closer range, encountered raiders coming ashore.[6]

To protect Maryland, the Provincial Convention created a revolutionary militia in late 1774. Implementing a request from the Continental Congress, the convention asked "gentlemen, freeholders, and other freemen" aged six-

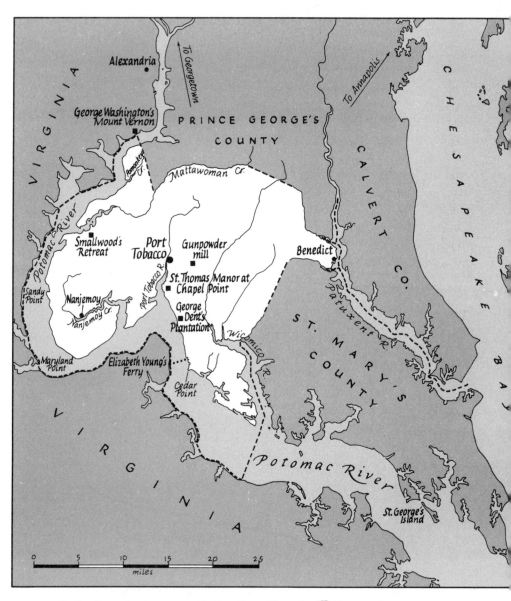

Defending the Potomac Valley from "Predatory" Warfare. After 1775 the Chesapeake and its magnificent rivers, an avenue of commerce during the colonial period, became an avenue of war whenever the British Navy chose to "harass & annoy" the inhabitants. This view of the Potomac river valley reinforces Thomas Stone's complaint in 1777 that Charles County "is so cut of Water that the [enemy] Ships can sail to any point much sooner than the Men, who have Arms, can reach it by marching."

teen to fifty *voluntarily* to organize companies, choose their own captains and other officers, and "use their utmost endeavors to make themselves masters of the military exercise."[7]

The response in Charles County was swift and enthusiastic. By early 1775 men were "forming companies with great diligence and alacrity" and "arming and training in every place." Such activity prompted Nicholas Cresswell to predict, "[T]hey will all be soldiers by and by." Just before sunset on a late winter's day, another visitor strode out to a field near Port Tobacco "& saw a Company of about 60 Gentlemen learning the military Exercise." A month later Lexington and Concord spurred determination "to prepare for our own Safety." And in May, when Virginia delegates to Congress ferried across the Potomac to the county, Port Tobacco militiamen met the luminaries at the beach, ceremoniously escorted them through the county, and left them in the good hands of the Prince George's militia.[8]

Following creation of the Continental Army and its first defeat, at the Battle of Bunker Hill in June of that year, Congress called for *all* able-bodied men to take up arms. The Maryland Convention obliged by ordering mandatory militia service. Henceforth free males and even indentured servants aged sixteen to fifty were required to join militia companies or be shunned as Tories. Each company included officers and seventy or more men who lived near one another and drilled together once a week, while eight companies formed a battalion, which mustered every month or two. Two battalions totaling approximately fifteen hundred men were organized in Charles County.[9]

To lead them, the convention commissioned two of its own members: Josias Hawkins and William Harrison. Hawkins had an easy familiarity with the men he was to command; he had once treated them so generously to alcoholic beverages during an election that he was expelled from the House of Delegates. No matter, the voters sent him back immediately and later elected him to extralegal committees and a militia captaincy. He also was a magistrate and owner of nearly three thousand acres of land. Harrison, although a less distinguished and wealthy gentleman, was the son of a prominent former legislator and justice. The convention also commissioned John Dent as brigadier general of all battalions on the lower Western Shore. His Charles County progenitors had sat in the Assembly since the seventeenth century, and he on the county court since the 1760s.[10]

While the convention reserved the power to choose battalion officers, militiamen continued to elect their own company officers, and here Charles County men combined deference with a measure of egalitarianism. As the full militia was getting organized in the fall of 1775, the rank and file consistently elected members of the patriot elite to be company captains. For example,

William Smallwood, English-educated and the son of a former legislator, was also a veteran of the Seven Years' War and since 1761 had represented the county in the colonial Assembly and revolutionary conventions. From Smallwood's Retreat on Mattawoman Creek, the forty-three-year-old bachelor presided over an estate of more than four thousand acres and was one of the wealthiest men in the county. Captain Francis Ware, who owned a smaller plantation near Port Tobacco, was nearly the same age as Smallwood and also an experienced legislator and a seasoned war veteran; he had commanded Maryland troops on the frontier during the last war. On the other hand, twenty-five-year-old John Hoskins Stone was new to the ways of war and politics, but his brother Thomas was a prominent revolutionary leader. Not all officers, especially junior-grade officers, came from elite families, however. And at least the appearance of egalitarianism prevailed after the convention ordered that "to avoid a needless and unsupportable expense," no one should "wear any uniform at exercise . . . but hunting shirts, the officers distinguishing themselves from the privates by different feathers, cockades, and the like, as fancy may direct."[11]

Once militiamen gained the power of electing company officers, they did not want to relinquish it, as a company raised in the Pomonkey area proved. The men claimed to be among the first in the county who "Steppd out in the Glorious cause of Liberty" in 1775 and had "with great diligence and care since perfected themselves in the Military Art and discipline, as far forth as could . . . be expected from the short time they . . . Exercisd." When the company was formed, the men elected John Dent as captain and Kenhelm Truman Stoddert as first lieutenant. When the Provincial Convention subsequently promoted Dent to brigadier general and Stoddert to battalion major, the militiamen interpreted that as a sign of approval. And when the county committee of observation asked them for recommendations to fill the vacated posts, a majority of the company voted to promote Henry Ward from second lieutenant to captain and General Dent's son George from ensign to first lieutenant. The company simply assumed that the committee would forward the names to Annapolis for commissioning.[12]

At that point egalitarianism and deference collided. In February 1776 the committee of observation, with General Dent presiding, approved the elevation of his son to second-in-command. But it ignored the militiamen's choice for captain and instead recommended Thomas Hanson Marshall, a former county justice. He did not belong to the company, but the gentleman was related to the Dents, Stodderts, and Harrisons. Ward, the militiamen's choice, was to remain a second lieutenant.[13]

Thoroughly displeased, a majority of the Pomonkey company complained to the Council of Safety that an incomplete committee had selected Marshall by no more than a two-vote margin, "thereby stopping the progress of Justice due to the merit of Inferior Officers that hath behaved themselves well." Pointing out that they had elected Ward by a majority of fifteen votes and that he was "a very proper person to entrust" with a captaincy, the militiamen asked that the commission be issued according to *their* choice, "which will be a means of keeping the said company in Harmony and Union . . . and will likewise remove all Suspicions of prejudice." The Council of Safety ignored the entreaty—as well as rules governing the militia—and commissioned Marshall. Gentry power, however modified under revolutionary conditions, remained formidable.[14]

No matter who exercised command, the militia had yet to demonstrate any ability to defend anyone. In fact, during the first two years of the war the home guard was so untrained, inexperienced, and untested that discipline broke down with distressing regularity. During the summer of 1775 Scotsmen at Port Tobacco joined the militia but then refused to bear arms, probably because of a false alarm that British troops were landing along the Patuxent River. Even General Washington heard about the incident. Wrote the "surprizd and vexed" commander in chief: "Why did they Imbark in the cause? what do they say for themselves? . . . are they admitted into Company? or kicked out of it? . . . I cannot say but I am curious to learn the reasons why men, who had subscribed, & bound themselves to each other, & their Country, to stand forth in defence of it, should lay down their arms the first moment they were called upon."[15]

Not until July 1776, the first month of America's declared Independence, did British forces actually offer people from the county a taste of the war. For some time Virginia's deposed royal governor, Lord Dunmore, and his loyalist followers had taken refuge in a "floating Town," nearly one hundred vessels gathered along the Virginia coast and protected by the British Navy. Increasingly racked with disease, short of arms, fresh water, and food, and also harassed by patriot forces, the Dunmore party and its protectors moved north into Potomac waters in mid-July and dropped anchor at St. George's Island, off St. Mary's County, Maryland. Immediately militia units converged on the nearby shore, and the Council of Safety ordered General Dent to take command. As soon as he arrived at camp, he sent for three militia companies from home. They were the first units from the county to see action in the war.[16]

They came to "a shocking place." While the two sides were "continually blasting away at each other," Dunmore's refugees were dying of disease so fast that the St. Mary's shoreline was "full of Dead Bodies chiefly negroes." "We are poisoned with the stench." And while poor men chafed at being away from their fields because "many have not any dependence but their [own] Labor," officers complained that "the militia do every duty so exceeding ill" because

JOHN DENT (CA. 1733–1809). *Appointed a justice of the county court in 1764, Dent first achieved elective office in 1774 as a delegate to the Provincial Convention of Maryland. At the beginning of the War for Independence, he was commissioned commander of a militia battalion, then brigadier general of militia units on the lower Western Shore. Dent remained a justice at least through 1799 and also represented Charles County in the legislature, 1781–82. From the collection of Sharon Gore Bolton. Photograph by John C. Kopp. Courtesy of the Southern Maryland Studies Center, Charles County Community College.*

SARAH MARSHALL DENT (1735–95). *The daughter of a gentry family from Prince George's County, Sarah Marshall married John Dent in 1754 and, during the next seven years, gave birth to five children. During the war she, like hundreds of white women in the county, had to manage at home whenever her husband and sons performed military duty. From the collection of Sharon Gore Bolton. Photograph by John C. Kopp. Courtesy of the Southern Maryland Studies Center, Charles County Community College.*

"the service is so very unknown to them." The Charles County units, having been urgently summoned to duty, arrived with little more than a few jugs, iron cooking pots, and provisions and soon sent entreaties home for "a small supply of cash" so that the men could buy food.[17]

Unable to find water on the island, the British commander, Captain Hamond, decided to fill his casks about a hundred nautical miles upriver, near where the freshwaters of the Potomac mix with the brackish waters of the bay. The site was off Sandy Point on the western edge of Charles County. To "harass & annoy the Enemy by landing at different places" along the way, he set out on July 20 in the flagship of the fleet, the forty-four-gun *Roebuck*, accompanied by three other warships, two tenders, and a row galley. The latter was a peculiar covered boat capable of raking the shoreline with cannon fire at close range. Trailed by two of the activated Charles County militia companies, the British "kept the Shores on both sides in continual alarms" as they proceeded upriver. Near Cedar Point on July 21, the galley dragged three boats away from Elizabeth Laidler's ferry, thereby cutting one of the few regular transportation links between tidewater Maryland and Virginia. Later that day, after firing eighteen-pound cannonballs at a house where Charles County "Rebels" reportedly were gathered, the expedition continued on to the watering place.[18]

On the morning of July 23, three militia companies under Colonel Harrison watched from Sandy Point as ten rowboats were launched from the *Roebuck* and joined the tenders and row galley. "It was every moment expected the enemy would land and attack us," wrote two of the observers. After raising "three loud huzzas," however, the landing party headed for a plantation on the Virginia shore because militiamen there, allegedly fortified by a "drinking Frolick," seemed "to bid . . . [the British] defiance." In short order His Majesty's troops drove off the militia and torched the plantation house, outbuildings, and stacks of grain.[19]

As smoke billowed into the summer sky, the men on the Maryland side of the river watched and waited. By early afternoon Harrison's forces had grown to three or four hundred men—and some sightseers. Having identified a stretch of beach where a landing party most likely would come ashore, Harrison ordered one company to advance down a hill and guard the area. All day he had been "very active and resolute, encouraging his men." Now he asked "if any one felt confused or under any panic, to candidly inform him and turn out of the ranks." One man did so.[20]

Soon enough the enemy tenders and row galley got under way and, about 150 yards offshore, opened fire on the detachment deployed at the beach. "Sundry great guns were discharged at us," and cannonballs and grapeshot "grounded within a few paces of us," militiamen remembered. Although the galley seemed to be positioning itself better to rake them with shot, Harrison did not order them to return fire because the boat was so well covered that "there was no living object to shoot at." When the galley closed to within eighty yards of the detachment and guns from the *Roebuck* and a schooner also opened fire, Harrison ordered a retreat. The men were "directed to scatter as they retreated through the old fields, to observe the flash of the enemy's cannon, and to fall down whenever they saw it.—The fire from the *Roebuck*, armed schooner, and gondola [the galley], grew very warm, and the frequent falling down of the men occasioned a general laughter.—We retreated to a fence at the edge of a wood, and lay behind it until the enemy's fire ceased."[21]

The following day people returned to the field and picked up grapeshot and cannonballs. Meanwhile, the warships remained off the county shoreline until July 26 but did not strafe it again. Putting the best face on what had happened, Colonel Hawkins informed state officials that the militia "have prevented the Enemy from landing or plundering if they intended it." Weary of "carrying on a sort of Piratical War," but convinced of the utility of such a war in the Chesapeake, Hamond soon left the region.[22]

How well the militia behaved at Sandy Point became grist for public discussion because several Virginians who were there accused the Charles County men of cowardice. According to their account, when Colonel Harrison shouted, "Come, let us march down" to the beach, "several replied, I can't bear to shoot a man; others, that their guns were out of order." The Virginians also alleged that the militia broke and ran under fire *before* Harrison signaled a retreat and that he "walked after them laughing . . . and never attempted to rally them." When this story circulated in Alexandria, one of the militia captains promptly posted a disclaimer in public places in the town. The allegations, he retorted, were a *"malicious, infamous falsehood."* Unchastened, the Virginians published their version of events in Alexandria and Baltimore newspapers.[23]

Thereupon Harrison decided to "publish a little too, as a piece of justice due myself and those whom I had the honour to command." Attacking the Virginians' veracity, he produced testimonials from seven spectators at Sandy Point. Alexandrians who had come down to watch the fight said that they "saw . . . nothing like cowardice; but on the contrary, a willing spirit seemed generally to prevail." Charles County spectators were more passionate: "[W]e think it a duty incumbent on us, and on every man, to rescue injured merit from undeserved reproach, and check any idle reports that may reflect disgrace on the American arms." Rather than behave in a cowardly manner, the militia had shown "the most undaunted courage and cool intrepidy" and "appeared spirited, brave, and ready to engage."[24]

Harrison's defense of his own actions and those of his men probably was persuasive. Admitting that he had ordered a retreat from the cannon assault, he asserted that "If I was wrong, I am chargeable with it and not the men— However, I thought it prudent," for "the chance of killing . . . [was] only on the side of the enemy." He depicted a dangerous situation at the beach, where the British alone had cannons and where the only escape route was fully exposed. "From the trial of the men at Sandy-Point," he concluded, "I entertain the highest opinion of their bravery in general, and were they equipped, as men going into battle should be, would risque my life with them, as soon as with any men in the world."[25]

The intensity with which Harrison and the others sprang to the militia's defense and rebutted charges of cowardice seems curiously exaggerated— until one realizes just how precarious was the military situation in Charles County during the summer of 1776. The prediction that "we must defend our plantations upon Potowmack with our Musquets" had come true. Against a heavily armed contingent of the strongest navy in the world, the county could mount only untested, inadequately armed militiamen whose previous martial experience consisted mostly of drilling in some field with their neighbors. Furthermore, in the moment of danger, those who were most experienced in the ways of war, or at least the most enthusiastic, had already left to join the Continental Army. William Smallwood and Francis Ware, veterans of the Seven Years' War, now commanded Maryland Continentals. An unknown number of men had volunteered as regular soldiers, and about 140 others filled two companies of the Flying Camp, a volunteer militia corps that augmented the army between July and December. Small wonder, then, that the home guard's performance at Sandy Point was less than glorious or that Colonel Harrison tried to uphold morale with his vigorous defense of the militia.[26]

Before the militia improved, however, it got worse. One company grew so "discontented and getting into confusion" in September that its captain resigned his commission and offered to enlist as a common soldier. More serious yet, Colonel Hawkins's battalion, comprising half the militia companies in the entire county, refused to muster. The men were drawn up in a line and ready to begin drill practice when an adjutant, a Scotsman, barked a command. According to Hawkins, "a great number of the soldiers broke their ranks and collected together in a crowd: upon which I instantly went amongst them to inquire into the reason of such extraordinary behavior: & some of them objected to their being mustered by a Scotchman, but the greater part declared that they would not be mustered by any adjutant at all, alledging that the province was run to a very great expense by employing adjutants and they thought it the duty of the officers to muster the Battalion." Hawkins and other officers used every argument they could think of "to shew them the absurdity of such conduct but to no purpose." Finally, in exasperation, he dismissed the battalion until he could report its "misbehaviour" to the Provincial Convention, to which he wrote, "I . . . hope it will not be long before some step is taken to reduce them to order."[27]

Hawkins, who had garnered the men's support in elections for provincial assemblyman, revolutionary committeeman, and militia captain, was at a loss to get them to obey orders that September. For the men, some of whom were poor and all of whom were feeling the economic consequences of revolution and war, adjutants were an unnecessary extravagance. As citizens, not subjects, of the new state of Maryland, they voiced their opinions and grievances even to the extent of disobeying commanding officers and challenging the rules under which the militia was organized. In the second year of the war, the home guard was not a disciplined corps. Nor had it convincingly defended Charles County from attack. Rather, its misbehavior gave proof to assertions, common among both American and British army officers, that militia units were, at best, seldom effective and, at worst, cowardly and useless.[28]

"MUCH INFESTED WITH THE PRIVATEERS AND CRUISERS OF THE ENEMY"

Nearly every year until 1783, enemy vessels returned to the Potomac and to the county, whose towns, inspection warehouses, and some of its finest plantations lay exposed on navigable waters. Consequently, from the Sandy Point skirmish in 1776 until the town of Benedict was sacked and partially burned in 1783 (*after* news of the peace treaty reached Maryland), the county was the scene of periodic destruction, looting, and sometimes frenzied defense efforts. If, at Sandy Point, men turned and ran without firing a shot, by the last years of the war, when the South was the principal theater of action, they were much more inclined to stand their ground and fight. Somehow they had learned to soldier.

Three principal factors account for the improved performance. First, British warships and privateers appeared often enough that people learned what to expect and how best to react. Secondly, in 1777 the state legislature created a new military post, that of county lieutenant. Thereafter each county had one, and he was responsible for coordinating defense preparations and supervising the militia. And thirdly, men who returned to Charles County after serving in the Continental Army usually came back as battle-hardened veterans.

War on the Potomac meant raiding, destruction of property, and pillaging of slaves and provisions. The county was never the site of battle between opposing armies, or a thoroughfare for British troops, as were parts of New Jersey. It never suffered military occupation, as did New York City, Philadelphia, and Charleston, and never knew civil war, as did the Carolina backcountry. A full-scale invasion of southern Maryland seemed imminent when Lord Cornwallis's army pushed north through Virginia in 1781, but it never happened because American and French forces trapped him at Yorktown. Periodic warfare in the Potomac river valley nonetheless caused "much injury" to nerves and property and "much expence by frequent calls for Militia."[29]

In the face of repeated incursions, Maryland officials rarely provided adequate assistance to localities. The state simply was so rife with waterways that it proved impossible to protect every locale. Nor could anyone accurately predict where marauders would strike. When rumors flew in 1779 that British warships had entered the bay, state officials could only warn the county lieutenants, "We have nothing yet that points out their Object, perhaps they may design to spread Destruction as wide as they can." Under such circumstances, raiders "grew more venturesome." By 1780, according to officials, "the Successes of small armed Vessels have invited a very formidable Enemy into our Bay," so that "Our Coast has lately been much infested with the Privateers and Cruisers of the Enemy . . . to the great Detriment of the Public." Appeals for help from the United States Navy were unavailing, aid from American privateers was inadequate, and alleged state impotence seemed a "disgrace." People living near the water's edge usually had to fend for themselves and hope that the state would send extra arms and ammunition in time to do some good. Even after the Yorktown campaign, sporadic raiding continued into 1783, when a thoroughly frustrated militia officer in St. Mary's County wailed, "It is really distressing to know the resources, and credit, of our State, will not furnish us, with the means of protection against the Enemys Barges, that are now in our Bay, & Rivers, plundering the Inhabitants, on the Shores, and keeping the whole of them, in constant alarm, and dread."[30]

Left largely to its own resources and strategies, each county organized its defenses under the direction of the county lieutenant. In Charles the obvious choice was Francis Ware, who combined military experience with popular appeal. (He, too, had been expelled from the colonial Assembly for treating the voters to spiritous liquors and was promptly reelected.) Ware rose to colonel and second-ranking officer in the Maryland Line of the army before ill health forced him to resign his commission and return home in early 1777. A few months later he was appointed county lieutenant, and he spent the rest of the war supervising local defense preparations and calling out the militia during emergencies. At such times he seemed indefatigable in directing the home guard.[31]

As Ware's career suggests, an exchange of manpower and know-how between the county and the Continental Army proved crucial to the militia's improved performance over the course of the war. From General Smallwood to the lowliest drummer, hundreds of local men served with the army. Despite the geographic expanse and shifting theaters of the war, as the soldiers experienced it from New York to the Carolinas, numerous links to home remained. Local people—troops and civilian spectators, too—continuously went back and forth between home and camp. Officers came back to the county on recruiting expeditions that lasted months at a time. Some Continentals wintered at home, a practice Smallwood endorsed because they might "refresh themselves in good winter quarters," tend to neglected private affairs, and "more readily than ever return [to camp] in the Spring." He himself was in the county and lent a hand during some of the worst raiding in 1781. Men who were discharged at the end of their enlistments sometimes came home for a while, then set out for camp again.[32]

Other veterans returned permanently because of war wounds, illness, or other reasons. Hence, after a musket ball shattered John Hoskins Stone's ankle at the Battle of Germantown in 1777, he resigned command of the First Regiment of the Maryland Line and later was busily engaged when the county was threatened. William Layman, an ensign in Stone's regiment, did not intend to leave army service when he came home to visit his mother and friends in 1779, but as he later recounted, "by her importunities he was prevailed upon . . . to stay with and attend to her business." Layman became a local army recruiter.[33]

For several hundred militiamen who never joined the army, even brief attachment to it was efficacious. In 1776 Charles County volunteers readily filled two companies of the Flying Camp of militia, which saw action with the Maryland Line in New York and New Jersey. The following year, after the British Army occupied Philadelphia and engaged the Continental Army in fierce combat at Brandywine and Germantown, two more companies from the county marched north to reinforce Smallwood. Their first encounter with British troops began with a retreat, but they rallied after a Continental officer arrived and threatened to "knock . . . the man that would not fight." Because "his appearance and talk to us encouraged us," according to one of the men, they marched forward to meet the enemy—who promptly retreated. In such ways did militiamen become more adept at soldiering. So, too, when they were commanded by Smallwood, a strict disciplinarian who shaped the state line into a brave, respected fighting unit. Although Continental officers always preferred regular soldiers over the militia, Smallwood noted that after a few weeks in camp, militiamen were "more orderly and regular . . . [and] somewhat better disposed and disciplined than I ever expected." Having

WILLIAM SMALLWOOD (1732–92). *Between 1761 and 1775 Smallwood represented Charles County in the colonial legislature and the revolutionary Provincial Convention. A veteran of the Seven Years' War, in January 1776 he received command of Smallwood's Battalion, from which evolved the Maryland Line of the Continental Army. As commander of the line, he led state troops in battle in New York, New Jersey, Pennsylvania, and South Carolina. A young Pennsylvania woman characterized him as "lively," possessed of "a truly martial air [and] the behaviour and manners of a gentleman," and "so good humor'd . . . [and] sensible I wonder he is not married." After the war Smallwood served as governor (1785–88) and member of the Maryland Senate (1791–92). Maryland Commission on Artistic Property Collection, SC1545-1054, Maryland State Archives.*

JOHN HOSKINS STONE (1750–1804). *The younger brother of Thomas Stone, John read law and began a mercantile career before receiving command of a regiment of Smallwood's Battalion in early 1776. He helped organize the Flying Camp that year, saw action with the Continental Army in New York and Pennsylvania, and received a severe leg wound at the Battle of Germantown in October 1777. After resigning his commission as colonel in the Maryland Line in 1779, Stone continued to support the war effort by assisting in the recruiting, training, and provisioning of Maryland troops. He represented Charles County in the legislature from 1785 to 1787 and was elected governor of the state in 1794. Maryland Commission on Artistic Property Collection, SC1545-1057, Maryland State Archives.*

tasted military life, and having fought at Princeton, Germantown, and Brandywine, or at Camden, Cowpens, and Guilford Courthouse, Ninety-Six and Eutaw Springs, or Yorktown, militiamen and regulars, together, were better prepared and steeled to defend the county from attack.[34]

"WELL DISPOSED TO GIVE BATTLE"

Successful resistance required not just men but arms and ammunition, and these were in short supply throughout the war. Because no fieldpieces were deployed in the county, any damage inflicted upon enemy warships was largely accidental. Nor was the supply of small arms ever adequate. When Colonel Ware tallied the militia's equipment in 1779, he counted fifty-eight muskets and forty-six bayonets—for fifteen hundred men—and about eighty pounds of good powder. Colonel Harrison, the battalion commander, believed that a few hundred well-armed men, no more than a fifth of the militia, could repel waterborne raiders. Without enough guns, however, "great Numbers are . . . obliged to be assembled to make up for [this] melancholy Want." Never was the deficiency overcome. Lacking adequate firepower, the militia always had to compensate with numbers. If it arrived in time, it could usually overpower landing parties but was no match for cannon assaults from gunships. On the other hand, while the British seemed invincible on the water, raiders became vulnerable as soon as they reached shore.[35]

The militia was called out whenever a naval squadron cruised off the county. Two encounters, in 1777 and 1781, were the most memorable and offer revealing, and different, glimpses of civilians coping with the war. In December 1777 a British squadron including the forty-gun *Phoenix*, thirty-four-gun *Emerald*, two tenders, and about a hundred marines dropped anchor near Sandy Point to take on fresh water and provisions. Thomas Stone, who was taking a respite from service in the Continental Congress, immediately informed state officials that "the Commander has issued a Manifesto signifying his Desire to exchange Gold & Silver for Provisions and in case the Inhabitants refuse [to] sell, his Resolution [is] to take by force every thing wanted by his King's Ships. They have done no [damage] in their Course up the River except by receiv[ing] some fugitive Negroes, but as they have been disappointed in their Expectations of trading, it is expected they will endeavour to pillage the Inhabita[nts] and destroy the exposed Tobacco Warehouses on their Re[turn]." Stone asked that sixty guns be dispatched to Port Tobacco as soon as possible because "Our people are well disposed to give Battle to [prevent?] Ravages wherever they may Land, but We have no Arms to equip Men for the Stations which ought to be guarded. And this County is so cut of Water that the Ships can sail to any point much sooner than the Men, who have Arms, can reach it by marching." State officials sent the muskets, then told Colonel Ware, "the scene of your Action will be so remote from us, that we shall not have it in our Power to assist you with our Advice, when you may require it."[36]

Ware, "extremely active" and "very attentive to his Duty" as county lieutenant, stationed militiamen at every place where British marines were likely to land, then waited. Reported Stone proudly: "[T]he Militia have shown great Readiness to [do] every thing which has been required of them" and were guarding the shoreline so well that "the Enemy will get no Provisions from this County." He spoke too soon.[37]

After taking on fresh water off Sandy Point, on December 9 the British squadron caught a fresh wind for its return down the river. But the ships' pilots being only slightly acquainted with the channel, the *Phoenix* ran aground several times and finally slammed solidly into the river bottom near Maryland Point. For three days British seamen removed ammunition to the other vessels until the *Phoenix* finally floated free. And during those same three days, exchanges were initiated between ship and shore.[38]

Colonel Harrison himself set the example. As he later explained, the captain of the *Emerald* asked for "a small Supply of Corn & Fodder to feed a Cow on, and a little Poultrie &c for his Cabbin. I granted him a few Bushells of I[ndian] Corn, some Fodder, a few Fowls, Piggs and some other Trifles—and, in Return, reciev'd a few Gallons of Spirits, with 2 Barrels of Salt—the former used by the Troops—the latter to be given in small Portions to the poor." Then it was Harrison's turn to deliver a request. Aware that several runaway slaves had boarded the *Emerald*, the colonel asked for their return, to which the ship's captain readily agreed. When a "thieving party" of three British seamen rowed ashore one night and almost immediately fell into the hands of sentries, Harrison promptly traded the rowboat for a barrel of salt and the captives for a like number of Americans held prisoner on board the ships.[39]

Still, dealing with the enemy had its limits. After the *Phoenix* was freed and the squadron got under way again, reports reached Annapolis that "many People on Patowmack," especially between Cedar Point and the Wicomico River in Charles County, were trading provisions for salt and other scarce commodities. Immediately the governor's Council lectured Ware: "Whatever temporary Convenience may result to Individuals from such a Practice, none can be ignorant how contrary it is to their Duty as Subjects to this State, or not foresee the pernicious Consequences. . . . if [the British] . . . are treated as half Friends, we may expect enough of their Company." Apprehension of extensive trading between ships and shore probably was exaggerated since only one man from Charles County was indicted for trading with the enemy.[40]

The episode nevertheless was instructive on several counts. No sensible person could doubt British resolve to buy provisions if possible and seize them if necessary. But men would have to come ashore to raid, and this time the militia was in place and determined to resist. Only after the battalion commander had victualed the captain's table and undertaken further exchanges— reasonable though they might have been—did civilians begin trading with the enemy. Tellingly, they wanted not British gold but staples that had become extremely scarce during the war: sugar, rum, and, especially, "very precious" salt.[41]

As the war in the South intensified, the enemy returned to Charles County not to trade but to raid. The worst pillaging and damage occurred during the first half of 1781, when British forces in Virginia, uncontested by an American army, wreaked wanton destruction across the state and appeared poised to move north into Maryland. Warned state officials: "Their object is plunder and after they have accomplished their Business in Virginia, it is more than probable they will visit us." Indeed, several hundred naval raiders soon descended, with a vengeance, on the Potomac river valley. Enemy brigs, sloops, schooners, barges, and even a frigate or two cruised at will, challenged only by winds and currents, all the way from the mouth of the river to the town of Alexandria. Laying waste to plantations and tobacco warehouses and threatening General Washington's Mount Vernon, a target sure to quicken any loyal British heart, the raiders "kept the Inhabitants on the Waters of Potomack in constant alarm," or at least "disquiet," for months.[42]

This action was part of a massive British naval assault intended to destroy as much property as possible beside the Chesapeake's principal rivers: the James, York, Rappahannock, and Potomac. Whether British marines or privateers, the intruders allegedly had orders to "burn and destroy all before them." They preferred to "land at unguarded places, plunder & destroy," then "[as] Soon as they see the Militia gathering they embark and go to another unguarded place." Wrote one eyewitness: "The scituation of the Inhabitants of Potom[a]k is very alarming & distressing." Conceded Maryland officials: "[T]he British continue superior on the water."[43]

In this, the valley's moment of greatest peril, the river was no better fortified against attack than at the beginning of the war six years earlier. There were no warning beacons, shoreline batteries, or lookout boats, much less anything powerful enough to stop ships of the Royal Navy. People in each county essentially had to take up muskets and fend for themselves with minimal help from the state. When, in January 1781, the governor's Council ordered county lieutenants to alert the entire militia "to march at a minutes Warning," Francis Ware immediately complied, then announced that "We have not more than 150 Stand of armes both public and private Within the County fit for Service." When he asked the state to "furnish us in such manner as to Enable us to oppose the Enemy With Spirit," the Council offered fifty muskets and two hundred pounds of powder, which Ware would have to fetch from Annapolis "as it will not be in our Power to send them to you." War on the Potomac was a most local affair.[44]

Thus armed, Charles County experienced a full measure of disruption and destruction. The entire militia was called out, and "none but the aged [were] left" at home for most of April. On the night of the second, a building containing eighteen thousand pounds of tobacco went up in flames at a plantation near Cedar Point—a prelude to what followed. Under cover of darkness on the night of the fifth, an enemy landing party plundered widow Elizabeth Young's ferry near the point (she was known to transmit military intelligence between Maryland and Virginia). At two o'clock in the morning the alarm sounded in Port Tobacco, and people roused themselves from slumber to learn that enemy barges were on the Port Tobacco River. The alarm almost certainly saved the town and its tobacco warehouse from attack, but estates on the river fared poorly in the hours before dawn. At the plantation of Walter Hanson, senior justice of the county court, the raiders seized valuable goods, "insulted the whole Family," and captured Hanson's son, an army officer home on leave. At St. Thomas Manor they torched a building and committed other "Devastages" ("not sparing the Church furniture"). At a nearby plantation they were prevented from landing by militiamen who had marched several miles to intercept them; from across the Potomac, Virginians "heard a good deal of firing." But mostly the intruders glided from place to place ahead of the militia until, in a grand finale, they burned the "elegant Seat" of George Dent, the former magistrate and legislator. A terrified Mrs. Dent fled into the night.[45]

The extent of the destruction along the Port Tobacco River, further raiding in the Nanjemoy area the following night, and reports that nearly three hundred men were amassed on warships and privateers off Charles County spurred people to get their movable property out of the way. On April 7 they also began taking hogsheads of tobacco out of the Cedar Point warehouse. As soon as the British noticed, however, three warships moved into position to rake the site with cross fire and a landing party captured the warehouse. Some militiamen arrived on the scene, attacked, and killed a sentry, but "the situation of these few men being too dangerous[,] they retired." Now it was the raiders' turn to carry off the tobacco, and they worked through the night loading it onto British vessels. Then they torched the warehouse.[46]

For several more weeks, warships maneuvered off the county while the militia maneuvered along the shore, thwarting some landings, capturing a few raiders, but not always able to prevent damage. Years later people recalled "the canonnading in the River," the "many roberys" and "immense property destroyed," and how they had "engaged in protecting the State from the invasion of the enemy" during 1781. Although reports pointing to a full-scale invasion via the Potomac eventually proved unfounded, what people experienced, and feared, was bad enough. Wrote General Smallwood from the county in early May: "The Inhabitants have been much alarmed, and have removed most of their Property from the water side. There has been nothing short of a State of confusion here for some time past."[47]

By all accounts, people in Charles and other counties on both sides of the Potomac wanted to offer stiffer resistance but were hampered by lack of munitions and accurate knowledge of the enemy's intentions. Within the county, people lauded the militia's "Alacrity and spirit" and its willingness to "Act with vigour." Although conceding superiority to brigs, frigates, and cannons, they knew that militiamen could prevail against "light ravaging parties," the "plundering Banditts." But they also regularly complained that "We are by no means prepared to prevent [the enemy's] . . . Designs taking Effect; having an extant of coast but few arms and less ammunition." Without advance warning and adequate munitions, "no Man's property on the Water can be secure and of Consequence the most valuable part of our Lands will be left uncultivated."[48]

The amount of state assistance extended in time of need seems remarkably meager. When faced with a military crisis, the county usually received some gunpowder and the loan of several dozen state-owned muskets. Yet even that was not assured because transport might not be available, state guns might be in use elsewhere, or they might arrive too late to do any good. Nor was the state of much help in conveying military intelligence. Amazingly, *after* the county had sustained intensive raiding in 1781, the governor's Council ordered Ware to call out the militia to protect the inhabitants and also to have all tobacco, livestock, and provisions moved out of harm's way. And only at the height of pillaging along the Potomac were plans forwarded to erect a fort and battery to interdict enemy vessels.[49]

Why did the state government not do more to protect and aid its own citizens? Answers to this question emerge only if one pulls back from the Potomac Valley and surveys the wider war. Whenever enemy vessels operated in Chesapeake waters or, as in 1781, a land invasion was anticipated, Maryland officials established military priorities. They had to, for the government's defensive capabilities were extremely limited, partly because of geography and partly because much of the state's war effort went to support the

Continental Army. From the early days of the conflict, when soldiers first marched north and took guns with them, munitions were in short supply in Maryland, and never more than in 1781, when the war built to its climax in the Chesapeake. As state officials usually reckoned dangers and defense priorities, the bay, the city and port of Baltimore, and the capital at Annapolis took precedence over other areas, especially those where enemy hit-and-run tactics often foiled successful resistance. Better to commit scarce military resources where they might do more good.[50]

With little assistance from the state, therefore, Charles County people worked together to resist threats to their home ground. Theirs was always a defensive posture. The militia did not attack enemy squadrons but instead watched and waited until raiders' targets seemed clear. Then, moving overland, militiamen tried to reach those targets in time, and with sufficient arms, to save property and persons. Although they did not consistently repel the enemy, they undoubtedly prevented even greater damage and chaos. And according to eyewitnesses, they behaved with spirit and alacrity. It is easy to fault the revolutionary militia for failing to deter and damage British forces, but quite another matter to assess what it had to work with and, with those resources, what it accomplished.

CHAPTER SIX

Prevailing on
the People

IN JUNE 1778 THE COUNTY ORPHANS' COURT APPRENTICED AN ELEVEN-
year-old lad to a militia captain named Walter Hanson, Jr., who promised to
teach "the said Orphan the Art of Manufacturing Gun powder" and, if the
opportunity arose, the less volatile trade of carpentry. Hanson needed the
boy's labor because he was building a powder mill on a tract of land he owned
near Port Tobacco. Soon the mill would be finished and, when fully opera-
tional, would produce at least twenty-five hundred pounds of cannon and
musket powder each week. That, in the fourth year of the war, would go a
long way toward supplying the "Battle powder" needs of the entire state.[1]

Hanson's venture had its origins in the summer of 1775, when the Provincial Convention appropriated funds to construct and operate a mill. Some
months later merchant Robert Townshend Hooe recommended Hanson to
the Council of Safety "in the Strongest Terms in my power" as "a Genius in
the mechanical Way," although he quietly confided to Hanson, "I hope I have
not said more than your Genius in the Mechanical way will very fully warrant." At public expense Hanson traveled to Pennsylvania to obtain from its
well-known armorers "a proper knowledge of Erecting & Making the Powder
Mill[,] also the Manufactory of Guns [or any]thing else that may be for the
P[ublic] good." Then, in June 1776, the Council authorized him and his

brother John to build a mill in Charles County. The province would try to furnish all necessary saltpeter and sulfur and, in return, would buy the gunpowder.[2]

Construction proceeded slowly because of the structure's great size, high costs of labor and materials, and difficulties in keeping the work going during wartime. Both Hansons were militia captains and "frequently called from Home to attend the Service of the Militia," while five of their laborers "disappointed them by quitting said Work and enlisting in the Army." In the summer of 1778—the same summer in which he acquired the orphan boy—Walter Hanson was scheduled to march new recruits to join the army in camp. But "I could not leave . . . without Sensure at that Time As many would say, POOR Fellow he has undertaking [*sic*] that which his Genius could not carry him through as many before him has done, and was glad of this Opertunity To leave the Mill." Fined at a court-martial in Port Tobacco for dereliction of duty, he argued that he had not marched off to "the Grand AMERICAN ARMY" because "it would be better for me to Continue and Compleat my grand under Taking."[3]

Regarding that undertaking, Hanson pronounced the mill nearly finished. Indeed, it would be running "If I could but get hands to assist me, in Carrying on the work." He confidently predicted nonetheless that soon he would be manufacturing gunpowder equal to any produced in Europe. Yet despite such optimism and an eventual state investment of at least £2,500, the mill never produced a single keg of powder. The problems encountered, and the state's success in locating other sources of supply, combined to stall the project just short of completion.[4]

The powder mill, albeit ultimately unsuccessful, formed a small part of war mobilization in Charles County—that is, the marshaling of human and material resources to further the American cause. For in addition to defending their lives and property during the war, to say nothing about just surviving from day to day, civilians were called upon to join the Continental Army and to support it with everything from bacon to bayonets. Whereas the war on the Potomac focused people's attention and energies on their locality, their home ground, manning and supporting the army raised their sights to the national level as did nothing else.[5]

During the first years of the United States—war years—only two national institutions existed: Congress and the army. The first was a distant entity, elected by the state legislatures and with no direct ties to the citizenry. The Continental Army, on the other hand, was the people's army, filled with fathers, husbands, and sons and with friends, neighbors, and kin. A woman who knit stockings for the military could take satisfaction in knowing that the work of her hands would warm soldiers' feet, just as a planter realized that grain he grew would ease their hunger. The army's ties to the local communities of America were extensive.

During the war the Maryland Provincial Convention and the successor state government received unprecedented, seemingly endless, and often urgent requests on behalf of the army. They in turn established basic guidelines, then delegated recruiting and provisioning to the counties. Initially citizens were asked only to *volunteer* their services and goods, but because of the scope and length of the war, in time they were *required* to support the army. Every household contributed something, and often someone.

Members of the gentry were at the forefront of the war effort in Charles County. They received the most coveted army commissions and, at home, oversaw the recruiting of soldiers and acquisition of war matériel. Yet just as the coming of the Revolution involved more men in politics and decision making, so the war also beckoned them to positions of public authority and trust. It furthered the process, begun in the 1760s, of drawing more and more white men into the public arena.

The war also altered the exercise of leadership. Traditionally members of the elite mediated between local people and the provincial government, as when they brought the transgressions of Sheriff Lee to the attention of the Assembly in 1769. During the war this role grew enormously. To meet the military needs of the Continental Army, recruiters and provisioners had to interact with the public on a large yet personal scale. The county lieutenant and Continental officers who came home on recruiting expeditions worked to persuade freemen to enlist, while provisioning agents scoured the countryside in search of blankets, clothing, food, horses, and other military supplies. In the process these men became the crucial link connecting the county to the war beyond its borders. They were pragmatic in mediating between the army's needs and citizens' ability or willingness to respond. Although, under the law, they had coercive powers to extract compliance, they preferred not to use those powers and, instead, in the words of one provisioner, did their best to "prevail on the people" for cooperation. And if prevailing did not yield the county's full portion of men and supplies, local war leaders explained the deficiencies and expected state officials and the army to understand.[6]

How effectively did the county's inhabitants assist the army? As would be expected, enthusiasm waxed and waned, individual efforts ranged from minuscule to magnanimous, and communal results varied from inadequate to impressive. On balance, and in light of the fact that Marylanders were little acquainted with warfare before the Revolution, the record of accomplishment was substantial, even impressive.

THE CITIZENS' ARMY

Because the Continental Army was composed of state lines, General Washington himself sometimes wondered whether "ours was *one* Army, or *thirteen*" or "a compound of *both*." Although hardly ideal from a military standpoint, the structure of the army reflected the nation's creation by the separate states as well as the pervasive localism of eighteenth-century America. In the Maryland Line, too, local attachments were strong. For much of the war, for example, Charles County men enlisted and served under officers who also were from the county, many of them relatives, neighbors, and friends. And local soldiers referred to native son William Smallwood, the only man ever to command the line, as "our General."[7]

The state first raised large numbers of Continental troops in 1776, when more than five thousand men volunteered for duty. Approximately fifteen hundred enlisted as regulars in several independent companies and a unit known as Smallwood's Battalion, while the rest were militiamen attached to the Flying Camp for six months. About the time the camp disbanded that December, the battalion and the independent companies merged to form the Maryland Line, which remained in the field for the rest of the war.[8]

For Marylanders, the campaign of 1776 was a period of *rage militaire*, when enough men were eager for a taste of life in the citizens' army that they more than filled the state's quota of troops. Transported on boats to the head of Chesapeake Bay, they marched the rest of the way on foot—through Wilmington and "Phillidelphy," across New Jersey, on to "York Island"—usually covering fifteen to twenty miles each day. As soldiers, most seemed "quite raw." Yet in a disastrous series of defeats at Long Island, White Plains, and Fort Washington, defeats that nearly destroyed the army, Maryland troops fought with such steadiness and courage that Washington, seeing them, allegedly cried out, "Good God, what brave fellows I must this day lose." Smallwood considered his men much superior to northern soldiers. New England officers, he complained, "instead of instructing their troops in the principles of military discipline, preparing and encouraging to meet their enemies in the fields and woods," trained them "to run away and to make them believe they never can be safe unless under cover of an intrenchment, which they would rather extend from the North to the South pole than risque an engagement."[9]

That autumn, as the days grew shorter and the nights colder, many Marylanders sickened "owing to our lying on the cold ground, without straw or plank" and sometimes even without blankets. Doctors were so scarce that "the neglect of the troops when sick discourages them more than any other circumstance." Some of the most lasting memories Charles County veterans had of the war were "how they had Suffered." Suffering stalked them even after they were discharged. Remembering the long walk home in December 1776, a militiaman wrote that "we had hard times getting home as we got nothing for our Service, and had sometime to Starve when we were not where we could beg." Their return to the county from New Jersey took twenty-three days.[10]

The *rage militaire* subsided as soon as men arrived home with tales of deprivation and carnage, and never again was recruiting accomplished as easily as in 1776. Thereafter the state line annually sought up to three thousand new recruits and reenlistments to augment troops already on active duty. But seldom was the line—or the rest of the army—at full strength, and this sometimes caused Smallwood, like General Washington, to despair. Where was "that boasted Valour, public Spirit & Patriotism, (which were so conspicuous in the mouth of every man at the commencement of this contest)?" Smallwood asked during the winter of Valley Forge. Alas, he wrote, "Professions are made, and Wars carried on, with more facility in a warm Room, than in the Field. Amidst all this boasted Patriotism the burthen has & must hang on a handful of worn out worried continentals."[11]

Partly because revolutionary rhetoric depicted European-style professional armies as threats to liberty, and largely because freeholders had the vote, the Assembly always hoped that volunteers would man the Maryland Line. Seeking to avoid conscription and encourage long-term enlistments, the Assembly as of 1777 provided that anyone who voluntarily enrolled for three years would receive a cash bounty upon enlistment, choice of the unit in which he served, immunity from arrest and prosecution for small debts, and exemption from state taxes for seven years. The state also promised land bounties, pensions for disabled soldiers, and public assistance for needy families of military men and for survivors of those who died of wounds.[12]

Notwithstanding such enticements, enlistments plummeted in 1777. Reluctantly, therefore, the Assembly initiated a military draft, but only in emergencies and for short periods of time. Every militia company was divided into eight "classes," which, in rotating order, could be drafted for up to two months' duty outside the state. Any man who was unwilling or unable to serve, however, could hire a substitute within three days of being drafted. That failing, officers were to find appropriate substitutes. Militia classes reinforced the army that year when British forces under General William Howe sailed up Chesapeake Bay, marched overland to occupy Philadelphia, and met Continental troops in fierce combat at Brandywine, Germantown, and other sites near the city.[13]

Emergency reinforcements did not, however, fill the Maryland Line. In 1777 it fielded only eleven hundred regulars and allegedly presented "a trifling figure" compared with other state lines. As the 1778 campaign approached, the governor confessed that "I do not know what Success we may have" in raising Maryland's quota of twenty-nine hundred recruits. But this time the Assembly tried to ensure that the line would operate at full strength and cast a wide net for recruits. If the number of volunteers proved inadequate, the ranks would be completed with vagrants, substitutes procured by militiamen, and conscripts. Each of these sources of manpower was tapped that year. Vagrants had no choice: They were simply rounded up, and each was "considered as a soldier enlisted." On the other hand, any two militiamen who produced an able-bodied substitute were exempt from army duty while he served. As a last resort, drafting began. Once again the militia was divided into classes, and if a class did not furnish an acceptable recruit, one of its members was drafted. This was the first time that Maryland channeled militiamen into regular army units.[14]

Still, the Assembly was so reluctant to coerce freemen into the army that it adopted elaborate procedures meant to encourage civilians to hire substitutes. In 1778 the total amount of property owned by the men of each militia class was supposed to be the same, so that no class bore an inequitable burden if it hired a substitute. Two years later all taxpayers, male and female, and even paupers were classed and became liable for hiring costs—and at an astonishing rate of up to 15 percent of the assessed value of their property. Explained the legislature: "[A]ll the citizens of this state should contribute a due proportion of property to procure troops for the support and defence of our country, or should render personal service in lieu thereof." Absent volunteers, that was a republican answer to the army's needs.[15]

From the army's perspective, the annual recruiting ritual in Maryland and other states yielded too few soldiers, too late in the season. Routinely the Maryland Line did not receive its full complement of recruits until a campaign was well advanced. In addition, each year the Assembly confronted anew the politically sensitive question of whether or not to draft. When drafting was not employed in 1779, state officials acknowledged that recruiting, although not "altogether without Success," fell "much short of our Wishes." Baron von Steuben, the German drillmaster credited with turning ragged Continentals into a disciplined fighting corps, delicately reminded Governor Thomas Johnson that "the earlier and longer the time for which the Men are Enlisted the more service they will render the Country."[16]

By then the major theater of war, and the Maryland Line, had shifted to the South. British forces occupied the capitals of Georgia and South Carolina, while violent confrontations among rival armies, loyalists, and patriot forces reverberated across the backcountry. The southernmost states might well be torn from the nation. Given command of the American Army in the South, and the unenviable task of trying to salvage the situation, was one of Washington's most talented generals, Nathanael Greene.[17]

Desperate for soldiers, Greene lobbied the states for recruits during the winter of 1780–81. He personally visited Maryland legislators and pressed them to reenact drafting. "If a draft could be once [more] accomplished," he forecast, "it would damp the hopes of the enemy more than ten Victories," save the southern army from "ruin," and prevent the "spread of desolation and horror." Faced with a request for nearly two thousand recruits for the coming campaign, the Assembly agreed to draft up to half of them out of the militia for up to three-year terms, but, as in the past, only if all other means of recruiting lagged.[18]

They did. In March 1781 Greene learned that notwithstanding his command's "disturbing and critical situation" as well as Smallwood's "extensive influence in the State of Maryland," not one soldier had yet been recruited. "I am at a loss to account for this very extraordinary delay," Greene fumed, and then warned of dire consequences for Maryland should the lower South be lost.[19]

Although Marylanders were not insensitive to the army's plight, their attention just then was focused closer to home, on the naval raiding in Chesapeake waters. Not until the danger subsided that summer did drafting resume. Then, suddenly, as American and French forces closed in on Lord Cornwallis's army at Yorktown, the martial spirit returned to Maryland. Boasted the governor's Council: "[O]ur People are resolute and determined[;] they feel that animating and noble spirit which diffused itself through all Ranks at the Commencement of this glorious Contest." When a regiment of the state line left Annapolis with a full complement of troops in September, the *Maryland Gazette* reported that "they are the best men enlisted in this state since the war [began]." The *rage militaire* returned because a decisive victory, which would finally secure the national independence proclaimed in 1776, seemed imminent.[20]

SOLDIERS OF THE REVOLUTION

The responsibility for filling the ranks of the Maryland Line devolved upon the counties, which received annual troop quotas from the legislature. Initially the committees of observation oversaw recruitment, but as of 1777, that task logically fell to the county lieutenants, the men who supervised military affairs in their respective localities. Usually working with Continental recruiting parties, the lieutenants helped procure, equip, and train troops and located food and quarters for them until they marched off to camp. Only by examining this process at the local level can one fully comprehend both the popular foundations of the army and the reasons why maintaining Continental troop strength was such an arduous undertaking.

Charles County men readily volunteered for duty in 1776, the first year of extensive recruiting in Maryland. Although the total number who served is unknown, a reasonable estimate would be about 15 to 20 percent of able-bodied freemen—an impressive proportion of the free male population. Those who joined Smallwood's Battalion of regulars usually enlisted in John Hoskins Stone's company, which they helped fill within a few weeks of its establishment. When the Flying Camp of militia was created to reinforce the army in New York, volunteers filled the county's quota, two companies, in less than a month. A lieutenant who began recruiting on July 1, for example, met his quota of twenty men on the sixteenth. One among them ever afterward recalled that "in July 1776 he volunteered and entered the Services of the United States as a soldier of the Revolutionary army." The woman who sewed his soldier's clothes proudly watched "him take leave of his friends & started on his March to the Army."[21]

Besides the eagerness with which Charles County men volunteered in 1776, the *rage militaire* was manifest in the scramble for officers' commissions. In that scramble gentry status and connections weighed heavily. Men like Smallwood and Ware, possessed of both military credentials and political connections, readily obtained their high Continental commissions. For those aspirants with no wartime experience and only recent military training, it helped to hold a militia command, and it was essential to have patrons with access to the Provincial Convention, which granted appointments. Hence, when John Hoskins Stone sought to move up from militia captain to regular army officer, he suggested that convention members from Charles and St. Mary's counties could speak "for his character & ability." He won a coveted captaincy. Another young man received command of a company in the Flying Camp after his father had contacted influential acquaintances, including Daniel of St. Thomas Jenifer, president of the Maryland Council of Safety. The letter that Jenifer received read as follows: "My son Tommy being desirous to take an Active Part in the present unhappy Contention . . . permit me therefore to ask your Interest for Him, who I hope will not dishonor your Friendship." Yet another successful candidate for a commission allegedly performed so well "in the cause of liberty" as a militia captain that he enjoyed "the good wishes of his County." Whatever their military prowess or potential, would-be army officers needed access to the convention and the backing of patrons, especially Smallwood and Ware, members of the convention, and the county's Continental congressman, Thomas Stone.[22]

So many men aspired to commissions in 1776 that not all could be accommodated, as the military careers of two scions of the gentry, young William Courts and his cousin Richard Hendley Courts, illustrate. William dreamed of a lieutenancy, and in January 1776 his guardian asked Smallwood "to use your Interest in giting a Commission for Billey Courts in the Service if any Troops Should be Raised here." Fearful that Smallwood had forgotten the request, the guardian soon renewed it. Unable to claim military expertise on behalf of his ward, he emphasized promise and wealth: "Billey is anxious to be in the Service therefore must beg the favour of you to use your Interest for him. . . . [H]is property you know is very Considerable which Should be an inducement for the Convention to prefar him, and [I] am persuaded his Conduct will be Such as will be of Service to the Cause and a Credit to his particular friends." After this effort failed—allegedly because "particular friends were out of the Convention at the time of appointing the officers"— the guardian tried again: Not only was William sober and capable of improvement, but "his Estate is Considerable, which [I] am persuaded will be one weighty Reason with those in power in the Choice of officers." Smallwood must not have promoted Courts energetically because he entered the army as a cadet. He was captured in August 1776 at the Battle of Long Island (the first in which Maryland units fought) and exchanged several months later. Finally promoted to the coveted lieutenancy in April 1777, Courts immediately resigned from the army. He had seen enough of soldiering.[23]

When William's cousin Richard Hendley Courts solicited a commission, he claimed more preparation and experience but was not successful in becoming an officer. In early 1777 he said that he had served as a first lieutenant in the militia "ever since these Calamitous Times commenced" and had gone to "much trouble and great Expence in acquiring the Military Art, which I now want to put in practice." He also emphasized that his estate was "sufficient to Support me," a distinct advantage in an army that often went unpaid for months. Disappointed in his hope of becoming an officer, Courts served as a Continental surgeon's mate for nearly two years, then spent most of the rest of the war on board a privateer. (Years later his widow was still trying to collect his military pay.)[24]

Whatever else enticed men into the army, calculations about their prospects in civilian life during "these convulsed times" influenced decisions to seek commissions or enlist as common soldiers. An unpromising outlook at home might well nudge a man into the military. For example, one applicant wanted "any office in the Service, I shall be ever satisfied with a Sergeant, rather than be out of employ, which has been the case this sometime [past] oweing to the Stopage of Merchandizing." Others probably were in difficult financial straits, since they mortgaged property to creditors shortly before they enlisted. For their part, Samuel McPherson and James Farnandis were awaiting inheritances. In 1775 McPherson's father bequeathed him 175 acres of land but stipulated that he was not to use any of it "till my two Daughters Chloe and Anna Shall Marry or Die . . . they . . . shall have my Dwelling house and all my Land as long as they live Single." When Farnandis's father died the same year, he left his widow, during her lifetime, and his four daughters, while they remained single, joint use of his entire estate. James had to content himself with the gift of a feather bed and the knowledge that someday, if he lived long enough, one hundred acres would descend to him. Facing extended waits for their legacies, these sons of middling planters joined the army as ensigns.[25]

For Daniel Jenifer Adams, military life offered not just an escape from bleak economic prospects at home but also a chance to redeem a tarnished reputation. In the early 1770s creditors successfully sued him for delinquent debts. Then, in 1773, Adams inherited about five hundred acres from his father, but with the proviso that he must satisfy the deceased man's creditors. Ambitious and persuasive, Adams looked beyond his encumbered fields and dreamed of extricating himself by turning a profit in the West Indies trade. He managed to mount a voyage to the Indies, but it ended in financial disaster, and George Washington, who had a stake in the venture, successfully sued to recover his losses. After deeding all his property to Washington in December 1775, Adams hoped that "Sir, after my giving up every thing I have to you, you will let me at liberty." Immediately thereafter he joined the army. Commissioned a third lieutenant in a company of regulars in early 1776, a brigadier major in the Flying Camp the following summer, and a major in the Maryland Line in December, Adams gained the reputation and respect denied him in civilian life. Observed a superior officer after he and his men fought against the British Army in New York: "Major Adams's good conduct spirit and Alacrity on all occasions, both in and out of Action since he has been in this army, leaves me no Room to doubt, but he is the good Soldier."[26]

The combination of motives that induced men to try their hand at soldiering undoubtedly was endless, ranging from the naive enthusiasm of a William Courts to the desperation of a Daniel Jenifer Adams. To all, the army offered wider horizons than they had known, a chance to see with their own eyes what the new nation looked like and how other Americans lived, and, above all, a tangible, critically important way in which they could protect and advance the Revolution. These attractions of military service persisted throughout the war. Yet, for many men the hazards and deprivations of the citizens' army soon enough overshadowed its advantages.

"PILLAGED OF OUR YOUTH"

Recruiting for the Maryland Line began in winter or early spring, when officers returned to the state, often to their home counties, seeking soldiers for the coming campaign. For 1777 their orders read, "With the utmost diligence recruit all the able bodied freemen you can, convicts who are not married to natives of this Country excepted." Yet even with such a broad definition of "freemen," each recruiter, it was expected, would enroll only eight or ten men. These small-scale operations eased civilians' transition to military life. They frequently remained near home for a while to be outfitted, inoculated against smallpox, and at least minimally trained before marching off to camp.[27]

Beginning in 1777, recruiting became a remarkably tedious annual ritual in Charles County and many other localities. In 1779 a recruiting party was stationed in the county from March through July; the following year, from January to August. The annual quota of Continentals (exclusive of militia reinforcements) varied. Surviving but incomplete records indicate that in any single year after 1776, the army called upon the county for no fewer than eighty-three or more than 145 men. Compared with the available pool of manpower, these were substantial numbers.[28]

The militia, approximately fifteen hundred freemen ages sixteen to fifty, constituted that pool of manpower. In reality, however, those in their forties and fifties were less likely, and able, to become soldiers than were men in their late teens through about their mid-thirties. Therefore, the viable reservoir of military manpower was considerably smaller than fifteen hundred, and it was continually diminished by men on active duty, those who returned home sick or wounded, and those who died. By 1781 Francis Ware, although promising to "do every thing in my power to promote the Service," was not optimistic about recruiting for the forthcoming campaign. "It appears to me," he wrote, "that we shall be able to Raise but very few Recruits in this County this year, having heretofore been much pillaged of our youth." A planter underscored that point when he was drafted a short time later, notwithstanding a "weakly . . . Constitution" and "a Humour in his Eye which renders him inca[pa]ble to bear the fatigues of a Campaign." He was forty-nine years old.[29]

From 1777 onward, Ware and Continental recruiters never found enough volunteers to meet the county's troop quotas. With that year used as an example, by mid-March only nineteen fresh recruits had rendezvoused at Port Tobacco. Colonel Hawkins subsequently twice mustered his militia battalion, about 750 men, seeking volunteers, then apologetically reported that "forty six Men were all that cou'd be prevailed on to enroll themselves. . . . [T]he Batta[lion] was not more than half full at either of the meetings." The county thereafter met its troop quotas only when the Assembly authorized hiring substitutes and drafting out of the militia.[30]

Even then, success was never guaranteed. When Ware carefully noted recruiting results for 1778, the pyramid that the Assembly envisioned—with an exceedingly large proportion of volunteers, a smaller tier of substitutes, and few or no draftees—was only a vision. Ware's tabulation was as follows:

Volunteers		1
Recruits (volunteers)		4
Vagrants		0
Hired substitutes		
for 9 months	13	
for 3 years	24	
duration of the war	5	42
Furnished by [militia] classes for 9 months		59
Draftees		
joined the army	12	
discharged or excused	19	
not joined the army	8	39
		145

For draftees who refused to march, courts-martial were held in Port Tobacco. Some were excused from service, the rest fined but not otherwise punished. Out of thirty-nine draftees, only twelve actually entered the army.[31]

Probably no man went to greater lengths to avoid Continental duty than a laborer named Richard Clark. In May 1778 he bound himself as an indentured servant for seven years, promising to be "true and trusty" to his master and to "behave himself in all respects as a good and faithfull servant should or ought to do." In return, the master agreed to find and pay for an able-bodied substitute if Clark was selected "in the draught of men presently to be sent to the Continental Army."[32]

Conventional wisdom holds that whereas the army initially attracted a broad spectrum of freemen, including substantial property holders, its ranks soon were filled with economically marginal men. The county's troop quota raised in 1778 lends credence to this view, although the men's economic ranking cannot be determined with complete certainty. The names of all 145 of them have survived, but the closest fairly complete property lists for the county (land in 1774, total assessed wealth in 1782) are four years removed from the year of recruitment. In addition, because of duplicate names within kin groups, one cannot be sure that a Continental recruit is the same person noted in the property records. When we allow for these limitations, comparison of the data is suggestive, albeit inconclusive. The few volunteers and nearly all hired substitutes were landless men who owned only modest amounts of personal property. The same held true for the fifty-nine recruits furnished by militia classes. If we assume an exact match between them and the 1782 tax records, we find that only one-third were household heads and all but one or two were landless men whose personal wealth was less than £50, usually less than £25. Several were classified as paupers. It is not hard to imagine the members of a militia class, aware that they must either furnish a soldier or be subject to the draft, offering enough incentives to persuade a poor man to agree to army service. But in thirty-nine classes that year, persuasion failed. Again if we assume an exact match between the troop list and property records, we find that the draft picked up a few landowners, mostly men with holdings of about one hundred acres. They quickly were excused from service or bought their way out of the army. By 1778, therefore, Charles County was sending its most available men, those who did not own plantations. Still, they were not necessarily marginal individuals with few ties to the community. Because nearly half the recruits whose names do not appear in the property records had the same surnames as people who were listed there, some likely were younger sons who had not yet established themselves independently.[33]

In subsequent years a larger proportion of volunteers enlisted, but for someone like John Thompson, enlistment was barely voluntary. He and his wife were arrested and jailed in April 1780 for allegedly stealing a silver watch and a substantial amount of money. A month later a local magistrate asked the governor to dismiss the charges because "the proof I believe will not be suff[icien]t to convict them and Thompson wou'd make an Excellent Soldier and is willing to go as such." He left for the army even before the charges were dropped. One wonders whether the couple ever learned that the case against them was weak.[34]

Meeting troop quotas involved other forms of coercion as well. Continental recruiters spent some of their time apprehending and guarding deserters until they were returned to the army. The only Charles County man indicted for trading with the enemy during the war exchanged an almost certain conviction for military service. John Collins also had a choice—between the army and the gallows. In the fall of 1779 he was condemned to death—"Justly condemned," he admitted—for stealing a horse. Languishing in jail and suffering "much by being Naked and the Weather very Cold," Collins pleaded for a pardon because of his youth, his inexperience, and his hope "through the Blessing of God Almighty to become a good Christian and a Useful member of Society." Whether the governor was swayed more by Collins's hopes of reformation or by the suggestion that he "may perhaps be Serviceable either in the Army or Navy," the pardon was granted.[35]

Why was recruiting so difficult? Patriotic enthusiasm certainly waned as tales of combat and the hardships of camp life—filth, disease, exposure to the weather, inadequate supplies, and homesickness—drifted back from the army. But more was involved. Indeed, people needed to look no farther than Charles County to appreciate that life as a Continental would likely be one of deprivation.

Lack of uniforms and blankets impeded recruiting significantly. When Francis Ware was ordered to activate as many as 150 militiamen to march to Pennsylvania in 1777, he told the governor that the contingent "Will be Short of What your Excellency Expects owing in a great Measure to the peoples being very Sickly, and many of them so poore that they are not able as times are, to furnish Clothing Sufficient to Shelter Them from the inclemency of the Weather." During the winter of 1779–80, when General Smallwood wintered at home, he himself solicited blankets from civilians and urged state officials "in the strongest Terms that Supplies of Cloathing might generally be furnished to the Recruiting Office[r]s as nothing wou'd contribute more essentially to promote that Service than cloathing their Recruits upon their Inlistment." The state and the army furnished what they could, but outfitting new recruits remained a persistent problem.[36]

Feeding them sometimes proved equally difficult. Although food was generally available, local planters insisted upon immediate payment for provisions. If public funds ran out, officers had to reach into their own pockets. So when a deserter from Dunmore's loyalists spread smallpox to recruits at Port Tobacco in 1776 (he "was a day and night in company with all the Soldiers here; some combed his hair and others slept with him"), the commanding officer appealed for public funds to buy special rations. "I have expended almost all my own cash," he explained, "and when that is gone we may whistle for provision until we can get a fresh supply [of money]. The People here follow a very good rule, not trust us farther than they can see us." Three years later John Hoskins Stone, at home nursing war wounds but still advancing the Continental cause, bought corn for recruits at Port Tobacco. Then he warned state officials that "Our provision at this place is nearly exhausted and

it will be attended with inconvenience and great disad[van]tage to the recruiting Service unless a Supply can shortly be furnished us. . . . Provisions may be
bought here if money was furnished."[37]

The lesson for prospective soldiers seems obvious. If basic necessities were
scanty when they enlisted, what would happen later? And if planters demanded payment before they would furnish food to *their* recruits, how would
Charles County men fare among strangers? Ware, who as county lieutenant
was more knowledgeable than anyone else about the local recruiting situation,
believed that more men, especially poor men, would have volunteered had
they felt reasonably confident about receiving adequate food and clothing.[38]

Ware also identified another major obstacle to a volunteer army, and that
was the practice of hiring substitutes. Why would any man freely step forward if, by waiting, he would be paid to do so? When the governor's Council
exhorted the county lieutenants in 1778 that "We very much wish a proper
Spirit may diffuse itself throughout the State, so that the Number of Recruits
we want may be made up, by voluntary Inlistments," Ware retorted, "I
doubt We are To Expect but few voluntares—The indulgances Granted The
Militia in Regard to Substitutes having Greatly impeeded if not totally destroy[e]d the Recruiting Service." It was a vicious circle: Without enough
volunteers, substitutes were employed, but the financial incentives offered
substitutes discouraged volunteering.[39]

Finally, some families had trouble surviving when their men went off to
war, and this may well have deterred others from enlisting. Poignant petitions
for public assistance filed in the county court speak of impoverishment result-
ing from the loss of men's labor. The father of five young children, "the rest of
his sons to the number of five being now in the Continental Army," appealed
for aid. So did another father, a tenant farmer who said that he "has been at
the Expence of Raising Twelve Children . . . the most part of them Girls and
them that is with me Small." Without the labor of two sons who had entered
the army at age sixteen, he could not "get me & my family the necessaries of
Life." Nor could some wives left behind. A draftee left his spouse "with two
Small Children and big with the third" and nothing for support except their
own labor. She claimed to be "in a very distressed Situation . . . her Self and
Children must un[a]voidably Suffer Exceedingly unless relieved."[40]

Widows whose husbands "dyed in the Service of the united States" also
poured anxiety into their petitions for help. One had six children under the
age of fourteen "and nothing to Support them upon"; another had five and
"but little To Subsist on." Other widows despaired after they had lost the
labor of sons. A blind woman whose infirmities made her "unable to Labour
for a lively hood" had relied on three sons until they went to war. As of 1778,
two were "if Living[,] now in the Service of Their Country," while the third

had returned from the Flying Camp "rendered So infirm by the hardships of that Campaign" that he could not support himself, much less his mother. And after a seventeen-year-old youth, the "Chief Support" of his mother and eight siblings, was "drawn in" to the army, "the loss of his Labour and assistance . . . so much increased the difficulties of maintaining herself and family that she and they are much distressed." Most families were not so impoverished and managed to carry on without public assistance. Yet the plight of the petitioning families was well known and served as a warning to others.[41]

Striving to overcome these multiple problems, recruiters did their best to "prevail" upon the citizenry, appealing to duty or adventure here, obtaining pardons for criminal offenses there. But even as they exerted themselves on behalf of the army, they also functioned as spokesmen for the county, indicating what seemed possible and what did not. Francis Ware performed most effectively in this capacity. He worked hard to complete annual troop quotas,

SMALLWOOD'S RETREAT. *While commander of the Maryland Line, William Smallwood sometimes wintered in his native Charles County, where he helped raise military supplies. The modest size of Smallwood's Retreat, located near the confluence of Mattawoman Creek and the Potomac River, reflects its owner's bachelor status rather than his wealth and social standing. Photograph by Thomas N. Lee.*

to the point of tracking down "Sculkers that I have Not been able as yet to git hold off [*sic*]." On the other hand, he protected the county by offering excuses for incomplete quotas, complaining when state policies retarded voluntary enlistments, and getting the draft suspended when the county itself was under attack in 1781. Occasionally he even softened the impact of the recruiting laws or ignored them altogether, as when he stopped drafting before a troop quota was filled or settled for shorter terms of enlistment than the state prescribed. To judge from commentary in other Maryland counties, Charles did as well as or better than most in raising Continental troops. Recruiting never amounted to more than an imperfect system for satisfying the army's manpower needs. In that, it demonstrated the limits of what could be required of a people waging war in the name of liberty and independence.[42]

SUPPLYING THE ARMY

Efforts to supply the army encountered similar limits. Americans were subject to ample criticism during and after the war for being unresponsive, even uncaring, while soldiers went ragged, cold, and hungry. Indeed, the condition of Continental troops too often was deplorable, as officers of the Maryland Line regularly reported to state officials. Colonel Stone predicted during the summer of 1777 that men without blankets or tents would desert. "We have also suffered much for shoes," he wrote, and "shall also be very bare of all kinds of Cloathing by the winter." And as the army licked its wounds after the battles of Brandywine and Germantown, and the winter of Valley Forge beckoned, General Smallwood bemoaned the "ragged situation" of his Marylanders, as well as "the approaching season, & the improbability of procuring supplies of Cloathing." The situation only worsened after the line joined the southern campaigns. In 1780 troops in the Carolinas went hungry and half naked.[43]

The loudest allegations of neglect, naturally, came from the army, but those allegations produce a partial picture. Outfitting and feeding the military were new and extremely complicated undertakings, which involved communication and coordination among the army, Congress, state governments, and the localities where supply lines began. A full assessment of provisioning must evaluate what the army wanted and when, how the state governments and localities organized to obtain matériel, and what the capabilities and inclinations of the citizenry were at any given moment. A balanced account must also acknowledge that the American cause would not be advanced by widespread seizure of supplies from civilians—and certainly not by taking food from their mouths and the shirts off their backs. Washington was acutely aware that in a war fought partly to protect property rights, "an Army is not to be supported by measures of this kind." As with recruiting, securing supplies required prevailing upon the people in a variety of ways.[44]

Maryland relied heavily on the civilian population for supplies, although some also were purchased in Philadelphia or the West Indies, confiscated from the British military, or obtained from privateers. As with recruiting, the Provincial Convention and the state Assembly established general guidelines, then delegated actual procurement to the counties. Here, too, public policy underwent a transition from voluntary to required participation. Through a process of trial and error, Maryland eventually developed a local supply system that Washington regarded as a model for other states.[45] Although always an imperfect and often an ad hoc system, it became more effective as the war progressed, and during the Yorktown campaign it produced spectacular results.

Marylanders first raised substantial amounts of supplies—voluntarily— during the *rage militaire* of 1776. With the county committees of observation exercising oversight, people were asked to arm and clothe the thousands of Continental recruits who enlisted that year. The public's contributions nevertheless were insufficient, and that delayed the departure of some troops for New York because "it would answer very little purpose to send [forward] . . . a Number of Men unarmed and unprovided with necessaries."[46]

The following year the Assembly took the first, tentative steps toward required civilian contributions when a critically important item—blankets—was in short supply. Collectors in every county were to visit each householder and ascertain how many blankets he or she owned beyond the family's needs for the winter. Each household was to contribute half its surplus, in exchange for a certificate of value redeemable for cash at the state treasury. Collectors had no authority to confiscate blankets, however. The only coercive power the legislature authorized was litigation in the county courts, a lengthy and uncertain process that would not warm soldiers' bodies.[47]

In other ways, too, the blanket law proved instructively defective. It failed to inaugurate a coordinated effort within counties; each collector worked independently. Furthermore, in choosing collectors, the Assembly tended to name commanding officers of the militia. They certainly appreciated military needs but also had other weighty responsibilities. In Charles County several declined to serve. These included Colonel Hawkins, because it would be "extremely inconvenient" for him to go door to door in search of blankets, and Colonel Harrison, because "I am at this Time in the Small Pox." Another man learned of his appointment only upon returning from the army and immediately wrote to the governor: "I have been absent from Home for the last nine Months . . . my own private Concerns require, from this Circum-stance, such immediate Attention as would render the Execution of the Com-mission not only inconvenient but injurious to me." If the state government was to obtain large amounts of war matériel from the civilian population, it had to devise a better system.[48]

In late 1777 the Assembly established the basic principles and administra-tive structure through which procurement thereafter proceeded. The state consistently preferred to acquire surplus goods, rather than those set aside for subsistence, but it was prepared to confiscate property if necessary. In every county, state-appointed provisioning agents organized collecting activities and had authority to buy or seize designated commodities, ranging from horses to hats. These men worked on commission. Initially the state pur-chased supplies with cash, but as military requisitions mounted and public coffers emptied, it sometimes resorted to interest-bearing certificates, which were nothing more than promises to pay (if the war ended favorably). In addition, the taxing power became an important instrument for transferring commodities from planters' fields to Continental quartermasters. To meet the immense supply needs of the southern campaigns of 1780 and 1781, people were required to pay state taxes with surplus wheat and encouraged to pay with meat, bacon, flour, and even horses. Since few households escaped taxa-tion, the responsibility for supporting the army thereby was extended even to the poor.[49]

Through 1779 Maryland's provisioning system functioned intermittently and only when the army requisitioned supplies. Delays were inevitable, and while civilians worked to produce and gather matériel, soldiers suffered. After Washington asserted that "Something of a more permanent and effectual nature must be done," Congress in 1780 began issuing annual quotas for which the states were entirely responsible. Quotas never accurately predicted all needs, but at least they informed state governments of the minimum expected of their citizens, and in Maryland they led to a continuous local supply system that lasted until the end of the war.[50]

With few exceptions (most notably when the army passed through Mary-land on the way south to Yorktown and needed boats and wagons for trans-port), the state adhered to the principle of buying or confiscating only surplus goods. These were defined as anything "over and above what is necessary for the common use and consumption," but the line between subsistence and surplus occasionally shifted. Hence before 1779 people were allowed to keep a full year's supply of food. Then, during some of the darkest days of the war, the Assembly limited each household to a four-month ration of flour. Even so, provisioning agents could not simply confiscate whatever they deemed a surplus. Rather, a communal decision of sorts, which shielded the public from

zealous agents and agents from the public, was required. A typical provisioning law stated that two or three "indifferent and reputable neighbours" had
to agree that contested items "may be spared without distress to the family."[51]

Maryland's performance in mobilizing military supplies was substantial,
sometimes even heroic. Yet from the vantage of Annapolis, the state might
have done better had the army done better. Two problems seemed virtually
insurmountable. First, during much of the war Maryland officials had little or
no forewarning of what the army wanted. Often the first word they received
about critically short supplies was an urgent entreaty, typically accompanied
by dire warnings of the army's possible collapse for lack of public support.
Only when news arrived in late 1779 that "Disolution of the Army for want of
Bread" was imminent did officials also learn that Continental granaries were
empty. In this instance the governor relayed the alarm to the state's inhabitants in a proclamation predicting that the army would "infallibly disband
unless the most speedy and Extraordinary exertions are made by this State."
Second, trying to fill the army's requisitions was often like shooting at a
moving target. One month the item most urgently wanted might be blankets,
the next meat, then flour or horses. By the time the state and localities could
react to one crisis, it might have subsided, but the next would be at hand.
Having coped with this situation year after year, the governor's Council
finally complained in 1780 that "numerous Demands, unexpectedly made, on
this State . . . interferes with the Mode chalked out by the Legislature to
obtain Supplies for the Continental Army and, we are apprehensive, will
procrastinate the Procurement of them." That said, people continued provisioning the army.[52]

"AMONG THE PEOPLE"

Charles County proved most successful in furnishing the simple goods that
clothed and sheltered the army and, above all, the food that sustained it. The
county yielded only modest amounts of clothing and other textiles, no doubt
because it had been a major importer of those items before the war. People
were better able to produce shoes because both cowhide and shoemakers were
at hand. And they supported the war effort with thousands of pounds of beef,
pork, corn, and wheat. From one year to the next, they produced increasing
amounts of supplies until, by the Battle of Yorktown, men and women were
working at a feverish pace and "Charles County Carts" laden with provisions
were a familiar sight along the dusty roads leading away from the county.[53]

Although every household contributed matériel, either voluntarily or otherwise, only a few men—gentry men—organized the local supply effort. Their energy, dedication, and diligence in going "among the people" were indispensable. They and their assistants knocked on doors, spotted surplus goods, elicited cooperation, and sometimes resorted to confiscation. They also monitored what the county was capable of producing, under what conditions, and balked when state actions seemed unreasonable.[54]

One local provisioner, Daniel Jenifer of Port Tobacco, accomplished more than any other. While his better-known brother, Daniel of St. Thomas Jenifer, sought wider horizons in state and national politics, Daniel Jenifer's world was Charles County. A merchant and large landowner, he had successfully moved from proprietary magistrate and sheriff to revolutionary committeeman. In 1777 he was appointed a judge of both the county court and the orphans' court. Between 1777 and 1781, usually with little or no advance notice, the state regularly appointed him a provisioner. His activities—and his uninhibited comments—offer a window onto the procurement of military supplies, including the satisfactions and frustrations associated with so new, ambitious, and complicated an undertaking.[55]

Jenifer was a dedicated provisioner who more than once sacrificed personal interests for the public good. In 1778, intending to visit the army, not supply it, he heard of critical shortages of meat and agreed "to postpone this jaunt"

DANIEL JENIFER (D. 1795). *A merchant and justice of the local court, Jenifer became the county's most energetic and resourceful collector of food and other supplies for the Continental Army. He is not to be confused with his better-known brother Daniel of St. Thomas Jenifer. The portrait is privately owned. Photograph by John C. Kopp. Courtesy of the Southern Maryland Studies Center, Charles County Community College.*

and "do the best I can for the [Continental] service." On another occasion, when horses were needed, he searched until scarcely able to "hold my head up having rode with a fever every day this week." He also took pride in what was accomplished, as when he boasted that "provisions can be as well cur'd in the State of Maryland as in . . . any part of the world," spoke of the "Neat Cattle" raised for the army, and bragged that shoes made at Port Tobacco would be "well executed" by laborers competing to "excell in doing their work well."[56]

On his first major assignment—buying blankets, cloth, clothing, and shoes during the winter of 1777–78—Jenifer displayed a combination of ingenuity, sensitivity to the community, attention to detail, and diligence which consistently characterized his provisioning work. He and several assistants did not fan out across the countryside, going from one dwelling to the next, because the majority of inhabitants had little or nothing to spare (at least if Francis Ware was correct that many were "not able as times are, to furnish Clothing Sufficient to Shelter Them from the inclemency of the Weather)." Instead the provisioners exerted themselves where they might best succeed, among substantial property owners. Jenifer went straight to the gentry and initially concentrated on the army's most needed item: blankets. On his first day of collecting, he called upon three merchants. Yield: a dozen blankets. Next he visited two of the wealthiest women in the county, including General Smallwood's sister Priscilla. Eight more blankets. On his way home he stopped at the general's plantation for two more. Jenifer knew what he was doing; it was the best day of blanket collecting he would have. Day after day thereafter he approached only those who belonged to the upper strata of the social order.[57]

In a pattern that often typified the local supply operation, most people sold a few items at a time, a pair of shoes and stockings here, a blanket or two there. One man distinguished himself by turning in 53 pairs of shoes, as did a woman who produced 14 pairs of stockings. The collectors did not uncover large surpluses even among substantial property owners, no doubt owing to several years of nonimportation and earlier efforts to outfit Continental recruits. In their first two months of collecting, Jenifer and his assistants gathered up 183 pairs of shoes, 138 pairs of stockings, 70 blankets, and 9 yards of cloth.[58]

The first requests for large amounts of food arrived, unexpectedly, in early 1778, when the main body of the army was in Pennsylvania and Delaware. From Valley Forge came a plea for the "virtuous yeomanry" of the states from New Jersey to Virginia to produce as much cattle and meat as possible for the coming campaign. When Jenifer was asked to buy fattened cattle and salted beef, pork, and bacon, he was not hopeful. "The prospect for the purchasing of provisions in this county is dreary," he announced in April. "Neither pork, or Salted beef is to be had at all, and I fear not more than 15 or 16 M wt.

[thousand pounds] of Bacon, if so much." Perhaps eight or ten head of cattle could be obtained. Promising nonetheless to do his best, he hired assistants to canvass every parish while he went "Round to every Man and Woman of consequence in the county and endeaver[ed] to prevail on them to furnish liberally." The results exceeded expectations, probably because the provisioners had Continental dollars in their pockets. In less than five weeks people sold nearly eighteen thousand pounds of bacon and promised another twenty-five hundred, which amounted to more than a pound for every man, woman, and child, free or slave, in the county. Planters also promised to fatten three hundred head of cattle and have them ready by autumn.[59]

At least as arduous as acquiring supplies was the task of caring for them while they remained in the county. Jenifer fussed over airing stockings "to prevent the Moth" and once advised state officials that "if the Woolens in the public Store are not Aired this Month and tobacco stored amongst them they will not be worth a Button." Livestock had to be fed and pastured, and he found this responsibility particularly burdensome. After filling the county's quota of thirty-seven horses in 1781, Jenifer had no place to put them except his son's "very valuable pasture." In less than two weeks the horses stripped the meadow bare, and "there not being a pasture worth a button to be had in the neighborhood," he had to arrange for grass to be cut and carried to them daily. Although he assigned people to watch the animals even at night, several times the tenders dozed off and the horses invaded a nearby meadow and cornfield. Jenifer also worried that the herd might be lost to enemy raiders. When the army wanted cattle on the hoof, he asked sellers to deliver them to a central location on an appointed day so that they could be driven out of the county immediately.[60]

Handling food presented further challenges. Beef and pork had to be salted down, barreled, and stored. And as the episode of trading with British warships in 1777 underscored, salt was extremely scarce. When state officials alerted Jenifer to "pressing Demands" for meat during the winter of 1780–81, he quickly lined up promises of twenty thousand pounds of beef and pork, only to see opportunity slip through his fingers when the state failed to send him salt. Preserving bacon was easier because hickory ashes, in his estimation "the best preservative (for bacon) that I know of," were locally available. Since meat collected in the county usually was carried to Port Tobacco, Jenifer's meat house there must have been filled to overflowing at times, his slaves likely contributed a full measure of their labor to the war effort, and townspeople surely were impressed with the army's appetite.[61]

Daunting difficulties arose in trying to integrate the local supply effort with state directives and the Continental Army's wishes. Synchrony rarely prevailed. Once large amounts of foodstuffs were requested, middling and poor planters needed time to respond because they ordinarily produced little surplus wheat and livestock. Gentry families were better positioned in that regard. For everyone, though, seasonal agricultural cycles meshed poorly with the military calendar. Troop numbers were highest, and food requirements greatest, between late spring and autumn. But the Maryland wheat crop did not come in until late June, and newly threshed grain was not available until early August. The situation with livestock was worse because range cattle typically lost up to a third of their weight during the winter months and were scarcely worth slaughtering until late summer. Fattened in the fall, they were normally killed in December and January.[62]

To complicate matters further, when supplies were successfully collected, they sometimes sat in storehouses because transportation was unavailable. With more than eighteen thousand pounds of bacon on his hands in early May 1778, Jenifer warned the governor that it "had better be sent for immediately, as in all probability when the weather turns warm it will spoil." Just then, however, Maryland officials were having "great Difficulties" obtaining boats to pick up provisions and carry them to the northern end of Chesapeake Bay, whence they would travel overland to the army. Not until late May did the first provision vessel load on the Potomac, and not until mid-June did the last of the bacon leave Port Tobacco. Two years later, when provisioners had several thousand bushels of grain and no way to get it to the army, they built their own grain-hauling boat.[63]

In their relations with the state and army, no problem frustrated local people more than being urgently summoned to produce some item, only to learn later that the army no longer wanted what they had worked to provide. In the spring of 1778 planters agreed to fatten three hundred head of cattle. But by the time they were ready several months later, the army was over-stocked with beef, all the meadows near Philadelphia reportedly were filled with livestock, and the Charles County cattle were not needed after all. The planters were disappointed in their expectations of Continental dollars; Jenifer lost his purchasing commission. In 1781, having with great effort acquired and pastured the county's quota of horses, he impatiently awaited orders to deliver them to the army. But when instructions finally arrived, he had to return fifteen to their original owners and continue caring for the rest, in case the army needed them later.[64]

At issue were not only the funds or tax relief that military procurement brought to the county's war-ravaged economy but also the credibility of the provisioners and the pride that they and others felt in tangibly supporting the cause of Independence. The sharpest illustration of this point occurred in August 1779, when officials in Annapolis learned that the Maryland Line sorely needed clothing and shoes. For the latter they turned to Charles

County and Daniel Jenifer, who immediately hired laborers to manufacture twelve hundred pairs of well-made shoes. Because "the men with whom I have contracted are poor, and only work from hand to mouth," he told the governor, he promised to pay half their wages in advance so they could "lay in their winter provisions, which will make them some amends for the inferiority of price at which they have undertaken the work." Once again, however, local people were disappointed. When the laborers met in Port Tobacco to receive leather and cash advances, they learned that the state would use soldiers to make shoes during the coming winter. Jenifer could not contain himself. The men "seem'd not a little Chagrin'd at the disappointment," which "perhaps may be a means of preventing their engaging so readily on a future Occasion." He had "endeavor'd to pacify them, as well as I cou'd and have paid those who wou'd receive pay for their loss of time." And with a trace of pique he announced that, since he had dismissed the men, Francis Ware, William Smallwood, and other army officers had applied to him for nine hundred additional pairs of shoes.[65]

While such problems originated outside the county, others were home-grown and reflected inevitable wartime tensions between public and private needs. Civilians faced a war of unknown duration amid severe economic disruption. "Every means of raising money is taken from the people by this unhappy Dispute" with England was the lament of 1775. Five years later the refrain ran, "As to money, there is very little in circulation with us at present." Few "are able to do more than pay their Taxes." Understandably some were reluctant to part with possessions or turned to profiteering.[66]

The extent of profiteering is impossible to measure, but it seems to have happened sporadically and mostly during the last years of the war, when Congress and the states were trying to keep the war effort going with massive emissions of paper money. Because the currency depreciated drastically, householders were tempted to charge as much as they could get for their commodities, even if they sold to speculators rather than provisioning agents. When planters asked £60 more per hundredweight for pork than Jenifer was offering, he opined that "They are in these scarce times very fickle and must be coaxed as well as paid." Where coaxing failed, he and other agents occasionally confiscated goods. When Thomas Howe Ridgate, the overly ambitious merchant who had gone bankrupt shortly before the war, demanded "extravagantly high" prices, payable in cash, for a "trifling" amount of goods, Jenifer confiscated the only items worth the trouble, 190 common felt hats. He suspected correctly that "Mr. Ridgate had more Goods but what has become of them he best knows."[67]

Profiteering bothered provisioners, for it threatened their ability to meet supply quotas. "I am greatly disappointed" with prospects for cattle collection, Jenifer wrote in September 1780. Worried lest planters renege on their agreements with him and sell to speculators instead, he lamented that "many pretences are made for the dissappointments" and "very little dependance is to be put in the promises of the people now a days." When Baltimore speculators, whose operations reached scandalous proportions, hired a local planter to buy up beef at inflated prices just as Jenifer was expecting people to bring him cattle for sale or as tax payments, he exploded: "[T]he Baltimorians are at their old tricks again: endeavoring to starve the Army." Even then, provisioners employed confiscation sparingly lest they alienate those whose cooperation they sought.[68]

Profiteering was an extreme result of an attitude that persisted throughout the war. That is, no matter how worthy the cause or pressing the need, local people did not regard military supplies as charitable donations. Much of the success of the procurement system depended upon the availability of money, even badly depreciated money. *Something* could be bought with it. When troops were first raised, the Council of Safety asked the committee of observation "to procure from the House-Keepers . . . all the Blankets or Rugs that they can with any Convenience spare," on a promise of future payment, and also to provide housing, firewood, and provisions for Continental recruits then at Port Tobacco. Speaking on behalf of the populace, the committee refused: "Your Requisition for purchasing Blankets and Ruggs in this county cannot be readily complied with without ready money, as also the subsistance of the soldiery in this county." Jenifer, too, pressed state officials for cash. It was, he assured them, "a powerful Argument, and the sooner it arrives the better"; "fill my hands" with money "so as to enable me to fulfill my contracts." Provisioners might be "Remarkably industrious and diligent," but without cash in hand they found householders resistant to their requests.[69]

Jenifer therefore balked when the state expected him to obtain supplies entirely with interest-bearing certificates, or promises to pay: "It will, I believe be in my power to prevail on the people to take half Certificates but their necessities are such, that they must have some money." Among the troubles that plagued his horse-collecting efforts in 1781 was the lack of cash. Although planters promised enough animals to fill the county quota, they did not deliver, owing "to the Minds of the people being poisoned with regard to the validity of the [promissory] Certificates to be given for them." Walter Hanson, Jr., the unsuccessful gunpowder manufacturer, was particularly "abusive and busy in crying down the Cred[i]t of the pay." When Jenifer went looking for the horses, one man sent his out of the county, another hid his, and Hanson rode off on the mount he had promised the army. Others cooperated, including a "good whig" who gave up the only horse his wife could ride. But in the end Jenifer saw no alternative to confiscation, then described his distasteful experience: ". . . after much fatigue or exertion, trouble, and bearing much illiberal abuse; I have compleated the quota of Horses for this County (35 are already branded) tho' not all so good as I cou'd wish, some being impressed against my inclination. My intention was to have furnished the best in the County, but was defeated in my purpose. The No[.] wou'd have been compleated in a few days had it not have been for the Refractoriness of a few and the wickedness of others; in endeavouring by insinuations to down the Credit of the certificates." Those who withheld horses, he thought, "ought to be made immediate examples of," especially Hanson, "who deserves the Greater chastisem[en]t because he is, or ought to [be,] a Gent[leman]." Furthermore, anyone who undermined public confidence in the state's certificates "ought in my opinion to be made Smart." Whether out of anger at the treatment he had received or out of determination to serve the cause, Jenifer also wanted to replace the inferior animals he had gathered up in haste with "several very good ones . . . belonging to young fellows, who ought either to spare their Horses, or render personal Service" by joining the army.[70]

Despite such disillusioning episodes, Jenifer was an effective provisioner. Within two months of being appointed to collect foodstuffs in 1780, he had, according to Colonel Ware, "engaged all [the wheat] that was for sale in the county for the use of the army." His prices for cattle induced some planters in St. Mary's County to sell to him rather than their own provisioning agent, although Jenifer bought corn below rates offered nearby. No matter what he collected, he did indeed prevail upon the people to support the army. In September 1781, his thoughts turning to the drama shaping up at Yorktown, Jenifer relinquished his responsibilities. "I have a great inclination to go to the Southward," he wrote, "to have the pleasure of seeing a finishing Stroke put to the War."[71]

Yorktown

While Jenifer's labors in the cause of Independence were abating that September, others were working at a frenzied pace receiving and shipping wheat and beef, the dietary staples most wanted by the army. Several months earlier, Marylanders had been urged to redouble their efforts. Then, at the end of August, seven thousand American and French troops moved through the state, bound for Virginia. A week later news arrived that a French fleet, thirty-two ships strong, had entered the bay and landed another three thousand men near Yorktown. Maryland had to marshal immense amounts of additional grain and large herds of cattle to meet escalating military requirements.[72]

Directing the collection of food in Charles County during this period was Hezekiah Reeder, "a young Gent[lema]n of family and fortune" who had served as a second lieutenant in the Maryland Line. He encountered many of the same problems that had plagued his predecessors but also enjoyed advantages they did not. People sensed that the war was building to a climax, the siege of Yorktown occurred in early autumn, when food was most plentiful, and the French had hard currency to pay for it.[73]

All summer long, Reeder collected cattle. In June he quickly bought or seized a hundred head from plantations most exposed to naval raiding, but then the pace slowed for lack of cash. While fresh Continental recruits crowded into Annapolis and had to be fed, he managed to purchase only twenty-two head of cattle out of another hundred requested by the state. And these he delayed delivering to Annapolis because not only would the summer's heat cause the animals' weight to "fall away much by driving," but he had no money to hire drivers. Snapped Colonel Stone: "Forward the Cattle immediately—as they are now wanted." Then he confided to Reeder, "I have only two beeves at my plantation in Nanj[emo]y the only Beef I shall have for my family next winter, if you can procure your number without them it will be doing an essenial favor." Reeder sent what he had and immediately asked for more money. "The Collection . . . will come very high," he predicted, because the livestock would be gathered from throughout the county. As soon as the state obliged, he took up another twenty-nine head in one day. Thirty-nine men and women—everyone from General Smallwood to the old loyalist Richard Lee—finally sold over forty thousand pounds of beef on the hoof. Most sellers were in the upper strata of wealthholders but were no more willing than anyone else to relinquish property without immediate payment, even if they received only paper money.[74]

Then the French arrived, and suddenly money poured into the county. Reeder received orders to buy or confiscate another two hundred head of cattle plus all the bacon, wheat, and barreled meat he could acquire "without distressing the Owners." Although authorized to use the militia to ensure success, that was unnecessary. Cash was sufficient. No sooner did Reeder receive £500 than Stone advised him, "[W]hen you want more money, you will apply for it." Whether Reeder bought all the livestock the state requisitioned is unknown, but the accounts of three foremen whom he employed are illuminating. Between the beginning of September and the middle of November they, five of their boys, and another twenty-two men labored a total of 217 days to collect and brand cattle, search for strays, and drive herds north from the county toward Georgetown and army commissaries.[75]

Traveling the same route were wagons and carts laden with wheat and with flour and pork packed in newly made barrels. During the summer wheat had come slowly into the public stores; Reeder received twenty-five shipments from May to the end of August. Then, while Washington's army moved to entrap Cornwallis, people brought in more and more grain. Reeder took in over a hundred lots in September and October. One of the horses that Daniel Jenifer had purchased was thin of flank from treading the grain to separate out the chaff. Contributors spanned the spectrum of wealthholders, from landless Daniel McPherson, whose estate amounted to £10 10s., which nearly classified him as a pauper, to Robert Fergusson, whose assessed worth was £4,230. Fergusson's neighbors brought their grain to him, and he delivered it to Reeder along with his own. Some householders contributed more than once. The widow Clare Slye sent seven bushels on September 21 and another 150 the following week. General Smallwood's overseer came three times with wheat. The Jesuits of St. Thomas Manor came five times and turned in 338 bushels over a twenty-three-day period. Together, Charles County people were supplying the army at a rate of about a thousand bushels of wheat per month.[76]

On September 28, the day the French Army marched down to Yorktown, Richard Robey took four bushels of wheat to Reeder. On October 16—when people living in the county *heard* the tremendous cannonade a hundred miles to the south—Ignatius Luckett deposited five more. The next day, when the guns fell silent and the British asked for terms, William Lee had thirty-one bushels to spare. These scenes in Charles County were part of a tapestry woven throughout Maryland during those early autumn days, and when Washington saw it whole, he was moved to rare praise: "The supplies granted by the State are so liberal, that they remove any apprehensions of want."[77]

WHETHER WITH ENTHUSIASM, RESIGNATION, OR RELUCTANCE . . .

In evaluating the county's material support of the army, we must distinguish circumstances that were beyond civilians' control from those susceptible to their willingness or reluctance to cooperate. County people could not control the timing of Continental and state requests, the army's shifting supply needs, the fact that the climactic months of the war fortuitously coincided with the harvest season, or the weather. In countless other situations, people proved cooperative, whether in a small way, like building a grain-hauling boat, or in a major way, as when planters adjusted their agricultural output to match the army's appetite. Wheat had never been a major crop in the county, and it was so scarce in 1779 that state officials rightly anticipated little or none would be forthcoming. The following year, out of more than seventy-eight hundred bushels of grain the county dispatched to the army, approximately one-third was wheat. And during the Yorktown campaign thousands of bushels moved from planters' fields to Continental granaries. So, too, the county that originally produced few head of cattle furnished approximately four hundred for that campaign.[78]

Surely some inhabitants sought to avoid the obligations laid upon them, as instances of withholding horses attest. And some undoubtedly held out for higher prices than the provisioners offered. Yet what is most striking about mobilization of supplies in Charles County is that—whether with reluctance, resignation, or enthusiasm—people *did* mobilize. And they continued to do so even when the state and army reneged on requisitions, as happened with the canceled orders for cattle and shoes. Outright confiscation, such as Jenifer's seizure of hats and horses, was an extraordinary event, something to be commented upon. Nor is there evidence of organized public resistance, which would have prompted confiscation and commentary.

People's willingness to supply the army probably derived from several causes, not least of which was commitment to the Revolution. In addition, they were never required to surrender their last blanket or bushel of grain. Even during the Yorktown campaign, when the army's demands for contributions from Maryland were at their height, state officials affirmed that collections should not be so burdensome as to distress civilians. Supplying the army, moreover, was one way to obtain cash or pay the tax bill during a period of intense economic disruption. With the colonial export trade gone, military provisioning may have been the most important source of income for many families. And paying state taxes with surplus agricultural commodities probably was relatively painless for local households.

Even as people contributed their country goods to the common cause, they nevertheless wanted to be paid promptly for their efforts. Public virtue—if the definition of the term encompasses altruistic, voluntary, and cheerful self-sacrifice—was far less instrumental in generating supplies than was public money. That remained true from the beginning of the war, when an army officer at Port Tobacco said that without money his troops could "whistle for provisions," until the summer of Yorktown, when people handed over their livestock only when the provisioner handed over cash. This attitude was prevalent among substantial property owners as well as among those who had precious little to spare. Balancing their own interests and the army's during long years of war, people bargained for the best deals they could get. Only in an ideal, unreal world would they have behaved differently.[79]

Had the provisioning agents ignored local interests and operated arbitrarily, they would have turned their backs upon the recent, heady days of Independence, when the county's revolutionary leaders paid heed to the "vox populi." Furthermore, drastic methods of procurement might well have invited a revival of politics out of doors and the thwarting of civil authority, which were of very recent memory. Hence the provisioners served with sensitivity to the public mood, even as they criticized that mood. They had to negotiate between the populace and, beyond the county, the state and ultimately the army. And they recognized the public's awareness, born of the Revolution, of how much power it had.

Jenifer presents the extraordinary sight of a county court justice, a man whom people customarily approached with some degree of deference, going door to door asking householders to part with their humble possessions, receiving "illiberal abuse" from war-weary inhabitants, and worrying about moths devouring soldiers' stockings. He was not unique. Even General Smallwood collected blankets when he wintered at home. Their experiences, and those of Francis Ware and other members of the gentry who acted as provisioners and recruiters, cast into stark relief the changing nature of leadership in the county and, indeed, across revolutionary America. For just as surely as political ideology and the practice of politics out of doors pushed colonial elites in the direction of responsiveness and representativeness, so did their war-based activities. The war was an integral part of the transformations under way in America.[80]

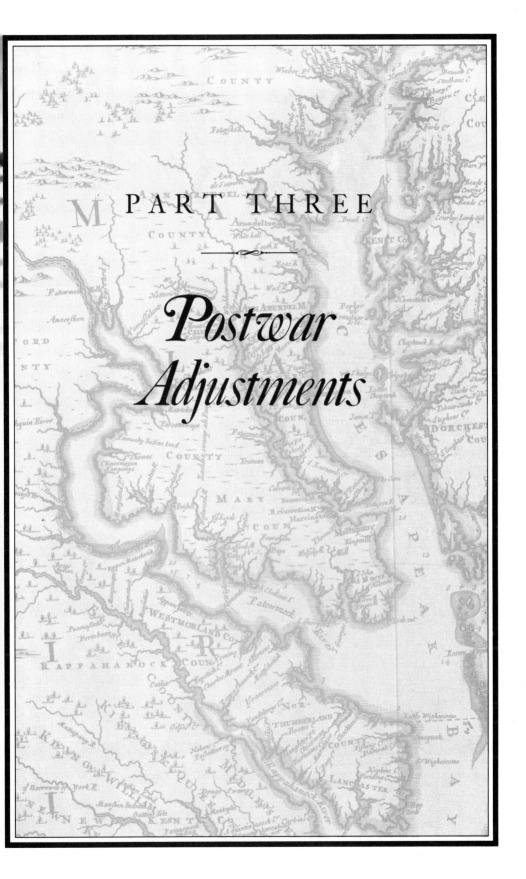

PART THREE

Postwar Adjustments

Prologue:
"All Rejoiced"

For nearly a year and a half after Cornwallis's army surrendered in October 1781, Americans looked for peace. No one knew whether it
was truly in the offing. Certainly not the six Charles County men who in 1782
joined the army for three years or the duration of the war. Certainly not local
men who were several hundred miles from home that year, living from hand
to mouth with the army in the Carolinas. And certainly not people who dwelt
along the shores of the county. Well after Yorktown, British vessels and
"bandity chaps"—pirates—plundered plantations, the tobacco warehouse at
Nanjemoy, and even the town of Benedict, to the "constant alarm, and dread"
of those in the way. "Are we likely to have Peace?" they wondered.[1]

So people waited and hoped. While James Tillard, who lost an arm at
Yorktown, and William Morrison, whose body ached from wounds received
at Camden, did so, they subsisted on half pay authorized by the county
orphans' court. The Reverend Isaac Campbell passed some of the time writing
a ponderous four-volume justification of the revolution his generation had
wrought, which argued that representative government was of divine, Old
Testament origin. Cloe, "about twenty-five years of age, a short, thick, well
made negro, very black, and flat nos'd," ran away when her master switched
her from housework to field work. Walter Hanson Jenifer, a physician, bought
property that the state had confiscated from a Scottish mercantile firm. Trust-

ees of Charlotte Hall School gathered for the first time in eight years and rededicated themselves to building and operating the school. And the "Polite Circle" at Port Tobacco gave itself over to "Mirth and Gaity," gossip about marriages and flirtations, and a ball at the widow Forry's, which disappointed her because only thirty-eight people came (and the female guests because only six were males). Finally, toward the end of March 1783, word of the peace treaty arrived and "all rejoiced."[2]

In the aftermath of the war, some tried, in the manner of the Charlotte Hall trustees and the young people at Port Tobacco, to resume plans and activities set aside during the conflict. Others, like Campbell, the black woman Cloe, and Jenifer, plumbed the promises, the opportunities, of Independence, whether political or economic, personal or communal. Eventually all could see, as Tillard and Morrison could never forget, that the war and its outcome had irrevocably changed their lives.

The full extent of the change was not clear until about 1800. Only then, when the postwar years could be seen as a whole, was it possible to assess what people in Charles County had gained and lost in the birth throes of the nation. Postwar developments never were entirely linear, for possibilities and setbacks, hope and heartbreak, accomplishments and failings often were intertwined. Yet ultimately the expectations and hopes of many in the county gave way to disappointment, sometimes to desperation. Independence brought with it an economic, social, political, and even psychological toll.

CHAPTER SEVEN

A Penchant
for Improvement

"Worthy Members of Human Society"

So far as such things can be measured, the gross contours of Charles County society seemed, at war's end, much as they had been at its beginning. The population had grown in the interim, from 15,875 to 17,724 persons, of whom 55 percent were whites. Most people continued to live on small or middling plantations. Port Tobacco, largest of the towns, counted only 99 residents in 1782. The ratio of slaves to whites remained highest in the southeastern sector of the county and generally decreased as one traveled north and west across it. Slightly less than half of all taxpayers owned slave labor, not much different from the late colonial period. So, too, free blacks were few. Of 484 blacks living in the Benedict area, for example, only "William a free negro" was not enslaved.[1]

The postwar county also retained its stratified, hierarchical social order. From pulpit to gallery, the seating of churchgoers presented a visual representation of rank, as did a gentry family's carriage passing a poor planter walking along the road. Data on wealth distribution confirm the visual impressions. Property—half of which lay in land, another third in slaves, as of 1782—was concentrated in the hands of a minority. The top tenth of taxpayers (with estates assessed at £878 or more) held 58 percent of the wealth. The top quartile owned 82 percent; the bottom quartile, less than 1 percent. From another perspective, per capita assessed wealth in white households was £464 in the top decile, £3 in the bottom quartile. Not surprisingly, the most prominent men, who bore surnames like Smallwood, Ware, Jenifer, Stone, Hanson, Hawkins, and Dent, also numbered among the wealthiest. Charles County was still a gentry-led society.[2]

Despite apparent continuities with the colonial past, however, the county was a transformed place. The Revolution, while not overturning social hierarchy, nonetheless changed it. If, from foundation to capstone, inhabitants still ranked from hoe-wielding slaves to officeholding gentlemen, the overall edifice was different. Among whites the gradations of freedom characteristic of the colonial order were narrowing. Independence erased legal distinctions between Protestants and Catholics, and it stopped the influx of unfree labor—that is, convicts and indentured servants. Expansion of the franchise and the development of political parties continued the process, dating from the 1760s, of drawing ever more men into the political arena. Although most women's lives revolved, as they had since time immemorial, around their roles as wives and mothers, the county's contingent of economically independent femes sole was growing. The domestic roles of all white women were accorded greater social importance. Therefore, on the complex continuum from slavery to freedom, white society, especially its men, was compressing nearer the freedom pole. That widened the divide between the white and black populations, for almost all African-Americans remained enslaved. Even so, potentially significant changes were under way for them as well. No longer did newly arrived, unassimilated Africans enter local slave quarters; the Atlantic slave trade to Maryland ended, effectively, during the war and, legally, in 1783. More important, the county was home to a small but growing population of free blacks. Only time would tell what free status would mean for them in a society so deeply divided along racial lines.[3]

In addition to an evolving social order, the postwar county also experienced a nearly palpable passion for improvement. Wherever one looked, residents busied themselves—and not only because they finally could attend to matters long neglected or postponed. More than that, they had shared in the creation of a new nation. Its potential many of them could envision; its future, and their own, they meant to help shape. Peace released people's energies to rebuild their economy, to perpetuate connections formed in the Revolution, to launch or further political careers, to better themselves and their surroundings. Even when they took up strands laid aside during the war, such as education or economic development, the scope of their efforts often was broader, more ambitious than it had been in the colonial period. As if revolution and war had taught them, as nothing else had, the value of organized

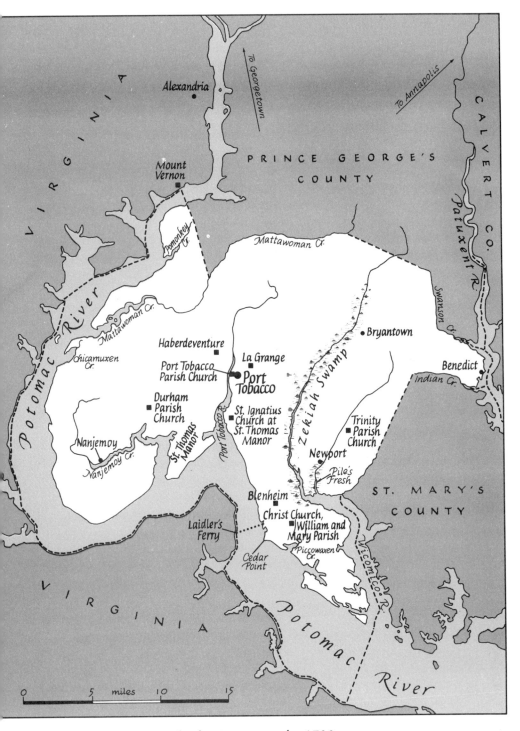

To Georgetown

To Annapolis

V I R G I N I A

Alexandria

Mount Vernon

PRINCE GEORGE'S COUNTY

CALVERT CO.

Patuxent R.

Potomac River

Mattawoman Cr.

Mattawoman Cr.

Piscataway Cr.

Swanson Cr.

Bryantown

Chicamuxen Cr.

Haberdeventure

La Grange

Port Tobacco Parish Church

Port Tobacco

Zekiah Swamp

Benedict

Indian Cr.

Durham Parish Church

St. Ignatius Church at St. Thomas Manor

Trinity Parish Church

Nanjemoy

St. Thomas Manor

Port Tobacco R.

Newport

Pile's Fresh

ST. MARY'S COUNTY

Nanjemoy Cr.

Blenheim

Christ Church, William and Mary Parish

Laidler's Ferry

Piccowaxen Cr.

Wicomico R.

Cedar Point

V I R G I N I A

Potomac River

0   5   miles   10   15

Charles County in the 1790s

undertakings, they turned to voluntary, collective actions and associations to accomplish their purposes. In this respect the county resembled many other communities in postwar America.[4]

Church membership and financial support became entirely voluntary, thanks to the 1776 Maryland Declaration of Rights, which disestablished the Church of England and placed all Christian denominations on an equal legal basis, and the 1785 decision of the Maryland General Assembly, with the county's delegates in unanimous agreement, to refuse to allocate state tax money to support religion. In the county, magistrates occasionally levied substantial fines on individuals who misbehaved on the Sabbath, but otherwise church and state were separate. Episcopal vestries did not choose public tobacco inspectors, as their Anglican predecessors had done, but they did choose their own ministers, as Anglican vestries had not. Thereupon the vestry of Trinity Church asserted that "no clergyman [will] be allowed to preach in either the church or chapel without the consent of a majority of the vestry." Worshipers continued to follow Church of England doctrine and liturgy, but only "as far as shall be consistent with the American revolution." Stripped of access to public tax monies, Episcopalians turned to private subscriptions to pay their ministers "a genteel salary," support congregation activities, and maintain church property. Some subscribers were more generous than others. One young man paid more in tavern fees for two days than he contributed for the "spiritual services" of the rector at Port Tobacco for a year.[5]

Disestablishment initially created difficulties for the Episcopal churches. In Durham Parish the vestry actually stopped functioning for three years, until communicants grew anxious about "all Parochial affairs, particularly the approaching ruin and destruction of the church." Aroused to action in 1791, they resurrected the vestry and began raising funds to "restore the spirit of their religion and the flourishing state Durham Parish was in previous to the late glorious revolution." Within months construction of an "elegant" church began on "the almost total Ruins of the old one." Within a year a visiting cleric reported that "the Spirit of Religion seems to be reviving" and that dissidents were in decline in Durham.[6]

Trinity Church underwent a difficult transition from mandatory public to voluntary private support. In 1779, when Protestants living within the borders of the parish were asked to pledge funds for the minister's salary, two-thirds responded favorably. The rest, especially those who lived more than a few miles from the church or were poor, were uninterested. One communicant promised five hundred pounds of tobacco yearly, but only if the Reverend Mr. Campbell, who had served the congregation for thirty years, continued to officiate. Based on this and other pledges received, Campbell's salary was set at approximately one-third the amount he had legally claimed as the Anglican rector. The vestry clearly regarded pledges as contracts and several times demanded arrearages and authorized "warrants for all those subscribers of Trinity Parish who have not paid their subscriptions." Retorted one man in 1783, he no longer belonged to the Episcopal Church "and therefore looked upon it as a hardship to be obliged any longer to pay for the support of a Clergyman of that Denomination."[7]

Campbell's death in 1784 precipitated a crisis. "Being destitute of the means of employing another minister or teacher," the vestry initiated a new subscription campaign and asked people to pay by poll, as in the colonial period, and to consider the value of their land when giving to the church. The response from the northern reaches of the parish was swift and unequivocal: "[T]he inhabitants of Benedict Hundred were not inclined to subscribe to the support of a clergyman" at Trinity Church. Thereupon the vestry engaged a

DURHAM PARISH CHURCH. *Originally a one-story structure and probably the oldest public building in Charles County, the church by 1790 approached "ruin and destruction." Thereupon the congregation raised funds to rebuild and expand the building and to return Durham Parish to its prerevolutionary "flourishing state." The brickwork, entrance, and window openings of the original structure remain identifiable. Photograph by Thomas N. Lee.*

schoolmaster and army veteran named Hatch Dent to read prayers every Sunday "and if he thinks proper a sermon." For this he received part of whatever money the vestry could collect. When Dent was ordained an Episcopal priest two years later, the vestry promptly hired him and agreed to pay him everything raised to support the minister—"after deducting the parochial charges." Heartened at again having a rector, the congregation began refurbishing the church and grounds.[8]

NOW
CATHOLIC
FREEDOMS

Unlike the Episcopalians, Roman Catholics required no transition to voluntarism. They responded energetically to the religious liberties gained during the Revolution. No longer restricted to hearing mass in private chapels, they built a large brick church adjacent to the priests' residence at St. Thomas Manor and named it for St. Ignatius, founder of the Jesuit order. It is still in service today. Religious liberty also beckoned native sons and daughters home from European monasteries and convents. Several priests returned and took up residence at the manor, while three nuns who belonged to the Matthews family returned home from a Carmelite convent in Belgium. Shortly after arriving in the county in 1790, on a hilltop three miles north of Port Tobacco, they founded the cloistered Monastery of Mount Carmel. It was the first religious community for women established in the United States.[9]

Neither the Catholic nor Episcopal churches were much threatened by evangelical Protestantism, and that distinguished the county from parts of Virginia and Maryland. Itinerant Methodist preachers periodically rode through, but the first Methodist church was not built until the 1830s. The Baptists were only slightly more successful. In about 1790 Virginia Baptists began proselytizing in Durham Parish—they may have sparked the renewed Episcopal activity there—but membership of the Nanjemoy Baptist Church, organized in 1793, remained below sixty, sometimes below thirty, until after the War of 1812. No other Protestant denominations established a church in the county until well into the nineteenth century. Although separation of church and state had dramatic effects, it did not significantly alter the denominational profile inherited from the colonial period.[10]

Like church activities, schooling reflected what might be called an "improving mentality" after the war. Besides delivering "very good Sermons," the Reverend "Mr. Hig—" at Port Tobacco introduced boys to "Latin grand Latin," while Hatch Dent and a son of the Reverend Campbell opened a school in Trinity Parish. At the same time, the Charlotte Hall trustees, including several Charles County men, planned the most ambitious educational project yet on the lower Western Shore. In 1785 they selected a design for the school building, advertised for workmen, and promised to furnish them 250,000 bricks and 2,500 bushels of lime for mortar. When finished, the school would house sixty boys, their instructors, and servants. No college-

ST. IGNATIUS CHURCH, AT ST. THOMAS MANOR (1798). *No longer restricted to hearing mass in private chapels, Roman Catholics began worshiping in the newly constructed church at St. Thomas Manor in the late 1790s. Photograph by Thomas N. Lee.*

THE MONASTERY OF MOUNT CARMEL (1790), *the first community of Roman Catholic women founded in the United States. After living here for four decades, the Carmelite order moved to Baltimore in 1831. This picture of the abandoned site was taken in the early twentieth century. Today cloistered nuns again reside at the restored monastery. Woodstock College Photographic Archive, Special Collections Division, Georgetown University Library, Washington, D.C.*

level institution was established in or near the county, so local people helped found St. John's College at Annapolis, and priests from St. Thomas Manor figured prominently in founding Georgetown University.[11]

Only once during the colonial period, so far as is known, did a benefactor establish a school for "those Children whose parents are incapable of bestowing an Education on them." Immediately after the war, a dying man left money to educate children in his neighborhood who were "objects of Charity." Another bequeathed all profits from the labor of four slave women and men, and their descendants "for Ever," to establish and maintain one or more charity schools in Durham Parish. Thus were some poor children—presumably only white children—to receive a chance to overcome their humble beginnings.[12]

A spirit of self- and social improvement also surfaced as Charles County people sorted out what it meant to be citizens living under a republican form of government. So potent was the ideology of the Revolution, and still so formative, that like Americans everywhere, local residents simply could not resist having their say about it. More than anything else, they lectured one another about behaving as the virtuous citizens upon whom the very survival of American representative government was supposed to depend.[13]

Their ideal of citizenship combined morality, piety, temperance, industry,

THE REVEREND FRANCIS NEALE (1756–1837). *A member of one of the county's most prominent Roman Catholic families, Francis Neale was educated in Europe and entered the Society of Jesus. He returned to America after the Revolution, served as president of Georgetown University from 1810 to 1812, and died at St. Thomas Manor in 1837. Courtesy of the Georgetown University Art Collection, Washington, D.C.*

and dedication to human progress. Women were lauded for "female virtue," including "unaffected piety" and "irreproachable deportment." Students at Hatch Dent's school worked on "moral improvement" in addition to academic subjects. Having signed the Declaration of Independence, Thomas Stone contemplated and discussed citizenly virtues for the rest of his life. When his youngest brother embarked upon a mercantile career in the 1780s, Stone admonished him as follows: "[B]e attentive to your Morals Conduct and Behavior in every Respect"; "do Nothing which would be improper for a Gentleman and a Man of the most enlarged Principles of Integrity. . . . I hope You will . . . by your prudence Industry and Honor establish such a Character as will recommend You to the Confidence and Esteem of all good Men"; and, finally, when the inexperienced younger man wanted to investigate mercantile opportunities in Baltimore, "You want steadiness thought & attention more than Knowledge and I am sure Baltimore is not the place to acquire these habits." Articulating some of the idealism of American republicanism, Stone wrote that "all men can distinguish clearly between Right and Wrong when not under the immediate influence of some seducing Passion." Reason and an innate moral sense destroyed "cobweb arguments weaved by interest or convenience," opined another brother.[14]

While "Attention and industry" were to be applauded and rewarded, indolence and inebriation were to be avoided and condemned. A "Citizen of Nanjemoy," having sobered up from a debauched evening at a friend's house, publicly warned against "that insinuating deity called Bacchus. . . . Young men will please to consider that drunkenness is an inlet to all wickedness, for when a man has no reason to direct him, he is prepared for any enormity." Devoid of reason, the inebriate was incapacitated "for self government." Thomas Stone urged his only son to "shun all giddy, loose and wicked company" and to seek that of "sober, virtuous and good people." Several local men, determined to stave off vice and ignorance wherever they could, became patrons of an orphans' school in Annapolis. There indigent youths might be raised with "the strictest attention to their morals," encouraged "to persevere in those virtuous principles which will make them amiable and worthy members of human society," and "early inured to habits of virtuous industry." Such was "the best and firmest foundation . . . for the prosperity and glory of the state."[15]

Private virtue thus led inexorably to public good. Dr. Walter Hanson Jenifer, eulogized in 1785 as a "steady friend to America, and the principles of our republic," was "distinguished for all those virtues which render men useful to society." Not only was he "a dutiful son, an affectionate husband, and an indulgent master," but he also treated the needy charitably, his neighbors benevolently, and the sick tenderly. As a magistrate he was "attentive, just, and independent" and utterly convinced that "no Man may be allowed to consider himself from his Family Wealth or Connections above the Law, or that he can be screened from Justice." Other republican men "conceived it to be their . . . duty" to vote, while revolutionary rhetoric accorded women the role of raising virtuous, public-spirited sons.[16]

Taken together, these commentaries on citizenly virtues and improvements struck an egalitarian note. The more widespread they were, among whites, the more likely was the daring experiment in self-government to succeed. And, mused Thomas Stone, "our Country . . . will be happy henceforth if properly governed." Yet even as public life became more inclusive both ideologically and in practice, a counterpoint arose in the form of avowedly elitist male secret societies. "The Brethren of Charles county" met at a tavern in Port Tobacco and in 1787 laid plans to establish a lodge in town. The next year members of the elite formed a debating (and dining) society.[17]

Because these groups left scant record of their existence, one can only speculate why they were created so soon after the war. As much as they likely manifested a penchant for improvement, they may also have been a gentlemanly reaction against egalitarian impulses. Another, and certainly not antithetic, possibility is that these societies were attempts to perpetuate the male camaraderie of the war years, when even men too sensible or scared to join the army nevertheless performed militia duty and probably talked to Continental recruiters, and when boys too young for military service almost certainly watched their elders muster and march off to fight. For decades afterward, men and boys no doubt filled many an hour with stories of battle and camp life. A man who was thirteen years old in 1778 claimed, more than fifty years later, that he "well remembers" the day his stepbrother "left home to join the Army, in the Maryland line in the North." Ever after, the veteran reminisced "of his services during the revolutionary War."[18]

No wonder, then, that the most elite and manly of the associations founded in the county—and across America—during the 1780s was the Society of the Cincinnati, a "fraternity" restricted to designated former Continental officers. Having persevered together "through the various stages of a war, unparalleled in many of its circumstances," they were now intent upon "cherishing our mutual friendships to the close of life." Nearly every Charles County veteran eligible to join the organization did so. At the head of the state society, and instrumental in its founding, was General Smallwood, who was as prickly about social rank as anyone in the county.[19]

The Few and the Many

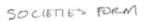
SOCIETIES FORM

Secret societies meeting behind closed doors, widespread discussion of everyone's need to be morally and civilly upright—private exclusiveness and public inclusiveness: These bespoke a major theme of the 1780s and 1790s. That is, from Port Tobacco to Philadelphia, relationships between the elites and the rest of the people often were uncertain, open to change, and tested. In a related development in the county, the status of major segments of the population—lesser planters, women, and some blacks—changed, too, and in ways that offered them hope of exerting, in varying degrees, greater control over their own destinies. They were, after all, living in revolutionary America.

The extent to which the Revolution and war already had tempered gentry dominance startled Alexander Hamilton, the Scottish tobacco factor, in 1784. Having abandoned the lower Western Shore for the Virginia frontier during the war, he returned that year and promptly branded the Charles County justices "Wiseacres of Magistrates" who too easily responded to the populace. Yet it was not a simple case of popular pressure and gentry retreat. Although tempered by political rhetoric and wartime realities, the power of the gentry—mostly the Protestant gentry—remained formidable, even as one among them named his estate Equality.[20]

Custom, habit, and property qualifications for officeholding blended to ensure their leadership. When freeholders elected a sheriff or legislator, parishioners a vestry, and supporters of St. John's College a representative on its governing board, they habitually chose members of the elite. Although the minimum property qualification for a seat in the lower house of the Assembly was £500 (a criterion that one-fifth of local male household heads could meet as of 1782), voters nearly always elected men with estates worth at least twice that amount, men who ranked in the upper tenth of the county's taxpayers. George Dent, a fifth-generation assemblyman and a perennial favorite among voters during the 1780s and 1790s, owned more than eighteen hundred acres of land and more than £1,100 in personal property at the start of his legislative career in 1782. Legislators like Dent, who had wealth and social standing, were best positioned to devote time to public affairs, intervene successfully on behalf of constituents, carry "great weight" in the Assembly, and whisper a suggestion in the governor's ear.[21]

Of the generation that was of age during the war, those who thereafter attained the highest public offices had impressive records in the army or Congress: General Smallwood and Colonel John Hoskins Stone each became governor of Maryland, while Thomas Stone was named a delegate to the

Mount Vernon Conference of 1785, the Annapolis Convention of 1786, and the Constitutional Convention of 1787. At the county level Colonel Francis Ware handily defeated all opponents in the sheriff's election in 1785. Even in parish churches, revolutionary service counted. When Durham congregants chose a ten-member vestry in 1791, six of the successful candidates had military titles of captain, major, or general.[22]

Taken as a whole, the elite dominated elective offices and the county court and virtually controlled access to appointive public offices. The magistrates themselves were responsible for all appointments made within the county, such as clerk of the court, constable, and keeper of the roads. For appointments made at a higher level—whether a tobacco inspectorship or, in the 1790s, a federal revenue collectorship—magistrates, Assembly delegates, and others among the elite routinely offered recommendations and advice to state and national officials.[23]

Surely the gentry advanced their own interests through those contacts. A candidate for a surveyorship in 1786 approached then Governor Smallwood "on the Strength of the Acquaintance that has been between us." Colonel Stone in 1789 personally pressed his application to sell property that the state had seized from loyalists. After officials declined the terms he offered, he told them, "[I]f I cou'd know the extent of this business and what were the determination of the [governor's] Council, . . . we might agree on such terms as wou'd be agreeable to them and myself, if there is no impropriety in it." Stone got the job. In a day when men mingled private and public business without provoking ethical questions, Daniel of St. Thomas Jenifer employed several relatives as clerks after he was appointed intendant of the revenue, the state's chief fiscal officer.[24]

Parallel to the self-interest they attended to, gentlemen officeholders pursued a vision of the public interest, a noblesse oblige that the Revolution actually intensified. Thomas Stone felt so burdened with poor health, family obligations, and work in the Maryland Senate that he debated curtailing a lucrative law practice "or declining all public engagements." The latter, he decided, "I cannot well reconcile it to myself to do and therefore shall narrow my professional Circuit." Zephaniah Turner, a merchant at Port Tobacco, persistently refused all entreaties from "very respectable neighbors" to seek a justiceship—until he became convinced that public convenience required two justices who lived in the town. Even when recommending members of the elite for vacant offices, the magistrates wielded influence with an eye toward public opinion. They tallied how far candidates lived from the courthouse, asked whether a justice was needed in a given neighborhood, and wondered whether prospective candidates were acceptable to the public. Walter Hanson, the senior magistrate, in 1784 nominated two men who he thought "would be agreeable to the people for the County Court," while he suggested another for the orphans' court who "has been . . . Commission[ed] before and well approved of." If the governor made the appointments, Hanson believed that "the Magistracy will . . . give great Satisfaction."[25]

Officeholders or not, the gentry continued the role—so sporadic before Independence and so practiced during the war—of interceding with officials in Annapolis on behalf of ordinary citizens. For example, when twenty-one freemen voted for Assembly delegates in 1783 (thinking that they were "acting in the Line of their duty as Good Citizens"), only to be fined because they had not taken a required oath of allegiance to the state, they immediately petitioned the governor for relief. Bolstering their plea were the signatures of thirty-two men, including four justices, the rector of Port Tobacco Church, Francis Ware, and other assorted gentlemen. Magistrates again interceded after a widow with small children was fined six hundred pounds of tobacco for selling liquor without a license. She thought that "a permit had been obtained from John Dent Esqr. one of the . . . Magistrates . . . to enable her family to sell liquor untill the meeting of Court, but in this found herself mistaken." At the urging of several magistrates the governor remitted her fine. Similarly, a young forger succeeded in getting criminal charges dropped because "several respected inhabitants" of the county attested that he had "always supported the Character of an honest man until now and never was Suspected of clandestine Dealings before, he is of good parents and A Very young man, which Circumstances induce us to hope his Reformation."[26]

Even a slave characterized as "a half witted easy Tempered Wench" worth only £20 might be the object of gentry intercession. Nan, identified as a laborer, was accused of trying to poison her master, a substantial planter named Mereval Moran, and six other members of his family. At "a very Just Trial" in Port Tobacco in March 1781, she was condemned to hang for attempting to murder Mrs. Moran. Convinced of Nan's guilt, her master nonetheless petitioned for a pardon on the grounds that he had "known her for many years and never knew or understood, that she was ever guilty of any such Offence before and believ[ed] . . . her not to have near her Share of common sence and that she never wou'd have thought of doing any One the least harm, had not she been influenced by a Certain Negro Peter, who Claimed her as his Wife, and Who . . . perfess[ed] . . . himself to be a Parson and a Conjuror." Perhaps swayed by Moran's assurance that Nan promised "for the future, [to] have more Regard for her Own Soul, as well as for the lives of Others, ever to be guilty of the like again," the governor pardoned her. Taking no chances, Moran sold her.[27]

But she was still in jeopardy. At August court Nan again was tried and condemned to death, this time for trying to murder another member of the

Moran family. In addition, the grand jury indicted her for the five other alleged poisoning attempts. Nan's new master hastily asked the governor for a second pardon and explained that "but few . . . Recomended [signed] my Petition[,] this was Owing to it's not being Offered. I dare say I cou'd git at least Twenty." The governor did not answer. A month later fifteen local men, none of them prominent, wrote to Annapolis on Nan's behalf. Again no reply. Two months later the elite finally intervened. A magistrate and the county clerk sent a third petition, and sundry planters also signed. This time one of the county's most distinguished citizens vouched for the petitioners. "I believe," Thomas Stone wrote, that the magistrate was "a good Man," the clerk "a Man of Sense and Integrity," and the other signers mostly "plain Country people . . . and I believe of good Characters." Finally the governor issued a pardon. The clerk himself gave a clue to what had happened: Since "there never is a Record made of the Evidence against a Criminal," the governor required information "from proper Authority." The rhetoric of the Revolution was egalitarian; the government of postwar Maryland was still tied to the hierarchical social order.[28]

But just as the many needed the few, the few increasingly needed the many, at least those men who owned a minimum of fifty acres or other property worth £30. They had the votes. And never, before the 1780s and 1790s, were there so many popularly elected public officials—county, state, and national—or so many elections. During the late colonial period freeholders had voted once each year for vestrymen and, whenever the governor called an election, for delegates to the lower house of the Assembly. After the war an expanded electorate voted for Assembly delegates (annually), sheriff (every three years), electors for the state Senate (five years), delegates to the convention that ratified the United States Constitution in Maryland (1788), federal congressmen (two years), and presidential electors (four years).[29]

Before 1789 voters were courted and perhaps intimidated with such time-honored electioneering practices as treating with drinks and having to vote aloud, viva voce, in the presence of the candidates. Into this pastiche of local political customs came, beginning in 1789, national elections and federal voting districts that transcended county lines. Party organization and disciplined voting soon followed. That year, in the first election for the United States Congress, county voters backed a published statewide ticket dedicated to supporting George Washington's presidency—with one exception. In a contest between two local men, George Dent and Michael Jenifer Stone, the former—who by then was speaker of the Maryland House of Delegates but was not on the ticket—triumphed with 79 percent of the vote. The following year, at a meeting presided over by General Smallwood, "deputies" from several counties again placed Stone's name on a statewide congressional slate, which they recommended "to the patronage and warm support of the people." Whether Dent succumbed to a desire for harmony, at a time when the word "party" carried pejorative connotations, or simply deferred to Smallwood, he immediately refused to run against Stone. At the Port Tobacco courthouse the electorate backed every candidate on the slate—and no one else. It was a stunning display of solidarity.[30]

As the national Federalist and Jeffersonian-Republican parties developed during the 1790s and crystallized around issues related to the Napoleonic Wars and the Jay Treaty with Britain (which was highly unpopular because it seemed to concede too much to America's recent enemy), county people fanned the flames of partisanship. Jeffersonianism, the more egalitarian and anti-British political philosophy, was incipient as early as the congressional elections of 1792, when "A Charles County Voter," writing in the *Maryland Gazette*, warned as follows: "We have among us at this day, a good deal of the old leaven of toryism. . . . [T]he tories stand forth, and endeavour to get into all our places of public trust. It is not the smiling countenance, the polite address, the handsome person . . . that can shew the heart. . . . Real whigs are commonly sorry courtiers—Real tories possess the arts of flattery . . . [and] servility. . . . Their principles are aristocratical in the greatest degree." That year Dent first won election to Congress, representing Charles, Calvert, and St. Mary's counties, and soon he led his native county into the Jeffersonian camp. While Washington tried to keep the nation out of the war then raging between Britain and France, Dent urged his constituents to prepare for it because "scarce a shadow of hope remains" of avoiding hostilities with the former mother country. Reminiscent of the 1770s, people gathered at Port Tobacco in 1794 and—addressing Dent as "Fellow-Citizen" in the French republican style—offered "our lives and fortunes" in support of "the freedom, dignity, and independence of America." That fall, with a resounding show of confidence from Charles County—88 percent of the vote—Dent won reelection. He ran unopposed there in 1796, the year in which Jay's Treaty rocked the Federalist cause. A disgruntled, suspicious local Federalist who traveled through the countryside during the campaign saw "people of all sorts, among others Characters passing the Stage who I took to be *Spyes* going to and fro rumouring false Reports tending to overthrow the Government."[31]

Such disdain for the mischief that surrounded the new politics resonated with people who wondered where the egalitarianism inspired by the Revolution was heading. In the late 1780s, when Maryland politics was severely agitated over paper money issues, the county's only signer of the Declaration of Independence could not fully embrace, even in public, the idea that "the great body of the people, left to form their opinions freely and without bias," never erred. In the early 1790s a petition circulated that advocated reversion to an appointed sheriff because, it read, the "zeal"—and probably alcoholic drinks—"diffused by the candidates among the people has diverted their attention from objects more important to the public." The "vices" of direct election, the document asserted, tended "to ruin the morals and the health— to waste the time and property—to disturb the harmony and good will of the community."[32]

There was no turning back, however. A candidate in Calvert County, which was in the same congressional district as Charles, described a scene in 1799 in which ordinary planters enjoyed political leverage their great-grandfathers had never known:

> The candidates . . . sat on a raised bench immediately behind the sheriff, so that each of them could see and be seen by every voter. . . . When a voter came up, every candidate began to solicit his vote, and press his own name upon him. . . . These scenes were occasionally enlivened by sallies of wit between the voter and the candidate, and sometimes the voter gave a pretty hard hit to a candidate whom he happened to dislike. But, however hard the hit, the candidate was obliged to take it in good humor, and treat it as a joke. . . . These . . . were days of no small anxiety to me,—the poll-books being open before us and the voting viva voce, and we were always aware of the exact number of votes that each candidate had received, and the ebbs and flows in his prospects, as his friends or the friends of other candidates came in.

Party competition for voters in Maryland led to universal adult white male suffrage as of 1801 and abandonment of all property qualifications for elective and appointive offices in 1810. The old political ideology, which insisted that only substantial property owners should vote and that only the most substantial should hold office, was dead. The electoral innovations, along with issue-oriented elections (as, for example, when the nation was agitated over President Jefferson's trade embargo in 1808 or war with Britain in 1812) drew as many as three-fourths of eligible voters to the polls in Charles County. And there they used ballots beginning in 1803. The revolutionary generation had created a modern electoral system.[33]

"Formed to Diffuse Serenity and Happiness"

While white men thus progressed toward an egalitarianism that startled Alexis de Tocqueville in the 1830s, their wives, sisters, and mothers inhabited a different world. Charles County women gained no political rights in the aftermath of the Revolution, nor would any of their daughters and few of their granddaughters. The law of coverture continued to deny wives the right to control property and otherwise defined them as nonpersons before the law. Female literacy rates continued to lag behind men's, even as women narrowed the gap. Hatch Dent's school and Charlotte Hall educated only males, although the benefactors who gave money and slaves to send poor children to school did not explicitly restrict their gifts to boys. Young bucks—whose world was wider and who were superior to women before the law—revealed just how superior they felt when they privately, gleefully traded pejorative witticisms about women who "will swallow flattery big enough to choake a dog," and a wealthy matron's "Fringe, lace—back, sides, hoops and *showing all for nothing*," and "the Mortification of the poor Little Girls" who had to dance together when not enough young men came to a ball.[34]

The "sphere in which [women] . . . moved" nonetheless differed in significant respects from its colonial counterpart. However much young bucks chortled among themselves, exemplary female traits were more publicly, precisely, and elaborately defined and commented upon, in order to "induce a more general imitation." Local women who died during the 1780s and 1790s were extolled as "affectionate and loving" wives, "tender and indulgent" mothers, "dutiful" daughters, "kind" mistresses, and "ever attentive and polite" hostesses, whose hearts were "ever awake to the afflictions of others" and "happy when [they] . . . could administer comfort." Where a man's epitaph might mention "his Learning as a Scholar [and] . . . his Wisdom as a Philosopher," a woman's mind—if it was mentioned at all—was "formed to diffuse serenity and happiness" in the household. Where a man might be remembered for "his Patriotism as a Citizen" and "the offices of Trust he has filled," a woman's highest virtues included "her *piety*, her *charity*, her *humility*." Before 1800 seeds of the cult of true womanhood—the nineteenth-century ideology that defined American women as pious, pure, domestic, and submissive—were germinating in Charles County.[35]

So, too, was the ideal that marriages should be happy and companionate, something more than practical arrangements. Although one young man was "industriously seeking for a companion" and "determined to have one against the fall," he found "one very difficult to be met with." The young women he courted may have resented being spoken of as if they were provisions to be stored against the winter. When a female friend of Michael Jenifer Stone's was contemplating marriage, he cautioned her to stop at "the brink and tremble at the Abiss" rather than slide into a "whirlpool of Misery." Stone, a younger brother of Thomas and John Hoskins Stone, did not marry until his mid-forties, by which time he had served as a state legislator and federal congressman and was an incumbent state district judge. The companionship and affection of his wife, Polly, inspired verbal rhapsody. "It is I know unreasonable," he wrote her,

> But I cannot command my Heart—It swells with impatience to see my gentle and true hearted girl—First of Honest Friends! How delightful is matrimony! The indulgence of our fondest wishes is the exercise of our best virtues—and to be happy is to be dignified. . . . The whole neighbourhood of Marlbro [Prince George's County] . . . has made free enough to tell me that I only wanted a good wife to render me quite respectable. There is no doubt but that a respectable and affectionate wife always adds to the importance of a man's character. He also adds to hers—and in this *more* than in any other duty in life they mutually exalt each other.[36]

Her husband's effusive language does not reveal whether Polly exercised greater autonomy and influence in her marriage than the law sanctioned and whether affectionate companionship also entailed mutual decision making. These questions are unanswerable for her and almost every other wife in the county, except for hints contained in documents designed to circumvent coverture and enable a few wives to control property. Two families marked the poles of what must have been a broad spectrum. At one extreme were Tabitha Britt and her husband, Henry, a shipwright by trade. Tabitha's father willed that his executors should hire out a male slave whose wages she was to receive. Incensed at this circumvention of his husbandly rights, and probably at Tabitha's determination to have the money, Henry Britt sued in the orphans' court at Port Tobacco. The judges decided that her father's final wishes took precedence over Henry's legal privileges. Unsatisfied, Henry got his revenge: He first prevailed upon Tabitha to sign over to her "trusty and well beloved Husband" full authority to receive and dispose of her property, then promptly sold the slave and pocketed the money. One wonders what powers of persuasion he used.[37]

At the opposite pole from the Britts were Katherine Hawkins and Richard Brown, her neighbor and betrothed. Here was a woman whose property and gentry status enabled her to guarantee that she would exercise significant autonomy as a wife. Before marrying in 1783, the couple signed a prenuptial agreement giving Katherine "full power" to possess, control, and dispose of all of her realty and personalty "as she may think fitt" and to specify the ownership of her slaves' descendants. To secure "the power over her own fortune," she relinquished her dower rights to Richard's estate. It was a smart decision because those rights were then worth less than half of her own fortune.[38]

The best that women could hope for, given the restraints of coverture, was a prenuptial agreement like Katherine Hawkins's, which was enforceable in chancery. Most wives in fact had to depend on informal agreements and their husbands' goodwill if they were to have a say in how the profits from the shirts and butter they made and sold, or the slaves they inherited, were spent. At the worst they were locked in marriages to men like Henry Britt, whom even a court decision did not deter. And they would remain so, for the Maryland legislature did not adopt a married woman's property act, granting wives control of assets, until well into the nineteenth century.[39]

As in the years preceding the Revolution, some women—a small but increasing proportion of them—were not married. Femes sole constituted 12.5 percent of taxpayers in 1782 and, in 1790, 16 percent of the household heads on large plantations, meaning those with more than twenty slaves. The largest slaveholder in the county was a woman who, with 115 blacks, held forty more than the next largest master, a man. Land and slave labor enabled some women to avoid "throwing the Die upon the Hazard of exceeding Happiness or Intence Misery." There is no evidence that their independent status provoked communal disapproval or hostility. Indeed, at least among some females, the femes sole seem to have been an inspiration.[40]

In the top tenth of wealthholders in 1782, the average value of unmarried women's property amounted to £1,943. They held proportionately less plantation land than men, although as many slaves and considerably more realty in the towns of Port Tobacco and Benedict. Content with a maternal inheritance that included two plantations, twenty-one slaves, and about three hundred head of livestock, Priscilla Smallwood had no need to marry. Content with a comfortable widowhood, Anne Neale and Judith Chase had not remarried since their husbands' deaths many years earlier and, in the interim, had conserved and enhanced their inheritances. Chase held nearly as much land and twice as many slaves as her husband owned when he died in 1755. When Neale was widowed in 1763, she acquired a life estate in 393 acres of land, on which stood the Port Tobacco inspection warehouse. Through the years she collected rent on every hogshead of tobacco stored at the warehouse, improved the buildings there, and increased her land- and slaveholdings. By 1782 she held 760 acres, eighteen slaves, and total property in the county valued at £2,929.[41]

Below the top tier of female taxpayers, women were quite evenly distributed, rather than clustered at the bottom, as was often the case in New England at the same time. Compared with men, they were slightly overrepresented in the top half of taxpayers and underrepresented in the bottom half. In every wealth quartile their average slaveholding was slightly above men's, as was their total assessed wealth in all but the top quartile of taxpayers. Every parish had women who had no assessed wealth but had others like Elizabeth Hall, who with four slaves raised cattle and crops on a one-hundred-acre leasehold, and Elizabeth McAttee, who owned no land but could readily support herself by hiring out her thirteen slaves. As the county's black population grew, moreover, an increasing proportion of women controlled and benefited from slave labor. That, together with growing literacy and the enhanced importance of female domestic roles, added up to some substantial gains for white women in the wake of the Revolution.[42]

"Free Forever"

Not every mistress and master unquestioningly accepted chattel slavery, for its persistence in a nation founded upon principles of human liberty was too ironic and troubling to ignore. Some Charles County slaveowners assuaged their doubts with self-serving assurances that they were "indulgent," "easy," "kind & humane," or that an occasional runaway "went off without any the least provocation either from her master or overseer." On the other hand, a particularly candid master commented that he "had never known a single instance of a negro being contented in slavery." If that was true, then 96 percent of the county's black people were discontented.[43]

Yet they, too, were living in revolutionary America, and if their contemporaries did not solve the problem of slavery, at least they defined it as a problem and confronted it as no previous generation had done. It was during the revolutionary period that northern states, beginning with Pennsylvania in 1780, adopted *gradual* emancipation of the slaves within their borders. Concurrently thousands of slaveowners, especially in the Chesapeake region, freed blacks through individual acts of manumission. The rise of free African-American communities in the United States consequently dates from this same period. And the very presence of free blacks raised hope and expectations among people still enslaved.[44]

After the war the county's free black population grew alongside the slave system. The only colonial count of free blacks and mulattoes, in 1755, showed 252 in Charles County. When the first federal census was taken in 1790, 404 were gathered into 132 households. In 1800, 571 free African-Americans lived in the county. It was a beginning.[45]

The 1790 census presents a still life of this rural population at the moment when many of its members had barely emerged from slavery. Descent from a mixed racial union was almost a prerequisite for inclusion: Nearly 90 percent of free black household heads were classified as mulattoes. The others—the "negroes" to the census takers—were thought to be entirely of African descent. Free black households were smaller than those of whites. Half had only one person, and sixty-six different surnames were recorded among the 132 households. In addition, the proportion of female household heads (one-third) was considerably higher than among whites.[46]

The relative newness of this freed population, and its rural nature, distinguished it from older, more developed urban black communities in places like Philadelphia or New York. Unlike urban blacks, recently freed persons in Charles County seldom remained part of white households. Only thirteen were living in six white families in 1790, and half of them were at General Smallwood's. Nor, considering the small size of the average household, could there have been much doubling up of families, which was one way urban free blacks made the transition to self-sufficiency. Yet in one telling respect the county's blacks duplicated a pattern found in the cities. That is, they often changed their names when they took up lives as free men and women. Forty-four percent of their surnames were not duplicated among local white families as of 1790. Although some were common English names (Carter, Upton, Webster, Ogle), others (Barjona, Goose, Featt) were not. Unlike some urban blacks, no Charles County family took a name like Carpenter or Mason to denote craft skills. Nor did any assume the name Freeman, perhaps because several white families carried the name, and one of them owned nineteen slaves. Two black families, however, adopted the name Wiseman.[47]

Freedom came to this emergent community in different ways during the postwar years. A handful were mulattoes born to white mothers. Such children customarily were bound out as servants until their thirty-first birthdays, then set free. Some blacks, contending that they were unlawfully held in bondage, successfully sued for release. Others ran away from their masters and created new lives for themselves. "From a sentiment of fond reverence" for their deceased parents and brother, the daughters of Thomas and Margaret Stone manumitted a slave family in 1793. And some whites took "into serious Consideration the injustice and Cruelty of keeping my fellow Creatures in perpetual slavery" and determined to set them "free forever"—or at least some of them. Whatever path blacks followed, the passage out of bondage could be long and was potentially perilous.[48]

Owners considering manumission confronted slaves' three-dimensional nature: They were human beings, laborers, and a capital investment. Humanitarian sentiment pointed toward immediate freedom. Economic considerations and the slaveowners' standards of living tugged in the direction of gradual manumission, not unlike the gradual emancipation enacted by states in the North. If material considerations prevailed over humanitarian ones, manumission was a lengthy process in which Charles County blacks essentially bought their freedom with their own labor. When a man named Ben died in 1790, his owner lamented, "I am very sorry for poor Ben, he was an honest faithful fellow, and I intended in the course of next year to have given him his liberty—as he had nearly paid for himself." Another master began his manumission grant by chastising the injustice of "perpetual Slavery," then proceeded to free all his blacks, but with the proviso that each had to serve him for up to twenty-two more years.[49]

Some blacks belonging to Samuel Hanson, and some of *their* descendants, remained enslaved even longer. His "two old Trusty and faithful Slaves Cato and Poll" were manumitted at his death, but the rest only gradually. To ease subsequent masters' "hard and burthensome" task of raising the young slaves—and any offspring they bore while still in bondage—Hanson ordered that they and "all such Issues and Descendants to the last Generation of them" would not walk free until their twenty-eighth birthdays.[50]

Even so, he undoubtedly regarded himself as an enlightened, generous master—and by contemporary standards he was. If Cato and Poll were unable to support themselves as free persons, Hanson required his executors to do so. When his bondwoman Sall bore children in 1791 and 1794, he named them Ann Liberty and Thomas Liberty. A different mother's baby he christened Samuel Liberty. Furthermore, he left strict instructions about the slave children's treatment and how they were to be prepared for lives in freedom:

> [N]one of the aforesaid Children . . . shall be sold, hired or by any other means disposed of out of the State of Maryland at any time during their time of Service, and . . . the Masters or owners of the said Children shall give to each of them three hundred days schooling, I mean that they shall actually go to School so many days; The females between the Age of fourteen and sixteen and the males between the age of Eighteen and twenty one Years, and on failure of either of these particulars, by the person or persons who may have a right to the said Childrens service, such right shall be thereby forfeited, and such Children from thence forth shall receive full and ample freedom.

Upon manumission, moreover, they were to receive the same freedom dues—clothing and tools—accorded indentured servants during the colonial period. Hanson's slaves needed the legal protection he gave them, for his body was scarcely in the grave when his executor advertised the sale of "A Number of valuable SLAVES, among whom are a carpenter, shoemakers, and several very promising boys."[51]

In another case a mistress who desperately wanted to manumit a bondwoman failed to do so. Neighbors who saw Ann Cornish during the last weeks of her life disagreed about her mental state. One woman refused to "swear any body . . . was in their senses," yet believed that Cornish was lucid except "when she drank a little too much and then she talked a little idle." Another neighbor heard Cornish recount what happened at a wedding fifty years earlier. Other visitors, however, contended that her memory was "very defective," that she "cou'd not say her prayers," refused to say the catechism, "spoke of a complaint in her head," or seemed "to be a little in liquor." Indeed, said one observer, she was so drunk that a woman in the house was obliged to put her to bed.[52]

Drunk or sober, forgetful or not, the dying woman had one compelling desire: She wanted to free a slave named Juda. Certainly she had tried, but according to Juda, the man who wrote Cornish's will had objected that "it was a pretty story to leave such a fine wench free." As death drew near in 1783, Cornish complained that "she coud not die unless her Will was altered" to free Juda "if the law woud allow it." A son-in-law claimed that "it coud not be done, but promis'd Ms Cornish if the law wou'd allow it to set Juda free and told Juda if the law woud not allow it that he would build her a house" on the plantation that his wife was about to inherit from her mother. Protesting that she was being "tormented . . . out of her life" and could not please her heirs, Cornish willed the slave to her son-in-law and then died. Juda just missed crossing the threshold to freedom.[53]

At that very moment a select group of Charles County slaves was determined not to await manumissions that might never come but to attempt crossing the threshold to freedom through litigation. These were men and women who claimed descent through the female line of Eleanor Butler (Irish Nell), a seventeenth-century servant who, over the objections of Lord Baltimore, had married Charles, an African slave. Even though a grandson and great-granddaughter of hers had sued for their freedom—unsuccessfully—in the late colonial period, other descendants renewed the effort after Independence in what they hoped would be a more favorable climate. By 1784 freedom petitions from several slaves who used the surname Butler had advanced from the county court to the General Court of the Western Shore. If they or any of several hundred descendants of Irish Nell then living on the shore were to succeed, the court would have to be convinced that they—and their forebears back to Nell—had been unlawfully held in bondage because she was white and not herself a slave.[54]

In 1784 the court made a test case of the petition of Mary Butler of Prince George's County, who had previously belonged to masters in Charles and St. Mary's counties. The fact that she was the daughter of the prewar litigants perhaps encouraged her master because those litigants had failed. He argued that the earlier decision should bar Mary Butler "from any Relief on her present petition." This time, however, the General Court in 1787 and, upon appeal, the Maryland Court of Appeals agreed with her contention that she was "entitled to Liberty." The judges ruled that documentary proof of marriage between Irish Nell and the African did not exist, and therefore, "without a Conviction [proof] in a Court of Record of Irish Nell's having intermarried with a Slave, she could not become a Slave, nor could her Issue become Slaves by Virtue of such Intermarriages." No matter how long they had been held in bondage, they were not slaves.[55]

The decision was a dramatic vindication of the Butlers' argument, dating from at least a generation before the Revolution, that they were illegally enslaved. It did not, however, free them all. The Maryland decision merely established the legal precedent upon which others claiming descent from Irish Nell could press their suits. Nor did the decision move whites who knew the lineage of their Butler slaves to manumit, for the 1790 federal census enumerated only eight free Butlers in all of Charles County.[56]

Blacks using the name, therefore, soon inundated the General Court with freedom petitions. At the October 1791 term the docket listed petitions involving more than forty-four men and women held in slavery in the county. Three years later more than one hundred petitions were pending, including some from blacks who used the surname Shorter or Thomas and who also claimed descent through the female line of a white woman. "When the Butlers got free by Judgment of the General Court," complained a white woman, "it was the common talk of the neighbourhood that several other families, the Shorts [Shorters] and Mingoes now called Thomas's, would probably petition." By 1800, when just thirteen cases from the county remained on the General Court docket, many of the petitioners had entered the ranks of free blacks.[57]

The grandchildren and great-grandchildren of Irish Nell who won their freedom suits benefited enormously from the colorful vignettes that several generations of blacks and whites had told about her, ever since the day Lord Baltimore allegedly "asked her how she would like to go to bed to a Negro" and she replied "that she rather go to bed to Charles than his Lordship." Again and again, as people recounted stories about the Irishwoman who had married a "saltwater negro" and helped populate the lower Western Shore, they perpetuated a collective memory of her and her descendants. In addition, some of the whites who in the 1760s gave depositions about the family had personally known Nell's children, while *their* parents had known Nell. In the absence of documentary proof of Nell's offspring, her descendants might not have gained their liberty had not white people entered their knowledge of the family into the public record.[58]

By the early 1790s Butlers who already were free tried to help those who were not by testifying to their lineages. In 1791 Joseph Butler, "a Free man of

colour" in his fifties, testified in the case of *Thomas Butler v. Jezreel Penn* that
the plaintiff was the great-grandson of Irish Nell. Rather than stop there,
however, Joseph Butler entered into the record the names of six of the plaintiff's brothers and sisters, three of whom were suing for their freedom, and
seven children of one of the sisters, whom he had "known ever since they
were children at the breast" and all of whom had freedom petitions pending.
So there could be no confusion, he also identified the masters. Sarah Butler,
the sister of Thomas, belonged to Penn; her sons were "William who has
Petitioned against Joseph Neale, Lewis who has petitioned against John Laidler, Clement who has petitioned against Jezreel Penn & George who has
petitioned against Jezreel Penn"; her daughters were suing for freedom from
three different masters. Aided by lawyers willing to take their cases, the
Butlers were mounting a concerted effort to gain their liberty.[59]

Encouraged by the Butlers' success, slaves using the name Shorter began,
about 1790, to petition for their freedom. Their task was more difficult because the collective memory about their family was less sharply etched than
that concerning the Butlers. As a result, the Shorter lineage was not as well
established, and sworn testimony was contradictory on cardinal points. The
conflicting evidence came from both whites and free blacks and did not divide
along racial lines.

Like the Butlers, the Shorter family originated in St. Mary's County and,
over the course of a century, had spread into Charles and other Western Shore
counties. Unquestionably they had been considered slaves for several generations. William Gibson, born about 1720, remembered a slave named Jane, who
was "shrunk with Age" and "ordered and commanded by Mr. Neale & Mrs.
Neale, & they used to receive what she earned by her labour." Unquestionably, too, the family was mulatto and had been so for several generations.
Parents and grandparents of the 1790s petitioners were variously described as
"dark mulatto," "yellow," "a tolerably bright Mulatto," or with hair "on the
curly order, but between the hair of a Negro & white person." The crucial
question, though, was whether the white progenitor had been male or female.
Only if it were the latter, and only if the petitioners could prove descent from
her, could they hope to escape slavery.[60]

The petitioners began their lineage with a white servant named Elizabeth
Shorter who allegedly married a slave named "little Robin." As of 1702 both
were living in the household of Anthony Neale of Charles County. The
petitioners claimed descent through one of Elizabeth's daughters: Mary
(Moll), Patty, and Jenny (Jane).[61]

The Neales and others, however, either adamantly denied the genealogy or
did not know enough to substantiate it. Jeremiah Neale, born about 1739,
swore that he never heard "there was a white woman in Anthony Neale's

family who had mulatto children," while Leonard Neale, born about 1747, testified, "I never knew, neither did I ever hear that any Negroe under the name of Short or Shorter was descended from a white Woman. I have simply heard that the Negroes under that Denomination pretended to such a descent." Old William Gibson agreed: He knew nothing of a white woman named Elizabeth Shorter and "thinks if any such Person had lived in the Family, he must have known it." Nor, he added, had any of the Neales' slaves alleged such descent until about 1790. Interjected Leonard Neale: "[A] Negroe Woman now belonging to Me calling herself Short did formerly sue for her liberty in Charles County Court on that Score, but . . . she was discarded by the Court as laying in a pretence, that was perfectly groundless."[62]

The petitioners' use of the surname Shorter also was challenged. Sixty-nine-year-old Elizabeth Neale asserted that "she never heard of the name of Shorter until about the time of the Butler's getting free," and someone else deposed that he "never heard that Patt or any of her descendants called themselves Shorter or had any claim to their freedom until the Butlers first petitioned," after which some blacks told him that Patt's descendants "were as much intitled to their freedom as the Butlers." Several witnesses testified that the family name was not Shorter but Short, and intimated that it was linked only to the height of Jenny, the alleged daughter of the white female progenitor. People living in the 1790s remembered Jenny. William Hill, a free black born about 1726, had known her as a "Flux Doctor" and manager of a mill owned by the Neales, while two white men affirmed that by the 1740s "she was past labour" and "doubled with age." Undeniably, too, Jenny was "a remarkably short, squat Woman," so short that she could not hoist a bag of flour onto a horse's back. Hill said, "he thinks he never saw a shorter Woman."[63]

In the scenario that the Neales, other masters defending against freedom suits, and people who corroborated their testimony constructed, no white woman named Elizabeth Shorter had ever lived in the Neale household, none of the petitioners was known to be descended from a free white woman, and they had not adopted the name Shorter until after the Revolution. Carefully calling them negroes rather than mulattoes, Leonard Neale summarized the defendants' position: "I have no knowledge whatever of any right that any of the Negroes called Shorters have to liberty." They simply "pretended" to be descended from a white woman.[64]

Other evidence created a far different scenario. People who had personally known Jenny and her sisters remembered that they were called both Short and Shorter—the former, perhaps, because they carried the genes of the slave named "little Robin," and the latter, perhaps, because Robin married a white servant named Elizabeth Shorter. Although neither Jenny nor anyone else ever told William Hill, the free black, that she should be free, he observed that she "had great liberty in going about & attending people sick with the Flux in the Neighbourhood" and that people approached her, not her master, when they wanted her healing skills. Although Samuel Collins had not known Jenny, he often heard, about the time of her death in 1762, that she was entitled to freedom. And if no one remembered whether Jenny herself had said the same thing, her sisters certainly had. Recalled a sixty-seven-year-old mulatto named Henny Butler in 1793, Patty Shorter "would always talk about her Freedom when she was made mad by any of the [Neale] family." Said a free mulatto born about 1720: "Moll claimed h[e]r Freedom as being the Daughter of a white Woman."[65]

But were Moll, Patty, and Jenny Short or Shorter the daughters of a white servant named Elizabeth Shorter? No one born after 1720 could remember, not even William Hill, whose memories of Jenny were graphic. The freedom suits might well have faltered on the point had not eighty-three-year-old William Simms, born in 1709, tottered into a tavern at Port Tobacco in 1792 and, in a deposition, recounted some boyhood memories:

[W]hen he was a lad he knew a woman by the name of Betty Short and he has seen her twice or oftener at his fathers who then lived near Zachiah Swamp in Charles County; that the said Betty Short was a white woman and it was generally understood was not a Country born woman, but from what Country she came he has forgot: he remembers very well to have seen her playing at ball at his fathers with some Girls and boys that she would catch the ball in her Apron and what makes the deponent recollect her more strongly, he remembers that in taking hold of her Apron to catch the ball she pulled up her Petticoat with her Apron and he saw above her knees.

The Betty Short about whom Simms reminisced was in her thirties or forties when he knew her early in the century, lived with the Neales as far as he knew, and "did not appear to have any stain of the Mulatto in her." She matched the description of the progenitor whom the Shorter petitioners claimed.[66]

Once again the General Court of the Western Shore selected a test case, that of Basil Shorter against Henry Rozier of Prince George's County. Steadfastly denying the Shorter scenario, undoubtedly worried because of the Butlers' success, and hoping that a jury would accept his word over that of free blacks and mulattoes, Rozier threw himself upon the country. He lost the case. Basil Shorter—and other slaves who subsequently persuaded the court that they, too, were related to Elizabeth Shorter—walked free beginning in 1794.[67]

For Charles County masters and mistresses, the whole process must have been disconcerting at best. Depending upon how many Butlers or Shorters tended their fields and washed their linens, they were threatened with substantial property losses. While some stood to lose only one slave, one master had five suits pending against him in the early 1790s, another fifteen, and the solvency of William and Mary Church was threatened because thirty-six glebe slaves were petitioning for release. In addition, suits cost money and—because in 1789 several children of a Butler woman were sold out of Maryland before her suit was heard—judicial supervision of the defendants. When Agnes Butler sued her master in 1791, the General Court required him to post £50 as security that he would not send her out of the state or "obstruct her from attending this Court from time to time in support of her Petition of Freedom . . . and in the meantime to feed, cloath and use her well and pay whatever Satisfaction the Court shall adjudge for the Services of the said Agnes Butler from this Term to the time of Judgment, with costs."[68]

Even though slaveholders were liable to pay successful petitioners' legal fees and wages from the day they filed their respective suits, many owners delayed the proceedings. One waited more than a year until five cases pending against him were ready for trial, then pleaded no contest. Henrietta Shorter's attorney filed her claim in November 1790, but not until three years later did her master post the required recognizance bond, and then only after being cited for contempt of court. Not until the May term 1795 was she adjudged a free woman. After Teresa Shorter brought suit in 1792 to free herself and her five children, she encountered a delay of more than three years because her mistress ignored summonses and contempt citations and allegedly could not be found by the Charles County sheriff. Result: Between 1792 and 1795 the petitioner and her children spent a total of twenty more years in slavery. Although most masters were not so intransigent, it was not unusual for them to wait until a case proceeded to trial before they acknowledged that they could not refute the petitioner's right to freedom.[69]

The existence of the county's expanding free black community did not go unnoticed among slaves who were unable to claim descent from a white woman and whose masters had no intention of manumitting them. Compared with the colonial period and the war years, the number of local runaways advertised in the *Maryland Gazette* doubled in the five years after Yorktown and steadily increased thereafter. More than before, runaways were black as well as mulatto, and for the first time a few slave women and children joined the outflow. Yet the number of runaways sought in the advertisements, fifty-five from 1782 through 1796 and never more than eight in any one year, probably was a testament to the deterrent powers of the slave system and, conversely, masters' toleration of temporary absences. Tall, slender twenty-seven-year-old George took "his usual walks," for example, at Daniel of St. Thomas Jenifer's quarter and in the vicinity of Port Tobacco. Only when his master suspected that George might have set out for Baltimore, "as he once before attempted," did a runaway ad appear in the *Gazette*.[70]

Slaveowners often expected their runaways to "be harboured" in or near the county, wherever—like carpenter Jess or "smart sensible" Clara—they had spouses or "a great correspondence" of friends and family. Hoping that wayward slaves would return of their own accord, owners also sometimes waited months before advertising. One planter did not resort to the *Gazette* until ten months after Jem, who was "pretty well made, of a very black complexion . . . [with] small red eyes, and remarkable white teeth," failed to return from Cob Neck or Nanjemoy, "where he has a great many relations and connexions."[71]

To his chagrin, the president of the Continental Congress tried to locate a slave who ran away *to* Charles County in 1782. John Hanson, Jr., was born and lived in the county until 1773, then moved to the Maryland frontier, assumed a prominent role in revolutionary politics, and in 1781 was elected president of Congress. He owned a slave named Ned Barnes, who worked for the family, made shoes, and was sometimes hired out to individuals, a poorhouse, and a gun manufactory. During the winter of 1782 Ned ran away to Charles County, where he had a wife. Hanson vowed that he would "never be plagued by a runaway negro," but plagued he was. For two months he intermittently turned from the affairs of state to the whereabouts of Ned. Eventually informed that he was at a plantation in the county, Hanson decided to sell Ned there, as it "Will be to no purpose" to send him back to the frontier.[72]

Even as some runaways continued the old pattern of staying near family members or friends who lived on local plantations, a new dynamic was emerging: Fugitives sought to pass as free men and women in Annapolis, Baltimore, Alexandria, Georgetown, or even Pennsylvania and New York. Each had a growing free black community in which plantation runaways might be concealed or given new identities. Because Peter, who ran away in 1784, was "a sensible fellow," according to his owner, he "probably will endeavor to pass as a free man." When tawny-toned Elizabeth "eloped" in 1786, her owner suspected she would try "to pass as far as possible from her native place, and that as a free person." "Supposed he will make for Baltimore or Philadelphia," "I suspect he is gone to Annapolis or George-town," and "as he has been used to going by water, may attempt to pass for a free man and get on board some vessel," mused the masters of other runaways from the county. Isaac, who knew how to write "a reputable hand," set out in 1790 "with an intention of going to some one of the northern states, where he should be entitled to his freedom." And Will, a groom who dressed "remarkably neat" and was "well known to gentlemen of the turf, having rode for several purses in Virginia and Maryland," took a horse in 1795 and headed for Delaware, where he hoped to live free. Slaveholders regularly offered rewards gauged to whether runaways were captured in the county, within Maryland, or outside the state.[73]

In addition to having free-black centers to run to, local runaways took advantage of the increased movement of people—strangers—that accompanied the War for Independence and did not abate entirely thereafter. Mulatto Daniel Cain set out in 1782 and, warned his master, "intends to pass as a free man, and is either going to camp or to sea." Three years later "impudent," smallpox-scarred Sam, who used several aliases and had run away to Philadelphia and the West Indies during the war, struck out again in the guise of a free man.[74]

In the 1790s, as members of the Butler and Shorter families gained their liberty through the courts, some local runaways tried to improve *their* chances for freedom by assuming one of those names. Not content to await the outcome of a pending petition, a young man calling himself Will Shorter left his master, who warned that he "is remarkable cunning and artful, of a good address when spoken to; it is presumed he will . . . endeavour to pass for a free man." Another master believed that his runaway would probably "attempt to pass as a free man under the name of Butler." And a third notified the public that "A YOUNG MULATTO WOMAN left my plantation some weeks ago, and (as I am since informed) has been about Annapolis passing for one of the Butlers."[75]

Unlucky slaves escaped, were dragged back, and escaped again. George was being brought back in handcuffs from the jail in Chester County, Pennsylvania, when he managed to break away and, it was thought, probably headed for New York "in hopes of his freedom." Philip Briscoe's Will, who gave his master a "down roguish look," was equally determined when he ran away in August 1783. Briscoe predicted that "he will try to get to Philadelphia, as he has been heard to say that he would try to get there; he has a brother that lives there." Furthermore, "he will make a stout resistance before he will be taken, and if taken will get away" unless "well secured." Will was captured, but Briscoe turned him over to the Charles County sheriff as an incorrigible who might take flight again. He did. In March 1784 someone set fire to the jail and released him. "He had round his neck when he made his escape," laconically droned the sheriff, "a pair of pot-hooks with a long chain fastened to them, and a pair of hand cuffs on."[76]

To the dismay of their masters, runaways did everything they could to maximize their chances of success. A fortunate few managed to acquire passes, written permission for them to move about unmolested. Blacksmith Bob went off from Port Tobacco with "a written permission, signed by . . . his former master, to hire himself wherever he chose." In an unusual incident, four slaves left their home plantation together in 1788. Besides mantles and hats, the two women carried forged passes, "one of them on brown paper, badly wrote and spelt." Three bondmen, each the property of a different Charles County master, escaped in June 1794 and were still at large the following autumn, thanks partly to passes "it is supposed wrote by one of the black men, as he writes a pretty good hand."[77]

The clothing slaves carried away was particularly important, for it could be changed and exchanged as they tried to avoid detection. Although Daniel Cain escaped in new garments and laced shoes, his master considered him "likely [to] change his dress, as he is an artful fellow and a notorious liar." Jacob's overseer expected him to "change his cloaths, if he can get others at any rate, even by stealth." A mulatto fugitive was loaded down with "an osnabrig coat and overalls, London brown superfine broad cloth coat, a white linen jacket, two striped jackets, a pair of yellow lasting breeches, white and brown thread stockings, white and brown linen shirts, new shoes and metal buckles." Yet he was no match for a bondman named Sam, who one June day carried off a dark blue broadcloth great coat with a red velvet cape, three other coats, four waistcoats, three pairs of breeches, four shirts, two pairs of white stockings, several handkerchiefs, and a pair of boots. Nor for Clara, whose runaway wardrobe included jackets made of linen, calico, cotton, and country cloth, purple and white petticoats, as well as shifts, shoes, stockings, aprons, handkerchiefs, an old felt hat, and, around her neck, a favorite brass cross. All this suggests that slaves planning to run away saved, borrowed, and took, from masters and each other, against the time when they would attempt their escapes.[78]

If slaveowners were ignorant of what escapees wore and carried with them, so much the better. Blacksmith Bob's master knew only that "he took with him a variety" of clothes and "generally ties his hair behind." Walley, an African or West Indian who spoke "bad English, so that it can be hardly understood" and who was "remarkably fond of dress," made off with many garments his master could not describe. Other owners found themselves in the same predicament.[79]

Some fugitives' clothing, appearance, and behavior seemed so unexceptional that little could be said about them in runaway advertisements. Others had a missing tooth, a fierce look, a twisted grin, or a "pleasing countenance when in a good humour" which, masters hoped, would give them away. Still others had distinctive mannerisms and physical features that might make it difficult for them to live free for long. Seventeen-year-old Vick, who ran away from Port Tobacco with her child and hoped to exist as a free Butler, would be wise to hide the large lump on her stomach, and Daniel Cain would prudently cover "the scars or marks of some stripes he received some time ago (not for his goodness)" across his back, but a man named Basil could hardly conceal that he was "crippled in one of his arms . . . so that it stands wide from his side, and is very perceivable." Nor could Jacob do much about the leg that swelled "and som[e] times break[s] out in sores" or his remarkable "gait": "His knees and ancles frequently . . . rub, and the calves of his legs twist out, which cause them to be wide between them." Runaway John, on the other hand, had "a remarkable long swinging walk." Perhaps Aaron would marshal the willpower to overcome his "great propensity to strong drink," which rendered him "when intoxicated . . . extremely quarrelsome and impertinent," but what was Phill Carter to do about his "round face, full of pimples" or ankles that "crack very much when he walks"?[80]

Then there were the scars. Not every slave bore marks from past accidents, fights, or abuse, and some bore only small ones that might go undetected. Others' bodies, however, had been severely injured and disfigured. One master described the "remarkable scars" a runaway received when someone tried to murder him with a knife: "[O]ne of these scars is below his upper lip, another from the upper part of his right cheek across his neck, and two others across the back part of his neck, which have left marks resembling those frequently seen on Africans." Another had a deep gash on his leg, an ax cut not yet fully healed. For her part, Henny had smallpox scars, holes in her ears, one scar that ran from elbow to wrist, "nearly as broad as a dollar, and another raised into a ridge nearly two inches in length, at the lower and back part of her neck."[81]

The chances for a successful, permanent escape nevertheless were greater in the late eighteenth century than ever before. Having seen a bit of the world and broken out of two jails during the war, "a cunning artful fellow" ran away again after bragging "that he can break out of any gaol" and intended to pass for free. Toby, said to be "remarkably active, fond of waiting in public or private houses, a good groom, and a very handy fellow by water," headed north through Prince George's County in July 1784. By the following October his master confessed, "[I]t is uncertain by this date where his notions may have led him." A year later, despite increasingly detailed runaway advertisements, Toby remained at large, openly frequented Annapolis, and was probably working as a boatman on Chesapeake Bay. With monotonous regularity—more than forty times—Bob's master advertised to no avail, even though the fugitive blacksmith was seen at the Annapolis races and traveling toward Baltimore. Notwithstanding his blotchy complexion and creaky ankles, Phill Carter, who ran away with a large sum of stolen money and then returned to his home plantation and took a horse, bought trade goods and hawked them in Alexandria, Georgetown, and Annapolis.[82]

Such fugitives succeeded through their own wits and because free black communities, into which they could meld, were growing all along the Atlantic coast. As the owner of Osten, who ran away in 1796, wrote, "[I]t is probable he will push to George-town, he is acquainted with almost every negro and free mulatto of that town, he is likewise well acquainted with the free mulattoes and negroes of Charles and St. Mary's counties." In his quest for freedom Osten might call upon scores of free people who themselves had once known bondage and consequently were exquisitely sensitive to what was at stake. Charles County slaveholders, on the other hand, were learning firsthand that the very existence of free blacks undermined the institution of slavery.[83]

From slaves to squires, the Revolution had transformed the complex gradations of freedom characteristic of the colonial social order. Blacks, through their own efforts and with assistance from some whites, had mounted a strong challenge to the perpetual enslavement so unquestioned before the war. Among whites, bound labor had virtually vanished; men in the aggregate enjoyed greater political power; women, higher status; and everyone, religious liberty. The relative equilibrium of the late colonial society was gone, and no one could foretell how far revolutionary change would extend.

CHAPTER EIGHT

The Price of Nationhood

In 1785 Colonel Francis Ware ran for sheriff and won handily with 548 votes, compared with 149 cast for the runner-up. Before assuming office, he and several sureties posted a customary performance bond of two hundred thousand pounds of marketable tobacco, an immense sum. It was their pledge to the state of Maryland that Ware would faithfully discharge the duties of his office. Already ranked in the top tenth of local wealthholders, he could anticipate enriching his estate with the fees he would receive for performing those duties during his three-year term.[1]

Less than two years after the election, however, Ware stood convicted in the General Court of owing more than £14,000 to the state, on which interest was accruing at the rate of 10 percent per year. Subsequently he suffered the humiliation of seeing part of his plantation as well as slaves, livestock, and even furniture seized and auctioned off. Ware's sureties also lost property to the state, and to compensate them, he signed over all of his book debts in 1789. Trustees assumed control of the rest of his plantation. When they advertised it for sale in 1793 and 1794 to satisfy his creditors, Ware was a tenant on the land that so recently had helped secure his position at the apex of his society. By 1800 the former legislator, officer in the Maryland Line, county lieutenant, and sheriff was "reduced to extreme indigence."[2]

In ordinary times Ware's insolvency might have resulted from personal mismanagement, overextension, or even corruption. But the 1780s and 1790s were not ordinary times in Charles County, and Ware was guilty of none of these. Instead he painfully learned that both the war and American Independence—no matter how glorious the victory or exhilarating the prospect of building a new nation—had created intractable economic and political problems in the lower Potomac Valley. Ware's difficulties, rather than unique, were emblematic. Neither he nor anyone else in the county had foreseen the toll that political independence and nationhood would exact. At war's end they had been more optimistic.

LUCRATIVE PURSUITS

During the war, people from the county traveled over hundreds of miles of unfamiliar territory, passed through towns they had never heard of before, saw cities like Philadelphia and New York for the first time, and encountered everything from Yankee accents to Carolina drawls. In sum, whether they soldiered or went to sea, carted military supplies to Georgetown or accompanied husbands elected to Congress, they returned home with a better awareness of America, a keener interest in events beyond their immediate purview, and contacts that sometimes lasted a lifetime. Even those who never left the county experienced a wider slice of life through the increased activity and movement of people that accompanied the war.[3]

With such widened horizons, and with a penchant for improving everything from politics to the wall surrounding Trinity Church, inhabitants looked forward to postwar economic recovery and development. Wider horizons, an inclination toward improvement, and visions of economic well-being: That was not a bad combination with which to enter the postwar era. Local people variously sowed bumper crops, worked to repair wartime damages, promoted or resisted an attempt to replace Port Tobacco as the county seat, forged new commercial partnerships and connections, and joined other Marylanders and Virginians in an ambitious, risk-laden project to open the continent to settlement and trade by linking the Potomac with the headwaters of the Ohio River system.

Even in 1782, when not one ship "in which any prudent Man cou'd venture his Property" came up the Potomac, and when the tobacco market in the county was characterized as dull and prices so low that they could hardly sink much lower, the general mood was optimistic. Plantation land and Port Tobacco town lots changed hands briskly. European manufactured items, as many as merchants managed to acquire, sold well because people were tired of "Country Produce." To be sure, tobacco brought only 15s. per hundredweight on the Potomac, but no one expected such prices to persist. Anticipating they might soon triple, planters were interested in lending tobacco in the hope that "the Borrower will most probably pay a great deal more in Value than he receives."[4]

Following news of the peace treaty, commercial activity quickened. "Trade properly conducted," predicted Thomas Stone, "will certainly be the most lucrative pursuit in America." Tobacco prices doubled in 1783, to 30 or 35s. paid in cash, while the profits on manufactures were so high that one eager merchant traveled all the way from Port Tobacco to New York during the winter of 1783–84 to buy a cargo of goods. Then he hastened to get the merchandise transported home and sold before the 1784 shipping season, when great quantities of European goods and a "Cloud of Merchants foreign and Domestick" were expected to inundate the Chesapeake.[5]

Most people assumed that Port Tobacco would remain the county's principal trading center because of its location at the intersection of all the main roads and its amenities—the courthouse, church, ordinaries, and stores that brought country people and travelers to town. In short, the town was "a most convenient stand for any merchant who proposes to carry on the purchase of tobacco, or any other produce of this part of Maryland." When young Walter Stone, weary of a clerkship in Philadelphia, contemplated a mercantile career, he naturally thought of returning to Port Tobacco, where, a friend advised, the social life was "the most agreeable . . . I know Philad[elphi]a not excepted." The town was so genteel that geese and swine were not allowed to run loose and, if they did, could be shot on sight.[6]

A notice in the *Maryland Gazette* in August 1783 therefore came as a surprise. "Sundry inhabitants" of Charles County, it seemed, intended to petition the General Assembly to move the county seat to Chapel Point, at the mouth of Port Tobacco Creek, where the Jesuits had attempted to found a town before the war. Thomas Howe Ridgate, whose business was based in the old town, swiftly got "many respectable Inhabitants" to sign a counterpetition to keep the court at Port Tobacco and prohibit any town from being built on Catholic land. Somehow he mislaid the document before he could dispatch it to Annapolis, and this provoked complaints that the Port Tobaccoans had "negligently managed" their interests. Thereupon Thomas Stone—who thought that moving the county seat was an "absurd and unjust" idea meant only to "answer the Convenience of a few to whom the point is more convenient than the present Town"—mounted the town's defense.[7]

Stone conveyed to legislators every plausible reason he could think of why Port Tobacco should remain the county seat, including a *Protestant* church, a courthouse that "might be made good with a little Repairing," and the investments and improvements residents had made. In contrast, he argued, "it is impossible that there can be a Town of any Consequence at Chappel point, because there is no Subject to export which will bring any considerable trade & because there is no reason to expect Manufacturers to settle there." He foresaw only eight hundred hogsheads of tobacco and not a shipload of wheat being exported from the point unless Port Tobacco burned to the ground or "unless people from distant parts bring these Commodities to the new Town merely for the sake of incurring an expense." Finally, because no public meeting to discuss the proposed relocation had been called, "the Sense of the county has never been fairly taken."[8]

Persuaded, the Assembly kept the county seat at Port Tobacco. New mercantile establishments soon opened. Rachael Forry tended to guests' needs at her inn. Dr. James Craik, home after directing the Continental Army hospital during the siege of Yorktown, advertised for an apprentice in surgery and physic. And mail carried from as far as New Hampshire and Georgia regularly passed through.[9]

Sensing boom times in 1784, planters refused cash offers of up to 40s. per hundredweight for tobacco because they rightly expected that when large cargoes of European goods arrived during the spring, storekeepers would pay even more, in exchange for their merchandise. People sowed immense crops of leaf that year—"the greatest crop of Tobacco . . . that ever was made in America," thought Alexander Hamilton. "I never saw such quantitys growing before." During the summer, as Irish linen, earthenware dishes, salt, rum, and a host of other imported items became readily available, Patuxent tobacco soared to 50s. per hundredweight, Potomac to 45. Buyers nevertheless snapped up every hogshead brought to market, for the demand in Europe was brisk. Plans were afoot to rebuild the Cedar Point inspection warehouse destroyed during the war and to erect another nearby. Inhabitants talked as if, despite the late unpleasantness with Britain, "business will be carried on in the same manner it was during the former connection."[10]

They had some justification. The British government, eager to revive trade with America, in 1783 agreed that Chesapeake tobacco would be handled and taxed as in the colonial period. Within the county the operations of Robert Fergusson, a Scottish merchant who opened a store at Port Tobacco and assigned a factor to St. Mary's County, recalled the colonial system. He was a partner in the firm of Henderson, Fergusson and Gibson, successor to the largest prewar tobacco firm, John Glassford and Company. The operations of the indigenous Hooe, Harrison and Company also echoed the colonial era. Like its prewar predecessor, Hooe, Stone and Company, the firm maintained stores at Alexandria and Port Tobacco and dealt in tobacco and grain.[11]

Yet an important new element was present alongside the old. Before 1776, lines of trade joined Charles County directly to ports in Europe, the West

Indies, and Africa. By 1784 several local entrepreneurs were trying to enter a larger *American* commercial network than had existed before Independence, one utilizing acquaintances and connections formed during the war years. In essence, county merchants would sometimes import European goods through mercantile houses in American port cities and, in turn, would act as agents of such firms when buying and shipping tobacco and other staples. There was talk of a string of "crop ports" beginning at Port Tobacco and extending down the Potomac and up the bay to Baltimore.[12]

Several members of the Stone family created the Charles County sector of this new network between 1782 and 1786. In the beginning they seemed inclined to develop ties with Philadelphia, where Thomas Stone and his brother Walter had spent several years, respectively, in Congress and in the office of Robert Morris, the superintendent of finance of the United States. At war's end, when Walter was planning to leave the city, he received advice to "mention to all the Merchants you are intimate with that you could purchase wheat flour Tobacco Porke Corn etc.a in Maryland—and Sell goods." His "most advantageous Scheme" would be a partnership with a Philadelphia importer "who should supply you with Goods at Portobacco or Benedict where you might buy Tobacco & other Country produce very cheap." By 1784 Stone had returned to Port Tobacco and, with his brothers Michael Jenifer and John Hoskins, opened a store under the name of John H. Stone and Company. The firm rapidly forged a commercial network that linked the river valley from St. Mary's County to Alexandria with buyers and suppliers in Philadelphia, Annapolis, and Baltimore. Moreover, the firm established mercantile connections in London.[13]

The brothers' plans were ambitious. Hoping to conduct business exclusively with "reputable" planters "who we know," by early 1785 they were buying wheat and assembling individual cargoes of up to one hundred thousand pounds of Maryland and Virginia tobacco. They sold leaf at cost plus shipping charges and intended to reap their profits from a 100 percent markup on imported goods. Reluctant to tie up capital by selling merchandise on credit, they meant to extend it for no more than six months. The company's headquarters at Port Tobacco featured two rooms "completely fitted for a retail store . . . a large counting-room and lodging-room for clerks," and spacious storage areas.[14]

In 1785 John Hoskins Stone, the Continental army officer, approached Tench Tilghman of Baltimore, formerly an aide-de-camp to General Washington, about a possible mercantile connection. Tilghman then was buying Chesapeake tobacco on behalf of Robert Morris of Philadelphia, who had a contract to supply the French. When Stone offered to trade Potomac leaf for bills of exchange payable in London, Tilghman promptly told Morris that "he may be depended on for what he undertakes, and has it in his Power to furnish more Tobo than any other man upon the Maryland side of Potow [Potomac] riv[e]r." Thereafter the Stone firm was Tilghman's preferred contact in the lower Potomac Valley. Thomas Howe Ridgate and John Halkerston, a former army officer who lived in Port Tobacco, were drawn into the same nexus. Its potential benefit for the local economy seemed enormous: In December 1785 alone, Tilghman sent $4,000 gold into Charles County for tobacco purchases.[15]

"Joy! Joy! Joy!"

To some local men a revived and partially reoriented trade was only part of a much broader mosaic, one composed of dreams, plans, and projects that collectively would make the Potomac the busiest, most important river in America. With its headwaters nearly touching those of the Ohio River system, the Potomac stirred in many the vision that—if only its course from the fall line at Georgetown, Maryland, to its upper reaches were made navigable—a vast sector of the continent could be settled, cultivated, linked politically and commercially with the eastern states, and thereby secured to the new nation. To George Washington, who articulated the fullest idea of what was possible, a "new empire" was there for the making in the West. In the 1780s he foresaw the wharves of Alexandria and Georgetown piled high with wheat grown in the Ohio country and furs traded at Detroit. By the 1790s his vision encompassed a military fort on the Maryland shore, in Prince George's County, guarding an inland waterway on which stood the national capital, commercial entrepôts, thriving farms, and a federal armory where the Shenandoah River joins the Potomac at Harper's Ferry.[16]

Partaking of the same vision and trusting that development of the upper valley would benefit the entire valley, members of the Charles County gentry supported the nation's first large-scale internal improvement project, the Potomac Company. Chartered by the Maryland and Virginia legislatures in 1784–85 to make the river navigable for about 175 miles above Georgetown and, furthermore, to build a twenty-mile road linking the headwaters of the Potomac and Ohio rivers, the company began soliciting private subscriptions in early 1785. Because shares cost £100 sterling each, only substantial property holders could afford to buy stock in a work allegedly "fraught with . . . universal advantages." Hence the Charles County subscribers—including Jenifers and Hansons, three Stone brothers, and even old Richard Lee—constituted a roster drawn from the elite. "If the scheme is properly executed," Thomas Stone believed, "I have the most sanguine expectation that it will fully succeed to the Wishes of those who are anxious to promote the Wellfare of these States and to form a strong Chain of connection between the Western and atlantic governments." By western governments he meant the territories and states to be established beyond the Appalachian Mountains, under the land ordinances passed in 1784–87 by the Continental Congress. Those ordinances, which determined how the huge transmontane West would be settled and governed, constitute one of Congress's most enduring accomplishments.[17]

In the 1790s, as construction began on a national capital city located a few miles upriver from the county, Marylanders envisioned not only the seat of the new federal government but also a bustling commercial center. A visitor to the District of Columbia opined that, "if Ohio River traffic can be routed as these people wish, I think Washington will become incontestably one of the biggest cities in North America." Among Charles County men hoping he was right was Michael Jenifer Stone, who, as a congressman in 1790, had written that "my . . . object is to fix the Seat of Congress Where the Interests of the Union point out.—That Spott I think is on the Banks of the Potowmack." When Congress voted to move the federal capital to the Chesapeake, Stone had exulted, "Joy! Joy! Joy!"[18]

By the early 1790s such buoyancy did not always come easily to Charles County inhabitants. If American nationalism, regional pride, and economic optimism had inspired in them ambitious plans to develop the District and the river on which it stood, other forces—far less favorable—also pressed upon local people. Behind Stone's seemingly unbridled enthusiasm lay a profound sense of relief, perhaps even an expectation of salvation from assorted ills that now plagued the county. For the boom times of the immediate postwar years all too soon collided with intractable problems. Alongside dreams of a prosperous and politically important Potomac Valley, many residents experienced moments of despair. Amid trying times, local people kept trying. Yet even as their individual fortunes and prospects rose and fell, their society lost much ground, and much vitality, during the last years of the century. This long and complicated story begins with unpaid debts and taxes and ends with demographic upheaval and the passing of the revolutionary generation. The county's history from 1785 to 1800, moreover, is part of a broader one: the history of a new nation's emergence and an old empire's end.

DEBT, DEPRESSION, AND TUMULTS

When the war came and trade with the mother country ceased, Charles County inhabitants owed thousands of pounds of tobacco and money to

English and Scottish merchants. As early as 1774, avoiding those debts was regarded as a patriotic act. At one Scottish store alone—Cunninghame, Findlay and Company at Port Tobacco—the prewar accounts of about 350 persons remained unsettled in 1777. In subsequent years lawsuits pending on behalf of British creditors were quashed through a simple legal device: The defendants merely asked the Charles County court to require the plaintiffs to post security, which would guarantee payment of the costs of litigation. Since no creditors or their representatives came forward—there being a revolution in progress—they automatically lost the cases. Intoned the justices in a typical suit: "Cunninghame Findlay and Company being Solemly called to come and give Security for the payment of the Costs aforesaid comes not but makes default." The state government also abetted debtors by permitting them to pay into the state treasury, with dramatically depreciated paper money, what they owed British creditors. Such facile maneuvers help explain why the British government insisted that the Peace of Paris protect its subjects' right to recover prewar debts, in full and at sterling value.[19]

Fortified by the treaty, agents of British creditors were active in Maryland by late 1783. Some came only to collect debts. Others, like Alexander Hamilton, factor for James Brown and Company, also wanted to revive the Scottish trade. At first the agents were solicitous. They "requested" people to "settle their accounts," asked for partial payments immediately and bonds to secure the rest, and pleaded that "those who have it not in their power to pay at present, I expect will *at least* come and renew their obligations." Some debtors obliged. Many did not.[20]

Hamilton, that inveterate, though hardly unbiased, chronicler of characters and conditions on the lower Western Shore, found debt collection in Charles County "a damned business for an old grey hair'd man to be pestered with." Not that he harbored great expectations. "Collecting debts in this world was att all times a very fatiguing as well as a dissagreeable business," he complained in March 1784, but "it is now greatly more so" because the rule of law was relaxed during the Revolution and "A relaxation of Law always vitiates the Morals of Mankind." Furthermore, because planters "generaly" assumed that the break with Britain had canceled the debts, their protection in the Peace of Paris was "a Stroke so unexpected that it has created a general amazement." Hamilton's best hope was that favorable tobacco prices would induce "the people who are willing" to remit part of what they owed.[21]

Convinced that "Collection will be a work of time" and unhappy at having "to be troublesome to those who owe by teazing them for payment," he persisted in the face of "sorry excuses." Feeling that he "dare not yet use threats ex[c]ept to some whom I know well," he knew William Hanson, a former Charles County sheriff, well enough to threaten him with a lawsuit.

The Scotsman also broached a topic about which the peace treaty was unclear: interest. To a gentleman who was well endowed with silver plate, slaves, and over five hundred acres of land, Hamilton wrote, "I must again intreat you will pay me your debt, if not the whole at least the Interest of it." From another debtor he expected to receive interest because "I told him he must pay."[22]

Local people had other ideas, however, and in the summer of 1784 the justices and jurors of the Charles County court rejected British creditors' attempts to collect interest. A furious Hamilton wrote to Robert Fergusson at Port Tobacco: "The dread bodys has taken it into their heads, especially your County Gentry, to refuse to pay the Interest. It is said some of your Wiseacres of Majestrates has determined that point. How they may reconcile this conduct with their oaths to do justice according to the Laws of the Land, is, you may say, another affair." Because court records for the 1780s are missing, no one knows how the court justified its action, but one argument then circulating held that the war was Britain's fault, that it prevented Marylanders from earning the money needed to pay interest on their debts, and therefore that the British government should be liable to the creditors. While Thomas Stone prepared to argue in the General Court against accrual of wartime interest, Hamilton found that "Interest is the Cry . . . [and people] will not pay it." He also feared that "if that point be given up, they will refuse to pay the principal." The court had made "the business with debtors living in that County extremely troublesome and they can pay nothing they say 'till next year." Collections during the remainder of 1784 were "trifling." The court's "troublesome precedant," Hamilton was certain, made a bad situation infinitely worse, and he foresaw "nothing but plague and trouble for many years to come in this business."[23]

More than prewar indebtedness soon plagued the lower Western Shore. When Hamilton wrote, imports and credit were plentiful and planters received good prices, often in cash, for their tobacco. In late 1785, however, the Chesapeake economy sank into a severe depression. Glib predictions of Britain's willingness to resume the "former connection"—the commercial connection—with an independent America had proved dead wrong. Instead, even as planters bought large cargoes of imported goods (draining specie from the economy and increasing indebtedness), the British government barred Americans from the lucrative West Indies trade (thereby denying them significant earnings with which to pay for European goods). In addition, overproduction of tobacco satiated British demand and depressed prices, while Robert Morris's monopolistic contract with the French had a comparable effect. Amid low commodity prices and contracted credit, Marylanders had not yet developed adequate alternate markets for their staples. Then, too, the state's monetary policy of retiring large amounts of paper money emitted during the war had a deflationary effect on the economy.[24]

The situation in Maryland was typical—in broad strokes, if not every detail—of the country as a whole. For the passage from colonial status through war to independent nationhood was accompanied by profound economic dislocations, many of which were not fully remedied until the nineteenth century. Although few reliable analyses have been published, preliminary work suggests that the young nation suffered severe economic contraction between 1775 and 1790, on the order of the Great Depression of the 1930s, and that Americans during the 1780s generally knew more depression and stagnation than expansion. The southern states suffered most, undergoing drastic declines in per capita wealth (exclusive of slaves) and exports. Events in Charles County reveal the wrenching complexity, and the wide-ranging consequences, of the postwar economic crisis.[25]

Like the rest of the state, the county endured acute depression during 1786. Early in the year Tench Tilghman and Company sharply reduced its cash advances for tobacco purchases from local planters. Notwithstanding a location "well known to be equal, if not superior, to any in Charles county," a mercantile firm at the head of the Wicomico River closed its doors. By midsummer John Hoskins Stone had decided that his firm needed to reduce inventories, virtually cease offering credit, and otherwise minimize risks. Several months later he groaned, "[N]ever was money so hard to procure, I have been disappointed in every one of my resources, nor is there any such thing as attaining it at present for debts."[26]

Exacerbating the economic situation were several other problems. Among them was Henry Harford, the bastard son and heir of the last Lord Baltimore. After the war he claimed compensation for his lost province, including uncollected quitrents and the rents on proprietary lands that the state had confiscated as loyalist property. By Harford's reckoning, occupants of the manor lands in Charles County owed him more than £700 sterling in back rents *through 1784*, and landowners at least triple that amount in quitrents. Harford found the lower house of Assembly surprisingly unresistant to his claim, but in early 1786 Thomas Stone spoke "exceedingly strenuous" against it in the Senate and carried the day. Another and far more intractable source of anxiety was Maryland's public debt, incurred in prosecuting the war and maintaining republican state government. At war's end, most counties were in arrears in paying taxes to the state treasury, but Charles had the highest outstanding balance—more than £50,000 in several currencies then in circulation. That was in a county whose white population then numbered just under ten thousand people. Collecting delinquent taxes and subsequent levies would not be easy while Marylanders complained that "We are really in a most deplorable situation."[27]

Economic distress produced dramatic consequences in 1786 and 1787. At the state level, the most famous of these was agitation for paper money, which pitted the two houses of the Assembly against each other. While the lower house actually courted public pressure on this issue, the Senate successfully resisted it. As a result, the Maryland upper house, with its indirect method of election and lengthy terms of office, was seen as a counterweight to popular excesses and served as a model for the United States Senate and the electoral college under the Constitution of 1787. At the county level, several courts, including the one at Port Tobacco, adjourned their spring 1786 sessions to delay the day when debtors had to settle their accounts or go to jail. In June the most serious riot in postwar Maryland broke out at the Charles County courthouse.[28]

On the morning of June 12, 1786, the day the court was scheduled to convene, ten of twelve incumbent justices stayed away and thereby prevented a quorum. The two who appeared were Chief Justice Walter Hanson, who had been on the bench since the 1740s and had been active locally in the Revolution, and John Dent, a member of the court since the 1760s and a brigadier general of the militia early in the War for Independence. A third justice was needed to complete the quorum, but the morning passed, and none appeared. Finally, someone suggested that Hanson and Dent send for another magistrate, a common procedure. Yet "these two Gentlemen never moved one Step to forward the Execution of Justice," according to one of the attorneys who was present. Hanson and Dent later contended that they did not summon an additional magistrate because only Samuel Hanson, Jr., a war veteran and nephew of the chief justice, was within nine miles of Port Tobacco. Since he was then serving as a public tobacco inspector, " 'twas Understood that he Apprehended he could not Serve in the double Capacity of a Justice of the peace and Inspector." Two attorneys nevertheless sent an urgent message asking the younger Hanson to hurry to the courthouse. He did, only to announce that he "did not Choose" to join the court " 'til he rode home to Consult the Constitution and form of Government" about his "double Capacity"—a question that seems not to have bothered him until that day. He did not return to Port Tobacco until late in the afternoon, just as the elder Hanson and Dent were on the verge of adjourning the court. They probably regretted his arrival.[29]

When the three magistrates finally got down to business, sitting beside them on the bench were Sheriff Ware, Colonel Josias Hawkins, and Henry Massey Hanson. Neither this Hanson nor the colonel was a court official, and their presence on the bench suggests the easy familiarity among the gentry that characterized court days in eighteenth-century Maryland. Attorney John Allen Thomas, himself a former legislator, justice of St. Mary's County, and Continental officer, undoubtedly was eager to proceed, for he had filed one hundred suits that session on behalf of Alexander Hamilton's tobacco firm. No other lawyer practicing in Charles County had brought so many suits, and friends familiar with Thomas's "Early, and Active part to Accomplish the Revolution" allegedly were shocked—so shocked that some men decided to thwart the litigation. Walking to the courthouse that afternoon, Hawkins heard rumors that several people "threat'ned to Use Mr. Jno. Allen Thomas very rudely for bringing a great number of suits for British Creditors against the inhabitants of s[ai]d County."[30]

Proceeding down a docket that, by all accounts, was loaded with debt cases, the magistrates began with several defendants who had already lost their suits and faced imprisonment because they had not settled their debts. After ordering them jailed, the court abruptly reversed itself and asked the creditors' attorneys whether they *really* intended to send people to debtors' prison. Thereupon Chief Justice Hanson reportedly said that "he could not bear to send a Man to Gaol for debt" (although he had been doing just that for forty-five years). Furthermore, he expressed the hope that the legislature would exempt from prison any debtor who surrendered his effects to his creditors, especially "at a time when Debts to a most Enormous amount that have lain Dormant ever since the commencement of the War without any demand made or any person Empower'd to receive are now called for with such Rapidity that the Gaols must be filled with Wretched and Unhappy Debtors." Unmoved, Thomas persevered. After he delivered what he politely called an "Expostulation," the court returned to the docket and, as evening came on, again began sentencing delinquent debtors to jail. Thomas was sure that Hanson's soliloquy had "no Purpose under Heaven but . . . shewing the Sense of the Court, and to rouse the People."[31]

Roused they were. Sometime after taking a seat on the bench, Hawkins noticed approximately ten men lined up on the courthouse green and warned Hanson that "he fancyed that he would soon have some disagreeable company, & Mr. Hanson replyed he supposed so." The crowd quickly grew to a hundred, then rushed the courtroom "in a most riotous and tumultuous Manner" and demanded that Thomas remove his name from every British suit he had filed, an act that would render them moot. By now the mob was convinced that no other attorney would dare represent British creditors, so that with the court openly sympathetic to postponing debt litigation, only Thomas blocked the way. He, however, refused to strike his name from the docket. Thereupon a middling planter named William Ward threatened to use

"Arbitrary power," a compatriot named Joseph Nelson "spoke to some men that stood near him & bid them come on boys," and the mob pressed forward to the bar. As Thomas later told the story, "the Rioters immediately advanced and laid violent hands" on him. All Nelson and Ward publicly admitted to was taking Thomas by the coat and hand. On this point memory somehow failed the presiding justices and Hawkins, but they vividly recalled the beleaguered attorney beating a hasty retreat to the bench, ensconcing himself between the chief justice and the sheriff, and throwing himself on "the Protection of the Law and the Court."[32]

There are several versions of what happened next, and why. Thomas accused the justices of sitting "perfectly silent and apparently indifferent, not once endeavouring by Persuasion Expostulation, Threats, or even by Commanding the Officers of the Court to preserve the Peace, to rescue . . . [him] from the impending Danger." Instead the court allowed the mob to force him to submit to its demand. A shaken Thomas believed that the chief justice and Dent, "so far from discountenancing such riotous Conduct, were actually behind the Curtain supporting it" and that Hanson particularly had incited the mob, "for this very humane tender hearted Old Gentleman who a few Minutes before could not bear to see a Man goe to Gaol for debt, could sit in Court perfectly unmoved, and forgetful of his Humanity & of his Oath, see a fellow Citizen assaulted and shamefully abused by a riotous and tumultuous Mob, without using one single Effort to prevent it."[33]

The justices' version of what happened was slightly more heroic. Disclaiming any prior knowledge, much less incitement of the riot, they described themselves as "Apprehensive some Mischief was Intended to Mr. Thomas." Concluding it would be futile to order Sheriff Ware "to raise a Superior force" to quell the disturbance because "nine tenths of the Multitude the[re] present were Engaged in it," the justices took a different approach. While the chief justice counseled the rioters "not [to] be so violent" and "not to be out of temper but keep the Peace[,] observing to them that he was glad to See them all perfectly sober," John Dent tried to persuade Thomas "to Save his Person." Assured that the hapless attorney would probably satisfy it, a quieter but no less determined mob waited until Thomas, feeling very alone in the packed courtroom, agreed to drop the debt cases. The rioters then dispersed as Hanson loudly proclaimed that filing so many lawsuits was "shameful."[34]

Thomas's client, Alexander Hamilton, was in Port Tobacco but not at the courthouse during the uproar. He thought he escaped injury only because the mob could not find him. Upon returning home to Prince George's County, he learned that a man named Walter Smallwood "has been here boasting of his Exploits at the head of the Liberty Boys of Charles County" and that he and others were threatening to break into Hamilton's house to seize and burn account books and other evidence of indebtedness. Several weeks later the old Scotsman still suspected he might be assassinated and announced, "I have made my Will."[35]

In words echoed during the 1780s from Massachusetts to South Carolina, from Shays's Rebellion to the Camden court riot, Hamilton attributed the Charles County episode and continuing harassment to "some radical Deffect in our Constitution." Magistrates who disregarded their oaths actually encouraged "dangerous risings," he charged, and under the 1776 state constitution the governor lacked power to hold "the most worthless part of the Society" in check. "I am affraied by aiming at too much Liberty we shall lose it altogether," he confided to Fergusson. "You are a Republican and so must I be, and I am, with the greatest deference & respect to the established Mode of Government, of opinion that in the Nature of things it cannot long subsist in this Continent."[36]

Attorney Thomas offered his own interpretation of events. Three days after the riot he sent a memorial to Governor Smallwood and the Council, in which he first refuted any suspicion of loyalist sympathies by recalling, correctly, his "early and active Part in his Country's Cause" and his "utmost Endeavours to accomplish the Revolution." He then asked for an investigation of the justices' conduct and promised that he would bring the rioters' actions to the attention of an unspecified "Tribunal." Thomas justified these measures "not only from the Injury he has received in his own Person and Fortune, but also from the Injury the Community at large thro[ugh] him has received." And he framed what was at stake in unequivocal terms: "[I]f Proceedings of this kind pass unnoticed . . . all civil Liberty is at an End."[37]

Others agreed. Governor Smallwood reportedly was "much displeased with this affair" in his home county and "determined to have it searched to the bottom." According to Hamilton, "the independent & honest part of the Society"—that is, people attached to law, the state constitution, and peace—"are exceedingly alarmed at the Consequences of this affair and wish he may as far as the Constitution will allow him, act with a decided vigour in putting a Stop to such behaviour in the bud." On July 13 Smallwood issued a strongly worded proclamation emphasizing that "riotous Proceedings" like those at Port Tobacco threatened the welfare of the state and "are highly Criminal and punishable with severe Pains and Penalties." Admonishing "all Persons to refrain from committing such Violences and Outrages," he promised strict enforcement of the laws, urged all sheriffs and magistrates "to be vigilant and active in suppressing such disorderly and tumultuous Assemblies," and exhorted the citizenry to support those efforts. He then ordered Sheriff Ware to read the proclamation at the courthouse and other public gathering places and to pepper the county with printed copies. In addition, the proclamation was disseminated throughout the state in the *Maryland Gazette*.[38]

The governor's subsequent handling of the riot did not match the ardor of his denunciation, for the executive in revolutionary Maryland, as in other states, was notably limited. He and the Council asked, but could not require, the accused justices, the clerk of court, the sheriff, and Thomas to appear at an inquiry in Annapolis on August 10. The summonses simply read, "[W]e expect you'l attend."[39]

Imperiously—as if they were sitting on the colonial court—the justices refused. Walter Hanson declined to go to Annapolis on the ground that age and infirmities had long since prevented him from traveling more than ten miles from home. Nor did his presumably healthier colleagues deign to appear. Instead, the three men offered a single written response to Thomas's accusations. In addition, the chief justice persuaded the other men seated at the bench during the riot—Ware, Hawkins, and Henry Massey Hanson—to volunteer sworn depositions.[40]

The accused justices mounted a three-pronged defense. First, they held themselves up as examples of rectitude and impartiality. Pointedly mentioning his forty-five years on the bench, the elder Hanson asserted that in all that time "many worthy Gentlemen Eminent in their profession have practic'd the Law at our Bar . . . and I dare say that neither my self or any of my associates were ever thought wilfully failing in their duty Until we Unfortunately happened to disoblige Mr. Thomas." All three men were particularly incensed at Thomas's suggestion that Samuel Hanson, on the court less than a decade, was under the influence of his senior colleagues. The younger Hanson's retort was laden with republican rhetoric: As an officer in the war he had "Servd the public in a much higher Station" than county justice; to intimate that "he was so much of a Cypher as to have no Oppinion of his own or was under the Influence of any one living" was "very Ungenteel," to say the least.[41]

The second prong of the defense was that the courthouse had been the scene of "such Uproar and Confusion" during the riot, and the mob so large, that it would have been futile for the justices to "command the peace"—a telling admission that they had not read the riot act, ordered the mob to cease and desist, and, that failing, called out a posse. Commanding the peace "would not have answered any good purpose," mused Hawkins, because the rioters seemed "determined & sober." Asked what might have happened had a posse been called out, Henry Massey Hanson answered that "the consequence must have been Very bad, and that in his Oppinion Nothing More could have been done then what was done by the Court." The justices agreed, even as they offered assurances that "nothing in our power ever has or shall be wanting to discourage all . . . Unlawful assemblys."[42]

The coup de grace of their defense was a concerted effort to undermine Thomas's credibility. The justices labeled him passionate, angry, and so skilled at elocution that he might mislead "an ordinary Judicature," and they cautioned that he might surfeit the forthcoming inquiry with "Surmises, Conjectures or Suppositions" and exaggerations. Rather than attack their behavior, Thomas owed them thanks for saving his life, for which Walter Hanson took sole credit because he had calmed the crowd. Surely Thomas would withdraw his memorial once he read their answer—"Unless his Intention be to get us displaced, and the Commission of the Peace filld up with Members a little more plyable, and Suple, and more ready to come to his Measures."[43]

Despite their bravado the justices obviously were worried about the forthcoming inquiry. Dent even quizzed two leaders of the mob, Nelson and Ward, in the presence of several gentlemen and extracted a statement that he had not encouraged the rioters. Chief Justice Hanson was uneasy, too, because on August 3 he volunteered that if Thomas wanted his name reinstated on the one hundred debt cases, "I dare say he will meet with no hindrance from the Court." He did not reveal what the court intended to do if another riot ensued.[44]

When the governor and Council met on August 10, their only options under the state constitution were either to exonerate the justices of misconduct or to remove them from office. They had to decide, moreover, without being able to question the justices. Thomas, their accuser, came, and *he* questioned the panel. Are magistrates bound to suppress rioting? Of course, was the answer. Are magistrates bound to see that rioters are apprehended? Yes, "on proper Information" (not otherwise defined). And had the Charles County magistrates done anything to apprehend the culprits? The panel replied, "It may be asked has Mr. Thomas obliged to have them arrested?— or could the Justices have done it."[45]

In the end Smallwood and the Council declined "to exercise the only constitutional power we have with regard to persons in the Judicial Department[,] that of displacing them," and pronounced the Charles County magistrates not guilty "of any wilfull violation of their duty." No one could read that statement as commendation. The only person praised, and then rather faintly, was Thomas, whose questioning of the justices' conduct "manifested a becoming Zeal & Regard for Order & good Government."[46]

If the justices were not excoriated, the riot was. Its immediate impact and potential dangers for the administration of justice in Maryland simply could not be ignored. British debts may have been the ostensible cause, but suspicion was widespread that all debts—and even the payment of taxes—were in jeopardy. In the wake of the riot, moreover, the county court system throughout the state nearly ground to a halt. One observer commented in mid-August that "scarcely any of the Courts have since met to proceed with Business, nor is it expected they will do more than just meet & adjourn the Courts which by Law are to be held in most of the Counties this Month." The likeness to events of 1765 and 1775 was clear. This time, however, the riot and court closings threatened not the British and proprietary governments but the new republican state. Should this state prove impotent, what would replace it? Hence the alarm beneath the strident language of Smallwood's July 13 proclamation—and in a notice that twenty grand jurors on the Eastern Shore placed in the *Maryland Gazette* in September 1786. Promoting the Port Tobacco riot to a "dangerous insurrection"—one "excited, raised and committed, by a set of infatuated men in Charles county"—they warned that such disorder would have "dangerous and fatal consequences . . . if not timely discountenanced and suppressed." Under a government with a written constitution and laws adequate to address citizens' legitimate grievances, there could be no pretext for tumult. As a means of protest, rioting and court closings had lost legitimacy in Maryland.[47]

For the gentlemen justices, the entire episode carried a loud message. No matter how understandable or regrettable local problems might be, the wider community would not tolerate perceived threats to the welfare and survival of the young state government. During the fall of 1786 a chastened Charles County court "severely reprimanded & fined" the riot leaders, after which Hamilton reported, "they are quiet but do not pay any better." In 1787 the General Assembly recognized the Peace of Paris, including the debt clause, as legal within Maryland. By December, when the postwar depression was still so severe that public officers went unpaid and John Hoskins Stone lamented that "our Affairs wear such a Gloomy Aspect," calm nonetheless prevailed at the courthouse. Fergusson informed Smallwood that in a court session lasting more than two weeks, "much business was done, and the sitting Magistrates gave much consent to the Bar and Suitors. In short we have the pleasing prospect of our Court business in this County being in an agreeable situation soon to the satisfaction of all concerned." Not all: Dent and Walter Hanson stayed home.[48]

The episode at Port Tobacco was a classic eighteenth-century riot. The mob was disciplined and determined, had a specific objective, and disbanded rapidly once that objective was attained. Town dwellers and local planters closed ranks behind the rioters and the justices, whose behavior protected everyone from British debt litigation. No one came forward to name the members of the mob, to support Thomas's version and interpretation of events, or to provide a detailed narrative of those events from beginning to end. Finally, it was a common form of early American riot because what sparked it was a problem for which no legal remedy then existed.[49]

The riot broke out, it will be remembered, as the court reluctantly began consigning debtors to jail—the only possible judicial response in cases where creditors had earlier obtained judgment and the defendants proved unable to pay. During the colonial period such insolvents languished in dark, dank confinement or were sold into indentured servitude to satisfy their creditors. As Walter Hanson perceived, however, such measures seemed inappropriate for the freemen of a republican state. At the courthouse shortly before the mob formed, he "wish'd the Wisdom of the Legislature could fall upon some Expedient to Exempt the Body of a free Citizen from Imprisonment for Debt." Responding to intense public pressure, the Assembly did just that when it passed the state's first comprehensive bankruptcy act in May 1787. Charles County insolvents promptly sought refuge in it.[50]

TAXES AND TRAVAIL

While local people were absorbing lessons about public order, state officials were offering another: about fiscal responsibility. During the war the legislature abandoned poll taxes and instituted ad valorem state taxes based on wealth. In each county a board of tax commissioners appointed a salaried collector. Benjamin Cawood, who held the post in Charles County from 1779 until the end of the war, operated much like the local army recruiters and procurers of military supplies. That is, he did not always take up the full amount of taxes that were due. Although such leniency undoubtedly pleased people who were struggling with the economic burdens of the war, it also contributed to Maryland's immense public debt. By 1780 Cawood's arrearages stood at more than three hundred thousand pounds of tobacco. Revenue officers in other counties also had difficulty with collections, but by 1781 Cawood's arrearages were the largest in the state.[51]

While the war dragged on, government officers did not press the issue. Afterward, determined to support the state's financial position with more than good intentions, they moved in earnest to collect or secure outstanding balances. As a result, Cawood was called to account. In 1784 the state filed suit on his performance bond, the legal instrument in which he and his sureties pledged more than £11,000 for the faithful execution of his office. If taxpayers would not pay Cawood, the state would collect from him and his sureties.[52]

A measure of panic soon emanated from Charles County. When Robert

Brent realized that the state proposed to seize more than £3,000 of his property because "I was unfortunately drawn in to be a Security for Mr Cawood as collector," he appealed to Daniel of St. Thomas Jenifer, then the chief fiscal officer of Maryland and the man whose efforts to improve public finances were largely responsible for Brent's distress. With the specter of poverty suddenly looming before him, his wife, and their seven children, he pleaded with Jenifer to "Take Compassion on me and the Rest of the Gentl[me]n that are taken in with me and give us all the Indulgence that you Possoble can it being the only Chance to Save us poor Securitys and our famalys from Utter Ruining." Brent no doubt spoke the truth when he promised to "push" Cawood immediately and "use Every method [that] Lays in my power to gitt him to make a finish of his Arrears." He also begged Jenifer to allow Cawood time to settle his accounts, asked what "Indulgence" the sureties might obtain, and then quickly and quietly transferred much of his property to a life estate in his daughters' names.[53]

Cawood himself was more composed by the time he approached Jenifer in May 1784. By laboring "under a very heavy burthen" since 1780, he claimed, he had reduced his liability from three hundred thousand pounds of tobacco to eighteen thousand. He asked the state not to charge interest on the unpaid portion and, in lieu of tobacco, to accept paper money. Apparently Cawood somehow managed to settle his accounts, for no record of seizure and sale of his or Brent's property has been found. His successors were not so fortunate.[54]

Charles Mankin began his three-year term as tax collector in 1783 and, aided by high postwar tobacco prices, collected everything due for the year. Then, as economic depression settled over the Chesapeake, he, too, fell into arrears. An energetic, insistent official who sometimes used "very Improper Language," Mankin started seizing delinquents' property in lieu of taxes, but that proved a useless way to raise revenues because everyone boycotted his distress sales. Although he managed to move Charles from dead last to midway among Maryland counties in terms of tax arrearages, he left office owing almost £10,000 in uncollected taxes.[55]

By now Maryland officials were growing impatient. In May 1786 the state treasurer contemplated whether to bring suit on the performance bonds of delinquent collectors and, within the year, did so. Because Mankin and former collectors from other counties were still in arrears in 1787, the governor pressed them to send remittances at once. Unable to oblige, Mankin soon was defending his honor against rumors that he had converted county tax money to Virginia real estate. In 1789 the state foreclosed on him and two sureties, including Francis Ware, who had pledged money to guarantee that Mankin would fulfill his collecting duties. When their property was auctioned off that

September, Mankin lost everything: two hundred acres of land (aptly named Mankin's Venture and Mankin's Folly), six lots in Port Tobacco, and all his slaves, livestock, and furniture. The sureties lost another four hundred acres and two slaves. Because no one offered a reasonable price for the property, the state bought most of it at the appraised value and later attempted, with mixed results, to resell it. All of it, however, did not entirely cover Mankin's arrearages; as of late 1789 he still owed the state more than £4,000 in back taxes.[56]

Well before anyone knew for sure that Mankin and his sureties were headed toward financial disaster, no one wanted to succeed him in office. The burdens of tax collecting were too heavy, the potential consequences of failure too high. Ultimately the county board of tax commissioners persuaded one of its members to take the job. He was Hoskins Hanson, also a justice of the peace. Another commissioner reluctantly agreed to act as security. Filling the position was so difficult, asserted the board, "that one of the Commissioners became Collector, and another of them security for him, which wou'd not have happened if any other person cou'd have been got to undertake the Collection."[57]

It was Hanson's sorry task to deal with Charles County taxpayers during the depths of the depression. Not even his status as a magistrate helped him succeed. As of November 1786, toward the end of his first year in office, people owed him £7,146. Because of abysmal collection rates throughout Maryland, the Assembly began working on legislation to suspend tax payments temporarily, and even before it passed, John Hoskins Stone intimated that Hanson should cease collecting at once. "It will be hard on our people to force them to Pay," Stone argued, "when there is no collections in any other part of the State."[58]

No one forced them to pay, then or after the Assembly's reprieve expired in May 1787. As of June 30 the state treasurer had yet to see a single shilling of 1786 tax money from Charles County. Indeed, the commissioners had not even submitted the assessment lists. "We think it high time it was done," fumed the governor, "& request you to do it immediately that the Collector may be called on for Payment." The commissioners' reply: Their "extraordinary exertions" notwithstanding, the lists must have gone astray.[59]

For their agreement, however unenthusiastic, to aid the state government, Hanson and his securities suffered the same fate as Mankin and his. Predictably by now, the state sued on his performance bond and in 1789 auctioned off nearly a thousand acres of Hanson's land. His securities lost well over twelve hundred additional acres.[60]

Such disasters, which were not unique to the county during the 1780s, obviously could not continue if the state hoped to retain any tax collectors. In late 1789 the Assembly therefore halted the distress sales. Shortly thereafter it also designated an agent to arrange with collectors appointed since 1783 a schedule whereby they could remit their arrearages and interest within fifteen months. If they paid the appraised value, they could even reclaim title to property the state bought in 1789 and still retained. Neither Hanson nor Mankin seems to have met those terms because property seized from them and their sureties subsequently was offered for sale.[61]

Parallel to and, in Charles County, entwined with the tax collectors' travails were those of the sheriffs. Their ability to exact revenues for which they were legally responsible—including county tax levies, court fines, lawyers' fees, and marriage, peddlers', tavern, and liquor licenses—also suffered during the 1780s. And that placed in jeopardy their large performance bonds. Worse, three men successively elected sheriff—Benjamin Cawood (1779–82), Charles Mankin (1782–85), and Francis Ware (1785–88)—stood in double jeopardy, the first two because they served as both sheriff and tax collector and Ware because he agreed to act as surety for Mankin. Public offices that would have enhanced their wealth in better times, instead impoverished them and some of their sureties during the 1780s.[62]

Ware's downfall began when Mankin defaulted on his tax collections. In April 1787 the General Court ordered the county coroner to seize property from Ware to help cover the arrearages. (The court could not follow customary procedure and contact the sheriff because Ware *was* the sheriff.) By then he was also in trouble for defaulting on his own collections. In early 1789, shortly after leaving office, he assigned all monies owed him to his sureties. They apparently forestalled foreclosure by indemnifying the state on his behalf and then, to redeem their losses, tried to pry shillings from planters' purses. At that they proved no more adroit than Ware and eventually advertised his remaining property for sale. But no one would buy it, perhaps because the sureties were allowing him to live as a tenant on his former land.[63]

While the travails of the county sheriffs and tax collectors were the most sensational, at least one other class of public officers experienced similar problems. These were tobacco inspectors at whose warehouses British raiders had destroyed or stolen tobacco "during the tumults of the late war." Because they stored planters' tobacco until shipment, inspectors, too, had to post performance bonds and assume personal liability for losses. Compensating planters for hogsheads destroyed at the Chicamuxen warehouse exhausted one inspector's wealth and landed him in debtors' prison. Only the 1787 Maryland bankruptcy law effected his release. The estates of deceased inspectors were equally liable, as two widows sadly learned when they petitioned for relief. The Assembly turned a deaf ear to their plea for a county-wide levy to reimburse planters for property destroyed in raids on the Pomonkey and

Nanjemoy warehouses. Not even acts of war absolved local officials from the obligations of their performance bonds.[64]

If one steps back and views the officers' difficulties in a broader context, one sees them caught in a revolution that had yet to run its course. During the war American Independence hung in the balance; during the 1780s republican government was at stake. From 1775 to 1783 the state government depended on the counties to support the war with everything from fresh recruits to newly harvested wheat, but whether and how quotas of men and supplies were filled depended upon the people who organized the local war effort. When the state first enacted ad valorem taxation, householders could pay in commodities sorely needed to feed the army. After the war the state wanted taxes paid promptly and in currency, not wheat or pork, for without regularly collected revenues—not just what local agents of the state managed to take up—the government could neither meet current expenses nor retire the war debt. And without regularly collected revenues, the state could no more maintain viable government than if the courts fell victim to mobs.

"When Taxes once become odious," mused a resident of Annapolis in 1784, "I believe we shall find too little Energy in our republican Government, to Enforce a Collection of them." The challenge to state officials during the 1780s was to prove that prophecy wrong even during bad times, no matter how much or little taxpayers, county collectors, and sheriffs cooperated. Although the Assembly sometimes temporarily deferred tax collections, it did not revoke them. Collectors and sheriffs either had to remit everything people owed or had to suffer the consequences. So, too, tobacco inspectors who "could not prevent" destruction at the hands of the British nevertheless had to indemnify planters for property destroyed at the warehouses. There was no recognition from the state that in circumstances beyond the control of local officials, the community should assume or at least share the burden.[65]

The system through which officeholders were called to account, the performance bond, had worked well during the colonial period, when relatively few demands were placed on it. In the wake of a costly and disruptive war, in the crisis over collection of public revenues, the system broke down. In Charles County and elsewhere in Maryland during the 1780s, public offices involving collection of revenues became paths to personal financial ruin.

No one could have been more shocked by this than Francis Ware, who did as much as any man in the county to forward the Revolution. In 1787, just as the state moved against him, his property was assessed at nearly £2,300. By the early 1790s he was too poor to qualify to vote, much less hold offices that so recently had been his for the asking. The old soldier's fortunes never recovered. In 1800 friends and acquaintances asked the legislature to authorize a county tax for his support, but it rejected the stigma of public relief for a man who had served in the Maryland Line with "distinguished bravery and fidelity." Instead the Assembly, citing Ware's ill health and "misfortunes arising from those acts of benevolence which the duties of society often render indispensable," granted him half pay for life at the rank of lieutenant colonel.[66]

Imagine the tensions created when "the duties of society" caught Ware and other local officers between the citizenry and a determined state government. Certainly Robert Brent was not the only surety who, abruptly confronted with the prospect of ruin, "pushed" the man whose performance bond he had signed. Nor could Thomas Stone have been the only attorney who let the sheriff know that "I must have what is due Me" in fees. And certainly the sheriffs and tax collectors pushed the citizenry in turn, as Joseph Nelson learned. At November court 1780 Nelson pleaded no contest to a charge of pulling Virlinda Haislope from her horse, tearing her Clothing, and "making use of many threats to Accomplish his Designs." Assessed a £30 fine, he petitioned the court to remit it and, when Sheriff Cawood came by to collect, announced that he did not owe it. There the matter rested until Cawood got in trouble with the state. He then reappeared and demanded payment in specie that, because of postwar deflation, reportedly was worth six times the value of the original fine. One of the leaders of the courthouse riot, it will be recalled, was named Joseph Nelson.[67]

Although the sheriffs and collectors pressed citizens hard at times—as Cawood did in confronting Nelson, and Mankin in seizing delinquent taxpayers' possessions—the huge balances on their books when they left office suggest their lack of success. Householders who owed taxes, fees, and fines to the state or county were not without recourse. One was the communal cohesiveness Mankin encountered when he tried to sell delinquents' property but discovered that no one would even attend the sales. Then, too, some delinquents adopted a more individualistic approach: They simply ran away.[68]

From the vantage of local officers, *they* bore the brunt of concerted efforts by the state government to set things right after the war, by both ensuring fiscal responsibility and, in the case of the courthouse riot, quelling public disorder. The state also intervened in a third area, the size and composition of the county court and the orphans' court. In 1786—the year of acute depression, the riot, and no tax collections—the state reduced the number of magistrates, "not from any Doubt of their Sufficiency to discharge the Trust," the governor assured them, but for the sake of efficiency. The following year the justices of the orphans' court asked the governor to fill vacancies on that body with whomever he "Judge[d] most proper," all the while assuming that he would choose from among the magistrates in order of seniority. When he did not, Walter Hanson, whose seniority made him chief justice of both local courts, was outraged and warned that the slight would "give great umbrage to the Gent who had by Custom a right to expect the appointment."[69]

By the time Hanson vented his anger in the autumn of 1787—at the very moment when a stronger national government was being launched—public officeholding and the conduct of public business were in disarray in Charles County. The combination of a county court under a cloud; former tax collectors, sheriffs, and tobacco inspectors in default and heading toward insolvency with their sureties in tow; and state intervention in the composition of the local courts alternately overwhelmed and infuriated an elite that previously had been content to exercise power and garner the status it accorded. Now Hanson sighed: "I heartily wish our County . . . could be at Peace and the Publick business Carried on in a regular and Constant manner."[70]

The gentry reacted to the perils of officeholding, republican style, with a rash of resignations and refusals to serve. Whether citizens could obtain public services, even access to the courts, became problematic. Colonel William Harrison declined appointment to the orphans' court. It could not always raise a quorum. After less than a year in office a tobacco inspector resigned with the explanation that "the business [is] So Very Fatiging & Perplexing, think my Self not Equal to the Task." His successor did not last a year. Keeping an incumbent coroner became as difficult as finding a tax collector.[71]

Someone had to serve as county coroner because "the frequency of accidents which happen on the water" meant that bodies regularly washed ashore and, furthermore, because "the business of that office has very much increased owing to the delinquencies of Sheriffs and Collectors." In early 1787 the state appointed Francis Boucher Franklin, who promptly resigned. His successor soon asked to be excused. A third man resigned, citing old age and infirmities (which did not prevent him from accepting the same post several years later, after a measure of tranquillity had returned to the county). Next, Charles Mankin—despite or perhaps because of his desperate financial straits—volunteered: "I should be glad to serve." His letters of recommendation were unenthusiastic. Delinquent as both sheriff and tax collector, he was not appointed coroner. In 1789 Franklin finally consented to serve again, but then the state foreclosed on Mankin, Ware, and their sureties. After three months in office he gave up because "ever since my appointment I have had to serve most of the precepts [writs] against the sheriffs & their deputies which has been attended with great risque and trouble."[72]

As for the magistrates, they staged something of a strike because of the appointment of nonmagistrates to the orphans' court in 1787. The governor's action "has given great Offense" and allegedly was widely regarded as illegal, according to Justice Samuel Hanson. Hoskins Hanson, passed over for an orphans' court appointment, thought himself "ill used"—and understandably so. For what disqualified him for the appointment was the tax collectorship that he had accepted only reluctantly and that soon was to cost him nearly a thousand acres of land because of his defaults. So incensed was Hanson that he threatened not to serve in the magistracy, and his was not an idle remark. Soon most of the justices refused to perform their duties. Observed Samuel Hanson in October 1787: "At present it is very difficult & troublesome to get Business done from the remoteness [from the courthouse] of the few Magistrates who will do it." The spirit of noblesse oblige faltered when the magistrates thought themselves under attack.[73]

The county court sank into lassitude. Several justices either resigned or, because they lived "remote" from the courthouse, seldom appeared on the bench. Those in attendance in December 1787 reported, "[I]ts with much difficulty the Court business can be Carried on in the manner it ought to be." In early 1789 Daniel Jenifer stated, "Tho it should seem from looking over the list of Magistreates, there are enough in this County, Yet . . . from a variety of Circumstances, it often happens that a sufficient number to conduct the business is not found on the Bench." Accomplishing out-of-court business was even more difficult, especially since fewer magistrates meant enlarged jurisdictions.[74]

The Assembly solved the problem—not by honoring requests from the county for more magistrates but by drastically altering the court. In 1790 the Assembly created five circuit courts in Maryland, each composed of a chief judge and two associate judges from each county in the judicial district. The old county courts were reduced to three men each—the chief circuit judge and the associate judges from that county—and any one of them could conduct judicial business. No longer did justices of the peace sit on the bench. Their duties became largely administrative: levying local taxes, overseeing tobacco inspection, and issuing licenses.[75]

In Charles County reorganization of the judiciary was the last act of a drama begun the day of the courthouse riot. When the curtain fell, the single most important center of local power, gentry power, was dramatically changed. The old court had survived the proprietary regime's demise, Independence, and the war. It succumbed, as did the revenue officers, to the disarray of the 1780s and the agenda of Maryland's postwar government.

The new court reinvigorated the administration of local justice, but lassitude among other officials continued into the 1790s. The county sheriff was late in submitting polling results in the presidential election of 1792. A man opened a store and sold liquor without a license (for which he was fined) because he could not find anyone to issue the license. Roads became impassable, in one case because the overseer was in jail for debt. And in 1794 state officials waited in vain for the justices of the peace to recommend a slate of tobacco inspectors, then finally asserted, "[A]s we have been at a loss to understand your intentions, we would recommend a stricter attention in future to . . . your duty in this particular."[76]

Although the breakdown of local government in the county may have been more severe than elsewhere in Maryland (the courthouse riot was the most serious civil disturbance of the postwar years), it was far from unique. The Assembly several times postponed tax collections because collectors in many counties were in arrears and unable to fulfill their obligations. The state's prodding of local officials and seizure and sale of their property also occurred in many counties. And the 1790 law that reorganized the courts cited widespread problems of inefficiency and lack of uniformity in the administration of justice. The exquisite difficulties, the wrenching transformation of local government and officeholding in the postwar county, formed parts of a much larger mosaic, one that spanned the entire state.[77]

The disarray in local government may also go far toward explaining Marylanders' willingness to embrace a stronger national government under the Constitution of 1787—one that could effectively maintain order and foster American economic development. They scarcely needed Shays's Rebellion in Massachusetts to convince them that the Revolution had been enormously destabilizing and that the bold experiment in self-government was threatened. When elections for the state's ratifying convention were held in the spring of 1788, all but three counties chose delegations that supported the Federal Constitution. Charles County voters sided solidly with the majority.[78]

A DIMINISHING BOUNTY

If postwar dislocations and readjustments wreaked havoc with the morale, status, and fortunes of the county's officeholders, they had a lot of company. In one way or another, everyone in the county experienced substantial stress after 1785. Besides debts and taxes that would not go away, a state government that would not relent, and trade that did not fully revive, inhabitants worked land and fished waters that were not as bountiful as in the colonial period. Generations of planters had used fields sequentially for tobacco, corn, and wheat, with decreasing fertility until the land was restored by lying fallow for some years. But growers disrupted the cycle, first when the tobacco trade collapsed and the army begged for grain during the war, and again when the trade languished during the 1780s, then collapsed at the outbreak of the Napoleonic Wars in 1793. The consequences of changed agricultural practices were both economic and environmental.

Robert Fergusson, the Port Tobacco merchant, chronicled the decline of tobacco cultivation. The problem was not that the land was incapable of yielding good crops, for leaf harvested in the county sometimes surpassed that grown in surrounding areas. While loading a cargo in 1792, Fergusson informed his business partner that "I can with truth say a parcel of better Tobacco from the Warehouses of this Neighborhood I think never went from my hands, especially that from Portobacco." At the same time, he bewailed the "wretched condition of the Tobacco Trade [that] makes us rather think of a curtail than an extension of our business." The problem with tobacco was not land and leaf but a stagnant trade.[79]

What Fergusson labeled "this adverse time for business" soon worsened. In 1792 he fretted over "the obstinate stagnation" of the European market. Not even a drought and short crops from Maryland to Georgia seemed to "make any impression on the sales of Tob[acc]o in Europe." The following year he bemoaned a new threat to the Chesapeake's economic vitality: "[D]isagreeable intelligence" pictured the French revolutionary army overrunning the Low Countries and sealing off the Rhine River. The best foreign markets for Potomac tobacco were now "the seat of war" and remained so during the Napoleonic era. Planters reacted by cutting production. Fergusson calculated that they would bring less than three hundred hogsheads to the public warehouse near Port Tobacco in 1793. Before the War for Independence, "the q[uanti]ty annually inspected here was 1000 Hhds [hogsheads]."[80]

Prudent growers sowed other cash crops. With wheat bringing a dollar per bushel locally, stores stocked up on scythes and reaping hooks. Pre-1793 advertisements for plantations often claimed that, as one seller put it, "This land is particularly adapted to the produce of wheat, indian corn and tobacco." Post-1793 notices referred to thriving orchards and "soil well adapted to the produce of grain, and particularly to that of wheat and rye," but seldom mentioned tobacco. Some people planted grasses and in other ways tried to maintain soil fertility. Others did not, and hurt the land. Plowing associated with wheat cultivation did the same.[81]

The tenant farms of St. Thomas Manor provide the best-documented example of how severe the damage could be when traditional tidewater agricultural methods were abandoned. For most of the colonial period the tenancies were family farms with few indentured servants and even fewer slaves. Notwithstanding more than a century of cultivation, long-fallow agricultural practices replenished the soil and maintained crop yields. Tenants had incentives to conserve and improve the farms because they held lifetime leases and because sons often succeeded their fathers. After the Revolution the Jesuits rapidly converted the farms to short-term leases, carrying higher rents, in order to realize immediate income. Only slaveholders more interested in exploitation than careful husbandry could afford them. The newcomers worked more land, and much more intensively, than earlier tenants; swiftly exhausted the soil and timber; and allowed buildings, fences, and orchards to deteriorate. By 1800 the farms no longer produced enough food or building materials to support the occupants.[82]

Many other tracts suffered a similar fate. By the mid-nineties some land-owners advertising their plantations for sale were curiously silent about what crops would grow there. They spoke of good fencing, "salubrious and pleas-ant" water, level land, valuable woods, fine meadows, adequate dwellings, and even the distance to the new national capital, but not a word about tobacco, grain, or any other cash crop. To a northerner traveling the road from Port Tobacco southeast to the Potomac, the countryside seemed bleak. Exhausted fields, which he mistakenly blamed on tobacco cultivation, lay abandoned and produced only sedge grass so coarse that cattle avoided it.[83]

Rains rived overworked fields with gullies. Runoff from the land turned streams brown and choked them with silt. That was not an entirely new phenomenon in the county. In 1773 an effort was made to relocate Pile's warehouse because it was "extremely inconvenient to those in trade, on account of the creek's being fill'd up in such manner that the craft taking off the tobacco are often detained for want of water." After the war what had been a serious inconvenience became an ecological disaster. Wharves from Mattawoman Creek to the Wicomico River became landlocked. One problem was solved, though. Flooding, probably intensified by rapid runoff associated with changed land-use patterns, swept away Pile's warehouse in July 1788. The flood also destroyed the rebuilt inspection warehouse at Cedar Point.[84]

Large amounts of silt-laden runoff entering the Potomac River adversely affected its ecology. True, some still boasted about "capital fisheries," "fine fish, oysters, and crabs . . . caught in abundance," and "the great fishery of Patowmack" lying offshore. But the Jesuits began supplementing slave diets with fish caught off the Carolina coast. And when a landowner advertised three herring and shad landings for rent in the Pomonkey area in 1789, a rejoinder foretold the future. The owner claimed that the landings were "long noted for the quantity of fish taken at them," featured a smooth, clear shore-line for drying and good houses for curing, and attracted "numerous custom-ers by land and water." Immediately someone countered, "Profitable fisheries have been formerly carried on there, but now the time is past, and not likely to return."[85]

AMID TRYING TIMES

Past times unlikely to return: That theme ran through much of life in Charles County toward the end of the eighteenth century. Even as people

went about customary activities—from marking land boundaries to ostraciz-
ing a woman suspected of being "a Fornicatress, strumpet, and prostitute"
who would "converse unlawfully . . . with . . . either white, or Black"—in
countless ways they also responded to the changed circumstances of their
lives and society.[86]

Optimistic plans and projects taken up just after the war—signs of dedication to improving the society—frequently were delayed. Consider the building of Charlotte Hall School. In 1785 the trustees chose the architectural plan
and advertised for workmen. Then the depression hit and construction
lagged. The brickmaker could not get the trustees to accept or pay for thousands of bricks they had ordered. With the building not yet started, the
trustees adjourned in 1788 and did not reconvene for almost five years. As of
1795 the school was only half finished because of lack of money. Whereas the
trustees had expected to realize more than £1,000 sterling from sale of the
colonial free school lands in Charles, Prince George's, and St. Mary's counties,
they actually received much badly depreciated Continental money. According
to one observer, had not people "dealt thus fraudulently with the visitors
[trustees], Charlotte Hall would . . . be richly endowed." Private benefactors,
too, did not always fulfill their pledges.[87]

Still, the trustees persisted and ultimately succeeded. Not only did they
anticipate the school building being ready by the end of 1795, but they also
congratulated themselves that their "exertions for the promotion of this laud-
able institution promise fair that it will in a short time become a flourishing
seminary of learning." By the early nineteenth century, Charlotte Hall accommodated up to 120 students, 70 as boarders, and supported a teaching staff of
5, including a French instructor. A departing student sighed in 1808: "I
cannot help expressing the regret I expect to feel not only at leaving a place,
which the residence of nearly six years has rendered almost as familiar and
natural as a home, and where I have formed several strong and lasting attachments among my fellow-pupils, but also at parting with my faithful Instructors." The school survived until the mid-twentieth century.[88]

Perhaps because Charlotte Hall was so long abuilding, parents in the Nanjemoy area approached the president of the College of New Jersey for help in
finding someone to instruct twenty to twenty-five boys in English and Latin,
writing and arithmetic, geography, surveying, and navigation. "The District
of Nanjemoy like every other place in the Southern States," they wrote before
Charlotte Hall opened, "is at a great loss for an instructor of Youth." A
qualified person who agreed to stay four years would receive £245 plus room,
board, and washing "fitting for his station."[89]

Other groups that persisted amid trying times were Episcopal and Catholic
congregations. Construction of St. Ignatius Church and the restoration and
expansion of Durham Church were completed in the 1790s. While the large

St. Ignatius structure symbolized Catholics' attainment of religious liberty in Maryland, the refurbishing of Durham was meant to encourage "A more Strict adherance [to the] Tenets of our persuasion, and a more uniform attendance and fixed attention to our publick Devotion." That doctrinal matters were in a "lethargic and relaxed" state seemed "no less obvious, than the damaged s[tate] of the church and parochial affairs since the commencement of the Revolution." A clerical visitor soon pronounced the situation much improved.[90]

Extensive work at Trinity Church dragged on for years. Since 1786 the vestry had been committed to renovating the sanctuary and churchyard. However, financial chaos in the county—to which the tax-collecting situation graphically attested—forced suspension of fund raising until the end of 1789. Meanwhile, the walls and roof of the old structure were dismantled, and materials saved for the reconstruction. Hoping to attract funds, the vestry voted to conduct a lottery and optimistically decided to build a church large enough to hold the congregation. Because too little money was raised, a smaller church was finally begun in 1791. Two years later it was far enough along that Thomas John Claggett, Episcopal bishop of Maryland, came to

TRINITY PARISH CHURCH, *as rebuilt beginning in 1791. Photograph by Thomas N. Lee.*

consecrate the building and confirm thirty-one communicants, three of them enslaved blacks. But thereafter enthusiasm dimmed. At the end of the century Trinity Church stood in "unfinished condition" for lack of funds, and it no longer had a resident rector because the Reverend Hatch Dent had left to become principal of Charlotte Hall School. He returned to the parish only to preach.[91]

Alongside these communal efforts, individuals tried to overcome adverse economic conditions. And in reacting to their own adversities, individuals cumulatively reshaped the larger society in profound ways, as the experiences of slaves demonstrate. To begin with one example, Thomas Stone was a prudent man not given to risky ventures. He nonetheless imbibed enough postwar optimism to invest in land, the great mill near Port Tobacco, an ironworks at Baltimore, and the Potomac Company. During the depression, as he struggled to remain solvent, his slaves suffered the consequences. In April 1785 the blacks he owned in Charles County lived in at least four separate groups: Four men and a girl were with an overseer, "Vilet & child hired out. Ann & child, Will, Marget at the Mill—Sal[,] Guss, young Clare hired out." As the depression intensified and Christmas Day approached—the day when contracts for slave hire often began—he told his brother Walter, "I shall have some Negroes to hire next Year, Carpenter Tom . . . Bob . . . Sal for any thing above her Victuals & Clothes, Violet d[itt]o & Ann, Heth . . . Guss. . . . I should be very glad to sell some of these if proper prices could be had. The Children of Clare I would not sell. You may advertise Negroes to hire."[92]

Later, at his town house in Annapolis, Stone was feeling desperate and urged Walter, "I want Money exceedingly & must request You to receive as much as You can for Me." His plans for the slaves were still unsettled: "I really do not know what to do with the Negroes." Now he wanted to hire out Violet, Heth, Tom, and Ann, as well as "Sall unless a good price can be got for sale of her, & Bob. . . . Guss & Clare to be hired unless Guss can be sold." A bondman at Stone's mill was to remain there, but another, who was hired out, was to join him "as soon as his time is out." Stone no longer needed to worry about Marget; she was dead. Heth and Sal, at least, soon were hired out, but almost immediately Stone asked their new masters to release one of them, for he wanted another slave in Annapolis. The world in which his blacks lived and moved and tried to hold together some semblance of family and community was constantly changing in the mid-1780s.[93]

So, too, was the world of many other local blacks. Even as some entered the ranks of free blacks through freedom suits, manumissions, and running away, the vast majority remained enslaved, their destinies inextricably joined to those of their masters. For sale: "one NEGRO WOMAN"; "two likely NEGROES"; "A Negro Carpenter, And Several Negro Women and Children"; "twelve valuable NEGRO SLAVES, consisting of men, women and children"; "will be EXPOSED to PUBLIC SALE . . . BETWEEN 15 and 20 likely healthy young country-born SLAVES"; "UPWARDS of twenty valuable NEGROES, consisting of likely young fellows, breeding women, boys, and girls"; "TWENTY-TWO NEGROES . . . all valuable and hearty, except one"; "TWENTY-FIVE negroes"; "twenty-nine negroes, with their increase"; "THIRTY very likely NEGROES"; "THIRTY-NINE NEGROES, men women and children"; "UPWARDS of fifty likely and valuable NEGROES." And on and on. The largest group of blacks was put up for sale by the executors of General Smallwood's estate. When "the Angel of death . . . summoned" him in 1792, he left a large estate but had "run in debt more than was imagined." Every one of his slaves—there were fifty-six of them in 1790—was auctioned off to satisfy his creditors.[94]

The cumulative effect of masters' decisions was rapid dispersal of the African-American population, both within and beyond the county's borders. Locally, slaveholding expanded to more and more plantations. In less than a decade it jumped about a third, from 46.5 percent of property owners in 1782 to 60 percent of household heads as of 1790. Charles thereby earned the dubious distinction of having the highest proportion of slaveholding households of any county in Maryland. Because sellers extended as much as two years' of credit, buyers could envision paying at least partly with the profits of the blacks' labor. That may explain what seems to have been an exodus from large to small plantations.[95]

Planting families that added a slave or two, or acquired them for the first time, might anticipate somewhat higher incomes, lightened manual labor, and the enhanced status that came with owning blacks. Here was opportunity amid the economic turmoil of the postwar era. On the other hand, the relocated slaves had to adjust to new surroundings, the demands and idiosyncrasies of new owners, and, perhaps, greater difficulties in maintaining family and communal ties. Yet, other slaves who were sold had no hope at all of perpetuating such ties. Spanish slave ships carried some of them away, and Americans from as far south as Georgia came to Charles County and bought bond labor. Leaving loved ones behind must have been as wrenching for these people as the passage from Africa had been for their forebears.[96]

Even if an owner sold off or hired out every slave, he or she might fail to stave off financial ruin. A startling number of the elite, not just officeholders, slipped into insolvency after 1785. The downfall of a man like Thomas Howe Ridgate was almost predictable. Overextended in trade and forced into bankruptcy before the war, he repeated the scenario afterward, so that his debts amounted to approximately twice his assets when he died unexpectedly in 1790. At an auction of his personal property his widow, Elizabeth, moved among the crowd, buying furniture for herself and child, and she had to sue to secure her dower rights to the real estate. Ridgate's demise helped bankrupt his largest creditor, Robert Morris of Philadelphia, whose claim against the estate was £8,800 sterling in 1796.[97]

If Ridgate's financial ruin was predictable, Gerard B. Causin's was not. He represented the promise of the Revolution for Roman Catholics in Maryland. Scion of a family that arrived from France during the 1630s, Causin's grandfather rose to Charles County magistrate, militia officer, and provincial assemblyman, then was barred from office after 1689 because of his religion. The family retired to private life at Causin Manor overlooking the Potomac, and there Gerard lived on 750 acres of prime land with an ever-increasing number of slaves. Given his lineage and wealth, he was one of the county's most prominent Catholics and could reasonably expect to gain public office with the Revolution.[98]

He did. After collecting money locally for the war effort, Causin won election to the lower house of Assembly in 1780, and three years later he was appointed a county tax commissioner. He also joined the board of trustees of Charlotte Hall School. And then the promise of the Revolution withered for him. At least partly because of business connections with Ridgate, Causin by 1789 was facing financial ruin. He tried to extricate himself by selling his plantation and slaves, but that year, with the state auctioning off sheriffs', tax collectors', and sureties' property, he could not dispose of much. The seventy-five slaves attributed to him in the 1790 federal census, the second-largest lot in the county, belied his desperate situation. Soon he deeded the manor and thirty-nine blacks to Alexander Hamilton, the tobacco factor, to satisfy a debt. Hamilton could not sell the land either. So Causin, like Francis Ware, became a tenant on the very plantation that had recently made him one of the wealthiest men in his society. Like Ware, he remained trapped in insolvency.[99]

A number of propertied women also suffered spectacular financial decline. Judith Chase, whose assessed worth was over £1,300 in 1782, left only "some effects" at her death in 1790 and many claims against the estate. Rachael Forry, the tavernkeeper, had a reputation as "a pains taken Woman rather Cautious than otherwise," but she made a fatal error. Having purchased the confiscated John Glassford and Company store in Port Tobacco, she needed money to pay for it and sensed opportunity in a small parcel of merchandise that a stranger, Patrick McGuire, brought to town in 1781. Too quickly she not only agreed to sell the goods but was persuaded to sign a document that illiteracy prevented her from reading. Her verbal agreement to sell on consignment and take a percentage of the profit became, on paper, a contract to purchase the goods outright, at highly inflated prices and for tobacco rather

RIDGATE (CHIMNEY) HOUSE. *One of the finest buildings in Port Tobacco when it was constructed about 1770, the house passed to a succession of owners after the heavily indebted Ridgate died in 1790. By the 1930s it, along with much of the town, was deteriorated and abandoned. After 1895 Port Tobacco no longer served as the county seat, and even the Episcopal church was removed, stone by stone, to the new seat at La Plata, a few miles to the east. Courtesy of the Maryland Historical Society.*

than paper money. "The common Voice of the People" rightly concluded that Forry had been cheated by the "Villianous" contract and "had Compleatly ruined herself." McGuire, on the other hand, "boasted that he had cleared forty thousand weight of Tobacco Since [he] had come to Charles County," all at her expense. The contract was adjudged legally binding. Forry paid McGuire more than seventy thousand pounds of tobacco but was still in debt to him. And in 1789, following her death, her Port Tobacco property was auctioned off for his benefit.[100]

Life is filled with kindnesses and betrayals, with rising hopes, dashed expectations, and ambivalent outcomes, and an impression of unrelieved decline and desperation would distort the truth. For alongside people who lost everything were others who lived well. That certainly was true of the family of Gustavus Richard Brown, the physician who had prescribed noxious medicine for the Englishman Nicholas Cresswell just before the war. After serving in the Continental Army, Brown returned to the county and built Rose Hill, a stately, gracious home overlooking the Port Tobacco River. Fascinated with botany, he designed gardens and boxwood plantings that today still suggest the beauty of his world. Yet even as Rose Hill stood witness to continuing gentility, signs of impoverishment were unrelenting.[101]

Prewar travelers, including Cresswell, wrote of the county's "pleasant" landscape and cultivated fields, hospitable people who "appear to live very well and [to be] exceedingly happy," and slaves who seemed to forget, or at least ignore, "their miserable condition" while singing and dancing together on Sundays. Now compare those evocations with the only extended account of a journey through the county in the 1790s. Isaac Weld, having made his way south to Port Tobacco, did not find a bustling market town. Its wooden buildings he pronounced "very poor." The fieldstone Episcopal church, once "an ornament to the place . . . is now entirely out of repair; the windows are all broken, and the road is carried through the church-yard, over the graves, the paling that surrounded it having been torn down." As he proceeded farther south, following the route taken by countless overland travelers before him, Weld thought that "the country . . . wears a most dreary aspect." In addition to worn-out fields, "the remains of several good houses," now abandoned, imparted an air of loneliness, which was reinforced because "the face of a human being is so rarely met with."[102]

About twelve miles from Port Tobacco, at a Potomac River ferry, he discovered "one of those old dilapidated mansions that formerly was the residence perhaps of some wealthy planter, and at the time when the fields yielded their rich crops of tobacco would have afforded some refreshment to the weary traveller." Now "it was the picture of wretchedness and poverty." Although the house served as a tavern, scarcely a bite of food could be bought, and Weld passed his time watching the many slaves who lived in nearby "huts." To him the blacks seemed wretched and half starved, with the women and men clothed in rags "and the children . . . running about stark naked." Once—and not long ago, he realized—"the country was . . . very different."[103]

Frustrations over the assorted and seemingly endless ills that plagued Charles County inhabitants finally were vented against an old enemy, Great Britain. Congressman George Dent provided the spark in the spring of 1794, shortly after the outbreak of war in Europe caused the county's tobacco trade to collapse once more. In a letter to his lower Western Shore constituents, Dent accused Britain of violating the nation's honor and integrity, especially by seizing American merchant vessels on the high seas. He also voiced a complaint that came straight out of the Potomac Valley—"our commerce, from whence great part of our resources have hitherto flowed, [is] being almost annihilated"—and he called upon people to return to "habits of economy and domestic manufacture, which, in a trial similar to that now threatened, was wisely and successfully exerted." The congressman almost seemed eager for the United States to be "driven from the shade of peace, and

ROSE HILL (CA. 1784). *After returning home from the Continental Army, Dr. Gustavus Richard Brown built Rose Hill, the finest example of early Federal architecture in the county. The house site commands a stunning view of the Port Tobacco river valley. Photograph by Thomas N. Lee.*

forced to a solemn appeal to arms in vindication of violated rights, and in defence of every thing dear to freemen."[104]

Dent struck a nerve—and stirred memories twenty years in the making. Charles County "citizens" (as distinguished from the colonists of 1774 and 1775) gathered at the courthouse on April 4, 1794, this time to consider European and American affairs "so far as they relate to us." When Britain's "cruel and unjust" war against America ended, they self-servingly maintained, "we generously dropt all resentment for injuries past . . . and gave her the most valuable part of our trade." Yet now the English king was "arrogantly" attempting "to prescribe boundaries to the American commerce" and had a "wicked design of ruining our country." To thwart such a fate, the participants mutually pledged their lives and fortunes to "support the freedom, dignity and independence of America" and pass it on to their descendants "as pure as we now hold it." Those were the words of men to whom the Revolution had bequeathed a large measure of political freedom, but whose economic well-being had been battered again and again since the 1770s. The price of nationhood came high in Charles County.[105]

Epilogue

Even as men on the courthouse green almost certainly raised their fists and shouted huzzahs that day in 1794, people they had known as neighbors and kin were absent from the scene. And from the county. The place no longer had a hold on them. Its Atlantic commerce in shambles, Charles County was also becoming a backwater of the new nation. Stagecoach lines now regularly crossed Maryland but not the county. A post road still connected Maine with Georgia but no longer passed through Port Tobacco. Congress had rerouted it westward through Baltimore, Georgetown, and Alexandria. Georgetown also was the site of the first bridge to span the Potomac. Not until the twentieth century would one link the county, where the river was much wider, to the Virginia shore. And although someday the river might be fully navigable above the fall line, thereby placing the county on a major artery into the transmontane West, for now the Potomac Company's monumental project was slowed by engineering and financial problems.[1]

Beckoning people away from the county were millions of acres of virgin land secured to the states and nation in the 1783 peace treaty with England. With the exception of American Independence, no other treaty provision was more important for the subsequent history of the United States. While inhabitants of the Chesapeake tidewater struggled with debts, taxes, depression, and diminished productivity, prosperity seemingly lay across the mountains, from the Gulf Coast to the Ohio country. An advertisement published in the *Maryland Gazette* shortly before the Charles County riot captured the lure of the West:

> to be sold, leased, or rented . . . tracts of 160, 400, 500, 700, 800, and 1000 acres each . . . on the waters of Little Kanhawa [in western Virginia]. . . . These lands are of the first quality, rich, level, well watered, abounding in sugar trees, poplar, walnut, locust, wild cherry, oak, and other valuable timber. There are fine fish and wild fowl in the streams; deer and turkies in the woods; many good mill seats. . . . There is an easy communication with the Ohio, Pittsburg, and soon will be with the Patowmack. From the richness of the soil and southern situation, the winters are milder than common. A long time will be allowed to purchasers. Good tobacco or cotton, which may be easily raised, will be taken in payment; encouragement will be given to industrious planters, farmers, and tradesmen, to go and settle there; and it is not to be doubted, but that many people who are forced to pay heavy rents and tend poor worn-out lands, which produce little or nothing, will avail themselves of an immediate opportunity of providing for their families in a rich, fertile soil, where the necessaries of life can be easily raised.

To apply, see Mr. West in Prince George's County.[2]

There were other enticements. Cross into the West or go to the Gulf Coast in search of opportunity, just as your European forebears crossed the Atlantic. Or if gruesome reports of Indian resistance dampen your enthusiasm, go no farther than western Maryland. If that prospect is not pleasing, why not move to Baltimore, now "the great port of this State"? Or try Alexandria, Georgetown, the new federal city. Enter a lottery for a chance to win a lot in the District of Columbia. See Beal Turner at Port Tobacco for tickets. Come and hear what a man born in the county, just returned from Georgia, has to say about the southeastern United States. The possibilities seemed endless.[3]

People abandoned the county in droves, part of a massive outmigration from the eastern seaboard during the early national period. By the mid-1790s, according to the traveler Isaac Weld, parts of the countryside seemed "as if it had been deserted by one half of its inhabitants," who "find it more to their interest to remove to another part of the country . . . than to attempt to reclaim these exhausted plains."[4]

Some of those who left traveled short distances and settled down for the rest of their lives. James Craik moved from his graceful country house, La Grange, and opened a new medical practice in Alexandria, Virginia. From there he regularly rode out to Mount Vernon to tend the maladies of aging

General Washington and his family and slaves. Samuel Hanson and his wife, Mary, settled in Alexandria, too, but then moved on to the District of Columbia, where the old soldier talked about his military exploits until his dying day. Down the road, in Georgetown, lived yet another Hanson, Anne, who had married a merchant. And down the road from them was Georgetown University, where priests from St. Thomas Manor taught and prayed.[5]

Others migrated much farther, sometimes in stages (one man said he got "in a habit of moving from place to place"), sometimes with relatives and friends from home. A son of Mary and Samuel Hanson went to Kentucky. Elijah Clark, born in the county, left after the war and moved successively to Virginia, eastern Tennessee, then Kentucky. Richard Blandford, who enlisted in the army at Bryantown in 1776, was living in Kentucky half a century later, as were his brother and the woman who had sewn his soldiers' clothes. Three men who served in the militia together left Charles County for the North Carolina backcountry. Far from the scene of their military service they basked in—and exaggerated—their contributions "to the Cause of liberty." Perhaps Zachariah and Mildred Robey Burch migrated the farthest. Married in the county in 1787, they moved to Kentucky for a while, then to Missouri. He died there in 1844. She survived until, at age ninety-one in 1856, she was "feeble, and liable at any time to drop off." The revolutionary generation reached far across the continent.[6]

Both the propertied and the poor left the Potomac shores. John Hoskins Stone, governor of the state in the mid-nineties, moved to Baltimore. Richmond attracted George Gray, who had traded at Port Tobacco both before and after the war. George Dent, the epitome of the county's brand of Jeffersonianism, left politics in disgust because President Jefferson did not appoint him treasurer of the United States. Dent went to Georgia in 1802. Another politician, Henry Hendly Chapman, stayed on longer, representing the county in the Assembly much of the time between 1787 and 1815. But then he, too, departed.[7]

Of the poor and middling whites, the free blacks, and the slaves who either were sold out of the county or whose masters relocated, little is known about how they fared. Questions far outnumber answers. What became of Thomas Dehaney, convicted of assault and battery in the local court, who "quit the state, never more to return," in exchange for remission of his fine? How many Charles County blacks became part of antebellum Baltimore's vibrant African-American community? What brought old Clement Edelin to Illinois about 1820, and why was he reduced to selling his gun to buy food and thereafter depending "on the charity of my neighbours"? Were the lives of slaves marched into the Deep South better or worse than what they had known in the county? And how did Eleanor Glasgo's experiences in the new state of

Kentucky fit into broader patterns of American development? The answers to these and countless other questions about the women and men who left the Potomac shores after the Revolution lie in the histories of communities all across America.[8]

Within the county the cumulative effects of individual actions again produced dramatic social change. During the last decade of the eighteenth century, the population reversed the pattern of over a hundred years: It stopped growing. Between 1700 and the first federal census in 1790, the population had increased more than sevenfold, to over twenty thousand people. During the 1790s it dropped 7 percent, and that was merely the beginning. On the eve of the Civil War the number of inhabitants was about 20 percent less than in 1790. Only after World War II did the county's population again equal and then surpass what it had been during Washington's presidency—a century and a half earlier. Demographic data alone bespeak massive change during the postrevolutionary years.[9]

Between 1790 and 1850 the number of whites dropped by an astonishing 44 percent, the greatest loss of any county in Maryland, but the number of blacks remained unchanged. As outmigration enticed or dragged people away, the white majority that had existed since the seventeenth century was rapidly replaced by a black majority. And because the free black population never grew beyond a thousand—freed men and women apparently sought opportunities elsewhere—nearly all Charles County blacks remained in bondage. Slaves accounted for 60 percent of the local population after 1810. While Maryland as a whole had a large proportion of free blacks by the Civil War, the county did not.[10]

People born in Charles County after 1800 inherited a different world from the one the revolutionary generation had known. Gone were the intensity of the nation's formative years, the expansive commercialism, and the self-assured gentry leadership. Drained of many of its people and much of its economic vitality, the county slipped quietly into the nineteenth century.

PROSPECT FROM THE ENTRANCE
HALL OF ROSE HILL. *Photograph by John C.
Kopp. Courtesy of the Southern Maryland Studies
Center, Charles County Community College.*

APPENDIX

———— ∞ ————

STATISTICAL TABLES

TABLE 1

The Population of Charles County, 1700–82

Year	Whites		Blacks		Total
	N	%	N	%	
1700					2,808
1710	2,791	81	638	19	3,429
1733					6,770[a]
1755	8,095	62	4,961[b]	38	13,056
1775					15,875[a]
1782	9,804	55	7,920	45	17,724

SOURCES: Russell R. Menard, "Five Maryland Censuses, 1700 to 1712: A Note on the Quality of the Quantities," *WMQ*, 3d ser., 37 (1980): 616–26; 1733 List of Taxables, Charles County, in the Maryland State Papers, Ser. Z: Scharf Collection (S1005), box 96, folder 1, Maryland State Archives, Annapolis; "An Account of the Number of Souls in the Province of Maryland, in the Year 1755," *Gentleman's Magazine* (London), 34 (1764): 261; Evarts B. Greene and Virginia D. Harrington, *American Population before the Federal Census of 1790* (New York: Columbia University Press, 1932), 131; *American Museum, or, Universal Magazine* 7 (1790): 159. See also Lorena S. Walsh, "The Historian as Census Taker: Individual Reconstitution and the Reconstruction of Censuses for a Colonial Chesapeake County," *WMQ*, 3d ser., 38 (1981): 242–60.

[a] Based on a 1:2.5 ratio of taxables to the whole population. See U.S. Bureau of the Census, *Historical Statistics of the United States: Colonial Times to 1970*, 2 vols. (Washington, D.C.: U.S. Government Printing Office, 1975), 2:1152.

[b] Includes 428 mulattoes.

TABLE 2

The Population of Charles County, 1790–1860

Year	Whites	Free Blacks	Slaves	Total
1790	10,124	404	10,085	20,613
1800	9,043	571	9,558	19,172
1810	7,398	412	12,435	20,245
1820	6,514	569	9,419	16,502
1840	6,022	819	9,182	16,023
1860	5,796	1,068	9,653	16,517

SOURCES: [U.S. Census Office, 1st Census, 1790], *Return of the Whole Number of Persons within the Several Districts of the United States, According to "An Act Providing for the Enumeration of the Inhabitants of the United States"* . . . (Philadelphia: Childs & Swaine, 1791), 47; U.S. Census Office, 2d Census, 1800, *Return of the Whole Number of Persons within the Several Districts of the United States* (Washington, D.C.: William Duane & Son, 1802), 66; U.S. Department of State, *Aggregate Amount of Each Description of Persons within the United States . . . in the Year 1810* (Washington, D.C., 1810); U.S. Census Office, Population Schedules of the 4th Census of the United States, 1820, Record Group 29, Microcopy 33, reel 40, National Archives and Records Service, Washington, D.C.; U.S. Census Office, 6th Census, 1840, *Compendium of the Enumeration of the Inhabitants and Statistics of the United States, as Obtained at the Department of State, from the Returns of the Sixth Census* (Washington, D.C.: Thomas Allen, 1841), 28–31; U.S. Census Office, 8th Census, 1860, *Population of the United States in 1860; Compiled from the Original Returns of the Eighth Census* (Washington, D.C.: Government Printing Office, 1864), 210–14.

TABLE 3

Census of Charles County, 1755

Status	Whites	Mulattoes	Blacks	Total
Free	7,241	239	13	7,493
Hired or indentured servants	548			548
Convicts	306			306
Slaves	____	189	4,520	4,709
Totals:	8,095	428	4,533	13,056

SOURCE: "An Account of the Number of Souls in the Province of Maryland, in the Year 1755," *Gentleman's Magazine* (London), 34 (1764): 261.

Table 4

Distribution of Adult Slaves by Household Units, 1758[a]

Size of Slave Group	Households	Slaves		Mean N of Slaves per Household
		N	%	
None	382			
1–5	219	490	50.9	2.24
6–10	36	259	26.9	7.19
11–20	12	166	17.2	13.83
Above 20	2	48	5.0	24.00
Totals:	651	963	100.0	3.58[b]

SOURCE: 1758 Charles County tax lists for the following hundreds: East Newport, Lower Durham Parish, Lower William and Mary Parish, Pomonkey, Upper Trinity Parish, and West Port Tobacco Parish, in Secretary in Maryland, Tax Lists (S244), Maryland State Archives, Annapolis.

[a] The tax lists on which this table is based survey approximately 43 percent of the adult slave population as of 1758. The lists come from every area of the county and include jurisdictions with substantially different proportions of households containing adult slaves, from a low of 32.1 percent in Lower Durham Parish to a high of 65.1 percent in Lower William and Mary Parish. The total adult slave population as of 1755 was 2,227 persons, of whom fewer than 2 percent were nontaxables. "An Account of the Number of Souls in the Province of Maryland, in the Year 1755," *Gentleman's Magazine* (London), 34 (1764): 261.

[b] For households with taxable slaves.

TABLE 5

Number and Valuation of Slaves, by Age-Group and Gender, 1782

Age/Gender Category	N	%	Assessed Value[a]	% of Assessed Value
Under age 8	2,693	34.0	£26,913	9.5
Ages 8–14	1,293	16.3	32,300	11.4
Males, ages 14–45	1,516	19.1	105,470	37.2
Females, ages 14–36	1,324	16.7	84,990	30.0
Males above 45 and females above 36	1,094	13.8	33,705	11.9
Totals:	7,920	99.9	£283,378	100.0

SOURCE: Summary Accounts of the Valuations of the Assessments in the Several Counties Returned by the Commissioners of the Tax, 1782, Maryland State Papers, Ser. Z: Scharf Collection (S1005), box 95, folder 56, Maryland State Archives, Annapolis. See also Jean Butenhoff Lee, "The Problem of Slave Community in the Eighteenth-Century Chesapeake," *WMQ*, 3d ser., 43 (1986): 345–54. The statutory basis of the 1782 assessment is Maryland General Assembly, *Laws of Md. . . . [Nov. Session 1781]* (Annapolis: Frederick Green [1782]), chap. 4.

[a] In Maryland currency. Slaves were rated at £10 per child under age eight, £25 per child aged eight to fourteen, £70 per male aged fourteen to forty-five, and £60 per female aged fourteen to thirty-six. Artisans, females above thirty-six, males above forty-five, and slaves whose state of health diminished their value were individually appraised.

TABLE 6

Distribution of the Slave Population by Household Units, 1782[a]

Slaves in Household	Households	Children Under 14		Males Age 14–45		Females Age 14–36		Older[b]		Total Slaves
		N	%	N	%	N	%	N	%	
1	172	73	42.4	47	27.3	32	18.6	20	11.6	172
2–5	273	410	45.3	165	18.3	195	21.6	134	14.8	904
6–10	174	719	53.2	256	18.9	240	17.8	137	10.1	1,352
11–20	112	824	50.5	296	18.1	267	16.4	245	15.0	1,632
21–60	45	651	48.2	267	19.8	234	17.3	199	14.7	1,351
Totals:	776	2,677	49.5	1,031	19.1	968	17.9	735	13.6	5,411

SOURCE: 1782 Charles County Tax Assessment Lists, Maryland State Papers, Ser. Z: Scharf Collection (S1005), box 96, folders 7–10, 12–17, Maryland State Archives, Annapolis.

[a] The 5,411 slaves counted in the extant 1782 lists constituted 68.3 percent of the total enslaved population (N = 7,920) then living in the county. "Population in Maryland—1782," *American Museum, or, Universal Magazine* 7 (1790): 159.

[b] Males above age forty-five, females above age thirty-six.

TABLE 7

Land Distribution, 1753 and 1774

| Acres | Landowners[a] | | | |
| | 1753 | | 1774 | |
	N	%	N	%
100 or less	190	27.7	169	23.7
101–200	178	26.0	213	29.9
201–500	183	26.7	202	28.3
500–1,000	93	13.6	87	12.2
1,001–2,000	37	5.4	31	4.4
Above 2,000	5	0.7	11	1.5
Totals:	686	100.1	713	100.0

SOURCES: 1753 and 1774 Charles County Debt Books, in Land Office, Debt Books (S12), Maryland State Archives, Annapolis.

[a] Data are for the entire county, but with proprietary holdings excluded.

NOTE: Mean tract size: 343 acres in 1753, 352 acres in 1774. Median tract size: 199 acres in 1753, 189 acres in 1774.

TABLE 8

Tobacco Shipped from the Inspection Warehouses, 1763–76[a]

Warehouse	N Hogsheads									
	1763	1764	1765	1766	1767	1768	1769	1774	1775	1776
Benedict	947	753	716	712	386	569	740	352	844	1
Cedar Point	560	583	647	413	412	396	381	334	645	—
Chicamuxen	623	591	590	460	425	502	400	176	491	49
Nanjemoy	371	433	428	484	495	293	452	370	652	106
Pile's	1,036	797	868	702	935	639	637	769	1,595	87
Pomonkey	462	602	715	601	599	421	393	599	855	208
Port Tobacco	971	1,070	1,003	1,041	902	804	1,003	344	1,302	324
Totals:	4,970	4,829	4,967	4,413	4,154	3,624	4,006	2,944	6,384	775

SOURCE: Charles County Court, Tobacco Inspection Proceedings (C680), vols. 70–71 (1755–69, 1774–86), Maryland State Archives, Annapolis.

[a] Shipping records do not exist for 1770–73, the years when the tobacco inspection law lapsed in Maryland.

Appendix

Table 9

Average Price of Tobacco Shipped from
the Inspection Warehouses, 1766–76[a]

Warehouse	Average Price per Hundredweight (in Shillings/Pence)					
	1766	1767	1768	1769	1774	1776
Benedict	19/6	26/6	25/6	26/2	17/8	12/
Cedar Point	18/4	26/1	26/8	29/1	17/8	—
Chicamuxen	20/4	27/8	24/5	28/6	18/	17/6
Nanjemoy	19/	27/5	25/	30/6	17/10	17/
Pile's	19/6	26/6	27/10	30/8	17/	16/8
Pomonkey	18/3	27/11	26/6	28/1	—	—
Port Tobacco	20/2	27/5	27/6	30/6	18/5	—

Source: Charles County Court, Tobacco Inspection Proceedings (C680), vols. 70–71 (1755–69, 1774–86), Maryland State Archives, Annapolis.

[a] Price records begin in 1766 but do not exist for 1770–73, the years when the tobacco inspection law lapsed in Maryland.

TABLE 10

Value of Assessed Property in Charles County, 1782[a]

Property	Assessed Valuation[b]
Land	£420,058
Slaves	283,378
Horses and black cattle[c]	73,114
Silver plate	2,374
Other assessed property	63,136
Total:	£842,060

SOURCE: Summary Accounts of the Valuations of the Assessments in the Several Counties Returned by the Commissioners of the Tax, 1782, in Maryland State Papers, Ser. Z: Scharf Collection (S1005), box 95, item 56, Maryland State Archives, Annapolis.

[a] "A Note on the 1782 Tax Assessment Lists," pp. 283–86, describes the origin and nature of the property valuations made that year.

[b] In Maryland currency. Amounts rounded off to the nearest £.

[c] 6,411 horses, 18,019 black cattle.

TABLE 11

Wealth Distribution, 1782[a,b]

Assessed Property	Wealthholder Category				
	Top Decile[c]	Top Quartile[d]	Upper Middle Quartile[e]	Lower Middle Quartile[f]	Bottom Quartile[g]
Land	£183,321	£238,226	£27,380	£3,992	£95
Town lots	3,680	6,510	490	200	0
Slaves	101,871	159,780	29,732	4,070	275
Silver plate	1,100	2,330	1,101	0	0
Horses and black cattle	19,066	31,328	10,212	6,834	1,817
Other assessed property	18,588	29,421	8,109	4,669	820
Totals:	£327,626	£467,595	£77,024	£19,765	£3,008
Mean wealth per taxpayer	£1,950	£1,119	£183	£47	£7
% of assessed wealth	57.7	82.4	13.6	3.5	0.5

SOURCE: 1782 Charles County Tax Assessment Lists, Maryland State Papers, Ser. Z: Scharf Collection (S1005), box 96, items 1–10, 12–17, Maryland State Archives, Annapolis.

[a] Data cover ten of fourteen hundreds, in which 65.9 percent of the white and 68.3 percent of the slave population lived. "A Note on the 1782 Tax Assessment Lists," pp. 283–86, describes the origin and nature of the property valuations made that year.

[b] In Maryland currency; St. Thomas Manor and tobacco stored in public warehouses not included. Includes seventeen estates owned by heirs and three by mercantile firms.

[c] Estates valued at £878 and above.

[d] Estates valued at £335 and above.

[e] Estates valued at £83–£334.

[f] Estates valued at £19–£82.

[g] Estates valued to £18.

TABLE 12

Per Capita Wealth in White Households, 1782[a]

Wealthholder Category	Whites in All Households in Decile or Quartile		Total Assessed Wealth[b]	Per Capita Assessed Wealth[b]
	N	%		
Top decile[c]	706	10.9	£327,626	£464
Top quartile[d]	1,971	30.5	467,595	237
Upper middle quartile[e]	1,844	28.6	77,024	42
Lower middle quartile[f]	1,648	25.5	19,765	12
Bottom quartile[g]	990	15.3	3,008	3

SOURCE: 1782 Charles County Tax Assessment Lists, Maryland State Papers, Ser. Z: Scharf Collection (S1005), box 96, items 7–10, 12–17, Maryland State Archives, Annapolis.

[a] Data cover ten of fourteen hundreds, in which 65.9 percent of the white and 68.3 percent of the slave population lived. "A Note on the 1782 Tax Assessment Lists," pp. 283–86, describes the origin and nature of the property valuations made that year.

[b] In Maryland currency; St. Thomas Manor and tobacco stored in public warehouses not included.

[c] Estates valued at £878 and above.

[d] Estates valued at £335 and above.

[e] Estates valued at £83–£334.

[f] Estates valued at £19–£82.

[g] Estates valued to £18.

TABLE 13

Comparison of Male and Female Wealthholders, 1782[a,b]

Wealthholder Category	Males		Females	
	N	%	N	%
Top decile[c]	145	10.1	16	7.8
Top quartile[d]	353	24.5	52	25.4
Upper middle quartile[e]	352	24.4	63	30.7
Lower middle quartile[f]	369	25.6	48	23.4
Bottom quartile[g]	368	25.5	42	20.5
Totals:	1,442	100.0	205	100.0

SOURCE: 1782 Charles County Tax Assessment Lists, Maryland State Papers, Ser. Z: Scharf Collection (S1005), box 96, items 7–10, 12–17, Maryland State Archives, Annapolis.

[a] Data cover ten of fourteen hundreds, in which 65.9 percent of the white and 68.3 percent of the slave population lived. "A Note on the 1782 Tax Assessment Lists," pp. 283–86, describes the origin and nature of the property valuations made that year.
[b] Estates attributed to heirs not included.
[c] Estates valued at £878 and above.
[d] Estates valued at £335 and above.
[e] Estates valued at £83–£334.
[f] Estates valued at £19–£82.
[g] Estates valued to £18.

TABLE 14

Comparison of Male and Female Landholders, 1782[a]

Size of Acreage	Males		Females	
	N	%	N	%
100 acres or less	170	29.2	32	35.1
101–200 acres	178	30.6	34	37.4
201–300 acres	80	13.7	9	9.9
301–500 acres	82	14.1	10	11.0
501–1,000 acres	54	9.3	6	6.6
1,001–3,400 acres	18	3.1	—	——
Totals:	582	100.0	91	100.0

SOURCE: 1782 Charles County Tax Assessment Lists, Maryland State Papers, Ser. Z: Scharf Collection (S1005), box 96, items 7–10, 12–17, Maryland State Archives, Annapolis.

[a] Data cover ten of fourteen hundreds, in which 65.9 percent of the white and 68.3 percent of the slave population lived. "A Note on the 1782 Tax Assessment Lists," pp. 283–86, describes the origin and nature of the property valuations made that year.

TABLE 15

Women's Share of Total Wealth and Real Estate, 1782[a]

	Total Assessed Wealth[b]			Plantation Land			Town Lots		
	All Wealth-holders	Women		All Wealth-holders	Women		All Wealth-holders	Women	
Wealth-holder Category	Mean Value	Mean Value	% of Total Wealth	Mean Value	Mean Value	% of Total Land	Mean Value	Mean Value	% of Total Lots
Top decile[c]	£1,950	£1,943	9.5	£1,091	£1,012	8.8	£22	£104	45.1
Top quartile[d]	1,119	994	11.1	570	438	9.6	16	32	25.5
Upper middle quartile[e]	183	187	15.3	65	58	13.4	1	3	33.7
Lower middle quartile[f]	47	57	13.7	10	13	15.9	0.5	0	0
Bottom quartile[g]	7	9	11.9	0.2	0	0	0	0	0

SOURCE: 1782 Charles County Tax Assessment Lists, Maryland State Papers, Ser. Z: Scharf Collection (S1005), box 96, items 7–10, 12–17, Maryland State Archives, Annapolis.

[a] Data cover ten of fourteen hundreds, in which 65.9 percent of the white and 68.3 percent of the slave population lived. "A Note on the 1782 Tax Assessment Lists," pp. 283–86, describes the origin and nature of the property valuations made that year.

[b] In Maryland currency; St. Thomas Manor and tobacco stored in public warehouses not included. Includes seventeen estates owned by heirs and three by mercantile firms. N wealthholders = 1,667; N women wealthholders = 205.

[c] Estates valued at £878 and above.

[d] Estates valued at £335 and above.

[e] Estates valued at £83–£334.

[f] Estates valued at £19–£82.

[g] Estates valued to £18.

TABLE 16

Women's Share of Slaves, 1782[a]

Wealthholder Category	Mean N of Slaves	
	All Wealthholders[b] (N = 1,667)	Women (N = 205)
Top decile[c,d]	16.1	16.4
Top quartile[e]	10.5	11.2
Upper middle quartile[f]	2.0	2.6
Lower middle quartile[g]	0.3	0.7
Bottom quartile[h]	0.03	0.05

SOURCE: 1782 Charles County Tax Assessment Lists, Maryland State Papers, Ser. Z: Scharf Collection (S1005), box 96, items 1–10, 12–17, Maryland State Archives, Annapolis.

[a] Data cover ten of fourteen hundreds, in which 65.9 percent of the white and 68.3 percent of the slave population lived. "A Note on the 1782 Tax Assessment Lists," pp. 283–86, describes the origin and nature of the property valuations made that year.

[b] St. Thomas Manor and tobacco stored in public warehouses not included. Includes seventeen estates owned by heirs and three by mercantile firms.

[c] In Maryland currency.

[d] Estates valued at £878 and above.

[e] Estates valued at £335 and above.

[f] Estates valued at £83–£334.

[g] Estates valued at £19–£82.

[h] Estates valued to £18.

A NOTE ON THE 1782 TAX ASSESSMENT LISTS

One day between mid-February and mid-March of 1782, John Morton, who lived in Benedict Hundred in Charles County, went to Hezekiah Billingsly's plantation and announced that he had come to assess Billingsly's worldly goods. The man's principal asset was the land on which he lived, a 229-acre tract called Whitson Monday. Sixty acres were cleared, and a dwelling house and tobacco house, both in "midling" condition, stood on the land. Morton declared the real estate worth £1 Maryland currency per acre. Three slaves lived on the place: a child old enough to help with chores and do a little field work, a woman no more than thirty-six years of age, and an older slave who was lame. Morton set their combined value at £105. Billingsly's next most valuable species of property, to use the term common at the time, was his livestock: four horses and six head of cattle appraised at £37. Did he own any silver plate? No, came the answer. Well, then, what about other assessable property? Morton looked it over and valued it at £18, which brought Billingsly's total assessed worth to £389. On that amount he owed a tax of £8 15s. 1d., which he could pay in cattle, pigs, barreled pork, wheat, flour, tobacco, bar iron, or money, in any combination that suited him. Finally, the assessor noted that Billingsly was the only free adult male living in the household and that two other white people also lived there. His work at Whitson Monday completed, Morton moved on to other plantations until he had viewed and valued all of the taxable property and counted every inhabitant in Benedict Hundred.[1]

This scene was repeated in every household in Maryland during the winter of 1782 because, in the seventh year of the War for Independence, the state needed to furnish supplies to the Continental Army and meet other public expenses. At its November 1781 session, therefore, the General Assembly passed "An act to raise the supplies for the year seventeen hundred and eighty-two." All property was subject to a uniform tax rate of 45s.

Maryland currency per £100 with the following exceptions: money, clothing, plantation and artisans' tools, and the provisions, livestock excepted, that would feed the property owner's household for the year; all assets of the county, state, and national governments, the churches, publicly supported schools, and men who could prove at least three years of service in the Continental Army; and belongings of certain refugees from war-ravaged southern states. Each free, able-bodied bachelor above age twenty-one whose assessed property was worth £10 or less was to pay a higher tax of 15s. on the ground that he "should contribute in some degree towards the expences of government and the support of the war." Everyone else of comparable means was declared a pauper and exempt from taxation.[2]

The tax law designated five men of property and prudence in every county to serve as commissioners of the tax, and they in turn appointed an assessor in every hundred, a man who promised to value his neighbors' assets with neither "favour or affection, nor . . . hatred, malice, or ill will." No later than March 20, 1782, each assessor had to visit the households in his hundred and calculate assessments according to property values specified by the Assembly. These measures supposedly ensured equitable treatment and insulated the assessment from rampant wartime inflation. All land, houses, and improvements were to be appraised at their sale value in 1774. Fixed rates were to be applied to most of the slave population: £10 for each child under eight years of age, £25 for children eight to fourteen years, £60 each for females fourteen to thirty-six years, and £70 for males between fourteen and forty-five. Artisans, who customarily were more valuable than field hands, as well as females beyond age thirty-six, males beyond forty-five, and slaves in poor health had to be appraised individually. The law set the value of silver at 8s. 4d. per ounce, bar iron at £30 per ton, and all other property, including tobacco not yet delivered to an inspection warehouse, at the amount it would have brought if sold in 1774.

Since the assessors were to visit every plantation, country crossroad, and town within their respective jurisdictions, the Assembly also required them to produce a census. In addition to organizing the slave population into the aforementioned age and gender groups, assessors were to count the number of free males above eighteen years of age and the total number of white inhabitants for whom each property holder was responsible. Further opportunity was lost when the legislature permitted rather than required the assessors to obtain from every householder a record "of the names and occupations of all free male persons above eighteen years of age, as shall sojourn or lodge in their respective houses." The Charles County assessors did not produce such an account.

Once assessors completed their work and delivered their tax lists to the county commissioners, the latter heard citizens' complaints and decided whether to adjust valuations. In Charles County most such complaints involved real estate. After disputed assessments were settled, and no later than April 10, 1782, a clerk in each county drew up a final, approved account, organized by hundreds, and sent it to the House of Delegates in Annapolis. In addition to recording individuals' property and assessments, the account noted the number and assessed worth of all hogsheads stored at the public warehouses, on which purchasers, not producers, paid the tax.

Such was the origin of a magnificent set of tax lists that cataloged the wealth and population of every household in Maryland less than six months after the guns fell silent at Yorktown. Thanks to the avid collecting habits of Maryland's most prolific nineteenth-century historian, J. Thomas Scharf, many of the lists survived public neglect and eventually were deposited at the Maryland Historical Society, which later relinquished custody to the Maryland State Archives. Of the fourteen hundreds into which Charles County was divided in 1782, lists are extant for ten of them, in which lived 6,457 whites and 5,411 blacks, or two-thirds of those population groups. The hundreds are as follows: Benedict, Upper Durham Parish, East and West Newport, Pomonkey, Lower William and Mary Parish, and the Upper, Upper East, Lower East, and Town hundreds of Port Tobacco Parish. Missing are the accountings for Bryantown, Lower Durham, West Port Tobacco, and Upper William and Mary hundreds. No section of the county is unrepresented in these records. They describe the holdings of 1,687 property owners, some of whom, because they were paupers or long-term army veterans, escaped taxation but not the assessor's notice. The lists also contain valuations of tobacco stored at four inspection warehouses.[3]

Of comparable scope and value are 1783 assessment records for the county. They are organized according to seven newly designated taxing districts, and only the list for the Sixth District, encompassing the Lower, East, and Town hundreds of Port Tobacco Parish, is missing. Supplementing these documents is a set of land tax lists that indicate the owner, acreage, and assessed worth of every tract; the number of acres classified as arable, meadow, and woodland; brief descriptions of soil quality and of the kinds and condition of improvements on the land; and a cryptic indication of its location, such as "Wicomico," "forrest," or "near Newport."[4]

These sources constitute a treasure trove for historians concerned with eighteenth-century social stratification, wealth and poverty, slaveownership, the adult labor force, household size, female-headed families, and the age structure of the black population. Computer-based analysis of the 1782 data was conducted at the Academic Computing Center of the University of Virginia, using the Statistical Package for the Social Sciences (SPSS).

NOTES

1. 1782 Charles County Tax Assessment Lists, in Maryland State Papers, Ser. Z: Scharf Collection (S1005), box 96, item 8, Maryland State Archives, Annapolis. Morton qualified for the post on February 16 and turned in his assessments on March 20. Charles County Commissioners of the Tax, Minutes for 1782, ibid., item 11. Information about the condition of Billingsly's plantation comes from the 1783 Land Tax List, ibid., item 19.

2. Unless otherwise noted, all information about the tax assessment of 1782, including quoted matter, comes from the act as printed in Maryland General Assembly, *Laws of Md. . . . [Nov. Session 1781]* (Annapolis: Frederick Green [1782]), chap. 4. An additional amount of property was potentially exempt from taxation because local

tax commissioners were authorized to suspend payment from persons who had "exerted [themselves] in favour of the freedom and independence" of Maryland and had been driven from their homes or lost property at the hands of the British. According to the commissioners' minutes, no such exemptions were granted in 1782 in Charles County. Scharf Collection, box 96, item 11.

3. See Table 1 supra for total population as of 1782. The surviving Charles County lists are in the Scharf Collection, box 96, items 7–10, 12–17; the commissioners' minutes for 1782 are ibid., item 11. Wealth totals for the entire county are in Summary Accounts of the Valuations of the Assessments in the Several Counties Returned by the Commissioners of the Tax, 1782, ibid., box 95, item 56, and are reproduced in Table 10 supra.

4. Microfilm copies of the 1783 Maryland tax assessment lists are available at both the Maryland State Archives and the Maryland Historical Society. The 1783 Land Tax Lists for Charles County are in the Scharf Collection, box 96, items 1, 3, 18–20, 25, 28. The tax commissioners' minutes for that year are ibid., item 24.

NOTES

---∞---

ABBREVIATIONS

The following abbreviations are used throughout the notes.

Arch. Md.   William H. Browne et al., eds., *Archives of Maryland*, 73 vols. to date (Baltimore: Maryland Historical Society, 1883–1972, and Annapolis: Maryland State Archives, 1990–)

Assessment Lists   Charles County Tax Assessment Lists

Chancery Records   Chancery Court. Chancery Records (S517), MSA

CCCR   Charles County Court. Court Records (C658), MSA

CCDB   Charles County Debt Books, in Land Office. Debt Books (S12), MSA

CCLR   Charles County Court. Land Records (C670), MSA

CCW   Charles County Register of Wills. Wills (C681), MSA

Cresswell, *Journal*   Nicholas Cresswell, *The Journal of Nicholas Cresswell, 1774–1777* (New York: Dial Press, 1924)

Executive Papers   Maryland State Papers, Series A: Executive Papers (S1004), MSA

Laws of Md. . . .   Maryland. General Assembly, *Laws of Maryland, Made and Passed at a Session of Assembly* . . . (Annapolis: Frederick Green [1777–91]). Each citation includes the appropriate Assembly session.

LC   Library of Congress, Washington, D.C.

Md. Gazette   *Maryland Gazette* (Annapolis)

Md. Hist. Mag.   *Maryland Historical Magazine*

MHS   Manuscripts Division, Maryland Historical Society Library, Baltimore

MSA   Maryland State Archives, Hall of Records, Annapolis

Papenfuse et al., eds.,   Edward C. Papenfuse et al., eds., *A Biographical Dictionary of the*
Biographical Dictionary   *Maryland Legislature, 1635–1789*, 2 vols. (Baltimore: Johns Hop-
                                   kins University Press, 1979, 1985)

Pardon Papers   Governor and Council. Pardon Papers, 1777–1800 (S1061), MSA

Pforzheimer Papers   Maryland State Papers, Series B: Pforzheimer Papers (S995), MSA

Red Books   Maryland State Papers: Red Books (S989), MSA

Ridgate Letter Book   Thomas Howe Ridgate Letter Book (1771–72), typescript in the
                                   Arents Collection, Rare Books and Manuscripts Division, New
                                   York Public Library, New York, N.Y.

Scharf Collection   Maryland State Papers, Series Z: Scharf Collection (S1005), MSA

WMQ   *William and Mary Quarterly* (3d series unless otherwise indicated)

INTRODUCTION

1. Father Joseph Mosely to his sister, Sept. 1, 1759, "Letters of Father Joseph Mosley,
   1757–1786," ed. E. I. Devitt, *Woodstock Letters* 35 (1906): 40; Invoice and Letter
   Book, 1771–74, 1792–93, Port Tobacco, Md., in the John Glassford & Co. Papers,
   container 61, Manuscript Division, LC; Buchanan & Simson (Glasgow) to Fraser &
   Wharton, Nov. 30, 1759, Buchanan & Simson Letterbook, 1759–61, CS96/507,
   Scottish Record Office, Edinburgh (used with permission of the Keeper of the
   Records of Scotland). See also George Fisher, *The American Instructor: or, Young
   Man's Best Companion* . . . , 14th ed. (New York: H. Gaine, 1770), 335.
2. Lewis Evans, *A General Map of the Middle British Colonies, in America* ([Philadelphia]:
   engraved by James Turner, 1755); Dennis Griffith, *Map of the State of Maryland. Laid
   down from an actual Survey of all the principal Waters, public Roads, and Divisions of the
   Counties therein* . . . (Philadelphia: J. Wallace, 1795); Samuel Lewis, *The State of
   Maryland, from the best Authorities* (n.p. [ca. 1795]); [Anderson, Scoles, et al.], *The
   States of Maryland and Delaware from the latest Surveys, 1799* (New York: I. Low, 1799);
   "Royal Mail Routes and Post Offices, 1774," in *Atlas of Early American History: The
   Revolutionary Era, 1760–1790*, ed. Lester J. Cappon, Barbara Bartz Petchenik, and
   John Hamilton Long (Princeton: Princeton University Press, for the Newberry
   Library and the Institute of Early American History and Culture, 1976), 32.
3. Cresswell, *Journal*, 1, 11, 16–19, 22, 26, 42, 54–57.
4. Adam Gordon, "Journal of an Officer Who Travelled in America and the West
   Indies in 1764 and 1765," in *Travels in the American Colonies*, ed. Newton D. Mereness
   (New York: Macmillan, 1916), 408; "Journal of a French Traveller in the Colonies,
   1765, II," *American Historical Review* 27 (1921): 70; Hunter D. Farish, ed., *Journal and
   Letters of Philip Vickers Fithian, 1773–1774: A Plantation Tutor of the Old Dominion*, new
   ed. (Williamsburg, Va.: Colonial Williamsburg, 1957), 97. For a hyperbolic account
   by a man who lived briefly in the county before the Revolution, see John F. D.
   Smyth, *A Tour in the United States of America* . . . , 2 vols. (London: G. Robinson, J.
   Robson, and J. Sewell, 1784), 2:144–45, 178, 183.
5. The author agrees with Fred Anderson's assessment that "failure to understand the
   enormous consequences" of the War for Independence "is the most persistent
   problem—and the greatest challenge—facing historians of the American Revolu-

tion today" and with John Shy's argument for the need to overcome a "characteristic tendency" to isolate military history from the political and social components of the Revolution. Anderson, "Bringing the War Home: The Revolutionary Experience of Newport and New York," *Reviews in American History* 15 (1987): 583; Shy, "American Society and Its War for Independence," in *Reconsiderations on the Revolutionary War: Selected Essays*, ed. Don Higginbotham (Westport, Conn.: Greenwood Press, 1978), 72–82; see also idem, *A People Numerous and Armed: Reflections on the Military Struggle for American Independence* (New York: Oxford University Press, 1976), 197; John J. McCusker and Russell R. Menard, *The Economy of British America, 1607–1789* (Chapel Hill: University of North Carolina Press, for the Institute of Early American History and Culture, 1985), 358–59. Recent studies that treat the wartime experiences of ordinary men and women, and the impact of war and revolution upon their lives, include Robert A. Gross, *The Minutemen and Their World* (New York: Hill & Wang, 1976); Christopher M. Jedrey, *The World of John Cleaveland: Family and Community in Eighteenth-Century New England* (New York: W. W. Norton & Co., 1979); Linda K. Kerber, *Women of the Republic: Intellect and Ideology in Revolutionary America* (Chapel Hill: University of North Carolina Press, for the Institute of Early American History and Culture, 1980); Mary Beth Norton, *Liberty's Daughters: The Revolutionary Experience of American Women, 1750–1800* (Boston: Little, Brown, & Co., 1980); John C. Dann, ed., *The Revolution Remembered: Eyewitness Accounts of the War for Independence* (Chicago: University of Chicago Press, 1980); Joy Day Buel and Richard Buel, Jr., *Way of Duty: A Woman and Her Family in Revolutionary America* (New York: W. W. Norton & Co., 1984), chaps. 5–6; Shy, "Hearts and Minds in the American Revolution: The Case of 'Long Bill' Scott and Petersborough, New Hampshire," *A People Numerous and Armed*, 165–79; Alfred F. Young, "George Robert Twelves Hewes (1742–1840): A Boston Shoemaker and the Memory of the American Revolution," *WMQ* 38 (1981): 561–623; Joseph S. Tiedemann, "Patriots by Default: Queens County, New York, and the British Army, 1776–1783," *WMQ* 43 (1986): 35–63; Laura L. Becker, "The American Revolution as a Community Experience: A Case Study of Reading, Pennsylvania" (Ph.D. diss., University of Pennsylvania, 1978). The essential guide to the literature on the Revolution is Ronald M. Gephart, comp., *Revolutionary America, 1763–1789: A Bibliography*, 2 vols. (Washington, D.C.: Library of Congress, 1984). For Maryland, see Robert J. Brugger, *Maryland: A Middle Temperament, 1634–1980* (Baltimore: Johns Hopkins University Press, in association with the Maryland Historical Society, 1988), 732–37.

6. Isaac Weld, Jr., *Travels through the States of North America, and the Provinces of Upper and Lower Canada, during the Years 1795, 1796, and 1797*, 4th ed., 2 vols. (London: John Stockdale, 1807; New York: Augustus M. Kelley, 1970), 1:139.

Part One: THE COLONIAL SOCIETY

Prologue: Within the Bounded Oaks

1. Recent overviews of the founding of Maryland are in Aubrey C. Land, *Colonial Maryland: A History* (Millwood, N.Y.: KTO Press, 1981), chaps. 1–2, and Robert J. Brugger, *Maryland: A Middle Temperament, 1634–1980* (Baltimore: Johns Hopkins

University Press, in association with the Maryland Historical Society, 1988), chap. 1. The leading authority on the early history of Charles County is Lorena S. Walsh, whose valuable assistance the author gratefully acknowledges. See her doctoral dissertation, "Charles County, Maryland, 1658–1705: A Study of Chesapeake Social and Political Structure" (Michigan State University, 1977), and publications cited in note 3 below. Also consult Margaret Brown Klapthor and Paul D. Brown, *The History of Charles County, Maryland* (La Plata, Md.: Charles County Tercentenary, 1958), chap. 1. On St. Thomas Manor and the Jesuits, see Walsh, "Land, Landlord, and Leaseholder: Estate Management and Tenant Fortunes in Southern Maryland, 1642–1820," *Agricultural History* 59 (1985): 373–96; Joseph Zwinge, "The Jesuit Farms in Maryland," *Woodstock Letters* 40 (1911): 181–84; and Gerald P. Fogarty, Joseph T. Durkin, and R. Emmett Curran, *The Maryland Jesuits, 1634–1833* (Baltimore: Maryland Province of the Society of Jesus, 1976). Evidence of early white settlement patterns is drawn from Augustin Herrman's map of *Virginia and Maryland As it is Planted and Inhabited this present Year 1670 Surveyed and Exactly Drawne* . . . (London: Herman and Within-brook, 1673) and the Charles County Rent Roll, Lib. 26 (1753–75), in Land Office, Rent Rolls (S18), MSA; these sources also site Indian villages. Work on the indigenous peoples of the lower Western Shore includes the report of the Jesuits in Maryland to the English Province of the Society of Jesus, 1642, in *Narratives of Early Maryland, 1633–1684*, ed. Clayton C. Hall (New York: Charles Scribner's Sons, 1910), 136–37; Alice L. L. Ferguson and Henry G. Ferguson, *The Piscataway Indians of Southern Maryland* (Accokeek, Md.: Alice Ferguson Foundation, 1960); Wayne E. Clark, "The Origins of the Piscataway and Related Indian Cultures," *Md. Hist. Mag.* 75 (1980): 8–22; James H. Merrell, "Cultural Continuity among the Piscataway Indians of Colonial Maryland," *WMQ* 36 (1979): 548–70; and Charlotte W. Rickenbaker, "The Yaocomico Indians: Part of the Piscataway Tribe of Southern Maryland" (unpublished paper, 1977), on deposit in the files of the Historical Society of Charles County (850046), at the Southern Maryland Studies Center, Charles County Community College, La Plata, Md. Indian-white relations are discussed in J. Frederick Fausz, "Merging and Emerging Worlds: Anglo-Indian Interest Groups and the Development of the Seventeenth-Century Chesapeake," in *Colonial Chesapeake Society*, ed. Lois Green Carr, Philip D. Morgan, and Jean B. Russo (Chapel Hill: University of North Carolina Press, for the Institute of Early American History and Culture, 1988), 47–98; W. Stitt Robinson, "Conflicting Views on Landholding: Lord Baltimore and the Experiences of Colonial Maryland with Native Americans," *Md. Hist. Mag.* 83 (1988): 85–97; and James Axtell, "White Legend: The Jesuit Missions in Maryland," *Md. Hist. Mag.* 81 (1986): 1–7. The term "Portobacke" appears on a map entitled *Noua Terrae-Mariae Tabula*, 1635; 2d ed. (London: John Ogilby, 1671). The meanings of local Indian names evoke the landscape: Chicamuxen, high land nearby; Mattawoman, where one goes pleasantly; Potopaco (Portobacco), jutting of the water inland; and Pomonkey, twisting in the lands. *Times-Crescent* (La Plata, Md.), May 23, 1979.

2. Walsh, "Charles County, Maryland, 1658–1705," 2–3, 19; Edward B. Mathews, *The Counties of Maryland: Their Origin, Boundaries, and Election Districts* (Baltimore: Johns Hopkins Press, 1907), 474–77; *Arch. Md.* 19:213–14, 26:428–29, 46:140–42; Mary Ross Brown, *An Illustrated Genealogy of the Counties of Maryland and the District of Columbia as a Guide to Locating Records* (Baltimore: French-Bray Printing Co., 1967),

25; Richard L. Hall and Earle D. Matthews, *Soil Survey of Charles County, Maryland* (Washington, D.C.: Soil Conservation Service, U.S. Department of Agriculture, in cooperation with the Maryland Agricultural Experiment Station, 1974), 1. Within its irregular borders the county extends about thirty-two miles from east to west, twenty-eight from north to south. An earlier Charles County, created in 1650 along the Patuxent River, was abolished four years later. *Arch. Md.* 3:259–60, 308.

3. Extensive research in the seventeenth-century public records of Charles County has contributed materially to historians' understanding of the early Chesapeake. My description of life in the county before 1720 is a brief synthesis based on the writings of scholars whose work, beginning in the 1970s, employed innovative methodologies and fostered a renaissance in Chesapeake studies. See especially Walsh, "Charles County, Maryland, 1658–1705"; idem, "Servitude and Opportunity in Charles County, Maryland, 1658–1705," in *Law, Society, and Politics in Early Maryland*, ed. Aubrey C. Land, Lois Green Carr, and Edward C. Papenfuse (Baltimore: Johns Hopkins University Press, 1977), 111–33; idem, "The Historian as Census Taker: Individual Reconstitution and the Reconstruction of Censuses for a Colonial Chesapeake County," *WMQ* 38 (1981): 242–60; idem, "Staying Put or Getting Out: Findings for Charles County, Maryland, 1650–1720," *WMQ* 44 (1987): 89–103; Walsh and Russell R. Menard, "Death in the Chesapeake: Two Life Tables for Men in Early Colonial Maryland," *Md. Hist. Mag.* 69 (1974): 211–27. Studies based in part on Charles County data include Carr and Walsh, "The Planter's Wife: The Experience of White Women in Seventeenth-Century Maryland," *WMQ* 34 (1977): 542–71; Gloria L. Main, *Tobacco Colony: Life in Early Maryland, 1650–1720* (Princeton: Princeton University Press, 1982); idem, "Maryland and the Chesapeake Economy, 1670–1720," in *Law, Society, and Politics in Early Maryland*, ed. Land et al., 134–52; Menard, *Economy and Society in Early Colonial Maryland* (New York: Garland Publishing, 1985); idem, "British Migration to the Chesapeake Colonies in the Seventeenth Century," in *Colonial Chesapeake Society*, ed. Carr et al., 99–132; idem, "Immigrants and Their Increase: The Process of Population Growth in Early Colonial Maryland," in *Law, Society, and Politics in Early Maryland*, ed. Land et al., 88–110; idem, "From Servant to Freeholder: Status Mobility and Property Accumulation in Seventeenth-Century Maryland," *WMQ* 30 (1973): 37–64; idem, "The Maryland Slave Population, 1658 to 1730: A Demographic Profile of Blacks in Four Counties," *WMQ* 32 (1975): 29–54; idem, "From Servants to Slaves: The Transformation of the Chesapeake Labor System," *Southern Studies* 16 (1977): 355–90; Menard, P. M. G. Harris, and Lois Green Carr, "Opportunity and Inequality: The Distribution of Wealth on the Lower Western Shore of Maryland, 1638–1705," *Md. Hist. Mag.* 69 (1974): 169–84; and two essays in *The Chesapeake in the Seventeenth Century: Essays on Anglo-American Society*, ed. Thad W. Tate and David L. Ammerman (Chapel Hill: University of North Carolina Press, for the Institute of Early American History and Culture, 1979): Walsh, " 'Till Death Us Do Part': Marriage and Family in Seventeenth-Century Maryland," 126–52, and Carr and Menard, "Immigration and Opportunity: The Freedman in Early Colonial Maryland," 206–42. Useful summaries incorporating recent scholarship on the early Chesapeake are John J. McCusker and Russell R. Menard, *The Economy of British America, 1607–1789* (Chapel Hill: University of North Carolina Press, for the Institute of Early American History and Culture, 1985), chap. 6; Allan Kulikoff, *Tobacco and Slaves: The Development of Southern Cultures in the Chesapeake, 1680–1800*

(Chapel Hill: University of North Carolina Press, for the Institute of Early American History and Culture, 1986), chap. 1; Jack P. Greene, *Pursuits of Happiness: The Social Development of Early Modern British Colonies and the Formation of American Culture* (Chapel Hill: University of North Carolina Press, 1988), chap. 4; Land, *Colonial Maryland: A History*, chaps. 2, 4; Carr, Menard, and Louis Peddicord, *Maryland . . . at the Beginning* (Annapolis: Hall of Records Commission, 1984); Brugger, *Maryland: A Middle Temperament, 1634–1980*, chaps. 1–2. See also the introductory essays in Tate and Ammerman, eds., *The Chesapeake in the Seventeenth Century*, 3–50, and Carr et al., eds., *Colonial Chesapeake Society*, 1–46, as well as Anita H. Rutman, "Still Planting the Seeds of Hope: The Recent Literature of the Early Chesapeake Region," *Virginia Magazine of History and Biography* 95 (1987): 3–24.

4. In addition to the sources cited in note 3, Darrett B. Rutman and Anita H. Rutman vividly convey the complexities of family life in " 'Now-Wives and Sons-in-Law': Parental Death in a Seventeenth-Century Virginia County," in *The Chesapeake in the Seventeenth Century*, ed. Tate and Ammerman, 153–82. Main, *Tobacco Colony*, chaps. 4–7, is based on extensive research on the housing and material possessions of planters in Charles and five other Maryland counties. Cary Carson describes Sarum, a surviving early Charles County dwelling, in "The 'Virginia House' in Maryland," *Md. Hist. Mag.* 69 (1974): 191–95, as does J. Richard Rivoire in *Homeplaces: Traditional Domestic Architecture of Charles County, Maryland* (La Plata, Md.: Southern Maryland Studies Center, Charles County Community College, 1990), 36–41.

5. For discussion of the lack of town development, see Lois Green Carr, " 'The Metropolis of Maryland': A Comment on Town Development along the Tobacco Coast," *Md. Hist. Mag.* 69 (1974): 139–45. Probing analyses of the nature and extent of social and communal interactions among early settlers are in Lorena S. Walsh, "Community Networks in the Early Chesapeake," and Michael Graham, "Meetinghouse and Chapel: Religion and Community in Seventeenth-Century Maryland," in *Colonial Chesapeake Society*, ed. Carr et al., 200–41, 242–74, respectively. The founding of Anglican churches and parishes is covered in Percy G. Skirven, *The First Parishes of the Province of Maryland: Wherein Are Given Historical Sketches of the Ten Counties & of the Thirty Parishes in the Province at the Time of the Establishment of the Church of England in Maryland in 1692* (Baltimore: Norman, Remington Co., 1923), 133–34, and Nelson W. Rightmyer, *Maryland's Established Church* (Baltimore: Church Historical Society, for the Diocese of Maryland, 1956), 141–43. Difficulties faced by the early establishment are the subject of Graham, "Churching the Unchurched: The Establishment in Maryland, 1692–1724," *Md. Hist. Mag.* 83 (1988): 297–309.

6. Walsh, "Charles County, Maryland, 1658–1705," especially 373–80; idem, "Servitude and Opportunity in Charles County, Maryland, 1658–1705," 115–28; idem, "Staying Put or Getting Out," 89–103; Donnell M. Owings, "Private Manors: An Edited List," in *Material for the Study of Maryland Manors*, comp. Montgomery Schuyler (New York: Order of Colonial Lords of Manors in America, 1944), 43–57; Carr and Walsh, "The Planter's Wife," 560–61.

7. Russell R. Menard, "Five Maryland Censuses, 1700 to 1712: A Note on the Quality of the Quantities," *WMQ* 37 (1980): 618; idem, "The Maryland Slave Population, 1658 to 1730," 32, 43; Walsh, "Staying Put or Getting Out," 98–102. The following sources help place Charles County developments in broader contexts. An index of Chesapeake prices of servants and slaves, 1641–1720, is in Menard, "From

Servants to Slaves: The Transformation of the Chesapeake Labor System," 372. Philip D. Curtin's influential thesis that blacks had greater immunities to malaria and yellow fever because of the African disease environment, and therefore were more likely than Europeans to survive in the New World, is contained in his "Epidemiology and the Slave Trade," *Political Science Quarterly* 83 (1968): 190–216. See also Darrett B. Rutman and Anita H. Rutman, "Of Agues and Fevers: Malaria in the Early Chesapeake," *WMQ* 33 (1976): 56–57, for a suggestive comment on a possible link between mortality rates and economic polarization. Persuasive evidence of the increasing disparity between the resources of greater and lesser planters emerges from Gloria L. Main's tabulation of the mean personal wealth of men's estates probated in six Maryland counties, including Charles, between 1656 and 1719. Main, *Tobacco Colony*, 54.

8. A detailed examination of this process is in Lorena S. Walsh, "The Development of Local Power Structures: Maryland's Lower Western Shore in the Early Colonial Period," in *Power and Status: Officeholding in Colonial America*, ed. Bruce C. Daniels (Middletown, Conn.: Wesleyan University Press, 1986), 53–71. The provincial perspective is presented in David W. Jordan, "Maryland's Privy Council, 1637–1715," in *Law, Society, and Politics in Early Maryland*, ed. Land et al., 65–87, and "Political Stability and the Emergence of a Native Elite in Maryland," in *The Chesapeake in the Seventeenth Century*, ed. Tate and Ammerman, 243–73. The Courts family was one of few in Charles County that began in indentured servitude and advanced to gentry status by the early eighteenth century. Papenfuse et al., eds., *Biographical Dictionary* 1:237–38.

9. Brugger, *Maryland: A Middle Temperament, 1634–1980*, 52–56; Lois Green Carr and David W. Jordan, *Maryland's Revolution of Government, 1689–1692* (Ithaca, N.Y.: Cornell University Press, 1974).

CHAPTER ONE: JOHN ELGIN'S WORLD

1. CCW, Libs. AC4 (1734–52), fols. 258–59, AE6 (1767–77), fols. 64–65, 106; 1733 List of Taxables, Charles County, Md., in the Scharf Collection, box 96, folder 1; CCDB, 1753 and 1774, fols. 74 and 28, respectively; 1755 List of Taxables, Lower Durham Parish, in Secretary in Maryland, Tax Lists (S244); and Durham Parish Vestry Minutes, 1774–1824, fol. 17, in the Christ Church, Old Durham Parish Collection (S2604), Special Collections, all at MSA; Samuel Elgin pension file, Revolutionary War Pension and Bounty-Land Warrant Application Files, Record Group 15, Microcopy 804, reel 910, National Archives and Records Service, Washington, D.C. Population data for the colonial period are in Tables 1, 3, and 4 of the Appendix. The main roads as of 1762 are identified in CCCR, Lib. M3 (1762–64), fols. 106–08. Analysis of white kin networks as of 1733 is in Jean Butenhoff Lee, "The Social Order of a Revolutionary People: Charles County, Maryland, 1733–86" (Ph.D. diss., University of Virginia, 1984), 141–44. Blacks attested to familiarity with their lineages in the General Court of the Western Shore, Judgment Records (S497), Lib. JG27 (May Term 1795), fols. 33–35, MSA. John Elgin lived until 1780. Durham Parish Vestry Minutes, 1774–1824, fol. 7.

2. Joseph Mosley to his sister, Oct. 5, 1760, in "Letters of Father Joseph Mosley, 1757–1786," ed. E. I. Devitt, *Woodstock Letters* 35 (1906): 43; CCW, Libs. AC4, fols.

215–16, AD5 (1752–67), fols. 243–48. The nationalities of whites in the county as of 1790 are summarized in [W. S. Rossiter], comp., *A Century of Population Growth: From the First Census of the United States to the Twelfth, 1790–1900* (Washington, D.C.: U.S. Bureau of the Census, 1909), 272.

3. *Md. Gazette*, Aug. 4, 1747; Thomas Howe Ridgate to Zephaniah Turner, Oct. 7, 1771, and to John Barnes, Nov. 6, 1771, Ridgate Letter Book, 31, 46; Civil Office Index, in the Legislative History Project Collection (SC1138), Special Collections, MSA; Cresswell, *Journal*, 18.

4. Hunter to Mr. Corbey, undated, Father George Hunter's Letter Book, 1760, fol. 4, in Maryland Province Archives of the Society of Jesus, 2.W, Special Collections Division, Georgetown University Library, Washington, D.C.

5. Darold D. Wax, "Black Immigrants: The Slave Trade in Colonial Maryland," *Md. Hist. Mag.* 73 (1978): 30–45; Philip D. Curtin, *The Atlantic Slave Trade: A Census* (Madison: University of Wisconsin Press, 1969), 72–75, 85–92, 282–84, and chaps. 4, 7; Paul E. Lovejoy, "The Volume of the Atlantic Slave Trade: A Synthesis," *Journal of African History* 23 (1982): 473–501; James A. Rawley, *The Transatlantic Slave Trade: A History* (New York: W. W. Norton & Co., 1981); Mahdi Adamu, "The Delivery of Slaves from the Central Sudan to the Bight of Benin in the Eighteenth and Nineteenth Centuries," and Paul Lovejoy and Jan S. Hogendorn, "Slave Marketing in West Africa," in *The Uncommon Market: Essays in the Economic History of the Atlantic Slave Trade*, ed. Henry A. Gemery and Jan S. Hogendorn (New York: Academic Press, 1979), 163–80, 213–35; Roland Oliver, *The African Experience* (New York: HarperCollins Publishers, 1992), chap. 10; Joseph C. Miller, *Way of Death: Merchant Capitalism and the Angolan Slave Trade, 1730–1830* (Madison: University of Wisconsin Press, 1988), especially chap. 11 on the experience of enslavement and transport to the Western Hemisphere.

6. *Md. Gazette*, Aug. 16, 1759, Sept. 24, Oct. 29, 1761; Buchanan & Simson (Glasgow) to Halliday & Dunbar, Oct. 19, 1759, and to Arthur & Benjamin Haywood, Nov. 14, 1759, Buchanan & Simson Letterbook, 1759–61, CS96/507, Scottish Record Office, Edinburgh (used with permission of the Keeper of the Records of Scotland); Ridgate to Clay & Midgley, Nov. 21, 1771, and to Barnes, Dec. 2, 1771, Ridgate Letter Book, 43–44, 77; Wax, "Black Immigrants," 31–38.

7. Table 1, Appendix. For discussions of natural increase, see Lorena S. Walsh, "Charles County, Maryland, 1658–1705: A Study of Chesapeake Social and Political Structure" (Ph.D. diss., Michigan State University, 1977), 74; Russell R. Menard, "The Maryland Slave Population, 1658 to 1730: A Demographic Profile of Blacks in Four Counties," *WMQ* 32 (1975): 38–45; and Jean Butenhoff Lee, "The Problem of Slave Community in the Eighteenth-Century Chesapeake," *WMQ* 43 (1986): 342.

8. The 1778 Charles County Constables' Census, in *Maryland Records: Colonial, Revolutionary, County and Church*, comp. Gaius M. Brumbaugh, 2 vols. (Baltimore: Williams & Wilkins Co., 1915, 1928; Baltimore: Genealogical Publishing Co., 1967), 1:295–312; Cresswell, *Journal*, 19, 56; Samuel Grahame to Samuel Grahame, Dec. 5, 1772, Chancery Records, 1792–93, fol. 66.

9. Charles County Rent Roll, Lib. 26 (1753–75), in Land Office, Rent Rolls (S18), MSA; 1782 Assessment Lists, Scharf Collection, box 96, folders 7–10, 12–17; CCW, Lib. AE6, fols. 134–37; CCDB, 1774; Table 7, Appendix.

10. The proprietary lands were laid out in manors named Calverton, Chaptico, Pangaiah, and Zachiah. Henry Harford claim, American Loyalist Claims, A. O. 12/79, fols. 132–40, A. O. 13/61, fols. 91–92, Public Record Office (microfilm in the Manuscript Division, LC); Leonard Calvert, "Answers to the Queries published in the London Chronicle Dated Sept. 16–19, 1758," Calvert Papers (MS. 174), no. 595, fols. 2–3, MHS; quitrent accounts with the rent roll keeper of the Western Shore, Proprietary Account Book, Calvert Papers, no. 933, fols. 4–6; Charles A. Barker, *The Background of the Revolution in Maryland* (New Haven: Yale University Press, 1940), 140–41. See also Clarence P. Gould, *The Land System in Maryland, 1720–1765* (Baltimore: Johns Hopkins Press, 1913) and, for proprietary lands, Gregory A. Stiverson, *Poverty in a Land of Plenty: Tenancy in Eighteenth-Century Maryland* (Baltimore: Johns Hopkins University Press, 1977).

11. CCDB, 1774; Table 7, Appendix.

12. John Ewing to Samuel Purviance, May 29, 1785, in *Maryland Reports . . . of the Most Important Law Cases . . . 1700 to 1799*, comp. Thomas Harris, Jr., and John McHenry, 4 vols. (New York: I. Riley, 1809–13; Annapolis: Jonas Green, 1818) 1:570; Carroll to William Graves, Aug. 14, 1772, "A Lost Copy-Book of Charles Carroll of Carrollton," *Md. Hist. Mag.* 32 (1937): 218; Johann David Schoepf, *Travels in the Confederation [1783–84]*, trans. Alfred J. Morrison, 2 vols., 1911 (New York: Bergman Publishers, 1968), 2:27. One local planter solved the problem by bequeathing his neighbor twenty-five acres "which the lines of my Land Takes from him." CCW, Lib. AD5, fols. 357–58.

13. On boundary stones and posts, see CCW, Lib. AD5, fol. 245, and Charles County Rent Roll, Lib. 26, fols. 136, 141. On Poynton Manor, consult Land Office, Patent Records (S11), Lib. AB&H, fol. 425, MSA; minutes of the county tax commissioners, 1783, Scharf Collection, box 96, folder 24; and Donnell M. Owings, "Private Manors: An Edited List," in *Material for the Study of the Maryland Manors*, comp. Montgomery Schuyler (New York: Order of Colonial Lords of Manors in America, 1944), 47–48.

14. Schoepf, *Travels in the Confederation* 2:27; William Eddis, *Letters from America*, ed. Aubrey C. Land (Cambridge: Belknap Press of Harvard University Press, 1969), 64.

15. CCCR, Libs. T3 (1770–72), fol. 617, N3 (1764–66), fol. 721.

16. Ibid., Libs. K3 (1760–62), fols. 152, 224, 303, 307, M3 (1762–64), fols. 4, 5, 504, 507, Q3 (1767–70), fol. 499, T3, fol. 617.

17. Ibid., Libs. I3 (1759–60), fol. 428, K3, fols. 300–03, N3, fol. 380, P3 (1766–67), fol. 264, U3 (1772–73), fol. 442.

18. Maryland Province Archives of the Society of Jesus, 101.N.3, 101.N.5. Over the fifteen years from 1759 through 1773, 113 "viewings" of land to perpetuate the boundaries were entered in the court records.

19. Adam Gordon, "Journal of an Officer Who Travelled in America and the West Indies in 1764 and 1765," in *Travels in the American Colonies*, ed. Newton D. Mereness (New York: Macmillan, 1916), 407–08; Philip Padelford, ed., *Colonial Panorama 1775: Dr. Robert Honyman's Journal for March and April* (San Marino, Calif.: Huntington Library, 1939), 2, 4; 1783 Charles County Land Tax Lists, Scharf Collection, box 96, folders 18–20, 25, 28, box 98, folders 1, 3; Grahame to Grahame, July 3, 1773, Chancery Records, 1792–93, fols. 67–68; Henry Harford claim, American Loyalist Claims, A. O. 12/79, fols. 132–33, 138–40. The major soil associations and

characteristics are discussed and located in Richard L. Hall and Earle D. Matthews, *Soil Survey of Charles County, Maryland* (Washington, D.C.: Soil Conservation Service, U.S. Department of Agriculture, in cooperation with the Maryland Agricultural Experiment Station, 1974).

20. 1783 Charles County Land Tax Lists, Scharf Collection, box 96, folders 18–20, 25, 28, box 98, folders 1, 3; CCW, Libs. AC4, fols. 152–53, 186–88, 203–06, 233–35, AD5, fols. 18–20, 81–82, 360–64, AE6, fols. 29, 136, AF7 (1777–82), fols. 62, 242; Gordon, "Journal," 408; Cresswell, *Journal*, 18. Original boundary trees mentioned in the Charles County Rent Roll, Lib. 26, reveal the composition of the virgin forest. Recent interpretations that stress the rationality and environmental conservatism of long-fallow cultivation in the Chesapeake are Lorena S. Walsh, "Land, Landlord, and Leaseholder: Estate Management and Tenant Fortunes in Southern Maryland, 1642–1820," *Agricultural History* 59 (1985): 385, and Carville Earle, "The Myth of the Southern Soil Miner: Macrohistory, Agricultural Innovation, and Environmental Change," in *The Ends of the Earth: Perspectives on Modern Environmental History*, ed. Donald Worster (New York: Cambridge University Press, 1988), 175–78, 192–98. The author wishes to thank David O. Percy for sharing his insights on the rationality of agricultural practices in the eighteenth-century Chesapeake.

21. CCW, Libs. AD5, fols. 2–4, 223, 252–53, AE6, fol. 81; CCCR, Lib. T3, fol. 435; St. Thomas Manor Rent Book (1755–1812) and George Hunter's Day Book Memoranda, 1763–69, in Maryland Province Archives of the Society of Jesus, 172.B, 172.C, respectively.

22. Cresswell, *Journal*, 17–18; Grahame to Grahame, July 3, 1773, Chancery Records, 1792–93, fol. 68; John Brown to Alexander Hamilton, Oct. 11, 1773, Hamilton Papers, 1760–1800 (MS. 1301), MHS. Other contemporary descriptions of tobacco production are in *The American Museum, or Repository of Ancient and Modern Fugitive Pieces, Prose and Poetical* (Philadelphia), 1 (1787): 135–37; Thomas Jefferson, "On Tobacco Culture," in *The Papers of Thomas Jefferson*, ed. Julian P. Boyd et al., 25 vols. to date (Princeton: Princeton University Press, 1950–), 7:209–12; Thomas Anburey, *Travels through the Interior Parts of America: In a Series of Letters, by an Officer*, 2 vols. (London: William Lane, 1789; New York: Arno Press, 1969), 2:386–89. See also Gloria L. Main, *Tobacco Colony: Life in Early Maryland, 1650–1720* (Princeton: Princeton University Press, 1982), 31–35, and Arthur Pierce Middleton, *Tobacco Coast: A Maritime History of Chesapeake Bay in the Colonial Era* (Newport News, Va.: Mariners' Museum, 1953), 99–102. Lorena S. Walsh has calculated mean annual outputs of tobacco per laborer, which in the late colonial period ranged from a high of 1,078 to a low of 808 pounds. I am indebted to Dr. Walsh for sharing this information from her essay entitled "Slave Life, Slave Society, and Tobacco Production in the Tidewater Chesapeake," in *Cultivation and Culture: Labor and the Shaping of Slave Life in the Americas*, ed. Ira Berlin and Philip D. Morgan (Charlottesville: University Press of Virginia, forthcoming). In 1763 the Maryland Assembly directed that hogsheads must contain a minimum of 1,000 pounds of tobacco. Thomas Bacon, comp., *Laws of Maryland at Large, with Proper Indexes: Now first Collected into One Compleat Body, and Published from the Original Acts and Records . . .* (Annapolis: Jonas Green, 1765), Oct. Session 1763, chap. 18.

23. Information on the mix of crops and other plantation products may be found in estate inventories and administration accounts; for example, CCW, Lib. AF7, fols.

94, 139–40, 147–48, 197. Economic diversification is treated in John J. McCusker and Russell R. Menard, *The Economy of British America, 1607–1789* (Chapel Hill: University of North Carolina Press, for the Institute of Early American History and Culture, 1985), 124–33, and Lois Green Carr and Lorena S. Walsh, "Economic Diversification and Labor Organization in the Chesapeake, 1650–1820," in *Work and Labor in Early America,* ed. Stephen Innes (Chapel Hill: University of North Carolina Press, for the Institute of Early American History and Culture, 1988), 144–88. On exports, see, in addition to sources cited below, the British customs records for exports from the Northern Potomac and Patuxent naval districts, 1768–73, in Customs 16/1, Public Record Office (microfilm in the Virginia Colonial Records Project, reel 276, at the Tracy W. McGregor Library, Manuscripts Division, University of Virginia Library, Charlottesville). Charles was one of several counties whose commodities cleared through those naval offices; only aggregate data are available. For tobacco shipped from Maryland and Virginia, see U.S. Bureau of the Census, *Historical Statistics of the United States: Colonial Times to 1970,* 2 vols. (Washington, D.C.: U.S. Government Printing Office, 1975), 2:1177–78, 1189–91. Jacob M. Price has pointed out that just before the Revolution, Maryland and Virginia accounted for more than 60 percent of colonial exports to England and Scotland. "The Economic Growth of the Chesapeake and the European Market, 1697–1775," *Journal of Economic History* 24 (1964): 496. On the importance of grain exports from the Chesapeake, see David Klingaman, "The Significance of Grain in the Development of the Tobacco Colonies" and "Food Surpluses and Deficits in the American Colonies, 1768–1772," *Journal of Economic History* 29 (1969): 268–78, and 31 (1971): 553–69, respectively; and Paul G. E. Clemens, *The Atlantic Economy and Colonial Maryland's Eastern Shore: From Tobacco to Grain* (Ithaca, N.Y.: Cornell University Press, 1980).

24. Grahame to Grahame, July 3, 1773, Chancery Records, 1792–93, fols. 68–69.

25. Ibid., fol. 68; Mosley to his brother, July 30, 1764, "Letters of Father Joseph Mosley," 44.

26. Grahame to Grahame, July 3, 1773, Chancery Records, 1792–93, fol. 68; Cresswell, *Journal,* 25; Robert Carter to William Diggs, July 21, 1774, Robert Carter Letterbook, May 1774–May 1775, fol. 26, Robert Carter Papers, William R. Perkins Library, Duke University, Durham, N.C. On damaged wheat, see *Md. Gazette,* Jan. 31, 1760, June 30, 1763, and estate inventories in CCW, Lib. AF7, fols. 171–72, 224, 258–60, 382–85, 617–22. Limitations of time and technology prevented more thorough gleaning, an observation for which the author is indebted to Lorena S. Walsh. Husbandry is the subject of David O. Percy's "Agricultural Labor on an Eighteenth-Century Chesapeake Plantation" (paper presented at a conference on "The Colonial Experience: The Eighteenth-Century Chesapeake," Baltimore, Md., 1984).

27. Hunter, Day Book Memoranda, 1770–85, fols. 3–4, 8, 15; CCLR, Lib. V3 (1775–82), fols. 588–91; *Md. Gazette,* Oct. 20, 1763, May 17, 1764, Aug. 5, 1773. A mill allegedly "long esteemed one of the best" in the county is described at some length in *Md. Gazette,* Oct. 23, 1777. References to milldams and water mills occasionally appear in CCW, as in Lib. AE6, fols. 8–10, 146–49, 153–54.

28. Cresswell, *Journal,* 20; Mosley to his sister, Sept. 1, 1759, "Letters of Father Joseph Mosley," 41; orphans' court proceedings, in CCW, Lib. AF7; "Journal of a French

Traveller in the Colonies, 1765, II," *American Historical Review* 27 (1921): 76; CCW, Lib. AF7, fols. 358–60; Joseph Scott, *A Geographical Description of the States of Maryland and Delaware* (Philadelphia: Kimber, Conrad & Co., 1807), 42.

29. Cresswell, *Journal*, 55, 57; Mosley to his sister, Sept. 1, 1759, "Letters of Father Joseph Mosley," 40–41; Isaac Weld, Jr., *Travels through the States of North America, and the Provinces of Upper and Lower Canada during the Years 1795, 1796, and 1797*, 4th ed., 2 vols. (London: John Stockdale, 1807; New York: Augustus M. Kelley, 1970), 1:140–41. Late colonial fisheries are mentioned in *Md. Gazette*, Oct. 13, 1763, Oct. 8, Dec. 17, 1772, Mar. 4, 1773; CCCR, Lib. U3, fol. 261; and Chancery Records, 1784–86, fol. 312.

30. Carr and Walsh, "Economic Diversification and Labor Organization in the Chesapeake, 1650–1820," 145–49. Plantations rarely were self-sufficient in fiber production. Chesapeake production of flaxseed that was shipped to Ireland remains an unexplored subject, but see Thomas M. Truxes, *Irish-American Trade, 1660–1783* (New York: Cambridge University Press, 1988), 107. For encouragement of flax growing in Maryland, see *Md. Gazette*, July 5, 26, 1745, and an act passed at the time of the Stamp Act agitation, in *Arch. Md.* 59:267–69. Thomas Anburey described cotton cultivation in Virginia in *Travels through the Interior Parts of America* 2:423–27.

31. *Arch. Md.* 37:588–89; Russell R. Menard, "The Tobacco Industry in the Chesapeake Colonies, 1617–1730: An Interpretation," *Research in Economic History* 5 (1980): 109–77.

32. The leading authority on the Chesapeake tobacco trade during the eighteenth century is Jacob M. Price, whose writings include "The Rise of Glasgow in the Chesapeake Tobacco Trade, 1707–1775," *WMQ* 11 (1954): 179–99; "Economic Growth of the Chesapeake," 496–511; *France and the Chesapeake: A History of the French Tobacco Monopoly, 1674–1791, and of Its Relationship to the British and American Tobacco Trades*, 2 vols. (Ann Arbor: University of Michigan Press, 1973); and *Capital and Credit in British Overseas Trade: The View from the Chesapeake, 1700–1776* (Cambridge: Harvard University Press, 1980). See also Vertrees J. Wyckoff, *Tobacco Regulation in Colonial Maryland* (Baltimore: Johns Hopkins Press, 1936) and, for the tobacco inspection act of 1747, *Arch. Md.* 44:595–638. The outlines of the boom cycle that began in Maryland in 1766 and ended abruptly in the late summer of 1772 are given in Jean H. Vivian, "The Poll Tax Controversy in Maryland, 1770–76: A Case of Taxation *with* Representation," *Md. Hist. Mag.* 71 (1976): 158. The boom is documented in Table 9, Appendix; see also Charles County Court, Tobacco Inspection Proceedings (C680), vol. 70 (1755–69), fols. 231–307. Also consult Allan Kulikoff, *Tobacco and Slaves: The Development of Southern Cultures in the Chesapeake, 1680–1800* (Chapel Hill: University of North Carolina Press, for the Institute of Early American History and Culture, 1986), 119–22.

33. Donnell M. Owings, *His Lordship's Patronage: Offices of Profit in Colonial Maryland* (Baltimore: Maryland Historical Society, 1953), 64–65; *Md. Gazette*, Aug. 4, 1757, Aug. 16, 1759, Jan. 29, 1761, Oct. 20, 1763, Mar. 15, Apr. 5, May 17, 1764, July 19, 1770.

34. Lewis Evans, *A General Map of the Middle British Colonies, in America* ([Philadelphia]: engraved by James Turner, 1755); William Faden, *The North American Atlas, Selected from the Most Authentic Maps, Charts, Plans, &c. Hitherto published* (London: William Faden, 1777); *Md. Gazette*, Mar. 2, 1769, Feb. 13, 1777, May 26, 1796; John F. D. Smyth claim, American Loyalist Claims, ser. 2, A. O. 13/62, fol. 237; CCCR, Lib.

Y3 (1778–80), fols. 466–70; CCW, Libs. AC4, fols. 252–55, AD5, fols. 243–48; Grahame to Grahame, July 3, 1773, Chancery Records, 1792–93, fol. 68; Ethel R. Hayden, "Port Tobacco, Lost Town of Maryland," *Md. Hist. Mag.* 40 (1945): 261–76. Annual export figures for each inspection warehouse in the county, 1755–69, are in Charles County Court, Tobacco Inspection Proceedings, vol. 70. My figures are for the period after the Seven Years' War; see Table 8, Appendix. For discussion of river ports in the eighteenth-century South, see Jacob M. Price, "Economic Function and the Growth of American Port Towns in the Eighteenth Century," *Perspectives in American History* 8 (1974): 123–86; Carville Earle and Ronald Hoffman, "Staple Crops and Urban Development in the Eighteenth-Century South," *Perspectives in American History* 10 (1976): 7–78; and Middleton, *Tobacco Coast*, 40–42.

35. *Md. Gazette*, May 28, June 22, 29, 1748, Aug. 16, 1759, Jan. 31, 1760; CCW, Lib. AC4, fols. 151–52; 1754 List of Taxables, Charles Town [Port Tobacco], Md., in Secretary in Maryland, Tax Lists; *Arch. Md.* 50:15, 59; "Journal of a French Traveller," 70.

36. Hunter D. Farish, ed., *Journal and Letters of Philip Vickers Fithian, 1773–1774: A Plantation Tutor of the Old Dominion*, new ed. (Williamsburg, Va.: Colonial Williamsburg, 1957), 97, 109; Cresswell, *Journal*, 19–20; Honyman, *Colonial Panorama 1775*, 3–4; CCCR, Libs. I3, fol. 264, T3, fols. 497–98, 591, U3, fols. 454–56; *Md. Gazette*, Oct. 13, 20, 1763, Oct. 18, 1764, Jan. 23, Apr. 9, 1772.

37. The author wishes to thank the Museum of Early Southern Decorative Arts, Winston-Salem, N.C., for sharing information on Charles County artisans. Store customers are named in ledgers, invoices, inventories, and letter books, Port Tobacco, Md., in John Glassford & Co. Papers, containers 21, 56–62, Manuscript Division, LC; and list of balances due the Port Tobacco store of Cunninghame, Findlay & Co., Sept. 1, 1777, A.O. 13/29, Public Record Office (microfilm in the Virginia Colonial Records Project, reel 250).

38. Thomas Stone to Hunter, Oct. 3, 1771, and Hunter's undated petition to the Assembly, Maryland Province Archives of the Society of Jesus, 101a.Z.1, 101a.Z.2; *Md. Gazette*, Oct. 10, 1771; *Arch. Md.* 63:12.

39. Nanjemoy: Cresswell, *Journal*, 17; *Md. Gazette*, Aug. 16, 1759, May 25, 1773. Newport: Journal, 1768–76, Newport and Port Tobacco, Md., in John Glassford & Co. Papers, container 21; *Md. Gazette*, Sept. 18, 1760, Mar. 22, May 17, 1764, Mar. 3, Aug. 11, 1774; Jacob M. Price, "Buchanan & Simson, 1759–1763: A Different Kind of Glasgow Firm Trading to the Chesapeake," *WMQ* 40 (1983): 25; Table 8, Appendix.

40. *Md. Gazette*, July 24, 1760, Apr. 30, Oct. 29, 1761, July 15, 1762, Aug. 2, 1764; Table 8, Appendix.

41. T. H. Breen, "An Empire of Goods: The Anglicization of Colonial America, 1690–1776," *Journal of British Studies* 25 (1986): 467–99; " 'Baubles of Britain': The American and Consumer Revolutions of the Eighteenth Century," *Past and Present* 119 (1988): 73–104; Lorena S. Walsh, "Urban Amenities and Rural Sufficiency: Living Standards and Consumer Behavior in the Colonial Chesapeake, 1643–1777," *Journal of Economic History* 43 (1983): 109–17; Carr and Walsh, "The Standard of Living in the Colonial Chesapeake," *WMQ* 45 (1988): 137–42, 151; McCusker and Menard, *The Economy of British America, 1607–1789*, chap. 13.

42. Invoice and Letter Book, 1771–74, 1792–93, Port Tobacco, Md., in John Glassford

& Co. Papers, container 61, fols. 2–9; Price, "The Rise of Glasgow," 179–99; idem, *France and the Chesapeake* 1:588–617. The Potomac Valley was the only section of Maryland where the tobacco trade expanded until the Revolution, according to Price, "Economic Growth of the Chesapeake," 510.

43. In the depression year of 1773, for example, Jamieson Johnston & Co. at Glasgow shipped Gray goods with an inventoried value of £762. Invoice and Letter Book, 1771–74, 1792–93, Port Tobacco, Md., in John Glassford & Co. Papers, container 61, fols. 2–9, 44–47.

44. Ibid., fols. 2–9.

45. *Md. Gazette*, June 28, 1745, Jan. 25, 1749; Buchanan & Simson to George Maxwell, Nov. 7, 1759, and to Messrs. Fraser & Wharton, Nov. 30, 1759, Buchanan & Simson Letterbook, 1759–61; James Lawson to Hamilton, Jan. 31, 1764, Hamilton Papers; Lawson to James Dunlop, Sept. 23, 1767, James Lawson Letter Book, CS96/1200, Scottish Record Office (used with permission of the Keeper of the Records of Scotland); Grahame to Grahame, July 3, 1773, Chancery Records, 1792–93, fol. 68; John M. Hemphill, "Freight Rates in the Maryland Tobacco Trade, 1705–1762," *Md. Hist. Mag.* 54 (1959): 36–58; Kulikoff, *Tobacco and Slaves*, 127–29.

46. Lawson to Hamilton, Jan. 31, Oct. 18, 1764, Hamilton Papers. Lawson calculated that by inflating the price of goods 25 percent "for Charges," the factor would drop his cost of tobacco from 6/ to 4/6 sterling per hundredweight. Price explains "Mark-ups and Profit Margins in the Chesapeake Trade" in *Capital and Credit in British Overseas Trade*, 149–51.

47. Lawson to Hamilton, Apr. 28, 1762, Jan. 13, 1763, Hamilton Papers.

48. For the amassing of mercantile wealth among Marylanders, see Aubrey C. Land, "Economic Base and Social Structure: The Northern Chesapeake in the Eighteenth Century," *Journal of Economic History* 25 (1965): 639–54; idem, "Economic Behavior in a Planting Society: The Eighteenth-Century Chesapeake," *Journal of Southern History* 33 (1967): 469–85; Main, *Tobacco Colony*, 81, 87–90; and Edward C. Papenfuse, *In Pursuit of Profit: The Annapolis Merchants in the Era of the American Revolution, 1763–1805* (Baltimore: Johns Hopkins University Press, 1975), chaps. 1–2.

49. Jacob M. Price, "One Family's Empire: The Russell-Lee-Clerk Connection in Maryland, Britain, and India, 1707–1857," *Md. Hist. Mag.* 72 (1977): 167–77, 179; Ethel R. Hayden, "The Lees of Blenheim," ibid., 37 (1942): 199–207; Owings, *His Lordship's Patronage*, 122, 161; Philip Richard Fendall to James Russell, Aug. 13, 26, 1774, Russell Papers, bundle 3, and James Forbes to Russell, Feb. 21, 1774, bundle 6, Coutts & Co., London (microfilm in the Virginia Colonial Records Project, reel M-235, at the Colonial Williamsburg Foundation Library, Williamsburg, Va.); Papenfuse et al., eds., *Biographical Dictionary* 1:318–19, 323, 2:526–27. James Russell's wife and Philip Richard Fendall's mother were sisters. An Annapolis resident wrote to Ann Lee Russell in London as follows: "Your Taste in fine Things is so much admir'd, that the first Question now ask'd by the Ladies at the Opening of a New Cargo, is whether you had the Choosing of the Embroider[y], Laces, Caps . . . they need only this Recommendation, so much your Choice has become the Standard of Taste in Annapolis." Nicholas Maccubbin to Lee, Russell Papers, bundle 13.

50. Chancery Record 11, DD2, fols. 390–438; Buchanan & Simson Letterbook, 1759–61; Buchanan & Simson Invoice Book, 1755–61, CS96/503, fol. 196, Scottish Record Office (used with permission of the Keeper of the Records of Scotland); *Md. Gazette*,

Sept. 4, 1760; CCW, Lib. AF7, fols. 92–93, 346–56, 393; Price, "Buchanan & Simson," 24–25, 29–31.

51. Price, "Buchanan & Simson," 4–41; idem, ed., *Joshua Johnson's Letterbook, 1771–1774: Letters from a Merchant in London to His Partners in Maryland* (London: London Record Society, 1979), xi–xii.

52. *Md. Gazette*, Oct. 25, 1759, Aug. 9, 23, 1764, June 27, 1765, Oct. 9, 1766, Oct. 1, 1767, Mar. 24, 1768, Sept. 14, 1769; Papenfuse et al., eds., *Biographical Dictionary* 1:454–55, 2:485–86. The earliest reference found to the Jenifer and Stone partnership is a bond dated May 26, 1765, in the William Cooke Papers (MS. 195), MHS; the earliest known reference to Hooe, Stone & Co. is dated Sept. 17, 1768, in Journal, Newport and Port Tobacco, Md., in the John Glassford & Co. Papers, container 21. Zephaniah Turner, a prominent local planter, apparently was a silent partner in the firm from 1768 to 1770 and in the latter year sold his share for £500 sterling. He recorded his net gain on the investment as £220. The Hooe-Stone-Jenifer partnership was formed June 11, 1771, and when Frederick Stone died in 1773, his share of the firm was worth £1,127 sterling. Zephaniah Turner Account Book, 1764–72, fols. 39, 63, Manuscript Division, LC; Deeds of Conveyance, Lib. S3 (1770–75), fol. 600, CCLR; CCW, Libs. AE6, fol. 170, AF7, fols. 162–66.

53. Hooe, Stone & Co. Invoice Book, 1770–84, Rare Books and Manuscripts Division, New York Public Library, Astor, Lenox, and Tilden Foundations, New York, N.Y. An advertisement for town lots, published in the *Md. Gazette*, Feb. 24, 1763, extolled the commercial virtues of Alexandria. Contemporary descriptions are in Fred Shelley, ed., "The Journal of Ebenezer Hazard in Virginia, 1777," *Virginia Magazine of History and Biography* 62 (1954): 401–02, and Howard C. Rice, Jr., and Anne S. K. Brown, trans. and eds., *The American Campaigns of Rochambeau's Army, 1780, 1781, 1782, 1783*, 2 vols. (Princeton and Providence: Princeton University Press and Brown University Press, 1972), 1:73, 159.

54. Hooe, Stone & Co. Invoice Book, 1770–84, fols. 1–7. The best-documented account of a Maryland merchant who established himself in London is Price, ed., *Joshua Johnson's Letterbook.* See also idem, "One Family's Empire," 174, and Papenfuse, *In Pursuit of Profit*, chap. 2.

55. Papenfuse et al., eds., *Biographical Dictionary* 1:114–16; *Md. Gazette*, July 19, Aug. 23, 1770, May 27, 1773; Ridgate to J. Barnes, Aug. 31, 1771, and to Clay & Midgley, Sept. 30, 1771, Ridgate Letter Book, 3, 22.

56. Ridgate to J. Barnes, Aug. 31, Sept. 19, Oct. 7, Nov. 6, 1771, to Turner, Sept. 19, Oct. 7, 1771, to Abraham Barnes, Oct. 7, 1771, to Thomas Johns, Nov. 6, 1771, to Alexander McPherson, Nov. 6, 1771, to Josh [John?] Gwinn, Nov. 6, 1771, and to William James, Dec. 9, 1771, Ridgate Letter Book, 1, 4, 10–11, 13, 24–25, 29, 32, 52, 61–64, 90.

CHAPTER TWO: DEGREES OF FREEDOM

1. CCW, Lib. AC4 (1734–52), fols. 315–17; Jonathan Boucher, *A View of the Causes and Consequences of the American Revolution; in Thirteen Discourses, Preached in North America between the Years 1763 and 1775* (London, 1797; New York: Russell & Russell, 1967), 186. The English social order is the subject of Roy Porter, *English Society in the Eighteenth Century* (London: Allen Lane, 1982), chap. 2, and J. C. D. Clark, *English*

Society, 1688–1832: Ideology, Social Structure, and Political Practice during the Ancien Regime (New York: Cambridge University Press, 1985). Summary statements are in Jack P. Greene, *Pursuits of Happiness: The Social Development of Early Modern British Colonies and the Formation of American Culture* (Chapel Hill: University of North Carolina Press, 1988), 105–11, and Carl Bridenbaugh, *Vexed and Troubled Englishmen, 1590–1642* (New York: Oxford University Press, 1967), 16–17. On the long tradition of property rights in persons, consult David B. Davis, *The Problem of Slavery in Western Culture* (Ithaca, N.Y.: Cornell University Press, 1966), chaps. 3–4. Rhys Isaac offers a richly nuanced interpretation of Virginia's hierarchical society in *The Transformation of Virginia, 1740–1790* (Chapel Hill: University of North Carolina Press, for the Institute of Early American History and Culture, 1982), part 1.

2. Isaac, *The Transformation of Virginia, 1740–1790*, chap. 8; Keith Mason, "Localism, Evangelicalism, and Loyalism: The Sources of Discontent in the Revolutionary Chesapeake," *Journal of Southern History* 56 (1990): 23–38; T. H. Breen, *Tobacco Culture: The Mentality of the Great Tidewater Planters on the Eve of the Revolution* (Princeton: Princeton University Press, 1985); Allan Kulikoff, *Tobacco and Slaves: The Development of Southern Cultures in the Chesapeake, 1680–1800* (Chapel Hill: University of North Carolina Press, for the Institute of Early American History and Culture, 1986), 263, 300; Ronald Hoffman, *A Spirit of Dissension: Economics, Politics, and the Revolution in Maryland* (Baltimore: Johns Hopkins University Press, 1973); David C. Skaggs, "Maryland's Impulse toward Social Revolution, 1750–1776," *Journal of American History* 54 (1968): 771–86; idem, *Roots of Maryland Democracy, 1753–1776* (Westport, Conn.: Greenwood Press, 1973); John C. Rainbolt, "A Note on the Maryland Declaration of Rights and Constitution of 1776," *Md. Hist. Mag.* 66 (1971): 421–23.

3. In addition to illustrations of dwellings reproduced in this volume, see J. Richard Rivoire, *Homeplaces: Traditional Domestic Architecture of Charles County, Maryland* (La Plata, Md.: Southern Maryland Studies Center, Charles County Community College, 1990) and Maryland Historical Trust, *Inventory of Historic Sites in Calvert County, Charles County, and St. Mary's County*, rev. ed. (Annapolis: Maryland Historical Trust, 1980), 57–109. Isaac, *The Transformation of Virginia, 1740–1790*, adeptly uses visual images to evoke social differences. The utility of land and tax records for portraying wealth distribution is dependent upon their accuracy and inclusiveness. Advantages and limitations of probate records are discussed in Lois Green Carr and Lorena S. Walsh, "Inventories and the Analysis of Wealth and Consumption Patterns in St. Mary's County, Maryland, 1658–1777," *Historical Methods* 13 (1980): 81–82; Gloria L. Main, "The Correction of Biases in Colonial American Probate Records," *Historical Methods Newsletter* 8 (1974): 10–28; idem, "Probate Records as a Source for Early American History," *WMQ* 32 (1975): 89–99. An example of a wealth distribution "pyramid" for Maryland is in Robert J. Brugger, *Maryland: A Middle Temperament, 1634–1980* (Baltimore: Johns Hopkins University Press, in association with the Maryland Historical Society, 1988), 781; cf. Carr and Walsh, "Economic Diversification and Labor Organization in the Chesapeake, 1650–1820," in *Work and Labor in Early America*, ed. Stephen Innes (Chapel Hill: University of North Carolina Press, for the Institute of Early American History and Culture, 1988), 149n.

4. "An Account of the Number of Souls in the Province of Maryland, in the Year 1755," *Gentleman's Magazine* (London), 34 (1964): 261. Data from the census are reproduced in Table 3 of the Appendix.

5. In order, the quotations are from a statement of Thomas Stone, Dec. 20, 1781, Pardon Papers, box 1, folder 82; undated letter from Richard Lee, Jr., to [British claims commissioners], in American Loyalist Claims, ser. 2, A. O. 13/40, fols. 100–01, Public Record Office, London (microfilm in the Manuscript Division, LC); Cresswell, *Journal*, 26. The statement about slaves is based on Charles County Sheriff, Account Book, 1769 (C649), at MSA, which records the levies assessed on the taxables of 438 male taxpayers. Only 4 had at least 20 taxables, including both slaves and white men. Land distribution data are from the CCDB, 1774, as summarized in Table 7 of the Appendix. The 713 "owners" listed in the Debt Book included 585 men, 38 women, 87 sets of heirs, and 3 institutions. Genealogical relationships among gentry families are traced in Harry Wright Newman, *Charles County Gentry* (Washington, D.C.: Harry Wright Newman, 1940).

6. *Md. Gazette*, Aug. 14, 1777; CCDB, 1774, fol. 57; Lee to [British claims commissioners], undated, American Loyalist Claims, ser. 2, A. O. 13/40, fols. 100–01; bill of complaint filed by Samuel Hanson, May 10, 1788, in Chancery Records, 1791–92, fol. 258.

7. The best collections of photographs of eighteenth-century dwellings are at the Southern Maryland Studies Center at Charles County Community College, La Plata, Md., and in the Historic American Buildings Survey files, Prints and Photographs Division, LC. Descriptions of the dwellings are in Rivoire, *Homeplaces: Traditional Domestic Architecture of Charles County, Maryland* and Maryland Historical Trust, *Inventory of Historic Sites in Calvert County, Charles County, and St. Mary's County*, 57–109. The 1783 Charles County Land Tax Lists, in the Scharf Collection, box 96, contain a brief description of each plantation. Additional information on Haberdeventure (also Habre de Venture) is in Don Swann, *Colonial and Historic Homes of Maryland*, 2d ed. (Baltimore: Johns Hopkins University Press, 1975), 32, and Aubrey A. Bodine, *Chesapeake Bay and Tidewater*, 3d ed. (Baltimore: Bodine & Associates, 1967), 64. For Margaret Brown Stone's dowry, see CCW, Lib. AD5 (1752–67), fols. 221–23. Blenheim, which burned during the nineteenth century, is described in [Mary Xavier Queen], *Grandma's Stories and Anecdotes of "Ye olden Times": Incidents of the War of Independence, etc.* (Boston: Angel Guardian Press, 1899), 125–27, 138, but see especially Rivoire, *Homeplaces: Traditional Domestic Architecture of Charles County, Maryland*, 10–11.

8. Every known gentleman whose will was filed for probate between 1740 and 1784 signed his name. Jean Butenhoff Lee, "The Social Order of a Revolutionary People: Charles County, Maryland, 1733–86" (Ph.D. diss., University of Virginia, 1984), 240. The most complete documentation of signature literacy for local men during the eighteenth century is in the oaths of fidelity to the state of Maryland, which are recorded in CCCR, Lib. X3 (1774–78), fols. 641–51. Of the county's free white males, age eighteen and above, 89 percent (N = 1,590) subscribed to the oath between January and April 1778; 1,068 (67 percent) signed their names while the others used marks. Male literacy rates rose gradually between the 1730s and the 1780s, according to probate evidence presented in Lee, "The Social Order of a Revolutionary People," 238. Gustavus Richard Brown's education is particularly well documented, including his thesis, *Disputatio physica inauguralis, de ortu animalium caloris* (Edinburgh, 1768), which is in the Rare Books and Special Collections Division, LC, and his medical diploma, which is in the Vertical File at MHS. See also CCW, Lib. AD5, fol. 221, and J. M. Toner, "A Sketch of the Life of Dr. Gustavus

Richard Brown of Port Tobacco, Maryland . . . ," *Sons of the Revolution in the State of Virginia Quarterly Magazine* 2 (1923): 12–23; George W. Corner, ed., *The Autobiography of Benjamin Rush: His "Travels through Life" together with his Commonplace Book for 1789–1813* (Princeton: Princeton University Press, for the American Philosophical Society, 1948), 43–44, 66; James Thacher, *American Medical Biography: or Memoirs of Eminent Physicians Who have Flourished in America*, 2 vols. (Boston: Richardson & Lord, 1828), 1:71. The educations of other young gentlemen from the county are mentioned in Hunter D. Farish, ed., *Journal and Letters of Philip Vickers Fithian, 1773–1774: A Plantation Tutor of the Old Dominion*, new ed. (Williamsburg, Va.: Colonial Williamsburg, 1957), 206; *Virginia Gazette* (Williamsburg), Oct. 28, 1773; and Papenfuse et al., eds., *Biographical Dictionary* 2:527, 741.

9. *Arch. Md.* 31:297–98; CCCR, Lib. Y3 (1778–80), fol. 596; Philip Ludwell Lee to [a brother], July 25, 1771, July 24, 1777, in the Lee Family Papers, 1638–1867 (Mss1 L51 f243–57), Virginia Historical Society, Richmond; John Hanson certificate, Apr. 1, 1748, in the Kremer Collection (850028), Southern Maryland Studies Center, Charles County Community College; will of Gustavus Brown, Dec. 9, 1755, CCW, Lib. AD5, fols. 219–34; *The Maryland Almanack For the Year of our Lord, 1761* (Annapolis: Jonas Green, 1760), 7. Riding chairs are mentioned in CCW, Libs. AD5, fols. 72–73, 221, AE6 (1767–77), fols. 133–34, and elsewhere. Thoroughbred horses owned by Charles countians are noted in CCW, Lib. AE5, fols. 242–43; *Md. Gazette*, Mar. 22, 1764; and J. Reaney Kelly, " 'Tulip Hill,' Its History and Its People," *Md. Hist. Mag.* 60 (1965): 370.

10. *Md. Gazette*, Feb. 3, 1748; *Arch. Md.* 32:355; Cresswell, *Journal*, 17–20, 23, 55.

11. Cresswell, *Journal*, 22–26.

12. Philip Richard Fendall to James Russell, Aug. 26, 1774, Russell Papers, bundle 3, Coutts & Co., London (microfilm in the Virginia Colonial Records Project, reel M-235, Colonial Williamsburg Foundation Library, Williamsburg, Va.); Boucher, *A View of the Causes and Consequences of the American Revolution*, 198; *Md. Gazette*, Feb. 15, 1787, Oct. 18, 1804; Cresswell, *Journal*, 26.

13. *Arch. Md.* 56:135–36; *Md. Gazette*, Mar. 25, Sept. 2, 1762; Joseph T. Wheeler, "Booksellers and Circulating Libraries in Colonial Maryland," *Md. Hist. Mag.* 34 (1939): 111–37.

14. *Arch. Md.* 34:740–44, 64:377; CCDB, 1750, fol. 40; memorial of former schoolmaster Francis Walker, Dec. 1777, in American Loyalist Claims, ser. 2, A. O. 13/40, fol. 230; *Md. Gazette*, June 4, 18, 30, 1772, Aug. 18, 1774. The free school was about a mile from Port Tobacco.

15. *Md. Gazette*, June 30, Nov. 5, 1772, May 27, 1773, Dec. 23, 1784; *Arch. Md.* 64:85, 336, 344, 377–79; Henry Tubman's account of payments to Charlotte Hall School, undated, Executive Papers, box 31, folder 132.

16. Thornton Anderson, "Eighteenth-Century Suffrage: The Case of Maryland," *Md. Hist. Mag.* 76 (1981): 143; *Arch. Md.* 30:612–17; CCW, Lib. AD5, fols. 219–34; Charles County Register of Wills, Inventories, 1753–66 (C665), fols. 203–09, MSA; Papenfuse et al., eds., *Biographical Dictionary* 1:242.

17. Donnell M. Owings, *His Lordship's Patronage: Offices of Profit in Colonial Maryland* (Baltimore: Maryland Historical Society, 1953); CCCR, Libs. I3 (1759–60) through X3 (1774–78). The structure and functions of county government are explained in Lois Green Carr, "The Foundations of Social Order: Local Government in Colonial Maryland," in *Town and County: Essays on the Structure of Local Government in the*

American Colonies, ed. Bruce C. Daniels (Middletown, Conn.: Wesleyan University Press, 1978), 72–94, and James S. Van Ness, "The Maryland Courts in the American Revolution: A Case Study" (Ph.D. diss., University of Maryland, 1967), 25–55.

18. CCCR, Libs. I3 through X3; "Maryland in 1773," *Md. Hist. Mag.* 2 (1907): 362; Owings, *His Lordship's Patronage*, 2; CCCR, Libs. I3, fol. 560, P3 (1766–67), fol. 151, T3 (1770–72), fol. 593.

19. CCCR, Lib. I3, fols. 21, 176, 264–69, 337, 359.

20. Ibid., fols. 21, 256, 426, Lib. K3 (1760–62), fols. 146, 588.

21. Ibid., Libs. I3, fol. 536, K3, fol. 405, M3 (1762–64), fol. 56; *Arch. Md.* 32:360.

22. *Arch. Md.* 46:428–30, 446–47, 557.

23. Papenfuse et al., eds., *Biographical Dictionary* 2:526–29; Owings, *His Lordship's Patronage*, 20n, 65–67, 122, 161; Rivoire, *Homeplaces: Traditional Domestic Architecture of Charles County, Maryland*, 10; Richard Lee, Sr., to [Thomas Gage?], July 4, 1774, Thomas Gage Papers, William L. Clements Library, University of Michigan, Ann Arbor. Rivoire, in a personal communication to the author, states that he believes Philip Lee (d. 1744) began building Blenheim and that his son Richard saw it finished. The "large and commodious" Lee town house in Annapolis is described in *Md. Gazette*, Feb. 26, 1784.

24. Rainbolt, "A Note on the Maryland Declaration of Rights and Constitution of 1776," 423. The CCDB, 1774, enumerated 585 male landowners, and the 1778 constables' census listed 1,787 free males aged eighteen and older. CCCR, Lib. X3, fols. 641–51. The proportion of Catholics in the population is unknown. Inventory valuations of slaves during the late colonial period are in CCW, Lib. AF7, fols. 10–12, 144–45, 167–68 and passim. The Assessment Lists for 1782, in the Scharf Collection, box 96, provide evidence for slaveownership among nonlandowners. Women's acquisition of real and personal property through parental bequests is analyzed in Jean Butenhoff Lee, "Land and Labor: Parental Bequest Practices in Charles County, Maryland, 1732–1783," in *Colonial Chesapeake Society*, ed. Lois Green Carr, Philip D. Morgan, and Jean B. Russo (Chapel Hill: University of North Carolina Press, for the Institute of Early American History and Culture, 1988), 306–41. On the franchise in colonial Maryland, see Anderson, "Eighteenth-Century Suffrage: The Case of Maryland," 141–58.

25. Vestry elections and activities are recorded in "Abstracts of Early Protestant Episcopal Church Records of Charles County, Maryland" (undated typescript, Martha Washington Chapter, Daughters of the American Revolution, Washington, D.C.) and the Durham Parish Vestry Minutes, 1774–1824, in the Christ Church, Old Durham Parish Collection (SC2604), Special Collections, MSA. Also consult Gerald E. Hartdagen, "The Vestry as a Unit of Local Government in Colonial Maryland," *Md. Hist. Mag.* 67 (1972): 363–88. A staunch defense of viva voce voting is in *Md. Gazette*, Nov. 10, 1791. James Haw explores ecclesiastical patronage in "The Patronage Follies: Bennet Allen, John Morton Jordan, and the Fall of Horatio Sharpe," *Md. Hist. Mag.* 71 (1976): 134, 137–44.

26. The length of each General Assembly elected between 1749 and 1773 is given in Papenfuse et al., eds., *Biographical Dictionary* 1:54–67. Property qualifications for election to the House of Delegates were not imposed until 1776. Thornton Anderson, "Maryland's Property Qualifications for Office: A Reinterpretation of the Constitutional Convention of 1776," *Md. Hist. Mag.* 73 (1978): 329–31.

27. *Md. Gazette*, Nov. 28, Dec. 19, 1754; Michael Earle to "Jemmy," Dec. 28, 1754,

Corner Collection (MS. 1242), MHS; *Arch. Md.* 50:605–07; Papenfuse et al., eds., *Biographical Dictionary* 2:522–23. The author wishes to thank Edward C. Papenfuse for bringing the Earle letter to her attention.

28. *Arch. Md.* 46:429–30.

29. Ibid., 430.

30. Ibid., 430, 557–58.

31. *Md. Gazette*, Oct. 17, Nov. 21, 1771. The colony's colorful election practices are the subject of Robert J. Dinkin, "Elections in Proprietary Maryland," *Md. Hist. Mag.* 73 (1978): 129–36.

32. Reference to women of consequence, in the subtitle, comes from Daniel Jenifer to Gov. Thomas Johnson, Apr. 1, 1778, Red Books, vol. 20, fol. 99. Quotations: CCW, Libs. AC4, fols. 185–86, AD5, fol. 287, AE6, fol. 121. Data on literacy among all female testators and witnesses to wills filed in the county between 1740 and 1784 are in Lee, "The Social Order of a Revolutionary People," 238–39. Examples of court directives regarding girls are in CCW, Lib. AF7, fols. 134, 229, 263–64. Cf. boys: Lib. AF7, fols. 2, 173–74, 228. Richard Lee's daughter Alice complained about female education in a Dec. 20, 1774, letter to Richard Potts: ". . . Greek (such is the ungenerous regulation of you Lords of the Creation) is a Language we females are not allowed to be versant in. . . . I think we females ought to have an exclusive right to the Tree of Knowledge, since Mother Eve was the first that took possession thereof—which you know is all the right that the Europeans have to America." Potts Papers (MS. 1392), MHS.

33. Quotation: Alice Lee to William Lee, Sept. 27, 1772, Edmund Jennings Lee Papers (Mss1 L5113 a18), at the Virginia Historical Society, Richmond. English common law restrictions on married women were observed in Maryland. See Elie Vallette, *The Deputy Commissary's Guide Within the Province of Maryland, together With plain and sufficient directions for Testators to form, and Executors to perform their Wills and Testaments* . . . (Annapolis: Ann Catharine Green & Son, 1774), especially 82–83, 97, 143–46; William Blackstone, *Commentaries on the Laws of England*, ed. Stanley N. Katz, 4 vols. (Chicago: University of Chicago Press, 1979), 2:433–36; *The Laws Respecting Women*, foreword by Shirley Raissi Bysiewicz (London, 1777; Dobbs Ferry, N.Y.: Oceana Publications, 1974). Norma Basch, *In the Eyes of the Law: Women, Marriage, and Property in Nineteenth-Century New York* (Ithaca, N.Y.: Cornell University Press, 1982), chaps. 1–2, is an excellent description of the legal status of early American women. Also informative are Marylynn Salmon, *Women and the Law of Property in Early America* (Chapel Hill: University of North Carolina Press, 1986) and two classic works, Julia C. Spruill, *Women's Life and Work in the Southern Colonies* (Chapel Hill: University of North Carolina Press, 1938), chap. 16, and Richard B. Morris, *Studies in the History of American Law*, 2d ed. (Philadelphia: J. M. Mitchell Co., 1959), chap. 3. A work that tends to downplay the legal disabilities of femes covert is Joan R. Gundersen and Gwen Victor Gampel, "Married Women's Legal Status in Eighteenth-Century New York and Virginia," *WMQ* 39 (1982): 114–34. On women's awareness of the hazards of marriage, see Mary Beth Norton, *Liberty's Daughters: The Revolutionary Experience of American Women, 1750–1800* (Boston: Little, Brown, & Co., 1980), chap. 2. On the absence of divorce in colonial Maryland, consult Mary Keysor Meyer, comp., *Divorces and Names Changed in Maryland by Act of the Legislature* (n.p., 1970), iv. A recent overview of the literature on colonial women is Mary Beth

Norton, "The Evolution of White Women's Experience in Early America," *American Historical Review* 89 (1984): 593–619.

34. Of 941 household heads in 1733, 35 were women. Surviving lists for 1758 name 46 out of 642 householders. And of 713 landholders identified in 1774, 38 were female and another 87 were "heirs," which surely included some women. 1733 List of Taxables, Charles County, Md., in the Scharf Collection, box 96, folder 1; 1758 tax lists for the following hundreds: East Newport, Lower Durham Parish, Lower William and Mary Parish, Pomonkey, Upper Trinity Parish, and West Port Tobacco Parish, in Secretary in Maryland, Tax Lists; CCDB, 1774. Female planters: CCCR, Lib. I3, fols. 34, 88–89; CCW, Libs. AD5, fols. 248–49, AE6, fol. 2; *Md. Gazette*, Mar. 18, 1762; Mary Mackall to James Russell, July 2, 1774, and Elizabeth Pile to Russell, Sept. 20, 1774, Russell Papers, bundles 14–15. Tenants: St. Thomas Manor Rent Book (1755–1812), fols. 1, 5, 8, 9, 14, and passim, in the Maryland Province Archives of the Society of Jesus, 172.B, Special Collections Division, Georgetown University Library, Washington, D.C.; CCW, Lib. AC4, fols. 179–81. Ferries: *Md. Gazette*, Dec. 16, 1773; Farish, ed., *Journal and Letters of Philip Vickers Fithian*, 109; Cresswell, *Journal*, 17. Mill operators: CCW, Lib. AD5, fols. 143–48. Creditors: CCW, Libs. AC4, fols. 175–76, AD5, fols. 122–24; women frequently appear as creditors in estate inventories, although not as often as men. Land transactions: Charles County General Index to Land Records, BGS1 (1658–1832), MSA. The warehouse owner was Ann Neale, and the quitrent collector, Margaret Brookes. CCW, Lib. AD5, fols. 243–48; Proprietary Account Book, fols. 4, 6, 11, in the Calvert Papers (MS. 174), no. 933, MHS. Other economic activities are mentioned in CCW, Libs. AE6, fols. 50–51, 166–67, AF7, fols. 244–46.

35. Lee, "Land and Labor: Parental Bequest Practices in Charles County, Maryland, 1732–1783," 306–41.

36. Vallette, *Deputy Commissary's Guide*, 107–09, 119–20; CCW, Libs. AC4, fols. 125–26, 246–47, AD5, fols. 149–51. William Dent's 1756 will, in Lib. AD5, fols. 73–76, is a particularly full and explicit bequest of discretion to his wife.

37. CCW, Lib. AE6, fols. 269–70, 297.

38. Ibid., Libs. B1 (1782–85), fols. 72–73, 75, AD5, fols. 260–62, AE6, fol. 312, respectively.

39. Ibid., Libs. AC4, fols. 141–43, AD5, fols. 47–48, 234–36, AE6, fols. 49–50.

40. Vallette, *Deputy Commissary's Guide*, 119–20; CCW, Libs. AE6, fols. 259–61, AF7, fols. 152–53, 569–72. Of the sixty-eight widows who renounced wills in Charles County between 1740 and 1784, thirteen claimed dower rights to land only, another twelve claimed their thirds in personalty, and the remaining forty-three renounced the wills with regard to both kinds of property.

41. Lois Green Carr and Lorena S. Walsh, "The Planter's Wife: The Experience of White Women in Seventeenth-Century Maryland," *WMQ* 34 (1977): 555, 560; Walsh, " 'Till Death Us Do Part': Marriage and Family in Seventeenth-Century Maryland," in *The Chesapeake in the Seventeenth Century: Essays on Anglo-American Society*, ed. Thad W. Tate and David L. Ammerman (Chapel Hill: University of North Carolina Press, for the Institute of Early American History and Culture, 1979), 128, 132, 137; Gloria L. Main, *Tobacco Colony: Life in Early Maryland, 1650–1720* (Princeton: Princeton University Press, 1982), 92; Alexander Keyssar, "Widowhood in Eighteenth-Century Massachusetts: A Problem in the History of the Family,"

Perspectives in American History 8 (1974): 83–119; Laurel Thatcher Ulrich, *Good Wives: Image and Reality in the Lives of Women in Northern New England, 1650–1750* (New York: Alfred A. Knopf, 1982), 148; Joseph C. Miller, *Way of Death: Merchant Capitalism and the Angolan Slave Trade, 1730–1830* (Madison: University of Wisconsin Press, 1988), 290–94.

42. Hanson: CCW, Libs. AC4, fols. 110–12, AD5, fols. 280–81; Charles County Register of Wills, Inventories, 1735–52, fols. 147–51; CCDB for 1750 and 1753, fols. 10, 8, respectively. Chase: Jonathan Boucher to John James, Mar. 9, 1767, "Letters of Rev. Jonathan Boucher," *Md. Hist. Mag.* 7 (1912): 343; Papenfuse et al., eds., *Biographical Dictionary* 1:212. As of 1753 Jeremiah Chase owned 300 acres of land in Charles County, on which his widow had dower rights; by 1774 she held 578 acres. CCDB for 1753 and 1774, fols. 93, 25, respectively; 1782 Assessment Lists and 1783 Land Tax Lists, in the Scharf Collection, box 96, folders 15, 25, box 98, folder 1.

43. Forry: CCW, Lib. AE6, fols. 126–27; Journal of Proceedings, 1781 (S132), fols. 56, 107, and Sale Book of Confiscated British Property, 1781–85 (S124), fol. 6, in Commissioners to Preserve Confiscated British Property, Ledger and Journal, MSA; 1782 Assessment List for Port Tobacco Town Hundred, Scharf Collection, box 96, folder 12. Halkerston: book of unsold lottery tickets, in the Kremer Collection, item 38; *Md. Gazette*, Mar. 17, 1763, June 26, 1777; CCCR, Lib. T3, fol. 375; CCW, Lib. AF7, fols. 53–55, and, for the inventoried value of her estate (£826 Maryland currency), fols. 57, 317–18. The author is indebted to Lucia C. Stanton, of the Thomas Jefferson Memorial Foundation, for the Jefferson reference.

44. *Md. Gazette*, Dec. 26, 1771, Jan. 16, Mar. 19, Apr. 9, 1772, Mar. 25, 1773; Deeds of Conveyance, Lib. S3 (1770–75), fols. 621–23, CCLR; CCW, Lib. AF7, fol. 178; Papenfuse et al., eds., *Biographical Dictionary* 1:407.

45. Blacksmiths: CCCR, Lib. U3 (1772–73), fols. 392, 718. Housekeepers: CCW, Lib. AE6, fols. 131–32, 174–75, 182, 267–69. Schoolmasters: *Md. Gazette*, Dec. 23, 1776; Francis Walker Memorial, Dec. 1777, in American Loyalist Claims, ser. 2, A. O. 13/40, fol. 230. Seamstresses: CCW, Libs. AE6, fols. 307–08, AF7, fols. 45, 206. The quotation is from a statement of Thomas Stone, Dec. 20, 1781, Pardon Papers, box 1, folder 82.

46. CCW, Lib. AD5, fols. 46–47.

47. Undated petition of James Freeman to William Paca (850056), Southern Maryland Studies Center, Charles County Community College.

48. Table 7, Appendix. The top quartile of landholders held 64 percent of the acreage accounted for in CCDB, 1774. The other quartiles are as follows: second (189–387 acres), 20 percent; third (106–88 acres), 11 percent; bottom (2–106 acres), 5 percent. As of 1782, 46.5 percent of taxpayers held slaves. 1782 Assessment Lists, Scharf Collection, box 96, folders 7–10, 12–17. Reasonably detailed descriptions of local plantations may be found in CCCR, Libs. Q3 (1767–70), fol. 256, T3, fols. 596–97, X3, fol. 584. Tenancies are advertised in *Md. Gazette*, Apr. 30, 1761, Feb. 3, 1763, May 17, Oct. 4, 1767, Aug. 5, 1773. Plantation management is discussed in Carr and Walsh, "Economic Diversification and Labor Organization in the Chesapeake, 1650–1820," 144–88.

49. CCCR, Lib. I3, fols. 262–63. An export merchant once remarked that some of the finest tobacco in the county was grown by "the poorest planter whose ground so casts it up." Robert Fergusson to Alexander Henderson, May 21, 1792, Invoice and Letter Book, 1771–74, 1792–93, Port Tobacco, Md., in the John Glassford & Co. Papers, container 61, Manuscript Division, LC.

50. CCLR, Lib. V3 (1775–82), fols. 128–30, 209; St. Thomas Manor Rent Book (1755–1812), fols. 10, 12; St. Thomas Manor Account Book (1741–43), fols. 31, 43, in the Maryland Province Archives of the Society of Jesus, 172.A; CCW, Lib. AF7, fol. 242.

51. American Loyalist Claims, ser. 2, A. O. 13/62, fols. 232–38; CCCR, Lib. W3 (1773–74), fols. 109–11; Lorena S. Walsh, "Land, Landlord, and Leaseholder: Estate Management and Tenant Fortunes in Southern Maryland, 1642–1820," *Agricultural History* 59 (1985): 374–87. The proprietary tenants are named, and their tenancies described, in the Henry Harford claim, American Loyalist Claims, A. O. 12/79, fols. 132–40; see also Gregory A. Stiverson, *Poverty in a Land of Plenty: Tenancy in Eighteenth-Century Maryland* (Baltimore: Johns Hopkins University Press, 1977), 6, 43–48, 59, 69, 151.

52. St. Thomas Manor Rent Book (1755–1812), fols. 26, 30; contracts with William Hill, Jan. 10, 1760, and Richard Boulton, Oct. 19, 1761, in Maryland Province Archives of the Society of Jesus, 52.T.2, 52.T.3, respectively; CCLR, Lib. V3, fols. 236–37.

53. *Md. Gazette*, Feb. 10, 1763, Nov. 4, 1773; Chancery Records, 1784–86, fols. 317–19.

54. *Md. Gazette*, Mar. 30, 1748, Aug. 3, Oct. 5, 1758, June 26, 1760, Mar. 1, 1764, Nov. 19, 1772; Journal of John Littlejohn (typescript), 3, United Methodist Historical Society, Baltimore, Md.; CCCR, Lib. K3, fols. 99, 229; *Arch. Md.* 42:421–22, 425; Tommy R. Thompson, "Debtors, Creditors, and the General Assembly in Colonial Maryland," *Md. Hist. Mag.* 72 (1977): 74. General works on servants and convicts are Abbot Emerson Smith, *Colonists in Bondage: White Servitude and Convict Labor in America, 1607–1776* (Chapel Hill: University of North Carolina Press, for the Institute of Early American History and Culture, 1947); Richard Hofstadter, *America at 1750: A Social Portrait* (New York: Alfred A. Knopf, 1971), chap. 2; David W. Galenson, *White Servitude in Colonial America: An Economic Analysis* (New York: Cambridge University Press, 1981); A. Roger Ekirch, *Bound for America: The Transportation of British Convicts to the Colonies, 1718–1775* (New York: Oxford University Press, 1987); idem, "Exiles in the Promised Land: Convict Labor in the Eighteenth-Century Chesapeake," *Md. Hist. Mag.* 82 (1987): 95–122; and Kenneth Morgan, "The Organization of the Convict Trade to Maryland: Stevenson, Randolph & Cheston, 1768–1775," *WMQ* 42 (1985): 201–27.

55. *Md. Gazette*, May 11, 1748, Oct. 10, Nov. 21, 1771, Sept. 2, 1773, Mar. 16, 1775; CCCR, Libs. I3, fols. 537, 541, T3, fols. 590, 593, W3, fols. 94, 601; CCW, Lib. AC4, fols. 230–33. Two contemporary commentaries on abuse of servants, which claim that they were treated as severely as slaves or worse, are Joseph Mosley to his brother, June 5, 1772, "Letters of Father Joseph Mosley, 1757–1786," ed. E. I. Devitt, *Woodstock Letters* 35 (1906): 53–54, and William Eddis, *Letters from America*, ed. Aubrey C. Land (Cambridge: Belknap Press of Harvard University Press, 1969), 38–40. A few masters, however, manumitted servants or reduced their terms. CCW, Lib. AC4, fols. 147–49, 162–63, 179–81, 250–52, 366–67.

56. Spouses: *Md. Gazette*, Apr. 16, 1761, July 31, 1777. Servants: ibid., Apr. 23, 1761, May 22, 1772, June 30, July 28, 1774 (in addition to the runaway advertisements cited in the preceding note). Sons: CCW, Libs. AC4, fols. 233–35, 280–82, 350–52, AD5, fols. 72–73, 171–72. Sailors: *Md. Gazette*, Oct. 11, 1745, Oct. 23, 1760. Hired hands: St. Thomas Manor Account Book (1741–43), fol. 26; CCCR, Lib. U3, fols. 392–93. Debtors: CCCR, Lib. K3, fols. 433–34; Ledger, 1762–64, Port Tobacco,

Md., pt. 2, fols. 357–58, in John Glassford & Co. Papers, container 57. Extension of servant terms: CCCR, Libs. P3, fol. 641, U3, fols. 455, 603. Kenneth Morgan comprehensively examines "Convict Runaways in Maryland, 1745–1775," *Journal of American Studies* 23 (1989): 253–68.

57. CCLR, Lib. V3, fol. 485.

58. Memorandum of Father George Hunter, Dec. 20, 1749, in the Maryland Province Archives of the Society of Jesus, 202.A.7. The literature on slaving and on attitudes toward slavery and blacks is enormous. Useful general introductions are John B. Boles, *Black Southerners, 1619–1969* (Lexington: University of Kentucky Press, 1983); Peter J. Parish, *Slavery: History and Historians* (New York: Harper & Row, 1989); Philip D. Curtin, *The Rise and Fall of the Plantation Complex: Essays in Atlantic History* (New York: Cambridge University Press, 1990); and Donald R. Wright, *African Americans in the Colonial Era: From African Origins through the American Revolution* (Arlington Heights, Ill.: Harlan Davidson, 1990). Extended treatments include David B. Davis, *The Problem of Slavery in Western Culture* and its sequel, *The Problem of Slavery in the Age of Revolution, 1770–1823* (Ithaca, N. Y.: Cornell University Press, 1975); Winthrop D. Jordan, *White over Black: American Attitudes toward the Negro, 1550–1812* (Chapel Hill: University of North Carolina Press, for the Institute of Early American History and Culture, 1968); and James A. Rawley, *The Transatlantic Slave Trade: A History* (New York: W. W. Norton & Co., 1981).

59. CCCR, Lib. U3, fols. 145–46, 150–51. McAtee owned sixty-nine acres, according to CCDB, 1774, fol. 14.

60. Ira Berlin, "Time, Space, and the Evolution of Afro-American Society on British Mainland North America," *American Historical Review* 85 (1980): 44–78; Peter H. Wood, " 'I Did the Best I Could for My Day': The Study of Early Black History during the Second Reconstruction, 1960 to 1976," *WMQ* 35 (1978): 185–225; Jonathan L. Alpert, "The Origin of Slavery in the United States—The Maryland Precedent," *American Journal of Legal History* 14 (1970): 189–221; William M. Wiecek, "The Statutory Law of Slavery and Race in the Thirteen Mainland Colonies of British America," *WMQ* 34 (1977): 258–80; Hunter, "On the danger of relapsing into former Sins," undated sermon in the Eighteenth-Century Catholic Sermon Collection, Hu-5, Special Collections Division, Georgetown University Library; CCCR, Lib. I3, fol. 292.

61. An extended discussion of these points is in the author's "The Problem of Slave Community in the Eighteenth-Century Chesapeake," *WMQ* 43 (1986): 333–61, which takes issue with Allan Kulikoff, "The Origins of Afro-American Society in Tidewater Maryland and Virginia, 1700 to 1790," *WMQ* 35 (1978): 226–59, and idem, *Tobacco and Slaves*, chaps. 8–9. The quotation is from Provincial Court Judgment Records (S551), Lib. DD17, pt. 1, fol. 238, MSA.

62. Tables 1, 4, Appendix; "An Account of the Number of Souls in the Province of Maryland, in the Year 1755," 261; Lee, "The Problem of Slave Community in the Eighteenth-Century Chesapeake," 342–44. For a regional perspective on slave population density as of 1755, see Richard S. Dunn, "Black Society in the Chesapeake, 1776–1810," in *Slavery and Freedom in the Age of the American Revolution*, ed. Ira Berlin and Ronald Hoffman (Charlottesville: University Press of Virginia, for the U.S. Capitol Historical Society, 1983), 55.

63. Distribution of slavery was calculated from the 1754 tax list for the town of Port Tobacco and from the 1758 tax lists for the following rural hundreds: East Newport,

Lower Durham Parish, Lower William and Mary Parish, Pomonkey, Upper Trinity Parish, and West Port Tobacco Parish. The lists are in Secretary in Maryland, Tax Lists. The 1782 Assessment Lists, in the Scharf Collection, box 96, folders 7–10, 12–17, reveal slave distribution as of that year. A detailed statistical analysis of the 1758 and 1782 tax lists is in Lee, "The Problem of Slave Community in the Eighteenth-Century Chesapeake," 342–54.

64. Lee, "The Problem of Slave Community in the Eighteenth-Century Chesapeake," 353.
65. The quotations are from advertisements in the *Md. Gazette*, Dec. 13, 1764, Feb. 14, 1765, Jan. 30, 1772; and Robert Carter to Bennett Neale, Sept. 15, 1781, in the Robert Carter Letterbook No. 4 (1780–82, 1785–87), fols. 117–19, in the Robert Carter Papers, William R. Perkins Library, Duke University, Durham, N.C. Occupations of other female slaves in the county are noted in *Md. Gazette*, May 17, 1764, Jan. 31, 1765, Jan. 30, 1772, Jan. 18, 1776, and CCW, Libs. AD5, fols. 281–83, AF7, fols. 593–95. Men's work: *Md. Gazette*, Dec. 3, 1761, May 17, Dec. 13, 1764, Feb. 14, 1765, Apr. 9, 1772, Dec. 2, 1773, Jan. 18, 1776; CCCR, Lib. P3, fol. 300; CCW, Libs. AC4, fols. 227–29, 230–33, AE6, fols. 28–29; Chancery Records, 1784–86, fols. 311–12, 318. Children's tasks: *Md. Gazette*, Feb. 14, 1765; CCW, Lib. AC4, fols. 247–49.
66. General Court of the Western Shore, Judgment Records (S497), Lib. JG25 (Oct. Term 1794), fols. 251, 253–56, 276, 282, MSA.
67. Cresswell, *Journal*, 18–19; CCW, Lib. AC4, fols. 179–81, 327–31; CCCR, Lib. I3, fol. 440; J. H. Stone advertisement in the *Md. Gazette*, Sept. 25, 1788, which mentions marks "frequently seen on Africans." An example of blacks' detailed knowledge of lineages is in the General Court of the Western Shore, Judgment Records, Lib. JG27 (May Term 1795), fols. 33–35. The conjurer and chief is identified in a petition for clemency for Nan, a convicted murderess, Apr. 10, 1781, in the Pardon Papers, box 1, folder 82. Mr. William Diggs, a resident of Charles County, performs thatching as he learned it from members of his family, as shown in George W. McDaniel, *Hearth and Home: Preserving a People's Culture* (Philadelphia: Temple University Press, 1982), 86. Sensitive treatments of African influences upon African-American culture are Mechal Sobel, *The World They Made Together: Black and White Values in Eighteenth-Century Virginia* (Princeton: Princeton University Press, 1987); Peter H. Wood, *Black Majority: Negroes in Colonial South Carolina from 1670 through the Stono Rebellion* (New York: Alfred A. Knopf, 1974); and, for the antebellum period, Charles Joyner, *Down by the Riverside: A South Carolina Slave Community* (Urbana: University of Illinois Press, 1984); idem, *Remember Me: Slave Life in Coastal Georgia* (Atlanta: Georgia Humanities Council, 1989).
68. Cresswell, *Journal*, 18–19.
69. CCW, Libs. AC4, fols. 230–33, 247–49, 358–59, AD5, fols. 251–52; Daniel Jenifer Adams to George Washington, Mar. 15, 1775, George Washington Papers, ser. 4, microfilm reel 33, Manuscript Division, LC; Lund Washington to G. Washington, Jan. 17, 1776, *The Papers of George Washington*, ed. W. W. Abbot et al., *Revolutionary War Series*, 5 vols. to date (Charlottesville: University Press of Virginia, 1985–), 3:126. Evidence of local slaves' religiosity is exceedingly scarce but drew comment as early as the 1720s. Fulham Palace Papers, vol. 3, fols. 56, 151–52, in the Lambeth Palace Library, London (microfilm in the Manuscript Division, LC).
70. CCW, Libs. AE6, fols. 183–84, AD5, fols. 210–12, respectively. Other manumis-

sions are recorded ibid., Libs. AC4, fols. 213–15, 299–300, AD5, fols. 186–88, AE6, fols. 76, 198–99. Although such actions were forbidden under a 1752 statute, some masters continued to manumit. *Arch. Md.* 50:76.

71. CCW, Lib. AE6, fols. 125–26, 300–02.

72. Carr and Walsh, "Economic Diversification and Labor Organization in the Chesapeake, 1650–1820," 157–61.

73. The quotations are from Thomas Howe Ridgate to Zephaniah Turner, Feb. 10, 1772, Ridgate Letter Book, 122, and *Md. Gazette*, Jan. 18, 1776. Additional evidence is in CCCR, Lib. K, fols. 436–37; CCW, Libs. AC4, fols. 81–82, 167–68, 203–04, AD5, fols. 25–28, 95–98, 183–84, 281–83, 303–07, AE6, fols. 28–30, 81–82, 120–21, 167–68, 203–04, 219–24. Slave sales were sometimes recorded in CCLR, as, for examples, in Lib. V3, fols. 3, 10, 18–19.

74. Quotations: CCW, Libs. AC4, fols. 261–62, AD5, fols. 100–02, 287, AE6, fol. 93. See also Libs. AC4, fols. 118–19, 270–71, 278–79, 308–10, 358–59, AD5, fols. 12–13, 348, AE6, fols. 96–98, 122–24.

75. *Md. Gazette*, May 17, Dec. 13, 1764; Prerogative Court, Wills (S538), Lib. 32, fols. 163–67, MSA; Charles County Register of Wills, Inventories, 1766–73, fols. 1–22. Three of Fendall's relatives bought nine slaves and probably kept an elderly woman who was not sold. The other fourteen buyers included both local planters and men who have not been linked to Charles County.

76. The work stoppage is described in Chancery Records, 1784–86, fols. 318–19. Examples of slaves being indicted for thefts committed away from their home plantations are in CCCR, Libs. K, fol. 88, M3, fols. 2, 120, 286, 351, 498, P3, fols. 501, 641.

77. During the years 1745–49, 1760–64, and 1772–76, only twelve local slave runaways were advertised in the *Md. Gazette*. All were males. Long-distance runaways captured and jailed in Charles County are identified ibid., June 18, 1761, Jan. 31, 1764, Jan. 28, Feb. 25, July 29, Aug. 5, 1773. The local nature of slave flight during the colonial period is discussed in Kulikoff, *Tobacco and Slaves*, 343–44.

78. CCCR, Libs. K3, no fol., X3, fol. 17.

79. "Journal of a French Traveller in the Colonies, 1765, II," *American Historical Review* 27 (1921): 70; *Arch. Md.* 28:340, 33:287–88; Brugger, *Maryland: A Middle Temperament, 1634–1980*, 54–56; John Tracy Ellis, *Catholics in Colonial America* (Baltimore: Helicon Press, 1965), 344–59. British colonial statutes governing Roman Catholics are gathered together in Francis X. Curran, comp., *Catholics in Colonial Law* (Chicago: Loyola University Press, 1963).

80. CCW, Lib. AC4, fols. 120–22; undated sermon of George Hunter, in the Eighteenth-Century Catholic Sermon Collection, Hu-2. Roman Catholic chapels located in the county are mentioned in an abstract of the sheriff's report, Aug. 10, 1697, in the Fulham Palace Papers, vol. 2, fols. 108–09, and CCW, Libs. AD5, fols. 191–97, 275–76, 313–14, 345, AE6, fols. 11–12, 122–24, 141–42.

81. Mosley to unknown correspondent, Sept. 8, 1758, to his sister, Sept. 1, 1759, and to his brother, July 30, 1764, "Letters of Father Joseph Mosley," 39, 42, 45.

82. *Arch. Md.* 50:52; undated notes regarding St. Thomas Manor, in the Maryland Province Archives of the Society of Jesus, 52.W.3.

83. *Arch. Md.* 50:52, 198; CCW, Lib. AD5, fols. 243–48; Hunter to Mr. Scansbrick, undated, in Father George Hunter's Letterbook, 1760, fol. 8, Maryland Province Archives of the Society of Jesus, 2.W. On priests in the Neale family, see Margaret

Brown Klapthor and Paul D. Brown, *The History of Charles County, Maryland* (La Plata, Md.: Charles County Tercentenary, 1958), 69–70. On local Catholic women who entered European convents, see Constance FitzGerald, ed., *The Carmelite Adventure: Clare Joseph Dickinson's Journal of a Trip to America and Other Documents* (Baltimore: Carmelite Sisters of Baltimore, 1990), 10–16.

84. Hunter to Mr. Poyntz and to the Cambray and Aires convents, undated, Father George Hunter's Letterbook, 1760, fols. 2, 3, 6, 7.

85. Hunter to Scansbrick and to Poyntz, undated, ibid., fols. 8, 11.

86. *Arch. Md.* 22:96, 308, 50:199; Philip Lee to Giles Rainsford, July 25, 1725, and Rainsford to the Bishop of London, July 25, 1725, in the Fulham Palace Papers, vol. 3, fols. 76–77; Hunter memorandum, Dec. 20, 1749, Maryland Province Archives of the Society of Jesus, 202.A.7. See CCW, Lib. AD5, fols. 145–48, 361, for bequests contingent upon the Protestantism of heirs. On the other hand, the fascinating 1751 will of John Turton complained that "it is too Customary in this province of Maryland for busy persons to take away the Children of such whose fathers were protestants after their Decease from the mother who are Romans under a pretence & for fear the said Children should be brought up Romans which gives often Ill designing persons an Opportunity of not only Defrauding the poor Children of their Rights but likewise very Greatly Injurys the poor widow in takeing from her such assistance as she may Justly Expect." CCW, Lib. AD5, fols. 156–58.

87. "Proceedings of the Parochial Clergy," *Md. Hist. Mag.* 3 (1908): 369; "Journal of a French Traveller," 70.

88. *Md. Gazette*, Apr. 29, May 6, 1746; CCCR, Lib. Y2 (1744–45/6), fols. 509, 520; *Arch. Md.* 50:53, 57, 201.

89. *Arch. Md.* 28:355–57, 50:53. Molyneux was superintendent at St. Thomas Manor from 1740 to 1747. "Catalog of Members of the Maryland Mission of the Society of Jesus, 1634–1806," typescript in the Special Collections Division, Georgetown University Library.

90. *Arch. Md.* 50:201, 203.

91. Ibid., 28:357.

92. Ibid., 363; deed of St. Thomas Manor from Richard Molyneux to John Lancaster, Sept. 8, 1746, Maryland Province Archives of the Society of Jesus, 101.M.2; *Md. Gazette*, Feb. 10, Sept. 15, 1747.

93. *Md. Gazette*, Feb. 28, 1750, Nov. 4, 1754; *Arch. Md.* 46:593–94, 52:356–58, 376, 436, 440–49; "Proceedings of the Parochial Clergy," 364, 373–74, 384; Jean Butenhoff Lee, "Isaac Campbell (c. 1724–1784)," in *American Writers before 1800: A Biographical and Critical Dictionary*, ed. James A. Levernier and Douglas R. Wilmes, 3 vols. (Westport, Conn.: Greenwood Press, 1983), 1:266–68. Timothy W. Bosworth, "Anti-Catholicism as a Political Tool in Mid-Eighteenth-Century Maryland," *Catholic Historical Review* 61 (1975): 539–63, examines efforts of the lower house of the Assembly to curtail Catholicism during the 1750s.

94. *Arch. Md.* 31:122–23, 52:88–92; Rivoire, *Homeplaces: Traditional Domestic Architecture of Charles County, Maryland*, 7–9; *St. Ignatius Church, Chapel Point* ([Port Tobacco, Md.: St. Ignatius Church], 1982).

95. Douglas E. Leach, *Roots of Conflict: British Armed Forces and Colonial Americans, 1677–1763* (Chapel Hill: University of North Carolina Press, 1986), 81.

96. Proceedings of the court of oyer and terminer, June 10, 1755, in Charles County Court, Tobacco Inspection Proceedings, vol. 70, fols. 1–16; *Md. Gazette*, Apr. 10,

May 15, 1755; Boucher to James, Mar. 9, 1767, "Letters of Rev. Jonathan Boucher," 343; Papenfuse et al., eds., *Biographical Dictionary* 1:212; *Arch. Md.* 52:51.

97. Proceedings of the court of oyer and terminer, June 10, 1755, in Charles County Court, Tobacco Inspection Proceedings, vol. 70, fols. 1–16; *Arch. Md.* 31:69, 81; *Md. Gazette,* June 26, July 3, 10, 1755. See also the address of the House of Delegates, approved the day before the executions in Charles County, which expressed alarm at "the constant and unwearied Application of the Jesuits to proselyte, and consequently to corrupt and alienate, the Affections of our Slaves" during a time of "Danger from a powerful Foreign Enemy," the French. Some months later Gov. Horatio Sharpe informed the members of the lower house that he was "ready and willing to redress any Evils, which shall appear to be more than imaginary." *Arch. Md.* 52:159–60, 387. Mark J. Stegmaier, "Maryland's Fear of Insurrection at the Time of Braddock's Defeat," *Md. Hist. Mag.* 71 (1976): 467–82, explores the aftermath of the crushing defeat of British and colonial forces, at the hands of the French and their Indian allies, on July 9, 1755.

98. CCW, Lib. AE6, fols. 113–14; John F. D. Smyth, *A Tour in the United States of America . . .* , 2 vols. (London: G. Robinson, J. Robson, and J. Sewell, 1784), 2:181; CCCR, Lib. T3, fol. 66; Papenfuse et al., eds., *Biographical Dictionary* 1:204; *Arch. Md.* 63:12. The School de la haute ville operated from 1763 until at least 1765 and was supported with students' tuition (1s. Maryland currency per month) and the sale to St. Thomas Manor of spun wool and flax, woven "Negro" cloth, and knitted stockings. Students boarded at the school. George Hunter's Day Book Memoranda, 1763–69, fols. 3, 10, Maryland Province Archives of the Society of Jesus, 172.C.

Part Two: REVOLUTION AND WAR

Chapter Three: Primed for Revolution

1. Andrew Burnaby, *Travels through the Middle Settlements in North America in the Years 1759 and 1760, with Observations upon the State of the Colonies,* 3d ed. (London: printed for T. Payne, 1798; New York: Augustus M. Kelley, 1970), 153; John Adams to Hezekiah Niles, Feb. 13, 1818, *The Selected Writings of John and John Quincy Adams,* ed. Adrienne Koch and William Peden (New York: Alfred A. Knopf, 1946), 204.

2. Adams to Niles, Feb. 13, 1818, *Selected Writings,* ed. Koch and Peden, 204; Lawrence Henry Gipson, *The British Empire before the American Revolution,* 15 vols. (New York: Alfred A. Knopf, 1939–70), vols. 11–12; John Shy, *Toward Lexington: The Role of the British Army in the Coming of the American Revolution* (Princeton: Princeton University Press, 1965); Bernard Bailyn, *The Ideological Origins of the American Revolution* (Cambridge: Belknap Press of Harvard University Press, 1967); Carolyn Rabson, *Songbook of the American Revolution* (Peaks Island, Maine: NEO Press, 1974); Merrill Jensen, *The Founding of a Nation: A History of the American Revolution, 1763–1776* (New York: Oxford University Press, 1968); Pauline Maier, *From Resistance to Revolution: Colonial Radicals and the Development of American Opposition to Britain, 1765–1776* (New York: Alfred A. Knopf, 1972); Marc Egnal and Joseph A. Ernst, "An Economic Interpretation of the American Revolution," *WMQ* 29 (1972): 3–32; Ian R. Christie and Benjamin W. Labaree, *Empire or Independence, 1760–1776: A British-American Dialogue on the Coming of the American Revolution* (New York: W. W. Norton & Co., 1976);

Robert W. Tucker and David C. Hendrickson, *The Fall of the First British Empire: Origins of the War of American Independence* (Baltimore: Johns Hopkins University Press, 1982); Jack P. Greene, *Peripheries and Center: Constitutional Development in the Extended Polities of the British Empire and the United States, 1607–1788* (Athens: University of Georgia Press, 1986), chaps. 5–7. The text of the Declaratory Act is reprinted in Richard B. Morris, ed., *The American Revolution, 1763–1783* (New York: Harper & Row, 1970), 86–87.

3. Bailyn, *The Ideological Origins of the American Revolution*, chaps. 3–5; Maier, *From Resistance to Revolution*, chaps. 4–5; Gordon S. Wood, *The Creation of the American Republic, 1776–1787* (Chapel Hill: University of North Carolina Press, for the Institute of Early American History and Culture, 1969), pts. 1–2; David Ammerman, *In the Common Cause: American Response to the Coercive Acts of 1774* (Charlottesville: University Press of Virginia, 1974); John Phillip Reid, *Constitutional History of the American Revolution: The Authority of Rights* (Madison: University of Wisconsin Press, 1986).

4. Christie and Labaree, *Empire or Independence*, 163–241; Labaree, *The Boston Tea Party* (New York: Oxford University Press, 1964); Ammerman, *In the Common Cause*; Adams to Niles, Feb. 13, 1818, *Selected Writings*, ed. Koch and Peden, 204.

5. Standard sources for these subjects are Charles A. Barker, *The Background of the Revolution in Maryland* (New Haven: Yale University Press, 1940); Ronald Hoffman, *A Spirit of Dissension: Economics, Politics, and the Revolution in Maryland* (Baltimore: Johns Hopkins University Press, 1973); David C. Skaggs, *Roots of Maryland Democracy, 1753–1776* (Westport, Conn.: Greenwood Press, 1973); and Aubrey C. Land, *Colonial Maryland: A History* (Millwood, N.Y.: KTO Press, 1981). For individual offices and officeholders, see Donnell M. Owings, *His Lordship's Patronage: Offices of Profit in Colonial Maryland* (Baltimore: Maryland Historical Society, 1953); Papenfuse et al., eds., *Biographical Dictionary*; and Nelson W. Rightmyer, *Maryland's Established Church* (Baltimore: Church Historical Society, for the Diocese of Maryland, 1956).

6. Barker, *Background of the Revolution in Maryland*, chaps. 9–10; Hoffman, *Spirit of Dissension*, chaps. 2–6; Skaggs, *Roots of Maryland Democracy*, chaps. 6–7.

7. "Journal of a French Traveller in the Colonies, 1765, II," *American Historical Review* 27 (1921): 76; Barker, *Background of the Revolution in Maryland*, 256, 275–89; James Haw, "The Patronage Follies: Bennet Allen, John Morton Jordan, and the Fall of Horatio Sharpe," *Md. Hist. Mag.* 71 (1976): 134–50; Owings, *His Lordship's Patronage*, 168, 176; Horatio Sharpe to Cecilius Calvert, Aug. 16, 1765, and to Hugh Hamersley, Oct. 30, 1768, *Arch. Md.* 14:220, 546–47. Jenifer was commissioned a judge of the Provincial Court in 1766, rent roll keeper of the Western Shore in 1768, and, in the same year, his lordship's agent and receiver general.

8. Barker, *Background of the Revolution in Maryland*, 139–44, 224–33; idem, "Property Rights in the Provincial System of Maryland: Proprietary Revenues," *Journal of Southern History* 2 (1936): 230; Henry Harford's claim, American Loyalist Claims, ser. 2, A. O. 13/61, fols. 62, 71, Public Record Office, London (microfilm in the Manuscript Division, LC); *Arch. Md.* 34:122–23.

9. The Anglican establishment act is in *Arch. Md.* 24:265–73. The fullest treatment of the vestry is Gerald E. Hartdagen, "The Anglican Vestry in Colonial Maryland: Organizational Structure and Problems" and "The Anglican Vestry in Colonial Maryland: A Study in Corporate Responsibility," *Historical Magazine of the Protestant Episcopal Church* 38 (1969): 349–60, and 40 (1971): 315–35, 461–79. See also

Carol L. van Voorst, "The Anglican Clergy in Maryland, 1692–1776" (Ph.D. diss., Princeton University, 1978), 106, 145–46, 160–63, 174–75. Petitions of Charles County parishes to the Assembly, as well as legislative actions, are in *Arch. Md.* 46:461–62, 50:290–91, 526–27, 58:194–95, 516–17; *Md. Gazette,* June 17, 1773. A generally sympathetic history is Rightmyer, *Maryland's Established Church.*

10. Table 1, Appendix; William S. Perry, ed., *Historical Collections Relating to the American Colonial Church,* 5 vols., 1878 (New York: AMS Press, 1969), 4:334–37; Thomas John Claggett to Weeden Butler, July 1, 1768, in George B. Utley, *The Life and Times of Thomas John Claggett, First Bishop of Maryland and the First Bishop Consecrated in America* (Chicago: R. R. Donnelley & Sons, 1913), 20; Alexander Hamilton, *Gentleman's Progress: The Itinerarium of Dr. Alexander Hamilton, 1744,* ed. Carl Bridenbaugh (Chapel Hill: University of North Carolina Press, for the Institute of Early American History and Culture, 1948), 161; van Voorst, "The Anglican Clergy in Maryland," 163. Taxables included the free, indentured, and slave inhabitants above age sixteen, *except* white women, Anglican clergymen, and the poor who received public alms. Thomas Bacon, comp., *Laws of Maryland at Large, with Proper Indexes: Now first Collected into One Compleat Body, and Published from the Original Acts and Records . . .* (Annapolis: Jonas Green, 1765), acts of 1715 (chap. 15) and 1725 (chap. 4).

11. Horatio Sharpe's remark is quoted in Rightmyer, *Maryland's Established Church,* 198. For the Charles County clerics, see ibid., 169, 199–200, 204; Giles Rainsford to [the Bishop of London], Aug. 10, 1724, and Jacob Henderson to the Bishop of London, Apr. 25, 1735, Fulham Palace Papers, vol. 3, fols. 39, 176, Lambeth Palace Library, London (microfilm in the Manuscript Division, LC); *Arch. Md.* 44:291; CCCR, Lib. Y2 (1744–45/6), fol. 246, and vol. 41 (1746–47), fol. 2.

12. Rightmyer, *Maryland's Established Church,* 200–01, 213–14; *Md. Gazette,* Oct. 21, 1762, Apr. 28, June 16, Aug. 4, 1763; John MacPherson to George Gordon, Aug. 6, 1763, Vertical File, Archives of the Episcopal Diocese of Maryland, Baltimore.

13. *Arch. Md.* 61:357, 366–67, 465–68; *Md. Gazette,* May 28, 1772, Feb. 3, 1774, Mar. 7, 1776.

14. Isaac Campbell to the Bishop of London, Nov. 6, 1773, Fulham Palace Papers, vol. 22, fol. 90; *Md. Gazette,* Oct. 7, 1784; Jean Butenhoff Lee, "Isaac Campbell (c. 1724–1784)," in James A. Levernier and Douglas R. Wilmes, eds., *American Writers before 1800: A Biographical and Critical Dictionary,* 3 vols. (Westport, Conn.: Greenwood Press, 1983), 1:266–68; James F. Vivian and Jean H. Vivian, "The Reverend Isaac Campbell: An Anti-Lockean Whig," *Historical Magazine of the Protestant Episcopal Church* 39 (1970): 71–89. The earliest documented date for Campbell's school is 1763. See Annie Walker Burns, comp., *Abstracts of Wills of Charles and St. Mary's Counties, Maryland, 1744–1772* (Annapolis, 1937), 76.

15. MacPherson to the Bishop of London, Oct. 2, 1766, Thomas Thornton to same, Oct. 10, 1766, June 19, 1767, Thornton, Campbell, and John Eversfield to same, ca. July 1, 1767, Thornton, Campbell, and MacPherson to same, Nov. 5, 1773, Campbell to same, Nov. 6, 1773, in the Fulham Palace Papers, vol. 21, fols. 292–93, 273–75, vol. 22, fols. 88, 90, respectively.

16. Hugh Jones to the Bishop of London, Oct. 19, 1741, ibid., vol. 3, fol. 191; Rightmyer, *Maryland's Established Church,* 195; Haw, "The Patronage Follies," 137–44; Barker, *Background of the Revolution in Maryland,* 278–89; David C. Skaggs and Gerald E. Hartdagen, "Sinners and Saints: Anglican Clerical Conduct in Colonial Maryland," *Historical Magazine of the Protestant Episcopal Church* 47 (1978): 177–95; Skaggs,

ed., "Thomas Cradock's Sermon on the Governance of Maryland's Established Church," *WMQ* 27 (1970): 630–53.

17. John Doncastle to unknown correspondent, July 16, 1769, Stone Family of Maryland Papers, Manuscript Division, LC; "Journal of a French Traveller," 73; CCW, Lib. B1 (1782–85), fols. 438–43; John Sanderson and Robert Waln, Jr., *Biography of the Signers to the Declaration of Independence*, 9 vols. (Philadelphia: R. W. Pomeroy, 1823–27), 9:329.

18. Sanderson and Waln, *Biography of the Signers* 9:329; John M. Wearmouth, "Thomas Stone Biographical Sketch" (typescript, 1988), copy at the Southern Maryland Studies Center, Charles County Community College, La Plata, Md.; Allen Johnson et al., eds., *Dictionary of American Biography*, 22 vols. (New York: Charles Scribner's Sons, 1937–58), 18:84–85; Forensic Club of Annapolis Minutes (typescript), fols. 1, 48, 51–52, 54, 60–61, 95–96, in the George Forbes Collection (SC182), Special Collections, MSA; Barker, *Background of the Revolution in Maryland*, 59–60.

19. Jonathan Boucher, *A View of the Causes and Consequences of the American Revolution; in Thirteen Discourses, Preached in North America between the Years 1763 and 1775* (London, 1797; New York: Russell & Russell, 1967), 152, 181, 192–200. Anne Y. Zimmer emphasizes more positive aspects of the cleric's personality in *Jonathan Boucher: Loyalist in Exile* (Detroit: Wayne State University Press, 1978).

20. Cresswell, *Journal*, 19; Boucher, *A View of the Causes and Consequences of the American Revolution*, 152.

21. *Md. Gazette*, Apr. 18, 25, May 2, 30, 1765; Edmund S. Morgan and Helen M. Morgan, *The Stamp Act Crisis: Prologue to Revolution*, 2d ed. (New York: Collier Macmillan, 1963), chaps. 5–11; Maier, *From Resistance to Revolution*, chaps. 3–4; Hoffman, *Spirit of Dissension*, 50–52; Barker, *Background of the Revolution in Maryland*, 297–304; Daniel Dulany, "Considerations on the Propriety of Imposing Taxes in the British Colonies" (Annapolis, 1765), in *Pamphlets of the American Revolution, 1750–1776*, ed. Bernard Bailyn, with the assistance of Jane N. Garrett, 1 vol. to date (Cambridge: Belknap Press of Harvard University Press, 1965–), 1:598–658.

22. Quotation: *Md. Gazette*, Apr. 18, 1765; also consult the issues of Sept. 13, 1764, and Jan. 10, 1765. Proceedings of the August 1764 through June 1765 sessions are in CCCR, Libs. M3 (1762–64) and N3 (1764–66). Nearly three hundred pages of debt judgments entered at the August 1765 court are in Lib. N3, fols. 430–715, 721–23. The tax on attorneys and Thomas Stone's hurried admission to the courts are recorded in *Md. Gazette*, May 2, 1765; Annapolis Records No. 3 (1765–72), fol. 35, in Annapolis Mayors Court, Minutes (M44); Anne Arundel County Court, Judgment Records (1764–65), fol. 25 (C91); Prince George's County Court, Judgment Records, Lib. WW (1765–66), fol. 112 (C1231); Frederick County Court, Judgment Records, Lib. M (1763–66), fol. 502 (C810); all at MSA. Neil E. Strawser makes clear the leisurely pace at which Maryland lawyers established their circuits in "The Early Life of Samuel Chase" (M.A. thesis, George Washington University, 1958), chap. 4. After October 1765, recording of wills ceased until the following April. CCW, Lib. AD5 (1752–67).

23. CCCR, Lib. N3; Sharpe to Calvert, Nov. 11, Dec. 21, 1765, *Arch. Md.* 14:239–40, 253–54; *Md. Gazette*, Dec. 10, 1765; Barker, *Background of the Revolution in Maryland*, 306–09.

24. CCCR, Lib. N3, fols. 763–66; *Md. Gazette*, Apr. 3, 1766; Morgan and Morgan, *Stamp Act Crisis*, 226–27.

25. *Md. Gazette*, Apr. 3, 10, 1766; Maier, *From Resistance to Revolution*, 74–75; Morgan and Morgan, *Stamp Act Crisis*, 330–32; Hoffman, *Spirit of Dissension*, 36–38; CCCR, Lib. P3 (1766–67), fol. 2. Presentation of the homespun linen no doubt came in response to a statute passed at the height of the Stamp Act crisis, which provided monetary rewards, in every county, for the finest domestically produced cloth. *Arch. Md.* 59:267–69.

26. "Journal of a French Traveller," 73–74; Walter Dulany to Hamersley, Sept. 15, 1770, Dulany Papers (MS. 1265), box 5, MHS; H. Sharpe to William Sharpe [Oct. 1765], "Sharpe's Confidential Report on Maryland, 1765," ed. Aubrey C. Land, *Md. Hist. Mag.* 44 (1949): 126.

27. Christie and Labaree, *Empire or Independence*, 103–05; *Md. Gazette*, May 11, 25, 1769; *Arch. Md.* 62:458–62; H. Sharpe to Hamersley, Feb. 11, 1768, *Arch. Md.* 14:468; Robert Eden to Lord Hillsborough, June 23, 1769, "Correspondence of Governor Eden," *Md. Hist. Mag.* 2 (1907): 228; Hoffman, *Spirit of Dissension*, 83–90; Barker, *Background of the Revolution in Maryland*, 319–27. Nonimportation in Maryland nevertheless seemed stronger than what Virginians were prepared to undertake. James Robinson (Falmouth, Va.) to David Walker (Port Tobacco, Md.), July 11, 1770, in *A Scottish Firm in Virginia, 1767–1777: W. Cuninghame and Co.*, ed. T. M. Devine (Edinburgh: Clark Constable, for the Scottish History Society, 1984), 31–32.

28. *Virginia Gazette* (Williamsburg), Nov. 16, 1769; *Md. Gazette*, Nov. 30, 1769; George Mason to Richard Henry Lee, June 7, 1770, *The Papers of George Mason, 1725–1792*, ed. Robert A. Rutland, 3 vols. (Chapel Hill: University of North Carolina Press, for the Institute of Early American History and Culture, 1970), 1:119.

29. *Arch. Md.* 44:595–638, 62:90, 112, 123, 308; W. Dulany to Hamersley, Sept. 15, 1770, Dulany Papers, box 5. Maryland taxables are defined in note 10, supra. The following discussion is based on my article, published as Jean H. Vivian, "The Poll Tax Controversy in Maryland, 1770–76: A Case of Taxation *with* Representation," *Md. Hist. Mag.* 71 (1976): 151–76.

30. *Md. Gazette*, Dec. 6, 13, 1770, Feb. 21, Mar. 28, 1771; Eden to Hillsborough, Aug. 21, 1772, "Correspondence of Governor Eden," 297.

31. *Md. Gazette*, Dec. 13, 1770; *Arch. Md.* 62:301; Eden to the Earl of Dartmouth, Jan. 29, 1773, "Correspondence of Governor Eden," 301; William Fitzhugh to James Russell, Nov. 24, 1774, Russell Papers, bundle 6, Coutts & Co., London (microfilm in the Virginia Colonial Records Project, reel M-235, at the Colonial Williamsburg Foundation Library, Williamsburg, Va.); Vivian, "Poll Tax Controversy," 153–54. The debate between Dulany and Carroll appeared in *Md. Gazette* and is reprinted in Peter S. Onuf, ed., *Maryland and the Empire, 1773: The Antilon-First Citizen Letters* (Baltimore: Johns Hopkins University Press, 1974).

32. *Arch. Md.* 24:265; Vivian, "Poll Tax Controversy," 160–61, 163–66. The technical argument against the Anglican establishment act held that, because the English monarch William III died shortly before the royal governor of Maryland approved the statute, the act never enjoyed the force of law—despite having gone unchallenged for nearly seventy years. "A Constitutionalist," *A Reply to the Church of England Planter's First Letter Respecting the Clergy* (Annapolis: Anne Catharine Green, 1770).

33. *Md. Gazette*, Feb. 4, 1773.

34. Ibid., Feb. 25, 1773.

35. Ibid., Oct. 13, 1763, Feb. 23, 1764; Papenfuse et al., eds., *Biographical Dictionary* 1:417; *Arch. Md.* 62:399, 63:108, 114–15, 146, 154, 183, 190.

36. CCCR, Lib. Q3 (1767–70), fols. 307–08; *Arch. Md.* 32:337–39; Philip Padelford, ed., *Colonial Panorama 1775: Dr. Robert Honyman's Journal for March and April* (San Marino, Calif.: Huntington Library, 1939), 3; John Doncastle to unknown correspondent, July 16, 1769, Stone Family of Maryland Papers.

37. *Arch. Md.* 32:337–42, 62:469; CCCR, Lib. Q3, fols. 404–05.

38. Doncastle to unknown correspondent, July 16, 1769, and unknown correspondent to Doncastle, July 22, 1769, Stone Family of Maryland Papers; *Arch. Md.* 32:336–37, 341, 343, 62:45, 48, 51, 67–68, 73–74.

39. Richard Lee, Jr., claim, American Loyalist Claims, ser. 2, A. O. 13/40, fols. 100–01; *Arch. Md.* 32:336–37, 351–65, 367–68.

40. *Md. Gazette*, Mar. 4, 11, 1773.

41. Ibid.; CCCR, Lib. U3, fol. 161; Vivian, "Poll Tax Controversy," 175.

42. William West to John Barnes, 1772, Archives of the Episcopal Diocese of Maryland; CCCR, Lib. U3, fols. 1–2, 159–60.

43. CCCR, Lib. U3, fols. 161, 171, 285, 606.

44. Stone to unknown correspondent, Feb. 2, 1774, *Autograph Letters and Autographs of the Signers of the Declaration of Independence in the Possession of George C. Thomas* (Philadelphia: privately printed, 1908), n.p.; Stone to [Daniel of St. Thomas Jenifer?], May 20, 1776, in " 'The Dye Is Cast . . . ,' " ed. Dorothy S. Eaton and Vincent L. Eaton, *Library of Congress Quarterly Journal of Current Acquisitions* 14 (1957): 182–83.

45. Richard B. Sheridan, "The British Credit Crisis of 1772 and the American Colonies," *Journal of Economic History* 20 (1960): 161–86; Jacob M. Price, *Capital and Credit in British Overseas Trade: The View from the Chesapeake, 1700–1776* (Cambridge: Harvard University Press, 1980), chap. 7; idem, "One Family's Empire: The Russell-Lee-Clerk Connection in Maryland, Britain, and India, 1707–1857," *Md. Hist. Mag.* 72 (1977): 186–90; Thomas Howe Ridgate to Barnes, Dec. 18, 1771, and to Zephaniah Turner, Feb. 10, 1772, Ridgate Letter Book, 98, 139; Eden to Dartmouth, Aug. 19, 1773, "Correspondence of Governor Eden," 304; extract of a letter from England, *Maryland Journal, and Baltimore Advertiser*, Sept. 18–25, 1773; *Arch. Md.* 64:151–92. Perhaps dissatisfied with the rigors of the reinstituted public inspection system, thirty-six men and women asked the county court, at its March 1774 session, to dismiss the inspectors at Port Tobacco warehouse, on the ground that they were "inCompitent Judges of Tobacco, that from their want of Judgment in Tobacco many of the Inhabitants of Charles County have been injoured by their Tobacco being Condemned." The justices dismissed the petition. CCCR, Lib. W3, fol. 96.

46. Tables 8 and 9, Appendix; Vivian, "Poll Tax Controversy," 152–53; John J. McCusker and Russell R. Menard, *The Economy of British America, 1607–1789* (Chapel Hill: University of North Carolina Press, for the Institute of Early American History and Culture, 1985), 121 (fig. 6.1).

47. Ferdinand-M. Bayard, *Travels of a Frenchman in Maryland and Virginia with a Description of Philadelphia and Baltimore in 1791*, trans. and ed. Ben C. McCary (Williamsburg, Va.: Ben C. McCary, 1950), 152; list of balances due the Port Tobacco store of Cunninghame, Findlay & Co., Sept. 1, 1777, A. O. 13/9, Public Record Office (microfilm copy in the Virginia Colonial Records Project, reel 250, Colonial Williamsburg Foundation Library); Edward C. Papenfuse, *In Pursuit of Profit: The Annapolis Merchants in the Era of the American Revolution, 1763–1805* (Baltimore: Johns Hopkins University Press, 1975), 51–52; Ridgate to Barnes, Mar. 5, 1772, Ridgate Letter Book, 178.

48. The relevant proceedings are in CCCR, Libs. U3 and W3 (1773–74). The rever-berating effect of the financial panic is demonstrated in Sheridan, "The British Credit Crisis of 1772 and the American Colonies," 174–80, 183–85, and Price, *Capital and Credit in British Overseas Trade*, 131–37.

49. CCCR, Libs. U3 and W3. The August 1774 court session was typical: Of sixty-two debt judgments obtained by ten mercantile firms, Barnes & Ridgate accounted for twenty-eight.

50. Ridgate to Barnes, Aug. 31, 1771, Sept. 5, 19, 1771, Ridgate Letter Book, 4–7, 11–13; Jacob M. Price, ed., *Joshua Johnson's Letterbook, 1771–1774: Letters from a Merchant in London to His Partners in Maryland* (London: London Record Society, 1979), 13, 43, 45–46, 90.

51. Price, ed., *Joshua Johnson's Letterbook*, 50, 58, 61, 67–69, 82, 155.

52. *Md. Gazette*, May 27, June 3, Aug. 5, Sept. 2, 1773, Nov. 10, 1774, Oct. 12, 1775; CCCR, Lib. W3; CCLR, Libs. S3 (1770–75), fols. 412, 508, 532, 710–12, V3 (1775–82), fols. 15, 66–67, 78–81, 83–84, 88–90. As of 1786, the affairs of Barnes & Ridgate were not fully settled. *Md. Gazette*, Oct. 26, 1786.

53. Price, ed., *Joshua Johnson's Letterbook*, 58, 68, 69.

54. W. Dulany to Hamersley, Sept. 15, 1770, Dulany Papers, box 5.

CHAPTER FOUR: "LIBERTY MAD"

1. Cresswell, *Journal*, 16–18; *Md. Gazette*, Dec. 16, 1773; Papenfuse et al., eds., *Biographical Dictionary* 1:417–18; Hunter D. Farish, ed., *Journal and Letters of Philip Vickers Fithian, 1773–1774: A Plantation Tutor of the Old Dominion*, new ed. (Williamsburg, Va.: Colonial Williamsburg, 1957), 109.

2. Cresswell, *Journal*, 19; Philip Richard Fendall to James Russell, May 30, 1774, Russell Papers, bundle 3, Coutts & Co., London (microfilm in the Virginia Colonial Records Project, reels M-325, M-326, Colonial Williamsburg Foundation Library, Williamsburg, Va.).

3. Lawrence Henry Gipson, *The British Empire before the American Revolution*, 15 vols. (New York: Alfred A. Knopf, 1939–70), vol. 12, *The Triumphant Empire: Britain Sails into the Storm, 1770–1776*, 115–16, 148; Ian R. Christie and Benjamin W. Labaree, *Empire or Independence, 1760–1776: A British-American Dialogue on the Coming of the American Revolution* (New York: W. W. Norton & Co., 1976), 198–200; *Maryland Journal, and Baltimore Advertiser* (Baltimore), May 28, 1774; *Md. Gazette*, May 26, 1774; William Eddis, *Letters from America*, ed. Aubrey C. Land (Cambridge: Belknap Press of Harvard University Press, 1969), 86; Annapolis Committee of Correspondence to Peyton Randolph et al., May 25, 1774, Purviance Papers (MS. 1394), MHS.

4. Fendall to Russell, May 30, 1774, Russell Papers, bundle 3; John Hoskins Stone to Robert Christie, Jr., June 5, 1775, Miscellaneous Collection, William L. Clements Library, University of Michigan, Ann Arbor; Alexander Hamilton to James Brown & Co., May 28, June 13, 1774, "The Letterbooks of Alexander Hamilton, Piscataway Factor [1774–76]," ed. Richard K. MacMaster and David C. Skaggs, *Md. Hist. Mag.* 61 (1966): 158, 162, 164.

5. *Md. Gazette*, June 16, 1774; Fendall to Russell, June 15, 1774, Russell Papers, bundle 3; file of Charles County Court justices, in possession of the author.

6. *Md. Gazette*, June 16, 1774; Papenfuse et al., eds., *Biographical Dictionary* 1:68; file of Charles County Court justices; Fendall to Russell, June 15, 1774, Russell Papers, bundle 3. The county's fourth delegate to the Assembly, Robert Hendly Courts, died in 1774. Papenfuse et al., eds., *Biographical Dictionary* 1:238.

7. *Md. Gazette*, June 16, 1774; Fendall to Russell, June 15, 1774, Russell Papers, bundle 3.

8. Md. Provincial Convention, *Proceedings of the Conventions of the Province of Maryland, Held at the City of Annapolis in 1774, 1775, and 1776* (Baltimore: James Lucas & E. K. Deaver, 1836), 3–4; *Md. Gazette*, June 30, 1774; Ian R. Christie, *Crisis of Empire: Great Britain and the American Colonies, 1754–1783* (New York: W. W. Norton & Co., 1966), 86; William Fitzhugh to Russell, Aug. 3, 1774, Russell Papers, bundle 6; Gipson, *British Empire before the American Revolution* 12:116–18.

9. James Forbes to Russell, June 27, 1774, Russell Papers, bundle 6; Cresswell, *Journal*, 26; *Md. Gazette*, Aug. 11, 18, 1774; Charles County Committee of Correspondence to the Fairfax County, Virginia, Committee of Correspondence, Aug. 9, 1774, George Washington Papers, ser. 4, reel 33, Manuscript Division, LC; *Virginia Gazette* (Williamsburg), Aug. 24, 1774.

10. Samuel Hanson, Jr., to Russell, June 27, 1774, Basil Waring to Russell, June 25, 1774, Fendall to Russell, Aug. 13, 26, Sept. 14, 1774, Russell Papers, bundles 8, 18, 3, respectively.

11. Robert Carter to William Diggs, July 21, Aug. 25, 1774, Carter to John Digges, Aug. 27, 1774, Robert Carter Letterbook, May 1774–May 1775, fols. 26, 89, 91–92, in the Robert Carter Papers, Manuscript Department, William R. Perkins Library, Duke University, Durham, N.C.

12. Hamilton to James Brown & Co., May 28, Aug. 6, 1774, "Letterbooks of Alexander Hamilton," 61:158–59, 161, 308; Fendall to Russell, May 30, June 15, Aug. 13, 1774, Forbes to Russell, June 27, Aug. 31, 1774, Fitzhugh to Russell, Aug. 3, 1774, Russell Papers, bundles 3, 6.

13. Fendall to Russell, June 15, Nov. 15, 1774, Zephaniah Turner to Russell, Oct. 5, 1774, Charles Grahame to Russell, July 8, 1774, Russell Papers, bundles 3, 17, 20; Hamilton to James Brown & Co., Aug. 6, 1774, "Letterbooks of Alexander Hamilton," 61:309; Charles County Court, Tobacco Inspection Proceedings (C680), vols. 69 (1748–55) through 71 (1774–86). For quantities and the average price of tobacco shipped out of each warehouse in 1774, see Tables 8 and 9, Appendix. The figure of 12s. per hundredweight assumes a thousand-pound hogshead. John J. McCusker has calculated the August 1774 exchange rate between Maryland hard currency and British sterling as £1.68 to £1 (decimal scale). McCusker, *Money and Exchange in Europe and America, 1600–1775: A Handbook* (Chapel Hill: University of North Carolina Press, for the Institute of Early American History and Culture, 1978), 199.

14. Hamilton to James Brown & Co., Aug. 6, Oct. 31, 1774, "Letterbooks of Alexander Hamilton," 61:310–11, 319; Invoice and Letter Book, 1771–74, 1792–93, Port Tobacco, Md., fols. 2–74, John Glassford & Co. Papers, container 61, Manuscript Division, LC.

15. *Md. Gazette*, Sept. 29, 1774; Walter Hanson to Russell, Sept. 29, 1774, Thomas Hanson Marshall to Russell, Oct. 3, 1774, Francis Mastin to Russell, Oct. 4, 1774, Gerrard Fowke, Sr., to Russell, Nov. 9, 1774, Russell Papers, bundles 8, 14, 6, respectively. But see Fendall to Russell, Dec. 20, 1774, for an order for trade goods

worth £900, to be shipped to Maryland "as soon as matters between Great Britain and the Colonies are settled." Russell Papers, bundle 3.

16. *Md. Gazette*, June 16, Nov. 3, 1774; Christie and Labaree, *Empire or Independence*, 210–11.
17. Cresswell, *Journal*, 42.
18. *Md. Gazette*, June 16, Nov. 24, 1774.
19. Ibid.; file of Charles County justices; Papenfuse et al., eds., *Biographical Dictionary* 1:66, 68–69; Nelson W. Rightmyer, *Maryland's Established Church* (Baltimore: Church Historical Society, for the Diocese of Maryland, 1956), 142–43. Provincial Convention delegates: George Dent, John Dent, Samuel Hanson, Joseph Hanson Harrison, Josias Hawkins, Robert T. Hooe, Daniel Jenifer, Samuel Love, Thomas Hanson Marshall, William Smallwood, Thomas Stone, and Francis Ware.
20. *Md. Gazette*, Nov. 24, 1774; CCDB, 1774.
21. *Md. Gazette*, Nov. 24, 1774.
22. Alice Lee to Richard Potts, Feb. 11, 1775, Potts Papers (MS. 1392), MHS.
23. Lee to Potts, Dec. 20, 1774, ibid.; Md. Provincial Convention, *Proceedings*, 7–10; Jean Butenhoff Lee, "The Social Order of a Revolutionary People: Charles County, Maryland, 1733–86" (Ph.D. diss., University of Virginia, 1984), 50–51; *Md. Gazette*, Jan. 19, Mar. 16 et seq., 1775; Philip Padelford, ed., *Colonial Panorama 1775: Dr. Robert Honyman's Journal for March and April* (San Marino, Calif.: Huntington Library, 1939), 2; Fendall to Russell, Nov. 15, 1774, Forbes to Russell, Dec. 10, 1774, Fitzhugh to Russell, Jan. 6 [1775], Turner to Russell, Apr. 5, 1775, Russell Papers, bundles 3, 6, 17.
24. Md. Provincial Convention, *Proceedings*, 8; Fitzhugh to Russell, Jan. 6 [1775], Russell Papers, bundle 6; Hamilton to James Brown & Co., Dec. 23, 1774, "Letterbooks of Alexander Hamilton," 61:321; *Md. Gazette*, Feb. 2, 1775.
25. *Md. Gazette*, Jan. 19, 1775; A. Lee to Potts, Feb. 11, 1775, Potts Papers.
26. Cresswell, *Journal*, 17, 57.
27. Grahame to Russell, Apr. 3, 1775, Turner to Russell, Apr. 5, 1775, Fendall to Russell, Apr. 6, 1775, Russell Papers, bundles 20, 17, 3, respectively; [James Robinson] to William Cunninghame & Co., Mar. 31, Apr. 22, 1775, William Cunninghame & Co. Letter Book, 1774–77, National Library of Scotland, Edinburgh, used with permission of the library trustees (microfilm reel M-1342, Colonial Williamsburg Foundation Library).
28. *Md. Gazette*, Apr. 27, 1775; Daniel of St. Thomas Jenifer to "Gentlemen" (draft), Apr. 28, 1775, Stone Family Papers, in the possession of the Stone Family, La Plata, Md.; Fendall to Russell, May 4, 17, 1775, Russell Papers, bundle 5; Thomas Stone to Margaret Stone, Apr. 28, 1775, in John Sanderson and Robert Waln, Jr., *Biography of the Signers to the Declaration of Independence*, 9 vols. (Philadelphia: R. W. Pomeroy, 1823–27), 9:330.
29. Fendall to Russell, May 4, 17, 1775, Fitzhugh to Russell, May 6, 1775, William Carr to Russell, May 13, 1775, McPherson & Boarman to Russell, May 18, 1775, Philip Thomas Lee to Russell, May 30, 1775, Jamison Johnston & Co. to Russell, July 7, 1775, Russell Papers, bundles 5, 6, 2, 14, 11, 9, respectively; [Robinson] to William Cunninghame & Co., July 27, 1775, William Cunninghame & Co. Letter Book; Hamilton to James Brown & Co., June 30, 1775, "Letterbooks of Alexander Hamilton," *Md. Hist. Mag.* 62 (1967): 143, 145.
30. Hamilton to James Brown & Co., June 30, 1775, "Letterbooks of Alexander Hamil-

ton," 62:143, 145; Fendall to Russell, May 17, 1775, Samuel Love to Russell, May 20, 1775, Russell Papers, bundles 5, 11.

31. *Md. Gazette*, June 15, 1775.

32. Ibid. The committee of observation's less dramatic but no less rigorous interdiction of other imported goods can be followed in the Gilmor Papers (MS. 387.1), vol. 4, fols. 4, 38, MHS; entries for July 17 and 21, 1775, in the Journal of the Baltimore Committee of Safety, 1774–76, Peter Force Collection, ser. 8D, Manuscript Division, LC; *Md. Gazette*, Aug. 3, 1775.

33. *Arch. Md.* 11:5, 35, 37.

34. Ibid., 35.

35. Ibid., 37.

36. Ibid., 5, 14, 35–37.

37. Ibid., 15–16, 19–20; *Md. Gazette*, July 24, 1777.

38. See Chapter 5. John Shy emphasizes the militia's vital role in polarizing the population in *A People Numerous and Armed: Reflections on the Military Struggle for American Independence* (New York: Oxford University Press, 1976), 217–20.

39. Financial Records, Miscellaneous, fol. 2, in the Calvert Papers (MS. 174), reel 13, MHS; Charles County Register of Wills, Inventories (C665), 1774–75, fols. 223–26, MSA; CCCR, Lib. X3 (1774–78); Hamilton to James Brown & Co., Aug. 20, 1775, "Letterbooks of Alexander Hamilton," 62:151. In 1780 the Maryland Assembly formally abolished quitrents, with the explanation that it was "highly improper for, and derogatory to, the citizens of this sovereign and independent state, to pay quit-rent or tribute to the subject of a foreign prince" and that Marylanders "should hold their lands on equal terms with the citizens of the other states." *Laws of Md. . . . [Mar. Session 1780]*, chap. 18. Henry Harford's claim for his lost revenues is in American Loyalist Claims, ser. 2, A. O. 13/61, fols. 61–62, Public Record Office, London (microfilm in the Manuscript Division, LC).

40. *Arch. Md.* 11:16, 27–30, 32.

41. George Chalmers, memorial to the Commission of Enquiry into the Losses and Services of the American Loyalists, Oct. 14, 1783, American Loyalist Transcripts, vol. 35, fol. 16, Rare Books and Manuscripts Division, New York Public Library, Astor, Lenox, and Tilden Foundations, New York, N.Y.; Thomas Johnson to Horatio Gates, Aug. 18, 1775, in Edward S. Delaplaine, *The Life of Thomas Johnson: Member of the Continental Congress, First Governor of the State of Maryland, and Associate Justice of the United States Supreme Court* (New York: F. H. Hitchcock, 1927), 125; Richard Lee, Jr., claim [Mar. 1784], American Loyalist Claims, ser. 2, A. O. 13/40, fols. 100–01.

42. Extract of a letter from St. Mary's County, Jan. 12, 1776, in *Letters on the American Revolution, 1774–1776*, ed. Margaret W. Willard (Boston: Houghton Mifflin Co., 1925), 252–54; Richard Lee, Sr., to Russell [Oct.] 8, 17, 1775, Russell Papers, bundle 11; Papenfuse et al., eds., *Biographical Dictionary* 2:528.

43. Francis Walker claim [1777], American Loyalist Claims, ser. 2, A. O. 13/40, fols. 228, 230; Richard Lee, Jr., claim [1777–Mar. 1784], ibid., fols. 100–02, 107. By 1786 Lee was insane and a ward of his uncle James Russell. Ibid., fol. 109. See also R. Lee, Sr., to Russell, June 1, 1779, Russell Papers, bundle 11.

44. Papenfuse et al., eds., *Biographical Dictionary* 1:318–19; *Md. Gazette*, June 16, 1774, June 8, 1775; *Arch. Md.* 11:10, 62:462; CCCR, Lib. V3 (1775–82), fols. 47–49; R. Lee, Sr., to Russell, Sept. 12, [Oct.] 8, 17, 1775, Russell Papers, bundle 11. Fendall

eventually returned to America and by 1788 was living in Alexandria, Virginia. *Md. Gazette*, Nov. 20, 1788.

45. George Mason to the Md. Council of Safety, Nov. 29, 1775, *Arch. Md.* 11:93; John F. D. Smyth claim, American Loyalist Claims, ser. 2, A. O. 13/62, fols. 219, 234, 237–38; CCCR, Lib. V3, fols. 32–34. Smyth wrote the hyperbolic *A Tour in the United States of America . . .* , 2 vols. (London: G. Robinson, J. Robson, and J. Sewell, 1784). Harold Hancock attempts to disentangle fact from fancy in Smyth's writings in "John Ferdinand Dalziel Smyth: Loyalist," *Md. Hist. Mag.* 55 (1960): 346–58.

46. T. Stone to D. S. T. Jenifer, Apr. 24, 1776, in *Letters of Delegates to Congress, 1774–1789*, ed. Paul H. Smith et al., 19 vols. to date (Washington, D.C.: Library of Congress, 1976–), 3:581.

47. *Md. Gazette*, June 16, Nov. 24, 1774, Jan. 19, June 8, 15, Oct. 19, 1775. For loyalist insurrectionary activities on the Eastern Shore, see Ronald Hoffman, *A Spirit of Dissension: Economics, Politics, and the Revolution in Maryland* (Baltimore: Johns Hopkins University Press, 1973), 185–88, 197–203, 230–36, and Keith Mason, "Localism, Evangelicalism, and Loyalism: The Sources of Discontent in the Revolutionary Chesapeake," *Journal of Southern History* 56 (1990): 23–54. Emphasis on loyalism, however, obscures the extent to which even proprietary placemen became patriots. Anne Alden Allan, "Patriots and Loyalists: The Choice of Political Allegiances by the Members of Maryland's Proprietary Elite," *Journal of Southern History* 38 (1972): 283–92.

48. *Md. Gazette*, Oct. 14, 1784; Cresswell, *Journal*, 1.

49. CCCR, Lib. V3, fols. 52–54.

50. *Arch. Md.* 11:16, 27–28.

51. Ibid., 27; *Md. Gazette*, Oct. 19, 1775. Robert T. Hooe's role as a supplier for Maryland may be traced with the aid of Edward C. Papenfuse et al., comps., *An Inventory of Maryland State Papers*, vol. 1, *The Era of the American Revolution, 1775–1789* (Annapolis: Hall of Records Commission, 1977).

52. Hamilton to James Brown & Co., Aug. 2, 20, Oct. 30, 1775, "Letterbooks of Alexander Hamilton," 62:149, 151, 166; Fendall to Russell, May 30, 1774, Russell Papers, bundle 3.

53. CCCR, Lib. X3, fols. 48–68, 186–200; Hamilton to James Brown & Co., Aug. 2, 20, 1775, "Letterbooks of Alexander Hamilton," 62:148, 151; *Arch. Md.* 11:31–33.

54. Hamilton to James Brown & Co., Sept. 28, 1775, "Letterbooks of Alexander Hamilton," 62:162; *Md. Gazette*, Oct. 19, 1775.

55. *Md. Gazette*, Oct. 19, 1775.

56. CCCR, Lib. X3, fols. 514, 517, and passim. See also ibid., Lib. V3, fol. 118.

57. The governing elite's odyssey from the late colonial period to the 1790s is set forth in Jean Butenhoff Lee, "Lessons in Humility: The Revolutionary Transformation of the Governing Elite of Charles County, Maryland," in *"The Transforming Hand of Revolution": Reconsidering the American Revolution as a Social Movement*, ed. Ronald Hoffman (Charlottesville: University Press of Virginia, for the U.S. Capitol Historical Society, forthcoming).

58. *Arch. Md.* 11:30, 186–87, 280, 292, 530, 12:13, 39, 41, 55, 248.

59. *Md. Gazette*, July 4, 1776; Christie and Labaree, *Empire or Independence*, 227–28, 232; Don Higginbotham, *The War of American Independence: Military Attitudes, Policies, and Practice, 1763–1789* (New York: Macmillan, 1971), 116, 130–33; John E. Selby, *The Revolution in Virginia, 1775–1783* (Williamsburg, Va.: Colonial Williamsburg Foundation, 1988), 66, 82.

60. Mason to the Md. Council of Safety, Nov. 29, 1775, and J. Beall to D. S. T. Jenifer, Mar. 15, 1776, *Arch. Md.* 11:92–93, 251; T. Stone to [Washington], Jan. 16, 1776, Pierpont Morgan Library, New York, N.Y. Smyth's version of the plot is in his claim for compensation from the British government, in American Loyalist Claims, ser. 2, A. O. 13/62, fol. 194.

61. U.S. Continental Congress, *Journals of the Continental Congress, 1774–1789*, ed. Worthington C. Ford et al., 34 vols. (Washington, D.C.: U.S. Government Printing Office, 1904–37), 4:342; T. Stone to [D. S. T. Jenifer?], May 20, 1776, in " 'The Dye Is Cast . . . ,' " ed. Dorothy S. Eaton and Vincent L. Eaton, *Library of Congress Quarterly Journal of Current Acquisitions* 14 (1957): 182–83; Stone, Matthew Tilghman, and John Rogers to the Md. Council of Safety, June 11, 1776 (italics mine), *Arch. Md.* 11:478; *Md. Gazette*, July 4, 1776; Jenifer to Horatio Sharpe, June 22, 1776, quoted in Herbert E. Klingelhofer, "The Cautious Revolution: Maryland and the Movement toward Independence: 1774–1776," *Md. Hist. Mag.* 60 (1965): 297.

62. *Md. Gazette*, July 4, 1776. For the move toward Independence in Maryland during 1776, see Klingelhofer, "The Cautious Revolution," 268–307; Hoffman, *Spirit of Dissension*, chap. 7; and David C. Skaggs, *Roots of Maryland Democracy, 1753–1776* (Westport, Conn.: Greenwood Press, 1973), 174–80.

63. *Md. Gazette*, July 4, 1776.

64. Ibid., Nov. 24, 1774, Jan. 19, 1775, July 4, 1776; T. Stone to [D. S. T. Jenifer?], May 20, 1776, " 'The Dye Is Cast . . . ,' " ed. Eaton and Eaton, 183. Instructing colonial representatives, in theory and practice, is explored in Bernard Bailyn, *The Ideological Origins of the American Revolution* (Cambridge: Belknap Press of Harvard University Press, 1967), 170–73, and J. R. Pole, *Political Representation in England and the Origins of the American Republic* (Berkeley: University of California Press, 1971), 70, 72–73, 79–80.

65. *Md. Gazette*, July 4, 1776.

66. Ibid.; Klingelhofer, "The Cautious Revolution," 292, 303–06.

67. John Parke Custis to Washington, Aug. 8, 1776, George Bolling Lee Papers, 1732–1870 (Mss1 L5114 b1), Virginia Historical Society, Richmond; *Dunlap's Maryland Gazette or, The Baltimore General Advertiser* (Baltimore), Aug. 27, 1776; Md. Council of Safety to the Md. delegates in Congress, Aug. 16, 1776, *Arch. Md.* 12:212; Skaggs, *Roots of Maryland Democracy*, 179–84; Hoffman, *Spirit of Dissension*, 169–70.

68. Md. Council of Safety to the Md. delegates in Congress, Aug. 16, 1776, *Arch. Md.* 12:212; George W. Corner, ed., *The Autobiography of Benjamin Rush: His "Travels through Life" together with his Commonplace Book for 1789–1813* (Princeton: Princeton University Press, for the American Philosophical Society, 1948), 151; Richard Henry Lee to Patrick Henry, Aug. 20, 1776, *The Letters of Richard Henry Lee*, ed. James C. Ballagh, 2 vols. (New York: Macmillan, 1911, 1914; New York: Da Capo Press, 1970), 1:214; D. S. T. Jenifer to William Smallwood, Aug. 24, 1776, in *Papers relating chiefly to The Maryland Line during the Revolution*, ed. Thomas Balch (Philadelphia: T. K. Collins, 1857), 64–65; Hamilton to James Brown & Co., Dec. 23, 1774, "Letterbooks of Alexander Hamilton," 61:321.

69. Md. Council of Safety to Md. delegates in Congress, Nov. 29, 1776, *Arch. Md.* 12:491; Md. Constitutional Convention of 1776, *The Decisive Blow Is Struck: A Facsimile Edition of the Proceedings of the Constitutional Convention of 1776 and the First Maryland Constitution*, intro. Edward C. Papenfuse and Gregory A. Stiverson (Annapolis: Hall of Records Commission, 1977), n.p.; CCW, Lib. AF7 (1777–82), fols. 87–89, 382–83. See also John C. Rainbolt, "A Note on the Maryland Declaration of Rights

and Constitution of 1776," *Md. Hist. Mag.* 66 (1971): 420–35; J. R. Pole, "Suffrage and Representation in Maryland from 1776 to 1810: A Statistical Note and Some Reflections," *Journal of Southern History* 24 (1958): 218–21.

70. Md. Constitutional Convention of 1776, *The Decisive Blow Is Struck*, n.p.

71. File of Charles County Court justices; CCCR, Lib. X3, fol. 563; *Md. Gazette*, Nov. 24, 1774. Samuel Love was a justice in 1774, was active in extralegal politics, but, probably because of severe financial reverses, was not reappointed in 1777. Papenfuse et al., eds., *Biographical Dictionary* 2:547–48. When commissions were issued for the first justices of the new orphans' court, they went to five senior members of the county court (George Dent, John Dent, Samuel Hanson, Josias Hawkins, and Daniel Jenifer), while Chief Justice Walter Hanson was named register of wills. *Arch. Md.* 16:274; CCW, Lib. AF7, fols. 1–1a.

72. Papenfuse et al., eds., *Biographical Dictionary* 1:66, 76, 425–26, 2:741–42, 861; Md. Constitutional Convention of 1776, *The Decisive Blow Is Struck*, n.p.

73. Register of Civil Officers, 1777–1800, fol. 23, in Governor and Council, Commission Records (S1080), MSA; CCCR, Lib. X3, fol. 563; *Md. Gazette*, Nov. 24, 1774.

CHAPTER FIVE: WAR ON THE POTOMAC

1. "Journal of a French Traveller in the Colonies, 1765, II," *American Historical Review* 27 (1921): 72–73; Cresswell, *Journal*, 19, 42.

2. The quotation is from "Maryland in 1773," *Md. Hist. Mag.* 2 (1907): 358. The colony's role in the Seven Years' War, which was limited because of protracted disputes between Gov. Horatio Sharpe and the lower house of Assembly, is discussed in Charles A. Barker, *The Background of the Revolution in Maryland* (New Haven: Yale University Press, 1940), 205–13; Paul H. Giddens, "The French and Indian War in Maryland, 1753 to 1756," *Md. Hist. Mag.* 30 (1935): 281–310; and David C. Skaggs, *Roots of Maryland Democracy, 1753–1776* (Westport, Conn.: Greenwood Press, 1973), 113–15. For the county's involvement, see "A List of the Militia in Charles County . . . 1748," in Governor and Council, Colonial Muster Rolls (S962), MSA; *Arch. Md.* 42:238, 44:446, 464, 55:561–62; Mary K. Meyer, ed., "Genealogica Marylandia: Maryland Muster Rolls, 1757–1758," *Md. Hist. Mag.* 70 (1975): 224–25; and Margaret Brown Klapthor and Paul D. Brown, *The History of Charles County, Maryland* (La Plata, Md.: Charles County Tercentenary, 1958), 47–49. Fred Anderson, *A People's Army: Massachusetts Soldiers and Society in the Seven Years' War* (Chapel Hill: University of North Carolina Press, for the Institute of Early American History and Culture, 1984), is an excellent study of mobilization and wartime experiences of New England soldiers. Virginians' quite different experiences in the war are the subject of James Titus, *The Old Dominion at War: Society, Politics, and Warfare in Late Colonial Virginia* (Columbia: University of South Carolina Press, 1991). Informative surveys of the colonial military tradition include Howard H. Peckham, *The Colonial Wars, 1689–1762* (Chicago: University of Chicago Press, 1964); Douglas E. Leach, *Arms for Empire: A Military History of the British Colonies in North America, 1607–1763* (New York: Macmillan, 1973); idem, *Roots of Conflict: British Armed Forces and Colonial Americans, 1677–1763* (Chapel Hill: University of North Carolina Press, 1986); Don Higginbotham, *The War of American Independence: Military Attitudes, Policies, and Practice, 1763–1789* (New York: Macmil-

lan, 1971), chap. 1; and Lawrence D. Cress, *Citizens in Arms: The Army and the Militia in American Society to the War of 1812* (Chapel Hill: University of North Carolina Press, 1982), chap. 1. Valuable historiographic surveys are Higginbotham, "The Early American Way of War: Reconnaissance and Appraisal," in *War and Society in Revolutionary America: The Wider Dimensions of Conflict* (Columbia: University of South Carolina Press, 1988), 260–312, and E. Wayne Carp, "Early American Military History: A Review of Recent Work," *Virginia Magazine of History and Biography* 94 (1986): 259–84.

3. Recent works critical of the citizenry are Charles Royster, *A Revolutionary People at War: The Continental Army and American Character, 1775–1783* (Chapel Hill: University of North Carolina Press, for the Institute of Early American History and Culture, 1979) and E. Wayne Carp, *To Starve the Army at Pleasure: Continental Army Administration and American Political Culture, 1775–1783* (Chapel Hill: University of North Carolina Press, 1984). Jean Butenhoff Lee, "'They Will All Be Soldiers By and By': War and Society in Charles County, Maryland, 1775–83" (unpublished paper presented at the 1992 meeting of the Organization of American Historians, Chicago, Ill.) summarizes the principal themes and arguments presented in this and the following chapter.

4. Andrew Snape Hamond Autobiography; Hamond to Capt. Squire, Feb. 26, 1776, in A. S. Hamond Orders and Correspondence, 1771–77; Hamond to Hans Stanley, Aug. 5, Sept. 24, 1776, Hamond-Stanley Correspondence. These documents are in the Hamond Papers, 1766–1825 (#680), Tracy W. McGregor Library, Manuscripts Division, University of Virginia Library, Charlottesville.

5. Lund Washington to George Washington, Oct. 29, Nov. 5, 12, 14, 1775, in *The Papers of George Washington*, ed. W. W. Abbot et al., *Revolutionary War Series*, 5 vols. to date (Charlottesville: University Press of Virginia, 1985–), 2:256–57, 304, 357, 375.

6. Virginia Committee of Safety to the Md. Council of Safety, Jan. 27, Mar. 9, 1776, *Arch. Md.* 11:110, 228; Council to the Virginia Committee, Mar. 19, 1776, and to George Plater and John Dent, Mar. 19, 25, 1776, ibid., 11:263–64, 286; Dent to Council of Safety, Apr. 30, 1776, ibid., 11:394. The last mention of the beacon project is ibid., 11:449, 476.

7. Md. Provincial Convention, *Proceedings of the Conventions of the Province of Maryland, Held at the City of Annapolis in 1774, 1775, and 1776* (Baltimore: James Lucas & E. K. Deaver, 1836), 7–9. On the role of militias in the Revolution, see John Shy, *A People Numerous and Armed: Reflections on the Military Struggle for American Independence* (New York: Oxford University Press, 1976), 216–22; Higginbotham, *War and Society in Revolutionary America*, 106–31; Skaggs, *Roots of Maryland Democracy*, chap. 8; and Barry Windsor Fowle, "The Maryland Militia during the Revolutionary War: A Revolutionary Organization" (Ph.D. diss., University of Maryland, 1982).

8. *Md. Gazette*, Jan. 19, 1775; Cresswell, *Journal*, 57; Philip Padelford, ed., *Colonial Panorama 1775: Dr. Robert Honyman's Journal for March and April* (San Marino, Calif.: Huntington Library, 1939), 2; Samuel Love to James Russell, May 20, 1775, Russell Papers, bundle 11, Coutts & Co., London (microfilm in the Virginia Colonial Records Project, reels M-325, M-236, Colonial Williamsburg Foundation Library, Williamsburg, Va.); *Virginia Gazette* (Williamsburg), May 12, 1775, supplement. On the *rage militaire* at the beginning of the war, see Royster, *A Revolutionary People at War*, chap. 1.

9. Higginbotham, *War of American Independence*, 70–77, 82–95; Worthington C. Ford et al., eds., *Journals of the Continental Congress, 1774–1789*, 34 vols. (Washington, D.C.: U.S. Government Printing Office, 1904–37), 2:187–89; *Arch. Md.* 11:19–20; Md. Provincial Convention, *Proceedings*, 74, 76. Muster rolls for Charles County units, 1776–77, are printed in S. Eugene Clements and F. Edward Wright, *The Maryland Militia in the Revolutionary War* (Silver Spring, Md.: Family Line Publications, 1987), 158–65.

10. Md. Provincial Convention, *Proceedings*, 76–78; Papenfuse et al., eds., *Biographical Dictionary* 1:264, 419–20, 425–26; CCDB, 1774, fol. 60.

11. *Arch. Md.* 11:186–87; Papenfuse et al., eds., *Biographical Dictionary* 2:741–42, 784–85, 861; Charles County Sheriff, Account Book, 1769 (C649), MSA; CCDB, 1774, fols. 53, 67; CCCR, Libs. I3 (1759–60), fol. 257, N3 (1764–66), fol. 429; Meyer, "Genealogica Marylandia," 224–25; Md. Provincial Convention, *Proceedings*, 77.

12. Memorial of the Pomonkey Company to the Council of Safety, ca. Mar. 1, 1776, Red Books, vol. 13, fol. 148.

13. *Arch. Md.* 11:186–87; Papenfuse et al., eds., *Biographical Dictionary* 2:575–76. Marshall's sister was married to General Dent.

14. Memorial of the Pomonkey Company to the Council of Safety, ca. Mar. 1, 1776, Red Books, vol. 13, fol. 148; *Arch. Md.* 11:206.

15. Alexander Hamilton to James Brown & Co., Aug. 29, 1775, in "The Letterbooks of Alexander Hamilton, Piscataway Factor: Part III, 1775–1776," ed. Richard K. MacMaster and David C. Skaggs, *Md. Hist. Mag.* 62 (1967): 154; G. Washington to L. Washington, Aug. 20, 1775, in *The Papers of George Washington*, ed. Abbot et al., *Revolutionary War Series* 1:334–35.

16. Council of Safety to Dent, July 15, 1776, and to Richard Barnes, July 15, 1776, *Arch. Md.* 12:49–50; Barnes to Council of Safety, July 13, 1776, Jeremiah Jordan to Council of Safety, July 15, 1776, Dent to Council of Safety, July 16, 1776, William Harrison to unknown correspondent, July 19, 1776, and Josias Hawkins to Daniel of St. Thomas Jenifer, July 26, 1776, ibid., 12:43–44, 51, 60–61, 83, 125–26; Hamond to Sir Peter Parker, June 10, 1776, and to Stanley, Aug. 5, 1776, in the A. S. Hamond Orders and Correspondence, 1771–77, and the Hamond-Stanley Correspondence, respectively, in the Hamond Papers. Accounts pertaining to the deployment of Charles County militia units are in Maryland State Papers, ser. D: Revolutionary Papers (S997), box 1, items 14/20, 22, 35, MSA; Alexander McPherson account, July 20, 1776, Revolutionary War Military Records (MS. 1146), MHS; Council of Safety to Treasurer, Sept. 3, 1776, *Arch. Md.* 12:255. See also John M. Luykx, "Fighting for Food: British Foraging Operations at St. George's Island," *Md. Hist. Mag.* 71 (1976): 212–19, and W. Hugh Moomaw, "The Autobiography of Captain Sir Andrew Snape Hamond, Bart., R.N., 1738–1823, Covering the Years 1738–1793" (M.A. thesis, University of Virginia, 1953). A chronology of naval activity during the war is in Ernest M. Eller, ed., *Chesapeake Bay in the American Revolution* (Centreville, Md.: Tidewater Publishers, 1981), xxi–xxxv.

17. Quotations: Thomas Price to Council of Safety, July 23, 26, 1776, Hawkins to Jenifer, July 26, 1776, and John Allen Thomas to Plater, July 29, 1776, *Arch. Md.* 12:98, 122, 126, 136–37; Richard Henry Lee to Landon Carter, July 21, 1776, in *The Letters of Richard Henry Lee*, ed. James C. Ballagh, 2 vols. (New York: Macmillan, 1911, 1914; New York: Da Capo Press, 1970), 1:209. See also list of Dunmore's fleet, July 10, 1776, Jordan to Council of Safety, July 17, 1776, Dent to Council of Safety,

July 19, 1776, *Arch. Md.* 12:24–25, 65–66, 83–84; John Hanson receipt, Oct. 11, 1776, Md. State Papers, ser. D., box 1, item 14/21.

18. Diary-Memoir of Captain Sir Andrew Snape Hamond, July 20, 1776, Hamond Papers; Dent to Council of Safety, July 20, 1776, Josias Beall to Jenifer, July 24, 1776, Hawkins to Jenifer, July 26, 1776, *Arch. Md.* 12:87, 111, 125–26; master's log of HMS *Roebuck*, July 21, 1776, in *Naval Documents of the American Revolution*, ed. William Bell Clark et al., 9 vols. to date (Washington, D.C.: U.S. Naval History Division, Department of the Navy, 1964–), 5:1172.

19. Master's log of HMS *Roebuck*, July 23, 1776, and deposition of John Matthews and William Stoddert, Oct. 18, 1776, in *Naval Documents of the American Revolution*, ed. Bell et al., 5:1194, 6:1324; John Parke Custis to G. Washington, Aug. 8, 1776, George Bolling Lee Papers, 1732–1870 (Mss1 L5114 b1), Virginia Historical Society, Richmond; Diary-Memoir of Captain Sir Andrew Snape Hamond, July 23, 1776, and A. S. Hamond Autobiography, in the Hamond Papers; Dean C. Allard, "The Potomac Navy in 1776," *Virginia Magazine of History and Biography* 84 (1976): 424; Council of Safety to Md. delegates in Congress, July 26, Aug. 2, 1776, *Arch. Md.* 12:119, 162.

20. *Virginia Gazette* (Williamsburg), Sept. 6, 1776; Matthews and Stoddert deposition, Oct. 18, 1776, *Naval Documents of the American Revolution*, ed. Bell et al., 6:1324.

21. Matthews and Stoddert deposition, Oct. 18, 1776, *Naval Documents of the American Revolution*, ed. Bell et al., 6:1324–26.

22. Ibid., 1325; master's log of HMS *Roebuck*, July 24–26, 1776, ibid., 5:1250; Hawkins to Jenifer, July 26, 1776, *Arch. Md.* 12:126; and, in the Hamond Papers, Hamond to Stanley, Aug. 5, Sept. 24, 1776, and to Capt. Montagu, Aug. 6, 1776, Hamond-Stanley Correspondence and A. S. Hamond Orders and Correspondence, 1771–77, respectively, and Diary-Memoir of Captain Sir Andrew Snape Hamond, July 25–29, 1776.

23. *Dunlap's Maryland Gazette or, The Baltimore General Advertiser* (Baltimore), Aug. 20, 1776; *Virginia Gazette* (Williamsburg), Sept. 6, 1776; *Md. Gazette*, Nov. 7, 1776.

24. *Md. Gazette*, Nov. 7, 1776.

25. Ibid.

26. L. Washington to G. Washington, Nov. 14, 1775, *The Papers of George Washington*, ed. Abbot et al., *Revolutionary War Series* 2:375; Rieman Steuart, *A History of the Maryland Line in the Revolutionary War, 1775–1783* (n.p.: Society of the Cincinnati of Maryland, 1969), 2–5, 8, 154–56.

27. Charles Somerset Smith to Matthew Tilghman, Sept. 9, 1776, and Hawkins to Tilghman, Oct. 7, 1776, *Arch. Md.* 12:262–63, 325.

28. Papenfuse et al., eds., *Biographical Dictionary* 1:425–26; *Arch. Md.* 11:187; Higginbotham, *War of American Independence*, 7; idem, *War and Society in Revolutionary America*, 107–09. The state legislature retained adjutants when it passed a comprehensive militia law. *Laws of Md. . . . [June Session 1777]*, chap. 17.

29. R. H. Lee to [William Whipple?], June 26, 1779, *The Letters of Richard Henry Lee*, ed. Ballagh, 2:81.

30. Quotations: Council (as of 1777 the governor's Executive Council) to Patrick Henry, Feb. 14, 1778, to county lieutenants, May 17, 1779, and to the Md. delegates in Congress, July 28, 1780, *Arch. Md.* 16:499, 21:396, 43:238; Barnes to Gov. Thomas Sim Lee, Sept. 20, 1780, ibid., 45:113; Barnes to Gov. William Paca, Mar. 1, 1783, Executive Papers, box 47, items 115A&B. Representative commentaries

about British threats to Chesapeake Bay and the Potomac River system, as well as efforts to repel them, are in Council to the county lieutenants, Aug. 18, 1777, to Thomas Jefferson, Aug. 28, 1780, to John Dorsey, Dec. 20, 1780, to John Stewart, Dec. 31, 1780, and to Zedekiah Walley, Sept. 24, 26, 1782, *Arch. Md.* 16:338, 43:269, 45:247–48, 258, 48:267, 269; *Md. Gazette*, Nov. 17, 1780; Ignatius Fenwick to Gov. Thomas Johnson, Dec. 24, 1777, Feb. 12, 1778, Executive Papers, box 8, item 179, box 10, item 64; Barnes to Johnson, Dec. 20, 1777, Feb. 10, 1778, George Cook to Johnson, Dec. 22, 1777, Red Books, vol. 17, fol. 97, vol. 21, fol. 13, and vol. 14, fol. 71, respectively; Robert T. Hooe to T. S. Lee, Dec. 21, 1780, Maryland State Papers: Brown Books (S991), vol. 5, fol. 31, MSA.

31. Steuart, *History of the Md. Line,* 143; Papenfuse et al., eds., *Biographical Dictionary* 2:861; commission to Ware, July 1, 1777, *Arch. Md.* 16:304. Ware still held the post as of 1786, according to the Council Letter Book, 1780–87, fol. 498, in Governor and Council, Letterbooks (S1075), MSA. Legislation establishing the position of county lieutenant is in *Laws of Md. . . .* [*June Session 1777*], chap. 17.

32. Glimpses of the "neighborliness" of military service for men from the county appear in the George Dent pension file, Revolutionary War Pension and Bounty-Land Warrant Application Files, Record Group 15, Microcopy 804, reel 798, National Archives and Records Service, Washington, D.C.; Richard H. Courts to John Hanson, Jan. 24, 1777, Red Books, vol. 19, fol. 69; Samuel Chase to Johnson, Oct. 10, 1777, *Arch. Md.* 16:395; and *The Journal and Occasional Writings of Sally Wister*, ed. Kathryn Zabelle Derounian (Madison, N.J.: Fairleigh Dickinson University Press, 1987), 45–46. Civilian visits to camp are recorded in the Michael Jenifer Stone Account Book, Port Tobacco, Md., fol. 14, in the Kremer Collection (850028), item 21, Southern Maryland Studies Center, Charles County Community College, La Plata, Md.; CCW, Lib. AF7 (1777–82), fols. 64–65; and Daniel Jenifer to Johnson, Apr. 1, Aug. 31, 1778, Red Books, vol. 20, pt. 1, fol. 99, and pt. 2, fol. 67 (hereafter D. Jenifer, to distinguish him from his brother Daniel of St. Thomas Jenifer). For winter furloughs, see William Smallwood to Council of Safety, Oct. ?, 1776, to Johnson, Jan. 20, 1779, and to T. S. Lee, Apr. 23, 1780, *Arch. Md.* 12:361–62, 21:279, 43:479–80; Council to Smallwood, Apr. 27, 1780, *Arch. Md.* 43:155; and Samuel Hanson to Johnson, May 27, 1777, Executive Papers, box 7, item 130. Preference for "old Regular Troops" during crises is expressed in Council to John Hoskins Stone, May 31, 1779, *Arch. Md.* 21:432. On community within the Continental Army, see Holly A. Mayer, "Belonging to the Army: Camp Followers and the Military Community during the American Revolution" (Ph.D. diss., College of William and Mary, 1990).

33. J. H. Stone to Johnson, May 27, 1779, Red Books, vol. 25, fol. 66; John Layman file, Revolutionary War Pension and Bounty-Land Warrant Application Files, reel 1534; *Arch. Md.* 43:54. The National Genealogical Society's *Index of Revolutionary War Pension Applications in the National Archives* (Washington, D.C.: National Genealogical Society, 1976) is indispensable for locating veterans' files. Particularly engaging portions of these records, but none from Charles County, are published in John C. Dann, ed., *The Revolution Remembered: Eyewitness Accounts of the War for Independence* (Chicago: University of Chicago Press, 1980).

34. Quotations: Samuel Elgin file, Revolutionary War Pension and Bounty-Land Warrant Application Files, reel 910; Smallwood to Johnson, Oct. 14, 1777, *Arch. Md.* 16:398. Charles County enlistment lists for the Flying Camp are in the Revolutionary War Military Records; published lists are in *Arch. Md.* 18:31–33. Local men's

reminiscences of where they fought are in the pension files of Leonard Bean (reel 189), Jesse Boswell (293), Richard Blandford (265), William Bruce (384), John Carrol (481), Elijah Clark (552), Samuel Elgin (910), Robert Halkerston (1157), and Belain Posey (1956), in the Revolutionary War Pension and Bounty-Land Warrant Application Files. A brief synopsis of the major battles in which the Maryland Line fought is in Steuart, *History of the Md. Line*, 154–66.

35. Return of Military Stores in Charles County belonging to the State of Maryland, Apr. 1779, Executive Papers, box 20, item 17A; Harrison to Johnson, Dec. 14, 1777, Red Books, vol. 18, fol. 18; Ware to T. S. Lee, Sept. 9, 1780, Jan. 16, 1781, *Arch. Md.* 45:89, 47:24.

36. Thomas Stone to Johnson, Dec. 9, 1777, Red Books, vol. 4, pt. 1, fol. 81; Council to Ware and to T. Stone, Dec. 9, 1777, *Arch. Md.* 16:431–32.

37. T. Stone to T. S. Lee, Dec. 11, 1777, and to Johnson, Dec. 13, 1777, Red Books, vol. 4, pt. 1, fols. 83–84.

38. T. Stone to Johnson, Dec. 13, 1777, and Harrison to Johnson, Dec. 14, 1777, ibid., vol. 4, pt. 1, fol. 84, and vol. 18, fol. 18.

39. T. Stone to T. S. Lee, Dec. 11, 1777, and Harrison to Johnson, Dec. 14, 1777, ibid., vol. 4, pt. 1, fol. 83, and vol. 18, fol. 18.

40. Council to Ware and Barnes, Dec. 21, 1777, *Arch. Md.* 16:440. The proceedings against Edward Smoot for trading with the enemy are ibid., 16:444, 21:145; CCCR, Lib. X3 (1774–78), fol. 616; and Executive Papers, box 8, item 178. The only other local indictments involved two men who helped a loyalist from Georgetown board a British vessel lying off the county. CCCR, Lib. X3, fols. 615–16.

41. CCCR, Lib. X3, fol. 616; Alice Lee to unknown correspondent, Apr. 26, 1778, Potts Papers (MS. 1392), MHS.

42. Quotations: Council to county lieutenants, Jan. 11, 1781, and Barnes to T. S. Lee, Feb. 18, 1781, *Arch. Md.* 45:270, 47:75. American expectations regarding British plans for the Potomac River valley may be followed in John Peyton to T. S. Lee, Jan. 12, 1781, Hooe to T. S. Lee, Jan. 17, 18, 1781, Peter Wagoner to William Deakins, Apr. 6, 1781, and Council to the Marquis de Lafayette, Apr. 8, 1781, ibid., 47:13–14, 26, 28–29, 170, 45:383, respectively.

43. R. H. Lee to Samuel Adams, June 19, 1779, and to [Whipple?], June 26, 1779, *The Letters of Richard Henry Lee*, ed. Ballagh, 2:75, 81; J. Skinker to Jefferson, Apr. 11, 1781, *Calendar of Virginia State Papers and Other Manuscripts . . . Preserved in the Capitol at Richmond*, ed. William P. Palmer et al., 11 vols. (Richmond: Virginia State Library, 1875–93), 2:27; Council to Lafayette, Apr. 12, 1781, *Arch. Md.* 45:394. For additional contemporary comments about enemy plundering along the Potomac, see R. H. Lee to Arthur Lee, Aug. 31, 1780, *The Letters of Richard Henry Lee*, ed. Ballagh, 2:200; letters to T. S. Lee from Joseph Wilkinson, Nov. 9, 1780, Samuel Smith, Jan. 25, 1781, Robert Armstrong, Jan. 26, 1781, and Barnes, Feb. 16, Apr. 3, 1781, *Arch. Md.* 45:173, 47:37–39, 72–73, 159–60; *Md. Gazette*, Mar. 15, 1781; and Jordan et al. to Barnes, Apr. 3, 1781, *Arch. Md.* 47:160.

44. Council to county lieutenants, Jan. 11, 1781, and to Ware, Jan. 19, 1781, Ware to T. S. Lee, Jan. 16, 1781, *Arch. Md.* 45:270, 281, 47:24; T. Stone to T. S. Lee, Apr. 23, 1781, Emmet Collection, Rare Books and Manuscripts Division, New York Public Library, Astor, Lenox, and Tilden Foundations, New York, N.Y.

45. Quotations: Belain Posey file, Revolutionary War Pension and Bounty-Land Warrant Application Files, reel 1956; D. Jenifer to T. S. Lee, Apr. 8, 1781, *Arch. Md.* 47:172–73; Skinker to Jefferson, Apr. 11, 1781, *Calendar of Virginia State Papers*, ed.

Palmer et al., 2:27. Other descriptions are in Stephen West to T. S. Lee, Apr. 1, 1781, Beall to T. S. Lee, Apr. 7, 1781, Council to Lafayette, Apr. 8, 1781, and to Andrew Buchanan, Apr. 8, 1781, *Arch. Md.* 47:157–58, 168, 45:383–84, respectively; *Md. Gazette*, July 12, 1781; Henry Lee to Jefferson, Apr. 9, 1781, and Edmund Read to Jefferson, Apr. 10, 1781, *Calendar of Virginia State Papers*, ed. Palmer et al., 2:22, 25–26; Samuel Hanson file, Revolutionary War Pension and Bounty-Land Warrant Application Files, reel 1184. Requests for provisions to feed militiamen during the weeks of crisis are in Executive Papers, box 43, items 44E–44Q. Use of Elizabeth Young's ferry for intelligence purposes is documented in *Arch. Md.* 43: 198, 47:13–14, while the ferry facilities are described in *Md. Gazette*, July 4, 1782.

46. D. Jenifer to T. S. Lee, Apr. 8, 1781, *Arch. Md.* 47:173; H. Lee to Jefferson, Apr. 9, 1781, *Calendar of Virginia State Papers*, ed. Palmer et al., 2:22.

47. Quotations: pension files of Samuel Hanson (reel 1184), Belain Posey (1956), and John Shaw (reel 2161), Revolutionary War Pension and Bounty-Land Warrant Application Files; Smallwood to T. S. Lee, May 8, 1781, *Arch. Md.* 47:235. Continuing apprehensions about a full-scale British invasion of Maryland are expressed in Hooe to T. S. Lee, May 31, 1781, Council to county lieutenants, June 1, Aug. 4, 1781, *Arch. Md.* 47:261, 45:453, 455, 544, respectively; and George Mason to Pearson Chapman, May 31, 1781, *The Papers of George Mason, 1725–1792*, ed. Robert A. Rutland, 3 vols. (Chapel Hill: University of North Carolina Press, for the Institute of Early American History and Culture, 1970), 2:688–89. Not until August 9, after state officials learned that British forces were at Yorktown, Virginia, was Francis Ware notified that "it is not the Intention of the Enemy to invade this State at this Time." James McHenry to T. S. Lee, Aug. 6, 1781, and Council to Ware, Aug. 9, 1781, *Arch. Md.* 47:394, 45:552, respectively.

48. The quotations are in letters to Gov. T. S. Lee from D. Jenifer, Apr. 8, 1781, and T. Stone, Apr. 17, 23, 1781, *Arch. Md.* 47:173, 198, and Emmet Collection. Evidence of Maryland and Virginia militia units' efforts to resist the raiders, despite being poorly armed, comes from Mason to George Mason, Jr., June 3, 1781, *The Papers of George Mason, 1725–1792*, ed. Rutland, 2:693; J. Rogers et al. to Council, Apr. 11, 1781, and letters addressed to Gov. Lee from S. West, Apr. 10, 12, 1781, J. Beall, Apr. 15, 17, 1781, and R. T. Hooe, June 9, 1781, *Arch. Md.* 47:180, 177–78, 184–85, 188, 192–93, 277, respectively.

49. Return of Military Stores in Charles County belonging to the State of Maryland, Apr. 1779, Executive Papers, box 20, item 17A; Harrison to Johnson, Dec. 14, 1777, Red Books, vol. 18, fol. 18; Council to Ware, May 31, 1779, Apr. 9, 10, 1781, to Md. counties, Apr. 11, 1781, to Beall, Apr. 9, 11, 1781, and to George Keeports, Apr. 27, 1781, *Arch. Md.* 21:433, 45:385, 389, 392, 386–87, 391, 418, respectively; Council proceedings, Apr. 9, 10, 1781, *Arch. Md.* 45:384, 387.

50. Council to John Hancock, Apr. 21, 1777, to Ware, May 31, 1779, to Lafayette, Apr. 12, 1781, and to Special Council, Eastern Shore, June 1, 1781, *Arch. Md.* 16:221–22, 21:433, 45:394, 454.

CHAPTER SIX: PREVAILING ON THE PEOPLE

1. The mill stood on a wooded two-hundred-acre tract and was, according to the 1783 Land Tax List, "So well known that description is unnecessary." CCW, Lib. AF7 (1777–82), fols. 173–74; Walter Hanson, Jr., to Gov. Thomas Johnson, Sept. 8,

1778, Red Books, vol. 21, fol. 59; 1782 Assessment List for the lower east hundred of Port Tobacco Parish, Scharf Collection, box 96, item 15; 1783 Charles County Land Tax List, 6th District, Scharf Collection, box 98, item 1. All of these materials are at MSA.

2. *Arch. Md.* 11:24, 29–30, 337, 463, 534; Council of Safety to Md. delegates in Congress, Apr. 18, 1776, ibid., 11:341; Robert Townshend Hooe to W. Hanson, Jr., Mar. 19, 1776, John and Walter Hanson Papers (MS. 1579), MHS.

3. Md. House of Delegates, *Votes and Proceedings of the House of Delegates of the State of Maryland. October Session, 1777* . . . [Annapolis: Frederick Green, 1778], 23–24; *Arch. Md.* 11:186; W. Hanson, Jr., to Johnson, Sept. 8, 1778, Red Books, vol. 21, fol. 59; petition to the General Assembly [1790], John and Walter Hanson Papers; "A List of Recruits, Substitutes and Draughts Furnished in Troops for the Continental Army," 1778, Revolutionary War Military Records (MS. 1146), MHS.

4. W. Hanson, Jr., to Johnson, Sept. 8, 1778, Red Books, vol. 21, fol. 59; *Arch. Md.* 16:431; and the following items in the John and Walter Hanson Papers: report of Gabriel Duvall, Nov. 27, 1777, Thomas Gassaway to J. Hanson and W. Hanson, Jr., Mar. 10, 1780, petition to the General Assembly [1790], and two undated indentures for monies lent by the state. The Assembly apparently gave up on the mill in 1779, when it authorized sale of the public saltpeter. *Laws of Md. . . . [Nov. Session 1779]*, chap. 28.

5. Little has been published on war mobilization. Works that address the questions of who joined the army and why include John R. Sellers, "The Common Soldier in the American Revolution," in *Military History of the American Revolution: Proceedings of the Sixth Military History Symposium, USAF Academy* (Washington, D.C.: U.S. Government Printing Office, 1976), 151–61; Edward C. Papenfuse and Gregory A. Stiverson, "General Smallwood's Recruits: The Peacetime Career of the Revolutionary War Private," *WMQ* 30 (1973): 117–32; Mark E. Lender, "The Social Structure of the New Jersey Brigade: The Continental Line as an American Standing Army," in *The Military in America: From the Colonial Era to the Present*, ed. Peter Karsten (New York: Free Press, 1980), 27–44; and Don Higginbotham, *War and Society in Revolutionary America: The Wider Dimensions of Conflict* (Columbia: University of South Carolina Press, 1988), 285–88. On the mobilization of matériel, consult Erna Risch, *Supplying Washington's Army* (Washington, D.C.: U.S. Government Printing Office, 1981); James A. Huston, *Logistics of Liberty: American Services of Supply in the Revolutionary War and After* (Newark: University of Delaware Press, 1991); Laura L. Becker, "The American Revolution as a Community Experience: A Case Study of Reading, Pennsylvania" (Ph.D. diss., University of Pennsylvania, 1978); and the only thorough study of a single state, Richard Buel, Jr., *Dear Liberty: Connecticut's Mobilization for the Revolutionary War* (Middletown, Conn.: Wesleyan University Press, 1980). Works critical of civilians at war are E. Wayne Carp, *To Starve the Army at Pleasure: Continental Army Administration and American Political Culture, 1775–1783* (Chapel Hill: University of North Carolina Press, 1984) and Charles Royster, *A Revolutionary People at War: The Continental Army and American Character, 1775–1783* (Chapel Hill: University of North Carolina Press, for the Institute of Early American History and Culture, 1979). An exploratory examination of the effect of mobilization on American economic development is in Janet Riesman, "The Origins of American Political Economy, 1690–1781" (Ph.D. diss., Brown University, 1983), chap. 6.

6. Daniel Jenifer to Gov. Thomas Sim Lee, July 22, 1780, *Arch. Md.* 45:21. (Hereinaf-

ter D. Jenifer is used to distinguish Daniel Jenifer from his better-known brother, Daniel of St. Thomas Jenifer. Unless otherwise indicated, all Lee references in this chapter are to Thomas Sim Lee, who served as governor from 1779 to 1782.)

7. George Washington to John Sullivan, Dec. 17, 1780, *The Writings of George Washington from the Original Manuscript Sources, 1745–1799,* ed. John C. Fitzpatrick, 39 vols. (Washington, D.C.: U.S. Government Printing Office, 1931–44), 20:488; George Dent file, Revolutionary War Pension and Bounty-Land Warrant Application Files, Record Group 15, Microcopy 804, reel 798, National Archives and Records Service, Washington, D.C. "Lineages" of the state lines are collected in Robert K. Wright, Jr., *The Continental Army* (Washington, D.C.: Center of Military History, U.S. Army, 1983), 195–315.

8. *Arch. Md.* 18:4, 29, 76–77; Rieman Steuart, *A History of the Maryland Line in the Revolutionary War, 1775–1783* (n.p.: Society of the Cincinnati of Maryland, 1969), 1–25.

9. Quotations: Council of Safety to Md. delegates in Congress, July 26, 1776, *Arch. Md.* 12:119; John Carrol and Samuel Elgin files, Revolutionary War Pension and Bounty-Land Warrant Application Files, reels 481, 910; Steuart, *History of the Md. Line,* 154; William Smallwood to Council of Safety, Oct. ?, 1776, *Arch. Md.* 12:363. Information on Charles County companies in the Flying Camp is in Thomas Hanson to Daniel of St. Thomas Jenifer, July 23, 1776, Thomas Ewing to Council of Safety, Aug. 18, 1776, and Council of Safety to Ewing, Aug. 19, 1776, *Arch. Md.* 12:106, 219, 221. Preparations to send state troops northward to join the army are reported in Council of Safety to Md. delegates in Congress, July 19, Aug. 16, 1776, *Arch. Md.* 12:80, 211–12. Descriptions of battles in which they fought are in *Md. Gazette,* Sept. 5, 1776; Smallwood to [Matthew] Tilghman, Oct. 12, 1776, *Arch. Md.* 12:338–43; Higginbotham, *The War of American Independence: Military Attitudes, Policies, and Practice, 1763–1789* (New York: Macmillan, 1971), 152–62; Steuart, *History of the Md. Line,* 154–56.

10. John Allen Thomas to Council of Safety, Sept. 4, 1776, and Ewing to Council of Safety, Oct. 13, 1776, *Arch. Md.* 12:256, 347–48; Richard Blandford and Samuel Elgin files, Revolutionary War Pension and Bounty-Land Warrant Application Files, reels 265, 910.

11. Smallwood to Johnson, Nov. 8, 1777, *Arch. Md.* 16:414. For troop strength in units commanded by officers from Charles County, see the muster rolls of William Bruce's and James Farnandis's companies, in Compiled Service Records of Soldiers Who Served in the American Army during the Revolutionary War, Record Group 93, Microcopy 881, reel 397, National Archives and Records Service. For the army as a whole, consult Charles H. Lesser, ed., *The Sinews of Independence: Monthly Strength Reports of the Continental Army* (Chicago: University of Chicago Press, 1976). Recruitment quotas for Maryland are in *Laws of Md.* . . . [*Oct. Session 1777*], chap. 8; *Laws of Md.* . . . [*Mar. Session 1778*], chap. 5; *Laws of Md.* . . . [*Nov. Session 1779*], chap. 36; *Laws of Md.* . . . [*June Session 1780*], chaps. 10, 26; and *Laws of Md.* . . . [*Oct. Session 1780*], chap. 43.

12. *Laws of Md.* . . . [*Feb. Session 1777*], chap. 3; *Laws of Md.* . . . [*June Session 1777*], chap. 8; *Laws of Md.* . . . [*Oct. Session 1777*], chap. 8; *Laws of Md.* . . . [*Oct. Session 1778*], chap. 14; *Laws of Md.* . . . [*Nov. Session 1779*], chap. 36; *Laws of Md.* . . . [*Mar. Session 1780*], chap. 2; *Laws of Md.* . . . [*June Session 1780*], chap. 10. In *War and Society in Revolutionary America,* 274–83, Higginbotham discusses recent scholarship that

"raises doubts whether the provincials were as 'ideological' about standing armies as they have been described by historians of Anglo-American commonwealth or radical whig thought." Cf. John Todd White, "Standing Armies in Time of War: Republican Theory and Military Practice during the American Revolution" (Ph.D. diss., George Washington University, 1978) and Lawrence D. Cress, *Citizens in Arms: The Army and the Militia in American Society to the War of 1812* (Chapel Hill: University of North Carolina Press, 1982), chap. 3.

13. *Laws of Md.* . . . [*June Session 1777*], chap. 17; *Laws of Md.* . . . [*Oct. Session 1778*], chap. 15; Smallwood to Johnson, Sept. 11, 1777, and Council (as of 1777 the governor's Executive Council) to Francis Ware, Oct. 3, 1777, and to Andrew Buchanan, Oct. 3, 1777, *Arch. Md.* 16:369–70, 388, 390; Steuart, *History of the Md. Line*, 157–58; Higginbotham, *War of American Independence*, 183–88.

14. John Hoskins Stone to Johnson, July 24, 1777, and Johnson to Smallwood, Dec. 31, 1777, *Arch. Md.* 16:319–20, 452; *Laws of Md.* . . . [*Mar. Session 1778*], chap. 5.

15. *Laws of Md.* . . . [*Mar. Session 1778*], chap. 5; *Laws of Md.* . . . [*June Session 1780*], chap. 10; *Laws of Md.* . . . [*Oct. Session 1780*], chap. 29.

16. Council to Md. delegates in Congress, June 4, 1779, and to Washington, July 9, 1779, and Baron von Steuben to Johnson, Sept. 24, 1779, *Arch. Md.* 21:442, 469, 536–37.

17. Higginbotham, *War of American Independence*, 352–66; Steuart, *History of the Md. Line*, 160–64. One of the most compelling accounts of the effects of warfare in the interior is A. Roger Ekirch, "Whig Authority and Public Order in Backcountry North Carolina, 1776–1783," in *An Uncivil War: The Southern Backcountry during the American Revolution*, ed. Ronald Hoffman, Thad W. Tate, and Peter J. Albert (Charlottesville: University Press of Virginia, for the U.S. Capitol Historical Society, 1985), 99–124. Even more graphic statements are in John C. Dann, ed., *The Revolution Remembered: Eyewitness Accounts of the War for Independence* (Chicago: University of Chicago Press, 1980), 174–233.

18. Nathanael Greene to Lee, Nov. 10, 1780, and Mordecai Gist to the committee appointed to consider Greene's request, Nov. 14, 1780, *Arch. Md.* 45:176–77, 183; *Laws of Md.* . . . [*Oct. Session 1780*], chap. 43. The critical shortage of troops induced the Assembly to specify that "any able bodied slave, between sixteen and forty years of age, who voluntarily enters into the service . . . with the consent and agreement of his master, may be accepted as a recruit."

19. Greene to Smallwood, Mar. 31, 1781, and to Lee, Apr. 7, 1781, in the Nathanael Greene Papers, William L. Clements Library, University of Michigan, Ann Arbor.

20. Council to Congress, Aug. 4, 1781, and James McHenry to Lee, Aug. 6, 1781, *Arch. Md.* 45:542, 47:394; *Md. Gazette*, Sept. 13, 1781.

21. Quotations: Richard Blandford file, Revolutionary War Pension and Bounty-Land Warrant Application Files, reel 265. His enlistment is recorded in the muster role of Henry Boarman's company, July 1776, Revolutionary War Military Records. In addition to muster roles from the county, this collection contains recruiting warrants, enlistment returns, and certificates of men's fitness to serve. In 1776 one of seven independent companies was raised in Charles and Calvert counties, the Flying Camp contained two Charles County companies, and additional local men enlisted in Smallwood's Battalion. Steuart, *History of the Md. Line*, 3–4, 8; *Arch. Md.* 18:5–7, 31–33. The population at risk for army duty is estimated from the 1778 oath of fidelity to the state, to which 1,590 Charles County men subscribed; they con-

stituted nearly 90 percent of the free adult male population. CCCR, Lib. X3 (1774–78), fols. 641–51; 1778 constables' census, in Gaius M. Brumbaugh, comp., *Maryland Records: Colonial, Revolutionary, County and Church*, 2 vols. (Baltimore: Williams & Wilkins Co., 1915, 1928; Baltimore: Genealogical Publishing Co., 1967), 1:297–312.

22. Quotations: J. H. Stone to the Provincial Convention, n.d., Red Books, vol. 32, pt. 1, fol. 14; Samuel Hanson to D. S. T. Jenifer, June 11, 1776, ibid., vol. 15, fol. 74; Josias Hawkins, Thomas Contee, and Smallwood to Council of Safety, Jan. 17–18, 1776, in Maryland State Papers: Blue Books (S990), vol. 4, fol. 77, MSA. Supporting evidence is from Steuart, *History of the Md. Line*, 93, 137; *Arch. Md.* 11:186–87, 16:13–14; Hugh Gardner to D. S. T. Jenifer, Apr. 18, 1776, Red Books, vol. 16, fol. 3; S. Hanson to John Hall, June 11, 1776, Executive Papers, box 1, item 70; John Dent and John Parnham to Council of Safety, Nov. 10, 1776, *Arch. Md.* 12:432; J. H. Stone to Commissioners for the State of Md., Dec. 8, 1776, Miscellaneous Collection, William L. Clements Library. Endorsements from influential men in the county were employed throughout the war. See Thomas Stone to Tilghman, Oct. 11, 1776, Gratz Collection, Historical Society of Pennsylvania, Philadelphia; undated recommendation from T. Stone, Gustavus Scott, and R. T. Hooe, in the Etting Collection, Historical Society of Pennsylvania; Ware to Smallwood, Apr. 13, 1780, Maryland State Papers: Brown Books (S991), vol. 5, fol. 5, MSA; and Smallwood to Lee, Apr. 18, 1780, *Arch. Md.* 43:473–74.

23. Samuel Love to Smallwood, Dec. 26, 1775, and to D. S. T. Jenifer, Mar. 21, 1776, Red Books, vol. 12, fols. 120, 7, respectively; Steuart, *History of the Md. Line*, 69. The lands to which Courts was heir are described in CCCR, Lib. T3 (1770–72), fols. 145–47, and CCDB, 1774, fol. 14. Cf. the more successful military career of William Bruce, who entered Smallwood's Battalion as a rifleman in early 1776, was commissioned a lieutenant in the Maryland Line that December and a captain in 1779, and served until 1783. In 1818 Bruce was remembered as "a meritorious revolutionary Soldier distinguished for his long faithful and Constant duties during that glorious contest." William Bruce file, Revolutionary War Pension and Bounty-Land Warrant Application Files, reel 384; Steuart, *History of the Md. Line*, 62.

24. Richard Hendley Courts to John Hanson, Jan. 24, 1777, Red Books, vol. 19, fol. 69; R. H. Courts file, in the Revolutionary War Pension and Bounty-Land Warrant Application Files, reel 664.

25. Gardner to D. S. T. Jenifer, Apr. 18, 1776, Red Books, vol. 16, fol. 3; CCCR, Lib. V3 (1775–82), fols. 84–88; Jean Butenhoff Lee, "Land and Labor: Parental Bequest Practices in Charles County, Maryland, 1732–1783," in *Colonial Chesapeake Society*, ed. Lois Green Carr, Philip D. Morgan, and Jean B. Russo (Chapel Hill: University of North Carolina Press, for the Institute of Early American History and Culture, 1988), 321; *Arch. Md.* 12:16. Farnandis remained in the army until 1779, McPherson until the end of the war. Steuart, *History of the Md. Line*, 80, 110.

26. CCCR, Lib. T3, fols. 298–99, 714–16; CCW, Lib. AE6 (1767–77), fols. 179–80; CCLR, Lib. V3 (1775–82), fols. 60–61; Donald Jackson and Dorothy Twohig, eds., *The Diaries of George Washington*, 6 vols. (Charlottesville: University Press of Virginia, 1976–79), 3:120, 172, 240–41, 304; Daniel Jenifer Adams to Washington, Mar. 15, 1775, George Washington Papers, ser. 4, microfilm reel 33, Manuscript Division, LC; Steuart, *History of the Md. Line*, 49; Rezin Beall to Council of Safety, Aug. 27, 1776, *Arch. Md.* 12:243; Charles G. Griffith to the Provincial Convention, Oct. 8, 1776, Red Books, vol. 11, fol. 92. Adams resigned from the army in 1779 and

later claimed to be "one of those unfortunate officers, that laid down my Commission more for the want of money to support my rank in the Army, than any other cause." Adams to Washington, June 25, 1790, George Washington Papers, ser. 7, reel 119.

27. H. Gardner recruiting warrant, Nov. 16, 1776, Council of Safety to John Hancock, Jan. 21, 1777, [Executive] Council to Washington, Mar. 26, 1779, *Arch. Md.* 12:452, 16:69, 21:329–30; Washington to J. H. Stone, Jan. 8, 1777, in *The Writings of George Washington from the Original Manuscript Sources, 1745–1799,* ed. Fitzpatrick, 6:478– 79; J. H. Stone to Joseph Ford, ca. early 1777, Etting Collection. In 1777 the legislature repealed authorization to enlist servants and apprentices. *Laws of Md. . . . [June Session 1777],* chap. 10.

28. The 1779 recruiting season is documented in Council to Washington, Mar. 26, 1779, recruiting orders to Farnandis, July 1, 1779, *Arch. Md.* 21:329–30, 433; and letters to Gov. Johnson from J. H. Stone, Apr. 9, July 12, 1779, W. Bruce, June 12, 1779, and Samuel McPherson and Bruce, July 22, 1779, Red Books, vol. 25, fols. 68, 58, and vol. 20, fols. 98, 102, respectively. For the 1780 season, see Council to recruiting officers, Jan. 3, 1780, recruiting orders, Jan. 11–12, 1780, Council to the commissaries for Charles and St. Mary's counties, Mar. 11, 1780, *Arch. Md.* 43:47–48, 53–55, 106; disbursement of recruiting money for Charles County, Jan. 16, 1780, Executive Papers, box 21, item 130A; Ware to Lee, Aug. 3, 1780, *Arch. Md.* 45:40; and Samuel Jones's list of new recruits, Aug. 23, 1780, Red Books, vol. 33, fol. 2. Troop quotas assigned to the county are in *Laws of Md. . . . [Oct. Session 1777],* chap. 8; *Laws of Md. . . . [Mar. Session 1778],* chap. 5; *Laws of Md. . . . [Nov. Session 1779],* chap. 36; and *Laws of Md. . . . [June Session 1780],* chap. 10.

29. Ware to J. H. Stone, Mar. 20, 1781, and John Simmes to Lee, June ?, 1781, *Arch. Md.* 47:136, 331.

30. Joseph Marbury to Gist, Mar. 12, 1777, ibid., 16:170–71; Hawkins to Johnson, July 5, 1777, Red Books, vol. 18, fol. 89; Francis Ware's account of disbursements to recruiters in 1777, dated May 12, 1780, Executive Papers, box 18, item 79.

31. Ware, "A List of Recruits, Substitutes and Draughts Furnished in Troops for the Continental Army," 1778, Revolutionary War Military Records; W. Hanson, Jr., to Johnson, Sept. 8, 1778, Red Books, vol. 21, fol. 59; proceedings against Ignatius Baggot, November Court 1778, CCCR, Lib. Y3 (1778–80), fol. 166. According to an unsigned document entitled "Number and State of the Troops raised in Maryland from the Year 1776 . . . ," May 14, 1782, most of those who entered service in 1778 were nine-month draftees. Executive Papers, box 40, item 61. A substitute cost one local man £424 in 1780. Michael Jenifer Stone Account Book, Port Tobacco, Md., fol. 9, in the Kremer Collection (850028), item 21, Southern Maryland Studies Center, Charles County Community College, La Plata, Md.

32. CCLR, Lib. V3, vol. 258.

33. Ware, "A List of Recruits, Substitutes and Draughts Furnished in Troops for the Continental Army," 1778, Revolutionary War Military Records; CCDB, 1774; 1782 Assessment Lists, Scharf Collection, box 96, folders 7–10, 12–17. One of the most frequently cited arguments for the marginal socioeconomic status of Continental soldiers is that of Papenfuse and Stiverson, who examined a roll of 308 men who enlisted in Maryland in 1782. Yet their findings cannot be considered representative of either the state or the war as a whole. Not only were these troops raised *after* the Battle of Yorktown, but a large proportion came from Baltimore and the surround-

ing area. (Only six men listed Charles County as their place of residence.) Furthermore, linkages between many recruits and property-holding data on the 1783 state tax assessment lists are possible rather than proved, and the authors eliminated men with common surnames because of the difficulty with linkages. Papenfuse and Stiverson, "General Smallwood's Recruits," 120–23; list of men recruited Feb.– Sept. 1782, in the Smallwood Papers (MS. 1875), MHS. That many Continentals were men of modest means seems undeniable, particularly after early euphoria gave way to the harsh realities of army life. See, for example, Sellers, "The Common Soldier in the American Revolution," 154; Lesser, "The Social Structure of the New Jersey Brigade," 30; and Robert A. Gross, *The Minutemen and Their World* (New York: Hill & Wang, 1976), 147–53. What remains unclear are the motivations that prompted men, and even boys, to enlist, as well as how they fared economically after the war. The inadequacy of simple correlations between wealthholding and enlistment is clear from Natasha A. Larimer's "A Manly Spirit: The Politicization and Militarization of Boys in Revolutionary Massachusetts" (M.A. thesis, University of Wisconsin—Madison, 1993), chap. 4.

34. "Men enrolled in Charles County by Capt. Joseph Marbury . . . 1780," *Arch. Md.* 18:333; Marbury recruiting return, Apr. 20, 1780, ibid., 43:478; D. Jenifer to Lee, May 13, 26, 1780, *Arch. Md.* 43:493, 501–02; indictment of Joseph and Jane Thompson and Noli p seqr granted June 13, 1780, Executive Papers, box 18.

35. Ware to Lee, Sept. 9, 1780, *Arch. Md.* 45:89–90; bond of William Smoot, Dec. 23, 1777, Executive Papers, box 8, item 178; CCCR, Lib. X, fol. 616; pardon of Smoot, June 22, 1778, *Arch. Md.* 21:145; John Collins file, in the Pardon Papers, box 1, folder 37.

36. Council to Ware, Sept. 1, Oct. 3, 1777, to the commissaries for Charles and St. Mary's counties, Mar. 11, 1780, to Marbury, Mar. 24, 1780, and to Smallwood, Apr. 18, 1780, *Arch. Md.* 16:357, 388, 43:106, 119, 144–45; Smallwood to Lee, Mar. 7, 9, Apr. 15, 1780, ibid., 43:443–46, 471–72; Ware to Johnson, Oct. 13, 1777, and J. H. Stone to Johnson, Apr. 9, 1779, Red Books, vol. 18, fol. 62, and vol. 25, fol. 68.

37. Bennett Bracco to James Tilghman, June 26, 1776, to Mr. Ridgely, July 2, 1776, and to Council of Safety, July 16, 1776, *Arch. Md.* 12:125, 11:543, 12:59, respectively; J. H. Stone to Johnson, Apr. 9, May 27, 1779, Red Books, vol. 25, fols. 68, 66, respectively.

38. Ware to Johnson, Oct. 13, 1777, Red Books, vol. 18, fol. 62.

39. Council to county lieutenants, Apr. 12, 1778, *Arch. Md.* 21:32; Ware to Johnson, Apr. 22, 1778, Red Books, vol. 20, pt. 1, fol. 9. At the end of the war Francis Ware listed several hundred property holders who had been assessed for hiring substitutes, by militia classes, but who had not yet paid. Executive Papers, box 48, items 6/2–6/3.

40. CCCR, Libs. X3, fol. 710, Y3, fols. 22, 20, respectively. Also see ibid., Lib. X3, fols. 711–12; and for a woman who lived at St. Thomas Manor and persuaded the Council to release her recently drafted son ("the only support of myself and two daughters very small"), *Arch. Md.* 45:551–52, 47:388–89, and George Hunter et al., Day Book Memoranda, 1770–85, in Maryland Province Archives of the Society of Jesus, 172.D, Special Collections Division, Georgetown University Library, Washington, D.C.

41. CCCR, Lib. Y3, fols. 20–23. See also *Arch. Md.* 47:464–65.

42. Quotation: Ware to J. H. Stone, Sept. 2, 1781, with returns of men drafted in June

and July, *Arch. Md.* 18:376–77. Ware's mediating role may be traced in his letters to Johnson, Oct. 13, 1777, Apr. 22, 1778, Red Books, vol. 18, fol. 62, and vol. 20, pt. 1, fol. 9; to Lee, Oct. 30, 1780, enclosing "A Return of Recruits furnished by several Classes . . . ," 1780, Revolutionary War Military Records; to J. H. Stone, Mar. 20, 1781, *Arch. Md.* 47:136; and Richard Barnes to Lee, July 28, 1780, and Gerard B. Causin to T. Stone, May 7, 1781, *Arch. Md.* 45:33, 47:233. A sampling of commentary on problems with recruiting elsewhere in Maryland is found in the Barnes letter cited above; Council to R. Dallam, May 14, 1778, Benjamin Mackall IV to Uriah Forrest, July 28, 1780, and J. Beall to Lee, July 30, 1780, *Arch. Md.* 21:82, 45:32–33, 35–36.

43. J. H. Stone to Johnson, July 24, 1777, Smallwood to Johnson, Nov. 8, 1777, and to Lee, Oct. 31, 1780, *Arch. Md.* 16:319, 413, 45:167.

44. Washington to Jonathan Trumbull, Jan. 8, 1780, *The Writings of George Washington from the Original Manuscript Sources, 1745–1799*, ed. Fitzpatrick, 17:366. The army's perceptions of inadequate civilian support are important themes in Royster, *A Revolutionary People at War* and Carp, *To Starve the Army at Pleasure.*

45. Washington to Trumbull, Jan. 8, 1780, *The Writings of George Washington from the Original Manuscript Sources, 1745–1799*, ed. Fitzpatrick, 17:367; Jean Butenhoff Lee, "Prevailing on the People: War Mobilization in Charles County, Maryland, 1775–81" (unpublished paper on deposit at the Southern Maryland Studies Center, Charles County Community College). The latter is a longer, more detailed treatment of efforts to collect matériel than appears in this chapter.

46. Md. Provincial Convention, *Proceedings of the Conventions of the Province of Maryland, Held at the City of Annapolis in 1774, 1775, and 1776* (Baltimore: James Lucas & E. K. Deaver, 1836), 8–9; *Arch. Md.* 11:30; Council of Safety to county committees of observation, Mar. 23, 1776, and to Md. delegates in Congress, July 19, 1776, *Arch. Md.* 11:280, 12:80.

47. *Laws of Md. . . . [Feb. Session 1777]*, chap. 3.

48. Ibid.; Md. House of Delegates, *Votes and Proceedings . . . February Session, 1777 . . .* [Annapolis: Frederick Green, 1777], 63–65; William Harrison to Johnson, Apr. 27, 1777, Hawkins to Johnson, May 4, 1777, S. Hanson to Johnson, May 27, 1777, Executive Papers, box 7, items 24C, 26B, 130; Council to Jenifer & Hooe, May 13, 1777, *Arch. Md.* 16:250.

49. *Laws of Md. . . . [Oct. Session 1777]*, chap. 4; *Laws of Md. . . . [Mar. Session 1778]*, chap. 1; *Laws of Md. . . . [Nov. Session 1779]*, chap. 32; *Laws of Md. . . . [Mar. Session 1780]*, chap. 25; *Laws of Md. . . . [June Session 1780]*, chaps. 21, 25; *Laws of Md. . . . [Oct. Session 1780]*, chap. 25; *Laws of Md. . . . [May Session 1781]*, chaps. 3, 24. During the war the Assembly imposed ad valorem taxes on all real and personal property except tools, food for subsistence, and a few other essential items. Adult, able-bodied males who did not have families, were not serving in the army, and did not have taxable property nevertheless paid a designated amount. As of 1781 any other persons whose ratable property did not exceed £10 Maryland currency were declared paupers and exempt from taxation. *Laws of Md. . . . [Nov. Session 1779]*, chap. 35; *Laws of Md. . . . [Oct. Session 1780]*, chap. 25; *Laws of Md. . . . [Nov. Session 1781]*, chap. 4.

50. Washington to Trumbull, Jan. 8, 1780, *The Writings of George Washington from the Original Manuscript Sources, 1745–1799*, ed. Fitzpatrick, 17:366; Worthington C. Ford et al., eds., *Journals of the Continental Congress, 1774–1789*, 34 vols. (Washington, D.C.: U.S. Government Printing Office, 1904–37), 16:196–201. Maryland's

original quota, subsequently amended, amounted to four million pounds of beef, twenty thousand barrels of flour, two hundred tons of hay, fifty-six thousand bushels of corn or forage equivalent, and a thousand hogsheads of tobacco.

51. *Laws of Md. . . .* [*Oct. Session 1777*], chap. 4; *Laws of Md. . . .* [*Mar. Session 1778*], chap. 1; *Laws of Md. . . .* [*Nov. Session 1779*], chap. 32; Council to D. Jenifer, Sept. 4, 1781, *Arch. Md.* 45:613.

52. Quotations: Ephraim Blaine to Lee, Dec. 8, 1779, Lee's proclamation to the citizens of Maryland, Dec. 29, 1779, and Council to the president of Congress, July 27, 1780, *Arch. Md.* 43:381–82, 43, 235, respectively. Urgent entreaties on behalf of the army are in Francis Dana et al. to Johnson, Feb. 16, 1778, Council to Horatio Gates, Feb. 18, 1778, Gates to Johnson, Feb. 23, 1778, Washington to Lee, Dec. 16, 1779, and Council to county purchasers, Sept. 28, 1780, and to county commissioners and sheriffs, Dec. 29, 1779, ibid., 16:503, 505–06, 519, 43:386–87, 307, 43–44, respectively. Examples of canceled requests are in Council to purchasers of wagons and horses, Nov. 1, 1780, and to the Md. delegates in Congress, Nov. 22, 1780, ibid., 43:347, 45:221, respectively. See also the Council's assertion, July 24, 1780, that "the Failure of the Supply required is not imputable to Supineness or unwillingness in this State to render every Assistance, but to the Want of Time to execute the Laws and in some Measure to the Scarcity of Money to answer the various Demands incessantly made on the People." Ibid., 42:228. For an overview of one of the worst provisioning crises, see S. Sydney Bradford, "Hunger Menaces the Revolution, December, 1779–January, 1780," *Md. Hist. Mag.* 61 (1966): 1–23.

53. Stephen West to Lee, Apr. 1, 1781, *Arch. Md.* 47:157; J. B. Lee, "Prevailing on the People."

54. Benjamin Douglass to Lee, Mar. 4, 1780, *Arch. Md.* 43:442; J. B. Lee, "Prevailing on the People."

55. Papenfuse et al., eds., *Biographical Dictionary* 2:484–85. Jenifer's provisioning appointments are documented in *Arch. Md.* 16:426, 551, 43:215, 45:462; *Laws of Md. . . .* [*Oct. Session 1780*], chap. 25; *Laws of Md. . . .* [*May Session 1781*], chap. 5. Glimpses of his mercantile career appear in CCLR, Lib. L3 (1761–65), fols. 132–33, and *Md. Gazette*, May 21, 1761, May 23, 1765.

56. D. Jenifer to Johnson, Apr. 1, 1778, Red Books, vol. 20, pt. 1, fol. 99, in reply to the Council's letter to the county purchasers, Mar. 27, 1778, *Arch. Md.* 16:555; to Johnson, Sept. 26, 1779, Executive Papers, box 15, item 46; and to Lee, Oct. 7, 1780, June 30, 1781, *Arch. Md.* 45:137, 47:325.

57. Ware to Johnson, Oct. 13, 1777, Red Books, vol. 18, fol. 62; D. Jenifer's account of clothing purchased for the army, Dec. 2, 1777–Feb. 2, 1778, accounts of assistant collectors John Mathews, Thomas Harris, John Morton, and Dr. Walter Hanson Jenifer (Daniel Jenifer's son), and Jenifer's invoice to the Council, Feb. 3, 1778, ibid., vol. 20, pt. 1, fols. 69–74.

58. Ibid.

59. "An Address to the Inhabitants of New Jersey, Pennsylvania, Delaware, Maryland and Virginia," Feb. 18, 1778, *Arch. Md.* 16:513; D. Jenifer to Johnson, Apr. 1, 13, May 5, 1778, Red Books, vol. 20, pt. 1, fols. 99, 96, and pt. 2, fol. 7, respectively.

60. D. Jenifer to Johnson, May 5, 1778, Red Books, vol. 20, pt. 2, fol. 7, and to Lee, Oct. 7, 1780, June 30, July 15, 1781, *Arch. Md.* 45:137, 47:324, 349–50.

61. Council to purchasing commissaries in Charles and other counties, Dec. 27, 1780, Council to D. Jenifer, Jan. 19, 1781, Jenifer to Lee, Jan. 15, 17, 1781, *Arch. Md.*

45:255, 281, 47:19, 25; Jenifer to Johnson, Apr. 1, 1778, Red Books, vol. 20, pt. 1, fol. 99. The meat house is mentioned in CCCR, Lib. Y3, fols. 466, 469. The number of slaves Jenifer owned in 1778 is unknown. He was assessed for seventeen taxables of all kinds in 1769 and for nineteen slaves in 1783. Charles County Sheriff, Account Book, 1769 (C649), MSA; Papenfuse et al., eds., *Biographical Dictionary* 2:484.

62. The author is indebted to Lorena S. Walsh for information on Chesapeake agricultural cycles.

63. D. Jenifer to Johnson, May 5, 1778, Red Books, vol. 20, pt. 2, fol. 7; Council to Thomas Clagett, May 25, 1778, Johnson to Capt. Ross, May 27, 1778, Council to county purchasers of provisions, June 6, 1778, and to Jenifer, June 12, 1778, *Arch. Md.* 21:110–12, 124–25, 133; Bennett Dyson's procurement account, Apr. 1, 1780, Executive Papers, box 18, fol. 3; Douglass to Lee, Apr. 1, 1780, and Dyson to Lee, June 20, 1780, *Arch. Md.* 43:461, 518.

64. D. Jenifer to Johnson, May 5, Aug. 31, 1778, and Blaine to Johnson, Sept. 9, 1778, Red Books, vol. 20, pt. 2, fols. 7, 67, 74; Council to Jenifer, Sept. 12, 1778, July 13, 1781, *Arch. Md.* 21:202, 45:501; Jenifer to Lee, June 13, July 10, 15, 25, 1781, and Council to collectors of horses, July 12, Sept. 29, 1781, *Arch. Md.* 47:289, 341, 349–50, 368, 45:499, 629. Other examples of canceled orders for supplies include Council to purchasers, May 13, June 20, 1778, *Arch. Md.* 21:80, 142.

65. Washington to Johnson, Aug. 26, 1779, Council to Smallwood, Sept. 24, 1779, *Arch. Md.* 21:504–05, 535–36; D. Jenifer to Johnson, Sept. 19, 26, 1779, Executive Papers, box 15, items 35, 46.

66. Alexander Hamilton to James Brown & Co., Oct. 30, 1775, "The Letterbooks of Alexander Hamilton, Piscataway Factor [1774–76]," ed. Richard K. MacMaster and David C. Skaggs, *Md. Hist. Mag.* 62 (1967): 166; Causin to Lee, Sept. 11, 1780, *Arch. Md.* 45:93. Statistical analysis of the wartime economy is lacking, partly because of inadequate records and a variety of currencies then in circulation, but ample narrative evidence speaks of economic distress in Charles County. The most revealing comments include "the Situation of the times [1776] are such . . . that Sales of Land cannot be made," "hard Metals have disappeared," "there is no money in this County," "the Spirit of the times . . . rendered it extremely Disagreeable and even hazardous to refuse or doubt the Credit of bills issued by Congress," and—in reference to state law that made paper money legal tender in payment for debts—"not knowing how to shun the Ruin which threatned his fortune by means of paper payments . . . Your Orator was obliged to yield to the times and has found himself most iniquitously defrauded of a great Part of the Earning of a life of Industry and care" and "I have been one of those unfortunate Ones, who have Suffered very considerably by the depreciating Paper Currency heretofore made a legal tender & which I have received in [lieu of] payment of Gold & Silver debts to the amount of 1500 or 2000£." CCW, Lib. AF7, fols. 289–90; Samuel Hanson (of Samuel) to William Tilghman, Sept. 4, 1779, William Tilghman Papers, Historical Society of Pennsylvania; D. Jenifer to Lee, July 15, 1781, *Arch. Md.* 47:349; *Samuel Hanson v. James Slater*, in Chancery Records, 1791–92, fols. 257–58; Parnham to Duvall, May 14, 1782, Executive Papers, box 34, fol. 47. The surety bonds required of executors of estates, which reached as high as £100,000 in 1780, attest to rampant inflation. CCW, Lib. AF7, fols. 505–06. Local efforts to cope with chaotic wartime economic conditions ranged from mortgages in which repayment depended on resumption of the export trade to private and public exhortations to uphold the

value of paper money. CCCR, Lib. V3, fols. 73–75; *Md. Gazette*, Aug. 16, Sept. 6, 1781.

67. Quotations: D. Jenifer to Lee, Jan. 15, June 30, 1781, and Council to Jenifer, June 15, 1781, *Arch. Md.* 47:19, 324–25, 45:476, respectively. Also consult Jenifer to Lee, June 13, July 25, 1781, and Council to Jenifer, July 17, 1781, ibid., 47:289, 368, 45:507, respectively. Background information on wartime paper money emissions and controversies is in Kathryn L. Behrens, *Paper Money in Maryland, 1727–1789* (Baltimore: Johns Hopkins University Press, 1923), 56–74; E. James Ferguson, *The Power of the Purse* (Chapel Hill: University of North Carolina Press, for the Institute of Early American History and Culture, 1961); and Ronald Hoffman, *A Spirit of Dissension: Economics, Politics, and the Revolution in Maryland* (Baltimore: Johns Hopkins University Press, 1973), 210–14, 250, 255–56.

68. Stephen Compton to D. Jenifer, Sept. 23, 1780, and Jenifer to Lee, Sept. 26, 1780, *Arch. Md.* 45:122–23; J. B. Lee, "Prevailing on the People."

69. Council of Safety to county committees of observation, Mar. 23, 1776, and to the committee of Charles County, Mar. 30, 1776, and George Dent to the Council of Safety, Apr. 2, 1776, *Arch. Md.* 11:280, 300, 305; Jenifer to Johnson, Apr. 1, 1778, Sept. 19, 1779, Red Books, vol. 20, pt. 1, fol. 99, Executive Papers, box 15, item 35; Jenifer to Lee, Oct. 7, 1780, *Arch. Md.* 45:137.

70. D. Jenifer to Lee, July 22, 1780, June 13, 30, 1781, *Arch. Md.* 45:21, 47:289, 324–25.

71. Letters to Lee from F. Ware, Sept. 9, 1780, J. Ford, Oct. 6, 1780, July 24, 1781, and D. Jenifer, Sept. 11, 1781, *Arch. Md.* 45:89–90, 136, 47:36, 487.

72. Higginbotham, *War of American Independence*, 380; Council to county commissaries, June 9, Aug. 30, Sept. 5, 1781, and to Thomas Nelson, Sept. 7, 1781, *Arch. Md.* 45:469, 590, 603, 609.

73. Marbury to Gist, Mar. 12, 1777, Council to Washington, Sept. 19, 1781, ibid., 16:170–71, 45:619; Steuart, *History of the Md. Line*, 122; Red Books, vol. 32, pt. 1, fol. 75; D. S. T. Jenifer to unknown correspondent, Sept. 18, 1781, Dreer Collection: Members of Congress, 3:12, Historical Society of Pennsylvania.

74. Quotations: Hezekiah Reeder to J. H. Stone, Aug. 14, 1781, and to James Brice, Aug. 20, 1781, Stone to Reeder, Aug. 16, 1781, *Arch. Md.* 47:420, 431, 423, respectively. Additional evidence is in Council to commissaries in Charles and adjacent counties, June 9, Aug. 17, 20, 1781, to D. Jenifer, Aug. 5, 1781, and to Reeder, Aug. 6, 23, 1781, Reeder to Lee, June 18, Aug. 22, 1781, ibid., 45:469, 569, 572, 544–45, 546, 579, 47:300, 439, respectively; Reeder's account of cattle purchased July 16– Sept. 4, 1781, and John Crisall to Reeder, Aug. 23, 1781, Executive Papers, box 23, item 23, and box 43, item 37L.

75. Council to county commissaries, Aug. 30, Sept. 5, Oct. 16, 1781, and to county lieutenants, Sept. 6, 1781, *Arch. Md.* 45:590–91, 603, 644, 605–06, respectively; J. H. Stone to Reeder, Sept. 8, 1781, ibid., 47:481; accountings to Reeder by Edward Kerrick, Oct. 22, 1781, Thomas Hopewell, Nov. 14, 20, 1781, and John Vardin, Oct. 29, 1781, Executive Papers, box 23, items 25/1–5, box 42, item 12.

76. D. Jenifer to Lee, Oct. 5, 1781, *Arch. Md.* 47:513–14; Lee to Reeder, Oct. 16, 1781, Maryland State Papers, ser. C, box 1, item 56, MSA. Certificates showing shipments discussed in the text are in the Executive Papers, box 42, items 15/42, 15/44–46, 15/50–51, 15/54–55, and box 43, item 45/O; and in an account of wheat received at Robert Fergusson's plantation, Sept. 11–Dec. 1, 1781, Executive Papers, box 42, items 14/2–3. By using the numbers on the certificates dated Sept. 1 through Oct.

30, I estimate that those that have survived constitute about 75 percent of all certificates issued during those months. The amount of wheat tallied in the extant certificates ranged from 2 to 121 bushels per lot and totaled 1,489 bushels. Hundreds of wheat certificates issued in Charles County between 1780 and 1783 are in the Executive Papers. The essential key for locating them is Edward C. Papenfuse et al., comps., *An Inventory of Maryland State Papers*, vol. 1, *The Era of the American Revolution, 1775–1789* (Annapolis: Hall of Records Commission, 1977). Information on the assessed worth of persons to whom wheat certificates were issued in September and October 1781 is based on the 1782 Assessment Lists, Scharf Collection, box 96, folders 7–17. Records of the amounts of bacon and pork collected are too scanty to permit any conjecture about the county's collection of those commodities, but see Executive Papers, box 42, items 15/32–33, 16/22, 16/24.

77. Executive Papers, box 23, item 24/7, box 42, item 15/46, box 43, item 45/K; Blaine to Lee, Sept. 27, 1781, Washington to Lee, Oct. 12, 1781, James Calhoun to Council, Oct. 15, 1781, *Arch. Md.* 47:507, 521, 524. Reference to the cannonade at Yorktown being "distinctly heard in Charles County" is in Charles Carroll of Carrollton to Charles Carroll of Annapolis, Oct. 15, 1781, in the Carroll Papers (MS. 206), vol. 7, no. 675, MHS. The author is indebted to Ronald Hoffman and Sally D. Mason, editors of the Carroll papers, for assistance in locating this letter.

78. Council to purchasers in Charles and Calvert counties, June 1, 1779, Thomas Richardson to Lee, June 10, 1780, *Arch. Md.* 21:437–38, 43:512; Bennett Dyson's account of provisions procured, Apr. 1, 1780, account book of purchases made by the commissioners under the act for the immediate supply of the army [1780], John Muschett's account of provisions collected in 1780, Executive Papers, box 18, item 3, box 21, item 130A, box 42, item 10/1, and, in the same collection, the following receipts for corn: Benjamin Sergeant to Muschett, June 17, July 29, 1780, John Betts to Muschett, July 7, Aug. 14, 1780, box 42, items 10/2–5.

79. Bracco to Ridgely, July 2, 1776, *Arch. Md.* 11:543.

80. D. Jenifer to Lee, June 30, 1781, ibid., 47:324. Insightful contemplations about the impact of the war on American society are in John Shy, "American Society and Its War for Independence," in *Reconsiderations on the Revolutionary War: Selected Essays*, ed. Don Higginbotham (Westport, Conn.: Greenwood Press, 1978), 72–82, and Charles Royster, "Founding a Nation in Blood: Military Conflict and American Nationality," in *Arms and Independence: The Military Character of the American Revolution*, ed. Ronald Hoffman and Peter J. Albert (Charlottesville: University Press of Virginia, for the U.S. Capitol Historical Society, 1984), 25–49.

PART THREE: POSTWAR ADJUSTMENTS

PROLOGUE: "ALL REJOICED"

1. List of men recruited Feb.–Sept. 1782, Smallwood Papers (MS. 1875), MHS; Nathanael Greene to Thomas Sim Lee, Apr. 28, 1782, Nathanael Greene Papers, William L. Clements Library, University of Michigan, Ann Arbor; Thomas Stone to Walter Stone, July 16, 1782, Stone Family of Maryland Papers, fol. 74, Manuscript Division, LC; Francis Adams's certification of British plundering at Nanjemoy, Apr. 20, 1782, Executive Papers, box 36, item 81B; depositions of Phillip Ferguson et al.,

Feb. 21, 1783, regarding raiding at Benedict, Red Books, vol. 32, pt. 2, fol. 15; Richard Barnes to William Paca, July 7, 1782, Feb. 8, 17, Mar. 1, 1783, Red Books, vol. 26, fol. 7, vol. 9, fol. 39, and Executive Papers, box 47, items 93, 115A&B, respectively.

2. Orphans' court proceedings, in CCW, Lib. B1 (1782–85), fols. 24, 47; account of payments to disabled soldiers, Aug. 15, 1782–Sept. 4, 1784, Executive Papers, box 46, item 117; Isaac Campbell, *A Rational Inquiry into the Origin, Foundation, Nature and End of Civil Government, shewing it to be a Divine Institution, Legitimately deriving its Authority from the Law of Revelation only, and not from the Law of Nature, as hath heretofore been generally held by Writers, from Time supposed immemorial* (Annapolis: Frederick Green [1787?]), the only known copy of which is in the Archives of the Episcopal Diocese of Maryland, Baltimore; Jean Butenhoff Lee, "Isaac Campbell (c. 1724–1784)," in *American Writers before 1800: A Biographical and Critical Dictionary*, ed. James A. Levernier and Douglas R. Wilmes, 3 vols. (Westport, Conn.: Greenwood Press, 1983), 1:266–68; *Md. Gazette*, Jan. 30, Mar. 20, 1783; Walter Hanson Jenifer purchase of property confiscated from Cunninghame, Findlay & Co., July 27, 1782, Executive Papers, box 35, item 17; Record Book of Charlotte Hall School, Lib. A (1774–1805), fol. 4, in the Charlotte Hall School Collection (850078), Southern Maryland Studies Center, Charles County Community College, La Plata, Md.; James Craik, Jr., to W. Stone, July 2, 1782, in Ethel R. Hayden, "Port Tobacco, Lost Town of Maryland," *Md. Hist. Mag.* 40 (1945): 269–70; T. Stone to W. Stone, Mar. 30, 1783, Signers' Collection, Special Collections Department, John Work Garrett Library, Johns Hopkins University, Baltimore.

CHAPTER SEVEN: A PENCHANT FOR IMPROVEMENT

1. Table 1, Appendix; 1782 Assessment Lists, Scharf Collection, box 96, items 7–10, 12–17; Jean Butenhoff Lee, "The Problem of Slave Community in the Eighteenth-Century Chesapeake," *WMQ* 43 (1986): 342–48.

2. Journal of the Vestry, Trinity Parish, "Abstracts of Early Protestant Episcopal Church Records of Charles County, Maryland" (typescript, Martha Washington Chapter, Daughters of the American Revolution, Washington, D.C., n.d.), 89; Tables 10–12, Appendix; 1782 Assessment Lists, Scharf Collection, box 96, items 7–10, 12–17.

3. James M. Wright, *The Free Negro in Maryland, 1634–1860* (New York: Longmans, Green & Co., 1921; New York: Octagon Books, 1971), 37–38.

4. Examples of postrevolutionary voluntary associations are discussed in Robert A. Gross, *The Minutemen and Their World* (New York: Hill & Wang, 1976), 173–75, and Suzanne Lebsock, *The Free Women of Petersburg: Status and Culture in a Southern Town, 1784–1860* (New York: W. W. Norton & Co., 1984), 195–213.

5. Declaration of Rights, Article 33, in Md. Constitutional Convention of 1776, *The Decisive Blow Is Struck: A Facsimile Edition of the Proceedings of the Constitutional Convention of 1776 and the First Maryland Constitution*, intro. Edward C. Papenfuse and Gregory A. Stiverson (Annapolis: Hall of Records Commission, 1977), n.p.; *Md. Gazette*, Dec. 9, 1784, Nov. 24, 1785, May 21, 1789; John Gwinn's list of men fined for breaking the Sabbath, Feb. 21, 1784, Pforzheimer Papers, box 1, item 107; Journal of the Vestry, Trinity Parish, "Abstracts of Early Protestant Episcopal

Church Records," 92; Michael Jenifer Stone Account Book, Port Tobacco, Md., fol. 14, in the Kremer Collection (850028), item 21, Southern Maryland Studies Center, Charles County Community College, La Plata, Md. John C. Rainbolt treats the legislative history of disestablishment and the issue of public support for all denominations in "The Struggle to Define 'Religious Liberty' in Maryland, 1776–85," *Journal of Church and State* 17 (1975): 443–58, while Episcopal adjustments to disestablishment are considered in Arthur Pierce Middleton, "From Daughter Church to Sister Church: The Disestablishment of the Church of England and the Organization of the Diocese of Maryland," *Md. Hist. Mag.* 79 (1984): 189–96, and Sandra R. Dresbeck, "The Episcopalian Clergy in Maryland and Virginia, 1765–1805" (Ph.D. diss., University of California, Los Angeles, 1976), 254–409. Cf. the more dramatic struggle over disestablishment in Virginia in Merrill D. Peterson, *Thomas Jefferson and the New Nation: A Biography* (New York: Oxford University Press, 1970), 133–45, and Rhys Isaac, *The Transformation of Virginia, 1740–1790* (Chapel Hill: University of North Carolina Press, for the Institute of Early American History and Culture, 1982), chap. 12.

6. Durham Parish vestry minutes, quoted in Margaret Brown Klapthor and Paul D. Brown, *The History of Charles County, Maryland* (La Plata, Md.: Charles County Tercentenary, 1958), 73–74; Hatch Dent to the Committee on the Protestant Episcopal Church in Maryland, June 1, 1792, Vertical File, Archives of the Episcopal Diocese of Maryland, Baltimore.

7. Journal of the Vestry, Trinity Parish, "Abstracts of Early Protestant Episcopal Church Records," 76–81, 84, 86, 92; Evarts B. Greene and Virginia D. Harrington, *American Population before the Federal Census of 1790* (New York: Columbia University Press, 1932), 131. Campbell's 1775 salary was calculated at thirty pounds of tobacco for each of fifteen hundred taxables.

8. Journal of the Vestry, Trinity Parish, "Abstracts of Early Protestant Episcopal Church Records," 92–94; Rev. Ethan Allen, *Clergy in Maryland of the Protestant Episcopal Church since the Independence of 1783* (Baltimore: James S. Waters, 1860), 17.

9. *St. Ignatius Church, Chapel Point* ([Port Tobacco, Md.: St. Ignatius Church], 1982); John Carroll to Charles Plowden, Feb. 23, 1779, in Joseph Zwinge, "The Jesuit Farms in Maryland," *Woodstock Letters* 42 (1913): 137; Clare Joseph Dickinson, *The Carmelite Adventure: Clare Joseph Dickinson's Journal of a Trip to America and Other Documents*, ed. Constance FitzGerald (Baltimore: Carmelite Sisters of Baltimore, 1990); *The Restorers of Mount Carmel in Maryland* (Port Tobacco, Md., n.d.). See also John Tracy Ellis, *Catholics in Colonial America* (Baltimore: Helicon Press, 1965), 404–15; Thomas O'Brien Hanley, *The American Revolution and Religion: Maryland, 1770–1780* (Washington, D.C.: Catholic University of America Press, 1971), chap. 7; and Jack D. Brown et al., *Charles County, Maryland: A History* (n.p.: Charles County Bicentennial Committee, 1976), 102–30.

10. Denominational histories are in Brown et al., *Charles County, Maryland: A History*, 131–96. On the Virginia Baptists, see Isaac, *The Transformation of Virginia, 1740–1790*, especially chap. 8 and pp. 299–302. A recent, perceptive examination of Methodism in Maryland is Doris E. Andrews, "Popular Religion and the Revolution in the Middle Atlantic Ports: The Rise of the Methodists, 1770–1800" (Ph.D. diss., University of Pennsylvania, 1986).

11. Margaret Stone to "Dr Uncle," Apr. 22, 1785, Conway Collection, Rare Book and Manuscript Library, Columbia University, New York, N.Y.; *Md. Gazette*, Dec. 25,

1783, May 13, July 8, 1784, May 5, June 2, Sept. 15, 1785, June 29, 1786; Tench F. Tilghman, *The Early History of St. John's College in Annapolis* (Annapolis: St. John's College Press, 1984).

12. CCW, Libs. AD5 (1752–67), fols. 120–22, AF7 (1777–82), fols. 512–13, B1 (1782–85), fol. 190.

13. Essential to the discussion of American republicanism is Gordon S. Wood, *The Creation of the American Republic, 1776–1787* (Chapel Hill: University of North Carolina Press, for the Institute of Early American History and Culture, 1969). Useful guides to the voluminous literature on the subject are Robert E. Shalhope, "Toward a Republican Synthesis: The Emergence of an Understanding of Republicanism in American Historiography" and "Republicanism and Early American Historiography," *WMQ* 29 (1972): 49–80, and 39 (1982): 334–56. Lance Banning, "Jeffersonian Ideology Revisited: Liberal and Classical Ideas in the New American Republic" and Joyce Appleby, "Republicanism in Old and New Contexts," *WMQ* 43 (1986): 3–19 and 20–34, are keys to the scholarly debate on the influence of republican ideology on subsequent American development, but see Pauline Maier's welcome comment that "by now, if any conclusions can be said to have emerged, they are that the distinctions drawn by modern historians were all but irrelevant to eighteenth-century Americans." *From Resistance to Revolution: Colonial Radicals and the Development of American Opposition to Britain, 1765–1776* (New York: W. W. Norton & Co., 1991), x. Daniel T. Rodgers, "Republicanism: The Career of a Concept," *Journal of American History* 79 (1992): 11–38, offers a penetrating critique of recent scholarship on the subject. Shalhope seeks to reconcile divergent views in *The Roots of Democracy: American Thought and Culture, 1760–1800* (Boston: Twayne Publishers, 1990).

14. Nellie Grant Ross, comp., "Charles County, Maryland Tomb-Stone & Bible Records" (typescript, Martha Washington Chapter, Daughters of the American Revolution, Washington, D.C., n.d.), 66; *Md. Gazette*, Dec. 25, 1783, Feb. 24, 1785, Nov. 11, 1790, Nov. 29, 1792; Thomas Stone to Walter Stone (in order quoted), Mar. 30, 1783, Oct. 8, 1781, Dec. 3, 1783, Apr. 21, 1782, in the Signers' Collection, Special Collections Department, John Work Garrett Library, Johns Hopkins University, Baltimore, the Fogg Collection at the Maine Historical Society, Portland, the Conway Collection, and the Stone Family of Maryland Papers, fol. 60, Manuscript Division, LC, respectively; Michael Jenifer Stone to unknown correspondent (transcript), n.d., Kremer Collection, item 17A.

15. T. Stone to W. Stone, May 24, 1783, Pequot Collection, Beinecke Rare Book and Manuscript Library, Yale University, New Haven, Conn.; *Md. Gazette*, Apr. 7, 1791; T. Stone to Frederick Stone [late Sept. or early Oct. 1787], in John Sanderson and Robert Waln, Jr., *Biography of the Signers to the Declaration of Independence*, 9 vols. (Philadelphia: R. W. Pomeroy, 1823–27), 9:332–33.

16. Quotations: *Md. Gazette*, Dec. 22, 1785; Walter Hanson Jenifer et al. to the governor of Maryland [1785], Pardon Papers, box 3, folder 10; John Roby et al. to Gov. William Paca, Sept. 17, 1783, Executive Papers, box 47, item 38, respectively. Pathbreaking scholarship on the ideological importance accorded motherhood in postwar America is in Linda K. Kerber, *Women of the Republic: Intellect and Ideology in Revolutionary America* (Chapel Hill: University of North Carolina Press, for the Institute of Early American History and Culture, 1980), chap. 9, and Mary Beth

Norton, *Liberty's Daughters: The Revolutionary Experience of American Women, 1750–1800* (Boston: Little, Brown & Co., 1980), 247–50, 298–99.

17. T. Stone to W. Stone, Apr. 8, 1783, Stone Family of Maryland Papers, fol. 81; *Md. Gazette*, Dec. 6, 1787; Klapthor and Brown, *History of Charles County*, 75–76.

18. Samuel Hanson file, Revolutionary War Pension and Bounty-Land Warrant Application Files, Record Group 15, Microcopy 804, reel 1184, National Archives and Records Service, Washington, D.C.

19. *Md. Gazette*, June 10, 1784, June 8, 1786, Oct. 21, 1790; William Smallwood to Otho Holland Williams, Feb. 10, 1784, Gilmore Papers (MS. 387.1), vol. 3, fol. 96, MHS; Rieman Steuart, *A History of the Maryland Line in the Revolutionary War, 1775–1783* (n.p.: Society of the Cincinnati of Maryland, 1969).

20. Alexander Hamilton to Robert Fergusson, July 17, 1784, and to John Anderson, Oct. 18, 1784, in David C. Skaggs and Richard K. MacMaster, eds., "Post-Revolutionary Letters of Alexander Hamilton, Piscataway Factor: Part 2, July–October 1784," *Md. Hist. Mag.* 65 (1970): 20, 31. Equality belonged to Michael Jenifer Stone.

21. This paragraph is based on comparison of civil officeholders and vestrymen with the 1782 Assessment Lists, Scharf Collection, box 96, items 7–10, 12–17, and slaveholding as reported in [U.S. Census Office, 1st Census, 1790], *Heads of Families at the First Census of the United States Taken in the Year 1790: Maryland* (Baltimore: Genealogical Publishing Co., 1965), 47–55. See also Table 13, Appendix. On property qualifications for the Assembly and sheriff, see the Constitution of 1776, Articles 2, 42, in Md. Constitutional Convention of 1776, *The Decisive Blow Is Struck*, n.p. For members of the legislature and their wealth, see Papenfuse et al., eds., *Biographical Dictionary*; the sketch on George Dent is in 1:263–64. Vestry elections are recorded in Journal of the Vestry, Trinity Parish, "Abstracts of Early Protestant Episcopal Church Records," 76, 85, 90, 95. Sheriffs elected between 1777 and 1800 are listed in Register of Civil Officers, 1777–1800, fols. 23, 91, 154, 159, 208a, 148a, and Register of Civil Appointments since the Year 1793 . . . , fol. 346, both of which are in Governor and Council, Commission Records (S1080), MSA. The quotation in the text is from T. Stone to W. Stone, Dec. 9, 1783 (transcript), Conway Collection; Thomas Stone was the first local man elected to the governing board of St. John's College.

22. Papenfuse et al., eds., *Biographical Dictionary* 2:741–42, 784–88; Register of Civil Officers, 1777–1800, fol. 159; Klapthor and Brown, *History of Charles County*, 74.

23. Constitution of 1776, Article 47, in Md. Constitutional Convention of 1776, *The Decisive Blow Is Struck*, n.p. From the Executive Papers: Walter Hanson to Thomas Sim Lee, Oct. 7, 1782, box 38, item 20; Hanson to Daniel Jenifer, May 24, 1784, box 50, item 16; justices of the Charles County orphans' court to Smallwood, Feb. 12, 1787, box 62, item 111; G. Dent et al. to Smallwood, Dec. 17, 1787, box 66, item 103. John Hoskins Stone and M. J. Stone to Smallwood, May 6, 1786, Etting Collection: Governors of States, vol. 2, fol. 56, Historical Society of Pennsylvania, Philadelphia; M. J. Stone to George Washington, undated, and J. H. Stone to Washington, June 15, 1789, George Washington Papers, ser. 7, microfilm reel 123, Manuscript Division, LC.

24. Theophilus Hanson to Smallwood, May 7, 1786, Executive Papers, box 59, item 123; J. H. Stone to John Davidson, n.d., Mar. 29, Apr. 8, 1789, Maryland State Papers: Blue Books (S990), vol. 3, fols. 26–28, MSA; salary receipts from Jenifer

relatives employed in the intendant's office are included in Executive Papers, box 50, items 80B, 80C, box 54, items 16/20, 19/4, 25/14.

25. T. Stone to W. Stone, Apr. 21, 1782, Dec. 3, 1783 (transcript), Stone Family of Maryland Papers, fol. 61, and Conway Collection, respectively; Zephaniah Turner to Gov. John Eager Howard, May 6, 1789, appointment and commission list for Charles County, Mar. 9, 1786, and W. Hanson to Daniel of St. Thomas Jenifer, May 24, 1784, Executive Papers, box 68, item 156, box 59, item 71, and box 50, item 16, respectively.

26. Roby et al. to Paca, Sept. 17, 1783, Executive Papers, box 47, item 38; Pardon Papers, box 2, folder 34, box 3, folder 78.

27. Pardon Papers, box 1, folder 82. In 1782, Moran owned 271 acres, three slaves, and total property valued at £504 in Benedict Hundred. 1782 Assessment Lists, Scharf Collection, box 96, item 8.

28. Pardon Papers, box 1, folder 82.

29. Constitution of 1776, Articles 2, 14, 42, in Md. Constitutional Convention of 1776, *The Decisive Blow Is Struck*, n.p.; *Md. Gazette*, Dec. 6, 1787. Analysis of the 1782 Assessment Lists would not produce an accurate estimate of the percentage of enfranchised adult males because of property specifically excluded from assessment and because, to avoid the effects of wartime inflation, 1774 values were assigned to most assets. See "A Note on the 1782 Tax Assessment Lists" in the Appendix.

30. *Md. Gazette*, Jan. 1, 22, 1789, Sept. 23, 30, Oct. 28, 1790; sheriff's certification of election returns in Charles County, in Election Returns, Jan. 7–10, 1789, Presidential Electors and Representatives to Congress, and Election Returns, Oct. 4–7, 1790, Representatives to Congress, both of which are in Governor and Council, Election Returns (S106), MSA. On political alignments and factions before adoption of the U.S. Constitution, consult Jackson T. Main, *Political Parties before the Constitution* (Chapel Hill: University of North Carolina Press, for the Institute of Early American History and Culture, 1973), chap. 8, and Norman K. Risjord, *Chesapeake Politics, 1781–1800* (New York: Columbia University Press, 1978), 138–48.

31. *Md. Gazette*, Sept. 6, Nov. 1, 1792, Apr. 17, 1794; sheriff's certification of election returns in Charles County, in Election Returns, Oct. 6–9, 1794, Representatives to Congress, and Election Returns, Oct. 3–6, 1796, Representatives to Congress; John Courts Jones to Matthew Blair, Apr. 24, 1796 (Mss2 J7185 a1), Virginia Historical Society, Richmond; Papenfuse et al., eds., *Biographical Dictionary* 1:264, 2:497–98. See L. Marx Renzulli, Jr., *Maryland: The Federalist Years* (Madison, N.J.: Fairleigh Dickinson University Press, 1972), chap. 4, and Risjord, *Chesapeake Politics, 1781–1800*, 517–19, 522, 542–46, 563–72, for the statewide context. National political developments may be followed in John C. Miller, *The Federalist Era, 1789–1801* (New York: Harper & Row, 1960); Felix Gilbert, *To the Farewell Address: Ideas of Early American Foreign Policy* (Princeton: Princeton University Press, 1961); Richard Hofstadter, *The Idea of a Party System: The Rise of Legitimate Opposition in the United States, 1780–1840* (Berkeley: University of California Press, 1969), chaps. 2–3; Lance Banning, *The Jeffersonian Persuasion: Evolution of a Party Ideology* (Ithaca, N.Y.: Cornell University Press, 1978); and Drew R. McCoy, *The Elusive Republic: Political Economy in Jeffersonian America* (Chapel Hill: University of North Carolina Press, for the Institute of Early American History and Culture, 1980).

32. T. Stone to the Printers, 1787, *Md. Gazette*, Apr. 5, 1787, reprinted in Melvin

Yazawa, ed., *Representative Government and the Revolution: The Maryland Constitutional Crisis of 1787* (Baltimore: Johns Hopkins University Press, 1975), 84; *Md. Gazette*, Oct. 27, 1791.

33. Samuel Tyler, ed., *Memoir of Roger Brooke Taney, LL.D.: Chief Justice of the Supreme Court of the United States* (Baltimore: John Murphy & Co., 1872), 82–83. Cf. John Hoskins Stone's confidence about being elected to Maryland's constitutional ratifying convention of 1788: "I do not in the least dread or fear an injury from any of the lower Class in Charles County, for very few there are indeed in that grade who are not more or less under obligations to me." J. H. Stone to W. Stone, Dec. 27, 1787, Stone Family Correspondence, 1782–91, in the Arents Collection, Rare Books and Manuscripts Division, New York Public Library, Astor, Lenox, and Tilden Foundations, New York, N.Y. Voter behavior is examined in J. R. Pole, "Suffrage and Representation in Maryland from 1776 to 1810: A Statistical Note and Some Reflections," *Journal of Southern History* 24 (1958): 218–25; idem, "Constitutional Reform and Election Statistics in Maryland, 1790–1812," *Md. Hist. Mag.* 55 (1960): 275–92; and David A. Bohmer, "Voting Behavior during the First American Party System: Maryland, 1796–1816" (Ph.D. diss., University of Michigan, 1974). Both authors provide county-level data. Bohmer (p. 90) misses the shift to Jeffersonian-Republicanism in Charles County.

34. CCW, Libs. AF7, fols. 512–13, B1, fol. 190; *Md. Gazette*, Dec. 25, 1783; M. J. Stone to [W. Stone] (transcript), Mar. 12, 1782, Kremer Collection, item 16; James Craik, Jr., to W. Stone, July 2, 1782, in Ethel R. Hayden, "Port Tobacco, Lost Town of Maryland," *Md. Hist. Mag.* 40 (1945): 270. The statement about literacy rates is based on analysis of all wills filed for probate in Charles County between 1740 and 1784. Signature literacy rates for female testators rose from 18.2 percent of wills dated 1732–47, to 28.1 percent of those dated 1764–73, to 37.7 percent of those dated 1774–83. Comparable rates for male testators during the years specified were 61.3, 66.9, and 68.5 percent. Because wills typically are biased in favor of age and wealth, these figures are suggestive rather than representative of the entire population. Jean Butenhoff Lee, "The Social Order of a Revolutionary People: Charles County, Maryland, 1733–86" (Ph.D. diss., University of Virginia, 1984), 237–39. An overview of postrevolutionary changes in women's legal status is Marylynn Salmon, "Republican Sentiment, Economic Change, and the Property Rights of Women in American Law," in *Women in the Age of the American Revolution*, ed. Ronald Hoffman and Peter J. Albert (Charlottesville: University Press of Virginia, for the U.S. Capitol Historical Society, 1989), 447–75; see also idem, *Women and the Law of Property in Early America* (Chapel Hill: University of North Carolina Press, 1986).

35. *Md. Gazette*, Feb. 24, 1785, June 7, 1787, Nov. 11, 1790, Apr. 4, 1793; Ross, comp., "Charles County, Maryland Tomb-Stone & Bible Records," 66. This material strongly supports Ruth H. Bloch, "The Gendered Meanings of Virtue in Revolutionary America," *Signs: Journal of Women in Culture and Society* 13 (1987): 37–58. Also see Linda K. Kerber, " 'History Can Do It No Justice': Women and the Reinterpretation of the American Revolution," in *Women in the Age of the American Revolution*, ed. Hoffman and Albert, 29–42. The classic study of nineteenth-century prescriptive commentary on female behavior is Barbara Welter, "The Cult of True Womanhood, 1820–1860," *American Quarterly* 18 (1966): 151–74.

36. Craik to W. Stone, July 2, 1782, in Hayden, "Port Tobacco," 270; M. J. Stone to unknown correspondent (transcript), n.d., and to [Polly Stone], Apr. 2, 1793, Kremer Collection, items 17A–B; Papenfuse et al., eds., *Biographical Dictionary* 2:785–86. See Lebsock's insightful, cautionary discussion of companionate marriage in *The Free Women of Petersburg*, chap. 2.

37. CCW, Lib. AF7, fols. 145, 476; CCLR, Lib. V3 (1775–82), fols. 495, 515–16.

38. CCCR, Lib. Z3 (1782–86), fols. 34–36; 1782 Assessment Lists, Scharf Collection, box 96, item 15.

39. The state first passed a married women's property act in 1843, according to Elizabeth Bowles Warbasse, *The Changing Legal Rights of Married Women, 1800–1861* (New York: Garland Publishing, 1987), 155–59.

40. 1782 Assessment Lists, Scharf Collection, box 96, items 7–10, 12–17; Table 13, Appendix; [U.S. Census Office, 1st Census, 1790], *Heads of Families*, 47–55; M. J. Stone to unknown correspondent (transcript), n.d., Kremer Collection, item 17A. By comparison, 3.7 percent of household heads were female in 1733, and 7.2 percent in 1758. 1733 List of Taxables, Charles County, Md., Scharf Collection, box 96, item 1; 1758 Charles County Tax Lists for Lower Durham, East Newport, Pomonkey, West Port Tobacco, Upper Trinity, and Lower William and Mary hundreds, in Secretary in Maryland, Tax Lists (S244), MSA.

41. 1782 Assessment Lists, Scharf Collection, box 96, items 7–10, 12–17; Tables 14–16, Appendix. Priscilla Smallwood: CCW, Libs. AF7, fols. 520–21, B1, fols. 409–11; 1782 Assessment Lists, Scharf Collection, box 96, item 9; Papenfuse et al., eds., *Biographical Dictionary* 2:739–40. Judith Chase: CCDB, 1753, fol. 93; Charles County Register of Wills, Inventories (C665), 1753–66, fols. 53–55, MSA; 1782 Assessment Lists, Scharf Collection, box 96, item 15. Anne Neale: CCW, Lib. AD5, fols. 243–48; CCDB, 1753, fol. 22; Charles County Court, Tobacco Inspection Proceedings (C680), vol. 71 (1774–86), fol. 30 and elsewhere, MSA; 1782 Assessment Lists, Scharf Collection, box 96, item 15.

42. 1782 Assessment Lists, Scharf Collection, box 96, items 7–10, 12–17; Tables 13, 15–16, Appendix. Cf. Alexander Keyssar, "Widowhood in Eighteenth-Century Massachusetts: A Problem in the History of the Family," *Perspectives in American History* 8 (1974): 83–119.

43. *Md. Gazette*, Jan. 30, 1783, Dec. 22, 1785, Nov. 12, 1789, Apr. 4, 1793; deposition of Mary Threlkeld, Mar. 25, 1793, Stone Family Papers, in possession of the Stone Family, La Plata, Md.; George W. Corner, ed., *The Autobiography of Benjamin Rush: His "Travels through Life" together with his Commonplace Book for 1789–1813* (Princeton: Princeton University Press, for the American Philosophical Society, 1948), 151; [U.S. Census Office, 1st Census, 1790], *Return of the Whole Number of Persons within the Several Districts of the United States, According to "An Act Providing for the Enumeration of the Inhabitants of the United States," Passed March the First, One Thousand Seven Hundred and Ninety-One* (Philadelphia: Childs & Swaine, 1791), 47.

44. Arthur Zilversmit, *The First Emancipation: The Abolition of Slavery in the North* (Chicago: University of Chicago Press, 1967); Ira Berlin, *Slaves without Masters: The Free Negro in the Antebellum South* (New York: Random House, 1974), chaps. 1–2; David B. Davis, *The Problem of Slavery in the Age of Revolution, 1770–1823* (Ithaca, N.Y.: Cornell University Press, 1975); Gary B. Nash, *Race and Revolution* (Madison, Wis.: Madison House, 1990); Donald R. Wright, *African Americans in the Colonial Era: From*

African Origins through the American Revolution (Arlington Heights, Ill.: Harlan Davidson, 1990); idem, *African Americans in the Early Republic, 1789–1831* (Arlington Heights, Ill.: Harlan Davidson, 1993); and William Freehling's seminal essay, "The Founding Fathers and Slavery," *American Historical Review* 77 (1972): 81–93. The winter 1989 issue of *Md. Hist. Mag.*, vol. 84, is devoted to the history of African-Americans in Maryland in the late eighteenth and early nineteenth centuries.

45. "An Account of the Number of Souls in the Province of Maryland, in the Year 1755," *Gentleman's Magazine* (London), 34 (1764): 261; [U.S. Census Office, 1st Census, 1790], *Return of the Whole Number of Persons within the Several Districts of the United States*, 47; U.S. Census Office, 2d Census, 1800, *Return of the Whole Number of Persons within the Several Districts of the United States* (Washington, D.C.: William Duane & Son, 1802), 66.

46. [U.S. Census Office, 1st Census, 1790], *Heads of Families*, 47–55.

47. Ibid. For the transition from slavery to freedom in urban areas, see Gary B. Nash, "Forging Freedom: The Emancipation Experience in the Northern Seaport Cities, 1775–1820," in *Slavery and Freedom in the Age of the American Revolution*, ed. Ira Berlin and Ronald Hoffman (Charlottesville: University Press of Virginia, for the U.S. Capitol Historical Society, 1983), 3–48.

48. CCLR, Libs. N4, fol. 165, V3, fol. 582; CCW, Lib. B1, fols. 127–28, 378; 1782 Assessment Lists, Scharf Collection, box 96, items 9, 14. The author is indebted to J. Richard Rivoire for calling the Stone manumission to her attention.

49. Zilversmit, *The First Emancipation: The Abolition of Slavery in the North*, 124–37 and chap. 7; J. H. Stone to W. Stone, Nov. 27, 1790, Stone Family of Maryland Papers, fol. 247; CCLR, Lib. V3, fols. 64–65.

50. Chancery Records, 1796, fol. 424.

51. Ibid., fols. 424, 427–28; *Md. Gazette*, Dec. 4, 1794; Hanson died possessed of twenty-six slaves. Papenfuse et al., eds., *Biographical Dictionary* 1:408.

52. CCW, Lib. B1, fols. 104–06, 108, 110.

53. Ibid., fols. 105, 108, 119–20. Cornish's inventoried estate was valued at £520 Maryland currency, including nine slaves. She also owned 515 acres of land. Ibid., fols. 160–61; 1782 Assessment Lists, Scharf Collection, box 96, item 9.

54. For the prewar litigation, see Thomas Harris, Jr., and John McHenry, comps., *Maryland Reports, Being a Series of the Most Important Law Cases, Argued and Determined in the Provincial Court and Court of Appeals of the Then Province of Maryland, from the Year 1700 down to the American Revolution* (New York: I. Riley, 1809), 371–84. Depositions used in both the original and postrevolutionary freedom suits are in Provincial Court, Judgment Records (S551), Lib. DD17, pt. 1, fols. 233–44, MSA. The General Court superseded the Provincial Court in 1777.

55. Court of Appeals, Judgment Records (S381), Oct. Term 1787, fols. 1–5, 20–21, 40, MSA. At issue was a 1663 statute, repealed in 1681, that held that any white woman marrying a bondman would become a slave, as would their children. The decision in *Butler v. Boarman*, decided in the Provincial Court in 1770, accepted the marriage of Eleanor Butler to Charles and held that their children born *after* repeal of the 1663 law nevertheless were slaves because the marriage occurred before repeal. Harris and McHenry, comps., *Maryland Reports*, 371–84, 605.

56. Provincial Court, Judgment Records, Lib. DD17, pt. 1, fol. 239; [U.S. Census Office, 1st Census, 1790], *Heads of Families*, 48.

57. General Court of the Western Shore, Dockets (S492), Oct. Term 1791, May Term 1795, May Term 1800, MSA; General Court of the Western Shore, Judgment Records (S497), Lib. JG27 (May Term 1795), fol. 40, MSA.

58. Provincial Court, Judgment Records, Lib. DD17, pt. 1, fols. 233–44; quotations on fols. 238, 240.

59. General Court of the Western Shore, Judgment Records, Lib. JG13 (Oct. Term 1791), fol. 31.

60. Ibid., Lib. JG25 (Oct. Term 1794), fols. 250–52, 254–56, 272–73, 280, 289.

61. Ibid., fols. 243, 247–48, 252–56, 300.

62. Ibid., fols. 254–56, 264–65, 275.

63. Ibid., fols. 251, 253–56, 282, 286, 289.

64. Ibid., fols. 264–65.

65. Ibid., 247, 250–54, 267, 292, 298; ibid., Lib. JG27, fols. 33–34, 39.

66. Ibid., Lib. JG25, fols. 262, 288.

67. Ibid., fols. 299–300. For other suits that resulted in emancipation, see ibid., Lib. JG27, fols. 21–29, 37–42. Unsuccessful suits are ibid., fols. 29–37.

68. General Court of the Western Shore, Dockets, May Term 1795; General Court of the Western Shore, Judgment Records, Libs. JG13, fols. 26–29, JG25, fols. 244, 298, JG27, fols. 42–48.

69. General Court of the Western Shore, Judgment Records, Libs. JG13, fols. 26–29, JG27, fols. 24–29, 42–48.

70. Quotation: *Md. Gazette*, Nov. 2, 1786. The number of runaways advertised in 1760–64 was five, and for 1772–76, six. Thirteen absent slaves were sought in 1782–86 issues of the *Gazette*. A sensitive reading of northern and southern newspapers is Jonathan Prude, "To Look upon the 'Lower Sort': Runaway Ads and the Apprearance of Unfree Laborers in America, 1750–1800," *Journal of American History* 78 (1991): 124–59.

71. *Md. Gazette*, Dec. 2, 1790, Dec. 13, 1792, Mar. 27, 1794.

72. Papenfuse et al., eds., *Biographical Dictionary* 1:405–06; John Hanson, Jr., to Philip Thomas, Feb. 14, 23, Mar. 5, 15, 18, Apr. 10, 27, 1782, in the John Hanson Papers (MS. 1785), MHS. Ned's activities, earnings, and expenses from 1776 to 1779 may be traced in the John Hanson Ledger (MS. 1785.1), MHS.

73. In order quoted: *Md. Gazette*, July 22, 1784, July 27, 1786, Aug. 28, 1794, June 16, 1796, June 14, 1787, Oct. 28, 1790, Jan. 21, 1796. For rewards offered according to the distance runaways managed to cover before capture, see ibid., Aug. 28, 1783, July 22, 1784, Dec. 2, 1790, May 17, Dec. 13, 1792.

74. Ibid., Dec. 12, 1782, July 28, 1785.

75. Ibid., May 17, June 28, Jan. 19, 1792, respectively.

76. Ibid., Nov. 6, Aug. 28, 1783, Apr. 8, 1784, respectively.

77. Ibid., Nov. 15, 1787, Apr. 17, 1788, Oct. 24, 1794.

78. Ibid., Dec. 12, 1782, July 22, 1784, Sept. 25, 1788, June 23, 1791, Dec. 13, 1792, respectively.

79. Ibid., Nov. 15, Oct. 11, Apr. 26, 1787, May 26, 1796, respectively.

80. In order: ibid., Feb. 14, 1793, Dec. 2, 1790, June 23, 1791, Jan. 19, 1792, June 20, 1793, Dec. 12, 1782, June 6, 1793, July 22, 1784, June 28, Jan. 19, 1792, May 22, 1794.

81. Ibid., Sept. 25, 1788, July 28, 1785, Mar. 6, 1791, respectively.

82. In order: ibid., July 22, Aug. 5, Nov. 11, 1784, Sept. 22, Oct. 13, 1785, Oct. 16, 1788, Sept. 18, 1794.
83. Ibid., Aug. 18, 1796.

CHAPTER EIGHT: THE PRICE OF NATIONHOOD

1. Papenfuse et al., eds., *Biographical Dictionary* 2:861; Register of Civil Officers, 1777–1800, fol. 159, in Governor and Council, Commission Records (S1080), MSA. Ware's performance bond is lost, but see that of Sheriff Edward Boarman in CCCR, Lib. Y3 (1778–80), fol. 24. In 1782 Ware's property in the county was assessed at £1,335 Maryland currency, including 404 acres of land valued at £303 and twenty-four slaves valued at £905. 1782 Assessment List for the lower east hundred of Port Tobacco Parish, Scharf Collection, box 96, item 15.
2. Loose Papers, 1779–88, in General Court of the Western Shore, Judicials (S509), MSA (the Judgment Records of the court are missing for 1786 and 1787); William Kilty to John Kilty, Sept. 10, 1789, Red Books, vol. 23, fol. 93; *Md. Gazette*, Feb. 12, 1789, Apr. 28, 1791, Dec. 26, 1793, Sept. 4, 18, 1794; Gaius M. Brumbaugh, comp., *Maryland Records: Colonial, Revolutionary, County and Church*, 2 vols. (Baltimore: William & Wilkins Co., 1915, 1928; Baltimore: Genealogical Publishing Co., 1967), 2:403.
3. The Stone family epitomized the broadened awareness and contacts ushered in with the Revolution. See, for example, *The Papers of Robert Morris*, ed. E. James Ferguson et al., 7 vols. to date (Pittsburgh: University of Pittsburgh Press, 1973–), 2:206, 208, 285, 290, for political connections; Peter and Isaac Wikoff to Thomas Stone, Dec. 6, 1781, Apr. 29, 1783, William Cooke Papers (MS. 195), box 1, MHS, for legal business; "Rusticus" [Daniel Brodhead] to Walter Jenifer Stone, Dec. 30, 1782, Gratz Collection, Historical Society of Pennsylvania, Philadelphia, for social life; and T. Stone to Walter Stone, July 16, 1782, Apr. 8, 1783, Stone Family of Maryland Papers, fols. 71–74, 81–83, Manuscript Division, LC, and Michael Jenifer Stone to Tench Coxe, May 4, June 14, 1789, Tench Coxe Papers, Historical Society of Pennsylvania, for mercantile connections.
4. George Mason to George Mason, Jr., Jan. 8, 1783, in *The Papers of George Mason, 1725–1792*, ed. Robert A. Rutland, 3 vols. (Chapel Hill: University of North Carolina Press, for the Institute of Early American History and Culture, 1970) 2:760; T. Stone to W. Stone, Apr. 21, July 16, 1782, Stone Family of Maryland Papers, fols. 62, 71–72; CCLR, Lib. V3 (1775–82), fols. 565–625; sale of Cunninghame, Findlay & Co. property at Port Tobacco, in Executive Papers, box 35, item 17; Richard Harrison & Co. Ledger, 1779–83, fol. 264, Manuscript Division, LC.
5. T. Stone to W. Stone, Apr. 26, 1783, Gratz Collection; Alexander Hamilton to James Brown & Co., Jan. 25, Mar. 10, 1784, in David C. Skaggs and Richard K. MacMaster, eds., "Post-Revolutionary Letters of Alexander Hamilton, Piscataway Merchant: Part 1, January–June 1784," *Md. Hist. Mag.* 63 (1968): 26, 31; deposition of William Hunter, Mar. 12, 1784, Stone Family Papers (MS. 406), MHS; M. J. Stone to W. Stone, May 3, 1783, Stone Family of Maryland Papers, fols. 85–87.
6. T. Stone to Daniel of St. Thomas Jenifer, Dec. 9, 1783, Louis Bamberger Autograph Collection, New Jersey Historical Society, Newark; *Md. Gazette*, Oct. 16, 30, 1783, June 9, 1785; 1782 Assessment List for Port Tobacco town hundred, Scharf Collec-

tion, box 96, item 12; James Craik, Jr., to W. Stone, July 2, 1782, in Ethel R. Hayden, "Port Tobacco, Lost Town of Maryland," *Md. Hist. Mag.* 40 (1945): 269–70; *Laws of Md. . . . [Nov. Session 1782]*, chap. 4.

7. *Md. Gazette*, Aug. 28, Oct. 2, 1783; T. Stone to Jenifer, Dec. 9, 1783, Louis Bamberger Autograph Collection.

8. T. Stone to Jenifer, Dec. 9, 1783, Louis Bamberger Autograph Collection.

9. Hamilton to Robert Fergusson, July 17, 1784, "Post-Revolutionary Letters of Alexander Hamilton, Piscataway Factor: Part 2, July–October 1784," *Md. Hist. Mag.* 65 (1970): 20; Craik to W. Stone, July 2, 1782, in Hayden, "Port Tobacco," 270; *Md. Gazette*, Dec. 9, 1784, Oct. 5, 1786.

10. Hamilton to James Brown & Co., Jan. 25, Mar. 10, May 20, July 20, Oct. 2, 1784, "Post-Revolutionary Letters," 63:26, 30–31, 38, 42, 65:24, 28–29; Richard Harrison & Co. Ledger, fol. 326; inventory of Phillip Farguson's store goods, filed June 6, 1784, CCW, Lib. B1 (1782–85), fols. 326–28; *Md. Gazette*, Aug. 19, Sept. 23, 1784.

11. Charles R. Ritcheson, *Aftermath of Revolution: British Policy toward the United States, 1783–1795* (Dallas: Southern Methodist University Press, 1969), 19–20, which discusses British reinstitution of the duty on tobacco, as well as other measures dating from the colonial period; Hamilton to James Brown & Co., May 20, 1784, "Post-Revolutionary Letters," 63:37n, 41–42; CCLR, Lib. V3, fols. 599–600.

12. John Henry et al. to Gov. William Smallwood, Oct. 31, 1786, Red Books, vol. 10, fol. 54.

13. T. Stone to W. Stone, Apr. 21, July 16, 1782, M. J. Stone to W. Stone, May 3, 1783, John Hoskins Stone to W. Stone, undated, Stone Family of Maryland Papers, fols. 61–62, 71, 85–87, 329; Hanson Briscoe to W. Stone, Aug. 4 [1785?], ibid., loose papers; J. H. Stone to W. Stone, Mar. 5, 1785, and M. J. Stone to W. Stone, Mar. 29 [year unknown], Vertical File, MHS; J. H. Stone to W. Stone, July 7, 1786, Stone Family Papers, in possession of the Stone Family, La Plata, Md.; Jenifer to the treasurer of the Western Shore, Apr. 15, 1785, and J. H. Stone to Jenifer, Aug. 15, 1786, Executive Papers, box 54, item 18/15, box 55, item 27; *Md. Gazette*, June 9, 1785. For a stimulating discussion of the merchant community in postwar Philadelphia, see Thomas M. Doerflinger, *A Vigorous Spirit of Enterprise: Merchants and Economic Development in Revolutionary Philadelphia* (Chapel Hill: University of North Carolina Press, for the Institute of Early American History and Culture, 1986), chaps. 6–7. Regarding dramatically different commercial circumstances at Annapolis, consult Edward C. Papenfuse, *In Pursuit of Profit: The Annapolis Merchants in the Era of the American Revolution* (Baltimore: Johns Hopkins University Press, 1975), chaps. 4–5.

14. J. H. Stone to W. Stone, Feb. 10, 1785, and undated, Stone Family of Maryland Papers, loose papers and fol. 329, respectively; *Md. Gazette*, Sept. 16, 1790, June 18, 1795.

15. J. H. Stone to Tench Tilghman, June 12, 1785, in Benson J. Lossing, *Pictorial Field Book of the American Revolution* (1900), vol. 6, fol. 234 (used with permission of the Huntington Library, San Marino, Calif.); Tilghman to Robert Morris, Nov. 15, 1785, Tilghman & Co. to William Hunter & Co., Nov. 13, 1785, and to Thomas [Howe] Ridgate, Dec. 1, 1785, in the Tench Tilghman Letterbook, 1785–86, fols. 250, 249, 277, respectively; Tilghman to Morris, Mar. 16, 1786, Thomas R. Tilghman to Morris, May 10, 1786, and to J. H. Stone and Ridgate, May 17, 1786, and Tilghman & Co. to J. H. Stone & Co., June 28, July 5, 1786, in the Tench Tilghman

Letterbook, 1786–89, fols. 10, 50–51, 62, 104, 109, respectively. This material is part of the Tench Tilghman Letter and Account Books, 1784–98 (MS. 2690), MHS. See also Jacob M. Price, *France and the Chesapeake: A History of the French Tobacco Monopoly, 1674–1791, and of Its Relationship to the British and American Tobacco Trades*, 2 vols. (Ann Arbor: University of Michigan Press, 1973), 2:746, 771, 1097; Papenfuse, *In Pursuit of Profit*, 198–99; *Md. Gazette*, Sept. 7, 1786.

16. Jean Butenhoff Lee, "Laboring Hands and the Transformation of Mount Vernon Plantation, 1783–1799" (unpublished paper presented at a conference on Re-creating the World of the Virginia Plantation, 1750–1820," Charlottesville, Va., 1990); Merritt Roe Smith, *Harpers Ferry Armory and the New Technology: The Challenge of Change* (Ithaca, N.Y.: Cornell University Press, 1977), 28–30; *Fort Washington, Maryland* (Washington, D.C.: U.S. Department of the Interior, n.d.).

17. Douglas R. Littlefield, "Eighteenth-Century Plans to Clear the Potomac River: Technology, Expertise, and Labor in a Developing Nation," *Virginia Magazine of History and Biography* 93 (1985): 291–93, 305–06; Wilbur E. Garrett, "George Washington's Patowmack Canal: Waterway That Led to the Constitution," *National Geographic* 171 (1987): 716–53; *Md. Gazette*, Feb. 17, 1785; Records of the Potomac Company, Stock Ledger, 1787–1828, fols. 3, 13, 15, 17, 33, 37, 53, Record Group 79, National Archives and Records Service, Washington, D.C.; T. Stone to George Washington, Jan. 28, 1785, Etting Collection, Historical Society of Pennsylvania; Richard B. Morris, *The Forging of the Union, 1781–1789* (New York: Harper & Row, 1987), 220–32, 249–50.

18. *Diary of My Travels in America: Louis-Philippe, King of France, 1830–1848*, trans. Stephen Becker (New York: Delacorte Press, 1977), 24; M. J. Stone to Jenifer, June 24, 1790, and to W. Stone, June 24, 1790, Stone Family of Maryland Papers, fols. 215–21, 305. See also Lee W. Formwalt, "A Conversation between Two Rivers: A Debate on the Location of the U.S. Capital in Maryland," *Md. Hist. Mag.* 71 (1976): 310–21. A euphoric assessment of Maryland's place in the new nation is in the *Md. Gazette*, Nov. 20, 1794.

19. List of balances due the Port Tobacco store of Cunninghame, Findlay & Co., Sept. 1, 1777, A. O. 13/29, Public Record Office (microfilm in the Virginia Colonial Records Project, reel 250, Tracy W. McGregor Library, Manuscripts Division, University of Virginia Library, Charlottesville); Hamilton's list, including unpaid pre-1775 debts from the Benedict store of John Glassford & Co., May 24, 1785, Hamilton Papers, 1760–1800 (MS. 1301), MHS; CCCR, Lib. Y3, fols. 85, 99–103; Philip A. Crowl, *Maryland during and after the Revolution: A Political and Economic Study* (Baltimore: Johns Hopkins Press, 1943), 67–68; Ritcheson, *Aftermath of Revolution*, 63–65.

20. *Md. Gazette*, Oct. 2, 1783, Feb. 19, May 27, 1784, Feb. 23, 1786; Jacob M. Price, "One Family's Empire: The Russell-Lee-Clerk Connection in Maryland, Britain, and India, 1707–1857," *Md. Hist. Mag.* 72 (1977): 210–12.

21. Hamilton to James Brown & Co., Jan. 25, Mar. 10, 1784, and to Matthew Blair, Oct. 21, 1784, "Post-Revolutionary Letters," 63:26, 30–31, 65:35.

22. Hamilton to William Hanson, May ? [1784], to Walter Pye, May 14, 1784, to James Brown & Co., May 20, July 20, Oct. 2, 1784, and to Fergusson, July 17, 1784, ibid., 63:34, 35, 37, 65:23–24, 28, 20, respectively. Pye's estate was valued at £2,629 in the 1782 Assessment Lists, Scharf Collection, box 96, item 5. While the peace treaty

was silent about interest, the Assembly recognized it when postponing certain debt litigation "unless the debtor shall refuse or neglect to pay the interest due." *Laws of Md. . . . [Apr. Session 1782]*, chap. 55.

23. Hamilton to Fergusson, July 17, 1784, to James Brown & Co., July 20, Oct. 2, 1784, and to Blair, Oct. 21, 1784, in "Post-Revolutionary Letters," 65:20, 22–24, 28, 35; Hamilton to Fergusson, Feb. 12, 1785, Hamilton Papers; Richard Henderson to Edward Matthews, June 4, 1785, in Chancery Records, SHH No. 3 (1797–98), fol. 521.

24. Hamilton to James Brown & Co., Jan. 25, Oct. 2, 1784, "Post-Revolutionary Letters," 63:26, 65:28–29. On British policy, see Ritcheson, *Aftermath of Revolution*, 6–13; the Order-in-Council, July 2, 1783, barred American ships from the West India trade. John J. McCusker and Russell R. Menard survey postwar economic conditions in *The Economy of British America, 1607–1789* (Chapel Hill: University of North Carolina Press, for the Institute of Early American History and Culture, 1985), 367–77, while Morris, *The Forging of the Union, 1781–1789*, chap. 6, persuasively destroys attempts to minimize the extent of postwar economic distress. Cf. Merrill Jensen, *The New Nation: A History of the United States during the Confederation, 1781–1789* (New York: Alfred A. Knopf, 1950), 191–92, and Gordon S. Wood, *The Creation of the American Republic, 1776–1787* (Chapel Hill: University of North Carolina Press, for the Institute of Early American History and Culture, 1969), 394–95. On conditions in Maryland, consult Louis Maganzin, "Economic Depression in Maryland and Virginia, 1783–1787" (Ph.D. diss., Georgetown University, 1967), especially 25–27, 47–75, 80–90, 105–06; Crowl, *Maryland during and after the Revolution*, chaps. 3–4, and Smallwood to county tax collectors, Mar. 18, 1786, Executive Papers, box 56, item 49. Kathryn L. Behrens, *Paper Money in Maryland, 1727–1789* (Baltimore: Johns Hopkins Press, 1923) remains the standard treatment of that subject. On the French monopoly, see Price, *France and the Chesapeake*, vol. 2, chap. 27. Contemporary observations and complaints include Tench Tilghman to Morris, Nov. 12, 1785, Feb. 23, 1786, Tilghman Letterbook, 1785–86, fols. 249, 350, in the Tilghman Letter and Account Books; Wallace, Johnson, & Muir (Annapolis) to Alexander Ogg, Jan. 20, 1785, and to Wallace, Johnson, & Muir (London), Feb. 19, 1785, Wallace, Johnson, & Muir Letterbook (MS. 1180), fols. 128, 195, MHS; Thomas Jefferson to John Adams, July 9, 1786, in *The Papers of Thomas Jefferson*, ed. Julian P. Boyd et al., 25 vols. to date (Princeton: Princeton University Press, 1950–), 10:106.

25. McCusker and Menard, *The Economy of British America, 1607–1789*, 358–77.

26. Tilghman & Co. to Ridgate, Feb. 28, 1786, Tilghman Letterbook, 1785–86, fol. 355, in the Tilghman Letter and Account Books; Tilghman to Ridgate, Mar. 8, 18, 21, 1786, Tilghman Letterbook, 1786–89, fols. 5, 8, 14, ibid.; *Md. Gazette*, June 15, Sept. 28, 1786; J. H. Stone to W. Stone, July 7, Oct. 30, 1786, Stone Family Papers, in possession of the Stone Family, La Plata, Md., and Stone Family Papers, MHS, respectively.

27. Henry Harford's claim, in American Loyalist Claims, A. O. 12/79, fols. 96–97, Public Record Office, London (microfilm in the Manuscript Division, LC); *Md. Gazette*, Feb. 23, June 1, 1786; [J. Kilty], *History of a Session of the General Assembly of the State of Maryland, Held at the City of Annapolis, Commenced in November, 1785* ([Annapolis: Frederick Green, 1786]), 29; John Ridout to Horatio Sharpe, Jan. 28, 1786, Ridout Collection (SC371), in Special Collections, MSA; account of balances due

from county tax collectors for 1779–82, Pforzheimer Papers, box 1, item 78; *"To his Excellency the Governor, and the honorable Council of the State of Maryland, The Address of the Subscribers . . . ,"* undated, Broadside Portfolio 28, no. 20, Rare Book Division, LC.

28. On the agitation for paper money, constitutional questions raised, and the role of the state Senate, see Melvin Yazawa, ed., *Representative Government and the Revolution: The Maryland Constitutional Crisis of 1787* (Baltimore: Johns Hopkins University Press, 1975); Alexander Hamilton, James Madison, and John Jay, *The Federalist: A Commentary on the Constitution of the United States* (New York: Modern Library, 1937), 414–15; Robert G. McCloskey, ed., *The Works of James Wilson*, 2 vols. (Cambridge: Harvard University Press, 1967), 2:782; Wood, *Creation of the American Republic*, 251–55; and Crowl, *Maryland during and after the Revolution*, chap. 4. Alexander Hamilton, the tobacco factor, kept track of court closings. Hamilton to James Brown & Co., May 24, 1786, Letter Book, 1773–76, 1784–90, Piscataway, Md., in the John Glassford & Co. Papers, Manuscript Division, LC. The following account of the Charles County riot of 1786 was published, with slight modifications, as Jean Butenhoff Lee, "Maryland's 'Dangerous Insurrection' of 1786," *Md. Hist. Mag.* 85 (1990): 329–44. It is included here with permission.

29. Memorial of John Allen Thomas to Smallwood, June 15, 1786, Walter Hanson, John Dent, and Samuel Hanson, Jr., to Smallwood [July 1786], Executive Papers, box 59, items 2/3, 2/11. Every justice appointed to the court in 1786 is named in the Proceedings of the Council of Maryland, Nov. 27, 1784–Nov. 10, 1788, fol. 104, in Governor and Council, Proceedings (S1071), MSA. Samuel Hanson, Jr., was also known as Samuel of Samuel. Biographical sketches of the three justices are in Papenfuse et al., eds., *Biographical Dictionary* 1:264, 409–10.

30. W. Hanson, Dent, and S. Hanson, Jr., to Smallwood [July 1786], Executive Papers, box 59, item 2/11; depositions of Henry Massey Hanson, July 22, 1786, Francis Ware, Aug. 1, 1786, and Josias Hawkins, Aug. 1, 1786, ibid., items 2/14–16. On John Allen Thomas, see Papenfuse et al., eds., *Biographical Dictionary* 2:808–09; CCCR, Libs. X3 (1774–78), fols. 618–19, Y3, fol. 604; and George Plater to Washington, Nov. 9, 1789, George Washington Papers, ser. 7, vol. 27, fol. 38, Manuscript Division, LC.

31. Thomas to Smallwood, June 15, 1786, W. Hanson, Dent, and S. Hanson, Jr., to Smallwood [July 1786], Hawkins deposition, Aug. 1, 1786, Executive Papers, box 59, items 2/3, 2/11, 2/16.

32. Hawkins deposition, Aug. 1, 1786, H. M. Hanson deposition, July 22, 1786, deposition of John Muschett, Aug. 8, 1786, Thomas memorial, June 15, 1786, W. Hanson, Dent, and S. Hanson, Jr., to Smallwood [July 1786], ibid., items 2/16, 2/14, 2/13, 2/3, 2/11, respectively. William Ward served as a private in the Maryland Line from July 1778 through February 1779. His total assessed property in 1782 was £167 Maryland currency, including two slaves but no land. The only Joseph Nelson named in the tax records for that year owned one hundred acres but no other assessed property. Both men lived in Pomonkey Hundred. *Arch. Md.* 18:255; 1782 Assessment Lists, Scharf Collection, box 96, item 13.

33. Thomas memorial, June 15, 1786, Executive Papers, box 59, item 2/3.

34. W. Hanson, Dent, and S. Hanson, Jr., to Smallwood [July 1786], Hawkins deposition, Aug. 1, 1786, H. M. Hanson deposition, July 22, 1786, ibid., 2/11, 2/16, 2/14, respectively.

35. Hamilton to Fergusson, June 18, 1786, photocopy in Collection G333, MSA; Hamil-

ton to James Brown & Co., July 10, 1786, Letter Book . . . Piscataway, Md., fol. 73, John Glassford & Co. Papers. Hamilton may have been referring to Walter B. Smallwood, who in June 1781 enlisted in the army for a three-year term. *Arch. Md.* 18:392, 429.

36. Hamilton to Fergusson, June 18, 1786, Collection G333. Contemporary accounts of civil unrest during the 1780s are in the *Pennsylvania Mercury and Universal Advertiser*, June 8, 1787; John Dawson to Madison, Apr. 15, June 12, 1787, James McClurg to Madison, Aug. 22, Sept. 10, 1787, and Madison to James Madison, Sr., Sept. 4, 1787, and to Jefferson, Sept. 6, 1787, in *The Papers of James Madison*, ed. William T. Hutchinson, Robert A. Rutland, et al., 16 vols. to date (Chicago: University of Chicago Press, 1962–77; Charlottesville: University Press of Virginia, 1977–), 9:381, 10:47, 155–56, 165, 161–62, 164, respectively; "Diary of Timothy Ford, 1785–1786," *South Carolina Historical and Genealogical Magazine* 13 (1912): 193; and "John F. Grimke's Eyewitness Account of the Camden Court Riot, April 27–28, 1785," ed. Robert A. Becker, *South Carolina Historical Magazine* 83 (1982): 209–13. On Shays's Rebellion see David P. Szatmary, *Shays' Rebellion: The Making of an Agrarian Insurrection* (Amherst: University of Massachusetts Press, 1980), and Richard D. Brown, "Shays's Rebellion and the Ratification of the Federal Constitution in Massachusetts," in *Beyond Confederation: Origins of the Constitution and American National Identity*, ed. Richard Beeman et al. (Chapel Hill: University of North Carolina Press, for the Institute of Early American History and Culture, 1987), 113–27.

37. Thomas memorial, June 15, 1786, Executive Papers, box 59, item 2/3. When Thomas did not receive a prompt reply, he wrote Smallwood again, July 3, 1786, ibid., item 2/8.

38. Hamilton to James Brown & Co., July 10, 1786, Letter Book . . . Piscataway, Md., fol. 73, John Glassford & Co. Papers; Proceedings of the Council of Md., Nov. 27, 1784–Nov. 10, 1788, fol. 149; Smallwood to Ware, July 14, 1786, Council Letter Book, 1780–87, fol. 504, in Governor and Council, Letterbooks (S1075), MSA; *Md. Gazette*, July 20, 1786.

39. Smallwood to W. Hanson and Dent, to John Gwinn, to Ware, and to Thomas, July 12, 1786, to Samuel Hanson, Aug. 5, 1786, and to T. Stone, Aug. 10, 1786, Council Letter Book, 1780–87, fols. 503–05. Replies: Gwinn to Smallwood, July 17, 1786, deposition of William Thompson, July 24, 1786, Ware to Smallwood, July 25, 1786, Thomas to Smallwood [early Aug. 1786], Executive Papers, box 59, items 52, 2/5–7, respectively.

40. W. Hanson to Smallwood, Aug. 3, 1786, W. Hanson, Dent, and S. Hanson, Jr., to Smallwood [July 1786], Executive Papers, box 59, items 2/2, 2/11.

41. Ibid.

42. Ibid.; H. M. Hanson deposition, July 22, 1786, Ware and Hawkins depositions, Aug. 1, 1786, ibid., items 2/2, 2/11, 2/14–16.

43. W. Hanson to Smallwood, Aug. 3, 1786, W. Hanson, Dent, and S. Hanson, Jr., to Smallwood [July 1786], ibid., items 2/2, 2/11.

44. Muschett deposition, Aug. 8, 1786, W. Hanson to Smallwood, Aug. 3, 1786, ibid., items 2/13, 2/2, respectively.

45. Thomas to Smallwood, Aug. 12, 21, 1786, and Council hearing notes [Aug. 10, 1786], ibid., items 2/9A&B, 2/1, 2/10, respectively.

46. Council hearing notes [Aug. 10, 1786], ibid., item 2/10.

47. Hamilton to James Brown & Co., July 10, 1786, Letter Book . . . Piscataway, Md.,

fol. 73, John Glassford & Co. Papers; Ridout to Sharpe, Aug. 9, 1786, Ridout Collection; *Md. Gazette*, Sept. 21, 1786.

48. Hamilton to James Brown & Co., Jan. 21, June 9, 1787, Letter Book . . . Piscataway, Md., fols. 75–77, John Glassford & Co. Papers; Fergusson to John Stewart, Nov. 28, 1787, to Smallwood, Dec. 10, 1787, and to John Gibson, Dec. 23, 1787, Port Tobacco Letterbook, 1787–88, ibid., container 62; J. H. Stone to W. Stone, Dec. 27, 1786, Stone Family Papers, MHS. Curiously, the three justices who presided at the time of the riot, together with a fourth, Richard Barnes, tried to blame the court's huge backlog of cases on Thomas Stone. He had witnessed the riot and was called to the August 10 Council hearing. Whether he offered testimony is unknown, but the four justices subsequently published a notice in the *Md. Gazette* claiming that Stone's absences from court had "loaded and swelled" the docket "to a most enormous size" and that henceforth suits would not be carried over from one session to the next merely because counsel was not present. Stone, pointedly observing that "the *majority* of the justices" had not complained, published a rejoinder, whereupon three more justices sided with their colleagues to make a majority. Smallwood to T. Stone, Aug. 10, 1786, Council Letter Book, 1780–87, fol. 505; *Md. Gazette*, Dec. 14, 28, 1786, Mar. 1, 1787.

49. Pauline Maier, *From Resistance to Revolution: Colonial Radicals and the Development of American Opposition to Britain, 1765–1776* (New York: Alfred A. Knopf, 1972), chap. 1. Thomas P. Slaughter, "Crowds in Eighteenth-Century America: Reflections and New Directions," *Pennsylvania Magazine of History and Biography* 115 (1991): 3–34, suggests a typology of crowd actions.

50. W. Hanson, Dent, and S. Hanson, Jr., to Smallwood [July 1786], Executive Papers, box 59, item 2/11. Under the insolvency act passed at the April 1787 session of the legislature, debtors who deeded all their property to their creditors were absolved of the debts. *Laws of Md.* . . . [*Apr. Session 1787*], chap. 34; see also *Md. Gazette*, Mar. 21, 1793. Charles County debtors regularly availed themselves of the bankruptcy legislation, beginning in 1787. For example, *Md. Gazette*, Aug. 2, 23, Sept. 20, Oct. 11, Nov. 1, 15, 1787. At first, imprisonment was still possible until a debtor completed the proper bankruptcy procedures. In 1796 John Hoskins Stone, a native son of the county who was then governor, asked the Assembly to abolish imprisonment for debt. Papenfuse et al., eds., *Biographical Dictionary* 2:785. The confusing history of debtor relief in postrevolutionary Maryland is outlined in Peter J. Coleman, *Debtors and Creditors in America: Insolvency, Imprisonment for Debt, and Bankruptcy, 1607–1900* (Madison: State Historical Society of Wisconsin, 1974), 171–78.

51. CCCR, Lib. X3, fols. 529, 621; *Laws of Md.* . . . [*Nov. Session 1779*], chap. 35; *Laws of Md.* . . . [*Mar. Session 1780*], chap. 30; Benjamin Cawood's accounts of balances due from county tax collectors for 1779–82, and account of taxes collected in the counties for 1782 supplies, Nov. 16, 1782, Pforzheimer Papers, box 1, items 78, 102; Cawood to Jenifer, May 20, 1784, Red Books, vol. 32, fol. 37. On the state war debt, see the partly conjectural discussion of Edward C. Papenfuse, "The Legislative Response to a Costly War: Fiscal Policy and Factional Politics in Maryland, 1777–1789," in *Sovereign States in an Age of Uncertainty*, ed. Ronald Hoffman and Peter J. Albert (Charlottesville: University Press of Virginia, for the U.S. Capitol Historical Society, 1981), 134–35. Changing public policy regarding taxation is treated in Robert A. Becker, *Revolution, Reform, and the Politics of American Taxation, 1763–1783* (Baton Rouge: Louisiana State University Press, 1980), 212–17.

52. CCCR, Lib. Y3, fol. 621.

53. Robert Brent to Jenifer, Apr. 18, 1784, Executive Papers, box 46, item 96; CCW, Lib. AI10 (1788–91), fols. 291–92.

54. Cawood to Jenifer, May 20, 1784, Red Books, vol. 32, fol. 37; Thomas Harwood's list of balances due for taxes on the Western Shore, Dec. 16, 1788, Vertical File, MHS, shows nothing due from Charles County.

55. Petition of James Freeman to Gov. William Paca, undated (850056), in the Southern Maryland Studies Center, Charles County Community College, La Plata, Md.; Charles Mankin to Jenifer, Sept. 2, 1783, to [Jenifer?], July 27, 1784, and list of balances due from collectors for 1783–85, Executive Papers, box 46, item 65, box 50, item 21, and box 54, items 44A&B. Mankin's taxable wealth in 1782 was £573. 1782 Assessment Lists, Scharf Collection, box 96, item 15.

56. Harwood to Smallwood, May 10, 1786, Smallwood to county tax commissioners, May 18, 1786, and Council to the sheriffs of Charles and other counties, Apr. 15, 1789, Executive Papers, box 61, item 32, box 56, item 70, and box 67, item 35, respectively; Smallwood to county tax collectors for 1784–85, Mar. 22, 1787, Council Letter Book, 1780–87, fol. 521; Gov. John Eager Howard to W. Kilty, Apr. 11, 1789, and to Harwood, July 16, Oct. 1, 1789, James Brice to Harwood, June 26, 1789, Council Letter Book, 1787–93, fols. 34, 59–60, 73–74, 57, respectively, in Governor and Council, Letterbooks; W. Kilty to J. Kilty, Sept. 10, 1789, Red Books, vol. 23, fol. 93; *Md. Gazette*, Aug. 28, 1788, July 30, Aug. 13, Oct. 29, 1789, Apr. 28, Oct. 20, 1791, Aug. 2, 1792; account of taxes due from the Western Shore counties, Nov. 1, 1789, Pforzheimer Papers, box 1, item 171.

57. Charles County tax commissioners to Smallwood, July 16, 1787, Executive Papers, box 62, item 34.

58. Charles County tax commissioners' certification of the account of Hoskins Hanson, Nov. 27, 1786, ibid., box 62, item 35; J. H. Stone to W. Stone, Dec. 27, 1786, Stone Family Papers, MHS.

59. *Md. Gazette*, Feb. 1, 1787; Harwood's list of Western Shore counties [including Charles] from which no tax money was received in 1786, June 30, 1787, Executive Papers, box 64, item 110/2; Smallwood to the tax commissioners in Charles and other counties, July 6, 1787, Council Letter Book, 1780–87, fol. 528; Charles County tax commissioners to Smallwood, July 16, 1787, Executive Papers, box 62, item 34.

60. *Md. Gazette*, Apr. 30, 1789.

61. Howard to the sheriffs of Charles and other counties, Nov. 7, 1789, Howard to W. Kilty, Nov. 8, 1789, J. Kilty to W. Kilty, Nov. 23, 1789, Council Letter Book, 1787–93, fols. 77–78, 85; Council to the House of Delegates, Nov. 8, 1789, Executive Papers, box 67, item 97; *Md. Gazette*, Nov. 19, 1789, Jan. 7, July 22, Aug. 5, Sept. 30, 1790, Apr. 28, 1791, Jan. 5, 1792.

62. *Md. Gazette*, Feb. 26, 1789; Register of Civil Officers, 1777–1800, fols. 91, 154, 159; CCCR, Lib. Y3, fol. 601. Cawood's difficulties during the 1790s were partly related to revenues he had failed to collect in specie while serving as deputy sheriff in 1776. He could not collect that year, he told the Chancery Court in 1795, and thereafter people offered him depreciated Continental money. Chancery Records, 1795, fol. 461.

63. Order to the coroner of Charles County, Apr. 1787, in Loose Papers, 1779–88, General Court of the Western Shore, Judicials; W. Kilty to J. Kilty, Sept. 10, 1789, Red Books, vol. 23, fol. 93; *Md. Gazette*, Feb. 12, Oct. 29, 1789, Apr. 28, 1791, Dec. 26, 1793, Sept. 4, 18, 1794.

64. *Md. Gazette*, Oct. 11, 1787, Mar. 27, Sept. 18, Oct. 23, 1788, Sept. 19, 1793, Oct. 9, 1794.

65. John Beatty to Reading Beatty, Apr. 2, 1784, "Letters of the Four Beatty Brothers of the Continental Army, 1774–1794," ed. Joseph M. Beatty, Jr., *Pennsylvania Magazine of History and Biography* 44 (1920): 240–41; *Md. Gazette*, Oct. 23, 1788, Oct. 9, 1794.

66. Inventory of Ware's property, May 1, 1787, in Loose Papers, 1779–88, General Court of the Western Shore, Judicials; Brumbaugh, comp., *Md. Records* 2:403; Md. General Assembly, *Votes and Proceedings of the House of Delegates of the State of Maryland, November Session, 1800* (Annapolis: [Frederick Green, 1801]), 45, 61, 67.

67. Brent to Jenifer, Apr. 18, 1784, Executive Papers, box 46, item 96; T. Stone to W. Stone, Jan. 15, 1786, Stone Family of Maryland Papers, fol. 163; Pardon Papers, box 5, folder 57.

68. Mankin to [Jenifer?], July 27, 1784, and Charles County tax commissioners' certification of the account of H. Hanson, Nov. 27, 1786, Executive Papers, box 50, item 21, box 62, item 35.

69. Smallwood to the justices of Charles, Prince George's, and Cecil counties, Mar. 10, 1786, justices of the Charles County orphans' court to Smallwood, Feb. 12, 1787, W. Hanson to the justices of the orphans' court, Sept. 22, 1787, ibid., box 56, item 46, box 62, items 111, 71/1&2, respectively. For a governor's contention that many local officers lacked "diligence and circumspection," which was "very detrimental to the public interest," see Howard to the tax commissioners of several counties, including Charles, Jan. 13, 1790, in the Council Letter Book, 1787–93, fol. 89.

70. W. Hanson to the justices of the Charles County orphans' court, Sept. 22, 1787, Executive Papers, box 62, items 71/1&2.

71. William Harrison to Smallwood, Mar. 9, 1787, John N. Smoot to Smallwood, May 19, 1787, Charles County tax commissioners to Smallwood, July 16, 1787, Apr. 19, 1788, Daniel Jenifer to Howard, Feb. 16, 1789, ibid., box 62, items 118, 36, 34, box 64, item 143, box 68, item 155, respectively.

72. Letters to Smallwood from Benjamin Fendall, Dec. 5, 1787, John Sanders, Apr. 7, 1788, Charles Mankin, Apr. 20, 1788, R. Fergusson, Apr. 28, 1788, and Henry Barnes, June 20, 1788, ibid., box 62, item 50, box 66, items 76, 136, 118, 119 respectively; state of Maryland to Francis Boucher Franklin, Jan. 2, 1787, Franklin to Howard, Apr. 19, 1789, ibid., box 57, items 14, 15.

73. S. Hanson to Smallwood, Oct. 8, 1787, ibid., box 62, item 76.

74. Charles County justices to Smallwood, Dec. 8, 1787, D. Jenifer to Howard, Feb. 16, 1789, Zephaniah Turner to Howard, May 6, 1789, ibid., box 62, item 25, box 68, items 155, 156; Fergusson to Smallwood, Dec. 10, 1787, Port Tobacco Letter Book, 1787–88, in the John Glassford & Co. Papers.

75. *Md. Gazette*, Dec. 24, 1789; *Laws of Md.* . . . [*Nov. Session 1790*], chap. 33.

76. Gov. Thomas Sim Lee to the sheriffs of Charles, St. Mary's, and Frederick counties, Nov. 29, 1792, Council Letter Book, 1787–93, fol. 167; Pardon Papers, box 5, folder 35, box 6, folders 19, 52, 90; Randolph B. Latimer to J. Dent et al., Aug. 8, 1794, Council Letter Book, 1793–96, fol. 138, in Governor and Council, Letterbooks.

77. Bountiful evidence supporting the generalizations made in this paragraph is contained in state records and in the *Md. Gazette*, which published notices of sales of property seized from local officials and their sureties, as well as an astonishing number of bankruptcy notices from them.

78. L. Marx Renzulli, Jr., *Maryland: The Federalist Years* (Madison, N.J.: Fairleigh Dickinson University Press, 1972), 73–74, 76.

79. Fergusson to Alexander Henderson, Mar. 14, 22, 1792, Port Tobacco Invoice and Letter Book, 1771–74, 1792–93, in the John Glassford & Co. Papers.

80. Fergusson to A. Henderson, Mar. 20, June 14, Dec. 8, 1792, Feb. 10, Aug. 18, 1793, ibid.

81. Fergusson to A. Henderson, Dec. 8, 1792, May 22, June 17, 1793, ibid.; *Md. Gazette*, Aug. 27, 1789, Feb. 18, Sept. 23, 1790, July 7, 1791, Apr. 5, Sept. 18, 1794, June 18, July 30, 1795, May 26, 1796.

82. Lorena S. Walsh, "Land, Landlord, and Leaseholder: Estate Management and Tenant Fortunes in Southern Maryland, 1642–1820," *Agricultural History* 59 (1985): 373–96. Walsh's work is an important contribution to the revision of Avery O. Craven's thesis that tobacco cultivation caused postwar agricultural decline. Craven, *Soil Exhaustion as a Factor in the Agricultural History of Virginia and Maryland, 1606–1860* (Urbana: University of Illinois Press, 1925; Gloucester, Mass.: Peter Smith, 1965). See also Edward C. Papenfuse, "Planter Behavior and Economic Opportunity in a Staple Economy," *Agricultural History* 46 (1972): 297–311.

83. *Md. Gazette*, Jan. 5, 1792, July 17, Sept. 4, 1794, June 18, July 30, Oct. 29, 1795, May 26, Oct. 6, Nov. 10, 1796; Isaac Weld, Jr., *Travels through the States of North America, and the Provinces of Upper and Lower Canada during the Years 1795, 1796, and 1797*, 4th ed., 2 vols. (London: John Stockdale, 1807; New York: Augustus M. Kelley, 1970), 1:138–39. Weld was not the only traveler who found the lower Western Shore uninviting during the 1790s. See *Moreau de St. Méry's American Journey [1793–98]*, trans. and ed. Kenneth Roberts and Anna M. Roberts (Garden City, N.Y.: Doubleday & Co., 1947), 73–74.

84. *Md. Gazette*, Apr. 22, Aug. 26, 1773, Sept. 11, 1788. In 1986, when the author visited Araby (the eighteenth-century home of the Eilbeck family), in the northwestern sector of the county, the owner called attention to a field at the foot of a steep hill and adjacent to a highway. Several years earlier the owner had uncovered a wharf in that field, lending credence to the tradition that masted vessels once sailed where the highway now runs. The regional character of silting and other agricultural problems is treated in Henry M. Miller, "Transforming a 'Splendid and Delightsome Land': Colonists and Ecological Change in the Chesapeake, 1607–1820," *Journal of the Washington Academy of Sciences* 76 (1986): 173–87, and Carville Earle's provocative "The Myth of the Southern Soil Miner: Macrohistory, Agricultural Innovation, and Environmental Change," in *The Ends of the Earth: Perspectives on Modern Environmental History*, ed. Donald Worster (New York: Cambridge University Press, 1988), 175–210.

85. *Md. Gazette*, Oct. 28, 1784, May 17, 1787, Nov. 12, 26, 1789, Mar. 31, 1791; Weld, *Travels through the States* 1:140–41; Joseph Scott, *A Geographical Description of the States of Maryland and Delaware* (Philadelphia: Kimber, Conrad & Co., 1807), 9, 15; Walsh, "Land, Landlord, and Leaseholder," 393; Miller, "Transforming a 'Splendid and Delightsome Land,' " 182–85.

86. *Md. Gazette*, Jan. 12, 1797; Pardon Papers, box 5, folder 61.

87. *Md. Gazette*, May 5, 1785, Aug. 17, Nov. 16, 1786, May 7, 1795; minutes of the board of trustees, Record Book of Charlotte Hall School, Lib. A (1774–1805), fols. 11, 13, 16, 30, in the Charlotte Hall School Collection (850078), Southern Maryland Studies Center, Charles County Community College; Scott, *Geographical Description*, 55–56.

88. *Md. Gazette*, May 7, 1795; Scott, *Geographical Description*, 57; Ferdinand S. Campbell to John Campbell, Oct. 26, 1808, Campbell Family Papers, section 1, Virginia Historical Society, Richmond.

89. Fergusson to John Witherspoon, July 1, Sept. 12, 1793, Port Tobacco Invoice and Letter Book, 1771–74, 1792–93, John Glassford & Co. Papers. See also the Durham Parish vestry's agreement to have a school established at the glebe. Entry for Dec. 1798, Durham Parish Vestry Minutes, 1774–1824, in the Christ Church, Old Durham Parish Collection (SC2604), Special Collections, MSA.

90. *St. Ignatius Church, Chapel Point* ([Port Tobacco: St. Ignatius Church], 1982); entry for May 9, 1791, Durham Parish Vestry Minutes; Hatch Dent to the Committee on the Protestant Episcopal Church in Maryland, June 1, 1792, Vertical File, Archives of the Episcopal Diocese of Maryland, Baltimore.

91. Journal of the Vestry, Trinity Parish, in "Abstracts of Early Protestant Episcopal Church Records of Charles County, Maryland" (typescript: Martha Washington Chapter, Daughters of the American Revolution, Washington, D.C., n.d.), 75, 95–102.

92. T. Stone to W. Stone, July 16, 1782, Apr. 22, Nov. 24, 1785, Stone Family of Maryland Papers, fols. 72, 141, 147–48; CCLR, Lib. V3, fols. 590–91; Stock Ledger, 1787–1828, fol. 17, in Records of the Potomac Company.

93. T. Stone to W. Stone, Dec. 21, 1785, Jan. 15, 1786, Stone Family of Maryland Papers, fols. 156, 159–60, 163.

94. In order quoted: *Md. Gazette*, Sept. 16, 1790, Apr. 14, 1791, Dec. 24, June 11, 1789, Apr. 15, 1790, Feb. 3, Jan. 27, 1791, Dec. 5, 1793, Aug. 19, Sept. 23, 1790, Jan. 12, 1797; Fergusson to Thomas Leiper, Mar. 8, 1792, Port Tobacco Invoice and Letter Book, 1771–74, 1792–93, John Glassford & Co. Papers. For Smallwood's slaveholding, see [U.S. Census Office, 1st Census, 1790], *Heads of Families at the First Census of the United States Taken in the Year 1790: Maryland* (Baltimore: Genealogical Publishing Co., 1965), 54, and *Md. Gazette*, Nov. 15, 1792.

95. [U.S. Census Office, 1st Census, 1790], *Return of the Whole Number of Persons within the Several Districts of the United States, According to "An Act Providing for the Enumeration of the Inhabitants of the United States," Passed March the First, One Thousand Seven Hundred and Ninety-One* (Philadelphia: Childs & Swaine, 1791), 47; [W. S. Rossiter], comp., *A Century of Population Growth: From the First Census of the United States to the Twelfth, 1790–1900* (Washington, D.C.: U.S. Bureau of the Census, 1909), 289; 1782 Assessment Lists, Scharf Collection, box 96, items 7–10, 12–17; Jean Butenhoff Lee, "The Problem of Slave Community in the Eighteenth-Century Chesapeake," *WMQ* 43 (1986): 347. A sampling of credit terms offered for slaves is in *Md. Gazette*, Mar. 8, Oct. 18, 1787, Jan. 21, Apr. 15, Sept. 23, 1790, Jan. 27, 1791, Nov. 15, 1792, Dec. 5, 1793.

96. Out-of-state slave buyers, including the Spanish, are mentioned in Fergusson to James Lorimer, June 14, 1792, and to George Gray, Sept. 22, 1793, Port Tobacco Invoice and Letter Book, 1771–74, 1792–93, John Glassford & Co. Papers. A regional overview, which demonstrates that demographic change in Charles County was part of a broad trend, is in Richard S. Dunn, "Black Society in the Chesapeake, 1776–1810," in *Slavery and Freedom in the Age of the American Revolution*, ed. Ira Berlin and Ronald Hoffman (Charlottesville: University Press of Virginia, for the U.S. Capitol Historical Society, 1983), 49–82. Subsequent developments are the subject of Barbara J. Fields, *Slavery and Freedom on the Middle Ground: Maryland during the Nineteenth Century* (New Haven: Yale University Press, 1985).

97. CCW, Lib. AI10, fols. 410–31, 457–78; Chancery Records, 1796, fols. 123, 188, 208–10, 217; *Md. Gazette*, July 1, Aug. 5, 1790, May 26, Oct. 20, 1796; Fergusson to A. Henderson, Mar. 20, 1792, Port Tobacco Invoice and Letter Book, 1771–74, 1792–93, John Glassford & Co. Papers; Morris to W. Stone, Apr. 11, Aug. 8, 1790, Stone Family of Maryland Papers, fols. 201, 231. Claims against the prewar partnership of Ridgate and John Barnes remained unsettled at Ridgate's death. Barnes recovered financially and died in Washington County, Md., in 1800. Barnes & Ridgate Account, 1774–90 (Mss2 Un3 a22), Virginia Historical Society; Papenfuse et al., eds., *Biographical Dictionary* 1:115–16.

98. Papenfuse et al., eds., *Biographical Dictionary* 1:204; 1782 Assessment list for the lower east hundred of Port Tobacco Parish, Scharf Collection, box 96, item 15. Causin's assessed wealth that year was £4,328, including thirty-four slaves.

99. Papenfuse et al., eds., *Biographical Dictionary* 1:204; Gerard B. Causin to T. S. Lee, Sept. 11, 1780, *Arch Md.* 45:93; minutes of the board of trustees, Aug. 28, 1786, in Record Book of Charlotte Hall School, Lib. A, fol. 22; Chancery Records, 1796, fols. 217–18, 226; *Md. Gazette*, July 17, Oct. 16, 1788, Oct. 29, 1789, Sept. 23, 1790; [U.S. Census Office, 1st Census, 1790], *Heads of Families*, 48; Fergusson to Hamilton, Feb. 6, May 26, 1792, Port Tobacco Invoice and Letter Book, 1771–74, 1792–93, John Glassford & Co. Papers.

100. Chase: 1782 Assessment Lists, box 96, items 9, 15; Fergusson to Witherspoon, Sept. 12, 1793, Port Tobacco Invoice and Letter Book, 1771–74, 1792–93, John Glassford & Co. Papers. Forry: Journal of the Proceedings of the Commissioners Appointed to Preserve Confiscated British Property, 1781, fol. 107 (S132), MSA; 1782 Assessment Lists, box 96, item 12; Chancery Records, 1789–90, fols. 7–50; *Md. Gazette*, May 28, 1789.

101. Cresswell, *Journal*, 22–24; J. Richard Rivoire, *Homeplaces: Traditional Domestic Architecture of Charles County, Maryland* (La Plata, Md.: Southern Maryland Studies Center, Charles County Community College, 1990), 10, 26; Wyndham B. Blanton, *Medicine in Virginia in the Eighteenth Century* (Richmond: Garrett & Massie, 1931), 150.

102. Colonial eyewitness observations, which depict a more vibrant, more economically and environmentally healthy scene, include Cresswell, *Journal*, 17–19, 25–26; Adam Gordon, "Journal of an Officer Who Travelled in America and the West Indies in 1764 and 1765," in *Travels in the American Colonies*, ed. Newton D. Mereness (New York: Macmillan, 1916), 407–08; "Journal of a French Traveller in the Colonies, 1765, II," *American Historical Review* 27 (1921): 70; Hunter D. Farish, ed., *Journal and Letters of Philip Vickers Fithian, 1773–1774: A Plantation Tutor of the Old Dominion*, new ed. (Williamsburg, Va.: Colonial Williamsburg, 1957), 97, 109. Cf. Weld, *Travels through the States* 1:137–39.

103. Weld, *Travels through the States* 1:138–40.

104. *Md. Gazette*, Apr. 17, 1794.

105. Ibid.

EPILOGUE

1. *Md. Gazette*, July 19, Sept. 27, 1787, May 13, 1790, Mar. 8, 1792, June 11, 1795, Jan. 7, 1796; Douglas R. Littlefield, "Eighteenth-Century Plans to Clear the Potomac River: Technology, Expertise, and Labor in a Developing Nation," *Virginia Magazine of History and Biography* 93 (1985): 291–322. The 175-mile route dropped nearly

two thousand feet, four times the drop over the course of the longer Erie Canal. The Potomac also had several rapids and major obstructions, a winding and narrow course, and significant variations in water flow, depending upon climatic conditions. Littlefield makes a convincing case that Americans lacked the technological expertise to conquer the river in the eighteenth century. See also Wilbur E. Garrett, "George Washington's Patowmack Canal: Waterway That Led to the Constitution," *National Geographic* 171 (1987): 716–53. On the company's financial problems, see Douglas R. Littlefield, "The Potomac Company: A Misadventure in Financing an Early American Internal Improvement Project," *Business History Review* 58 (1984): 562–85.

2. *Md. Gazette*, Feb. 23, 1786. See also ibid., Apr. 8, June 10, 1790, Nov. 10, 1791, Mar. 12, 1795; Alexander Hamilton to James Brown & Co., May 20, 1784, in David C. Skaggs and Richard K. MacMaster, eds., "Post-Revolutionary Letters of Alexander Hamilton, Piscataway Merchant: Part 1, January–June 1784," *Md. Hist. Mag.* 63 (1968): 42.

3. *Md. Gazette*, Mar. 2, Oct. 5, 1786, Dec. 18, 25, 1788, Jan. 1, July 9, 30, 1789, Aug. 5, 1790, Aug. 4, Nov. 10, Dec. 8, 29, 1791, Jan. 5, Apr. 19, 1792, Apr. 4, Sept. 12, Nov. 7, Dec. 26, 1793, Feb. 6, 1794; J. Franklin Jameson, ed., "Letters of Phineas Bond to the Foreign Office of Great Britain, 1787, 1788, 1789," American Historical Association *Annual Report* (1896), 2:526; Robert Fergusson to Alexander Henderson, Dec. 8, 1792, Port Tobacco Invoice and Letter Book, 1771–74, 1792–93, John Glassford & Co. Papers, Manuscript Division, LC.

4. Isaac Weld, Jr., *Travels through the States of North America, and the Provinces of Upper and Lower Canada during the Years 1795, 1796, and 1797*, 4th ed., 2 vols. (London: John Stockdale, 1807; New York: Augustus M. Kelley, 1970), 1:139.

5. *Md. Gazette*, Feb. 1, 1787, Oct. 22, 1789, Apr. 24, 1794; Samuel Hanson of Samuel (d. 1830) to George Washington, Feb. 22, 1793, George Washington Papers, ser. 4, Manuscript Division, LC; Papenfuse et al., eds., *Biographical Dictionary* 1:409; Joseph Zwinge, "The Novitiate in Maryland," *Woodstock Letters* 44 (1915): 4–5; Samuel Hanson file, in the Revolutionary War Pension and Bounty-Land Warrant Application Files, reel 1184, Record Group 15, Microcopy 804, National Archives and Records Service, Washington, D.C.

6. Papenfuse et al., eds., *Biographical Dictionary* 1:409; files of Richard Blandford (reel 265), Zachariah Burch (reel 408), Elijah Clark (reel 552), and John Shaw (reel 2161), in the Revolutionary War Pension and Bounty-Land Warrant Application Files.

7. John Hoskins Stone to Thomas Willing, Jan. 14, 1799, Gratz Collection, Historical Society of Pennsylvania, Philadelphia; George Mason to John Mason, Aug. 17, 1791, in *The Papers of George Mason, 1725–1792*, ed. Robert A. Rutland, 3 vols. (Chapel Hill: University of North Carolina Press, for the Institute of Early American History and Culture, 1970), 3:1235; Papenfuse et al., eds., *Biographical Dictionary* 1:211–12, 263–64, 2:784–85.

8. Pardon Papers, box 3, folder 104; Clement Edelin and Richard Blandford files, Revolutionary War Pension and Bounty-Land Warrant Application Files, reels 896, 265, respectively.

9. Tables 1–2, Appendix; John L. Androit, comp., *Population Abstract of the United States*, 2 vols. (McLean, Va.: Androit Associates, 1983), 1:347.

10. Table 2, Appendix; Robert J. Brugger, *Maryland: A Middle Temperament, 1634–1980* (Baltimore: Johns Hopkins University Press, in association with the Maryland Historical Society, 1988), 781.

SELECT LIST OF SOURCES

BIBLIOGRAPHIC AND REFERENCE AIDS

Baldwin, Jane, comp. *The Maryland Calendar of Wills*. 8 vols. 1904–28. Reprint. Baltimore: Genealogical Publishing Co., 1968.

Brugger, Robert J. "Bibliographical Essay." In *Maryland: A Middle Temperament, 1634–1980*, 711–69. Baltimore: Johns Hopkins University Press, in association with the Maryland Historical Society, 1988.

Burns, Annie Walker, comp. *Abstracts of Wills of Charles and St. Mary's Counties, Maryland, 1744–1772*. Annapolis, 1937.

"Catalog of Members of the Maryland Mission of the Society of Jesus, 1634–1806." Special Collections Division, Georgetown University Library, Washington, D.C. Typescript.

Cox, Richard J. "A Bibliography of Articles and Books on Maryland History . . . [1974–76]." *Maryland Historical Magazine* 70 (1975): 211–33; 71 (1976): 449–64; 72 (1977): 288–314.

———. "A Bibliography of Articles, Books, and Dissertations on Maryland History . . . [1977–82]." *Maryland Historical Magazine* 73 (1978): 280–90; 74 (1979): 358–66; 75 (1980): 238–49; 76 (1981): 286–95; 77 (1982): 279–90; 78 (1983): 205–13.

———. "A Selected List of Recent Dissertations on Maryland History, 1970–1976." *Maryland Historical Magazine* 73 (1978): 180–85.

Cox, Richard J., and Larry E. Sullivan, eds. *Guide to the Research Collections of the Maryland Historical Society: Historical and Genealogical Manuscripts and Oral History Interviews*. Baltimore: Maryland Historical Society, 1981.

Curtis, Peter H., Anne S. K. Turkos, et al., comps. "Maryland History Bibliography . . . [1983–92]." *Maryland Historical Magazine* 82 (1987): 37–68; 83 (1988): 157–77; 84 (1989): 147–62; 85 (1990): 144–63; 86 (1991): 199–216; 87 (1992): 323–44; 88 (1993): 210–31.

Duncan, Richard R. "Master's Theses and Doctoral Dissertations on Maryland History." *Maryland Historical Magazine* 80 (1985): 261–76.

Duncan, Richard R., and Dorothy M. Brown, comps. *Master's Theses and Doctoral Dissertations on Maryland History*. Baltimore: Maryland Historical Society, 1970.

Evans, Charles, comp. *American Bibliography: A Chronological Dictionary of All Books, Pamphlets, and Periodical Publications Printed in the United States of America from the Genesis of Printing in 1638 down to and including 1820*. 14 vols. New York: P. Smith, 1941–59.

Gephart, Ronald M., comp. *Revolutionary America, 1763–1789: A Bibliography*. 2 vols. Washington, D.C.: Library of Congress, 1984.

Land, Aubrey C. "Bibliography." In *Colonial Maryland: A History*, 331–51. Millwood, N.Y.: KTO Press, 1981.

Learning Resource Center, Charles County Community College. *The Southern Maryland Collection*. La Plata, Md.: Charles County Community College, 1981.

Magruder, James M., Jr., comp. *Index of Maryland Colonial Wills, 1634–1777, in the Hall of Records, Annapolis, Md.: Reprinted with Additions and a New Introduction by Louise E. Magruder*. Baltimore: Genealogical Publishing Co., 1967.

Maryland State Archives. *A Guide to Government Records at the Maryland State Archives: A Comprehensive List by Agency and Record Series*. Annapolis: Maryland State Archives, 1991.

Minick, A. Rachel. *A History of Printing in Maryland, 1791–1800, with a Bibliography of Works Printed in the State during the Period*. Baltimore: Enoch Pratt Free Library, 1949.

National Genealogical Society. *Index of Revolutionary War Pension Applications in the National Archives*. Washington, D.C.: National Genealogical Society, 1976.

Owings, Donnell M. *His Lordship's Patronage: Offices of Profit in Colonial Maryland*. Baltimore: Maryland Historical Society, 1953.

Papenfuse, Edward C., Alan F. Day, David W. Jordan, and Gregory A. Stiverson, eds. *A Biographical Dictionary of the Maryland Legislature, 1635–1789*. 2 vols. Baltimore: Johns Hopkins University Press, 1979, 1985.

Papenfuse, Edward C., Gregory A. Stiverson, and Mary D. Donaldson, comps. *An Inventory of Maryland State Papers*. Vol. 1, *The Era of the American Revolution, 1775–1789*. Annapolis: Hall of Records Commission, 1977.

Pedley, Avril J. M., comp. *The Manuscript Collections of the Maryland Historical Society*. Baltimore: Maryland Historical Society, 1968.

[Rossiter, W. S.], comp. *A Century of Population Growth: From the First Census of the United States to the Twelfth, 1790–1900*. Washington, D.C.: U.S. Bureau of the Census, 1909.

Sellers, John R., Gerard W. Gawalt, Paul H. Smith, and Patricia Molen Van Ee, comps. *Manuscript Sources in the Library of Congress for Research on the American Revolution*. Washington, D.C.: Library of Congress, 1975.

Sellers, John R., and Patricia Molen Van Ee, comps. *Maps and Charts of North America and the West Indies, 1750–1789: A Guide to the Collections in the Library of Congress*. Washington, D.C.: Library of Congress, 1981.

Shaw, Ralph R., and Richard H. Shoemaker. *American Bibliography: A Preliminary Checklist, 1801–19*. 22 vols. New York: Scarecrow Press, 1958–66.

Shipton, Clifford K., and James E. Mooney, comps. *National Index of American Imprints through 1800: The Short-Title Evans*. 2 vols. Worcester, Mass.: American Antiquarian Society, 1969.

Steuart, Rieman. *A History of the Maryland Line in the Revolutionary War, 1775–1783*. N.p.: Society of the Cincinnati of Maryland, 1969.

U.S. Bureau of the Census. *Historical Statistics of the United States: Colonial Times to 1970.* 2 vols. Washington, D.C.: U.S. Government Printing Office, 1975.

Wheeler, Joseph T. *The Maryland Press, 1777–1790.* Introduction by Lawrence C. Wroth. Baltimore: Maryland Historical Society, 1938.

MAPS AND ATLASES

[Anderson, Scoles, et al.] *The States of Maryland and Delaware from the latest Surveys, 1799.* New York: I. Low, 1799.

Cappon, Lester J., Barbara Bartz Petchenik, and John Hamilton Long, eds. *Atlas of Early American History: The Revolutionary Era, 1760–1790.* Princeton: Princeton University Press, for the Newberry Library and the Institute of Early American History and Culture, 1976.

Charles County. N.p., n.d. (Early nineteenth-century print; copy at the Archives of the Episcopal Diocese of Maryland, Baltimore.)

"A Chart of the Coast of New York, New Jersey, Pensilvania, Maryland, Virginia, North Carolina, &c. . . . March 1, 1780. . . ." In *The Atlantic Neptune, Published For the use of the Royal Navy of Great Britain, By Joseph F: W: Des Barres Esq. Under the Directions of the Right Honble. the Lords Commissioners of the Admiralty.* London, n.d.

Evans, Lewis. *A General Map of the Middle British Colonies, in America.* [Philadelphia]: engraved by James Turner, 1755.

Faden, William. *The North American Atlas, Selected from the Most Authentic Maps, Charts, Plans, &c. Hitherto published.* London: William Faden, 1777.

Griffith, Dennis. *Map of the State of Maryland. Laid down from an actual Survey of all the principal Waters, public Roads, and Divisions of the Counties therein; describing the Situation of the Cities, Towns, Villages, Houses of Worship and other public Buildings. Furnaces, Forges, Mills, and other remarkable Places . . . By Dennis Griffith, June 20th, 1794.* Philadelphia: J. Wallace, 1795.

Herrman, Augustin. *Virginia and Maryland As it is Planted and Inhabited this present Year 1670 Surveyed and Exactly Drawne. . . .* London: Herman and Within-brook, 1673.

Lewis, Samuel. *The State of Maryland, from the best Authorities.* N.p. [ca. 1795].

Papenfuse, Edward C., and Joseph M. Coale III, comps. *The Hammond-Harwood House Atlas of Historical Maps of Maryland, 1608–1908.* Baltimore: Johns Hopkins University Press, 1982.

"The Village of Port Tobacco, Maryland as it is known to have appeared in the year 1892." (Copy at the Maryland State Archives, Annapolis. Map no. 184.)

PRIMARY SOURCES

I. MANUSCRIPTS

A. Maryland State Archives, Hall of Records, Annapolis

NOTE: Since the author completed the research for this book, the MSA reorganized, renumbered, and sometimes renamed its collections. In accordance with MSA policy, the author has adopted the new nomenclature and numbering.

Adjutant General. Militia Appointments (S348)
Annapolis Mayors Court. Minutes (M44)

Anne Arundel County Court. Judgment Records (C91)
Chancery Court. Chancery Records (S517)
Charles County Court
  Court Records (C658)
  Land Records (C670)
  Tobacco Inspection Proceedings (C680)
Charles County Register of Wills
  Inventories (C665)
  Wills (C681)
Charles County Sheriff. Account Book, 1769 (C649)
Commissioners to Preserve Confiscated British Property
  Ledger and Journal (S132)
  Sale Book (S124)
Frederick County Court. Judgment Records (C810)
General Court of the Western Shore
  Dockets (S492)
  Judgment Records (S497)
  Loose Papers. In Judicials (S509)
Governor and Council
  Colonial Muster Rolls (S962)
  Federal Election Returns, 1789–1803. In Election Returns (S106)
  Commission Records (S1080)
  Letterbooks (S1075)
  Pardon Papers (S1061)
  Proceedings (S1071)
Land Office
  Charles County Debt Books. In Debt Books (S12)
  Charles County Rent Roll, Lib. 26 (1753–75). In Rent Rolls (S18)
  Patent Records (S11)
Maryland State Papers
  Blue Books (S990)
  Brown Books (S991)
  Red Books (S989)
  Series A: Executive Papers (S1004)
  Series B: Pforzheimer Papers (S995)
  Series D: Revolutionary Papers (S997)
  Series Z: Scharf Collection (S1005)
Prerogative Court
  Testamentary Proceedings (S529)
  Wills (S538)
Prince George's County Court. Judgment Records (C1231)
Provincial Court. Judgment Records (S551)
Secretary in Maryland
  Charles County Tax Lists, 1734–58. In Tax Lists (S244)
Special Collections
  Civil Office Index. In the Legislative History Project Collection (SC1138)
  Durham Parish Vestry Minutes, 1774–1824. In the Christ Church, Old Durham Parish
    Collection (SC2604)

Forensic Club of Annapolis Minutes. Typescript. In the George Forbes Collection
  (SC182)
Ridout Collection (SC371)
Special Collections Microfilm
  Goldsborough Lists of Civil Officers of Maryland, 1637–1891 (M875)

B. Maryland Historical Society Library, Baltimore

Calvert Papers (MS. 174)
Carroll Papers (MS. 206)
William Cooke Papers (MS. 195)
Corner Collection (MS. 1242)
Dulany Papers (MS. 1265)
Federal Assessment, 1798 (Microfilm)
Gilmore Papers (MS. 387.1)
Hamilton Papers, 1760–1800 (MS. 1301)
John Hanson Ledger, 1775–82 (MS. 1785.1)
John Hanson Papers (MS. 1785)
John and Walter Hanson Papers (MS. 1579)
Potts Papers (MS. 1392)
Purviance Papers (MS. 1394)
Revolutionary War Military Records (MS. 1146)
Smallwood Papers (MS. 1875)
Stone Family Papers (MS. 406)
Tench Tilghman Letter and Account Books, 1784–98 (MS. 2690)
Vertical File
Wallace, Johnson, & Muir Letterbook (MS. 1180)

C. Southern Maryland Studies Center, Charles County Community College, La Plata, Md.

Charlotte Hall School Collection (850078)
Historical Society of Charles County Files (850046)
Kremer Collection (850028)
Petition of James Freeman (850056)

D. National Archives and Records Service, Washington, D.C.

Compiled Service Records of Soldiers Who Served in the American Army during the
  Revolutionary War. Record Group 93. Microcopy M881
Records of the Potomac Company. Stock Ledger, 1787–1828. Record Group 79
Revolutionary War Pension and Bounty-Land Warrant Application Files. Record Group
  15. Microcopy 804
U.S. Census Office. Population Schedules of the Fourth Census of the United States, 1820.
  Record Group 29. Microcopy 33

E. Manuscript Division, Library of Congress, Washington, D.C.

John Glassford & Company Papers
Richard Harrison & Company Ledger, 1779–83
Henry Riddell Account Book, 1777–80. In the Peter Force Collection, Series 8D

Stone Family of Maryland Papers
Zephaniah Turner Account Book, 1764–72
George Washington Papers

F. Other Repositories

Archives of the Episcopal Diocese of Maryland, Baltimore
  Vertical File
Boston University, Boston, Mass.
  Edward C. Stone Collection of the Autographs of the Signers of the Declaration of
    Independence
William L. Clements Library, University of Michigan, Ann Arbor
  Thomas Gage Papers
  Nathanael Greene Papers
  Miscellaneous Collection
Colonial Williamsburg Foundation Library, Williamsburg, Va.
  Virginia Colonial Records Project
Rare Book and Manuscript Library, Columbia University, New York, N.Y.
  Conway Collection
Coutts & Company, London
  Russell Papers. Microfilm: Virginia Colonial Records Project, Colonial
    Williamsburg Foundation Library, Williamsburg, Va.
Martha Washington Chapter, Daughters of the American Revolution, Washington, D.C.
  "Abstracts of Early Protestant Episcopal Church Records of Charles County, Mary-
    land." N.d. Typescript
  Ross, Nellie Grant, comp. "Charles County, Maryland Tomb-Stone & Bible Records."
    N.d. Typescript.
John Work Garrett Library, Johns Hopkins University, Baltimore.
  Signers' Collection
Georgetown University Library, Washington, D.C.
  Eighteenth-Century Catholic Sermon Collection
  Maryland Province Archives of the Society of Jesus
Lambeth Palace Library, London
  Fulham Palace Papers. Microfilm: Manuscript Division, Library of Congress, Washing-
    ton, D.C.
Maine Historical Society, Portland
  Fogg Collection
Mount Vernon Ladies' Association of the Union, Mount Vernon, Va.
  Lund Washington Papers
National Library of Scotland, Edinburgh
  William Cunninghame & Company Letter Books, 1767–77. Microfilm: Colonial Wil-
    liamsburg Foundation Library, Williamsburg, Va.
New Jersey Historical Society, Newark
  Louis Bamberger Autograph Collection
New York Public Library, New York, N.Y.
  American Loyalist Transcripts
  Emmet Collection
  Hooe, Stone & Company Invoice Book, 1770–84

Thomas Howe Ridgate Letter Book, 1771–72. In the Arents Collection
Stone Family Correspondence, 1782–91. In the Arents Collection
Historical Society of Pennsylvania, Philadelphia
    Tench Coxe Papers
    Dreer Collection
    Etting Collection
    Gratz Collection
    William Tilghman Papers
William R. Perkins Library, Duke University, Durham, N.C.
    Robert Carter Papers
    John Hoskins Stone Papers
    William Briscoe Stone Papers, 1774–1888
Pierpont Morgan Library, New York, N.Y.
    Thomas Stone Letter, 1776
Public Record Office, London
    American Loyalist Claims. Microfilm: Manuscript Division, Library of Congress,
        Washington, D.C.
    High Court of Admiralty Prize Papers. Microfilm: Virginia Colonial Records Project,
        Colonial Williamsburg Foundation Library, Williamsburg, Va.
Scottish Record Office, Edinburgh
    Buchanan & Simson Invoice Book, 1755–61
    Buchanan & Simson Letterbook, 1759–61
    James Lawson Letter Book
United Methodist Historical Society, Baltimore
    Journal of John Littlejohn
Virginia Historical Society, Richmond
    Barnes & Ridgate Account, 1774–90
    Campbell Family Papers
    Josias Hawkins Letter, 1866
    John C. Jones Letter, 1796
    Lee Family Papers, 1638–1867
    Edmund Jennings Lee Papers
    George Bolling Lee Papers, 1732–1870
    Richard Lee, Jr., Letter, 1774
    McDonald Family Papers, 1767–1951
    Thornton Family Papers, 1744–1945
University of Virginia Library, Charlottesville
    Hamond Papers, 1766–1825
    Virginia Colonial Records Project
Beinecke Rare Book and Manuscript Library, Yale University, New Haven, Conn.
    Pequot Collection

II. Printed Primary Sources

"An Account of the Number of Souls in the Province of Maryland, in the Year 1755."
    Gentleman's Magazine (London), 34 (1764): 261.
Bacon, Thomas, comp. *Laws of Maryland at Large, with Proper Indexes: Now first Collected into*

One Compleat Body, and Published from the Original Acts and Records, remaining in the Secretary's Office of the said Province. . . . Annapolis: Jonas Green, 1765.

Boucher, Jonathan. *A View of the Causes and Consequences of the American Revolution; in Thirteen Discourses, Preached in North America between the Years 1763 and 1775.* London, 1797. Reprint. New York: Russell & Russell, 1967.

————. *Reminiscences of an American Loyalist, 1738–1789.* New York: Houghton Mifflin Co., 1925.

Browne, William H., et al., eds. *Archives of Maryland.* 73 vols. to date. Baltimore: Maryland Historical Society, 1883–1972; Annapolis: Maryland State Archives, 1990–.

Brumbaugh, Gaius M., comp. *Maryland Records: Colonial, Revolutionary, County and Church.* 2 vols. Baltimore: Williams & Wilkins Co., 1915, 1928; Baltimore: Genealogical Publishing Co., 1967.

Campbell, Isaac. *A Rational Inquiry into the Origin, Foundation, Nature and End of Civil Government, shewing it to be a Divine Institution, Legitimately deriving its Authority from the Law of Revelation only, and not from the Law of Nature, as hath heretofore been generally held by Writers, from Time supposed immemorial.* Annapolis: Frederick Green [1787?].

Clark, William Bell, et al., eds. *Naval Documents of the American Revolution.* 9 vols. to date. Washington, D.C.: U.S. Naval History Division, Department of the Navy, 1964–.

Cresswell, Nicholas. *The Journal of Nicholas Cresswell, 1774–1777.* New York: Dial Press, 1924.

Dickinson, Clare Joseph. *The Carmelite Adventure: Clare Joseph Dickinson's Journal of a Trip to America and Other Documents.* Edited by Constance FitzGerald. Baltimore: Carmelite Sisters of Baltimore, 1990.

Eddis, William. *Letters from America.* Edited by Aubrey C. Land. Cambridge: Belknap Press of Harvard University Press, 1969.

Fithian, Philip Vickers. *Journal and Letters of Philip Vickers Fithian, 1773–1774: A Plantation Tutor of the Old Dominion.* Edited by Hunter D. Farish. New ed. Williamsburg, Va.: Colonial Williamsburg, 1957.

Gordon, Adam. "Journal of an Officer Who Travelled in America and the West Indies in 1764 and 1765." In *Travels in the American Colonies,* edited by Newton D. Mereness, 367–453. New York: Macmillan, 1916.

Hall, Clayton C., ed. *Narratives of Early Maryland, 1633–1684.* New York: Charles Scribner's Sons, 1910.

Hamilton, Alexander. "The Letterbooks of Alexander Hamilton, Piscataway Factor [1774–76]." Edited by Richard K. MacMaster and David C. Skaggs. *Maryland Historical Magazine* 61 (1966): 146–66, 305–28; 62 (1967): 135–69.

————. "Post-Revolutionary Letters of Alexander Hamilton, Piscataway Merchant . . . [1784]." Edited by Richard K. MacMaster and David C. Skaggs. *Maryland Historical Magazine* 63 (1968): 22–54; 65 (1970): 18–35.

Harris, Thomas, Jr., and John McHenry, comps. *Maryland Reports . . . of the Most Important Law Cases . . . 1700 to 1799.* 4 vols. New York: I. Riley, 1809–13; Annapolis: Jonas Green, 1818.

Honyman, Robert. *Colonial Panorama 1775: Dr. Robert Honyman's Journal for March and April.* Edited by Philip Padelford. San Marino, Calif.: Huntington Library, 1939.

Johnson, Joshua. *Joshua Johnson's Letterbook, 1771–1774: Letters from a Merchant in London to His Partners in Maryland.* Edited by Jacob M. Price. London: London Record Society, 1979.

"Journal of a French Traveller in the Colonies, 1765, II." *American Historical Review* 27 (1921): 70–89.

Lee, Richard Henry. *The Letters of Richard Henry Lee*. Edited by James C. Ballagh. 2 vols. New York: Macmillan, 1911, 1914; New York: Da Capo Press, 1970.

Maryland. Constitutional Convention of 1776. *The Decisive Blow Is Struck: A Facsimile Edition of the Proceedings of the Constitutional Convention of 1776 and the First Maryland Constitution.* Introduction by Edward C. Papenfuse and Gregory A. Stiverson. Annapolis: Hall of Records Commission, 1977.

Maryland. General Assembly. *Laws of Maryland, Made and Passed at a Session of Assembly . . . [1777–1790]*. Annapolis: Frederick Green [1777–91].

Maryland. Provincial Convention. *Proceedings of the Conventions of the Province of Maryland, Held at the City of Annapolis in 1774, 1775, and 1776*. Baltimore: James Lucas & E. K. Deaver, 1836.

Mason, George. *The Papers of George Mason, 1725–1792*. Edited by Robert A. Rutland. 3 vols. Chapel Hill: University of North Carolina Press, for the Institute of Early American History and Culture, 1970.

Mosley, Joseph. "Letters of Father Joseph Mosley, 1757–1786." Edited by E. I. Devitt. *Woodstock Letters* 35 (1906): 35–55.

Perry, William S., ed. *Historical Collections Relating to the American Colonial Church*. 5 vols. 1878. Reprint. New York: AMS Press, 1969.

"Population in Maryland—1782." *The American Museum, or, Universal Magazine* 7 (1790), 159.

"Proceedings of the Parochial Clergy." *Maryland Historical Magazine* 3 (1908): 257–73, 364–84.

Rush, Benjamin. *The Autobiography of Benjamin Rush: His "Travels through Life" together with his Commonplace Book for 1789–1813*. Edited by George W. Corner. Princeton: Princeton University Press, for the American Philosophical Society, 1948.

Schoepf, Johann David. *Travels in the Confederation [1783–84]*. Translated by Alfred J. Morrison. 2 vols. 1911. Reprint. New York: Bergman Publishers, 1968.

Scott, Joseph. *A Geographical Description of the States of Maryland and Delaware*. Philadelphia: Kimber, Conrad & Co., 1807.

Smith, Paul H., et al., eds. *Letters of Delegates to Congress, 1774–1789*. 17 vols. to date. Washington, D.C.: Library of Congress, 1976–.

Smyth, John F. D. *A Tour in the United States of America. . . .* 2 vols. London: G. Robinson, J. Robson, and J. Sewell, 1784.

[Stone, Thomas.] " 'The Dye Is Cast. . . .' " Edited by Dorothy S. Eaton and Vincent L. Eaton. *Library of Congress Quarterly Journal of Current Acquisitions* 14 (1957): 181–85.

[U.S. Census Office. 1st Census, 1790]. *Heads of Families at the First Census of the United States Taken in the Year 1790: Maryland*. Baltimore: Genealogical Publishing Co., 1965.

————. *Return of the Whole Number of Persons within the Several Districts of the United States, According to "An Act Providing for the Enumeration of the Inhabitants of the United States," Passed March the First, One Thousand Seven Hundred and Ninety-One*. Philadelphia: Childs & Swaine, 1791.

U.S. Census Office. 2d Census, 1800. *Return of the Whole Number of Persons within the Several Districts of the United States*. Washington, D.C.: William Duane & Son, 1802.

U.S. Census Office. 6th Census, 1840. *Compendium of the Enumeration of the Inhabitants and Statistics of the United States, as Obtained at the Department of State, from the Returns of the Sixth Census*. Washington, D.C.: Thomas Allen, 1841.

U.S. Census Office. 8th Census, 1860. *Population of the United States in 1860; Compiled from the Original Returns of the Eighth Census.* Washington, D.C.: Government Printing Office, 1864.

U.S. Continental Congress. *Journals of the Continental Congress, 1774–1789.* 34 vols. Edited by Worthington C. Ford et al. Washington, D.C.: U.S. Government Printing Office, 1904–37.

U.S. Department of State. 3d Census, 1810. *Aggregate Amount of Each Description of Persons within the United States . . . in the Year 1810.* Washington, D.C., 1810.

Vallette, Elie. *The Deputy Commissary's Guide Within the Province of Maryland, together With plain and sufficient directions for Testators to form, and Executors to perform their Wills and Testaments. . . .* Annapolis: Ann Catharine Green & Son, 1774.

Washington, George. *The Diaries of George Washington.* Edited by Donald Jackson and Dorothy Twohig. 6 vols. Charlottesville: University Press of Virginia, 1976–79.

———. *The Papers of George Washington.* Edited by W. W. Abbot et al. 20 vols. to date. Charlottesville: University Press of Virginia, 1976–.

———. *The Writings of George Washington from the Original Manuscript Sources, 1745–1799.* Edited by John C. Fitzpatrick. 39 vols. Washington, D.C.: Government Printing Office, 1931–44.

Weld, Isaac, Jr. *Travels through the States of North America, and the Provinces of Upper and Lower Canada during the Years 1795, 1796, and 1797.* 4th ed. 2 vols. London: John Stockdale, 1807; New York: Augustus M. Kelley, 1970.

Willard, Margaret W., ed. *Letters on the American Revolution, 1774–1776.* Boston: Houghton Mifflin Co., 1925.

Yazawa, Melvin, ed. *Representative Government and the Revolution: The Maryland Constitutional Crisis of 1787.* Baltimore: Johns Hopkins University Press, 1975.

III. NEWSPAPERS AND MAGAZINES

American Museum, or Repository of Ancient and Modern Fugitive Pieces, Prose and Poetical. Philadelphia: Mathew Carey, 1787–89.

American Museum, or, Universal Magazine. Philadelphia: Mathew Carey, 1790–92.

Dunlap's Maryland Gazette or, The Baltimore General Advertiser (Baltimore).

Gentleman's Magazine (London).

Maryland Gazette (Annapolis).

Maryland Journal, and Baltimore Advertiser (Baltimore).

Virginia Gazette (Williamsburg).

INDEX